THE HANDBOOK OF INTERNATIONAL INVESTING

Editor, Carl Beidleman

Probus Publishing Company
Chicago, Illinois

Library of Congress Cataloging in Publication Data

The Handbook of international investing.

Includes index.
1. Investments, Foreign. 2. Portfolio management. I. Beidleman, Carl R.
HG4538:H325 1987 332.6'73 86-22515
ISBN 0-917253-64-7

Library of Congress Catalog Card No. 86-22515

Printed in the United States of America

1 2 3 4 5 6 7 8 9 0

To Inge

PREFACE

In the last several decades advances in international transactions of all types have progressed at an exceptionally rapid pace. Observers of this recent growth in international activity sometimes remark that the world is getting smaller. The planet, of course, has not diminished; rather, the sphere of our activities has become worldwide. Improvements in technology, transportation, and communications; the relaxation of restraining regulations and controls; the trust and confidence developing between far-flung individuals and nations doing business with each other; better resources and procedures for conducting international transactions; a growing awareness of the many advantages of an international marketplace—each of these is a force impelling a competitive desire to pursue new opportunities on a global scale.

International investing has flourished in the recent overall surge of international activity. *The Handbook of International Investing* examines many of the factors responsible for this growing interest in international investing. It considers the scale of international investing, its advantages in terms of the risk/return trade-off, the ways in which it differs from domestic investing, and the concerns and difficulties one may encounter when investing abroad. The full range of material integral to this subject is unusually far-reaching; I have attempted to gather in this volume the basic knowledge intrinsic to the process of international investing. Wherever possible, the contributors have attempted to direct their material to the interests of individual and institutional investors alike. [Some chapters, however, study international investment process from the perspective of segments of the investment community, and examine the role of these segments in the community as a whole.]

The contributors are prestigious experts in the field of international investing, both scholars and practitioners. Their work is intended to provide a foundation and framework upon which serious investors can build. The *Handbook* will provide a useful guide for the uninitiated, as well as a handy reference for more experienced investors. It will also prove useful in advanced undergraduate and graduate university courses and executive development programs designed to teach the increasingly prevalent practice of international investment.

Commercial and investment banks, institutional investors and international organizations will find the *Handbook* an indispensible aid in training sessions for employees and clients.

The organization of the contents is discussed in Chapter 1 and need not be repeated here. However, a few words regarding the conception of the book are in order. In designing its content, I tried to place myself in the position of an uninformed investor seeking to evaluate the pros and cons of investing in international portfolios. This led to the realization of a need for the history and nature of international investment; in short, an assessment of what this ''new'' opportunity has to offer. This is the subject matter of Section I. The opportunities afforded by investing abroad come attended by a whole new class of risks—the evaluation of these risks and their management are the focus of Section II.

Section III describes many of the major instruments that can be utilized by international investors. It is followed by sections on opportunities to enhance yields by using cross-border transactions, alternative approaches different investors take to global investment, and accounting, tax, and legal issues. A summary of investment performance for international fixed income and equity securities rounds out the final section of the book.

Acknowledgment of assistance in research undertakings of this magnitude can never be complete. I am, of course, grateful to the individual contributors. I also wish to express my appreciation to Richard W. Barsness, Dean of the College of Business and Economics at Lehigh University, for establishing an environment in which efforts such as this can be accomplished. I am also grateful to many members of the community of investment and merchant bankers and international investors for generously sharing their perceptions of the international investment process. While it is not possible to name them all, a number of particularly knowledgeable and helpful individuals merit special thanks: Jeffrey D. Hanna of Salomon Brothers Inc; Jay A. Dirnberger of Julius Baer Investment Management; David Hopkins of Morgan Guaranty; Jessica Einhorn of The World Bank; Francoise Soares-Kemp of Credit Lyonnais; Eugene Mercy of Goldman Sachs; Donald R. Lessard of M.I.T.; Peter Dietz of Frank Russell Trust; David P. Pritchard, formerly of Citicorp London and now of Royal Bank of Canada; and Paul N. Leitner of AEA Investors, Inc. I am also grateful to Janice Schaeffer, who cheerfully typed the many drafts and assisted in the data analysis.

Probus Publishing was helpful throughout the process leading to the publication of this book, and made it a more enjoyable undertaking.

I wish to acknowledge the generous support of the Allen C. DuBois Professorship expense fund, which provided funds to defray research costs.

Finally, I thank my wife, Inge, for her confidence and encouragement during the continuing process that led to the completion of this book. She alone remembers when it all began and patiently waits to take the time to "smell the roses."

Any errors of omission or commission are mine.

Carl R. Beidleman
Bethlehem, Pennsylvania
January 1987

CONTENTS

Section II. Managing Risk in an International Portfolio

Section III. Instruments Available to International Investors

Section IV. Opportunities for Yield Enhancement in International Markets

SECTION I

International Investment Assessment

CHAPTER ONE

Dr. Carl R. Beidleman joined the Lehigh University faculty in 1967, was promoted to associate professor of finance in 1972, and was awarded the Allen C. DuBois Distinguished Professorship in Finance in 1975. He was named chairman of the Department of Management and Finance in 1975, a position which he held until 1978. In 1983 he was appointed the first chairman of the newly organized Department of Finance.

A native of Wilkes-Barre, PA, and a graduate of Lafayette College, Dr. Beidleman earned the M.B.A. degree at Drexel University and the Ph.D. at the Wharton School, University of Pennsylvania.

He is currently engaged in several research projects at Lehigh University, including business and economic studies related to the new Engineering Research Center for Advanced Technology for Large Structural Systems.

Dr. Beidleman has had articles published in the *Columbia Journal of World Business, Sloan Management Review, Euromoney, National Tax Journal, Journal of Business Finance, Financial Analysts Journal, Journal of Business Education, Managerial Planning, The Accounting Review,* and *Accounting and Business Research.*

He is a member of the boards of directors of the Martin Guitar Corp., Independence Bancorp Inc. and Bucks County Bank and Trust Co., and has served as a consultant to commercial banks, legal counsel and industrial firms.

INTRODUCTION TO INTERNATIONAL INVESTING

Carl R. Beidleman
DuBois Professor of Finance
Lehigh University
Bethlehem, Pennsylvania

INTRODUCTION

This initial chapter could as readily have been called a "Summary" and appeared at the end of the book. The objective is to begin with a brief summary of data on the aggregate size of several of the measurable indicators of international investment and to provide a rationale for the organization and content of the book and the intended contribution of each of the chapter authors. Moreover, this introductory material, will illustrate the relevance of the material contained in each of the chapters to the overall process of international investment. This is done in the hope that it may lead a reader more quickly to material in the body of the book in which he has particular interest. For others who wish to survey the entire book, this introductory chapter will help in the integration of the material with related subject matter and assist in the comprehension of material on various (related) subjects written by different writers with diverse writing styles and approaches.

SOME SUMMARY STATISTICS

To say that expansion in international portfolio investment activity has been brisk in the last decade is clearly an understatement. The chapters that follow contain detailed data on the size and development of the various international security markets and their representation across the globe. In order to bring the total size of the potential for international investment into perspective, it is fitting to briefly summarize the size of the major security markets and provide a few related statistics that may help bring this subject into clearer view.

The aggregate size of the world bond market at the end of 1985, measured in U.S. dollars, was $5.9 trillion. This compares with only $3.2 trillion at the end of 1980. The aggregate capitalization of exchange listed equity shares at the end of 1985 reached $4.3 trillion. This is up from $2.4 trillion at the end of 1980 and $3.1 trillion at the end of 1984. The advance in the value of equity capitalization in 1985 alone was 39.2 percent; a remarkable increase, due in part to the effect of the decline in the value of the U.S. dollar, which is used in the measurement process. Added together, the world equity and fixed-income markets in publicly traded securities tallied at $10.2 trillion at the end of 1985. This sum is approximately two-thirds of the GDP of market economies in 1985. The monumental size of these markets is astonishing when compared with the asset blocks of even the largest institutional investors.

Other summary statistics on indicators which help to accommodate the increase in international investment are also of interest. According to studies undertaken in March 1986 by their respective central banks, the foreign exchange trading volume of London, New York, and Tokyo has soared to $188 billion per day. The distribution of daily trading volume was $90 billion in London, $50 billion in New York, and $48 billion in Tokyo. Earlier estimates of trading volume put London at $25 billion in 1979, nearly doubling to $49 billion in 1984 with another near doubling to $90 billion in 1986. An earlier survey by the New York Federal Reserve Bank put the New York net trading volume at $26 billion per day in 1983, making the more recent rise to $50 billion a 92 percent increase. These rates of growth reflect the rapidly increasing demand for foreign exchange needed to accommodate the growth of international trade and investment.

Other evidence of foreign appetites for international securities can be seen in the recent strong increases in foreign purchases of U.S. equities. This statistic has remained about $5 billion per year during the early eighties but has been estimated at $20 billion for 1986 and projected at $30 billion for 1987. In the second quarter of 1986 the foreign sector was the largest single buyer of U.S. common stocks. This trend reflects the general interest of foreigners in the U.S. equity market. In the reverse direction, data show that the investment of U.S. pension money (ERISA) invested overseas more than quintupled from $5 billion in 1979 to $26 billion in 1985. Other data show that the level of international bonds floated in 1986 reached $241 billion, an increase of 51 percent from 1985, which in turn exceeded the prior year by more than 50 percent. All of these increases in portfolio investment shadow the stunted increase in U.S. direct investment abroad. That statistic increased by $19.7 billion in 1985 to a total of $232.7 billion, following only a $5.8 billion increase in 1984 and a slight decrease in 1983.

There are many reasons for the striking increase in interest in international portfolio investment. These include the improved risk-return relationship that off-shore investing offers and the increased recognition of these advantages by international investors. Certain institutional developments have also stimulated the awakened interest in international investment. The advent of currency swaps and interest-rate swaps which enable investors to invest in one currency and receive payments in another, or invest in one maturity and receive interest based on a different maturity; the rapid growth of floating-rate notes where yields are pegged to a market basis that can be adjusted to reflect prevailing market conditions; and the recent trends toward securitizing debt which results in a more attractive form of return than some conventional loans. Each of these forces that have kindled interest in international investment is examined in more detail in the chapters that follow. The next section provides a brief summary of the content of the balance of the book.

ORGANIZATION OF THE BOOK

The *Handbook of International Investing* has been designed to provide a thorough understanding of the process of investment in international securities. Its purpose is to inform interested investors about the returns and risk inherent in international investment. It begins and ends with an historical perspective providing information on the transitional process of international investment as well as recent performance of various markets in international securities. The book addresses each of the major aspects of risk faced by international investors and provides detailed discussions of how to manage each type of risk. The role of diversification and balanced portfolios is thoroughly covered in a manner that is helpful to both the novice and the experienced investor. International markets frequently provide opportunities for yield enhancement to informed investors. These factors are treated carefully in a series of chapters related specifically to alternative returns across multinational securities markets.

There has been extensive innovation in the instruments that are now included on the menu available for selection by international investors. This expanded set of opportunities is covered in a group of chapters that addresses many of the unique instruments that are available only to international investors as well as those instruments that are more broadly available in today's security markets. Another set of chapters covers typical strategies of institutional and private international investors and provides case studies of successful approaches to the problem of international investment. Management questions involving accounting, taxation, legal and other peripheral issues round out the book.

The book has been written by a combination of skilled practitioners and academics, each a specialist in his or her own field of international investment. In this way it brings together theory and practice in a combination that can be readily intelligible to practicing international investors. The book has been designed to provide a starting point for investors seeking to engage in the international markets for the first time. In this regard we have attempted to define terms and concepts so that they can be understood by prospective international investors. But the content of the book goes beyond the basic concepts and addresses many of the techniques and strategies used by advanced players in this rapidly growing market. As such, the book will provide a very valuable reference resource for even the most proficient international investors.

INTERNATIONAL INVESTMENT ASSESSMENT

The book begins with an assessment of international investing. Section I attempts to set the stage for the process before it is explored more deeply in the sections that follow. In Section I we first examine the historical background of international investment and its implications for modern international investors. In this chapter Irene Finel-Honigman develops the history of the process of international investment from medieval times. As she points out, many of the concepts are not new but have been used for centuries by international investors. Next, the more important terms used by international investors are defined. Here Kevin Salwen develops a brief but interesting glossary which shows how many of the terms are used in today's markets. In Chapter 4, Raj Aggerwal presents in considerable detail the wide range of alternatives currently available to investors interested in crossing national borders. This chapter provides a comprehensive menu of the forms which can be employed to accomplish an international investment presence.

In order to evaluate the potential scale of international portfolio investment, two chapters by Richard Segal, Kathryn Jonas and Mark Sladkus present current data on the size of the global fixed income and equity markets. These chapters develop more fully some of the summary data that I presented earlier in this chapter. The massive size of these markets in many countries presents a staggering potential to those who are just beginning to evaluate international investment opportunities. These chapters are followed by a very comprehensive review by Terry Mason covering the recent movements toward deregulation of world capital markets. To complete the assessment of recent innovations in international investment, Tran Hung has developed an excellent chapter outlining the swiftly developing trend toward securitization in international finance. With this background in hand, the reader is ready to consider the incremental dimensions of the risks associated with international investing and how to manage them. Material highlighting each of these supplemental risks together with the application of traditional and recently developed management tools is presented in Section II.

MANAGING RISK IN AN INTERNATIONAL PORTFOLIO

Section II begins with a chapter rooted in the macroeconomic aspects of foreign exchange risk. This dimension of the aggregate risk of investment may be avoided in certain domestic investment initiatives, but cannot escape careful consideration by international investors. Professor Laurent Jacque examines the forces that lead to changes in exchange rates and provides suggestions regarding overall policies that would be helpful in managing this highly pervasive component of risk faced by international investors. In the next chapter, Professor Christine Hekman deals with the same risk from a microeconomic perspective. Here she examines the way in which foreign exchange risk may impact on the performance of individual securities within an international portfolio. She then shows how foreign exchange risk can be managed, in part, within the confines of the choice of individual companies selected by an international investor.

Section II continues with a detailed analysis of the role of interest rate risk in international portfolios. Since much of international investment resides in fixed-income securities for which interest rate risk is most significant and since foreign exchange movements are closely related to relative movements in interest rates, the material contained in this chapter is particularly important to international investors. Samuel Weaver has integrated the difficult concepts of foreign exchange risk and interest-rate risk into this very readable chapter.

A third important component of the aggregate risk faced by all investors deals with the variability of returns to the investor. This risk, which is related to the risk of the individual enterprise, its creditworthiness, and the systematic behavior of the particular economy and culture in which the investment is domiciled, is frequently measured by the expected variability of returns from the investment. It has been couched domestically in terms of the capital asset pricing model (CAPM), with its emphasis on betas. The international version of the CAPM has, perhaps, even more robust possibilities for improvement in the risk-return trade-off than has a reasonably well balanced domestic portfolio. Adrian Lee leads us into the possibilities provided by well managed positions in international portfolios and shows how the imperfect correlation in currency movements themselves serves to reduce the risk of an international portfolio that is properly allocated among available assets and currencies.

Recent advances in derivative security products have provided the means to match asset and liability positions in various currencies and maturities in order to effectively hedge both foreign currency and interest rate risks. Lee Thomas carefully and methodically develops the role of futures and options in hedging foreign currency risk by providing easy to follow diagrams of the way in which foreign currency futures and options can be used to progressively alter the distribution of possible outcomes to a hedged portfolio. In the course of this development, he is also able to illustrate the near equivalence of certain futures and options strategies. In the next chapter, he applies some of the newly developed concepts of portfolio insurance in using option replication strategies to manage foreign currency exposures.

INSTRUMENTS AVAILABLE TO INTERNATIONAL INVESTORS

Whereas Section II dealt with the evaluation and management of the risk implicit in international portfolios, Section III treats many of the newly developed features and instruments now available to international investors. Since international investors frequently begin with an interest in fixed-income securities and since these issues make up the majority of the market available to international portfolio investors, we begin with them. Edward Hart discusses the characteristics of international fixed-income securities while at the same time explaining the use of fixed-income securities denominated in various currencies in an international portfolio. Hence this chapter is both a description of instruments with emphasis on euro and foreign bonds, and a basic introduction to the allocation of a fixed-income portfolio by currency.

A subset of international fixed-income securities that has witnessed spectacular growth through the first half of the eighties has been the floating-rate intermediate-term maturity bonds. These securities, with interest rates repriced at frequent intervals based on some market index, have been particularly attractive to investors with short-term liabilities and those who fear being locked in to a current rate for a long period. Gioia Parente has traced the development of the floating-rate market in recent years and presents a comprehensive discussion of its activity and relevance to both issuers and investors.

Most floating-rate issues are eurobonds, but not all eurobonds are floaters. Many eurobonds are fixed-rate and can be compared with domestic fixed-rate bonds of similar issuers. In the next chapter, Richard Segal provides a rigorous analysis of the determinants of the yield differential between eurodollar and domestic dollar bonds. This chapter should be of particular interest to those international investors that participate in arbitrage-type transactions to take advantage of abnormal differences in yields among securities. The chapter on long-term eurodollar bonds is followed by another by Gioia Parente highlighting recent developments in the short-term sector of the eurocurrency markets. Here she examines recent activity in the euronote and eurocommercial paper markets. These markets have experienced extensive growth in recent years as a result of liberalization of regulations and practices among investors. They provide an added dimension to the process of international investment by offering an outlet for short-term funds that has many of the advantages formerly provided only by eurobonds.

The euromarkets constitute a comprehensive set of potential investment media. Other means of classifying instruments that have appeal to international investors are covered in the chapters on special currency, special issuers, and special characteristics and terms of the issue. With the vast extent of creativity and ingenuity that exists in world capital markets, it is not possible to report on all of the new features available to international investors. We have, however, selected three significant areas of major interest to international investors that have become popular in recent years. First is the rapid growth in interest in european currency unit (ECU) denominated bonds. The ECU is based on a basket of european currencies and has the advantage that its movements in value reflect the weighted average movements in the value of its constituent currencies. Hence the ECU is more stable than its member currencies. Moreover, the interest rate on ECU instruments is market determined based on the interest rates of the similar maturity issues denominated in the member currencies. These unique characteristics make ECU instruments very desirable for certain investors. Edward Rappa, et al., have outlined the development of the ECU and its use as an investment currency and present a case study to illustrate its potential for international investors.

Much has been written regarding the characteristics of government and industrial issues of fixed-income securities. However, little has been seen on the nature of securities issued by supranational institutions. Because these issues have always been of special interest to international investors and have also grown in amount outstanding, it seemed desirable to develop a chapter to provide a better understanding of these instruments. Lizabeth Palumbo has accomplished this in a comprehensive discussion of supranational instruments for world portfolios.

The last chapter in Section III provides a necessary link between fixed-income instruments and equity securities. Here Michael Katz traces the application of warrants and conversion features to international fixed-income instruments. Their use has become quite popular of late and, under certain conditions, enables the international investor to introduce an added measure of currency flexibility within his portfolio. Katz provides easily understood numerical case studies of the use of equity securities in the context of international investment.

It is notable that we have not attempted to provide a chapter on international equities. While perhaps desirable, such a chapter would have been redundant. Equities are generally similar in most countries, are usually understood by domestic investors, and offer little to examine beyond the various elements of risk and risk management covered elsewhere in this handbook. Moreover, extensive material on the nature of equity markets has been provided in the chapters that deal with the size of the world equity market and the returns on international equities.

OPPORTUNITIES FOR YIELD ENHANCEMENT IN INTERNATIONAL MARKETS

Having examined many of the special attributes of instruments available to international investors, in Section IV we look at some of the opportunities that international markets offer for the enhancement of yields to investors. The prospects for yield enhancement are first examined in terms of whether international capital markets are fully integrated or fully segmented, for only if some degree of segmentation prevails would it be possible to obtain improved returns from properly managed international deployment of funds. Richard Pettway and Craig Tapley examine this question in a conveniently developed experiment and conclude that for actively traded securities in highly liquid markets a high degree of integration exists. Nevertheless, not all international securities are so actively traded and there are many situations in which significant yield enhancement is available to international investors.

The first illustration of yield enhancement available in international markets is based on a set of deep rooted market anomalies that enable investors to take advantage of improvements in yields that result from differential pricing in various national capital markets, including the euromarkets. In the chapter on yield enhancement using financial swaps, I attempt to show why deployment of funds into alternative currencies can lead to fully hedged, above market yields after the transaction cost necessary to put the requisite swaps in place. Case studies are used to illustrate the strategies involved.

In the next chapter, Adrian Lee develops an international application of modern portfolio theory to show how optimal currency hedging strategies can lead to risk-return combinations superior to those available in individual domestic markets. This is followed by a thorough discussion of American Depositary Receipts (ADRs) by Officer and Hoffmeister. This chapter provides informative material on the characteristics and use of the ADR and shows that the use of ADRs can lead to returns greater than those provided by the domestic market alone.

These examples of yield enhancement in international markets are far from exhaustive. As the new frontiers becoming available to international investors become more thoroughly explored, many more opportunities will unfold. International investment offers many new and untried avenues for enhanced returns for enterprising investors to uncover. Some initiatives will fail, but others, including many already undertaken, will provide handsome all-in returns (after the cost of risk management) to those who are persistent enough to investigate the possibilities.

INVESTORS IN INTERNATIONAL PORTFOLIOS

Section V considers the attributes and approaches of various types of investors in international securities. Until a few years ago cross-border investment activity was limited to very wealthy individual investors who employed the services of an investment advisor or trust department of a major institution, or to institutional investors who were daring enough to utilize foreign securities in their portfolios despite the increased fiduciary responsibilities that this practice entailed. More recently, however, international investment has become more attractive to both institutional and individual investors. The former have been driven to increased international investment by a number of forces including (in the United States) competitive pressure to obtain more attractive risk-adjusted yields and (in Japan and elsewhere) a lack of market availability for the huge flows of funds seeking investment. Individual investors have found it attractive to move funds abroad to obtain better returns and easier to do so through the use of regional, global and international mutual funds, ADRs and direct investment in multiple listed foreign securities.

The three chapters of Section V detail much of the material of special interest to these various sets of international investors. In the first chapter, Gavin Dobson, who has had extensive experience in an internationally active mutual fund organization, takes the perspective of the individual investor and lists his choices and opportunities when considering international investment alternatives. Next, Timothy Prince, who, similarly, has had widespread experience in managing a large international pension fund outlines an institutional investor's approach to international investment. Finally, Michael Rosenberg, whose firm provides a weekly advisory service to international investors, offers his views on global bond portfolio management.

PERIPHERAL ISSUES

As in any endeavor, there are always a number of loose ends that warrant attention but which don't fit conveniently with other related material. I have combined three of these important areas into Section VI under the rubric of peripheral issues. They consist of accounting procedures, alternative taxation practices, and various national legal codes as they affect the process of international investment.

To attempt an exhaustive and fully complete listing of the effects of these issues on the international investment process is far too ambitious (and lengthy) for an introductory handbook. Nevertheless, we have been able to provide a reasonably comprehensive treatment of the impact of each of these disciplines on international investors in the chapters of Section VI. Professor Frederick Choi, with his wide range of background in international accounting, explains the effects of alternative accounting procedures on international investment performance. Similarly, Frank Grey and Douglas Nakajima have painstakingly distilled the myriad of tax questions into an orderly discussion of taxation as an incentive or impediment to international portfolio investment. Moving to the legal implications of international portfolio investment, Anthony Bartolini, et al., place the issues inherent to international investment into the proper legal perspective of each of a number of representative host countries. While these chapters are not intended to make experts of their readers in any of these peripheral areas, they do provide a very valuable and essential insight that can be significant in an international investment (or disinvestment) decision.

SUMMARY

Section VII provides a true summary of the work. It again draws on historical data to provide a sense of how attractive it has been to invest in international securities. Thus it represents a thorough summary of how effective the process would have been over the last decade. Kathleen Weber and Susan Badyna provide an eight-year summary of the investment performance obtained by investing in short-term and long-term international fixed-income securities in the major capital markets of the world. In the last chapter, Professor Roger Ibbotson and Lawrence Siegel provide data on equity returns for each major stock market in the developed world. They also provide data on the correlation of returns across countries and related information on various aspects of each of the major world equity markets.

No attempt will be made here to interpret the attractiveness of the returns that have been available to international investors. That remains for interested investors to do for themselves. The implications are obvious. What is needed is for potential international investors to overcome fear and inertia by learning more about a promising process and its opportunities. Perhaps this book may make a small contribution in moving this process along.

CHAPTER TWO

Dr. Irene Finel-Honigman received her Ph.D. from Yale University in 1973. Since 1980, she has been Director of the French Language Program, Credit Lyonnais Bank, New York. Former Coordinator of French Language Projects for the New York City Commission to the United Nations, she taught at Georgetown University and Lehman College (C.U.N.Y.). She has lectured at the New York University Institute of International Business on the history and etymology of foreign exchange, the Hartwick Institute of Humanities in Management, the Ecole Superieure de Commerce de Lyon, and other institutions. A member of the Institute of Research in History, her publications have appeared in *Foreign Language Annals, Modern Fiction Studies, Contemporary French Civilization, French for Business and International Trade,* and *The French Review.*

A HISTORICAL PERSPECTIVE OF INTERNATIONAL INVESTORS AND INVESTMENTS

Dr. Irene Finel-Honigman
Credit Lyonnais
New York, New York

INTRODUCTION

On April 26, 1399 Francesco Datini's correspondent in Bruges advised the Florentine banking house to place its funds in the following fashion:

"It appears that there is an abundance of specie in Genoa, so do not send our money to Genoa, or only if you can get a very good price for it; put it rather in Venice or Florence or here in Bruges, or in Paris, or Montpellier, or wherever seems best to you."[1]

Since the fourteenth century, merchants, bankers and currency dealers (money handlers) have been interested in how and where to invest their gold and silver earnings and profits abroad. The growth of foreign exchange markets and investment strategies have been key factors in Western Europe's economic development. The resurgence of trade routes and Mediterranean commerce during the first three Crusades (1095-1192) revived merchants, moneyhandlers and mercenaries' circulation of goods and currency throughout the previously isolated and monometallic (silver) Northern European kingdoms and principalities.

Large seasonal markets, in Champagne and Flanders, religious fairs and trading houses became the forums which generated and put into circulation many of the negotiable instruments and transactional networks which still dominate modern investment. They acted as embryonic clearing houses where bills of exchange, discount notes, letters of credit, and short- and medium-term exchange contracts were instituted between merchant/bankers in France, Spain, Italy and the Low Countries. Long before the advent of the influential role of London and New York's international financial centers, Genoa, Venice, Amsterdam, Bruges and Antwerp dominated commerce and finance with active currency dealings, short term gold and silver contracts, and futures markets in commodities.

Today's investment sums are significantly larger than ever before in history: millions have become billions, and the abstraction of paper and electronic numbers have replaced the tangible species of gold and silver. Nevertheless, the philosophical interpretation of investment and foreign exchange remains familiar: "A single currency has now been imposed on most of the world: but is it any more of a universal phenomenon than the Spanish piastre was, or more recently, the pound sterling? The fact is that until the world does away with all currencies, they will be devalued and revalued against each other, and all of them together against commodities, whichever of them is chosen as the standard for measuring and payment in international exchanges."[2]

A historical perspective can provide a broader understanding of the attitudes, trends and concepts which influence present day financial markets and investments, and also can serve as a research basis for conjectural analysis of future economic and sociogeographic shifts and ideologies.

METHODOLOGY

In tracing the socioeconomic and cultural attitudes toward finance and profit, this study of international investors' European antecedents follows the precepts of economic and social historian Fernand

Braudel.[3] Braudel has described the evolution of economic history as influenced by the following factors:

1) the need for a symbiotic relationship between the marketplace and a competitive mercantile society.
2) a broader definition of capital and capitalism which preceded Marx and placed investment at home and abroad within a humanistic construct of trade, competitiveness and liberal economic policy.
3) the role and significance of the city or city state as a financial center: whereas a specific city becomes a financial nucleus: Genoa, Amsterdam, London and, after 1929, New York.

Braudel extrapolated from this gradual geoeconomic shift toward the West to a movement to the Pacific nations. This trend is indeed occurring, as witnessed by the growing importance of Tokyo, Hong Kong and Singapore, the leading roles of the dollar and the yen, and the choice of Tokyo for the May 1986 Economic Summit.[4]

In his final work *La dynamique du capitalisme* (1984), Braudel predicted a long-term cyclical return to the originators of Western capitalism, Italy and Spain.

DEFINITIONS AND ANTECEDENTS

The term *investment* derives from the Latin *investare* (to don, to put on). *Investment* was first used in a modern financial context (circa 1783) in relation to monies placed in the East Indies Trade Company: "...a portion of revenues of Bengall has been set apart to be employed in purchase of goods for exportation to England and this is called the Investment."[5]

Investment of "capital" separate from "goods" also appears in early nineteenth-century tracts, taxation documents and stock subscriptions in England, but the actual concept was already described in Renaissance exchange contracts used in the silver markets to distinguish fixed versus circulating capital.

Who were the first international investors and where did they originate? Political and religious unrest in the late Middle Ages and during the war-ridden Renaissance forced into political exile a wealthy urban merchant class. The "fuorisciti," exiled old noble families in Italian city states, reestablished themselves in other Italian and French cities and continued to trade and to transact currency deals with their former colleagues (Braudel, II, p. 167).

The functions of bankers, moneyhandlers and merchants often overlapped. In the late thirteenth century, the historian Raymond DeRoover documented that the Lombards in Italy, the Cahorsians in Bruges, and Jewish moneyhandlers in Italy and England (referred to in Boccaccio's *Decameron* and Chaucer's *Canterbury Tales*) were associated with short-term "usurious" transactions while the "banchi grossi" of Florence dealt in international trade and coordinated government and papal loans. In 1470 the House of Medici had branches with banking functions outside of Italy in Lyon, Bruges, Avignon and London. Account books were kept in *florins*, the official gold coin minted in Florence and convertible throughout Europe. An active foreign exchange market flourished in thirteenth- and fourteenth-century Venice, Florence and Genoa, whose ruling Doges and princes encouraged currency exports and generated large loans to support England's military expeditions against France.

The 1596 records of the Besancon fairs describe the proceedings of wealthy merchants, government emissaries, brokers and important moneychangers (banchieri de canto: exchange rate bankers) who came from Genoa, Spain and Florence to establish a club (a *syndicat*) that regulated the rates of exchange by decree (*decretudos*). From 60-200 men paid a hefty membership fee of 3,000 gold ecus for the privilege of deciding rates and closing deals worth 30 to 40 million ecus: "Four times a year it was the scene of decisive but discreet meetings, something like the International Bank of Basle in our day" (Braudel, Vol. 1, P. 91).

In the fifteenth and sixteenth centuries, the Jewish merchant class in Spain, forced into conversion, fled to Holland to escape the Inquisition. These *marranos* often reverted to Judaism and became integrated into a Dutch middle class with direct links to Spain and

Portugal. A century later French Protestant bankers and businessmen, exiled after Louis XIV's Revocation of the Edict of Nantes in 1682, also fled to Holland and continued dealings with their contacts in Bordeaux, La Rochelle and Paris. In strategically placed cities like Vienna and Leipzig money markets flourished as refugee centers and focal points for trade between the West and the Ottoman Empire.

THE ROLE OF INVESTORS IN THE RENAISSANCE

During the reign of Francois I in France (1517-1547) and the unification of Europe under the Holy Roman Empire (1519), large merchant investment houses emerged, led by powerful, energetic men whose demeanor, luxurious lifestyle and keen business sense were similar to today's Goldsmiths, Rothschilds, Schlumbergers and Rockefellers. The two most representative banker/trader/investors were Jacob Fugger of Augsburg and Thomas Gresham of London. Fugger dominated the entire European currency, silver and copper market from the 1520's to the 1550's. His influence extended throughout Europe and the Ottoman Empire with representative offices in Budapest, Cracow, Breslaw, Danzig, Nuremburg, Mainz, Cologne, Antwerp, Venice, Rome, Naples, Lisbon and Madrid. Painted by Durer, known and respected by kings, advisor to Charles V, Holy Roman Emperor, Fugger ruled his own vast commercial empire involved in banking, underwriting maritime and government loans, land, mining and business holdings. He had a monopoly on copper and silver mining with exclusive rights to control prices. In 1523, in one of the first recorded antitrust suits, the High Council of Cologne accused Fugger of monopolizing the industry and trade of Augsburg. He invoked the help of the Emperor and won back his rights to continue control of traffic in metals and currency. Fugger's advice to those seeking to invest in the Orient was "the principle is to invest one's capital into three parts: one third in land, one third in precious commodities and one third in business" (Petit-Dutaillis, p. 75-106).

Sir Thomas Gresham, Elizabeth I's financial advisor, began his career as negotiator of bills of exchange in London's Change Alley and dealer in Spanish short-term gold contracts. Titled by Elizabeth I in 1559 as ambassador to the Netherlands, he speculated between the florin and sterling on the Antwerp Exchange. He also began an active traffic in the Spanish state bonds *Juros* issued by Philippe II of Spain. Returning to England in 1566 Gresham created the Royal Exchange based on the Amsterdam Bourse.

Both Christopher Marlowe in his *The Jew of Malta* (1591-1592) and Shakespeare with his character Shylock in *The Merchant of Venice* were responding to an English public's awareness of and interest in the persona of the financier. But while plagued by associations with usury and antisemitic traits, this financier also was representative of a new internationalism and prosperity: "But yesterday two ships went from the town. Their voyage will be worth ten thousand crowns. In Florence, Venice, Antwerp, London, Seville, Frankfurt, Lubech, Moscow and where not, have I debts owning, and in most of these, great sums of money."[7]

THE "BELGIAN DENTIST" AND THE FIRST EUROBOND MARKET

Modern international investment still remains the realm of powerful institutions, but it is also an area of lucrative endeavor for the professional middle class: dubbed the "Belgian dentist" by the English press (see *Euromoney Anniversary Issue,* June 1984, "In Search of the Belgian Dentist").[8] This conservative bourgeois placed his carefully earned funds in safe, government-backed securities.

Now the "Belgian dentist" has found his counterpart in the American pediatrician, who also turns toward foreign investments: "Dr. Marvyn D. Cohen decided last year to try something new with some of the $200,000 he had saved for retirement. After hearing a lecture given by an investment specialist at Shearson Lehman Brothers Inc., the pediatrician from Columbus, Ga., decided to put a portion of his money into a mutual fund specializing in foreign investments.

'This economist said it was logical for Americans to be more world-minded, that we're not an isolated group,' said Dr. Cohen, who at the time had exclusively invested in various United States equities. 'It made good sense to me.'"[9]

Both the "Belgian dentist" and the American pediatrician are similar in complexion and mentality to their Dutch, Spanish or Genovese ancestors who invested in the first state-issued bonds. These instruments were backed by guarantee of the Spanish crown in the 1550's. Termed *Juros,* they subsidized international trade and investment in the Americas (Mexico and Peru) and short-term gold contracts.

RENAISSANCE CONCEPTS AND INSTRUMENTS: THE ECU

The development of economic theories was part of the Renaissance humanistic quest and discovery of knowledge in all fields. Philosophers and clerics discussed mathematics and applied new conceptual analyses to economic as well as semantic, literary, or theological phenomena. Montaigne, in his *Essais* (1598), discussed rates of exchange tables which had been published in Antwerp by Simon Stevins, a mathematician who had printed rules for computing simple and compound interest *(Tables of Interest Rules,* Plantin, 1582).

The Spanish cleric Tomas de Mercado wrote *Summa de tratos y contratos,* 1562, 1572 (Transactions and Contracts), in which he differentiated between the value versus the cost of money (silver) in different countries by comparing currency prices in Italy, Spain, France and Flanders. The Spanish bankruptcy of 1557 had repercussions in the Netherlands and France, where a weakened decentralized system needed to be strengthened and restructured. In 1576 a *Cour de Monnaies* (Monetary Tribunal) was set up under Jean Bodin's leadership. Bodin, jurist and humanist, wrote treatises on foreign exchange; called for a need to control prices and wages; established the relationship between trade and influx of currency; and described the need to establish an account money, the *Ecu*, to offset inflation of devalued money in circulation (*Response a Malestroict,* Paris: 1578).[10]

The European Currency Unit, the Ecu, introduced in April 1975 and created as the central unit of the European Monetary System in December 1978, has its etymological and conceptual roots in a French gold coin called ''ecu de marc'' and ''ecu de soleil,'' which served as a fixed account money for purpose of bookkeeping and settlement of foreign transactions. The historical ecu was imposed by Henri III in his ordinances of 1577 to help stabilize rampant inflation of the French *livre tounois* due to Spanish silver flooding the French money market. Between 1630 and 1680 ''there are more memoranda about money in seventeenth-century Spanish archives than there are in the hands of the International Monetary Fund today'' (Vilar, p. 15). As merchants and bankers became more sophisticated and knowledgable of trading instruments, rates and eurocurrency deals, countries had to impose restrictions on outflow of silver and to establish commissions and laws controlling the markets.

Braudel's study of Renaissance markets provided references to highly sophisticated exchange and reexchange (ricorsa) deals (similar to Swaps), kiting of checks, use of bills of exchange in lieu of credit facilities, extended bonds (Spanish ''Juros,'' French state ''rentes'') and speculation in commodity futures on the active Antwerp, Amsterdam and London exchanges. A 1643 traveler's guide described Antwerp ''into which there flowed every year 500 million in silver, 130 million in gold, not counting exchange currency which comes and goes like the tide'' (Braudel, III, p. 31).

THE DEVELOPMENT OF TRADING HOUSES

Amsterdam dominated the market through the seventeenth and mid-eighteenth century. The first Northern European state-chartered bank opened in Amsterdam in 1609, the Exchange opened in 1631, and then came the Dutch East Indies Company. Located next to each other in what became Europe's financial center, by 1657 the Dutch East Indies Company had sent abroad over 2 million florins in gold and silver. Speculation from all over Europe took place in Dutch East Indies shares and government stocks, "but what was new in Amsterdam was the volume, the fluidity of the market and the publicity it received and the speculative freedom of transactions" (Braudel, III, p. 101).

However, this market also involved what the Dutch called "windhandel," trade in the wind. Such transactions were similar to today's financial futures where "people were not content simply to buy and sell shares, speculating on their possible rise or fall, but where one could by means of various ingenious combinations speculate without having any money or shares at all" (Braudel, II, p. 101).

Italy during this period retained its position in the capital markets in Genoa and Venice. The Genoa *lire di banco* was an account money that circulated throughout Europe, held a constant weight of 0.328 grams of gold from 1675 to 1793, and encouraged investments in France, Austria, Bavaria, Lyon and Amsterdam (271 million in 1725 and 342 million in 1785) (Braudel, III, p. 173). Similar to the modern Eurodollar, the *lire di banco* offered a hedge against rate inflation and unstable domestic currencies. Venice in 1619 also set up a state bank, Banco Giro, which sought to control its accounts and attempted to regulate the outflow and circulation of its currency.

THE ROLE OF LONDON: EIGHTEENTH-CENTURY ECONOMIC EPICENTER

The creation of the Bank of England in 1694 effected a gradual shift in the worldwide financial center from Amsterdam to London. The Exchange, Change Alley and Lombard Street in London would dominate the global money market through the 1920's. Indeed, London's recent move toward deregulation and international trading—"The Thatcher government has recognized that the globalization of financial markets was an irresistable force" *(New York Times*, 12/22/85)—represents a return to London's historical position as world center for speculation, trade, government bonds, short- and long-term loans and free circulation of goods and capital.

Historically, London's global position was most strengthened by the trading houses: the South Sea Company (1711 charter), the East India Company (1726), Lloyds insurance and private investment house (1730)—which throughout the eighteenth century carried major subscriptions by foreign investors to government bonds. Also, England's prestige and influence in financial markets resided in part in its strong domestic currency, that never required monies of account to offset inflation and circulation instability. The British pound sterling, established under Sir Thomas Gresham in 1560 at 4 ounces sterling silver, held this ratio till 1920.[11]

England, like France in the 1780's and early 1790's, had an excess of specie in its bank vaults and was exporting nearly 7 million pounds sterling per year! In the eighteenth century, London's sound financial standing allowed its institutions to absorb the losses incurred in one of the first large-scale investment schemes: the South Sea Bubble (1715), based on the sale of paper shares for gold in a futures scheme to develop the South Seas.

FRENCH INVESTMENTS: CONCEPTS AND ATTITUDES

A far more serious economic and sociocultural disruption in the politically precarious, heavily endebted French economy occurred between 1718-1720. John Law, Scot gambler, speculator and part-time economist, wrote a tract in 1709 entitled *Money and Trade Considered,* in which he argued that the more money in circulation, the more prosperity a country would enjoy. Law advocated widespread circulation of paper money to counteract deficits in gold reserve. He came to Paris in 1718, received a royal charter to set up a bank and the trading house, Companie des Indes, selling paper shares in overseas investment in French Louisiana for gold. France was already involved in heavy speculation between gold and paper (billets) since the louis d'or devaluation in 1709. This type of speculation, "agiotage," was immensely popular and promoted Law's scheme. However, in 1720, when investors began to ask The Royal Bank for their return in specie, the "Mississippi Bubble" burst with large-scale bankruptcies. A traumatic backlash against investment, banking and finance inculcated in the French a wariness and isolationist attitude toward overseas investments, market speculation and state banks. France then did not export but instead hoarded its gold, and records from the 1750-1781 period describe large *imports* of Spanish and Dutch currency through Bordeaux and Lyon.

French and British attitudes and trends in investment reflect their cultural and socioeconomic views of money and power. The writings of Adam Smith (1776), The Italian Galiani (1750, translated into French 1821), Jean Baptiste Says' *Traite d'economie politique* (1803), and the philosophical theories of Auguste Comte and his disciple Saint Simon reevaluated the relationship of wealth to political power, societal reforms and prosperity. Money, "L'Argent," became a focal point of political stability and an essential criteria in a politically active middle class' quest for new values and identity after the French Revolution. In nineteenth-century French and English literature, theater and art (Balzac, Flaubert, Claretie, Dickens, Zola, Shaw),[12] fictional characters revolved around an economic axis where money—either inherited, earned or gained by speculation in the market—functioned as a subtext to all personal and societal relationships. However, where England continued its tradition of externalizing its economic perspective toward its colonial empire and maintaining its global role, France throughout the Second Empire (1852-1870) continued to focus on internal financial development and remained wary and prejudiced toward foreign investments. Even in the 1890's, right-wing French politicians and writers viewed involvement in market speculation, foreign exchange and international investment as subversive and "no longer...in solidarity with French destinies."[13]

In fact, the most important nineteenth-century French investors, bankers and "capitalists" were foreigners either by nationality or religion. The Pereire brothers, Jules Mires—whose large investment in the Ottoman Empire ended in fraudulent bankruptcy charges, and the Rothschilds represented international interests. The very active French Bourse of the 1830's and 1840's dealt mainly in domestic issues, and, even in the Second Empire, Mexican bonds sponsored by the government were the only popular foreign instruments. The prosperity and spirit of initiative in Napoleon III's Second Empire encouraged profits to be reinvested in businesses, in landownership (*la propriete*) and in careful estate management (*prudence dans la gestion du patrimoine*)[14]—all focusing on the internal rather than international economic development.

Only after defeat in the Franco-Prussian War was France able to turn to the outside world for new channels of investment. The devalued, cheap franc encouraged the influx of foreign money into France. By 1900 the Credit Lyonnais had established itself in Alexandria, Barcelona, Seville, Bruxelles, Constantinople, Geneva, Jerusalem, London, Madrid, Moscow, St. Petersburg and Smyrna.[15]

The development of French and English investment in their African and Asian empires was another form of sociocultural colonization. European money was exported to build schools, hospitals, roads, and to impress the language, culture and religion of the colonizer in an economic crusade.

The Third Republic before the First World War saw a vast increase in foreign investment; whereas foreign issues traded on the Paris Exchange were from only 15 countries in 1867-1868, in the 1910-1911 period they rose to 40 countries including Russia, Egypt, Japan and the United States (Plessis, p. 51).

However, a residual wariness toward foreign investments is still prevalent in today's markets. An *Expansion* article on May 16, 1986 on the Tokyo summit analyzed France's key weakness as "insufficiency of investments which explains the loss of certain sectors of the market (in France and abroad). . . ."

INTRODUCTION OF THE U.S. DOLLAR

The American Revolution had initiated the shift of European currencies toward the new continent. Before 1776, England kept a strict control over the Colonies' economy in order to eliminate trade competition and maintain dependence on British loans. As in medieval

Europe, currency remained unstable, with individual colonies minting their own coins. Accounts abroad were limited to bills of exchange sold to travelers returning to England, where they then could be traded in London or Amsterdam.

Holland continued to be the largest subscriber to overseas loans. Throughout the eighteenth century, Amsterdam was inundated by German sovereigns, French gold louis, and British silver after 1776. The Dutch invested in English funds and state loans, and in American shares. Braudel quoted the papers of Louis Greffulhe, head of a "counting house" and broker in 1778 in Amsterdam: " 'Your former clerk Bringley,' wrote Greffulhe to A. Gaillard in Paris, 'is up to his ass in Americans.' As for himself, Greffulhe, who had a finger in every promising pie, went in for speculation on the Stock Exchange in a big way, on commission. He acted for himself and for others, for Rodolphe Emmanuel Haller (who had taken over the old. . .bank), for Jean-Henri Gaillard, the Perregaux, the ubiquitous Panchauds, bankers in Paris and Geneva, for Alexandre Pictet, Philibert Cramer, Turrettini—all names written in gold in the ledgers of Protestant banking. The game was difficult and risky, with very large sums of money at stake. But in the end, if Greffulhe played it with such aplomb it was because he was staking other people's money. If they lost, it annoyed him, but it was no tragedy" (Braudel, II, p. 104).

The American Congress of 1778 established a continental currency (a paper money) and began to issue short-term treasury obligations. Beginning in 1781, attempts at regulation and centralization of the money supply culminated in the creation of the Bank of North America (1781) in Philadelphia and of the Bank of New York (1784). Currency legislation of July 3, 1789 defined the dollar's par value against the British Sterling, 1 pound sterling = 4.44 dollars. The ratio remained steady from 1792 to 1830, encouraging an active export of American dollars through London. The French consul to New York described a very modern economic community in 1810: "New York can be described as a permanent fair in which two-thirds of the population is always being replaced, where huge business deals are being made, almost always with fictitious capital and where luxury has reached alarming heights'' (Braudel, III, p. 406, Letter of October 27, 1810).

The theme of investment and speculation in domestic and foreign stocks also enterered the cultural realm of popular literature and theater. The French stage from the 1680's through the 1750's abounded in plays, essays and pamphlets on commodities, bankers, agiotage (Dancourt, *Les Agioteurs,* 1710); financial schemes (Le Sage, *Tucaret,* 1709); (Voltaire, *Lettres Sur le Commerce; Lettres Philosophiques X,* 1760). In England the works of John Locke, Daniel Defoe and Jonathan Swift focused on investment schemes, stock market transactions, and foreign exchange with references to the American Colonies' financial potential.[16]

THE DEVELOPMENT OF THE U. S. POSITION

The 1820-1920 period forced the United States to rapidly absorb experience and knowledge of foreign markets, to undergo the necessary cyclical crisis of economic and monetary restructurization, and to establish regulatory institutions and procedures in order to compete with European markets.

An influx of Dutch and French money helped finance the railroads, once America had overcome its own currency deficiencies and inadequate supply which ''caused the United States to be regarded as an international nuisance'' through the 1820's.[17] However, the widespread financial crisis of 1856-1857 on Wall Street and on the Paris Exchange frightened many Europeans, who divested themselves of American securities and curtailed the flow of capital to the United States.

The United States also was plagued by a continued bimetallic standard (established in 1792) while England by 1821 had accepted the standard formalized by the adoption of a gold standard for France, Italy, Belgium and Switzerland—the Latin Monetary Union of 1865. The United States finally adopted the gold standard in 1900. With a strong dollar promoting American investors to lend to China, Sweden, and Germany, as well as to Canada and South America, between the 1870's and 1929 the United States shifted from a debtor to a creditor nation.

The U.S. role, particularly in relation to France and England, changed drastically with the outbreak of World War I. The historian Margaret Myers judged this shift from London and Paris to New York to have been premature: "At the same time the war brought to the United States a flood of gold which pushed the dollar into the foreground of international finance, changed the direction of Federal Reserve development, and provided the basis for eventual inflation, stock market speculation, and collapse. . . . By the end of the war, foreign holdings of American securities had declined from 5.4 billion dollars in 1914 to 1.6 billion, and direct investment in American companies from 1.3 to .9 billion. Great Britain, which had held about 63 percent of all foreign-owned American securities, disposed of about three-fourths of them. France had owned only one-tenth as much as Britain, but sold off an even larger proportion. When their securities had been liquidated, the Allies had to borrow, and by the end of 1920 Great Britian owed the United States 4.2 billion dollars, France owed 3 billion, and Italy 1.6 billion" (Myers, p. 270).

As a result, U.S. loans issued in dollars (a primitive Eurodollar market) became extremely popular and seemingly profitable. Christine Stead's fictional account in *House of All Nations* (1938) described the role of American banks and interests in the Paris of 1930-1938, where the low cost of European securities in the aftermath of World War I attracted gullible U.S. investors. According to Margaret Myers' documentation, the total of foreign investment by Americans rose from 7 to 17 billion from 1920-1929 (Myers, p. 296). This rise was facilitated by the Edge Act of 1919 (amendment to the Federal Reserve Act of 1913), which allowed American corporations to issue foreign securities and open branch offices abroad.

REEVALUATION OF MONETARY CONTROLS

The crisis of 1929 forced a reevaluation of global money markets, and, like the English defaulting on Florentine loans in the bankruptcies of 1347, the Spanish crown default of 1577 and the Stock Market crash of 1857, the '29 crash promoted more stringent regulatory measures and a period of fixed rates, reduced investment and conservative attitudes. Each country needed to heal its wounds and strengthen its own economy before relaunching into foreign investments.

Recent emphasis on deregulation and a move toward an open global economy can be viewed as a reaction to overly stringent controls which are now judged as counterproductive to natural growth and discordant with international communications and electronic networks.

"The quantum increase in trading of financial instruments of all kinds, and the speed at which information on which trading decisions are based is supplied to institutions and individuals everywhere, has emasculated governments' powers to regulate their domestic money and capital markets from behind barricades that were established to protect them from events elsewhere. As a result, entire financial systems, and the regulations wrapped around them, that were built in the depression era of the 1930s (in the case of the United States) and in the postwar period (as in Japan) are swept by change" (*Euromoney,* "The Great Deregulation Explosion," October 1984).[18]

THE AMERICAN-JAPANESE CONNECTION

The United States has continued to influence the conditions of the money markets since World War II. The Bretton Woods Agreement of 1944 was countermanded by the Smithsonian Agreements of 1971 with its efforts to achieve greater stability, to control overactive fluctuations in foreign exchange, yet to keep open channels of cooperation between nations, to decrease isolation (even in Japan), and to increase global investment. This was followed by freely floating exchange rates among industrialized countries. Now "The Tokyo summit has laid the first cornerstone of a new international economic regime" (*Expansion:* Tokyo. . .May 16, 1986, p. 17).

Japan, with its combination of attitudes and American initiative, has become the new player in international finance. Like France in the eighteenth century and the United States in the nineteenth century, Japan has had to quickly adapt and assimilate modern market procedures and ideology. Historically, its ancient and insulatory civilization had encouraged merchant dynasties and had granted strong political power to a conservative, highly structured mercantile class. However, its rulers prohibited foreign trade between 1638 and 1868 by Imperial interdictions, encouraging literature and philosophy to scorn the mercantile profession and to retain a feudal ideology. Today, therefore, when "Investment Fever" is sweeping Japan—"For years, Mr. Kyu said, Japanese considered it shameful to talk about money. Now, he said, I'm in the center of money-crazy Japan"[19]—the country is reevaluating its economic identity and relations with western powers.

" 'Money fever,' as the Japanese call it, is rampant here as an increasingly affluent society discovers that there are other ways of amassing savings than simply depositing money in the bank" (Susan Chira, *New York Times,* March 29, 1986). And as described in a *New York Times* April 27, 1986 article: "Japan's emergence as a leading capital exporter is relatively recent," where in 1986 "So far this year the money has continued to flow overseas at the rate of about 7 billion a month."

CONCLUSION

As this historical overview illustrates, attitudes and policies toward international investment are closely linked to each nation's self image, cultural perceptions of commerce and profit, and socioeconomic needs in relation to other countries. Many of today's financial instruments used in the international investment market were first created during the Renaissance. The Ecu, the Eurobond, the eurodollar, and the futures concepts all have their antecedents in a highly sophisticated Western European merchant economy that allowed commerce to flourish and capital to continue circulating despite drawn-out religious wars and constant shifting of geopolitical alliances and borders.

Economic relationships can often bypass or transpass political conflicts and can create a substructure of international cooperation based on mutual interests and gain.

The vast schema and interrelated networks of international capital investment continue. The players change over the centuries, the methods of communication have become instantaneous, and the size of investment commitments has become truly massive; yet at its heart the modern investors' quest for wealth and discovery through knowledge of currencies and a spirit of risk-taking remains the same as when Jean Charter, cleric at the Abbey of Saint Denis, described the exploits of Jacques Coeur (1450), banker and investor of royal funds: "He invented the means and found all possible schemes in order to gain finances and to recover money in all places. . . ." (Petit-Dutaillis, p. 51).

NOTES

[1]Fernand Braudel, *The Perspective of the World, Civilization and Capitalism 15th-18th Century,* trans. Sian Reynolds (New York: Harper and Row, 1984) III, p. 101

[2]Pierre Vilar, *A History of Gold and Money 1450-1920,* (Barcelona: Anel, 1969, 1976) p. 17

[3]Fernand Braudel, *Civilization and Capitalism 15th-18th Century,* trans. Sian Reynolds (New York: Harper and Row, 1984) I, II, III; Fernand Braudel, *La dynamique du capitalisme* (Paris: Arthaud, 1985)

[4]References to this phenomenon in the recent press: "The New Global Top Banker: Tokyo and Its Mighty Money" (*New York Times,* April 27, 1986); "Investment 'Fever' Is Sweeping Japan" (*New York Times,* March 29, 1986); "Le Yen Imperial" (*Nouvel Economiste,* No. 532, May 2, 1986); "Tokyo consolide la croissance" (*L'Expansion,* May 16, 1986)

[5]*Oxford English Dictionary* Volume II (London: Oxford University Press, 1976) p. 1478. Burke 1783

[6]Georges Petit-Dutaillis, *Portraits de Banquiers* (Paris: La Revue Banque, 1982) p. 28; also see: Raymond de Roover, *The Rise and Decline of the Medici Bank* (Boston: Harvard University Press, 1963)

[7]Christopher Marlowe, *Plays and Poems,* introduction by Edward Thomas (New York: E.P. Dutton, 1950)

[8]"In Search of the Belgian Dentist" (*Euromoney Anniversary Issue,* June 1984); Paul Ferris, *The Master Bankers, Controlling the World's Finances* (New York: William Morrow and Co., 1984) Chapter 8, "Belgian Dentists" p. 235-250

[9]Scott Bronstein, "Americans Finding Buys Overseas" (*New York Times,* June 1, 1986)

[10]References to the humanists' interest in finance mentioned in Braudel (op. cit.); Vilar (op. cit.); Henri Pirenne, *Histoire economique et sociale du Moyen Age* (Paris: 1933); Marc Shell, *Money, Language and Thought* (London: University of California Press, 1982); Daniel Boorstin, *The Discoverers* (New York: Random House, 1983) p. 396-398

[11]George Rude, *Hanoverian London 1714-1808,* University of California Press *History of London* series, (Berkeley: University of California Press, 1971) p. 21-36

[12]References to bankers, financiers and foreign investments appear in Balzac, *Le Pere Goriot* (1834), *La Maison Nucingen* (1837), which parodies the John Law investment scheme, *Un Homme d'Affaires* (1845); Flaubert, *L'Education Sentimentale* (1869), with Dambreuse's investment schemes; Jules de Claretie,

Le Million (1882); Charles Dickens, *Little Dorrit* (1857), with Mr. Merdle's shady speculation in foreign monies, *Nicholas Nickleby* (1839); Emile Zola, *L'Argent* (1891), based in part on the banker Jules Mires' deals with the Ottoman Empire; Bernard Shaw, *Major Barbara* (1906)

[13]Maurice Barres, *Les Deracines* (Paris: Plon, 1954) p. 249. "Le Capital agiote detruit, devient de plus en plus international et aspire a n'etre pas solidaire des destinees francaises."

[14]Alain Plessis: "La Bourse et la societe francaise du Second Empire" (*Romantisme, L'Argent,* No. 40, 1983) p. 49-50

[15]*Histoire Generale de la Presse Francaise* (Paris: Presses Universitaires, 1969) p. 513; Bulletin du Credit Lyonnais: Agences a l'Etranger (1900)

[16]*A History of Parisian Drama 1700-1715,* (London: Lancaster Series, 1951); John Locke, *Several Papers Relating to Money, Interest, and Trade* (London: 1696); Daniel Defoe, *The Fortunes and Misfortunes of the Famous Moll Flanders* (London: 1722); Defoe, *The Chimera: or the French Way of Paying National Debts, Laid Open* (London: 1720); Defoe, *The Complete English Tradesman* (1726); Jonathan Swift, *Drapiers Letters* (1724)

[17]Margaret Myers, *A Financial History of the United States* (New York: Columbia University Press, 1970) p. 247

[18]Peter T. Kilborn, "Rare Moment for a Global Economy" (*The New York Times,* Sunday, April 27, 1986) p. 1, p. 28; Serge Bellanger, "La dereglementation dans le secteur bancaire et financier" (*Banque,* No. 460, April 1986)

[19]See note 4

BIBLIOGRAPHY

Arnould, Ambroise. *De la balance du commerce et des relations commerciales exterieures de la France dans toutes les parties du globe* (Paris, 1791, Seligman Collection)

Bellanger, Serge. *''La Dereglementation dans le secteur bancaire et financier''* (*Banque,* No. 460, April 1986)

Bergel, Clive. *''Alternatives''* (*Nouvel Economiste,* March 21, 1986)

Bertier, Eric. *''Les Options sur Eurodollars futures''* (*Banque,* No. 457, January 1986)

Braudel, Fernand. *Civilization and Capitalism, 15th-18th century Vol. I: The Wheels of Commerce, Vol. III: The Perspective of the World* (Harper and Row, New York, 1984)

Braudel, Fernand. *La dynamique du capitalisme* (Arthaud, Paris, 1985)

Charmat. *Sur la Finance, la Banque et l'Agiotage* (1789) (Seligman Collection)

Chiro, Susan. *''Investment Fever Is Sweeping Japan''* (*New York Times,* March 29, 1986); *''The New Global Top Banker: Tokyo and Its Mighty Money''* (*New York Times,* April 27, 1986)

Condorcet. *Discours Sur les Finances* (1792) (Seligman Collection)

Dancourt. *Les Agioteurs* (Paris, 1710)

David, Jacques. *Crise financiere et relations monetaires internationales* (Economica, Paris, 1985)

Defoe, Daniel. *Moll Flanders* (Houghton, Boston, 1959)

Dehem, Roger. *Histoire de la pensee economique des mercantilistes a Keynes* (Dunod, Pierres de l'Universite, Laval, Paris, 1985)

Denizet, Jean. *Le Dollar: Histoire du systeme monetaire international depuis 1945* (Editions Fayard, Paris, 1985)

DeRoover, Raymond. *Money, Banking and Credit in Medieval Bruges* (Harvard, 1948); *Gresham on Foreign Exchange* (Cambridge, 1949); *L'Evolution de la Lettre de Change* (14eme au 18ieme siecle) (1953); *The Bruges Money Market Around 1400* (1953); *The Rise and Decline of the Medici Bank* (1963)

Fallon, P.H., Adam, N.H., Ollard, H. *''The Great Deregulation Explosion''* (*Euromoney,* October 1980)

Feder, Barnaby *''Foreign Money Spreading to All Walks of U.S. Life''* (*New York Times,* December 29, 30, 31, 1985); *''The Global Money Market Summit in Tokyo''* (*New York Times,* May 4, 1986)

Ferris, Paul. *The Master Bankers' Controlling of the World's Finances* (William Morrow, New York, 1984)

Flobert, P. *Recherches sur les billets de la banque de Law* (1716-1720) (Seligman Collection)

Freeze, John. *The Cambistes Compendium of Two Familiar Practical Treatises on Bills of Exchange* (London, 1828)

Gilbert, J. *The History and Principles of Banking* (London, 1837) (Seligman Collection)

Gille, B. *Histoire de la Maison Rothschild* (Tome 1,2) (Droz, 1967)

Gother, Karl. *Die Stadtischen Wechsel Banken Deutschlands Mittel Alter und im 16 Jahr hundert* (Munich, 1932)

Guimberteau. *Reflexions sur le credit public et sur l'etablissement d'une banque* (1799) (Seligman Collection)

Kilborn, Peter. *"Rare Moment for a Global Economy"* (*New York Times,* April 27, 1986)

Le Fournier, Philippe. *Le nouveau nouveau monde* (Pluriel, Paris, 1985)

Le Goff, Jacques. *Marchands et banquiers au moyen age* (Paris, 1912)

Lee, Susan E. *"Gold, the Ultimate Burglar Alarm"* (*Forbes,* September 23, 1985)

Lehrman, Lewis. *"To Move Forward, Go Back to Gold"* (*New York Times,* February 9, 1986)

Locke, John. *Several Papers Relating to Money, Interest and Trade* (London, 1696)

Lohr, Steve. *"Britain Braces for a Financial Free-for-all"* (*New York Times,* December 22, 1985); *"Rolling in Money in London"* (*New York Times,* April 20, 1986)

Luthy, H. *La Banque Protestante en France de la Revocation de l'Edit de Nantes a la Revolution* (Paris, 1959)

Macleod, Alison. *"In Search of the Belgian Dentist"* (*Euromoney Anniversary Eurobond Issue,* June 1984)

Marlowe, Christopher. *Plays and Poems* (Dutton, New York, 1950); The Jew of Malta (1591-1592)

Mirabeau. *Denonciation de l'Agiotage* (1787)

Myers, Margaret. *A Financial History of the United States* (Columbia University Press, 1970)

Petit-Dutaillis, George. *Portraits de Banquiers* (Revue Banque, Paris, 1982)

Pirenne, Henri. *Histoire Economique et Sociale du Moyen Age* (Paris, 1963)

Prevost, Antoine. *Histoire du Chevalier des Grieux et de Manon Lescaut* (Garnier, 1965)

Rambure, Dominique. *"La Compensation des paiements en ecus"* (*Banque,* No. 443, October 1984)

Rivoire, Jean. *Histoire de la monnaie* (PUF, Coll: Que Sais-je) (Paris, 1985)

Rosecrance, Richard. *The Rise of the Trading State* (Basic Books, 1985)

Rosenberg, Nathan and Birdzell L.E. *How the West Grew Rich: The Economic Transformation of the Industrial World* (New York: Basic Books, 1986)

Ross, Ian M. *"Euro Issuance Facilities"* (*Banque,* No. 447, February 1985)

Rueff, J. *La Reforme du Systeme monetaire internationale* (Plon, 1933)

Shakespeare. *The Complete Plays and Poems of William Shakespeare* (Houghton Mifflin, 1942); *The Merchant of Venice* (1600); *A Comedy of Errors* (1594); *The Merry Wives of Windsor* (1601)

Spooner, Frank. *L'Economie mondiale et les frappes monetaires en France* (Paris, 1956)

Stead, Christine. *House of All Nations* (Holt, Rinehart, Winston, New York, 1938)

Swift, Jonathan. *Selected Prose and Poetry* (Holt, Rinehart, Winston, New York, 1966)

Tate, William. *A Manual of Exchange Forming a Complete Synopsis of the Calculations of Foreign Exchange* (London, 1829)

Valles, Jules. *L'Argent* (Ledoyen, 1857)

Vilar, Pierre (trans.). *A History of Gold and Money 1450-1920* (Barcelona, 1969, 1976)

Hallenstein, Immanuel (French trans.). *Le Mercantalisme et la consolidation de l' economie Monde Europeen (1600-1750)* (Flammarion, Paris, 1985)

Wright, John. *Europeans (1600-1750)* (Flammarion, Paris, 1985)

Wright, John. *The American Negotiator on the Various Currencies of the British Colonies* (1761) (Seligman Collection)

Zola, Emile. *L'Argent* (Fasquelle, Paris, 1891)

CHAPTER THREE

KEVIN G. SALWEN, based in New York, is The Wall Street Journal's Assistant Special Reports Editor. A 1979 graduate of Northwestern University's Medill School of Journalism, he joined Dow Jones & Co. in 1981 as an associate in the company's Corporate Relations Department. In 1983, he became a Wall Street Journal copy editor, and was named night chief copy editor the following year. He has held his current post since 1985.

TERMS OF INTERNATIONAL INVESTMENT*

Kevin G. Salwen
The Wall Street Journal
New York, New York

This chapter contains a list of the essential terms currently in use in international investment together with a brief description of their meaning and importance to international investors.

American Depositary Receipt (ADR) A security issued in the United States to represent shares of a foreign stock, allowing that stock to be traded in the United States. Foreign companies use ADRs, which are issued in U.S. dollars, to expand the pool of potential U.S. investors. ADRs are available in two forms for about 690 foreign companies: company sponsored, which are listed on an exchange, and unsponsored, which usually are held by the investment bank that makes a market in the ADR. Both forms are available to individual investors, but only company-sponsored issues are quoted daily in newspapers.

Individual investors often are better off buying ADRs than the underlying foreign-market security because ADRs put market risk, company risk, and currency risk in one neat package.

*Adapted from "Terms of Investment" published in the special edition on Global Finance and Investing of The Wall Street Journal on September 29, 1986.

Belgian Dentist A stereotype of the traditional Eurobond investor. This self-employed professional must report income, has a disdain for tax authorities, and likes investing in foreign currencies. Anonymous bearer Eurobonds fit the bill nicely because they are unregistered and, therefore, untraceable. Such individual investors don't mind paying a premium for Eurobonds because the bonds effectively are issued on a tax-free basis.

Bid/Asked Spread The difference between the bid and asked prices on certain securities or on the foreign-exchange market. The spread is reconciled by traders, called market makers, who quote a price at which they will buy or sell, effectively setting the price. Brokers, in contrast, merely match up the two sides of a transaction.

Big Bang The nickname for October 27, 1986 when the London markets in equities and government securities were liberalized, specifically by the elimination of fixed commissions on debt and equity dealings. In 1975, May Day brought competitive commissions to the U.S.; Big Bang arrived with even broader changes in London, including a new regulatory system for all types of investment. For brokerages, Big Bang brought the end of single-capacity trading, which required brokering and market making in stocks and bonds to be handled by separate firms. Shortly before Big Bang, the first foreign firms, including several from the United States and Japan, were allowed to become members of the London Stock Exchange.

Big Four The nickname given to Japan's major brokerages. Nomura Securities Ltd., Nikko Securities Ltd., Daiwa Securities Ltd., and Yamichi Securities Ltd. dominate equity and bond trading in Japan, and are seeking to expand their international presence, particularly in New York and London. Together, the Big Four control nearly 60 percent of the trading volume in the Tokyo Stock Exchange's first section. Although in late 1985 six foreign firms (four are U.S. owned, one is British, and one is from Hong Kong) gained entry to the Tokyo bourse, inroads into the Big Four's market share are expected to come slowly.

BIS (Bank for International Settlements) A Basel, Switzerland-based organization of central banks or financial institutions that serves two distinct but related functions. It provides a forum for the discussion of international monetary issues, and it acts as a central bank for central banks. In its second role, BIS holds deposits, keeps gold reserves and handles central bank deposits and withdrawals as a clearing bank.

Cedel S.A. With Euroclear Clearance System Ltd., one of the two main clearing systems for internationally traded securities, mostly Eurobonds, but also some equities. They provide an institutional system for the transfer of securities and payments between buyers and sellers of securities. The two provide an efficient network for clearing, but often charge steep financing and borrowing fees.

Convertible Notes One of two main equity-related debt issues (along with warrants) commonly available overseas. Convertibles allow bondholders to exchange the debt for a fixed amount of equity (stock) within a certain period. According to the OECD, growth of the equity-related issues market slowed somewhat in 1985—expanding only about 5.5 percent to $11.5 billion—as issuing by Japanese and U.S. companies rose only modestly.

Cross Rate The exchange rate between two foreign currencies, generally neither of which is the U.S. dollar. The dollar, however, is used as an interim step in determining the cross rate. For example, if an investor wants to sell Japanese yen and buy Swiss francs, he would sell yen against dollars and then buy francs with those dollars. So although the transaction is designed to be yen for francs, the dollar's rate could be affected by the moves.

European Currency Unit (ECU) A basket of ten European currencies devised in 1979 and intended to serve as a monetary unit for the European Monetary System (EMS). By charter, EMS members reevaluate the composition of the ECU every five years or when there has been a shift of 25 percent or more in the weight of any currency. The West German mark is the most heavily weighted currency in the basket, with the French franc, British pound, and Dutch guilder each comprising more than 10 percent of the currency. The least representative weights are the Greek drachma, Luxembourg franc, and Irish pound.

Only in the past few years has the ECU begun to gain importance in the nongovernment marketplace. ECU Eurobonds were first issued in 1981, and in 1985 ECUs were the fourth most widely used currency in the Eurobond market, behind Eurodollars, Euromarks, and Euroyen. But the ECU's growth is limited by the fact that it has no central bank to issue it.

Eurobonds For many multinational companies and governments, Eurobonds have become the primary way to raise capital. Each Eurobond typically is denominated in a particular currency, though in recent years, some Eurobonds have begun to pay interest in one currency and allow redemption in another. Eurobonds are issued outside the restrictions that apply to domestic offerings and are syndicated and traded mostly from London. Trading can and does take place anywhere there is a buyer and seller.

Eurodollar bonds—which are denominated in dollars—comprise the majority of the Eurobond market (71 percent in 1985), with a smaller share of the market in West German marks, Japanese yen, European Currency Units, British pounds, Canadian dollars, Dutch guilders, French francs, and Australian and New Zealand dollars. Eurobonds increasingly are sold in the United States, but only through a private placement or ninety days after a new issue is considered all-sold in Europe.

The new-issue market for Eurobonds has soared in recent years, jumping to $133.4 billion in 1985 from $47.9 billion in 1983. The actual amount of Eurobonds outstanding exceeds $550 billion, and market turnover in 1985 exceeded $2 trillion.

From the buyers' side, the Eurobond market is primarily an institutional investors' market; for individual investors, Eurobonds are often bought as a tax shelter.

Eurocurrency Money deposited in a financial center outside the country whose currency is involved. For instance, Eurodollars—the most widely used Eurocurrency—are U.S. dollars deposited on books outside the U.S. Usually used to settle accounts, Eurocurrencies provide a pure interest rate reflective of the underlying supply and demand. That's because they are free of reserve requirements and free of insurance costs. Because the interest rate is pure, Eurocurrencies are crucial to the foreign exchange markets.

First Section Japan's three largest stock exchanges (Tokyo,

Osaka, and Nagoya) are divided into two sections. The first section has strict company requirements on dividends and per-share earnings, while the second section is for smaller or new companies. Companies can move from the second section to the first section in three years. First-section stocks on the Tokyo Stock Exchange account for about 80 percent of all trading on the eight Japanese exchanges.

Floating-Rate Notes Debt instruments with variable interest rates. The notes are pegged to a fluctuating interest rate, such as the six-month Libor rate, and interest payments are redetermined periodically along with movements in that rate. Floating-rate note payments usually are made every six months. For holders, they provide protection against interest-rate rises, but they can be tough to hold during times of low rates. According to the OECD, floating-rate notes comprised about 23 percent of the $256.5 billion borrowed in 1985 on the international capital markets. Fixed rate, or straight, bonds accounted for 35 percent.

Foreign Bonds Unlike Eurobonds, foreign bonds are issued by foreign borrowers in a nation's capital market and traditionally are denominated in that nation's currency. Yankee bonds, for example, are mostly issued in the United States by a foreign country, bank, or company; in recent years, however, some Yankee offerings have been denominated in other currencies. Often, the country in which these bonds are issued will draw distinctions between them and bonds issued by domestic issuers, including different tax laws, restrictions on the amount issued, or tougher disclosure rules.

Foreign bonds often are nicknamed for the country of issuance: Yankee bonds (United States), Samurai bonds (Japan), Rembrandt bonds (the Netherlands), and Bulldog bonds (Britain). Partly because of tougher regulations and disclosure requirements, over the past several years the foreign-bond market hasn't grown with the vigor of the Eurobond market; some $31 billion of foreign bonds were issued in 1985, compared with $27.8 billion the year earlier. Nearly half of all foreign bonds are issued in Switzerland. (Technically, there are no Eurobonds in Swiss francs.)

Forward-Exchange Market Forward-exchange markets represent a way for companies to hedge against major swings in foreign-exchange rates. Say, for example, that a U.S. exporter expects to receive 500 million Japanese yen in six months from a Japanese customer, but thinks the yen will weaken against the dollar by that time. The exporter can protect his exchange rate by arranging to sell 500 million yen six months from now to a bank at a set price. That price might be less than the current value of yen but more than what the exporter figures that yen will be going for in six months. In this way, the exporter has protected himself against a steeper rise in the dollar.

Gilts Technically gilts are British and Irish government securities, although the term also includes issues of local British authorities and some overseas public sector offerings. Like U.S. Treasury issues, gilts have a primary market (for money initially raised by the government) and a secondary market. But while Treasury issues are traded over the counter, gilts are traded on the London Stock Exchange, primarily by institutions. Governments and local authorities raised roughly 19.4 billion British pounds in 1985, with turnover on the secondary market totaling nearly 285 billion pounds.

Group of Seven The group of seven is the recently enlarged version of the Group of Five. The original five—the United States, France, Japan, West Germany and Britain—meet several times a year to discuss economic issues. G-7, which includes Canada and Italy, convenes at the annual economic summit. The nations usually are represented by their finance ministers or central bankers.

Indexes Each major stock exchange has a set of indexes that gauge the market much as the Dow Jones Industrial Average or Standard & Poor's 500 meter New York Stock Exchange trading. Aside from the usual pitfalls of indexes, currency moves can make it difficult to judge real returns on the overseas barometers. Although several new indexes have been designed in the past few years to take foreign exchange into account, Morgan Stanley's Capital International provides the industry standard for the world's major markets.

Libor (London Interbank Offered Rate) The rate the most creditworthy banks charge one another for loans of Eurodollars in the London market. Libor is a cornerstone in the pricing of money-market issues and other short-term debt issues by both governments and corporate borrowers. Oftentimes, less creditworthy issuers will borrow at rates of as much as one percentage point over Libor.

OECD (Organization for Economic Cooperation and Development) A Paris-based group created in 1960 to promote world trade and the economies of its member nations. The organization currently is made up of 24 industrialized countries, mostly in North America and Europe, but including Japan and several other nations.

Settlement Date The date on which the exchange of money and securities actually takes place. For example, if an investor buys 1,000 shares of Michelin stock on the Paris bourse, the settlement date is the day when the seller physically hands over the stock and the buyer provides the money. On the smaller overseas stock exchanges, settlement problems abound, with trades often taking weeks to settle—compared with five days on the New York Stock Exchange. For that reason, U.S. brokerages frequently will shy away from trades on the smaller international bourses.

Swaps The market play that has revolutionized the way companies raise money overseas. There are two basic kinds of swaps: interest rate and currency. Interest-rate swaps typically exchange floating-rate payments for fixed-rate payments, allowing two companies to reduce their borrowing costs. In the fourth quarter of 1985 alone, $36 billion of interest-rate swaps were completed. Currency swaps are accords to deliver one currency against another currency at certain intervals. Often, both types of swaps are used in the same transaction when debt denominated in different currencies is swapped.

The swaps makes it easy to move money around the world, allowing issuers to pay the lowest possible interest rate on a debt security and then simply exchange it for the preferred form of debt.

Tokyo Stock Exchange The world's second-largest stock exchange (after the New York Stock Exchange), measured by market capitalization. Tokyo accounts for nearly half of the market capitalization of non-U.S. exchanges. Trades on the Tokyo exchange are executed by matching orders, instead of the auction method used on the New York Stock Exchange.

The fee structure for Japanese securities is fixed and relatively high. Although the fees are regulated, widespread discounting is available to institutional investors, with the lowest rates for branch offices of U.S. brokerages. The recent opening of Tokyo exchange memberships to six foreign firms portends even further discounting for institutions. However, individual investors are likely to continue paying high posted commissions.

Unlisted Securities Market (USM) The London Stock Exchange's second tier. As of August 1, 1986, 360 companies with market capitalization equivalent to more than $6.2 billion were listed on the USM. The market was set up in 1980 to make it easier for smaller companies to get listings on the London exchange and have access to capital. Because USM stocks lack liquidity, institutional play is minimal and share prices can be erratic and volatile. Trades of USM stocks are often more expensive than first-tier London stocks because fewer firms make markets in the securities.

Warrant An option that allows the holder to buy a company's stock or debt in the future at a specified price, usually above the current value of the debt or equity. Often, warrants are issued to sweeten a fixed-income offering, allowing the holder of a company's bond or preferred stock to buy that company's stock.

International investment is a rapidly evolving process and financial creativity continues to develop at a quickening pace. While not intended to be exhaustive, this listing of the major terms of international investment is intended to be helpful to those who are entering the realm of global investment for the first time and to serve as a ready reference for more experienced investors.

CHAPTER FOUR

RAJ AGGARWAL teaches undergraduate, graduate, and executive courses and does research in the areas of financial management, international business and international finance and accounting. In addition to John Carroll University, he has taught graduate courses in finance and international business at the Universities of Toledo, Michigan, South Carolina, and Hawaii.

Professor Aggarwal's publications include books such as *Financial Policies for the Multinational Company, The Management of Foreign Exchange, International Dimensions of Financial Management, International Business: Operating in the Global Economy* and *Advances in International Planning and Forecasting* (forthcoming) over fifty scholarly papers in journals such as *Journal of Banking and Finance.*

He is a member of the editorial boards of *The Journal of International Business Studies, Issues in International Business,* and *Akron Business and Economic Review* and he is a past associate editor of the *Journal of the Midwest Finance Association.* He has held a number of elected and appointed positions in scholarly organizations and has received numerous research grants. In 1984 he served as the Senior Fulbright Research Scholar for South-East Asia.

ALTERNATIVES FOR INTERNATIONAL PORTFOLIO DIVERSIFICATION

Raj Aggarwal*
John Carroll University
Cleveland, Ohio

INTRODUCTION

International portfolio investment has increased greatly in recent years. The purchase of foreign securities through cross-border investments is the most commonly know method for achieving international diversification. However, depending on the reasons and goals for international diversification, an investor has a number of alternative routes to follow. This chapter examines the major alternatives available for international portfolio diversification.

Goals and Reasons for International Diversification

There are a number of reasons why an investor may wish to diversify internationally. While there are some unique advantages of diversifying internationally, most reasons for undertaking international diversification are similar to the reasons for diversifying within a

*The author would like to thank James J. Padilla for research assistance and professors L. V. Conway and R. Rao for helpful comments.

single country. It should be noted that the benefits of international diversification depend on the segmentation of capital markets in different countries. If asset markets were perfectly integrated internationally and assets were priced in a global context, there would be few or no benefits from international diversification. There seems to be, however, considerable indirect evidence of international capital market segmentation so that significant benefits can be obtained from international diversification.

First, risks can be diversified and reduced. The risk of holding a portfolio of investments is generally less than the risk of holding a single investment. This condition is true as long as there is less than perfect correlation of returns among the investments making up the portfolio, a condition that is easily satisfied. Thus, since all investments are unlikely to always move in tandem, a portfolio of investments generally has less risk than each of the investments by themselves. In general, the lower the correlation among the various investments, the greater is the reduction of risk in a portfolio. Maximum risk reduction takes place when returns on investments in a portfolio are perfectly negatively correlated. In practice however, most investments in a single economy are influenced by factors common to that economy and exhibit a relatively high positive correlation of returns.

Consequently, not only is it rare to find investments that have negative correlations, but a certain proportion of the risk of most investments in a given economy cannot be eliminated by diversification. This common, undiversifiable risk is called the systematic risk, or beta, of that investment. By diversifying internationally, some of this systematic risk with respect to a given economy may be reduced further since foreign economies do not move in perfect tandem with each other or with a given domestic economy. Empirical evidence seems to point to fairly stable correlation matrices (especially in the long run) for capital market returns in different countries. As the data in Tables 1 and 2 show, equity and bond returns in different countries do not move in tandem and, as shown in the correlation matrices in Tables 3 and 4, there is considerable potential for risk reduction through international diversification. As the data in Table

TABLE 1 WORLD EQUITY RETURNS 1960-1980

Asset	*Annual Returns in U.S. Dollars* Compound Return (%)	Arithmetic Mean (%)	Standard Deviation (%)	*Year-End Wealth Index 1959=1.00*	*1980 Year-End Value In Billions U.S. $*
Non-U.S. Equities:					
Europe					
Austria	9.1	10.3	16.9	6.23	1.9
Belgium	9.2	10.1	13.8	6.39	10.0
Denmark	9.5	11.4	24.2	6.72	4.0
France	6.2	8.1	21.4	3.56	53.0
Germany	8.3	10.1	19.9	5.32	71.0
Italy	2.4	5.6	27.2	1.63	25.0
Netherlands	9.3	10.7	17.8	6.45	25.0
Norway	10.3	17.4	49.0	7.81	2.6
Spain	8.4	10.4	19.8	5.49	16.3
Sweden	8.4	9.7	16.7	5.40	12.2
Switzerland	10.2	12.5	22.9	7.74	46.0
United Kingdom	10.0	14.7	33.6	7.39	190.0
Europe Total	8.4	9.6	16.2	5.47	457.0
Asia					
Hong Kong*	24.6	40.3	61.3	11.24	38.0
Japan	15.6	19.0	31.4	20.86	357.0
Singapore*	23.2	37.0	66.1	9.96	24.3
Asia Total	15.9	19.7	33.0	22.29	419.3
Other					
Australia	9.8	12.2	22.8	7.12	60.0
Canada	10.7	12.1	17.5	8.47	113.0
Other Total	10.6	11.9	17.1	8.24	173.0
Non-U.S. Total Equities	10.6	11.8	16.3	8.23	1049.3
U.S. Total Equities	8.7	10.2	17.7	5.78	1380.6
World Total Equities	9.3	10.5	15.8	6.47	2429.9

*1970-1980.

Source: Ibbotson, R.G., R.C. Carr, and A.W. Robinson, (1982), "International Equity and Bond Returns," *Financial Analysts Journal*, (July-August), pp. 61-83

TABLE 2 WORLD BOND RETURNS 1960-1980

Asset	*Annual Returns in U.S. Dollars*			*Year-End 1980 Wealth Index 1959=1.00*
	Compound Return (%)	*Arithmetic Mean (%)*	*Standard Deviation (%)*	
Domestic Bonds:				
Austria	8.1	8.6	9.9	5.15
Belgium	7.7	8.1	9.4	4.75
Canada	3.3	3.5	6.3	1.99
Denmark	6.3	7.0	12.8	3.58
France	5.3	6.0	12.3	2.95
Germany	10.3	10.6	9.2	7.77
Italy	2.4	3.4	13.4	1.66
Japan	10.6	11.2	11.9	8.26
Netherlands	7.6	7.9	8.1	4.66
Spain	4.6	5.2	11.2	2.56
Sweden	6.2	6.4	5.9	3.57
Switzerland	8.4	9.1	12.4	5.48
United Kingdom	5.9	6.8	14.9	3.32
United States	4.2	4.3	5.4	2.36
Crossborder Bonds:				
Deutschemarks	10.4	10.8	9.5	7.97
Dutch Guilders*	11.6	11.9	8.5	1.93
Japanese Yen*	18.0	19.8	19.2	2.71
Swiss Francs*	15.5	16.7	16.0	2.38
U.S. Dollars	5.9	6.0	4.4	3.34
Other Currencies*	5.7	5.8	2.5	1.25

*Returns measured over the period 1975-1980; wealth index 1974=1.00.

**Returns measured over the period 1977-1980; wealth index 1976=1.00.

Source: Ibbotson, R.G., R.C. Carr, and A.W. Robinson, (1982), ''International Equity and Bond Returns,'' *Financial Analysts Journal,* (July-August), pp. 61-83

TABLE 3 CROSS CORRELATIONS OF WORLD EQUITY RETURNS 1960-1980

Annual U.S.-Dollar-Adjusted Total Returns

Series	*Austria*	*Belgium*	*Denmark*	*France*	*Germany*	*Italy*	*Nether-lands*	*Norway*
Austria	1.000							
Belgium	0.308	1.000						
Denmark	0.224	0.387	1.000					
France	0.155	0.559	0.259	1.000				
Germany	0.258	0.303	0.058	0.273	1.000			
Italy	0.180	−0.104	0.156	0.398	−0.004	1.000		
Netherlands	−0.012	0.567	0.342	0.484	0.537	0.031	1.000	
Norway	0.343	0.359	−0.100	0.188	−0.212	0.119	0.010	1.000
Spain	0.260	0.208	0.413	0.326	−0.075	0.338	−0.102	0.171
Sweden	−0.038	0.311	0.281	0.277	0.285	0.131	0.429	−0.100
Switzerland	0.454	0.465	0.134	0.444	0.700	0.129	0.658	−0.021
United Kingdom	−0.349	0.284	0.152	0.432	0.258	0.104	0.675	−0.136
Europe Total	−0.039	0.493	0.266	0.643	0.505	0.289	0.783	−0.039
Hong Kong	0.127	0.447	0.743	0.387	0.131	0.324	0.729	0.046
Japan	0.216	0.331	0.831	0.361	0.302	0.307	0.284	−0.257
Singapore	0.260	0.510	0.921	0.404	0.311	0.353	0.614	−0.157
Asia Total	0.211	0.337	0.845	0.365	0.281	0.314	0.308	−0.228
Australia	−0.241	0.281	0.213	0.504	0.321	0.420	0.766	0.089
Canada	0.239	0.623	0.341	0.441	−0.037	0.269	0.554	0.469
Other Total	0.029	0.544	0.329	0.528	0.157	0.363	0.743	0.358
Non-U.S. Total Equities	0.062	0.559	0.557	0.646	0.470	0.390	0.774	−0.114
U.S. Total Equities	−0.076	0.389	0.243	0.214	0.210	0.208	0.730	0.009
World Total Equities	−0.042	0.483	0.358	0.384	0.322	0.281	0.804	−0.043

Source: Ibbotson, R.G., R.C. Carr, and A.W. Robinson, (1982), ''International Equity and Bond Returns,'' *Financial Analysts Journal,* (July-August), pp. 61-83

TABLE 3 CROSS CORRELATIONS OF WORLD EQUITY RETURNS (cont.) 1960-1980

Annual U.S.-Dollar-Adjusted Total Returns

Series	*Spain*	*Sweden*	*Switzer-land*	*United Kingdom*	*Europe Total*	*Hong Kong*	*Japan*	*Singa-pore*
Spain	1.000							
Sweden	0.313	1.000						
Switzerland	0.127	0.233	1.000					
United Kingdom	−0.039	0.301	0.454	1.000				
Europe Total	0.178	0.471	0.712	0.882	1.000			
Hong Kong	0.418	0.376	0.563	0.487	0.598	1.000		
Japan	0.337	0.340	0.240	0.171	0.374	0.707	1.000	
Singapore	0.585	0.439	0.584	0.338	0.547	0.898	0.927	1.000
Asia Total	0.338	0.337	0.244	0.198	0.391	0.759	0.997	0.952
Australia	0.090	0.282	0.432	0.674	0.731	0.667	0.184	0.512
Canada	0.260	0.312	0.350	0.360	0.505	0.791	0.231	0.598
Other Total	0.195	0.340	0.432	0.550	0.676	0.800	0.247	0.609
Non-U.S. Total Equities	0.242	0.522	0.643	0.716	0.905	0.785	0.688	0.826
U.S. Total Equities	−0.115	0.398	0.454	0.617	0.627	0.814	0.216	0.579
World Total Equities	−0.015	0.470	0.557	0.703	0.774	0.848	0.385	0.700

Series	*Asia Total*	*Aus-tralia*	*Canada*	*Other Total*	*Non-U.S. Total Equities*	*U.S. Total Equities*	*World Total Equities*
Asia Total	1.000						
Australia	0.224	1.000					
Canada	0.280	0.577	1.000				
Other Total	0.296	0.863	0.907	1.000			
Non-U.S. Total Equities	0.704	0.704	0.586	0.717	1.000		
U.S. Total Equities	0.260	0.699	0.710	0.787	0.667	1.000	
World Total Equities	0.422	0.753	0.716	0.818	0.831	0.967	1.000

Source: Ibbotson, R.G., R.C. Carr, and A.W. Robinson, (1982), ''International Equity and Bond Returns,'' *Financial Analysts Journal,* (July-August), pp. 61-83

TABLE 4 CROSS CORRELATIONS OF WORLD BOND RETURNS 1960-1980

Annual U.S.-Dollar-Adjusted Total Returns

Series	*Austria*	*Belgium*	*Canada*	*Denmark*	*France*	*Germany*	*Italy*
Austria	1.000						
Belgium	0.853	1.000					
Canada	0.244	0.159	1.000				
Denmark	0.481	0.548	−0.010	1.000			
France	0.544	0.716	0.010	0.693	1.000		
Germany	0.823	0.771	0.179	0.217	0.427	1.000	
Italy	0.141	0.248	−0.225	0.426	0.530	−0.009	1.000
Japan	0.154	0.318	−0.172	0.358	0.276	0.265	0.239
Netherlands	0.884	0.928	0.211	0.448	0.644	0.862	0.036
Spain	0.344	0.309	−0.102	0.488	0.472	0.044	0.612
Sweden	0.586	0.630	0.264	0.418	0.281	0.338	−0.039
Switzerland	0.882	0.895	0.037	0.475	0.662	0.854	0.075
United Kingdom	−0.005	0.095	−0.147	0.121	0.099	0.125	0.288
United States	0.150	0.049	0.632	0.228	0.146	0.098	−0.132
Deutschemark Crossborder	0.853	0.810	0.215	0.342	0.546	0.938	0.018
Dutch Guilder Crossborder	0.935	0.980	0.289	0.463	0.665	0.872	0.233
Japanese Yen Crossborder	−0.060	0.274	−0.478	0.262	0.251	0.249	0.005
Swiss Franc Crossborder	0.749	0.842	0.105	0.421	0.673	0.905	0.286
U.S. Dollar Crossborder	0.172	0.154	0.250	0.442	0.169	0.157	0.083
Other Crossborder	0.194	0.434	−0.619	0.173	0.341	0.634	0.114

Source: Ibbotson, R.G., R.C. Carr, and A.W. Robinson, (1982), ''International Equity and Bond Returns,'' *Financial Analysts Journal,* (July-August), pp. 61-83

TABLE 4 CROSS CORRELATIONS OF WORLD BOND RETURNS (cont.)
1960-1980
Annual U.S.-Dollar-Adjusted Total Returns

Series	*Japan*	*Netherlands*	*Spain*	*Sweden*	*Switzerland*	*United Kingdom*	*United States*
Japan	1.000						
Netherlands	0.244	1.000					
Spain	−0.158	0.235	1.000				
Sweden	−0.183	0.631	0.440	1.000			
Switzerland	0.383	0.944	0.174	0.463	1.000		
United Kingdom	0.500	0.033	−0.128	−0.238	0.134	1.000	
United States	0.095	0.166	0.072	0.059	0.104	0.076	1.000
Deutschemark Crossborder	0.293	0.903	0.158	0.400	0.901	0.025	0.242
Dutch Guilder Crossborder	0.360	0.996	0.274	0.462	0.968	−0.198	0.025
Japanese Yen Crossborder	0.982	0.242	−0.481	−0.355	0.408	0.400	−0.061
Swiss Franc Crossborder	0.594	0.858	−0.047	−0.032	0.949	0.104	0.115
U.S. Dollar Crossborder	0.325	0.178	0.117	0.036	0.167	0.168	0.715
Other Crossborder	0.944	0.443	−0.553	−0.554	0.610	0.666	0.160

Series	*Deutschemark Cross-Border*	*Dutch Guilder Cross-Border*	*Japanese Yen Cross-Border*	*Swiss Franc Cross-Border*	*U.S. Dollar Cross-Border*	*Other Cross-Border*
Deutschemark Crossborder	1.000					
Dutch Guilder Crossborder	0.931	1.000				
Japanese Yen Crossborder	0.281	0.273	1.000			
Swiss Franc Crossborder	0.933	0.868	0.550	1.000		
U.S. Dollar Crossborder	0.288	−0.113	0.215	0.132	1.000	
Other Crossborder	0.624	0.500	0.917	0.786	0.683	1.000

Source: Ibbotson, R.G., R.C. Carr, and A.W. Robinson, (1982), ''International Equity and Bond Returns,'' *Financial Analysts Journal,* (July-August), pp. 61-83

5 indicate, the opportunities for risk reduction are much greater when investing in developing countries. Thus, international diversification offers opportunities for risk diversification and reduction that are not available when the investment universe is limited to a single economy.

Second, international diversification may also offer additional opportunities for achieving higher returns. The expanded set of investment alternatives available to the investor means that high return investments are more likely to be found by the internationally diversified investor as compared to an investor that is limited to only one country. As of June 1986, U.S. equities were valued at about $2.3 trillion, Japanese equities at about $1.4 trillion, and European equities at about $1.1 trillion. In Europe, the countries with the largest equity values were the United Kingdom at about $0.4 trillion followed by West Germany at about $0.2 trillion and by France, Italy, and Switzerland at about $0.1 trillion each (Capital International Perspective). Table 6 illustrates the growth in impor-

TABLE 5 CORRELATION BETWEEN U.S. MARKETS AND DEVELOPING COUNTRY MARKETS

Monthly Dollar Returns, 1976-1980

Country	Correlation
Spain	0.11
Hong Kong	0.27
Singapore	0.42
Argentina	−0.02
Brazil	−0.03
Chile	−0.18
Greece	−0.01
Jordan	0.34
Korea	0.23
Mexico	0.22
Thailand	−0.36
Zimbabwe	0.00

Source: Errunza, (1983), "Emerging Markets: A New Opportunity for Improving Global Portfolio Performance," *Financial Analysts Journal,* 39 (No. 5, September/October), pp. 51-58

tance of non-U.S. equity markets. As this table shows, non-U.S. stocks now account for 55 percent of the value of all global equities while they were only 29 percent just two decades ago.

Tables 7 and 8 provide another perspective regarding the growing importance of diversification. As Table 7 indicates, U.S. equi-

TABLE 6 TRENDS IN GLOBAL STOCK MARKET CAPITALIZATION
Percent of Total

Country	1966	1975	1978	1981	1986
United States	71	58	50	56	45
Europe	19	22	22	13	23
Japan	3	12	20	23	26
Canada	3	N/A	N/A	4	3
Other	7	8	8	4	3

Data are for the quarter ending March 31 each year.

TABLE 7 DISTRIBUTION OF WORLD INVESTABLE WEALTH - 1980

Asset Class	Market Value	Percent
U.S. Residential Real Estate	2,932.3	25.4
Foreign Domestic Bonds	1,723.6	15.0
Metals	1,681.9	14.6
U.S. Equities	1,380.6	12.0
U.S Farm Real Estate	828.7	7.2
U.S. Domestic Bonds	799.1	6.9
U.S. Business Real Estate	486.2	4.2
Europe Equities	457.0	4.0
Asia Equities	419.3	3.6
U.S. Cash	372.8	3.2
Crossborder Bonds	182.9	1.6
Canada & Australia Equities	173.0	1.5
Foreign Cash	90.7	0.8
Total World Investable Wealth	11,528.1	100.0

Source: Ibbotson, Roger G. and Laurence B. Siegel, (1983), "The World Market Wealth Portfolio," *International Investing*, edited by Peter L. Bernstein, (New York: Institutional Investor Books). Market values are in billions of U.S. dollars.

ties account for only 12 percent of global investible wealth and as Table 8 indicates, markets in some high-growth foreign countries have provided significantly higher rates of return than have investments in U.S. or European equities. Therefore, plans for international portfolio diversification should, wherever possible, include investments in assets other than foreign equities. Table 9 provides some additional details regarding the nature of stock exchanges in

TABLE 8 WORLD CAPITAL MARKET TOTAL ANNUAL RETURNS 1960-1980

	Compound Return	Arithmetic Mean	Standard Deviation
Equities			
United States	8.71%	10.23%	17.68%
Foreign			
Europe	8.43	9.63	16.16
Asia	15.93	19.71	33.04
Canada & Australia	10.56	11.92	17.07
Foreign Total	10.56	11.78	16.30
Equities Total	9.30	10.52	15.80
Bonds			
United States			
Corporate*	3.37	3.61	7.13
Government	4.51	4.61	4.74
United States Total	4.14	4.27	5.25
Foreign			
Corporate Domestic	9.12	9.43	8.36
Government Domestic	6.42	6.66	7.44
Crossborder	6.89	6.99	4.68
Foreign Total	7.34	7.57	7.13
Bonds Total	6.13	6.26	5.31
Cash Equivalents			
United States	5.46	5.48	2.20
Foreign	6.60	6.76	5.91
Cash Total	5.67	5.69	2.42

*Including preferred stock.

TABLE 8 WORLD CAPITAL MARKET TOTAL ANNUAL RETURNS (cont.) 1960-1980

	Compound Return	Arithmetic Mean	Standard Deviation
Real Estate**			
Business	7.67	7.73	3.73
Residential	8.72	8.79	4.04
Farms	13.22	13.42	6.79
Real Estate Total	9.49	9.55	3.65
Metals			
Gold	14.39	17.59	29.21
Silver	16.09	27.49	79.26
Metals Total	14.46	17.61	28.96
US Market Wealth Portfolio	8.37	8.50	5.25
Foreign Market Wealth Portfolio	8.40	8.76	8.91
World Market Wealth Portfolios			
Excluding metals	8.36	8.50	5.44
Including metals	8.92	9.07	5.70
US Inflation Rate	5.26	5.33	3.81

**United States only.

Source: Ibbotson Roger G. and Laurence B. Siegel. (1983), ''The World Market Wealth Portfolio,'' *International Investing* edited by Peter L. Bernstein, (New York: Institutional Investor Books), pp.16-46

TABLE 9 STOCK EXCHANGE OF SELECTED HIGH-GROWTH ASIAN COUNTRIES

Country	Date Estab.	No. of Companies	Market Capitalization	Turnover	P/E Ratio
Malaysia	1937	278	29,200	2,430	19.00
South Korea	1920	336	6,100	3,869	5.30
Taiwan	1962	121	8,790	8,300	13.25
Philipines	1927	149	600	125	3.80
Thailand	1960	95	1,700	448	7.50
Indonesia	1952	24	130	2	9.00

Data are for 1984 and in millions of U.S. dollars for market capitalization and turnover.

Asian countries that have had rapid growth in the past and are projected to have some of the highest growth rates over the next decade or two.

Markets in a number of countries are heavily influenced, regulated, and often subsidized by their governments. While these market imperfections may sometimes make it difficult to operate in such countries, they also create extraordinary profit opportunities not found in highly competitive markets. Examples of the opportunities created by government regulation include situations where a company can obtain subsidized funds, cost-controlled raw materials and other inputs, export subsidies, and markets for its outputs that are protected from competition. In addition, markets in a number of foreign countries are growing at a much faster rate than markets in other more mature economies. Investments in such foreign markets may offer opportunities for returns far higher than those available domestically.

Many capital markets, especially those outside the United States, United Kingdom, the Netherlands, and Japan may not be as efficient as markets in the major industrial countries. Asset prices in these markets may not reflect appropriate risk and return characteristics. This means that with careful analysis it may be more possible to find undervalued assets in such markets than in markets that are efficient. Further, investing overseas may offer tax advantages not available to purely domestic investors. Very few countries, other than the United States, even tax foreign source income. Because of an extensive network of tax treaties and other reasons, domestic taxation of foreign source income may be at a rate that is effectively zero or is much lower than the rate applicable to domestic investments.

Third, an additional consideration faced in an internationally diversified portfolio is the presence of both exchange rate risk and political risk. In addition to the returns and risks of the foreign investments in terms of their domestic currency, the international investor also faces losses or gains due to changes in the value of the currency in which these investments are denominated. However, if international markets are well integrated and purchasing power and interest rate parity conditions hold, currency risk can be considered to be unimportant, especially in the long run. This ideal viewpoint can become a problem, however, in cases of short investment horizons, significant deviations from parity conditions because of government regulations, or if the foreign investment has to be liquidated unexpectedly.

In such cases an investor should consider hedging the part of the portfolio exposed to changes in value because of changing foreign exchange rates. A number of financial instruments are available for this purpose including the forward sale or purchase of foreign currencies in the inter-bank foreign exchange market, futures contracts on foreign currencies and interest rates traded on organized exchanges, and call and put options on foreign currencies and on futures that are available in the inter-bank market or traded on organized exchanges. In certain cases, foreign exchange risk may also be hedged by holding offsetting positions in appropriate commodities (such as precious metals) or futures or options on these commodities. In recent years, the availability of these financial instruments has increased greatly, especially since there has been a rapid rise in the number of exchanges where such instruments are traded. Table 10 lists the major exchanges where such futures and options are traded.

In addition to foreign exchange risk, a foreign investor also faces possible losses because of political risks in the form of unexpected government regulations that influence the profitability of the investment or the ability to repatriate funds out of a country. On the other hand, foreign investments also provide the opportunity to diversify assets into preferred currencies and political habitats. The international investor must account for these risks and possible rewards in making the decision to invest overseas.

While international diversification offers greater opportunities for risk reduction and for higher returns, it also involves a number of difficulties that are not faced by a domestic investor. First, a number of the foreign markets may have regulations against foreign investors. Second, some of the capital markets outside the United States, Japan, and the United Kingdom may be thinly capitalized leading to a lack of liquidity and the ability to accumulate or unload positions quickly.

TABLE 10 WORLDWIDE FUTURES AND OPTIONS MARKETS

Exchange	Principal Contracts by Group										Date Opened	Trading Hours (Local Time)	Trading Hours CST (Chicago Time)
	Physical Commodities		Currencies		Interest Rates		Indexes		Metals				
	F	O	F	O	F	O	F	O	F	O			
Chicago Mercantile Exchange	•	•	•	•	•	•	•	•			1919	07.20-15.15	07.20-15.15
Chicago Board of Trade	•	•			•	•	•		•		1848	08.00-15.15	08.00-15.15
Kansas City Board of Trade	•						•				1856	09.00-15.15	09.00-15.15
Montreal Exchange				•		•					1984	09.00-16.00	08.00-15.00
New York Futures Exchange							•	•			1979	09.30-16.15	08.30-15.15
INTEX							•		•		1984	08.30-16.00	06.30-14.00
Bolsa de Mercadorios de Sao Paulo	•								•		1917	09.00-16.15	06.00-13.15
UFFE			•	•	•	•	•				1982	08.15-16.20	02.15-10.20
London Commodity Exchange	•										1964	09.45-17.00*	03.45-11.00

F=Futures
O=Options on Futures
*Intermittent Hours
**Estimated Hours

TABLE 10 WORLDWIDE FUTURES AND OPTIONS MARKETS (cont.)

Exchange	Principal Contracts by Group										Date Opened	Trading Hours (Local Time)	Trading Hours CST (Chicago Time)
	Physical Commodities		Currencies		Interest Rates		Indexes		Metals				
	F	O	F	O	F	O	F	O	F	O			
BIFFEX							•				1985	10.15-16.15**	04.15-10.15
Tokyo Financial Futures Exchange			•		•		•				1985	09.00-15.00**	19.00-01.00
SIMEX			•		•				•		1984	09.20-17.20	19.20-03.20
Hong Kong Futures Exchange	•								•		1977	09.50-14.50**	19.50-24.50
Sydney Futures Exchange	•		•	•	•	•	•		•		1960	09.30-15.45*	17.30-23.45
New Zealand Futures Exchange	•		•		•						1985	08.45-16.00	14.45-22.00
Mid America Commodity Exchange	•		•		•				•	•	1880	07.20-14.15	07.20-14.15
Chicago Rice and Cotton Exchange	•										1976	09.30-14.00	09.30-14.00
Commodity Exchange (COMEX)									•	•	1933	09.00-14.30	08.00-13.30

F=Futures
O=Options on Futures
*Intermittent Hours
**Estimated Hours

Source: Chicago Mercantile Exchange Annual Report, 1985

There may also be lengthy delays in settlement in some cases. Third, the amount, quality, and type of information that is available on publicly traded companies may be very limited and not comparable to the information available in other countries. Fourth, brokerage fees can also be considerably higher for making foreign investments.

Thus, international investing can offer a better risk-return combination than investing in domestic investments. However, investing internationally can also be more difficult and expensive than investing domestically. Therefore, it is particularly important to explore the different alternatives that are available to achieve international diversi-fication.

ALTERNATIVES FOR INTERNATIONAL DIVERSIFICATION

There are a number of ways a portfolio can achieve international diversification. First, investors can directly purchase shares or bonds of foreign companies through brokers in that foreign country. The foreign broker can be contacted directly or through the investor's domestic broker. Second, a number of equities are now beginning to be listed on a number of exchanges in different countries. These shares can generally be bought in those countries just like any other domestic share.

Third, international diversification can be achieved by buying shares in an appropriate open-end or closed-end mutual fund that is internationally diversified. Fourth, international diversification in a portfolio can also be achieved by investing in the bonds or shares of domestic companies that have undertaken significant direct investment in foreign countries. Each of these different approaches to international portfolio diversification has different costs and benefits for an investor. Therefore, each of these major alternatives for international portfolio diversification are next explored in greater detail.

Securities Traded in Foreign Markets

Cross-border investments in securities listed or traded in foreign countries have increased greatly in recent years. It has been estimated that U.S. residents bought $4.25 billion of foreign stocks in 1976. This number had jumped to an annual rate of $80 billion by the middle of 1986 (*Forbes,* December 15, 1986, p. 210). According to Lipper Analytical Services, overseas investments by U.S. pension funds have grown from about half a billion dollars in 1975 to over 21 billion dollars in 1985 while internationally diversified mutual funds grew from less than a fifth of a billion dollars to over 1.5 billion dollars in the same period. Further, it is estimated that these numbers are expected to have exploded to 44 and 7 billion dollars respectively by the end of 1986. In addition, over 10 billion dollars are expected to have been invested by the end of 1986 in global mutual funds. Undoubtedly, U.S. investors are finally discovering international diversification. Consequently, a number of mutual funds that take the index approach to international diversification are now also being offered to U.S. institutional investors. Table 11 summarizes the increasing international investments of U.S. pension funds.

The growth of international investments has been a two-way street. Although precise and reliable statistics are hard to obtain, it has been estimated that foreigners own over a trillion U.S. dollars worth of U.S. assets. About 20 percent of that is in the form of U.S. Treasury securities owned by foreign governments, about 6 percent is in the form of U.S. Treasury securities owned by private foreign investors, about 20 percent in portfolio investments in U.S. corporate securities, 20 percent in direct investments in U.S. businesses, and the remaining amount is in the form of bank deposits, agricultural

TABLE 11 FOREIGN INVESTMENT BY U.S. PENSION FUNDS

Year	Total Pension Assets	Foreign Investment	Percent
1980	413	3.4	0.8
1983	610	11.9	1.9
1984	640	15.7	2.5
1985	950	21.0	2.2
1990 (est)	2,000	80.0	4.0

Source: Rowely, Anthony, (1985), "All Roads Lead to Wall Street," *Far Eastern Economic Review,* (August 29), p. 61

land, and real estate (*Fortune,* December 22, 1986, p. 45). Foreign investment in the United States is expected to grow much faster than U.S. investment overseas as barriers to cross-border investments progressively come down. As an example, Japanese insurance companies were recently permitted to increase their maximum foreign holdings from 10 to 30 percent.

In spite of this increased activity in cross-border investing by institutional investors, the direct purchase of foreign securities is perhaps the least popular route taken by individual investors seeking international diversification. An institutional investor, on the other hand, may find this approach to international diversification quite acceptable and, perhaps, very profitable. There are a number of reasons for this difference in perspective.

First, the purchase of foreign securities involves not only domestic brokerage commissions but also the additional costs involved in the international clearing process and in brokerage fees paid to foreign brokers. Both of these factors are, however, being mitigated slowly by advances and developments in the international clearing process, at least among the major stock exchanges. A number of electronic network and computer-based clearing systems for shares traded on the major exchanges are currently being developed and implemented. As these developments and systems are extended to additional countries, delays and costs of cross-border clearing and security delivery should fall significantly.

Brokerage costs of buying foreign securities should also fall as a larger number of brokerage firms become international by buying seats on stock exchanges in different countries and by making equity investments in other brokers or in establishing a 'denovo' presence as a broker in a number of countries. These trends toward the greater internationalization of the larger brokerage firms have been accelerating in recent years as the major stock exchanges become increasingly deregulated. Thus, driven by the rapidly advancing technology of financial telecommunication and by the rising trend towards deregulation, the brokerage costs of buying foreign securities are likely to continue to fall not only for the institutional investor, but eventually also for the individual investor.

Second, the direct purchase of foreign securities also involves higher information costs. Information about the performance of a foreign company may be difficult and costly to obtain, particularly in the investor's home country. On-line screen services for foreign securities are generally inadequate and more expensive. Because of different cultural and accounting standards, the type and amount of information that is publicly available may also be limited and different from that which the investor is accustomed to analyzing. Therefore, in order to properly evaluate the information that is available publicly, the investor must be familiar with the accounting and financial disclosure standards and valuation practices of that foreign country and how they differ from comparable standards in the investor's country. For example, investors in Japan are accustomed to paying much higher price-earnings ratios (an average of 45 in late 1986) than are U.S. investors (an average of 17 for the S&P 500 at the same time period).

The investor must also be aware of information sources that are peculiar to that foreign country, including the role and availability of inside information. In a number of countries it is not illegal or unusual to use inside information in evaluating investments. Thus, cross-border investments in foreign securities generally involve very high information costs. This means that without the involvement of an institution to analyze, evaluate, and recommend a security, an individual is rarely going to find it cost-effective to invest in foreign securities. An institution can, however, by virtue of its economies of scale, spread this information cost over a much larger trading volume. Table 12 summarizes selected data regarding the nature of some of the major stock exchanges globally.

In conclusion, the widespread direct purchase of most securities on foreign stock exchanges has so far been primarily suitable only for or with the involvement of an institution so that the high information costs of investing internationally can be spread over a large trading volume. However, the brokerage and settlement costs of cross-border trades are likely to come down in the future. This decline of brokerage and settlement costs means that there is likely to be greater interest in cross-border investments in major companies

TABLE 12 INTERNATIONAL SECURITY EXCHANGES

Selected Trading Characteristics

Exchange	Membs	Lstngs	Trd Hrs	GMTime	Settle	Comm	Inside
Sydney	250	1,150	10:00-12:00 13:00-15:00	+10	10	N	P
Brussels	715	336	11:30-14:30	+1	1-14	F	NP
Sao Paulo	90	131	9:30-13:00	−4	3	F	P
Toronto	74	1,438	9:30-16:00	−5	5	N	P
Montreal	77	993	9:30-16:00	−5	1-5	N	P
Vancouver	49	2,000	6:30-16:00	−8	5	F	P
Copenhagen	75	N/A	10:30- 6:30	+1	3	F/N	P
Paris	45	1,430	10:00-17:00	+1	Varies	F/N	P
Frankfurt	2,181	6,082	11:30-13:30	+1	2	N	P
Hong Kong	678	323	10:00-12:30 14:30-15:30	+8	1	N	P
Milan	150	160	10:00-16:00	+1	3-45	F	NP
Tokyo	97	2,377	9:00-11:00MF 13:00-15:00MF 9:00-11:00S	+9	1-14	F	P
Korea	25	4,188	9:40-15:20	+9	2	F	P
Mexico	N/A	206	10:00-13:40	−6	2	F	P
Amsterdam	150	2,000+	10:00-16:30	+1	10	F/N	P
New Zealand	215	352	10:00-11:30 14:30-15:30	+12	10	N	P
Singapore	29	317	10:00-12:30 14:30-16:00	+8	1-7	F	P
Madrid	150	334	9:30-12:30	+1	3	F	NP
Stockholm	28	170	10:00-14:30	+1	5	F	NP
Zurich	25	2,577	10:00-12:30	+1	3-10	F/N	NP
Geneva	17	N/A	9:00-14:00	+1	3-10	F/N	NP
Taiwan	27	132	9:00-12:00MF 9:00-11:00S	+8	1	F	NP
London	5,191	5,500	9:00-15:30	0	1-10	N	P
New York	1,366	2,250	9:30-16:00	−5	5	N	P
American	864	788	9:00-16:15	−5	5	N	P
NASDAQ	All	4,136	9:30-16:00	−5	5	N	P

Explanatory Notes

N/A: Information not available or applicable
Membs: Number of exchange members
Lstngs: Number of securities listed
Trd Hrs: Trading hours in local time
GMTime: Local time difference with Greenwich Mean Time
Settle: No. of business days normally required to settle trades
Comm: Commissions, F=Fixed, N=Negotiable
Inside: Use of inside information
P=Prohibited, NP=Not prohibited

that make a specific effort to develop a global market for their securities. These companies can do that best by reducing information costs for investors by providing easily available information about their operations in a consistent and internationally acceptable format. Table 13 lists the largest fifty companies outside the U.S. along with

TABLE 13 FIFTY LARGEST COMPANIES OUTSIDE THE UNITED STATES - 1985

Company	Country	Industry	Revenue	Assets	Market Value
				($000,000)	
Royal Dutch/Shell	Netherlds	Oil & Gas	81.8	74.9	27.5
Mitsui & Co Ltd	Japan	Trading	72.1	23.8	2.1
Mitsubishi Corp	Japan	Trading	70.5	24.9	4.4
C Itoh & Co Ltd	Japan	Trading	59.6	20.0	2.0
Marubeni Corp	Japan	Trading	56.1	21.1	1.6
Sumitomo Corp	Japan	Trading	54.5	12.6	2.6
British Petroleum Co	UK	Oil & Gas	53.1	43.6	14.7
Nissho Iwai Corp	Japan	Trading	37.7	12.2	0.8
Toyota Motor Corp	Japan	Automotive	27.1	17.2	16.2
ENI	Italy	Oil & Gas	24.5	27.2	N/A
IRI Group	Italy	Multicompany	23.5	47.6	N/A
Nippon T & T Co	Japan	Communication	23.0	60.8	N/A
Hitachi Ltd	Japan	Multicompany	72.1	28.8	10.9
Unilever	Nether/UK	Food Process	21.6	13.5	7.8
Matsushita Electric	Japan	Consum Electr	20.9	21.6	11.4
Pemex-Petroleos Mex	Mexico	Oil & Gas	20.4	36.8	N/A
Toyo Menka Kaisha	Japan	Trading	20.2	6.4	0.5
Elf Aquitaine Group	France	Oil & Gas	20.1	22.2	2.7
TOTAL Group	France	Oil & Gas	12.3	12.2	1.2
Nissan Motor Co	Japan	Automotive	18.9	14.4	6.2
Nichimen Corp	Japan	Trading	18.2	6.9	0.4
Philips Group	Nethrlnds	Electr Equip	18.1	17.8	5.1
Volkswagen Group	Germany	Automotive	17.9	14.1	4.7
Siemens Group	Germany	Electr Equip	17.8	19.5	14.3
Daimler-Benz Group	Germany	Automotive	17.8	14.4	17.1
Kanematsu-Gosho Ltd	Japan	Oil & Gas	17.6	5.0	0.3
Deutsche Bundespost	Germany	Communication	17.2	57.1	N/A
Nestle	Switzerld	Food Process	17.2	12.1	10.5
Japanese Nat'nl Rlws	Japan	Transportn	16.9	75.5	N/A
Nippon Life Insuran	Japan	Insurance	16.2	2.3	N/A
BASF Group	Germany	Chem & Drugs	16.2	11.5	5.6
VEBA Group	Germany	Oil & Gas	16.1	13.1	4.7

Company	Country	Industry	Revenue	Assets	Market Value
				($000,000)	
Tokyo Electric Power	Japan	Utility	16.0	36.0	18.7
Petrobas SA	Brazil	Oil & Gas	16.0	12.9	0.7
Samsung Group	Korea	Multicompany	15.7	8.2	N/A
Bayer Group	Germany	Chem & Drugs	15.6	12.3	5.7
Toshiba Corp	Japan	Multicompany	15.3	17.6	4.9
National Iranian Oil	Iran	Oil & Gas	15.0	N/A	N/A
Electricite France	France	Utility	14.6	51.1	N/A
Hoechst Group	Germany	Chem & Drugs	14.5	11.1	6.1
PTT	France	Communication	14.3	N/A	N/A
Fiat Group	Italy	Automotive	14.2	18.8	4.8
Mitsubishi Heavy Ind	Japan	Indus Equip	14.2	14.3	5.1
B.A.T. Industries	UK	Multicompany	13.9	12.8	6.7
Imperial Chem Indus	UK	Chem & Drugs	13.9	12.0	7.1
Hyundai Group	Japan	Multicompany	13.9	8.5	N/A
Kuwait Petroleum	Kuwait	Oil & Gas	13.6	18.9	N/A
Renault Group	France	Automotive	13.6	13.9	N/A
Nippon Oil Co Ltd	Japan	Oil & Gas	13.5	6.3	4.1
Honda Motor Co	Japan	Automotive	12.8	9.3	5.4

Source: *Forbes,* July 28, 1986, pp. 176-193

their home country, industry, and three measures of size, i.e., revenues, assets, and market value.

Foreign Securities Traded Domestically

One aspect of the increasing globalization of money and capital markets is the large number of firms that are supporting the listing and trading of their securities in foreign capital markets. Even though the foreign security may trade and be listed domestically, its price generally tends to move more in tandem with its home market than with the domestic market. Thus, investment in such companies can offer significant opportunities for international diversification.

In recent years, a growing round-the-clock global market in securities of at least the major companies has also emerged. Except for a three-hour gap between the closing of the New York Stock Exchange (NYSE) and the opening of the Tokyo Stock Exchange (TSE) and a half hour between the closing of the Hong Kong Stock

Exchange (HKSE) and the opening of the Amsterdam Stock Exchange, the twenty-four-hour trading day is already covered by one leading exchange or another. Further, as indicated earlier, most of the major brokerage houses now have a presence on all of these major stock exchanges. As a consequence, the simultaneous offering of new security issues in a number of countries is becoming increasingly popular. In 1983, four companies raised $116.6 million in such offerings. These numbers jumped to twenty-six companies and $3,185.6 million in 1985 and the pace continues to increase (*The Wall Street Journal,* June 16, 1986, p. 13). Even the settlement problem is being solved rapidly for equities of some of the larger firms that are being traded internationally. For example, the clearing system—Cedel claims that nearly 700 internationally traded equities are currently being cleared through their electronic multi-currency system (*Euromoney,* October 1986, p. 125). Table 14 lists the major equities as identified by *Euromoney* magazine that are now being traded internationally in significant volumes outside their home country.

In addition, a number of stock exchanges in different countries are now, or are planning to be, linked electronically so that trades can be made simultaneously on different exchanges. As an example,

TABLE 14 SELECTED INTERNATIONAL EQUITIES - MULTIPLE LISTINGS

Company	Industry	Country	Exchange Listings	Market Value ($000,000)
IBM	Com	US	NY,TKY,TOR,ZUR,PAR,FRA,LDN,AMS	75,119
Exxon	Oil	US	NY,AMS,ZUR,FRA,PAR,LDN	35,897
General Elec	Ele	US	NY,AMS,LDN,ZUR,	25,522
General Motor	Aut	US	NY,AMS,PAR,TOR,LDN,TKY,ZUR,FRA	24,665
AT&T	Tel	US	NY,LDN,ZUR,AMS,PAR	18,736
Shell Oil	Oil	US	NY,AMS	17,200
Standard Ind	Oil	US	NY,LDN,TOR,ZUR	16,391
Sumitomo Bnk	Fin	Jap	TKY,OSA,KYO,HIR,SAP,ADR	16,234
Royal/Dutch	Oil	Net	AMS,ZUR,FRA,PAR,LDN,NY,LUX, NASDAQ,ADR	12,936
Toyota Motor	Aut	Jap	TKY,NAG,OSA,KYO,NGT,HIR,FKK, NASDAQ,SAP,ADR	12,336
Fuji Bank	Fin	Jap	TKY,ADR	11,976

Company	Industry	Country	Exchange Listings	Market Value ($000,000)
Eastman Kodak	Ele	US	NY,AMS,PAR,ZUR	11,910
DuPont	Chm	US	NY,AMS,PAR,FRA,ZUR	11,860
Mobil	Oil	US	NY,AMS,TOR,ZUR,LDN	11,086
Matsushita	Ele	Jap	TKY,OSA,NY,PAC,AMS,FRA,DUS,HK, ADR	10,873
Chevron	Oil	US	NY,AMS,VAN,LDN,ZUR	10,691
Atlantic Rich	Oil	US	NY,AMS,ZUR	10,667
British Pet	Oil	UK	LDN,ZUR,NY,PAR,FRA,AMS	10,284
Philip Morris	Con	US	NY,AMS,PAR,ZUR,FRA	9,965
Hitachi	Ele	Jap	TKY,LUX,FRA,AMS,PA,HK,NY,ADR	9,600
ProcterGamble	Con	US	NY,AMS,FRA,PAR,ZUR	9,518
Tokyo Ele Pwr	Utl	Jap	TKY,OSA,NAG,NGT	9,319
3M	Div	US	NY,ZUR,PAR,FRA,AMS	9,247
Texaco	Oil	US	NY,LDN,AMS,ZUR	9,025
RJ Reynolds	Con	US	NY,AMS	8,876
Hewlett-Pack	Ele	US	NY	8,667
Ford Motor	Aut	US	NY,TOR,ZUR,PAR,FRA,LDN,AMS	8,432
Shell Trans	Oil	UK	LDN,PAR,FRA,NY,BRU,ADR	8,372
Coca-Cola	Con	US	NY,ZUR,FRA	8,304
American Exp	Fin	US	NY,LDN,AMS,PAR,TOR,FRA,ZUR	8,028
British Telec	Tel	UK	LDN,NY,TOR,ADR	7,346
Merck	Drg	US	NY,AMS,PAR	6,951
General Elec	Ele	UK	LDN,PAR,ADR	6,947
Phillips Pet	Oil	US	NY,AMS,TOR,ZUR	6,928
Fujitsu	Ele	Jap	TKY,OSA,NAG,LDN,FRA,ZUR,BAS,GEN	6,895
Pfizer	Drg	US	NY,PAR,ZUR,LDN	6,742
NEC Corp	Ele	Jap	TKY,AMS,FRA,LDN,ADR,7 JAP EXCHS	6,665
Seimens	Ele	WG	MUN,BER,ZUR,BAS,GEN,PAR,AMS, BRU,VNA,ADR	6,608
Digital Equip	Ele	US	NY,LUX	6,403
Daimler-Benz	Aut	WG	DUS,HAM,MUN,HAN,ZUR,FRA,STU, BER,BRN,GEN,BAS,ADR	6,377
Bell Canada	Tel	Can	TOR,MON,FRA,PAR,AMS,NY,ZUR	6,016
BAT Ind	Con	UK	LDN,AMR,ADR	5,997
Nomura Sec	Fin	Jap	TKY,AMS,LUX,ADR	5,958
Boeing	Air	US	NY,LDN,AMS,ZUR	5,490
ICI	Chm	UK	NY,AMS,LDN,ZUR,VNA,ANT,BRA,PAR, LUX,OSL,BAS,GEN,LAU,FRA,ADR	5,389
Dow Chemical	Chm	US	NY,AMS,ZUR,FRA,TOR,LDN,PAR,TKY	5,386
SUN	Oil	US	NY,AMS,FRA,LDN,ZUR	5,357
Nissan Motor	Aut	Jap	TKY,FRA,NASDAQ,ADR,6 JAP EXCHS	5,300
Tenneco	Oil	US	NY,FRA,LDN,PAR,TOR,ZUR	5,278
Imperial	Oil	Can	TOR,VAN,MON,NY	5,130
Abbott	Drg	US	NY,LDN,ZUR,BAS,GEN	5,098
Fanuc	Ele	Jap	TKY	5,029

Source: *Euromoney*, May 1985

in April 1986, the NASDAQ established a real-time electronic satellite link with its counterpart in London, the Unlisted Securities Market (USM). Initially, this link means that the NASDAQ makes available quotes on its 300 most heavily traded stocks to brokers in London while U.S. members of the NASDAQ system have available quotes on the 300 most heavily traded London stocks. One result of this link is the increase in the number of U.S. companies, like Borland International, that are making their Initial Public Offerings (IPOs) in London rather than the United States.

While a number of U.S. companies are listed on foreign stock exchanges; attracted by the large and efficient U.S. capital market, a much larger number of foreign securities trade in the United States. U.S. trading of these foreign stocks has become very important for some of these foreign companies. As an example, Novo Industries of Denmark could not have expanded as it did without its sale of equities in New York. As another example, more shares of Britain's Imperial Chemical Industries and Japan's Sony Corporation are traded in New York than are traded in their home markets. A limited number of these foreign companies have satisfied the relatively stringent disclosure and reporting requirements of the U.S. Securities and Exchange Commission (SEC) for their shares to be listed directly on one of the U.S. stock exchanges.

Most foreign companies have chosen to avoid the expense of these requirements by listing or otherwise making available American Depository Receipts (ADRs) representing their shares. An ADR represents shares on deposit with an American financial institution which collects and passes on foreign dividends (after foreign withholding taxes and a small handling charge), takes care of stock splits, rights offerings (which are required to be liquidated) and other similar developments. Each ADR represents an appropriate number of shares so that it is priced in a range that is attractive to U.S. investors. The owner of an ADR has access to dividends and other rights associated with the underlying shares. Further, ADRs can always be converted into the underlying shares. However, holding foreign shares exposes an investor to foreign death taxes and legal requirements for transfer of ownership.

The shares of over a thousand foreign companies trade directly or as ADRs in the United States. (*Fortune,* December 22, 1986). Most of these ADRs trade on the Over The Counter (OTC) market. The largest number of ADRs or stocks traded on the OTC are from Japan, followed by those from Australia, the United Kingdom, and South Africa. Next are stocks from West Germany, Hong Kong, Singapore, France, Italy, Sweden, the Netherlands, Malaysia, Norway, Finland, and a number of other countries ranging from Botswana and El Salvador to Zambia.

In addition to the OTC, the New York Stock Exchange (NYSE) had fifty-three foreign companies from fifteen countries listed as of the end of 1984. Of the fifty-three companies listed on the NYSE, twenty-three were headquartered in Canada, eight in Japan, seven in the United Kingdom, three in the Netherland Antilles, two each in the Netherlands and in Panama, and one each in the Bahamas, Bermuda, British West Indies, Denmark, Israel, Philippines, South Africa, and Spain. The NYSE also listed twenty-one bond issues of fourteen foreign companies, eighty-eight bond issues of four international banks, and ninety-three bond issues of thirty-four foreign governments. Foreign bond issues represent over 5 percent of the value and number of the bonds listed on the NYSE. Thus, there were a total of 255 non-U.S. issues listed on the NYSE at the end of 1984. Similarly, the American Stock Exchange (ASE) has listed fifty-nine foreign securities (fifty-three stocks and six bonds). Of these fifty-nine, forty issues are for companies from Canada, five from Israel, four from the United Kingdom, three from the Philippines, two each from Japan and the Bahamas, and one each from South Africa, Mexico, and the Netherland Antilles. Interestingly, even though the foreign stocks listed on the ASE represent only 5 percent of the total number listed, they represent over 25 percent of the total value (end-1984).

The London Stock Exchange (LSE) has over 500 foreign listings and the Amsterdam Stock Exchange has almost 300 foreign listings. Stock exchanges in West Germany and in Switzerland also have a number of foreign listings and the Tokyo Stock Exchange (TSE) is now beginning to allow listings by foreign companies and it already (end-1986) has fifty-two such listings. Stock exchanges in other countries do not have significant numbers of listings by foreign companies. Table 15 is a representative list of the major stock exchanges and the number and proportion of foreign listings on each exchange. Although foreign listings have increased in many cases since this information was compiled, the list is still fairly representative of the relative popularity of foreign listings on these exchanges.

Thus, investors in the United States, the United Kingdom, the Netherlands, and to a lesser extent in West Germany and in Switzerland, can achieve international diversification relatively easily

TABLE 15 LISTINGS ON SELECTED EXCHANGES - 1980

Exchange	Total	Domestic	Foreign	% Foreign
American	892	837	55	6.2
Amsterdam	508	214	294	57.9
Basel	260	101	159	61.2
Brussels	377	255	152	40.3
Copenhagen	222	218	4	1.8
Assc of German	634	459	175	27.6
Geneva	273	98	175	64.1
Hong Kong	157	137	20	12.7
Johannesburg	508	481	27	5.3
London	3,141	2,659	482	15.3
Luxembourg	168	74	94	56.0
Madrid	496	494	2	0.4
Montreal	417	393	24	5.8
New York	1,570	1,533	37	2.4
Paris	761	586	162	21.3
Singapore	261	97	164	62.8
Sydney	1,031	1,007	24	2.3
Tokyo	1,417	1,402	15	1.1
Toronto	799	731	68	8.5
Vienna	101	66	35	34.7
Zurich	274	118	156	56.9

Source: Freund, William C. (1982), "The Internationalization of Stock Exchanges," *The Journal of Accounting, Auditing, and Finance* (Fall), 80-88

by purchasing securities of foreign companies that are listed and traded in their domestic markets. However, the number of such securities are usually limited compared to the total number of publicly traded securities available globally. In addition, in spite of easier availability of information on foreign securities trading on domestic markets as compared to other foreign securities, investors in these securities still face higher information processing costs compared to investors in domestic securities.

Internationally Diversified Mutual Funds

International Mutual Funds is probably the most popular route to international diversification undertaken by individuals and, perhaps, by some institutional investors. The high fixed costs of evaluating and investing in foreign securities can be spread over a large trading volume in a mutual fund. Therefore, one reason for the popularity of internationally diversified mutual funds may be the ease and low cost with which they provide international diversification. Their popularity persists in spite of the mixed evidence regarding the long-run superiority of internationally diversified mutual funds in providing a significantly higher risk-adjusted rate of return as compared to purely domestic investments.

Closed-end mutual funds invest a fixed pool of money while open-end mutual funds seek and invest continuing additional funds. A number of closed-end mutual funds that specialize in specific countries or regions have been introduced to U.S. investors in recent years. These include funds for Japan, Korea, Taiwan, India, Mexico, France, Italy, Germany, Nordic countries, Scandinavian countries, and Australia. Another approach to international diversification by investing in the equities of a specific country that are just becoming widely available is to invest in a futures contract on an index of stocks in that country. A number of these futures on indexes have now begun trading. For example, the Singapore International Monetary Exchange (SIMEX) has recently started trading futures on the Nikkei 225 stock average for Japanese stocks. A number of U.S. and foreign exchanges also trade futures on various stock indexes for the United States, United Kingdom, Hong Kong, and other major stock markets.

Internationally diversified mutual funds can either be closed-ended or open-ended. Open-end funds based in the United States are generally classified into two categories. Global funds invest in foreign and U.S. securities while International funds invest only in non-U.S. securities. In addition, while most such funds invest only in foreign equities, some invest only in foreign fixed-income securities and some invest in a mixture of equities and fixed-income securities. Table 16 is a list of U.S.-based open-end internationally diversified mutual funds. As this table indicates, there were at least twenty-two Global mutual funds available to U.S. investors and fourteen of them had assets over a hundred million dollars. Similarly there were thirty International mutual funds available to U.S. investors and thirteen of them had assets over a hundred million dollars.

Domestically Traded Multinational Corporations

International diversification can also be achieved by investing in multinational corporations (MNCs) that are traded in domestic capital markets. This is an indirect form of international diversification and its effectiveness depends on at least two advantages that may be enjoyed by an MNC.

First, because of economies of scale and possible competitive advantages in collecting and analyzing data on foreign investments, the MNC may have the ability to perform this diversification service at lower cost than can a portfolio investor. In addition, an MNC may be able to capture some benefits of international diversification through direct investment, which includes managerial control of foreign facilities, that cannot be captured through portfolio investment alone. As a matter of fact, it is contended that MNCs often have access to, and appropriate the best investments in foreign countries and such investments are not available to portfolio investors. Unfortunately, direct empirical tests of the effectiveness of the MNC as a vehicle for international diversification provide mixed results and do not provide an unambiguous guide for investors. In addi-

TABLE 16 INTERNATIONALLY DIVERSIFIED MUTUAL FUNDS
Available to U.S. Investors
(Data as of September 30, 1986)

Global Fund	Net Assets	International Fund	Net Assets
Templeton World	$3,213.1	Fidelity Overseas	$2,560.5
Templeton Growth	1,813.1	T Rowe Price Intl Fd	751.6
New Perspective	869.5	Scudder International	685.7
Templeton Global II	497.7	Trustees Commgld Intl	633.9
Pru-Bache Global	402.0	Merrill Lynch Pacific	445.4
Oppenheimer AIM	373.2	Templeton Foreign	186.6
Putnam Intl Equities	372.2	IDS International	227.7
Dean Witter World Wide	345.7	Kemper Intl Fund	184.3
Templeton Global I	301.5	Shearson Lehman Intl	168.8
MerrillLynch Intl Hldg	277.7	Alliance International	164.4
Shearson Global	263.2	Europacific Growth	159.6
Paine Webber Atlas	244.5	BBK International	149.0
United Intl Growth	205.3	FT International	104.5
Mass Finl Intl Hldgs	133.5	Transatlantic Fund	99.9
John Hancock Global	72.4	Keystone International	89.8
Thomson McKinnon Global	67.0	GT Pacific Growth	67.2
First Inv International	28.8	Fenimore International	65.9
GAM Global	14.5	Nomura Pacific Basin	53.1
Scudder Global	11.4	GAM International	24.9
Principal World	7.3	Canadian Fund	22.6
Alliance Global	3.5	Financial Port-Pacific	16.5
Freedom Global	0.1	GT International Growth	10.2
		Fund Trust International	9.2
		IVY International	9.0
		Sigma World	8.5
		GT Europe Growth	6.7
		GT Japan Growth	6.3
		Newport Far East	2.8
		Colonial Intl Eq Index	1.7
		Intl Cash-Eurocash	1.4

Net assets in millions of U.S. dollars.

tion, the portfolio investor has little control over the geographic spread and overall proportion of the foreign investments made by an MNC. Thus, investing in securities of domestically traded MNCs may not allow the portfolio investor to achieve the level of international diversification considered optimal for that investor.

An investor that would like to diversify internationally by investing in shares of MNCs can consider companies that have a large percentage of their sales, assets, or profits denominated in terms of a foreign currency. Unfortunately, there is wide variation in the degree to which this data is disclosed by U.S. and other MNCs. Nevertheless, Business International, *Business Week,* and *Forbes* publish annual lists of the largest multinationals with their percentage of foreign assets, sales, and profits. Table 17 lists the top 100 U.S.-based multinational companies and their foreign sales and incomes.

CHOOSING AMONG ALTERNATIVES

Before choosing any of the above alternatives for international diversification, an investor must review the need and suitability of seeking international diversification given the needs and goals of the investor. The percentage allocation that should go to foreign investments may be limited by fiduciary requirements and government regulations. Thus, as a first step, given the goals and restrictions on the portfolio, the investor should determine the percentage of the portfolio that should be allocated to foreign assets and the distribution between equities, fixed-income, real estate, and other asset categories and the frequency with which the portfolio is to be evaluated and adjusted. Having made these decisions, the investor is ready

TABLE 17 TOP 100 U.S. MULTINATIONALS
(1985 Foreign Sales and Income)
(Millions of Dollars)

Company	Sales	%	Inc.	%	Company	Sales	%	Inc.	%
Exxon	62750	71	3530	59	Honeywell	1646	25	141	24
Mobil	34982	59	1317	58	TransWorld Air	1607	44	162	211
Texaco	21864	47	900	49	Sperry	1595	28	256	48
IBM	21545	43	3084	47	Merck	1589	45	214	25
Ford Motor	15995	30	527	21	U. S. Steel	1578	8	542	40
Phibro-Salomon	15100	54	349	37	Sara Lee	1510	19	109	23

Company	Sales	%	Inc.	%	Company	Sales	%	Inc.	%
General Motors	14534	17	627	14	Texas Instr	1418	29	−4	−20
Du pont	11429	32	358	21	Caterpillar	1403	21	−16	−3
ITT	7327	37	560	67	Halliburton	1400	34	58	65
Chevron	7154	16	765	35	H. J. Heinz	1386	34	155	31
Dow Chemical	6326	55	382	60	Gillette	1375	57	233	58
Amoco	5984	21	785	40	W. R. Grace	1320	25	188	47
R. J. Reynolds	4462	26	398	18	Bristol-Myers	1315	28	213	24
Safeway	4260	22	133	31	TRW	1260	21	137	29
Schlumberger	4136	68	1107	110	McDermott	1250	39	71	−186
Occidental Petr	4068	25	1389	68	Control Data	1179	23	138	99
American Brands	3930	56	169	19	American Cyana	1170	30	150	60
Proctor Gamble	3625	26	96	15	Warner-Lambert	1162	41	286	39
Phillip Morris	3545	22	152	6	HNG/Internorth	1142	11	86	14
Eastman Kodak	3239	30	167	31	Kimberly-Clark	1135	27	106	20
Xerox	3207	36	170	45	Amerada Hess	1128	15	119	−46
Goodyear	3148	33	177	28	Dresser Indus	1080	26	88	−244
Phillips Petro	3125	20	1339	49	Firestone	1063	28	91	63
General Elec	3112	11	101	4	SmithKlineBeck	1055	31	174	24
United Technol	3071	20	284	24	American Home	1048	22	209	17
Coca-Cola	2996	38	611	53	Eli Lilly	1039	32	204	26
Hewlet Packard	2809	43	304	32	Continental	1031	20	1	0
Sun	2755	18	19	3	Rockwell Intl	957	8	122	10
American Exprs	2749	23	316	22	Pepsico	952	12	67	8
Beatrice	2689	21	211	23	Abbott Laborat	950	28	151	20
Tenneco	2665	17	202	14	PPG Industries	934	21	54	8
Union Carbide	2632	29	272	33	American Std	930	31	119	51
Dart & Kraft	2628	27	328	34	Quaker Oats	927	28	77	21
3M	2594	33	332	29	A&P	923	16	30	34
Pan Am	2591	74	50	−28	Westinghouse	904	8	67	9
Chrysler	2488	12	257	11	Deere	898	22	54	62
Johnson & Johsn	2431	38	476	41	Avon products	888	36	139	46
CPC Internatl	2373	56	199	54	Litton Indus	870	19	112	24
Colgate-Palmol	2354	52	133	40	Murphy Oil	867	34	108	85
F. W. Woolworth	2335	40	119	34	Kellog	855	29	58	21
American Intl	2253	39	364	93	United Brands	853	26	25	32
Burroughs	2203	44	273	45	Borden	832	18	76	19
GTE	2169	14	101	9	Champion Intnl	826	14	77	15
Atlantic Richfd	2138	9	96	29	Schering-Plough	803	42	99	29
Allied-Signal	2047	22	129	−46	Borg-Warner	800	20	78	20
NCR	1965	46	278	46	McDonald's	790	23	147	18
Monsanto	1923	29	216	55	CBI Industries	779	50	101	84
Unocal	1834	15	186	23	Ingersoll-Rand	755	29	51	23
Motorola	1818	27	76	40	Ralston Purina	753	13	33	5
Pfizer	1682	42	298	33	RCA	743	8	62	17

Source: *Business Week*, April 18, 1986, pp. 290-298. % is foreign sales and income as a percent of total sales and income. Negative numbers indicate companies with an overall loss.

to evaluate the approach that is best for achieving international diversification.

As the discussion in the prior sections indicates, each of the alternatives for international diversification has some advantages and disadvantages whose importance depends to some extent on the needs and skills of the investor. Thus, a particular approach that may be optimal for one investor may be quite unsuitable for another. In order to evaluate each of the above alternatives for a particular investment situation, the following factors should be considered as a minimum.

First, the ability and skill of the investor in identifying, gathering, and analyzing information on foreign investments should be considered. To seek out and invest in undervalued investments in foreign countries on a consistent basis, as discussed above, can be an expensive task requiring personnel who have the appropriate knowledge-base and ability that extends beyond that required for the analysis of domestic investments. Second, brokerage and transaction costs must be added to the information costs discussed above. These costs are generally higher for making investments in foreign countries and are lower for investing in domestically traded ADRs, mutual funds, and other securities. Third, in addition to the costs of international diversification, the investor must also consider the foreign exchange, political, liquidity, and other risks when investing overseas. Some of these risks, such as the currency risk, can be managed and, therefore, the investor's ability and skill in managing these risks should also be a consideration, especially since efficient markets tend not to reward risks that can be managed or eliminated. Balancing these costs and risks of international investments are the benefits such as risk diversification and an expansion in the opportunity set of possibly undervalued assets. Table 18 summarizes these considerations.

As this table indicates, investing directly in foreign assets and in foreign securities listed or traded domestically may involve costs and skills that generally make them unsuitable unless these costs can be spread over relatively large trading volumes. On the other hand, international diversification through investment in internationally diversified mutual funds or in domestically traded multinational

TABLE 18 INTERNATIONAL DIVERSIFICATION ALTERNATIVES
Costs and Benefits

Investment	Costs and Risks: Info Costs	Costs and Risks: Trans Costs	Costs and Risks: Forex Risks	Potential Benefits: Risk Reduction	Potential Benefits: Asset Selection
Foreign Assets	High	High	High	High	High
Foreign Securities Traded Domestically	Medium	Low	Medium	High	Medium
Mutual Funds					
Closed-end	Low	Medium	Medium	Medium	Medium
Open-end	Low	Medium	Low	Medium	Medium
Index Funds	Low	Low	High	Medium	Low
Multinationals	Low	Low	Low	Low	Medium

companies offers low-cost alternatives. However, as the table also indicates, these latter alternatives are not as attractive as the first two higher-cost alternatives with regard to the opportunities for realizing returns in excess of what may be appropriate given the portfolio risk. In addition, when using mutual funds and multinationals for international diversification, the investor may not have the opportunity to achieve the exact geographic distribution of assets that may be desired by or be optimal for that investor.

Thus, choosing the best approach for international diversification involves trade-offs between alternatives that are high cost but have potentially high returns versus alternatives that are low cost but may not be ideally suited given the needs of a portfolio and providing only limited opportunities for investments in undervalued assets.

CONCLUSIONS

This chapter has reviewed briefly the major alternatives available for international diversification. An investor can invest in assets in foreign countries, in foreign securities listed and traded domestically, in mutual funds that invest internationally, and in domestically traded multinational companies.

The first two of these alternatives require specialized and expensive expertise that can only be justified by institutional investors or in special cases such as when making large investments or when access to particular information is provided. Fortunately, internationally diversified mutual funds and domestically traded multinational companies offer low-cost alternatives for international diversification.

BIBLIOGRAPHY

Abrams, Richard K. and Donald V. Kimbal. "U.S. Investment in Foreign Equity Markets," *Economic Review,* Federal Reserve Bank of Kansas City, (April 1981), pp. 17-30

Adler, Michael. "Global Fixed-Income Portfolio Management," *Financial Analysts Journal,* (September/October 1983), pp. 41-48

Adler, Michael and Bernard Dumas. "International Portfolio Choice and Corporate Finance: A Synthesis, "*Journal of Finance,* 38 (No. 3, June 1983), pp. 925-984

Aggarwal, Raj. "Investment Performance of U.S.-Based Multinational Companies," *Journal of International Business Studies,* 11 (No. 1, Spring/Summer 1980), pp. 98-104

Aggarwal, Raj. "International Differences in Capital Structure Norms," *Management International Review,* 21 (No. 1, 1981), pp. 75-88

Aggarwal, Raj. "Exchange Rates and Stock Prices," *Akron Business and Economic Review,* 12 (No. 3, Fall 1981), pp. 7-12

Ayling, D. E. *The Internationalisation of the Stock Markets* (Aldershot, England: Gower Publishing Company Limited, 1986)

Agmon, Tamir and Donald Lessard. "Investor Recognition of Corporate International Diversification," *Journal of Finance,* 32 (September 1977), pp. 1049-1055

Biger, Nahum. "Exchange Risk Implications of International Portfolio Diversification," *Journal of International Business Studies,* (Fall 1979), pp. 64-74

Black, Fisher. "The Ins and Outs of Foreign Investment," *Financial Analysts Journal,* (May/June 1978), pp. 1-7

Choi, Frederick D. S., and Arthur I. Stonehill. "Foreign Access to U.S. Securities Markets: The Theory, Myth and Reality of Regulatory Barriers," *The Investment Analyst,* (July 1982), pp. 17-26

Chrystal, H. A. "A Guide To Foreign Exchange Markets," *Federal Reserve Bank of St. Louis Economic Review,* (March 1984), pp. 5-17

Cohen, Kalman, W. L. Ness, H. Okuda, R. A. Schwartz and D. K. Whitcomb. "The Determinants of Common Stock Returns Volatility: An International Comparison," *Journal of Finance,* (May 1976), pp. 733-751

Dufey, Gunter. "Institutional Constraints and Incentives on International Portfolio Investment," *International Portfolio Investment,* U.S. Department of the Treasury, OASIA 1975

Ehrlich, Edna E. "International Diversification by United States Pension Funds," *Federal Reserve Bank of New York Quarterly Review,* (Autumn 1981), pp. 1-14

Ehrlich, Edna E. "Foreign Pension Fund Investment in the United States," *Federal Reserve Bank of New York Quarterly Review,* (Spring 1983), pp.1-12

Errunza, Vihang R. "Gains From Portfolio Diversification into Less Developed Countries' Securities," *Journal of International Business Studies,* (Fall/Winter 1977), pp. 83-99

Eun, Cheol S., and Bruce G. Resnick. "Currency Factor in International Portfolio Diversification," *Columbia Journal of World Business,* (Summer 1985), pp. 45-53

Folks, William R. and Raj Aggarwal. *International Dimensions of Financial Management* (Boston: Kent Publishing Company, 1987)

Germany J. David, and John E. Morton. "Financial Innovation and Deregulation in Foreign Industrial Countries," *Federal Reserve Bulletin,* (October 1985), pp. 743-753

Gray, S. J., L. G. Campbell and J. C. Shaw (Editors). *International Financial Reporting: A Comparative Survey of* Accounting Practices in 30 Countries, (New York: St. Martin Press, 1984)

Greig, Katherine, Charles Hildeburnand and Quek Peck Lim. "The Surge in International Equities," *Euromoney,* (May, 1985), pp. 121-146

Grubel, Herbert G. "Internationally Diversified Portfolios: Welfare Gains and Capital Flows," *American Economic Review,* (December 1968), pp. 1299-1314

Hawawini, Gabriel. *European Equity Markets: Price Behavior and Efficiency,* New York: Solomon Brothers Center for the Study of Financial Institutions and the Graduate School of Business Administration of New York University, Monograph, (1984)

Hill, Joanne and Thomas Schneeweis. "International Diversification of Equities and Fixed-Income Securities," *Journal of Financial Research,* 6 (No. 4, Winter 1983), pp. 333-343

Ibbotson, Roger G., Richard C. Carr, and Anthony W. Robinson. "International Equity and Bond Returns," *Financial Analysts Journal,* (July/August 1982), pp. 61-83

Jacquillat, Bertrand and Bruno Solnik. "Multinationals Are Poor Tools for Diversification," *Journal of Portfolio Management,* (Winter 1978), pp. 8-12

Jorion, Phillipe. "International Portfolio Diversifications with Estimation Risk," *Journal of Business,* 58 (No. 3, July 1985), pp. 259-278

Kemp, Lynnette J. *A Guide to World Money and Capital Markets,* (New York: McGraw-Hill, 1982)

Kemp, Lynnette J. *The Wardley Guide to World Money and Securities Markets,* (London: Euromoney Publications, 1984)

Lessard, Donald R. "World, Country, and Industry Relationships in Equity Returns: Implications for Risk Reduction Through International Diversification," *Financial Analysts Journal,* (January/February 1976), pp. 32-38

Levy, H. and M. Sarnat. "International Diversification of Investment Portfolios," *American Economic Reveiw,* (September 1970), pp. 668-675)

Maldonado, Rita and Anthony Saunders. "International Portfolio Diversification and the Inter-Temporal Stability of International Stock Market Relationships 1957-1978," *Financial Management,* (Autumn 1981), pp. 54-63

Merjos, Anna. "Investors Ticket Abroad," *Barron's,* (April 30, 1984), pp. 24-26

Philippatos, G. C., A. Christofi and P. Christofi. "The Inter-Temporal Stability of International Stock Market Relationships: Another View," *Financial Management,* 12 (No. 4, Winter 1983), pp. 63-69

Rao, Ramesh and Raj Aggarwal. "Performance of U.S.-Based Internationally Diversified Mutual Funds," *Akron Business and Economic Review,* 18 (No. 4, Winter 1987).

Rosenthal, Leonard. "An Empirical Test of the Efficiency of the ADR Market," *Journal of Banking and Finance,* 7 (No. 1, March 1983), pp. 17-29

Shaked, Israel. "International Equity Markets and the Investment Horizon," *The Journal of Portfolio Management,* (Winter 1985), pp. 80-84

Shouse, Mary C. and Mary E. M. Zellerbach. "The Theory and Price of International Equity Funds," *Columbia Journal of World Business,* (Summer 1982), pp. 46-52

Solnik, Bruno H. "Why Not Diversify Internationally," *Financial Analysts Journal,* (July/August 1974), pp. 48-54

Solnik, Bruno H. and Bernard Noetzlin. "Optimal International Asset Allocation," *Journal of Portfolio Management,* 9 (No. 1, Fall 1982), pp. 11-21

Stehle, Richard F. "An Empirical Test of the Alternative Hypothesis of National and International Pricing of Risk Assets," *Journal of Finance,* (May 1977), pp. 493-502

Subrahmanyam, Marti G. "On the Optimality of International Captial Market Integration," *Journal of Financial Economics,* (March 1975), pp. 3-28

Thomas, Barbara S. ''Internationalization of the Securities Markets,'' *George Washington Law Review,* (January 1982), pp. 155-190

Waterhouse, Price. *World's Major Stock Exchanges: Listing Requirements* (1984)

van Agtmael, Antoine W. *Emerging Securities Markets,* (London: Euromoney Publicatons, 1984)

Von Furstenberg, George M. ''Incentives for International Currency Diversification by U.S. Financial Investors,'' *International Monetary Fund Staff Papers,* (September 1981), pp. 477-494

CHAPTER FIVE

RICHARD SEGAL is currently a research analyst in the International Bond Market Research group at Salomon Brothers International, Ltd., based in London, where he concentrates mainly on the Eurodollar and the Japanese, Canadian, and Dutch Government bond markets. He has also collaborated in the development of trading strategies for the above markets. Prior to his arrival at Salomon Brothers in 1983, Mr. Segal worked at the Gillette Company in Boston, Massachusetts. Mr. Segal received a degree in economics from the Massachusetts Institute of Technology in 1982. His major focus of study was international macroeconomic policy.

HOW BIG IS THE WORLD BOND MARKET?*

Richard Segal
Salomon Brothers Inc.
London, England

INTRODUCTION

One of the more noticeable trends of fixed-income investors over the past few years has been their increasing global orientation. U.S. investors have been investing abroad, and foreign—especially Japanese—investors have been investing in U.S. dollar-denominated securities as never before. While U.S. investors have some knowledge about the government and international bond sectors of major foreign bond markets, they have relatively little knowledge about the workings of other sectors, such as the markets for corporate and local government bonds. As a result, it is important for investors to have a complete grasp of all of the aspects of the world's major bond markets. Accordingly, this chapter presents and analyzes the world's thirteen largest bond markets, with major emphasis on the activity that occurred during 1985. Some of the more important features of the world's major bond markets are listed below.

*Revised from "How Big Is The World Bond Market?—1986 Update" published by Salomon Brothers Inc, June 9, 1986.

PROFILE OF THE WORLD BOND MARKET AT YEAR-END 1985

In 1985, a year marked by sharp declines in interest rates in the major international bond markets, the nominal value of publicly issued bonds in the world's thirteen major bond markets grew by 17 percent when measured by constant exchange rates—a slightly higher rate than in 1984. When measured in U.S. dollar terms, the increase was an exceptional 27 percent, reflecting the 16 percent depreciation of the dollar on a trade-weighted basis during the year.

In U.S. dollar terms, five bond markets—those of the Italian lira, French franc, Dutch guilder, Danish krone, and Deutschemark—grew by more than 40 percent, as each of these currencies appreciated by more than 15 percent versus the dollar during the year. Of all the major markets, only the Australian dollar sector decreased in U.S. dollar terms, contracting by 4 percent in 1985, a result of the sharp depreciation of the Australian currency. This contrasts with 1984, when the Australian sector was the fastest-growing non-U.S. dollar market.

Currency fluctuations accounted for most of the change in the relative size of the major markets during 1985. Three pairs of markets traded places in 1985: the Canadian dollar and the French franc, the Danish krone and the Swedish krona, and the Dutch guider and the Australian dollar markets.

After several years of increasing domination of local bond markets, the central government and government agency share of all outstanding bonds has begun to level off. In several countries, austerity programs, aided by falling inflation and interest rates, have reduced fiscal strains. A notable exception is the Italian lira market, in which the share of government and agency bonds to all lira bonds rose by 15 percentage points between year-end 1982 and 1985. In Switzerland, where the general government budget is nearly in balance, central government bonds comprise just 8 percent of all outstanding bonds. In contrast, the government and agency bonds' share of total bonds has been over 75 percent in the U.K. sterling, Belgian franc, Italian lira, and French franc bond markets.

FIGURE 1 SIZE OF MAJOR BOND MARKETS AT YEAR-END 1985
(Nominal Value Outstanding, Billions of U.S. Dollars Equivalent)[a]

Bond Market	Total Publicly Issued	As Pct. of Public Issues in All Markets	Central Gov't.	Central Gov't. Agency & Gov't. Guar.	State & Local Gov't.	Corp. (Incl. Cvts.)	Other Domestic Publicly Issued	Int'l. Bonds: Foreign Bonds	Int'l. Bonds: Euro-bonds	Private Place. and Unclass.
U.S. Dollar	**$3,119.0**	52.6%	$1,037.8	$623.5[b]	$606.2	$479.0	$32.6	$72.7	$267.2	$269.5
Japanese Yen	**1,082.9**	18.2	664.8	79.1	29.5	68.1	206.2	25.8	9.3	208.3
Deutschemark	**427.2**	7.2	84.2	15.1	11.1	1.0	267.7	48.0		205.5[c]
Italian Lira	**276.4**	4.7	203.7	12.2	—	3.1	57.1	0.2	0.1	—
U.K. Sterling	**210.8**	3.6	179.5	—	0.5	11.0	—	5.3	14.4	—
French Franc	**174.4**	2.9	47.7	87.1	3.1	33.5	—	1.6	1.5	—
Canadian Dollar	**131.0**	2.2	56.6	0.1	41.4	24.1	0.9	0.6	7.2	—
Belgian Franc	**112.0[d]**	1.9	52.7[d]	36.1[d]	—	6.7[d]	16.0[d]	0.3	0.3	—
Danish Krone	**102.0**	1.7	36.9	—	—	—	64.8	—	0.3	—
Swedish Krona	**101.7**	1.7	51.0	—	1.5	8.0	41.2	—	—	—
Swiss Franc	**76.6**	1.3	6.1	—	5.9	14.6	17.5	32.4	—	43.3
Dutch Guilder	**69.0**	1.2	41.2	—	3.4	16.2	—	5.2	3.0	54.9[c]
Australian Dollar	**50.2**	0.8	25.9	9.6	—	11.2	—	—	3.6	26.3
Total	**$5,933.2**		**$2,488.1**	**$862.8**	**$702.6**	**$676.5**	**$704.0**	**$499.0**		**$807.8[c]**
Sector as Pct. of Public Issues in All Markets		100.0%	41.9%	14.5%	11.8%	11.4%	11.9%	8.4%		

[a] Exchange rates prevailing as of December 31, 1985, are as follows: ¥200.20/US$, DM2.445/US$, Lira 1,668.75/US$, £0.6921/US$, Ffr7.505/US$, C$1.400/US$, Bfr49.967/US$, Dkr8.969/US$, Skr7.548/US$, Sfr2.078/US$, Dfl 2.756/US$ and A$1.464/US$.
[b] Includes mortgage pool issues.
[c] In addition, there exists an unspecifiable amount of privately placed issues of the private sector.
[d] As of October 31, 1985.

FIGURE 2 CHANGING SHARE OF CENTRAL GOVERNMENT AND INTERNATIONAL ISSUES IN EACH OF THE WORLD'S MAJOR BOND MARKETS

	Central Government and Government Agency Bonds						International Bonds					
Bond Market	**1980**	**1981**	**1982**	**1983**	**1984**	**1985**	**1980**	**1981**	**1982**	**1983**	**1984**	**1985**
U.S. Dollar	47.0%	48.7%	49.8%	52.2%	53.8%	53.3%	7.6%	8.1%	9.0%	9.3%	10.1%	10.9%
Japanese Yen	63.2	66.4	67.5	68.7	68.5	68.7	1.7	1.8	2.1	2.2	2.5	3.2
Deutschemark	18.8	16.8	18.6	20.0	21.7	23.2	12.6	11.6	10.8	10.1	10.2	11.2
Italian Lira	59.6	58.4	61.3	69.1	73.8	78.1	0.1	0.1	0.1	0.1	0.1	0.1
U.K. Sterling	91.2	91.9	90.6	89.8	92.5	85.2	0.9	1.5	2.3	3.9	6.7	9.3
French Franc	72.4	74.3	76.3	77.1	77.8	77.3	2.5	2.6	2.2	1.9	1.7	1.8
Canadian Dollar	35.6	36.3	37.1	38.4	41.1	43.3	3.4	3.3	3.5	3.7	4.4	6.0
Belgian Franc	79.0	77.7	77.3	77.4	78.7	79.3	0.4	0.3	0.3	0.2	0.3	0.5
Danish Krone	16.1	21.1	29.2	33.9	36.8	36.2	0.1	0.1	0.1	0.1	0.1	0.3
Swedish Krona	40.3	45.2	48.5	52.6	51.0	50.1	—	—	—	—	—	—
Swiss Franc	11.9	10.7	9.4	8.7	8.2	8.0	27.2	29.4	34.7	37.6	39.5	42.3
Dutch Guilder	33.1	38.7	45.0	52.8	58.2	59.7	9.9	9.5	9.9	10.4	11.0	11.9
Australian Dollar	NA	NA	NA	73.0	75.9	70.1	NA	NA	NA	0.7	0.9	7.2

NA Not available.

Within markets, the international bond sectors continued to be the fastest growing, as the pace of worldwide financial deregulation has picked up. Primary market activity on Euro- and foreign bond markets exploded in 1985, encouraged also by the downward trend in worldwide interest rates. New issue volume totaled US$165 billion, a 52 percent increase over the 1984 level, which had been the previous record. As a result, the volume of international bonds outstanding reached the equivalent of US$499 billion by year-end 1985, a surge of 57 percent. Slightly more than 68 percent of all international bonds was dollar-denominated at the end of 1985, compared with 75 percent the previous year. Interest rate and currency swaps spurred activity in several nondollar markets, such as the Japanese yen and Australian dollar markets. In addition, further financial liberalization led to the reopening of the Euro-French franc and Euro-Danish krone primary markets, as well as the issuance of foreign currency-denominated issues in various domestic capital markets.

United States

Slower economic growth, coupled with higher defense outlays and a one-time increase in federal housing assistance, led to a steepening of the U.S. federal budget deficit, from $175.3 billion in 1984 to $202.8 billion in 1985. Consequently, the volume of Treasury bonds outstanding surged by 19 percent during the year, reaching $1,037.8 billion. Government agency bonds outstanding also grew by a healthy 18 percent. The steady fall in interest rates during 1985 led to a rapid expansion in mortgage activity and to renewed popularity of fixed-rate mortgages. As a result, agency mortgage pool securties outstanding shot up by 28 percent.

In the municipal sector, uncertainty surrounding proposed legislation that would reduce the attractiveness to investors of state and local government securities led to record new issue volume during 1985. A flurry of issues was brought to market just before year-end, as many borrowers feared that the effective date of any new regulation would become retroactive to January 1, 1986. This late rush contributed to an 18 percent increase in the size of this market

FIGURE 3 U.S. DOLLAR BONDS OUTSTANDING
(Nominal Value, Dollars in Billions)[a]

	Governments		Federal Agency				Corporate		International Bonds	
End of Period	U.S. Notes & Bonds Total	Of Which Privately Held	Total	Of Which Mortgage Pools	Other Mortgage Secur.[a]	Municipals	Total	Of Which Public Issues (Incl. Cvts.)	Foreign Bonds (Yankee)[b]	Eurodollar Bonds
1970	159.8	81.5[c]	77.4	23.8	—	131.1	$185.5	117.1	14.1	NA
1975	205.7	108.7	126.1	28.5	—	208.3	301.5	220.8	25.3	NA
1976	257.3	150.4	140.7	40.7	—	230.0	332.1	238.9	33.9	NA
1977	298.8	171.6	163.8	56.8	—	261.8	365.7	256.3	38.9	NA
1978	325.8	191.0	200.5	70.4	—	293.7	394.1	269.9	43.1	NA
1979	358.1	211.8	247.8	93.5	—	320.6	428.2	290.8	47.0	NA
1980	407.1	252.6	282.9	113.6	—	352.0	465.4	319.2	47.8	63.8
1981	475.3	305.3	328.5	128.8	—	366.2	483.7	335.8	53.2	80.3
1982	569.6	389.8	390.6	178.6	—	415.6	516.1	356.6	59.9	113.4
1983	707.1	499.9	457.4	246.7	4.7	456.2	562.3	370.6	63.7	145.1
1984	873.0	625.7	529.7	293.8	16.2	513.9	643.0	409.0	67.6	195.9
1985	1,037.8	747.1	623.5	377.0	32.6	606.2	748.5	479.0	72.7	267.2

[a] Consisting of collateralized mortgage obligations, the first of which was issued in June 1983.
[b] Includes issues of Canadian borrowers and supranationals in the U.S. domestic market, as well as the traditional Yankee sovereign borrowers.
[c] Fiscal year ended September 30, 1970.
NA Not available.
Sources: Salomon Brothers Inc; Federal Reserve System, *Flow of Funds*; *Euromoney Inter-Bond Annual of 1978*; Association of International Bond Dealers; Orion Royal Bank Ltd.; and *Treasury Bulletin*.

during 1985. Meanwhile, attractive borrowing conditions encouraged issuance in the corporate market, in which the volume of publicity issued bonds outstanding increased by 17 percent to $479 billion.

The combination of falling interest rates and rapid financial innovation led to record new issue volume in the Eurodollar market in 1985, as new issuance soared by 51 percent year to year. Outstandings increased by 36 percent, which slightly topped the percentage increase registered in 1984. Issuance was the heaviest in the floating-rate note (FRN) sector, although it tailed off late in the year as the yield curve flattened. In addition, favorable issuing terms encouraged the refinancing of many outstanding FRNs. Keen underwriter competition and swap-related activity, as well as a plethora of new financing techniques, attracted issuers to the Eurodollar straight sector. New issue activity in the foreign dollar (Yankee) sector was quiet during 1985, especially compared with the record primary market activity in most of the other sectors of the U.S. dollar bond market. Outstandings in this sector rose by a modest 7.5 percent.

Japan

In 1985, a sudden drop in export growth led to a deceleration in economic growth, as real gross national product (GNP) expanded by 4.6 percent versus 5.1 percent in 1984. Despite calls for fiscal actions aimed at stimulating domestic demand, fiscal policy actually became more restrictive; central government current expenditures totaled ¥33.3 trillion in fiscal 1985, virtually the same as in the previous year. Government bonds outstanding rose by about 11 percent, to ¥133 trillion. This increase is slightly below that of 1984 and is the smallest rise in the past decade. Credit demands elsewhere in the domestic market were sluggish. Corporate bonds outstanding rose by 9 percent, as the booming equity market encouraged the issuance of convertible bonds.

Measures taken to internationalize the Japanese yen in order to raise its foreign exchange value dramatically affected the Euroyen and Samurai bond markets in 1985. Although the Samurai market

FIGURE 4 JAPANESE YEN BONDS OUTSTANDING
(Nominal Value, Yen in Billions)

End of Period	Governments Total	Governments Of Which Discount	Government-Guaranteed & Associated Organizations Total	Of Which NTT[a] Subs.	Of Which Other Pvt. Place.	Municipals Total	Municipals Of Which Pvt. Place.	Bank Debs.	Corporate (Public Issues) Total	Corporate Of Which Cvts.	International Bonds Foreign (Samurai)	International Bonds Euroyen
1970	3,597[b]	—	6,006	1,710[b]	2,292	1,748[b]	1,279[b]	6,174	2,980	157	6	—
1975	13,911	—	12,803	3,196[b]	6,992	6,346	5,462	15,510	6,477	1,132	183	—
1976	21,720	—	14,833	3,332[b]	8,287	8,613	7,353	17,779	7,105	1,035	245	—
1977	30,351	325	17,336	3,345[b]	9,912	10,874	9,203	20,165	7,741	1,069	534	30
1978	42,140	599	19,804	3,226[b]	11,352	13,228	10,989	22,429	8,449	1,272	1,240	45
1979	53,637	841	22,397	3,129	12,763	15,637	12,696	24,254	9,307	1,355	1,553	70
1980	67,336	1,204	25,464	2,878	14,593	17,093	13,506	26,049	9,818	1,199	1,784	125
1981	79,850[c]	1,397	28,921	2,760	16,751	18,242	14,081	27,782	10,808	1,384	2,251	205
1982	92,847[c]	1,541	32,606	2,612	18,772	19,217	14,571	30,955	11,357	1,656	2,874	322
1983	108,264[c]	1,760	35,866	2,220	20,375	19,849	14,782	34,844	11,659	2,210	3,427	385
1984	120,250[c]	2,177	38,068	1,919	21,985	20,678	15,147	38,790	12,556	3,132	4,171	749
1985	133,086[c]	2,495	42,564	1,657	25,071	20,878	14,971	41,290	13,643	4,445	5,174	1,855

[a] NTT bonds issued prior to April 1985 carry a Government guarantee. Due to the privatization of the company, subsequent issues are not guaranteed by the Japanese Government.

[b] Amounts outstanding at the end of fiscal year (March of the year following the year indicated; for example, fiscal year 1970 ended on March 31, 1971).

[c] Because of a revision of this series by the Bank of Japan, current figures concerning Government bonds are not exactly comparable with those prior to 1981.

Sources: *Bond Review* (a publication of the Bond Underwriters Association of Japan); *The Financial Times* (London); The Bank of Japan and Association of International Bond Dealers; and Orion Royal Bank Ltd.

expanded by 24 percent, activity in this sector was easily overshadowed by developments in the Euroyen market. At the end of 1984, issuing conditions were relaxed to allow any corporation rated A or better to issue Euroyen bonds, and for the first time, swap-related issues, floating-rate notes and zero-coupon bonds were allowed. In addition, issuance of Euroyen convertible bonds by Japanese corporations became popular. As a result, outstandings in the Euroyen market at the end of 1985 surged by 144 percent year to year. Other financial innovations during 1985 included the issuance of U.S. dollar- and ECU-denominated bonds in the Japanese domestic market and yen-denominated bonds in the U.S. domestic market. These financial liberalizations, as well as the strong appreciation of the yen, should also promote heavy issuance of yen-denominated international bonds over the next few years.

West Germany

The combination of falling interest rates and steady GNP growth in the period ending in 1985 has greatly improved West Germany's fiscal situation. The federal government budget deficit has narrowed from 4 percent of GNP in 1981 to about 1.3 percent of GNP in 1985, and despite tax cuts of DM11.0 billion scheduled for 1986, it should remain roughly unchanged in 1986. Nonetheless, the amount of federal government bonds outstanding increased by 19 percent during 1985, hitting DM205.9 billion. The increase in the size of the public bond sector has come at the expense of the schuldschein (private loan) sector. The 1984 removal of the withholding tax on foreign holdings of government bonds has reduced the schuldschein market's relative attractiveness to investors; therefore, its issuing cost advantage has disappeared.

The bank bond sector is still by far the largest sector of the Deutschemark bond market, accounting for 63 percent of all publicly issued bonds, although growth in 1985 in this sector was modest. Bank bonds outstanding increased by about 6 percent to DM654.6 billion.

FIGURE 5 DEUTSCHEMARK BONDS OUTSTANDING
(Nominal Value, Deutschemarks in Billions)

			Provinces & Municipalities						Schuldscheine (Private Loans)			
				Of Which						Of Which		
End of Period	Fed. Gov't. (Bund)	Gov't. Agency (Bahn & Post)	Total	Prov. (Lander)	Munic. (Gemeinden)	Bank Bonds[a]	Nonban Corp. (Industrial Bonds Inc. Cvts.)	Int'l. DM Bonds[b]	Total Public Sector[c]	Federal Gov't.[c]	Local Gov't. or Gov't. Agency[c]	Other[c]
1970	12.2	12.4	6.9	6.2	0.7	117.8	7.7	19.4	76.4	17.5	58.9	NA
1975	34.2	20.7	12.6	11.8	0.8	239.7	8.9	35.9	176.2	50.9	125.3	NA
1976	48.8	21.6	14.1	13.4	0.7	217.8	8.4	42.6	203.5	58.7	144.8	NA
1977	69.1	22.8	13.9	13.3	0.6	302.7	8.0	52.9	216.5	60.5	156.0	NA
1978	82.8	23.4	14.1	13.6	0.5	334.1	6.9	63.2	248.3	76.8	171.5	NA
1979	90.9	21.9	13.0	12.6	0.4	372.0	5.8	70.1	284.7	94.0	190.7	NA
1980	94.3	23.9	12.5	12.2	0.3	413.3	4.6	79.2	337.1	119.6	217.5	NA
1981	91.4	25.6	10.9	10.6	0.2	484.4	3.6	80.3	413.3	158.4	255.0	NA
1982	114.4	28.9	12.3	12.1	0.2	530.7	3.0	83.6	454.7	168.7	285.9	NA
1983	143.4	30.0	16.8	16.6	0.2	584.4	2.4	87.6	478.5	172.8	305.7	NA
1984	173.3	31.7	21.6	21.4	0.2	619.8	2.2	96.3	493.8	171.6	322.1	NA
1985	205.9	36.8	27.3	27.1	0.2	654.6	2.4	117.4	502.4	166.5	335.9	NA[d]

[a] Bank bonds include mortgage bonds, communal bonds, bonds of special-purpose banks, bonds of central giro institutions, and other bank bonds.

[b] The West German market does not distinguish between "Euro" and "Foreign" international bonds, and they are combined in this figure. The "international bond" total also includes "private placements," which in the Deutschemark market are often actively traded.

[c] The figures in these columns are, strictly speaking, bank loans to the public sector, and therefore represent upper limits on the volume of public authority schuldscheine. However, virtually all such loans are in schuldschein form.

[d] Precise figures on the outstanding volume of private sector schuldscheine are not available. The size of this market is roughly the same size as the Federal Government schuldschein market.

NA Not available.

Source: Deutsche Bundesbank.

In 1985, a series of financial deregulations, plus a weakening U.S. dollar, led to record issuance in the Euro-DM sector. The new issue volume of DM31.1 billion represents a 63 percent increase over the 1984 level, which had been the previous record. Close to 40 percent of the issuance occurred during the fourth quarter, when the decline of the dollar was steepest. Also, the volume of bond redemptions fell for the third consecutive year. As a result, the size of the Euro-DM market expanded by 22 percent, to DM117.4 billion.

Italy

Despite steady economic growth, falling inflation and lower interest rates, the Italian public sector deficit worsened substantially during 1985. Government revenues failed to keep pace with expenditures, as tax avoidance remained a problem. The 1985 borrowing requirement totaled 121.4 trillion lire, up from 95.4 trillion lire in 1984. As a result, public sector bonds outstanding increased by 38.6 percent during 1985 to 340 trillion lire. Despite its size, the public sector debt has historically been manageable, since Italy has a high private saving rate. Also, Italian Government bonds are popular with the general public because they are tax-free. Italian entities also borrow a fair amount on the international markets: Public and private sector nonfinancial entities have about US$42 billion of foreign debt outstanding. Meanwhile, private sector credit demands have been limited, partly because of "crowding out" by the public sector.

In keeping with the trend of worldwide financial liberalization, the international lira bond markets opened up during 1985. While supranational organizations have issued bonds on the domestic market in the past, the foreign lira market was virtually closed until 1985, when the European Investment Bank and the World Bank each issued two bonds. The first three Eurolira bonds—two of which were from U.S. corporations—were issued late last year. The high coupons may attract international investors to these markets in the future, but capital controls in Italy may hinder expansion of the international lira markets.

FIGURE 6 ITALIAN LIRA BONDS OUTSTANDING
(Nominal Value, Italian Lire in Billions)

End of Period	Public Sector[a]	Of Which Held by Bank of Italy	Government Agencies[b]	Special Credit Institutions[c]	Corporate Bonds	International Bonds	
						Foreign Bonds	Euro-lira
1970	NA	NA	NA	NA	NA	30	—
1975	28,600	13,588	10,143	32,777	956	44	—
1976	32,386	16,081	11,074	38,172	832	42	—
1977	49,687	24,882	12,200	43,731	1.007	40	—
1978	70,109	30,771	13,195	49,436	1,185	36	—
1979	79,689	27,759	13,844	54,693	1,201	32	—
1980	77,735	28,261	14,000	60,979	1,273	28	—
1981	85,509	29,647	14,009	68,863	1,981	24	—
1982	110,038	28,891	16,682	77,172	2,760	20	—
1983	181,009	30,393	18,015	85,134	3,820	16	—
1984	245,250	36,367	19,254	89,554	4,487	12	—
1985	339,857	45,051	20,355	95,254	5,130	400	225

[a] Includes direct Government debt, debt funded on behalf of Government agencies and local authorities, as well as issues of local authorities, Railway Administrations, and Government Credit Agencies. The vast majority of these issues comprise Central Government and Government-guaranteed issues.

[b] Includes issues of state-owned companies, such as ENEL, ENI, IRI, and Autostrade.

[c] Includes issues of special industrial, public works and real estate credit institutions for medium- and long-term finance.

NA Not available.

Sources: Banca D'Italia; Istituto Bancario San Paolo di Torino; and Banca Commerciale Italiana.

United Kingdom

Underspending by the local authorities, asset sales by the government and an unexpected increase in tax receipts from the consumer sector all led to a reduction in the public sector borrowing requirement (PSBR) for 1985. The PSBR for the 1985 fiscal year, which ended March 31, 1986, came to just £5.9 billion, compared with £7.1 billion for 1984. Heavy borrowing during the first three months of calendar 1985 spurred a large increase in government bonds outstanding, however: The volume of gilts outstanding rose by about £10 billion, to £124.2 billion. In November 1985, the Government discontinued the practice of overfunding (gilt issuance in excess of the borrowing requirement) as an instrument of monetary policy. As a result, the gilt market should grow slowly over the next few years.

There was almost no bond issuance by the local authorities and corporate entities in 1985: in fact, the volume of bonds outstanding in these two sectors actually declined during the year. Corporate borrowing is typically in the form of bank loans. Other funding is accomplished through the international markets, in which financial institution issuance of dollar- and sterling-denominated FRNs has been prominent.

Eurosterling bond issuance was a record £5 billion during 1985. The sharp increase in the value of sterling against the U.S. dollar encouraged issuance in this sector early in the year. In addition, a regulatory change late in 1985 led to an onslaught of Eurosterling FRN issues from U.K. building societies. As a result, the Eurosterling bond market doubled for the third consecutive year, reaching £10 billion.

France

Athough 1985's public sector deficit—2.6 percent of gross domestic product (GDP)—was changed little from 1984, contributions from various sectors differed markedly. Falling interest rates eased the debt service portion, while a much smaller surplus from the Social

FIGURE 7 U.K. STERLING BONDS OUTSTANDING
(Nominal Value, Pounds in Billions)

				International Bonds	
End of Period	Government Bonds (Gilts)	Local Authority Negotiable Bonds	Corporate Bonds	Foreign Bonds (Bulldogs)[a]	Eurosterling Bonds
1970	21.0	0.4[b]	5.5	NA	—
1975	34.3	1.1	6.6	NA	—
1976	40.6	1.1	6.6	NA	—
1977	51.8	1.2	6.3	NA	0.1
1978	57.0	1.2	6.0	NA	0.3
1979	68.2	0.9	5.6	NA	0.4
1980	81.7	1.0	5.3	0.1	0.7
1981	89.5	0.9	5.4	0.6	0.8
1982	95.3	1.0	6.2	1.3	1.2
1983	104.5	1.0	6.2	1.9	2.6
1984	114.1	0.8	7.9	2.9	5.4
1985	124.2	0.4	7.6	3.7	10.0

a Nominal value of bulldogs proper. The figures do not include those foreign and Commonwealth bonds issued much earlier and for which there is no active market. The first strict bulldog was the £75-million Denmark issue of 1980.
b At the end of the fiscal year, March 31, 1971.
NA Not available.
Sources: London Stock Exchange; Pember & Boyle; Central Statistical Office; *The Financial Times* (London); Association of International Bond Dealers; and Orion Royal Bank Ltd.

FIGURE 8 FRENCH FRANC BONDS OUTSTANDING
(Nominal Value, French Francs in Billions)

End of Period	Central Government	Government Agency & Government Guaranteed	Provincial & Municipal		Corporate (Cvts. and Variable Rate Incl.)	International Bonds	
			Total	Of Which Emprunts des Villes[a]		Foreign[b]	Euro-French Franc
1970	NA	NA	NA	NA	NA	NA	0.2
1975	14.1	141.1	8.7	6.2	59.7	0.9	4.2
1976	15.5	164.9	10.1	7.7	72.7	1.1	4.2
1977	22.5	179.9	11.4	9.2	85.2	1.4	4.4
1978	34.6	202.8	13.8	11.1	92.5	2.1	4.7
1979	48.0	230.6	15.5	12.4	98.2	2.4	6.0
1980	77.7	282.5	16.7	13.8	108.1	3.9	8.7
1981	100.7	321.6	15.0	12.0	116.6	4.1	11.1
1982	138.2	407.8	19.9	16.4	134.4	5.3	10.5
1983	184.8	484.0	21.2	17.4	161.5	6.4	10.1
1984	266.4	563.2	23.3	16.6	194.4	7.3	9.0
1985	357.7	654.0	23.0	15.8	251.7	11.8	11.0

[a] Securities issued jointly on behalf of several local borrowers.
[b] International organizations only, which account for almost all of the foreign issues outstanding.
NA Not available.
Sources: *L'Annee Boursiere* (a publication of the Paris Stock Exchange); *Euromoney Inter-Bond Annual of 1978; The Financial Times* (London); and Association of International Bond Dealers.

Security sector and a lower personal tax burden cut into the revenue side. Meanwhile, public sector bonds outstanding increased by 22 percent to Ffr 1,012 billion. As in recent years, the central government sector comprised the lion's share of this increase: Central government bonds outstanding increased by 34 percent to Ffr358 billion, while government agency and government-guaranteed bonds outstanding rose by 16 percent. The public sector also relies heavily on the international credit markets to fulfill its funding needs, as new external borrowings totaled Ffr35 billion in 1985. However, external borrowing is expected to fall drastically in 1986. The recently elected conservative Government is expected to privatize many state-owned firms over the next few years. This will have the effect of increasing the size of the corporate bond market, which is currently the third-largest sector of the French franc bond market.

The Euro-French franc primary bond market reopened in 1985 after several years of inactivity. Activity was limited, as the French Treasury closely monitored new issues, many of which were floated by French entities. Outstandings rose by just 22 percent, as several issues matured during the year. Growth was much stronger in the foreign French franc sector, where outstandings increased by 62 percent. Supranatural organizations accounted for most of the issuance in this sector in 1985.

Canada

Despite uneven performance across industry groups, the Canadian economy was robust overall during 1985, with real GNP growth of 4.3 percent. Strong performances by the residential and business construction sectors were moderated by slow growth in the export manufacturing industries. Still, the government fiscal situation worsened nominally during the year, partly because of acceleration of expenditure growth during the first half of the year. The federal budget deficit was C$31.5 billion for fiscal 1985, versus C$29.7 billion in 1984. As a result, the size of the Canadian Government bond market expanded by a strong 20 percent to C$79.4 billion.

FIGURE 9 CANADIAN DOLLAR BONDS OUTSTANDING
(Nominal Value, Canadian Dollars in Billions)

	Marketable Government Bonds			Provinces and Municipalities					International Bonds	
		Of Which			Of Which					
End of Period	Total	Direct Debt	Gov't. Guar.	Total	Prov. Direct & Guar.	Munic. Direct & Guar.	Corp. (Incl. Cvts.)[a]	Instits.[b]	Foreign	Euro-Canadian
1970	13.8	12.8	1.0	NA	NA	5.4	10.4	0.5	0.1	—
1975	15.7	15.1	0.6	21.7	14.2	7.5	19.1	0.9	0.2	0.7
1976	17.5	16.9	0.6	24.1	16.1	8.0	20.3	1.0	0.2	2.0
1977	21.3	20.8	0.5	26.8	17.8	9.0	22.9	1.0	0.2	2.7
1978	24.7	24.2	0.5	29.6	20.0	9.6	25.6	1.0	0.2	2.7
1979	31.5	31.0	0.5	32.4	22.1	10.3	26.8	1.1	0.1	3.2
1980	38.7	38.2	0.5	36.9	25.9	11.0	28.4	1.1	0.3	3.4
1981	43.0	42.9	0.2	40.2	29.0	11.2	30.3	1.1	0.3	3.6
1982	47.7	47.5	0.2	44.6	32.9	11.7	30.4	1.3	0.4	4.2
1983	55.0	54.9	0.2	49.7	37.5	12.2	31.0	1.2	0.6	5.2
1984	66.1	66.0	0.2	54.2	41.6	12.6	32.9	1.2	0.8	6.3
1985	79.4	79.3	0.1	58.0	45.2	12.8	33.8	1.3	0.8	10.1

[a] Includes some private placements.
[b] Includes hospitals, colleges and religious institutions.
Sources: Bank of Canada; *The Financial Times* (London); Association of International Bond Dealers; and Orion Royal Bank Ltd.

In contrast to the federal government, the provinces have become more fiscally austere over the past few years. Net issuance of foreign currency bonds was about level year to year at C$3.1 billion, but net issuance in Canada (including nonmarketables) fell off by 26.5 percent in 1985 to C$5.9 billion. Meanwhile, provincial bonds outstanding increased by a modest 9 percent to C$45.2 billion.

Primary market activity in the Euro-Canadian dollar market was heavy during 1985; new issue volume was up by 44 percent year to year. Swap-related activity was a key factor, as non-Canadian entities accounted for two thirds of the issue volume. Issues maturing, which were high in previous years, were almost nonexistent during 1985. As a result, this market had ballooned 60 percent by year-end to C$10.1 billion.

Belgium

Although the Belgian public sector borrowing requirement has improved in recent years, it stayed large at 10 percent of GNP in 1985. Partly because of tax surcharges and public expenditure cuts, economic growth was sluggish and the unemployment rate remained high. Consequently, public sector deficits have been high, reflecting substantial social benefit programs. Therefore, public sector borrowings have likewise been substantial. In 1985, public sector bonds outstanding rose by 19 percent, to Bfr2,812 billion, on top of a 15 percent expansion in 1984. In contrast, foreign currency debt of the public sector dropped by about 5 percent in 1985, to Bfr967 billion.

Private sector credit demands were modest in 1985. Financial institutions' issues outstanding rose by 10 percent, while nonfinancial corporate bonds outstanding expanded by 8 percent. The international Belgian franc bond markets remain tiny compared with their international counterparts. For example, there was no activity in the Euro-Belgian franc primary market in 1985. A few foreign entities did issue bonds on the domestic market in 1985, however.

FIGURE 10 BELGIAN FRANC BONDS OUTSTANDING

(Nominal Value, Belgian Francs in Billions)

		Of Which					International Bonds	
End of Period	Total Public Authority	Central Gov't.	Other Public Sector[a]	Government Agencies[b]	Financial Institutions[c]	Non-Financial Corporate	Foreign Bonds	Eurobonds
1970	525	NA	NA	317	65	64	—	—
1975	943	NA	137	584	135	160	—	4
1976	1,043	861	182	669	166	177	—	4
1977	1,211	989	222	828	211	188	—	6
1978	1,376	1,133	244	900	245	199	—	8
1979	1,526	1,258	268	974	297	207	—	12
1980	1,604	1,328	276	1,070	389	219	—	12
1981	1,620	1,355	265	1,168	467	231	—	11
1982	1,707	1,513	194	1,358	568	242	—	11
1983	2,058	1,855	203	1,488	663	294	—	10
1984	2,363	2,082	281	1,565	727	310	3	14
1985	2,812[d]	2,631[d]	181[d]	1,622[d]	799[d]	334[d]	16	14

[a] Includes issues of the local authorities, social security and state pension fund systems, plus debt incurred from certain off-budget expenses of the Central Government.

[b] Includes issues of public agencies and public financial institutions.

[c] Includes issues of commercial banks, private savings banks and mortgage and capital accumulation companies.

[d] As of October 31, 1984.

NA Not available.

Sources: National Bank of Belgium; Societe Generale de Banque; and Orion Royal Bank Ltd.

Denmark

During recent years, Denmark has made substantial progress in correcting some of the severe economic problems of the early 1980s. Real economic growth was close to 3 percent in 1985, compared with a 1980-82 average of just 0.5 percent. The consumer price inflation in 1985 was 3.6 percent, down from an average 11.5 percent from 1980-83. Most importantly, the central government budget deficit has fallen dramatically: It totaled Dkr55 billion in 1983, fell to Dkr28 billion in 1985, and is projected to be as low as Dkr10-14 billion in 1986. At the end of 1985, there were Dkr331 billion of Government bonds outstanding—a 13 percent increase for the year. This represents a rapid slowing from 1984, when outstandings grew at a rate of 27 percent. As a result of the recession years of the early 1980s, the Kingdom of Denmark carries the heaviest debt load of any of the Scandinavian countries. At the end of 1984, total government debt amounted to 74 percent of GDP, while net external debt totaled 38 percent of GDP.

The removal of capital controls in Denmark has led to the rapid development of the Euro-Danish krone bond market. Investors have been attracted by the high coupons and the limited currency risk, reflecting the inclusion of the krone in the EMS exchange rate mechanism. Issuers, meanwhile, are able to borrow at attractive rates through the use of currency swaps. As a result, the size of this market had grown from almost nil in 1984 to Dkr2.5 billion by the end of 1985.

Sweden

Despite strong domestic demand, real GDP growth in Sweden was a subdued 2.2 percent in 1985, as the net export sector contributed negatively to economic growth. Strict credit controls implemented in May 1985, which included increased short-term interest rates and higher taxes on automobile purchases, contributed to the moderation of economic growth during the second half of the year. Despite a slowdown in real Government spending, public sector debt continued

FIGURE 11 DANISH KRONE BONDS OUTSTANDING
(Nominal Value, Danish Kroner in Billions)

End of Period	Government Bonds	Mortgage Credit Bonds	Other Credit Institutions[a]	Euro-Danish Krone Bonds
1975	8.4	176.1	14.4	—
1976	12.3	204.6	16.7	—
1977	20.3	232.2	19.4	—
1978	32.1	264.4	21.6	—
1979	45.4	301.5	22.5	—
1980	69.4	335.6	22.3	0.1
1981	102.1	356.9	24.3	0.1
1982	167.8	379.0	27.8	0.1
1983	231.8	417.6	34.4	0.1
1984	293.5	468.3	38.0	0.1
1985	331.1	540.4	41.0	2.5

[a] Includes issues of ordinary and special series from the Ship Credit Fund, as well as issues of the Municipal Credit Institute.

Sources: Danmarks Nationalbank and the Copenhagen Stock Exchange.

FIGURE 12 SWEDISH KRONA BONDS OUTSTANDING
(Nominal Value, Swedish Kronor in Billions)

End of Period	Central Gov't.	Local Gov'ts.	Local Gov't. Credit Institutions	Housing Credit Institutions	Business Credit Institutions	Banks	Corporate (Enterprises)
1970	23.4	3.4	NA	NA	NA	NA	7.8
1975	54.8	5.3	NA	91.4	NA	1.3	13.3
1976	63.0	5.5	2.4	94.2	7.0	1.8	17.3
1977	69.1	5.9	2.4	105.6	8.1	1.6	21.3
1978	92.3	6.1	2.8	119.6	9.4	1.8	25.3
1979	112.7	6.7	2.9	133.2	10.2	1.5	30.1
1980	136.0	4.8	3.1	146.5	12.2	2.7	32.1
1981	188.9	4.7	3.3	165.8	16.0	4.4	35.1
1982	241.8	4.6	3.7	181.2	22.5	4.4	40.1
1983	319.6	4.6	4.3	201.6	27.6	4.6	45.0
1984	347.4	4.9	5.4	221.5	40.2	4.6	56.1
1985	384.8	4.9	6.2	261.8	44.4	4.6	60.7

NA Not available.
Source: Sveriges Riksbank.

to grow. Central Government bonds outstanding had reached Skr384.8 billion by the end of 1985—an 11 percent increase for the year.

Housing credit institution bonds outstanding soared by 18 percent in 1985, in part because of the relaxation of lending regulations by the Riksbank (Swedish central bank).

Conventional corporate bond issuance was modest in 1985, as outstandings rose by 8 percent to Skr60.7 billion. Because of the existence of capital controls, an international krona bond market has yet to develop.

Switzerland

Economic growth picked up in 1985, underpinned by an acceleration in exports and capital equipment investment. Real GDP expanded by 3.2 percent, versus 2.1 percent in 1984. The medium-term fiscal policy goal is a balanced general government budget. This was nearly achieved in 1985, as the public sector deficit, which includes the Confederation and the cantons and municipalities, was about Sfr1 billion, or 0.4 percent of GDP. Central government bonds outstanding increased by a modest 7 percent to Sfr12.7 billion. Meanwhile, outstanding bonds of the cantons and municipalities declined slightly during 1985.

New issue volume in the foreign Swiss franc market was a record Sfr16.8 billion in 1985, a 51 percent year-to-year jump. The Swiss franc's appreciation versus the U.S. dollar attracted investors to this sector, especially late in the year; 36 percent of the issuance occurred during the fourth quarter. However, growth in outstandings was limited to 17 percent, as the level of redemptions was high. New issuance in the private note market was virtually flat year to year at Sfr19.4 billion. Convertible bonds, most of which were issued by Japanese corporations, accounted for about 30 percent of the 1985 volume. Although there are no accurate figures about the size of the foreign note market, we estimate that outstandings stood at approximately Sfr90 billion at the end of 1985.

FIGURE 13 SWISS FRANC BONDS OUTSTANDING
(Nominal Value, Swiss Francs in Billions)

		Cantons and Municipalities					Foreign	
			Of Which					
End of Period	Government Bonds (Swiss Confederation)	Total	Cantonal	Municipal	Banks & Mortgage Institutions[a]	Nonbank Corporate[b]	Foreign Bonds	Foreign Notes (Private Placements)
1970	3.5	4.9	NA	NA	9.8	10.2	5.8	NA
1975	6.5	11.3	7.7	3.6	13.5	19.2	14.3	NA
1976	10.6	12.4	8.5	3.9	14.4	21.2	16.8	NA
1977	10.9	12.7	8.6	4.1	15.6	22.2	18.5	NA
1978	10.9	12.4	8.5	3.9	16.0	22.8	19.9	NA
1979	10.7	12.0	8.3	3.7	17.7	23.0	21.4	NA
1980	11.3	12.1	8.4	3.7	21.9	23.9	26.0	NA
1981	11.3	12.3	8.7	3.6	25.7	25.3	31.1	NA
1982	11.5	12.3	8.7	3.5	29.6	26.7	42.6	NA
1983	11.5	12.0	8.9	3.1	30.7	28.4	49.7	NA
1984	11.9	12.6	9.6	3.0	34.3	29.0	57.5	NA
1985	12.7	12.3	9.3	2.9	36.3	30.4	67.4	90E[c]

[a] Includes issues of cantonal banks and emissionszentrale (joint issuing associations, which may issue bonds on behalf of a group of municipalities), as well as issues of commercial banks and mortgage institutions.
[b] Includes issues of transportation, financial and industrial concerns, and electric utilities.
[c] Reliable figures for the outstanding volume of privately placed notes are not available. Based on new issue volume in recent years, this total is estimated to be around Sfr85-95 billion for the end of 1985.
E Estimate.
NA Not available.
Sources: Zurich Stock Exchange; Swiss Bank Corporation; and Swiss National Bank.

Netherlands

The Dutch Government has made some progress in the past few years toward its goal of lowering the public sector financial deficit, partly through a reorganization of the social security system and reductions in government spending. In addition, early repayment of loans by major building societies produced a one-time improvement in the financial deficit for 1985. However, falling natural gas prices will hurt government revenues in 1986, so the improvement in the budget situation may be short-lived. At 6.5 percent of net national income in 1985, the Dutch public sector deficit is high relative to other low-inflation countries. Central government bonds outstanding expanded by 14 percent, to Dfl 113.6 billion. Still, this represents a slowdown from recent years, considering that the size of the government bond market grew at an average annual rate of 34 percent from 1979-84. Credit demands elsewhere on the domestic market were limited in 1985, although public sector outstandings in the Onderhandse Leningen (private loan) market rose modestly.

Issuance in the Euro- and foreign guilder markets in 1985 was steady, but slightly below the record 1984 level. Growth in outstandings was strong, as these markets are still relatively undeveloped. Outstandings of foreign guilder bonds grew by 24 percent, while Euro-guilder bonds outstanding expanded by 15 percent. Financial liberalizations effective January 1, 1986—which include the abolition of term and repayment requirements on guilder bonds and the legalization of floating-rate notes—may spur issuance in these sectors starting in 1986.

Australia

The Australian economy was the most vigorous of the major industrial nations in 1985: Real economic growth totaled 5.7 percent. This occurred at some cost, however, as the Australian dollar depreciated by close to 30 percent on a trade-weighted basis during 1985, and the rate of inflation accelerated to nearly 10 percent during the second and third quarters of the year. In addition, the current account

FIGURE 14 DUTCH GUILDER BONDS OUTSTANDING
(Nominal Value, Dutch Guilders in Billions)

End of Period	Governments	Provincials and Municipals	Corporate	International Bonds		Onderhandse Leningen (Private Loans)		
				Foreign Bonds	Euroguilder Notes[a]	Central Government	Local Authorities	Other Domestic & Foreign
1970	12.8	NA	NA	NA	1.5	9.6	24.6	NA
1975	14.8	NA	17.0	2.0	5.1	19.6	38.6	NA
1976	16.6	13.0	18.9	2.1	5.2	24.1	40.9	NA
1977	18.1	13.5	23.4	2.3	5.5	28.1	42.3	NA
1978	20.2	13.1	28.3	2.5	5.7	34.9	42.5	NA
1979	22.9	12.5	33.4	2.7	5.1	41.1	44.7	NA
1980	28.8	12.0	37.6	3.1	5.4	49.2	46.6	NA
1981	38.2	11.2	39.9	3.9	5.5	58.6	50.7	NA
1982	54.8	11.0	44.0	6.1	5.9	68.0	54.5	NA
1983	76.1	10.8	42.2	8.4	6.6	77.1	55.7	NA
1984	99.6	10.0	42.7	11.5	7.3	84.3	56.2	NA
1985	113.6	9.4	44.6	14.3	8.4	93.8	57.5	NA[b]

[a] Euroguilder notes are issued by a private-placement procedure, but are actively traded over the counter and are therefore included with public issues here.

[b] Precise figures on the outstanding volume of private sector Onderhandse Leningen are not available. The size of this market is roughly twice as large as that for Central Government Onderhandse Leningen.

NA Not available.

Sources: De Nederlandsche Bank; *The Financial Times* (London); Amsterdam Stock Exchange; *Euromoney Inter-Bond Annual of 1978*; and Association of International Bond Dealers.

FIGURE 15 AUSTRALIAN DOLLAR BONDS OUTSTANDING
(Nominal Value, Australian Dollars in Billions)

End of Period	Commonwealth and State Government Bonds	Semi-Gov't. Authority Bonds Of Which		Local Gov't. Bonds Unlisted[b]	Corporate Bonds (Debenture Stocks)	Unlisted Corporate Debentures (Private Placements)	International Bonds
		Listed[b]	Unlisted[b]				
1975	17.1[a]	NA	NA	NA	4.0	NA	—
1976	18.7	NA	NA	NA	5.4	NA	—
1977	21.4	NA	NA	NA	6.4	NA	—
1978	21.5	NA	NA	NA	7.6	NA	—
1979	22.6	NA	NA	NA	8.6	NA	—
1980	24.2	NA	NA	NA	10.3	NA	0.1
1981	25.6	NA	NA	NA	12.2	NA	0.1
1982	23.0	NA	NA	NA	13.8	NA	0.1
1983	28.0	9.2	14E	5E	13.4	12E	0.3
1984	36.3	12.2	18.5E	6.3E	14.8	13.5E	0.6
1985	37.9	14.0	17E	7E	16.4	14.5E	5.2

a At the end of the financial year, June 30, 1975.
b There are no accurate figures available concerning the breakdown of semi-Government and local Government bonds outstanding between listed and unlisted debt, and between bonds denominated in foreign currencies. The total is approximately A$47.5 billion for year-end 1985.
E Estimate.
NA Not available.
Sources: Reserve Bank of Australia; Bain & Company; and Dominguez Barry Samuel Montagu.

deficit—although slightly improved from 1984—was still exceptionally high at A$7.9 billion. Meanwhile, Commonwealth Government bonds outstanding reached A$37.9 billion at year-end 1985, an increase of 4 percent. In contrast to this small increase, the Commonwealth raised a substantial amount of funds in the short-term market and through the issuance of nonmarketable savings bonds in 1985. The Commonwealth, the state governments and private corporations borrowed heavily on the international bond markets in 1985, raising the equivalent of US$5.8 billion abroad.

One of the most sudden developments in the international credit markets in 1985 was the Euro-Australian dollar bond market's rise to prominence. Outstandings in this market had reached A$5.2 billion by year-end, after being all but nonexistent in 1983. In addition, the worldwide liberalization of financial markets has led to the issuance of several Australian dollar issues on the U.S. domestic market in 1986.

SUMMARY

The collective size of the world's thirteen major bond markets stood at $5.9 trillion at the end of 1985, compared with only $3.2 trillion at the end of 1980. The share of government and government agency bonds to all outstanding bonds has been gradually rising, and now account for about 57 percent of all publicly-issued bonds outstanding, compared with about 51 percent at the end of 1981. International (Euro- and foreign) bond markets have become increasingly prominent, led by the proliferation of new financing techniques, such as currency- and interest-rate swaps and floating-rate notes.

There are many similarities—and some important differences—among the major markets. For example, the central government and government agency bond sectors are generally the dominant sectors of each local bond market. The Swiss bond market, in which the government bond market comprises less than 10 percent of all Swiss franc bonds outstanding, is the notable exception. On the other hand, the roles of corporate and international bond markets vary widely. Corporate bond markets are of substantial size in the U.S. dollar and Japanese yen bond markets. However, corporate bond markets are relatively miniscule in the Deutschemark and U.K. sterling bond markets, where private corporate borrowing is typically in the form of bank lending. In the Swiss franc bond market, the largest sector is that of international bonds. Meanwhile, international bond markets are relatively undeveloped in the Italian lira, Belgian franc and Swedish krona bond markets.

A number of markets have developed alternatives to conventional public bond issues. The most notable examples occur in the Deutschemark and Dutch guilder bond markets, where instruments—known as schuldscheine and onderhandse leningen, respectively—have been created. In the case of these instruments, which are essentially private loans, banks play the role of middlemen, as opposed to utlimate lenders or borrowers. Also, the size of the Swiss franc foreign note (private placement) market far outstrips that for publicly issued foreign bonds. However, the growth of these private placement markets has been slowing in recent years, as rapid worldwide financial deregulation has been encouraging public bond issuance.

CHAPTER SIX

KATHRYN JONAS joined Morgan Stanley in 1985 as an Associate. She has marketing, advertising and press relations responsibilities for the Morgan Stanley Capital International Perspective products. She received her A.B. in Government and American Studies at Smith College and graduated with an MBA from the Wharton School of Finance.

MARK SLADKUS, a Vice President in the Research department, has been with Morgan Stanley since 1982. He serves as the publisher and product manager for *Morgan Stanley Capital International Perspective.* Mark received his undergraduate training in Economics at Cornell University and earned his MBA in Finance and Marketing from the University of Chicago.

TRENDS IN INTERNATIONAL EQUITY MARKETS 1975-1986

Kathryn L. Jonas, Mark H. Sladkus*
Morgan Stanley Capital International
New York, New York

INTRODUCTION

This chapter explores trends in the international equity markets from December 31, 1976 through 1986. It endeavors to define what has changed and to investigate why these changes have occured. Based on an analysis of these trends it attempts to provide projections for the future course of events in the world's equity markets.

During the period 1975-1986 revolutionary changes have dramatically impacted security markets around the world. Market participants, observers, and commentators have witnessed frenzied activity in the world's equity markets. Unprecedented expansion was fueled by swings in the macroeconomic environment, the quickening pace of technological innovation, and the simultaneous destruction of old, and creation of new operating rules for individual country security markets.

It is not possible to view these three developments individually just as it is not possible to determine all of the casual relationships

*The authors gratefully acknowledge the helpful statistical assistance of Jennifer J. Matuschek.

among them. It is instructive, however, to reflect upon the changes in security markets in an effort to discern how changing macroeconomic factors, technological innovation, and deregulation combined to begin the transformation of many separate national economies into one global economy.

HOW BIG ARE THE WORLD'S EQUITY MARKETS?

Significant growth in size has characterized equity markets around the globe over the past decade. In 1976 the market capitalization (defined as number of shares outstanding times price per share) of major world stock markets totaled $1,178.1 billion. By year-end 1986 total world stock market capitalization expanded to $5,641.7 billion. Capitalization grew at a compound annual rate of 15.3% to more than quadruple in size during these eleven years.

While all markets grew in U.S. dollar terms, markets of each individual country grew at varying rates. Perhaps more significant is the fact that each individual country's proportion of the world equity total shifted over this time. Exhibit 1 illustrates the capitalization distribution of world equity markets in 1975, 1980 and 1986. Two prominent markets, the U.S. and Japan, exemplify the concurrent growth in absolute size and the shift in relative proportion, experienced by the world's stock markets.

In 1975, with a market capitalization equal to $683.6 billion, the U.S. represented a dominant 58% of the world equity market. By 1986 the U.S. market capitalization grew to $2,203.2 billion. However, the U.S. contribution to the total world market shrunk by 19% to represent only 39% of the much larger world equity market at year-end 1986. During these same years Japan's market capitalization grew from 135.1 billion U.S. dollars to 1746.2 billion U.S. dollars. In percentage terms Japan moved from 12% of the world equity total to 31%, more closely rivaling the U.S.

Yesterday's investor did not spend much time considering the world stock market price. He did not need to. He was able to capture over half the world's market capitalization by investing in only one

EXHIBIT 1 A. WORLD STOCK MARKET CAPITALIZATIONS
$U.S. 1,178 Billons: 1975

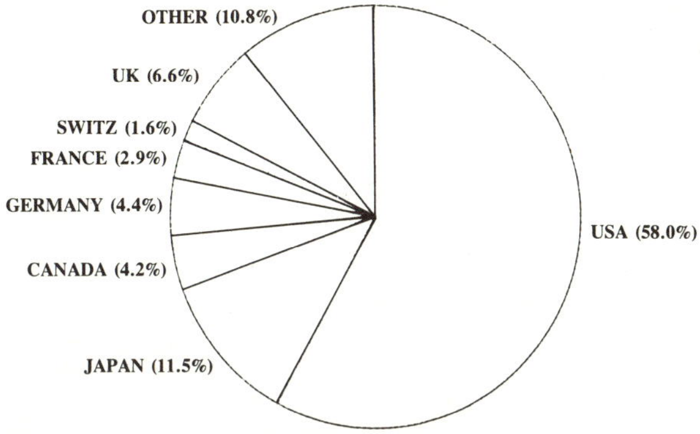

EXHIBIT 1 B. WORLD STOCK MARKET CAPITALIZATIONS
$U.S. 2,320.6 Billions: 1980

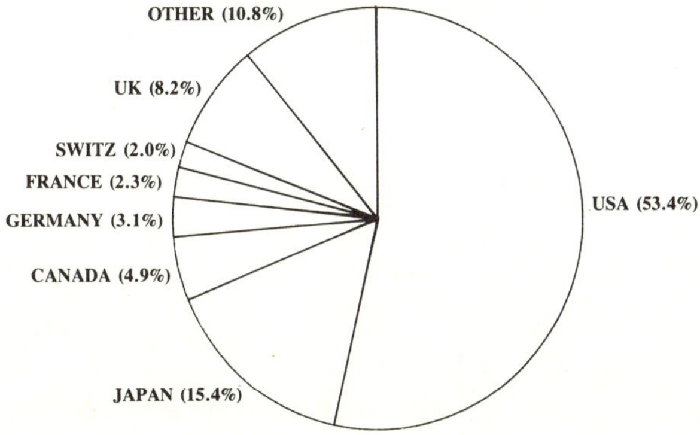

EXHIBIT 1 C. WORLD STOCK MARKET CAPITALIZATIONS
$U.S. 5,641.7 Billions: 1986

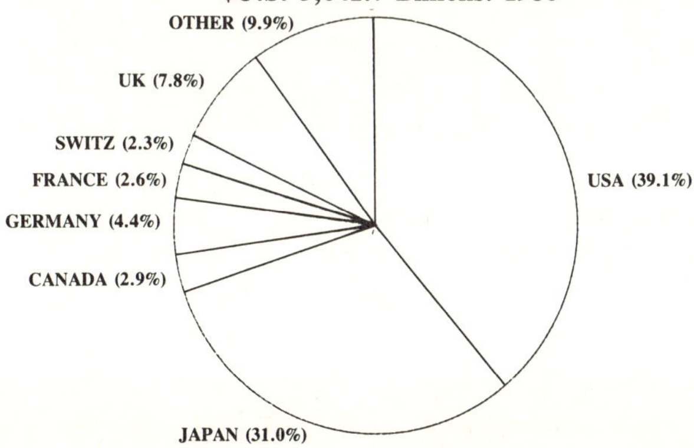

Source: Morgan Stanley Capital International Perspective, Geneva

country, the U.S.. The market capitalization of IBM alone was greater than the market capitalization of all but four countries. In contrast, today's investor would seriously limit his opportunities by remaining in only one market.

What has occured over the decade to change the realities of the equity marketplace? Very generally, the macroeconomic environment has shifted increasing the attractiveness of financial assets and resulting in greater capital flows into equity markets. Thus market expansion can be partly attributed to the basic laws of supply and demand, with more and more wealth chasing shares causing prices to rise.

The macroeconomic environment from 1975-1986 did not favor equity markets. High interest rates and rampant inflation placed financial assets in relative disfavor. Investors seeking high returns looked to real estate, gold and other hard assets. In the early 1980's restricted money supply growth and falling oil prices ignited a period of disinflation reversing the inflationary environment of the seventies. Lower oil prices and stricter monetary policies produced lower inflation which in turn caused interest rates to fall, increasing the attractiveness of equity markets. In 1982 the largest bull market in history began. As stock prices rose, companies turned to the equity markets to raise capital thereby increasing the number of shares outstanding. Many companies also found it attractive to go public which further contributed to the size of the markets. During the decade ending in 1985 markets around the world opened up to outside investors and some countries began to allow previously constrained local investors to explore foreign markets. Regulations limiting foreign participation began to be phased out in such markets as Japan, Sweden, Belgium and Finland. This openness has contributed to greater capital flows as investor's seek to find the best returns on a broader basis. In short, favorable macroeconomic conditions resulted in higher stock prices, and more shares outstanding, hence an expansion of market capitalization.

To explain the shift in country weightings within the world equity market, one has to examine each country's macroeconomic situation in more depth. For example, the U.S. economy experienced slower economic growth than other countries over the ten year period. Comparatively, countries with faster growing economies had faster growing stock markets therefore, not surprisingly, the U.S.' dominance has declined. Changes in exchange rates following the dissolution of the Bretton Woods agreement have also contributed to the shift in proportions within the world equity market. In Exhibit 1 the world equity market is expressed in U.S. dollar terms. In 1975 the dollar was much stronger than it was in 1986. If we hold constant the number of shares outstanding and calculate the market capitalization of Japan in 1975, 1980 and 1986 using consistent exchange rates we discover that currency explains a great deal of the shifting relative market capitalization.

Situations unique to individual markets can also explain shifts in relative market capitalization. In the U.S., for example, the Employee Retirement Income Security Act (ERISA) was passed in 1974 to safeguard employee pensions. ERISA allowed pension funds to diversify internationally. In the initial years after its passage the law was interpreted by some fund managers as a mandate to expand beyond U.S. borders and, in the later seventies, dollars began to flow from the U.S. market into other national stock markets. At the same time the domestic market began a phase marked by the major restructuring of many companies leading to privatization, merger, and stock buy-back programs causing outstanding shares to grow less rapidly in the U.S. market. The affect that these factors had on the overall expansion of individual equity markets is reflected in Exhibit 2 which presents the market capitalization growth rates for the major equity markets during 1975-1980, 1980-1986 and for the full 1975-1986 period.

HOW BIG ARE EQUITY MARKETS COMPARED TO NATIONAL ECONOMIES?

The growth trend seen in equity markets raises a number of questions. As stock markets have increased in total size have they also increased relative to the economy? Has stock market growth reflected actual

EXHIBIT 2 MARKET CAPITALIZATION OF MAJOR STOCK MARKETS 1975-1986

	Market Capitalization (In US$ Billion)			Percentage of Total		
	1975	1980	1986	1975	1980	1986
USA	683.6	1240.0	2203.2	58.0%	53.4%	39.1%
JAPAN	135.1	356.6	1746.2	11.5	15.4	31.0
UK	77.7	189.7	439.5	6.6	8.2	7.8
GERMANY	51.5	71.3	245.9	4.4	3.1	4.4
CANADA	49.5	113.3	166.3	4.2	4.9	2.9
FRANCE	34.5	52.8	149.5	2.9	2.3	2.6
ITALY	11.5	25.0	140.8	1.0	1.1	2.5
SWITZERLAND	18.6	45.5	132.4	1.6	2.0	2.3
AUSTRALIA	22.9	59.7	77.7	1.9	2.6	1.4
NETHERLANDS	15.6	24.5	73.3	1.3	1.1	1.3
HONG KONG	9.2	37.6	53.1	0.8	1.6	0.9
SWEDEN	9.5	12.2	48.5	0.8	0.5	0.9
SPAIN	29.4	16.3	41.6	2.5	0.7	0.7
BELGIUM	9.0	10.0	36.3	0.8	0.4	0.6
SINGAPORE/MAL	5.1	24.3	32.6	0.4	1.0	0.6
DENMARK	2.8	4.0	15.1	0.2	0.2	0.3
NORWAY	1.4	2.6	9.6	0.1	0.1	0.2
MEXICO	–	–	6.5	–	–	0.1*
AUSTRIA	1.4	1.9	5.3	0.1	0.1	0.1
WORLD	1,178.1	2,320.6	5,641.7	100.0%	100.0%	100.0%

	% Change in Market Capitalization			Compound Growth Rates of Market Capitalization		
	1975-80	1980-86	1975-86	1975-80	1980-86	1975-86
USA	81.4%	77.7%	222.3%	12.6%	10.1%	11.2%
JAPAN	164.0	389.7	1,192.5	21.4	30.3	26.2
UK	144.1	131.7	465.6	19.5	15.0	17.1
GERMANY	38.4	244.9	377.5	6.7	22.9	15.3
CANADA	128.9	46.8	236.0	18.0	6.6	11.6
FRANCE	53.0	183.1	333.3	8.9	18.9	14.3
ITALY	117.4	463.2	1,124.3	16.8	33.4	25.6
SWITZERLAND	144.6	191.0	611.8	19.6	19.5	19.5
AUSTRALIA	160.7	30.2	239.5	21.1	4.5	11.7
NETHERLANDS	57.1	199.2	369.9	9.4	20.0	15.1
HONG KONG	308.7	41.2	477.2	32.5	5.9	17.3
SWEDEN	28.4	297.5	410.5	5.1	25.9	16.0
SPAIN	–44.6	155.2	41.5	-11.1	16.9	3.2
BELGIUM	11.1	263.0	303.3	2.1	24.0	13.5
SINGAPORE/MAL	376.5	34.2	539.2	36.6	5.0	18.4
DENMARK	42.9	277.5	439.3	7.4	24.8	16.6
NORWAY	85.7	269.2	585.7	13.2	24.3	19.1
MEXICO	–	–	–	–	–	– *
AUSTRIA	35.7	178.9	278.6	6.3	18.6	12.9

*Back Data on Mexico Index not available

Source: Morgan Stanley Capital International Perspective, Geneva

economic growth? Analyzing growth rates for stock markets versus growth in gross domestic product, and measuring a stock market's percent of the gross domestic product within a country can provide answers to these questions. Exhibit 3 indicates that stock markets in all countries have grown faster than their underlying economies in general. Faster growth of the stock markets than of the real economy underscores the proposition that, over the decade, the macroeconomic environment has become more favorable for equity markets. However, the fastest growing economies still have the fastest growing markets. Up to this point, stock market capitalization has not reflected the size of a country's GDP relative to total world GDP. In 1975 when the U.S. represented 58% of the world equity market it represented 39.9% of world GDP. It can be argued that faster market capitalization growth by some countries is partly due to a "catch-up" process as market size began to more accurately reflect a country's participation within the world economy. Germany serves as a good example of this. As a country where companies have historically favored debt financing, Germany has doubled its market capitalization as a percent of GDP over the past ten years. This has resulted in a proportion of the total world equity market today which better reflects Germany's prominence in the total world economy.

Over the past decade, market capitalization has grown to be a larger share of gross domestic product in all countries except Spain. In Hong Kong, market capitalization now surpasses GDP.

HOW ACTIVE ARE THE WORLD'S EQUITY MARKETS?

It is notable that the turnover or trading activity that has been handled by the exchanges around the world has been increasing markedly. Exhibit 4 illustrates that all of the major markets had a much higher turnover than they did eleven years earlier. Looking at the changes from 1975-1980, 1980-1986 and 1975-1986 it is interesting to observe that Sweden grew the fastest (near 40%) over the decade while the U.S. and Japan grew at a compound annual

EXHIBIT 3 1985 GROSS DOMESTIC PRODUCT AND STOCK MARKET CAPITALIZATION

	gross domestic product		market capitalization		annual compound growth rate 1975-1985		
	US$ billion	US$ per capita	US$ billion	US$ per capita	GDP constant prices	GDP current prices	market capitalization
USA	3948	16681	1955	8260	3.4	9.9	11.0
JAPAN	1580	13164	909	7574	4.4	7.9	16.0
GERMANY	744	12193	179	2933	2.3	5.9	12.6
FRANCE	608	11065	79	1438	2.2	12.2	14.4
UNITED KINGDOM	504	8922	328	5806	1.6	12.7	19.8
ITALY	408	7142	65	1138	2.4	18.5	30.0
CANADA	336	13370	147	5850	2.9	10.8	17.0
SPAIN	183	4741	19	492	1.8	16.7	3.8
AUSTRALIA	152	9651	62	3937	3.1	12.8	16.2
NETHERLANDS	149	10290	52	3591	2.1	7.1	13.4
SWEDEN	113	13533	30	3593	1.5	11.1	18.1
SWITZERLAND	109	16925	90	13975	1.4	4.9	14.2
BELGIUM	95	9645	21	2132	1.7	7.5	11.2
AUSTRIA	79	10450	4	529	2.5	7.6	10.6
DENMARK	68	13307	13	2544	2.3	10.8	22.0
NORWAY	66	15904	10	2410	4.0	12.5	25.0
SINGAPORE/MALAYSIA	49	2753	20	1124	6.6	11.6	16.7
HONGKONG	34	6219	38	6951	9.0	19.2	21.0

The annual compound growth rates are calculated in local currencies.
1985 GDP estimates and 1985 market capitalizations are converted at year end exchange rates.

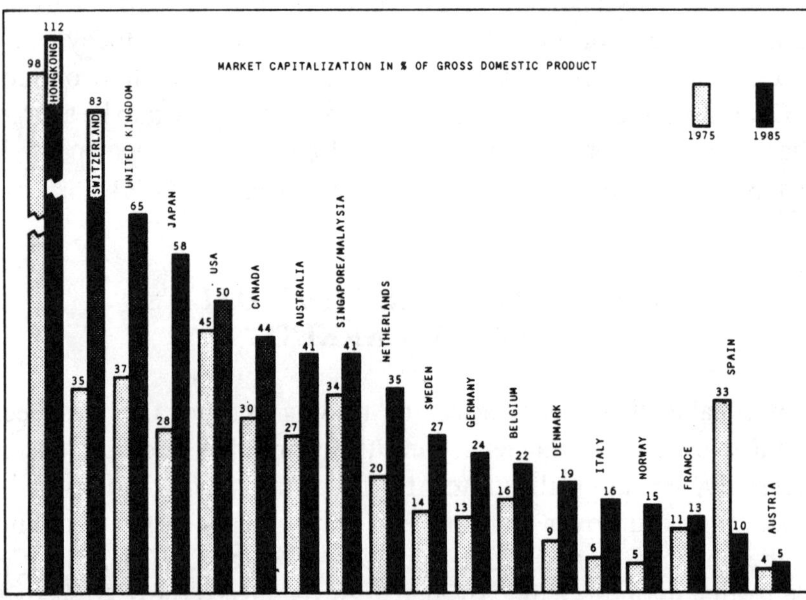

Source: Morgan Stanley Capital International Perspective, Geneva

EXHIBIT 4 TURNOVER ON MAJOR STOCK MARKETS 1975-1986

	Turnover in US$ Billion			Percentage of Total		
	1975	1980	1986	1975	1980	1986
USA	133.7	380.5	1373.8	55.4%	56.1%	47.8%
JAPAN	51.2	157.2	954.2	21.2	23.2	33.2
GERMANY	11.1	15.2	136.1	4.6	2.2	4.7
UK	19.6	36.0	133.3	8.1	5.3	4.6
CANADA	5.4	28.6	57.3	2.2	4.2	2.0
FRANCE	7.3	13.7	56.1	3.0	2.0	2.0
ITALY	2.1	8.1	44.9	0.9	1.2	1.6*
NETHERLANDS	2.5	5.0	29.8	1.0	0.7	1.0
AUSTRALIA	0.7	10.5	26.8	0.3	1.5	0.9*
SWEDEN	0.5	1.8	20.0	0.2	0.3	0.7
SPAIN	3.0	1.7	15.9	1.2	0.3	0.6*
HONG KONG	2.1	19.1	14.5	0.9	2.8	0.5
BELGIUM	1.3	2.1	6.6	0.5	0.3	0.2
S'PORE/MAL	0.8	3.7	5.0	0.3	0.5	0.2*
DENMARK	0.1	0.1	1.9	0.0	0.0	0.1
AUSTRIA	0.1	0.1	0.5	0.0	0.0	0.0
TOTAL	241.5	678.0	2876.7	100.0%	100.0%	100.0%**

*Changes in market coverage from 1975 to 1986 may distort turnover comparisons in these countries
**Totals may not add up due to rounding

	% Change in Turnover			Compound Growth Rates of Turnover		
	1975-80	1980-86	1975-86	1975-80	1980-86	1975-86
USA	184.6%	261.1%	927.5%	23.3%	23.9%	23.6%
JAPAN	207.0	507.0	1,763.7	25.2	35.1	30.5
GERMANY	36.9	795.4	1,126.1	6.5	44.1	25.6
UK	83.7	270.3	580.1	12.9	24.4	19.0
CANADA	429.6	100.3	961.1	39.6	12.3	24.0
FRANCE	87.7	309.5	668.5	13.4	26.5	20.4
ITALY	285.7	454.3	2,038.1	31.0	33.0	32.1*
NETHERLANDS	100.0	496.0	1,092.0	14.9	34.7	25.2
AUSTRALIA	1,400.0	155.2	3,728.6	71.9	16.9	39.3*
SWEDEN	260.0	1,011.1	3,900.0	29.2	49.4	39.8
SPAIN	-43.3	835.3	430.0	-10.7	45.2	16.4*
HONG KONG	809.5	-24.1	590.5	55.5	-4.5	19.2
BELGIUM	61.5	214.3	407.7	10.1	21.0	15.9
S'PORE/MAL	362.5	35.1	525.0	35.8	5.1	18.1*
DENMARK	0.0	1,800.0	1,800.0	0.0	63.4	30.7
AUSTRIA	0.0	400.0	400.0	0.0	30.8	15.8

*Changes in market coverage from 1975 to 1985 may distort compound growth rates in these countries

Source: Morgan Stanley Capital International Perspective, Geneva

rate closer to 25%. Events unique to individual markets can explain much of the dramatic growth. In Sweden, for example, stocks became a more popular investment vehicle over time, especially to foreign investors. The Swedish market, as a small market, keenly felt the inflow of foreign funds, particularly U.S. dollars. In addition, the Swedish government encouraged stock market participation by passing favorable tax regulations for investors.

Growth in turnover did not closely parallel growth in market capitalization. Unlike growth in size - where the U.S. contribution to the world equity picture has diminished significantly - the turnover in the highly liquid U.S. market as a proportion of total world turnover has remained a hefty 47.8%, down from 55.4% in 1976. This is partly attributable to the May 1975 deregulation of the U.S. markets. "May Day" as it was commonly called, signified the end of negotiated commission structures for buying and selling securities. This caused transaction costs in the U.S. to fall significantly and led to a rise in trading activity. This relaxation of fixed commissions is beginning to be repeated in other markets, for example London's October 1986 "Big Bang". Although it is too early to tell, preliminary indications suggest that London may also experience significant volume growth. At the same time Japan's liquidity has increased significantly, rising 1763.7% for the decade.

Several other factors leading to greater turnover on the exchanges include a favorable macroeconomic environment for stock trading, phasing out of regulations to encourage more players to participate in each market, and technological innovation enabling exchanges to more quickly process stock market turnover.

SOME OF THE BIG PLAYERS IN EACH MARKET

The largest companies around the world, whether Sumitomo Bank in Japan, Exxon in the USA or Daimler-Benz in Germany have become more and more familiar to investors. Exhibits 5, 6 and 7 display the ten top companies ranked by market capitalization in the major stock markets in 1975, 1980 and 1985. Exhibits 8, 9 and 10 illustrate the top companies ranked by market capitalization outside North America for the same three years. It is interesting to note Japan's ascendency during the decade. In 1975 there were no Japanese companies ranked in the top ten and by 1985 six of the top ten firms were Japanese. Only Royal Dutch Shell, British Petroleum and Daimler-Benz maintained their top ten status during this period.

GLOBALIZATION OF EQUITY MARKETS

In the mid-seventies the majority of investors viewed global investing as a technique which entailed more risk than reward. The predominence of the U.S. market (58% of total stock market capitalization), the heavily regulated and closed nature of foreign markets and the limited availability of information prevented the majority of investors from venturing beyond their own markets. However, over the past decade these barriers to global investing have been eroding.

The increasing interaction and interdependence of world economies over the past decade is a trend that is now being mirrored in financial markets. Increased information and communication resulting from technological innovation has made the world a smaller place. How is globalization affecting world equity markets?

One impact of globalization is greater interaction among world stock markets as information and capital flows increase. The increasing likelihood for corporations to raise capital in markets other than their own is evidence of this greater interaction. Companies are interested in raising capital in the markets they serve as well as the markets in which they are domiciled. They have broadened their perspective and now consider their options for raising capital to be more than a choice between domestic debt or equity instruments and

EXHIBIT 5 THE 10 LARGEST MARKET CAPITALIZATIONS AND THEIR SHARE OF NATIONAL STOCK MARKETS AUGUST, 1975

USA
total market capitalization = $ 657 billion

	$ million	% of total
I B M	27 020	4.1
AT & T	26 938	4.1
EXXON	19 289	2.9
EASTMAN KODAK	15 129	2.3
GENERAL MOTORS	14 237	2.2
SEARS ROEBUCK	9 450	1.5
DOW CHEMICAL	8 375	1.3
GENERAL ELECTRIC USA	8 105	1.2
PROCTER & GAMBLE	7 308	1.1
STANDARD OIL INDIANA	6 871	1.0
TOTAL TOP TEN	142 722	21.7

JAPAN
total market capitalization = $ 129 billion

	$ million	% of total
NIPPON STEEL	2 225	1.7
TOYOTA MOTOR	2 115	1.6
SONY	1 924	1.5
TOKYO ELECTRIC POWER	1 852	1.5
MATSUSHITA EL. IND.	1 694	1.3
SUMITOMO BANK	1 468	1.1
MITSUBISHI BANK	1 463	1.1
DAIICHI KANGYO BANK	1 450	1.1
SANWA BANK	1 445	1.1
FUJI BANK	1 441	1.1
TOTAL TOP TEN	17 077	13.1

UNITED KINGDOM
total market capitalization = $ 66.0 billion

	$ million	% of total
BRITISH PETROLEUM	4 150	6.3
SHELL T & T	3 702	5.6
I C I	2 644	4.0
BRITISH AMERICAN TOBACCO	1 545	2.3
UNILEVER LTD	1 350	2.0
GENERAL ELECTRIC UK	1 322	2.0
MARKS & SPENCER	1 313	2.0
BARCLAYS BANK	1 021	1.6
IMPERIAL GROUP	982	1.5
RIO TINTO ZINC	893	1.4
TOTAL TOP TEN	18 922	28.7

GERMANY
total market capitalization = $ 47.9 billion

	$ million	% of total
SIEMENS	3 320	6.9
DAIMLER BENZ	2 896	6.0
DEUTSCHE BANK	2 189	4.6
B A S F	1 844	3.9
HOECHST	1 844	3.9
BAYER	1 737	3.6
R W E	1 445	3.0
DRESDNER BANK	1 256	2.6
KARSTADT	1 187	2.5
VEBA	1 148	2.4
TOTAL TOP TEN	18 866	39.4

FRANCE
total market capitalization = $ 33.4 billion

	$ million	% of total
MICHELIN	973	2.9
AQUITAINE SNPA	901	2.7
SAINT-GOBAIN P-A-M	847	2.5
FRANCAISE PETROLES	689	2.1
PECHINEY - UGINE	636	1.9
CARREFOUR	585	1.7
AIR LIQUIDE	572	1.7
PERNOD-RICARD	554	1.7
SUEZ	531	1.6
RHONE-POULENC	518	1.6
TOTAL TOP TEN	6 806	20.4

SPAIN
total market capitalization = $ 28.0 billion

	$ million	% of total
TELEFONICA NACIONAL	4 032	14.4
IBERDUERO	2 144	7.6
BANCO CENTRAL	2 141	7.6
BANCO ESPANOL CREDITO	1 668	6.0
BANCO DE BILBAO	1 659	5.9
HIDROELECTRICA	1 340	4.8
BANCO HISP - AMERICANO	1 232	4.4
BANCO DE SANTANDER	1 141	4.1
DRAGADOS Y CONSTRUCCION	533	1.9
ESPANOLA DE PETROLEOS	520	1.9
TOTAL TOP TEN	16 410	58.6

AUSTRALIA
total market capitalization = $ 19.9 billion

	$ million	% of total
BROKEN HILL PROP	1 811	9.1
MIM HOLDING	758	3.8
CONZINC RIO TINTO	752	3.8
CSR	519	2.6
HAMERSLEY	496	2.5
BANK NEW SOUTH WALES	415	2.1
WESTERN MINING	376	1.9
MYER EMPORIUM	348	1.7
BOUGAINVILLE COPPER	314	1.6
NATIONAL BANK A'ASIA	214	1.1
TOTAL TOP TEN	6 003	30.2

SWITZERLAND
total market capitalization = $ 16.6 billion

	$ million	% of total
HOFFMANN-LA ROCHE	2 567	15.5
NESTLE	2 206	13.3
SCHWEIZ BANKVEREIN SBS	1 831	11.0
SCHWEIZ BANKGESELL UBS	1 603	9.7
CIBA-GEIGY	1 415	8.5
SCHWEIZ KREDITANSTALT	1 330	8.0
SANDOZ	657	3.9
SCHWEIZ RÜCKVERSICHERUNG	395	2.4
ALUMINIUM SUISSE	346	2.1
ZÜRICH VERSICHERUNG	345	2.1
TOTAL TOP TEN	12 695	76.5

NETHERLANDS
total market capitalization = $ 14.3 billion

	$ million	% of total
ROYAL DUTCH PETROLEUM	4 822	33.8
PHILIPS	1 614	11.3
UNILEVER NV	1 281	9.0
AMRO BANK	492	3.4
HEINEKEN	430	3.0
AKZO	414	2.9
ALGEMENE BANK	388	2.7
NATIONALE-NEDERLANDEN	325	2.3
HOOGOVENS	256	1.8
PAKHOED	217	1.5
TOTAL TOP TEN	10 239	71.7

ITALY
total market capitalization = $ 11.3 billion

	$ million	% of total
ASSICURAZIONI GENERALI	853	7.5
MONTEDISON	649	5.7
SIP	552	4.9
FIAT	404	3.6
STET	306	2.7
BANCA COMMERCIALE	280	2.5
ITALCEMENTI	269	2.4
BASTOGI	245	2.2
LEPETIT	244	2.2
CREDITO ITALIANO	240	2.1
TOTAL TOP TEN	4 042	35.8

SWEDEN
total market capitalization = $ 9.6 billion

	$ million	% of total
ERICSSON	849	8.9
SKF	672	7.0
VOLVO	557	5.8
ATLAS COPCO	437	4.6
ELECTROLUX	408	4.3
ASEA	387	4.0
SKANDINAVISKA ENSKILDA	310	3.2
SANDVIK	251	2.6
ALFA-LAVAL	246	2.6
GRANGESBERG	214	2.2
TOTAL TOP TEN	4 331	45.2

BELGIUM
total market capitalization = $ 9.4 billion

	$ million	% of total
PETROFINA	1 585	16.8
SOLVAY	529	5.6
INTERCOM	498	5.3
EBES	486	5.1
STE GEN DE BELGIQUE	412	4.4
UNION MINIERE	347	3.7
STE GEN DE BANQUE	316	3.3
KREDIETBANK	290	3.1
TRACTION & ELECTRICITE	238	2.5
BANQUE NAT BELGIQUE	214	2.3
TOTAL TOP TEN	4 915	52.1

Market capitalization is defined as the total number of shares outstanding times per share price (at mid August 1975). The 10 largest companies for all countries are selected from the 1600 companies included in the monthly issues of CAPITAL INTERNATIONAL PERSPECTIVE. The total market capitalization for each country is an estimate of the aggregate market value of all listed shares, excluding foreign securities and investment trusts. The total market capitalization of the USA refers to the New York Stock Exchange only, that of Japan to first section only. For industry classification of the above companies, see quarterly issues of CAPITAL INTERNATIONAL PERSPECTIVE.

Source: Morgan Stanley Capital International Perspective, Geneva

EXHIBIT 6 THE 10 LARGEST MARKET CAPITALIZATIONS AND THEIR SHARE OF NATIONAL STOCK MARKETS MAY, 1980

USA
total market capitalization: $ 979 billion

	$ million	% of total
AMERICAN TEL & TEL	37 348	3.8
I B M	31 952	3.3
EXXON CORP	28 605	2.9
STANDARD OIL INDIANA	15 331	1.6
MOBIL OIL	14 645	1.5
SCHLUMBERGER	14 096	1.4
GENERAL MOTORS	13 564	1.4
STANDARD OIL CALIFORNIA	12 186	1.2
GENERAL ELECTRIC	11 307	1.2
ATLANTIC RICHFIELD	10 768	1.1
TOTAL TOP TEN	189 802	19.4

JAPAN
total market capitalization: $ 302 billion

	$ million	% of total
TOYOTA MOTOR	6 283	2.1
NIPPON OIL	6 150	2.0
NISSAN MOTOR	4 670	1.6
NIPPON STEEL	4 202	1.4
TOKYO ELECTRIC POWER	4 040	1.3
MATSUSHITA ELECR IND	3 593	1.2
DAIICHI KANGYO BANK	3 457	1.2
MITSUBISHI CORP	3 364	1.1
SUMITOMO BANK	3 336	1.1
SANWA BANK	3 336	1.1
TOTAL TOP TEN	42 431	14.1

UNITED KINGDOM
total market capitalization: $ 155 billion

	$ million	% of total
BRITISH PETROLEUM	12 205	7.9
SHELL T & T	9 754	6.3
IMPERIAL CHEMICAL IND	4 877	3.1
GENERAL ELECTRIC	4 576	2.9
MARKS & SPENCER	2 646	1.7
GREAT UNIVERSAL STORES	2 288	1.5
BARCLAYS BANK	2 278	1.5
RIO TINTO-ZINC	2 039	1.3
B A T INDUSTRIES	1 876	1.2
LAND SECURITIES	1 811	1.2
TOTAL TOP TEN	44 350	28.6

GERMANY
total market capitalization: $ 78 billion

	$ million	% of total
SIEMENS	5 439	7.0
DAIMLER-BENZ	4 049	5.2
DEUTSCHE BANK	3 191	4.1
B A S F	3 161	4.1
BAYER	2 931	3.8
HOECHST	2 730	3.5
VEBA	2 604	3.3
VOLKSWAGENWERK	2 497	3.2
R W E	2 311	3.0
DRESDNER BANK	1 743	2.2
TOTAL TOP TEN	30 656	39.4

FRANCE
total market capitalization: $ 57 billion

	$ million	% of total
ELF AQUITAINE SNEA	6 059	10.6
DASSAULT-BREGUET	2 029	3.6
FRANCAISE PETROLES	1 661	2.9
AIR LIQUIDE	1 631	2.9
SAINT-GOBAIN-P.A.M.	1 106	1.9
THOMSON-CSF	918	1.6
MICHELIN	842	1.5
PARIS PAYS-BAS	826	1.5
ESSO FRANCAISE	822	1.4
CARREFOUR	820	1.4
TOTAL TOP TEN	16 714	29.3

AUSTRALIA
total market capitalization: $ 48 billion

	$ million	% of total
BROKEN HILL PROP	4 594	9.5
CONZINC RIOTINTO	2 158	4.4
C S R	1 855	3.8
M I M HOLDINGS	1 792	3.7
WOODSIDE PETROLEUM	1 286	2.7
HAMERSLEY HOLDINGS	1 084	2.2
WESTERN MINING	1 064	2.2
COMALCO	1 013	2.1
BOUGAINVILLE COPPER	1 006	2.1
BANK NEW SOUTH WALES	747	1.5
TOTAL TOP TEN	16 599	34.2

SWITZERLAND
total market capitalization: $ 45 billion

	$ million	% of total
NESTLE	4 654	10.3
SCHWEIZ BANKGESELL UBS	4 383	9.7
SCHWEIZ BANKVEREIN SBS	3 940	8.7
SCHWEIZ KREDITANSTALT	2 997	6.6
HOFFMANN-LA ROCHE	2 556	5.7
CIBA-GEIGY	2 396	5.3
OERLIKON BUHRLE	2 326	5.2
SANDOZ	1 310	2.9
ZURICH VERSICHERUNG	1 283	2.8
SCHWEIZ RUCKVERS	906	2.0
TOTAL TOP TEN	26 751	59.2

NETHERLANDS
total market capitalization: $ 23 billion

	$ million	% of total
ROYAL DUTCH PETROLEUM	10 799	46.1
UNILEVER	1 770	7.6
PHILIPS	1 531	6.5
ALGEMENE BANK	896	3.8
AMRO BANK	876	3.8
NATIONALE-NEDERLANDE	874	3.7
NED MIDDENSTANDSBANK	534	2.3
HEINEKEN	445	1.9
AKZO	360	1.5
AMEV	354	1.5
TOTAL TOP TEN	18 439	78.7

SPAIN
total market capitalization: $ 16 billion

	$ million	% of total
TELEFONICA NACIONAL	1 629	10.1
HIDROELECTRICA	1 084	6.7
BANCO CENTRAL	845	5.2
IBERDUERO	768	4.7
BANCO SANTANDER	721	4.4
BANCO ESPANOL CREDITO	658	4.1
BANCO HISPANO AMER	611	3.8
BANCO BILBAO	594	3.7
FECSA	466	2.9
UNION ELECTRICA	355	2.2
TOTAL TOP TEN	7 731	47.8

ITALY
total market capitalization: $ 15 billion

	$ million	% of total
ASSICURAZIONI GENERALI	1 632	10.9
FIAT	681	4.6
SIP	574	3.8
LEPETIT	534	3.6
MEDIOBANCA	468	3.1
ITALSIDER	455	3.0
MONTEDISON	396	2.7
STET	355	2.4
SME	347	2.3
BANCA COMMERCIALE	337	2.3
TOTAL TOP TEN	5 779	38.7

BELGIUM
total market capitalization: $ 13 billion

	$ million	% of total
PETROFINA	2 393	19.0
INTERCOM	1 252	10.0
EBES	908	7.2
SOLVAY	688	5.5
STE GENERALE DE BANQUE	471	3.7
UNERG	413	3.3
KREDIETBANK	399	3.2
ELECTROBEL	303	2.4
TRACTION ELECTRICITE	286	2.3
STE GENERALE DE BELGIQUE	270	2.1
TOTAL TOP TEN	7 383	58.7

SWEDEN
total market capitalization: $ 11 billion

	$ million	% of total
L M ERICSSON	510	4.7
ELECTROLUX	493	4.5
SKANDINAVISKA·ENSKILDA	454	4.2
SKANSKA CEMENTGJUTER	420	3.9
SANDVIK	414	3.8
SVENSKA HANDELSBANK	413	3.8
VOLVO	357	3.3
SVENSKA CELLULOSA	351	3.2
STORA KOPPARBERG	342	3.2
SKF	314	2.9
TOTAL TOP TEN	4 068	37.5

Market capitalization is defined as the total number of shares outstanding times per share price (at 26 May 1980). The 10 largest companies for all countries are selected from the 1600 companies included in CAPITAL INTERNATIONAL PERSPECTIVE. The total market capitalization for each country is an estimate of the aggregate market value of all listed shares, excluding foreign securities and investment trusts. The total market capitalization of the USA refers to the New York Stock Exchange only, that of Japan to First section only. For industry classification of the above companies, see quarterly issues of CAPITAL INTERNATIONAL PERSPECTIVE.

Source: Morgan Stanley Capital International Perspective, Geneva

EXHIBIT 7 THE 10 LARGEST MARKET CAPITALIZATIONS AND THEIR SHARE OF NATIONAL STOCK MARKETS APRIL, 1985

USA	$ million	% of total
IBM	77888	4.5
EXXON CORP	41381	2.4
GENERAL ELECTRIC	27040	1.6
AMERICAN TEL & TEL	21791	1.3
GENERAL MOTORS	21608	1.2
STANDARD OIL INDIANA	15402	0.9
DU PONT DE NEMOURS	13299	0.8
ATLANTIC RICHFIELD	12813	0.7
CHEVRON	12444	0.7
MOBIL	12435	0.7
TOTAL TOP TEN	256101	14.8
TOTAL STOCK MARKET	$ 1732 billion	

JAPAN	$ million	% of total
SUMITOMO BANK	14821	2.3
DAIICHI KANGYO BANK	14162	2.2
TOYOTA MOTOR CORP	13374	2.1
MITSUBISCHI BANK	13321	2.0
FUJI BANK	13233	2.0
SANWA BANK	12615	1.9
MATSUSHITA ELECT IND	10485	1.6
INDUSTRIAL BANK OF JAPAN	9280	1.4
HITACHI LTD	9047	1.4
TOKYO ELECTRIC POWER	8701	1.3
TOTAL TOP TEN	119039	18.2
TOTAL STOCK MARKET	$ 651 billion	

UNITED KINGDOM	$ million	% of total
BRITISH PETROLEUM	12340	5.0
BRITISH TELECOM	10080	4.1
SHELL T & T	9851	4.0
GENERAL ELECTRIC	6261	2.6
BAT INDUSTRIES	5919	2.4
IMPERIAL CHEMICAL	5838	2.4
BTR	5428	2.2
GLAXO HOLDINGS	5419	2.2
MARKS & SPENCER	4408	1.8
BEECHAM GROUP	3239	1.3
TOTAL TOP TEN	68783	28.0
TOTAL STOCK MARKET	$ 245 billion	

CANADA	$ million	% of total
BELL CANADA	6815	5.2
IMPERIAL OIL	6481	5.0
NORTHERN TELECOM	4030	3.1
SEAGRAM CO	3852	3.0
GULF CANADA	3372	2.6
TEXACO CANADA	3227	2.5
CANADIAN PAC ENTERPRISES	3226	2.5
CANADIAN PAC LTD	3128	2.4
ALCAN ALUMINIUM	2494	1.9
SHELL CANADA	2429	1.9
TOTAL TOP TEN	39054	30.1
TOTAL STOCK MARKET	$ 130 billion	

GERMANY	$ million	% of total
SIEMENS	8163	9.1
DAIMLER-BENZ	7369	8.2
ALLIANZ VERSICHERUNG	4449	5.0
DEUTSCHE BANK	4384	4.9
BAYER	3493	3.9
HOECHST	3435	3.8
BASF	2955	3.3
RWE	2252	2.5
MUNCHENER RUCKVERSICH	2010	2.2
VEBA	1958	2.2
TOTAL TOP TEN	40468	45.1
TOTAL STOCK MARKET	$ 90 billion	

AUSTRALIA	$ million	% of total
BROKEN HILL PROPRIETARY	4020	7.6
CRA	2202	4.2
WESTPAC	1255	2.4
MIM HOLDINGS	1096	2.1
ANZ GROUP HOLDINGS	1042	2.0
CSR	957	1.8
WESTERN MINING	925	1.8
NATIONAL AUSTRALIA BANK	824	1.6
COMALCO	807	1.5
SANTOS	800	1.5
TOTAL TOP TEN	13928	26.5
TOTAL STOCK MARKET	$ 53 billion	

FRANCE	$ million	% of total
AQUITAINE (ELF) SNEA	2429	5.0
AVIONS DASSAULT BREGUET	1651	3.4
AIR LIQUIDE	1639	3.4
L'OREAL	1050	2.2
MOET-HENNESSY	954	2.0
BSN-GERVAIS DANONE	919	1.9
FRANCAISE DES PETROLES	856	1.8
SANOFI	811	1.7
GENERALE DES EAUX	739	1.5
ESSO	697	1.4
TOTAL TOP TEN	11745	24.3
TOTAL STOCK MARKET	$ 48 billion	

SWITZERLAND	$ million	% of total
NESTLE	5381	11.7
SCHWEIZ BANKGESELL. UBS	4815	10.4
CIBA-GEIGY	3608	7.8
SCHWEIZ BANKVEREIN SBS	3587	7.8
HOFFMANN-LA ROCHE	2481	5.4
SCHWEIZ KREDITANSTALT	2428	5.3
SANDOZ	1577	3.4
ZURICH VERSICHERUNG	1227	2.7
SCHWEIZ RUCKVERSICHERUNG	1065	2.3
WINTERTHUR	987	2.1
TOTAL TOP TEN	27156	58.9
TOTAL STOCK MARKET	$ 46 billion	

NETHERLANDS	$ million	% of total
ROYAL DUTCH PETROLEUM	15774	43.4
PHILIPS	3428	9.4
UNILEVER	3156	8.7
NATIONALE-NEDERLAND	1876	5.2
AKZO	1252	3.4
ALGEMENE BANK NEDERLAND	1021	2.8
HEINEKEN	845	2.3
AMEV	779	2.1
AMRO BANK	772	2.1
AEGON	770	2.1
TOTAL TOP TEN	29673	81.5
TOTAL STOCK MARKET	$ 36 billion	

HONG KONG	$ million	% of total
HONGKONG SHANGHAI BANK	3231	10.0
HANG SENG BANK	1795	5.6
HONGKONG LAND	1554	4.8
HUTCHISON WHAMPOA	1521	4.7
CHINA LIGHT & POWER	1499	4.6
HONGKONG TELEPHONE	1301	4.0
HONGKONG ELECTRIC	1295	4.0
HONGKONG KOWLOON WHARF	1269	3.9
SWIRE PACIFIC	1266	3.9
CHEUNG KONG	800	2.5
TOTAL TOP TEN	15531	48.0
TOTAL STOCK MARKET	$ 32 billion	

ITALY	$ million	% of total
FIAT	2826	10.5
ASSICURAZIONI GENERALI	2726	10.1
STET	2045	7.6
SIP	1501	5.6
OLIVETTI	1489	5.5
SELM	1112	4.1
MONTEDISON	772	2.9
ALLEANZA ASSICURAZIONI	751	2.8
MEDIOBANCA	713	2.6
BANCA COMMERCIALE	698	2.6
TOTAL TOP TEN	14633	54.3
TOTAL STOCK MARKET	$ 27 billion	

SINGAPORE	$ million	% of total
OCBC OVERSEA CHINESE BK	2000	7.7
SIME DARBY	798	3.1
DEVELOPMENT BK SINGAPORE	773	3.0
UNITED OVERSEAS BANK	771	3.0
MALAYAN BANKING	702	2.7
SINGAPORE PRESS HOLDINGS	676	2.6
CONSOLIDATED PLANTATIONS	613	2.3
GENTING	561	2.1
STRAITS TRADING	449	1.7
KUALA LUMPUR KEPONG	444	1.7
TOTAL TOP TEN	7787	29.9
TOTAL STOCK MARKET	$ 26 billion	

SWEDEN	$ million	% of total
VOLVO	1871	9.2
ASEA	1253	6.1
ERICSSON	1188	5.8
SAAB-SCANIA	917	4.5
ELECTROLUX	909	4.5
PHARMACIA	801	3.9
ASTRA	710	3.5
SCA SVENSKA CELLULOSA	671	3.3
SKANDINAV. ENSKILDA BANK	642	3.1
SKANSKA	614	3.0
TOTAL TOP TEN	9576	46.9
TOTAL STOCK MARKET	$ 20 billion	

SPAIN	$ million	% of total
TELEFONICA NACIONAL	2469	17.2
HIDROELECTRICA ESPANOLA	856	6.0
IBERDUERO	725	5.1
BANCO DE SANTANDER	705	4.9
BANCO CENTRAL	632	4.4
BANCO ESPANOL DE CREDITO	603	4.2
BANCO DE BILBAO	428	3.0
UNION ELECTRICA-FENOSA	415	2.9
FECSA	341	2.4
BANCO HISPANO AMERICANO	299	2.1
TOTAL TOP TEN	7473	52.2
TOTAL STOCK MARKET	$ 14 billion	

BELGIUM	$ million	% of total
PETROFINA	1670	13.4
INTERCOM	1014	8.1
EBES	873	7.0
SOCIETE GEN DE BELGIQUE	596	4.8
GROUPE BRUXELLES LAMBERT	523	4.2
SOLVAY	513	4.1
UNERG	364	2.9
SOCIETE GEN DE BANQUE	359	2.9
KREDIETBANK	328	2.6
ROYALE BELGE VIE ACC.	301	2.4
TOTAL TOP TEN	6541	52.4
TOTAL STOCK MARKET	$ 12 billion	

Market capitalization is defined as the total number of shares outstanding times per share price (at 26 April 1985). The 10 largest companies for all countries are selected from the 1600 companies included in CAPITAL INTERNATIONAL PERSPECTIVE. The total market capitalization for each country is an estimate of the aggregate market value of all listed shares, excluding foreign securities and investment trusts. The total market capitalization of the USA refers to the New York Stock Exchange only, that of Japan to First Section only. For industry classification of the above companies, see quarterly issues of CAPITAL INTERNATIONAL PERSPECTIVE.

Source: Morgan Stanley Capital International Perspective, Geneva

EXHIBIT 8 COMPANIES OUTSIDE NORTH AMERICA WITH MARKET CAPITALIZATION OVER $1000 MILLION 1970 and 1975

RANK	COMPANY NAME	COUNTRY	MARKET VALUE 18 April 1975 US$ million	in % of country total	1 January 1970 US$ million	in % of country total	INDUSTRY GROUP	RANK
1	TELEFONICA NACIONAL	Spain	4 952	15	1 575	10	Telecommunications	1
2	ROYAL DUTCH	Netherlands	4 774	30	5 318	42	Energy	2
3	BRITISH PETROLEUM	UK	3 673	5	4 624	6	Energy	3
4	SHELL TRANSPORT & TRADING	UK	3 416	4	4 856	6	Energy	4
5	SIEMENS	Germany	3 313	6	1 386	4	Electrical & Electronics	5
6	DAIMLER BENZ	Germany	3 074	5	1 759	5	Automobiles	6
7	IMPERIAL CHEMICAL	UK	2 820	4	3 038	3	Chemicals	7
8	BANCO CENTRAL	Spain	2 457	8	708	4	Banking	8
9	IBERDUERO	Spain	2 445	8	1 014	6	Utilities	9
10	NESTLE	Switzerland	2 305	13	1 101	9	Food & Household Products	10
11	NIPPON STEEL	Japan	2 227	2	726	2	Steel	11
12	BASF	Germany	2 155	4	1 616	4	Chemicals	12
13	TOYOTA	Japan	2 102	2	805	2	Automobiles	13
14	BRITISH AMERICAN TOBACCO	UK	2 093	3	1 543	2	Other Consumer Non Durables	14
15	HOFFMANN-LA ROCHE	Switzerland	2 079	12	2 617	21	Health & Personal Care	15
16	DEUTSCHE BANK	Germany	2 063	4	1 094	3	Banking	16
17	BAYER	Germany	2 026	3	1 636	4	Chemicals	17
18	PHILIPS	Netherlands	1 946	12	1 983	16	Radio, TV, Appliances	18
19	BANCO ESPANOL DE CREDITO	Spain	1 939	6	996	6	Banking	19
20	HOECHST	Germany	1 934	3	1 879	5	Chemicals	20
21	TOKYO ELECTRIC POWER	Japan	1 844	1	694	1	Utilities	21
22	MARKS & SPENCER	UK	1 829	2	1 477	2	Merchandising	22
23	MATSUSHITA ELECTRIC INDUSTRIAL	Japan	1 804	1	1 673	4	Radio, TV, Appliances	23
24	SONY	Japan	1 777	1	804	2	Radio, TV, Appliances	24
25	MITSUBISHI BANK	Japan	1 722	1	576	1	Banking	25
26	SUMITOMO BANK	Japan	1 704	1	690	1	Banking	26
27	UNILEVER LTD	UK	1 689	2	1 393	2	Food & Household Products	27
28	SANWA BANK	Japan	1 681	1	480	1	Banking	28
29	FUJI BANK	Japan	1 672	1	576	1	Banking	29
30	BANCO DE BILBAO	Spain	1 659	5	432	3	Banking	30
31	SCHWEIZ BANKGESELLSCHAFT UBS	Switzerland	1 651	10	662	5	Banking	31
32	BROKEN HILL PROPRIETARY	Australia	1 630	8	2 635	8	Steel	32
33	SANKO STEAMSHIP	Japan	1 592	1	32	n	Shipping	33
34	PETROFINA	Belgium	1 588	16	375	6	Energy	34
35	CIBA-GEIGY	Switzerland	1 585	9	1 717	14	Chemicals	35
36	GENERAL ELECTRIC	UK	1 569	2	1 565	2	Electrical & Electronics	36

37	HIDROELECTRICA ESPANOLA	Spain	**1 554**	**5**	747	5	Utilities	37
38	RWE	Germany	**1 551**	**3**	1 481	4	Utilities	38
39	DAIICHI KANGYO BANK	Japan	**1 536**	**1**	383	1	Banking	39
40	UNILEVER NV	Netherlands	**1 475**	**9**	1 013	8	Food & Household Products	40
41	HITACHI	Japan	**1 419**	**1**	987	2	Electrical & Electronics	41
42	VEBA	Germany	**1 410**	**2**	810	2	Utilities	42•
43	DRESDNER BANK	Germany	**1 384**	**2**	702	2	Banking	43
44	BANCO HISPANO AMERICANO	Spain	**1 332**	**4**	709	4	Banking	44
45	SCHWEIZ KREDITANSTALT	Switzerland	**1 317**	**8**	476	4	Banking	45
46	BANCO SANTANDER	Spain	**1 282**	**4**	373	2	Banking	46
47	DE BEERS	South Africa	**1 272**	**n.a.**	2 911	n.a.	Other Consumer Durables	47
48	INDUSTRIAL BANK OF JAPAN	Japan	**1 253**	**1**	240	1	Banking	48
49	NISSAN MOTOR	Japan	**1 253**	**1**	400	1	Automobiles	49
50	BARCLAYS BANK	UK	**1 239**	**2**	758	1	Banking	50
51	COMMERCIAL UNION	UK	**1 229**	**2**	710	1	Insurance	51
52	NOMURA SECURITIES	Japan	**1 226**	**1**	210	n	Financial Services	52
53	SCHWEIZ BANKVEREIN SBS	Switzerland	**1 187**	**7**	611	5	Banking	53
54	KUBOTA	Japan	**1 169**	**1**	411	1	Machinery & Engineering	54
55	DISTILLERS	UK	**1 153**	**1**	1 084	1	Beverages	55
56	ANGLO AMERICAN GOLD INVEST.	South Africa	**1 152**	**n.a.**	56	n.a.	Gold Mines	56
57	KARSTADT	Germany	**1 130**	**2**	526	1	Merchandising	57
58	SNPA-PETROLES d'AQUITAINE	France	**1 129**	**3**	641	3	Energy	58
59	GREAT UNIVERSAL STORES	UK	**1 118**	**1**	1 161	1	Merchandising	59
60	KANSAI ELECTRIC POWER	Japan	**1 117**	**1**	511	1	Utilities	60
61	MITSUBISHI ESTATE	Japan	**1 092**	**1**	402	1	Construction & Real Estate	61
62	TOKYO MARINE & FIRE	Japan	**1 082**	**1**	213	n	Insurance	62
63	KAWASAKI STEEL	Japan	**1 079**	**1**	307	1	Steel	63
64	SAINT-GOBAIN PONT-A-MOUSSON	France	**1 073**	**3**	611	3	Building Materials	64
65	MITSUBISHI CORP	Japan	**1 072**	**1**	207	n	Other Services	65
66	HONGKONG & SHANGHAI BANK	Hong Kong	**1 057**	**15**	311	14	Banking	66
67	MITSUI & CO	Japan	**1 054**	**1**	181	n	Other Services	67
68	MICHELIN	France	**1 050**	**3**	757	3	Tires & Rubber	68
69	ITOH	Japan	**1 043**	**1**	145	n	Other Services	69
70	IMPERIAL GROUP	UK	**1 033**	**1**	1 218	1	Other Consumer Non Durables	70
71	MITSUI BANK	Japan	**1 025**	**1**	215	n	Banking	71
72	HONDA MOTOR	Japan	**1 022**	**1**	164	n	Automobiles	72
73	BANK OF TOKYO	Japan	**1 012**	**1**	116	n	Banking	73
74	NATIONAL WESTMINSTER BANK	UK	**1 004**	**1**	660	1	Banking	74
75	CHUBU ELECTRIC POWER	Japan	**1 001**	**1**	435	1	Utilities	75

The above table is based on the companies included in the quarterly issues of Capital International Perspective. A similar analysis of North American markets would show 111 US companies and 8 Canadian companies with market value over US$ 1 billion.
Market value is defined as shares outstanding times share price; prices and exchange rates are those applicable at date indicated. The columns "in % of country total" relate each company's market value to the total market value for its country as estimated by Capital International S.A.
n : negligible n.a. : not available

Source: Morgan Stanley Capital International Perspective, Geneva

EXHIBIT 9 COMPANIES OUTSIDE NORTH AMERICA WITH MARKET CAPITALIZATION OVER $2000 MILLION 1970 and 1980

RANK	COMPANY NAME	COUNTRY	MARKET CAPITALIZATION 28 October 1980 US$ million	28 October 1980 in % of country total	1 January 1970 US$ million	1 January 1970 in % of country total	INDUSTRY GROUP	RANK
1	BRITISH PETROLEUM	United Kingdom	19 252	9	4 624	6	Energy Sources	1
2	ROYAL DUTCH PETROLEUM	Netherlands	13 262	51	5 318	42	Energy Sources	2
3	SHELL T & T	United Kingdom	12 423	6	4 856	6	Energy Sources	3
4	GENERAL ELECTRIC	United Kingdom	7 613	4	1 565	2	Electrical & Electronics	4
5	TOYOTA MOTOR	Japan	6 933	2	805	2	Automobiles	5
6	ELF AQUITAINE SNEA	France	5 885	10	641	3	Energy Sources	6
7	BROKEN HILL PROP	Australia	5 677	10	2 635	8	Energy Sources	7
8	SIEMENS	Germany	5 477	7	1 386	4	Electrical & Electronics	8
9	NISSAN MOTOR	Japan	5 170	2	400	1	Automobiles	9
10	MATSUSHITA ELECTRIC INDUSTRIAL	Japan	4 919	1	1 673	4	Appliances & Household Durables	10
11	IMPERIAL CHEMICAL	United Kingdom	4 902	2	3 038	3	Chemicals	11
12	TOKYO ELECTRIC POWER	Japan	4 714	1	694	1	Utilities - Electrical & Gas	12
13	HONGKONG & SHANGHAI BANK	Hong Kong	4 569	12	311	14	Banking	13
14	NIPPON STEEL	Japan	4 478	1	726	2	Metals - Steel	14
15	DE BEERS	South Africa	4 362	n.a.	2 911	n.a.	Misc. Materials & Commodities	15
16	NIPPON OIL	Japan	4 186	1	78	n	Energy Sources	16
17	HITACHI LTD	Japan	4 132	1	987	2	Electrical & Electronics	17
18	SCHWEIZ BANKGESELLSCHAFT UBS	Switzerland	4 109	9	662	5	Banking	18
19	NESTLE	Switzerland	4 072	9	1 101	9	Food & Household Products	19
20	MITSUBISHI CORPORATION	Japan	4 011	1	402	1	Wholesale & International Trade	20
21	SCHWEIZ BANKVEREIN SBS	Switzerland	3 922	9	611	5	Banking	21
22	DAIMLER BENZ	Germany	3 881	5	1 759	5	Automobiles	22
23	MARKS & SPENCER	United Kingdom	3 717	2	1 477	2	Merchandising	23
24	DAIICHI KANGYO BANK	Japan	3 651	1	383	1	Banking	24
25	MITSUBISHI BANK	Japan	3 506	1	576	1	Banking	25
26	SUMITOMO BANK	Japan	3 498	1	690	1	Banking	26
27	FUJI BANK	Japan	3 498	1	576	1	Banking	27
28	SANWA BANK	Japan	3 498	1	480	1	Banking	28
29	SCHWEIZ KREDITANSTALT	Switzerland	3 483	8	476	4	Banking	29
30	R W E	Germany	3 359	4	1 481	4	Utilities - Electrical & Gas	30
31	DEUTSCHE BANK	Germany	3 253	4	1 094	3	Banking	31
32	BARCLAYS BANK	United Kingdom	3 212	2	758	1	Banking	32
33	KANSAI ELECTRIC POWER	Japan	3 209	1	511	n	Utilities - Electrical & Gas	33
34	SONY	Japan	3 078	1	804	2	Appliances & Household Durables	34
35	HONGKONG LAND	Hong Kong	3 061	8	n.a.	n.a.	Real Estate	35
36	C R A	Australia	3 058	5	2 872	9	Metals - Non Ferrous	36

37	GREAT UNIVERSAL STORES	United Kingdom	2 929	1	1 161	1	Merchandising	37
38	RIO TINTO-ZINC	United Kingdom	2 911	1	1 148	2	Metals - Non Ferrous	38
39	HOFFMANN - LA ROCHE	Switzerland	2 904	6	2 617	21	Health & Personal Care	39
40	HANG SENG BANK	Hong Kong	2 866	8	n.a.	n.a.	Banking	40
41	HONGKONG KOWLOON WHARF	Hong Kong	2 847	8	n.a.	n.a.	Business & Public Services	41
42	TOKIO MARINE & FIRE	Japan	2 820	1	213	n	Insurance	42
43	MIM HOLDING	Australia	2 774	5	1 654	5	Metals - Non Ferrous	43
44	NOMURA SECURITIES	Japan	2 683	1	210	n	Financial Services	44
45	BAT INDUSTRIES	United Kingdom	2 656	1	1 543	2	Beverages & Tobacco	45
46	BASF	Germany	2 627	3	1 616	4	Chemicals	46
47	ASSICURAZIONI GENERALI	Italy	2 619	1	650	5	Insurance	47
48	LAND SECURITIES	United Kingdom	2 581	1	442	1	Real Estate	48
49	NIPPON ELECTRIC	Japan	2 557	1	578	1	Electrical & Electronics	49
50	CHUBU ELECTRIC POWER	Japan	2 538	1	435	1	Utilities - Electrical & Gas	50
51	OERLIKON BUEHRLE	Switzerland	2 436	5	n.q.	n.a.	Aerospace & Military Technology	51
52	BAYER	Germany	2 428	3	1 636	4	Chemicals	52
53	NATIONAL WESTMINSTER	United Kingdom	2 407	1	660	1	Banking	53
54	VEBA	Germany	2 372	3	810	2	Utilities - Electrical & Gas	54
55	PETROFINA	Belgium	2 366	21	375	6	Energy Sources	55
56	BEECHAM GROUP	United Kingdom	2 326	1	732	1	Health & Personal Care	56
57	C S R	Australia	2 314	4	569	2	Multi - Industry	57
58	INDUSTRIAL BANK OF JAPAN	Japan	2 313	1	240	1	Banking	58
59	TOSHIBA	Japan	2 300	1	529	1	Electrical & Electronics	59
60	MITSUBISHI HEAVY	Japan	2 296	1	452	1	Machinery & Engineering	60
61	HOECHST	Germany	2 271	3	1 879	5	Chemicals	61
62	RACAL ELECTRONICS	United Kingdom	2 258	1	52	n	Aerospace & Military Technology	62
63	DASSAULT-BREGUET	France	2 250	4	n.q.	n.a.	Aerospace & Military Technology	63
64	KUBOTA	Japan	2 235	1	732	1	Machinery & Engineering	64
65	CIBA - GEIGY	Switzerland	2 221	5	1 717	14	Chemicals	65
66	FUJITSU	Japan	2 217	1	716	2	Data Processing & Reproduction	66
67	BOOTS	United Kingdom	2 208	1	497	1	Merchandising	67
68	VOLKSWAGENWERK	Germany	2 137	3	797	3	Automobiles	68
69	LONG TERM CREDIT BANK	Japan	2 113	1	n.q.	n.a.	Banking	69
70	GRAND METROPOLITAN	United Kingdom	2 069	1	243	n	Multi - Industry	70
71	UNILEVER	United Kingdom	2 050	1	1 393	2	Food & Household Products	71

The above table is based on the non-American companies listed in the quarterly issues of Capital International Perspective. A similar analysis of North American markets would show 95 US companies and 12 Canadian companies with market capitalization over US$ 2000 million.

Market capitalization is defined as shares outstanding times share prices; prices and exchange rates are those applicable at date indicated. The columns "in % of country total" relate each company's market capitalization to the total market capitalization for its country as estimated by Capital International S.A.

n: negligible n.a.: not available n.q.: not quoted

Source: Morgan Stanley Capital International Perspective, Geneva

EXHIBIT 10 COMPANIES OUTSIDE NORTH AMERICA WITH MARKET CAPITALIZATION OVER $2000 MILLION 1985

RANK	COMPANY NAME	COUNTRY	MARKET VALUE US$ million	RANK	COMPANY NAME	COUNTRY	MARKET VALUE US$ million
1	SUMITOMO BANK	JAPAN	17703	91	TOHOKU ELECTRIC POWER	JAPAN	3299
2	ROYAL DUTCH PETROLEUM	NETHERLANDS	16860	92	CANON	JAPAN	3251
3	DAIICHI KANGYO BANK	JAPAN	16857	93	TAKEDA CHEMICAL	JAPAN	3228
4	FUJI BANK	JAPAN	16245	94	ALL NIPPON AIRWAYS	JAPAN	3197
5	BRITISH TELECOM	U.K.	15989	95	UNILEVER PLC	U.K.	3183
6	MITSUBISHI BANK	JAPAN	15204	96	KIRIN BREWERIES	JAPAN	3174
7	BRITISH PETROLEUM	U.K.	14746	97	PRUDENTIAL CORP	U.K.	3173
8	TOKYO ELECTRIC POWER	JAPAN	14100	98	MERCEDES AUTOMOBIL	GERMANY	3139
9	DAIMLER-BENZ	GERMANY	13636	99	SEVEN ELEVEN	JAPAN	3104
10	SANWA BANK	JAPAN	13538	100	SHARP	JAPAN	3019
11	TOYOTA MOTOR CORP	JAPAN	13057	101	BASS	U.K.	2998
12	SIEMENS	GERMANY	11704	102	HONGKONG SHANGAI BANK	HONGKONG	2984
13	INDUSTRIAL BANK OF JAPAN	JAPAN	11342	103	GREAT UNIVERSAL STORES	U.K.	2975
14	SHELL T & T	U.K.	10785	104	MITSUBISHI ELECTRIC	JAPAN	2965
15	MATSUSHITA ELECT INDUSTRIAL	JAPAN	10137	105	KYUSHU ELECTRIC POWER	JAPAN	2935
16	HITACHI LTD	JAPAN	9698	106	TORAY	JAPAN	2929
17	NOMURA SECURITIES	JAPAN	8929	107	BANK OF YOKOHAMA	JAPAN	2917
18	MITSUI BANK	JAPAN	8767	108	YASUDA TRUST	JAPAN	2916
19	ALLIANZ	GERMANY	8078	109	DRESDNER BANK	GERMANY	2881
20	KANSAI ELECTRIC POWER	JAPAN	7935	110	TELEFONICA NATIONAL	SPAIN	2846
21	NESTLE	SWITZERLAND	7888	111	KYOCERA	JAPAN	2826
22	TOKAI BANK	JAPAN	7714	112	MITSUBISHI CHEMICAL	JAPAN	2758
23	NEC	JAPAN	7708	113	NIPPON EXPRESS	JAPAN	2731
24	LONG TERM CREDIT BANK	JAPAN	7667	114	ALLIED-LYONS	U.K.	2672
25	SCHWEIZ BANKGESELLSCHAFT UBS	SWITZERLAND	7600	115	NATIONALE-NEDERLANDEN	NETHERLANDS	2623
26	DEUTSCHE BANK	GERMANY	7499	116	KINKI NIPPON RAILWAY	JAPAN	2583
27	GLAXO HOLDINGS	U.K.	7301	117	AJINOMOTO	JAPAN	2574
28	BTR	U.K.	7080	118	SUMITOMO ELECTRIC	JAPAN	2560
29	FANUC	JAPAN	6685	119	OSAKA GAS	JAPAN	2542
30	FUJITSU	JAPAN	6676	120	COMMERZBANK	GERMANY	2496
31	BROKEN HILL PROPRIETARY	AUSTRALIA	6393	121	ROYAL INSURANCE	U.K.	2407
32	BANK OF TOKYO	JAPAN	6286	122	RIO TINTO-ZINC	U.K.	2406
33	MARKS & SPENCER	U.K.	6268	123	TOA NENRYO KOGYO	JAPAN	2404
34	GENERAL ELECTRIC	U.K.	6094	124	KUBOTA	JAPAN	2393
35	IMPERIAL CHEMICAL	U.K.	6020	125	TDK	JAPAN	2391
36	NISSAN MOTOR	JAPAN	5991	126	SEARS HOLDING	U.K.	2329
37	CHUBU ELECTRIC POWER	JAPAN	5958	127	ASSOCIATED DAIRIES GROUP	U.K.	2291
38	TOKIO MARINE & FIRE	JAPAN	5919	128	ANGLO AMERICAN CORP	SOUTH AFRICA	2289
39	MITSUBISHI TRUST	JAPAN	5802	129	ELF AQUITAINE SNEA	FRANCE	2286
40	BAT INDUSTRIES	U.K.	5701	130	DISTILLERS	U.K.	2282
41	SCHWEIZ BANKVEREIN SBS	SWITZERLAND	5697	131	BMW	GERMANY	2275
42	SUMITOMO TRUST	JAPAN	5434	132	LAND SECURITIES	U.K.	2267
43	MITSUBISHI ESTATE	JAPAN	5254	133	LLOYDS BANK	U.K.	2267
44	HONDA MOTOR	JAPAN	5145	134	IMPERIAL GROUP	U.K.	2264

45	CIBA-GEIGY	SWITZERLAND	5091
46	NIPPON STEEL	JAPAN	5054
47	FIAT	ITALY	4954
48	BAYER	GERMANY	4950
49	TAIYO KOBE BANK	JAPAN	4935
50	HOECHST	GERMANY	4929
51	NIKKO SECURITIES	JAPAN	4905
52	BASF	GERMANY	4860
53	TOSHIBA	JAPAN	4785
54	NIPPON DENSO	JAPAN	4672
55	MITSUBISHI HEAVY	JAPAN	4657
56	ITO YOKADO	JAPAN	4543
57	MITSUI TRUST	JAPAN	4513
58	ASSICURAZIONI GENERALI	ITALY	4451
59	DAIWA SECURITIES	JAPAN	4434
60	SONY	JAPAN	4376
61	ASAHI CHEMICAL	JAPAN	4286
62	HANSON TRUST	U.K.	4166
63	ASAHI GLASS	JAPAN	4159
64	BARCLAYS	U.K.	4095
65	SCHWEIZ KREDITANSTALT	SWITZERLAND	4013
66	GRAND METROPOLITAN	U.K.	3912
67	MITSUBISHI CORPORATION	JAPAN	3894
68	CABLE & WIRELESS	U.K.	3859
69	TOKYO GAS	JAPAN	3848
70	JAPAN AIR LINES	JAPAN	3790
71	DAIWA BANK	JAPAN	3787
72	MUNCHENER RUCKVERSICHERUNG	GERMANY	3745
73	HOFFMAN-LA ROCHE	SWITZERLAND	3727
74	NIPPON CREDIT BANK	JAPAN	3670
75	UNILEVER NV	NETHERLANDS	3665
76	FUJI PHOTO FILM	JAPAN	3662
77	MOCHIDA PHARMACEUTICAL	JAPAN	3618
78	NATIONAL WESTMINSTER	U.K.	3585
79	YAMANOUCHI PHARMACEUTICAL	JAPAN	3537
80	PHILIPS	NETHERLANDS	3525
81	RWE	GERMANY	3485
82	J. SAINSBURY	U.K.	3483
83	YAMAICHI SECURITIES	JAPAN	3459
84	NIPPON OIL	JAPAN	3454
85	KYOWA BANK	JAPAN	3446
86	VEBA	GERMANY	3442
87	BEECHAM GROUP	U.K.	3412
88	DAI NIPPON PRINTING	JAPAN	3355
89	STET	ITALY	3349
90	VOLKSWAGEN	GERMANY	3314

135	SUMITOMO CORP	JAPAN	2246
136	SIP	ITALY	2245
137	MANNESMANN	GERMANY	2239
138	BURTON GROUP	U.K.	2237
139	SANYO ELECTRIC	JAPAN	2236
140	SANDOZ	SWITZERLAND	2227
141	HOKKAIDO TAKUSHOKU	JAPAN	2224
142	MITSUI REAL ESTATE	JAPAN	2180
143	BOOTS	U.K.	2172
144	YASUDA FIRE & MARINE	JAPAN	2121
145	GREEN CROSS	JAPAN	2080
146	VOLVO	SWEDEN	2073
147	NIXDORF COMPUTER	GERMANY	2071
148	AIR LIQUIDE	FRANCE	2068
149	RICOH	JAPAN	2053
150	PETROFINA	BELGIUM	2038
151	MATSUSHITA ELECT WORKS	JAPAN	2027
152	ONO PHARMACEUTICAL	JAPAN	2025
153	NIPPON KOKAN	JAPAN	2024
154	BAYER HYPOTHEKEN BANK	GERMANY	2001

SUMMARY BY COUNTRY

country	number of cos	market capitalization US$ MM	in % of country(*)
PACIFIC	84	437879	47.2
JAPAN	82	428502	51.9
AUSTRALIA	1	6393	9.5
HONGKONG	1	2984	8.4
EUROPE	69	320389	43.6
U.K.	31	144419	46.7
GERMANY	18	86744	60.7
SWITZERLAND	7	36243	52.1
NETHERLANDS	4	26673	60.9
ITALY	4	14999	29.9
FRANCE	2	4354	7.1
SPAIN	1	2846	16.8
SWEDEN	1	2073	8.8
BELGIUM	1	2038	11.6
SOUTH AFRICA	1	2289	15.5
TOTAL OUTSIDE NORTH AMERICA	154	760557	45.3
USA	193	1048592	59.3
CANADA	12	41162	30.8
WORLD	359	1850311	51.7

The above tables are based on the companies listed in Capital International Perspective. The market capitalization is defined as shares outstanding multiplied by share price at 28/10/85.
(*) The column "in % of country" relates the total market capitalization of the relevant companies (those exceeding US$ 2000 million in market capitalization) to the estimated total market capitalization of the country in which they are domiciled.

Source: Morgan Stanley Capital International Perspective, Geneva

markets. Corporate treasurers realize they are faced with a choice between many complex financial instruments in any number of national equity or debt markets. The growing number of European and Japanese companies listing their equities on U.S. exchanges through the use of American Depositary Receipts (ADRs) underscores the growing interaction between world stock markets.

As companies began to cross list on various exchanges using instruments like ADRs they developed a growing interest in attracting investors directly to the domestic exchanges on which they are listed. These phenomena have in turn led to pressure, mainly in the US, for standardized disclosure practices among worldwide firms. In order for Japanese companies, for example, to list an ADR on a U.S. exchange they are required to conform to U.S. disclosure practices. Therefore, Japanese companies have modified their accounting procedures to report consolidated company earnings rather than the unconsolidated earnings formerly reported. Similarly, Japanese companies wishing to attract U.S. investors to their Tokyo listed securities have also started to modify their reporting standards in order to accommodate the foreign investors they seek. This initial movement toward standardized disclosure procedures has contributed to investor's greater understanding of securities beyond their domestic market. Deregulation of various markets has also increased investors understanding of "foreign" securities by accelerating the availability of information about equities from market to market.

As information began to flow more freely, investor's became aware of the superior returns available in national markets other than their own. The prevailing viewpoint began to change from one focusing on the risks of global investing to one favoring the rewards available through global diversification. The diversification theories applied in domestic markets were extrapolated to global markets. It has become clear that factors such as varying economic growth among nations, currency swings and limited dissemination of information, which many investors viewed as inhibiting global investment, more recently have become identified as market inefficiencies that could be translated into significant returns. As always, the lure of superior returns spurred investors to move into new areas.

FUTURE DEVELOPMENTS

Interaction among world stock markets appears to be continuing at a more rapid pace. Looking forward, it seems conceivable that this interaction is likely to lead to greater similarities among world stock markets. Exhibit 11 shows correlations for ten Morgan Stanley Capital International country indices relative to each other and relative to the world in local currency terms for two time periods, 1977-1982 and 1982-1987. A coefficient of 1.0 between two markets implies perfect correlation, meaning the factors affecting one market affect the other market in the same manner. A 0.0 coefficient suggests there is no relationship between the factors that affect a given pair markets. From 1977-1982 period correlations among markets was fairly weak, implying that returns to individual markets were caused by different forces. It is this argument that confirms the importance of holding a diversified global portfolio. As noted over the past decade, global investing has become increasingly important to the investor seeking to reduce investment risks specific to individual markets while maximizing returns on investment. It is interesting to consider how increased interaction among world stock markets will impact the importance of maintaining a diversified global portfolio.

In Exhibit 11, while the correlations among markets remains fairly low in both the 1977-1982 and 1982-1987 period, generally, the correlation among markets was somewhat greater during the 1982-1987 period. A dramatic increase in correlation occured between Japan and the World Index while at the same time a dramatic decrease occured between the U.S. Index and the World Index. Interestingly, correlation between Japan and U.S. markets increased over this time.

Although there is some evidence that correlation among markets is increasing it appears to be doing so at a slow rate. As long as correlation between markets is less than 1.0, there will continue to be advantages to global diversification. Country specific factors will always have a greater impact on the markets in the country in which they occur. However, it is increasingly important to understand the impact that these domestic events have on markets in other coun-

EXHIBIT 11 MATRIX OF MORGAN STANLEY CAPITAL INTERNATIONAL PERSPECTIVE INDICES IN LOCAL CURRENCY

COUNTRY		USA	Japan	UK	Germany	France	Switzerland	Australia	Sweden	Spain	S'pore/Mal	WORLD
USA	1/77-1/82	1.00	0.12	0.42	0.34	0.39	0.42	0.50	0.29	0.11	0.36	0.93
	1/82-1/87	1.00	0.30	0.61	0.24	0.44	0.55	0.32	0.28	0.21	0.35	0.90
Japan	1/77-1/82	0.12	1.00	0.38	0.36	0.22	0.34	0.17	0.21	0.17	0.17	0.39
	1/82-1/87	0.30	1.00	0.33	0.30	0.37	0.24	0.17	0.12	0.33	–0.01	0.63
UK	1/77-1/82	0.42	0.38	1.00	0.41	0.41	0.48	0.42	0.19	0.28	0.25	0.65
	1/82-1/87	0.61	0.33	1.00	0.32	0.49	0.44	0.35	0.26	0.24	0.26	0.69
Germany	1/77-1/82	0.34	0.36	0.41	1.00	0.18	0.47	0.29	0.13	0.05	0.24	0.48
	1/82-1/87	0.24	0.30	0.32	1.00	0.39	0.64	0.11	0.12	0.14	–0.08	0.40
France	1/77-1/82	0.39	0.22	0.41	0.18	1.00	0.20	0.30	–0.01	–0.08	0.06	0.47
	1/82-1/87	0.44	0.37	0.49	0.39	1.00	0.39	0.20	0.21	0.39	–0.02	0.58
Switzerland	1/77-1/82	0.42	0.34	0.48	0.47	0.20	1.00	0.32	0.32	–0.08	0.30	0.54
	1/82-1/87	0.55	0.24	0.44	0.64	0.39	1.00	0.25	0.32	0.11	0.04	0.60
Australia	1/77-1/82	0.50	0.17	0.42	0.29	0.30	0.32	1.00	0.09	0.20	0.32	0.62
	1/82-1/87	0.32	0.17	0.35	0.11	0.20	0.25	1.00	0.23	0.07	0.31	0.39
Sweden	1/77-1/82	0.29	0.21	0.19	0.13	–0.01	0.32	0.09	1.00	0.21	0.16	0.30
	1/82-1/87	0.28	0.12	0.26	0.12	0.21	0.32	0.23	1.00	0.15	0.18	0.33
Spain	1/77-1/82	0.11	0.17	0.28	0.05	–0.08	–0.08	0.20	0.21	1.00	0.16	0.20
	1/82-1/87	0.21	0.33	0.24	0.14	0.39	0.11	0.07	0.15	1.00	–0.12	0.34
Singapore/Mal	1/77-1/82	0.36	0.17	0.25	0.24	0.06	0.30	0.32	0.16	0.16	1.00	0.42
	1/82-1/87	0.35	–0.01	0.26	–0.08	–0.02	0.04	0.31	0.18	–0.12	1.00	0.25

Source: Morgan Stanley Capital International Perspective, Geneva

tries. While ten years ago global investing was a nascent concept, today the benefits of global investing are clearly apparent and many of the former barriers have disappeared. A macroeconomic environment favoring equity investment, the changes wrought from deregulating national markets and the increased speed of technology ensure that global investment will continue to provide greater opportunities and rewards for investors.

CHAPTER SEVEN

TERRY B. MASON has been employed by the E. I. Du Pont de Nemours and Company for ten years and has served as an International Equity Analyst in the Pension Fund Investment Department since June 1984. His responsibilities include European, Japanese, and other Pacific Basin equity markets. One area of concentration has been the broadly defined financial services industry as analyzed from a global perspective. Terry received his B.A. in political science from Glassboro State College in New Jersey and his MBA from Widener University in Pennsylvania. His primary outside interests are his wife JoAnne and his two sons Bryan and Justin.

DEREGULATION OF WORLD CAPITAL MARKETS

Terry B. Mason
E.I. Du Pont de Nemours & Company
Wilmington, Delaware

INTRODUCTION

When a money manager considers a commitment to the diversification afforded by international investing, a number of questions arise which are critical to the decision making process. Questions regarding risk-reward, liquidity, disclosure, transaction costs, taxation, repatriation of profits, and currency risks immediately come to mind, and indeed the answers to these questions will be an important factor at performance evaluation time. Moreover, the answers to these questions vary from country to country as a myriad of regulatory bodies establish laws intended to serve nationalistic economic goals of trade, monetary, and fiscal policy. Barriers have been erected which limit capital flow, maintain currency exchange advantage, fix commission rates on security transactions, limit access to security markets, and stifle free trade in goods and services. While serving the purposes of each individual nation these barriers have had an adverse effect on the world economy and the development of international financal and capital markets.

Today, however, we find ourselves in the midst of radical and rapid change that, ironically, is being accelerated by the same nationalistic sentiments that fostered the forces of regulation. In fear of being left behind in the expansion of the world's capital markets, nations are participating in a wave of change whose time has come—deregulation!

DEREGULATION

Deregulation is primarily the reduction or elimination of barriers which have inhibited the free interaction between various financial, corporate and national entities. Although the trend toward deregulation has been accelerating rapidly over the last few years, the seed of this financial and capital market revolution was actually planted in the early 1970's. When historians try to pinpoint the move toward deregulation, they will probably focus on 1971, when Richard Nixon closed the gold window. The result was, of course, the movement of the world's currencies toward a freely floating market. It is notable that there was no longer any restraint of the U.S. government's inflationary tendencies at that time in history.

As the world's largest economy, the implications of these actions resulted in changes in the U.S. financial system that were bound to spill over into the economies of the rest of the world. The entire process was further exaggerated by the inflation caused by the Arab oil embargo in 1973. In many ways, subsequent deregulation of the U.S. financial system in the late 1970's and early 1980's acted as a stimulus for the deregulation of financial and capital markets in other countries during this decade, with the reasons for change interrelated or coincident. Thus, the changes which occurred in the U.S. over the last ten years make it a microcosm of changes in today's world.

Reasons for Deregulation

Before examining these deregulatory changes, we should first determine the reasons for this trend; reasons vary from country to country but invariably can be reduced to a few primary causes. Since they are all somewhat interrelated, no particular ranking of importance is appropriate. The most common reasons are the growing internationalization of financial markets, high and variable interest rates, large government deficits, technological change, competition and nationalism. As a result of these factors, we have experienced an unprecedented explosion in financial innovation. In turn, new products stimulated by this innovation have brought new pressures on supervisory and regulatory bodies and influenced monetary and fiscal policy.

What stimulated this changing environment? In the late 1970's, as inflation grew in most industrialized nations, government deficits began to expand rapidly. As a result, countries were forced to stimulate the development of bond and money markets in an effort to finance their increasing national debt. In countries where immature markets existed, the authorities were forced to alter regulations and encourage market development so that government debt instruments could be sold more easily. An example of this phenomenon is the growth of the French bond market over the last ten years.

Examples of Deregulation

Deregulation played an important role in the expansion of the French capital market. In the late 1970's, the government was faced with the need to finance their large budget deficit. In an attempt to entice savers away from traditional investments in gold and real estate, the government enacted legal changes in 1978 and 1983 which greatly enhanced tax incentives for both holders and issuers of bonds. To entice the banking community, the authorities exempted loans financed by bond sales from credit ceilings. As a result, the French experienced a four-fold increase in the amount of gross and net bond issues between 1979 and 1984. But, as frequently happens, this activity in the bond market had an adverse impact on another sector. The banks began to experience disintermediation of funds as savers withdrew deposits and invested them in the bond market. To combat this, the banking industry began to offer mutual funds to be invested in short-maturity and variable-rate bonds.

The growth of these products was so outstanding that by early 1985, they accounted for nearly one-fifth of the total capitalization of the French bond market.

Thus deregulatory changes aimed at accomodating fiscal policy actually resulted in innovative new products in the financial markets which further expanded liquidity and participation by investors. In turn, these new products provided the incentives for further deregulation and new financial innovation. A similar scenario would be replayed many times around the world.

The Japanese provide a similar example. Japan's financial structure was probably the most regulated in the industrial world. Bank deposit rates were regulated and lending rates were tied to the Bank of Japan's discount rate. Because corporations depended almost entirely on bank loans for external financing, the Japanese bond market was poorly developed. Then, following the first oil shock in 1973, the environment began to change. As inflation accelerated, government deficits grew. The government required a syndicate of banks and securities firms which would accept newly issued government debt instruments at below market rates, hold them for a specified period, and then resell them in the secondary market. As resistance to this method of financing grew, the government was forced to introduce new medium-term instruments that were sold directly at public auction. It also reduced the holding period required before resale of long-term bonds.

Once again, financial innovation came to the rescue. A secondary market for long-term bonds evolved. Known as the "gensaki" market, this unregulated market was a short-term repurchase market based on long-term government bonds. Also, in 1980, the securities companies introduced the "chugoku" funds, medium-term government bond funds that offered rates of interest above those on fixed-rate bank deposits. As this disintermediation in the banking system, and the demand by individuals for higher returns on their investments, grew, the government was forced to allow banks to issue negotiable certificates of deposit to stem the competition from the securities companies. Today the CD market has taken its place along with the "gensaki" market as Japan's primary money market.

In addition, interest rate ceilings have been eliminated on large denomination time deposits and are scheduled to be removed on smaller deposits by 1987. Once again, deregulation stimulated financial innovation. As the examples of France and Japan show, economic conditions such as inflation, fiscal deficits, and high variable interest rates coupled with financial innovation of new products have prompted regulatory authorities to loosen their reigns. National fiscal pressures must also be addressed, as they influence the banking and financial structures of a country. Although efforts to solve domestic problems have clearly been the impetus that initiated the snowball of deregulation, numerous factors have led from domestic accommodation to today's worldwide phenomenon. We now turn to an examination of these factors.

GLOBAL DEREGULATION

Aside from the aforementioned movement to a floating exchange rate system, the elimination or relaxation of exchange and capital controls by most industrialized countries by early 1980 was probably the most important factor in facilitating investment flows into an integrated world financial market. The controls had originally been instituted to limit domestic money supply problems caused by capital flows into the deutsche mark and yen as the dollar weakened in 1973-78. Then, when the dollar subsequently strengthened after 1983, the absence of exchange controls allowed for massive capital flows out of Japan, Germany and the United Kingdom into dollar-denominated assets. There is ample evidence that the current account surpluses of these countries and their excess savings were invested abroad, particularly in the dollar. As a result, deregulation played an important role in the massive mobility of international capital and the resulting integration of world capital markets. This factor has had such an impact that several theories are evolving that contend that capital movements rather than trade have become the driving force of the world economy.

As a result of these massive flows, international growth in financial assets has reached an unprecedented level. To provide some perspective on the magnitude of financial activity that regulatory bodies face, a few facts may be helpful. The total amount of world trade in goods and services for 1985 was approximately 2.75 trillion dollars, including "invisible trade." Foreign exchange transactions in that year amounted to nearly $35 trillion, or twelve times the trade in goods and services. Securities transactions have expanded from $150 billion in 1979 to $1.5 trillion in 1984, a ten-fold increase. However, the London Eurodollar market transacted over $300 billion each working day, or approximately $75 trillion a year. This highly successful market is virtually unregulated, yet it is twenty-five times larger than the amount of total world trade.

Role of Technology

Technological change has been an additional stimulus toward deregulation and financial innovation. Computer technology has given financial institutions the ability to handle a tremendous number of transactions less expensively and more rapidly than at any time in the past. This has allowed these institutions to offer a wider variety of services in today's competitive environment. At the same time, the computer has provided for the rapid dissemination of information and ease of transactions that are vital to investor confidence. Today, information is passed instantaneously throughout the world by various news retrieval and quotation services, while transactions are simplified by the use of telex, facsimile, and electronic mail. As technology evolves, it will continue to be a factor in the expansion of international markets and in the enhancement of financial decisions. In turn, regulatory bodies will be under continued pressure to relax barriers in order to allow financial institutions to compete with counterparts in other nations.

International Integration of Markets

The predominant factor in the movement toward deregulation is probably the internationalization of the financial and capital markets and the international integration that has resulted. Various financial instruments have spread beyond their traditional markets and have broadened into different currency sectors, while new channels such as eurocommercial paper and international equities have opened up, allowing funds to flow directly between investors and borrowers in different countries. In addition, the dismantling of regulatory and tax barriers has given borrowers a greater choice of markets. Finally, the securitization of international lending has allowed a wider range of institutions to participate in the long-term credit market. The result of these changes is that the distinction between domestic markets and euromarkets is eroding as borrowing terms between the two move closer in line with one another. International markets are now acting as intermediaries between investors and borrowers in the same country, as when Japanese borrowers sell eurobonds to Japanese investors in London, or German borrowers sell Australian dollar eurobonds to German investors in New York. These developments have transformed international financial markets while providing flexibility to borrowers worldwide.

This flexibility is illustrated by R.J. Reynolds Industries' decision to refinance its $1.5 billion debt incurred in the acquisition of Nabisco Brands. Over a ten-week period, they were able to raise $650 million in Europe by way of various borrowing operations in Euroyen, Swiss francs, ECU's, Eurodollars and deutsche marks. All of these loans were later swapped into U.S. dollars, thus eliminating currency exposure. As a result, Reynolds' all-in cost was between fifteen and forty-five basis points below what it would have cost them to borrow domestically. In another example, Japanese firms have recently been extremely aggressive in issuing convertible securities denominated in Swiss francs. Financing initiatives such as these provide many interesting financing opportunities for corporate treasurers while further intensifying the pressure toward deregulation. Reglatory authorities fear that unless they liberalize rules, companies will finance in lower-cost, less restrictive money centers such as London and New York.

The trend toward dereglation is indeed a worldwide phenomenon, with all the major free economies participating to some degree. We next examine the various courses that these nations have taken in the process of deregulation by looking at a number of them in more detail.

UNITED STATES

As noted earlier, deregulation of foreign exchange markets in the U.S. actually began with the closing of the gold window by Richard Nixon in 1971, and the ensuing movement to floating exchange rates. However, in the subsequent period of rising inflation, one individual had an idea that would alter the financial services industry for the next two decades. Bruce Brent, of the Reserve Fund, realized that savers would seek a haven for their funds that would enable them to protect capital. Thus, in 1971, Brent and a partner established what is thought to be the first money market fund. The advantage of the money market fund was that it could operate outside the regulation that restrained the banking industry—Regulation Q. Reg-Q restricted the interest rate that banks and thrift institutions could pay on deposits. As a result, in an environment of double-digit inflation, money market funds grew faster than any other industry in the history of U.S. finance. Unfortunately, the money that was pouring into these funds was fleeing banks and other financial institutions, depriving them of their traditional low-cost deposits. As a result of this disintermediation of funds, many banks and thrifts found themselves with low-yielding assets, in the form of low-interest fixed-rate mortgages, on their books while inflation was escalating their cost of funds. Finally, in 1980, with the U.S. banking industry in shambles, Congress passed the ''Depository Institutions Deregulation and Monetary Control Act of 1980'' (DIDMCA).

This act altered the nature of the banking industry, as it included provisions which:

1) Subjected any depository institution offering transaction accounts to universal reserve requirements set by the Federal Reserve.
2) Opened the discount window at the Federal Reserve to all depository institutions.
3) Eliminated interest rate ceilings on deposits (Regulation Q) by 1986.
4) Permitted all depository financial institutions to offer Negotiated Order of Withdrawal (NOW) accounts.
5) Removed state usury ceilings on mortgage rates for three years.
6) Allowed thrift institutions to lend up to 20 percent of assets in consumer loans, commercial paper, and corporate debt securities.
7) Offered Federal Reserve services to members and non-members on an equal basis.

The enactment of DIDMCA allowed financial institutions to compete on an equal basis with one another. Inefficiencies in the system began to be eliminated and a consolidation of the industry resulted, with the weak and poorly managed institutions being purchased by the larger, better managed ones. Today, the rates paid by money market funds and bank money market accounts are only a few basis points apart, due primarily to FDIC protection of banks. In addition, banks were forced to actively manage their portfolios by matching assets and liabilities, providing for more stable and professionally managed institutions. The point here is that financial innovation (the money market funds) led to deregulation that resulted in a stronger, more competitive industry that is better suited to serve its clientele. This is exactly what is occurring on a larger scale throughout the world.

In the United States, two areas of regulation continue to impede banking activity. Interstate branching of banks is restricted by the McFadden Act (1927) and the Douglas Amendment to the Bank Holding Company Act (1970). However, financial innovation is eroding the geographic restrictions of these acts. Electronic funds transfer systems and the use of national credit cards have allowed banks to conduct business beyond state boundaries. The holding company umbrella has also enabled institutions to offer a wide array of financial services nationwide. Thus, existing loopholes are being pushed far beyond the original intentions of regulators, and it is probably only a matter of time before these acts are fully circumvented.

The second, and most important, regulation inhibiting banking activity from an international perspective is the Glass-Steagall Act (1933), which separates commercial and investment banking. Unlike the universal banks in Europe, such as Deutsche Bank, National Westminster, or the Swiss banks, U.S. banks are not permitted to underwrite the issuance of corporate securities, or to act as dealers. This law was intended to protect consumers from speculation by the banks or conflicts of interest between investment banking and commercial banking. Today, however, large investment bankers, such as Morgan Stanley and Goldman Sachs, and the giant financial conglomerates, such as Sears, Merrill Lynch, and Shearson-American Express, are providing virtually the same products as commercial banks with the exception of federally insured deposits. In defense, banks are beginning to infringe on the brokerage community. Citibank has purchased Vickers & Co., a British brokerage firm, while Bank of America has purchased a discount broker, Charles Schwab. As the lines of distinction begin to erode, the potential for deregulation improves. In the United States, the concept of universal banking may be closer than many anticipate.

Another important step in the deregulation of the U.S. financial structure was the advent of negotiated commissions on securities transactions. As the U.S. securities markets became more institutionalized, fixed commissions came under considerable pressure. Finally, on May 1, 1975, investors were permitted to negotiate commission rates with brokers. Mayday, as it was known, resulted in the demise of many firms who found it impossible to compete in the new environment. Meanwhile, the consumer benefited from improved cost and service as the industry consolidated, leaving only the more efficient, well-capitalized firms as survivors. This phenomenon is repeating itself today in many of the world's financial markets. In Japan, the brokerage community was forced to lower commission rates to large investors in 1985. In the United Kingdom, negotiated commissions began on October 27, 1986, when what was referred to as the "Big Bang" took place. In 1987, the Swiss, French, and Dutch plan to cut commissions to avoid losing business in their securities markets. As international investing continues to grow, regulatory agencies will increasingly have to choose between relaxing barriers to their markets or simply dropping out of the international financial revolution.

The United States has been leading the movement toward global deregulation. It's financial markets are the largest and most diverse in the world, and, accordingly, have been deregulated the most. Since there are no exchange controls, foreigners are encouraged to enter the markets, especially as borrowers. All credit facilities available to U.S. firms are also available to foreign firms. On June 27, 1984, the Tax Reform Act of 1984 repealed the 30 percent withholding tax on interest paid to foreigners on certain U.S. obligations. This provision has effectively abolished all withholding tax on interest and discount bearing securities. As a result, there is now little distinction between the domestic and Eurobond markets. In fact, in 1982 there were more Eurodollar bonds issued in the international market than there were corporate bonds in the domestic market.

The United States is also virtually unregulated in regard to currency. All residents and nonresidents are permitted to operate freely in the spot and forward foreign exchange markets. Additionally, non-residents are permitted to hold interest bearing demand and time deposit accounts in dollars or foreign currency, and most importantly, may repatriate all proceeds from investments without restrictions.

When one examines the financial structure in the United States, it becomes quite apparent that deregulation has provided new opportunities and a more efficient system than exists anywhere else in the world. The competitive pressures that have been exerted on foreign nations by the activity in the United States is an impetus for change internationally, and should ultimately lead to further deregulation. The one factor that could have an adverse effect on this trend is the protectionist sentiment that currently prevails in Congress.

Most analysts would agree that increased protectionism would be a major error which would only establish new retaliatory barriers and reverse the positive effects of deregulation. Protectionist legislation would serve only to delay the inevitable reduction in manufacturing employment in the United States caused by the maturation of other industrialized nations and the introduction of new technologies, while forcing the U.S. consumer to bear the cost. Instead, the United States should maintain its leadership role by setting an example and continuing to demonstrate the benefits of an unregulated global economy.

JAPAN

Prior to the 1980's, Japan's financial market stood as the most regulated system in the free world. However, beginning with the Foreign Exchange Liberalization Law of December 1980, a combination of market forces, external pressures, and computerization have succeeded in significantly opening up the capital market of the second largest democracy in the world. This is not to say that Japan has become a totally free system, on the contrary, the Japanese economic system still remains entangled in a web of bureaucracy in which change occurs in an evolutionary rather than a revolutionary fashion. Still, the fact remains that great strides have been taken toward liberalization that will ensure that Tokyo establishes itself as one of the world's major financial centers alongside New York and London.

From the view of an international investor, Japan has provided a lucrative investment vehicle, with equity returns which have far exceeded those of any other market in the world over the last fifteen years. However, it is critical to note that although the Japanese financial system seems quite similar to those in the West in terms of institutions and nomenclature, it functions quite differently. For this reason, and the fact that nearly 30 percent of the market capitalization of the Tokyo Stock Exchange Index is comprised of financial stocks, we will focus primarily on the deregulation that has occurred in this area.

The financial services industry in Japan includes various types of institutions: thirteen city banks (large money center banks), sixty-four regional banks, 427 consumer finance companies, 252 leasing companies, seven trust banks, three long-term credit banks, seventy-six foreign banks, twenty-three life insurance and twenty-three nonlife insurance companies, sixty-nine sogo banks, 456 shinkin banks, 448 credit institutions, and a myriad of credit associations and trade cooperatives.

Traditionally, these institutions and their operations have been subjected to very strict controls, including:

1) Restrictions on various interest rates, in particular deposit rates.
2) The segregation of various financial service areas, such as commercial banking, long-term finance, securities brokerage and related activities, the trust business, and the life and nonlife insurance businesses.
3) The segregation of domestic and overseas financial markets through strict foreign exchange controls.
4) Restrictions on market practices, such as in the definition of collateral requirements.

Much of this regulatory framework is now being dismantled or redesigned. In December 1980, the system of exchange controls was revised. Rather than most transactions being forbidden in principle but free in exceptional cases, most transactions are now free in principle but forbidden in exceptional cases. As a result, a number of controls have been relaxed or lifted since 1980. In May 1984, the *Report of the Japan—U.S. Ad Hoc Committee on Yen and Dollar Rates* set out a specific schedule for the elimination of some basic regulatory structures. The most important of these dealt with deregulation of deposit rates and Euroyen transactions, while others focused on the expansion of short-term money markets, such as yen-denominated Bankers' Acceptances; development of the corporate bond market through the establishment of more flexible rules for issuance; and approval of foreign banks as entrants into the highly restrictive and rapidly growing trust service market.

In a country where change usually progresses in a slow, methodical manner, what factors would initiate such dynamic deregulatory activity? There is no single factor that can be cited, but rather, a number of interrelated stimuli. The initial cause was probably the dramatic alteration of money flows that resulted from the first oil crisis in 1973. Business reduced capital expenditures which were, in turn, offset by increased public spending aimed at averting economic contraction. These expenditures were financed by issuance of government bonds which were imposed upon various financial institutions at below market rates. By the end of the 1970's, resistance by these intermediaries increased and various forms of financial innovation were introduced to provide relief. Eventually, restrictions were lifted and a new secondary market for government bonds rapidly developed to provide a new free-rate investment instrument. Coincident with this activity, individuals and businesses became more sensitive to the yields on their financial assets, preferring higher yielding open market instruments to the traditionally regulated bank deposit rates. This inadequacy in the financial structure had to be addressed. The only recourse was the dismantling of old restrictions and the advent of a new system of financial instruments capable of meeting the needs of a maturing society.

Additional international pressures began to appear, necessitating attention. The miraculous growth of "Japan Inc." in the post-World War II economy was beginning to cause problems. Europe and the United States were becoming more and more concerned with Japan's huge trade surplus and as a result, protectionist sentiment increased. To make matters worse, Japan's traditional labor cost advantage was being eroded and competition from Pacific Basin neighbors such as Korea, Singapore, Taiwan and Hong Kong was reducing Japanese dominance in the labor intensive basic industries. As Japan evolved into a technologically oriented economy, their competitors began to follow. Thus, the next step in the maturation of the Japanese economy was toward the service and financial industries. As the largest creditor nation in the world, the country was well positioned to fill a void that existed in the rapidly growing Pacific Basin. But, in order to assure success, continued deregulation was necessary. The success of Japan's efforts can be seen in the fact that in 1985, Japanese banks replaced U.S. banks as the largest international lenders, although their lending was mainly financed from the international interbank market.

Another area of particular importance to international investors is the securities market. As the second largest equity market in the world, the Tokyo Stock Exchange (TSE) provides the liquidity required for even the largest investors. In an important deregulatory move, Merrill Lynch, Goldman Sachs, Morgan Stanley, Jardine Fleming, Vickers da Costa, and S.G. Warburg became the first foreign members of the TSE in early 1986. As a result, they no longer have to pay 27 percent of their commissions to the Japanese TSE members who executed their trades in the past. In turn, the Japanese "big four" securities firms of Nomura, Daiwa, Nikko and Yamaichi are making their presence felt internationally. Nomura and Daiwa are currently attempting to become primary dealers in U.S. government securities. All four are actively seeking to become underwriters of foreign securities to be traded on the Tokyo Exchange. As worldwide deregulation continues, these Japanese brokers will be formidable competitors in the international capital markets.

Future deregulaton in Japan will progress as deemed necessary by the powerful Ministry of Finance (MOF). This regulatory body has been instrumental in allowing change to occur in an orderly fashion while still serving governmental policy requirements. For example, since the G-5 agreement of September 1985, the yen has appreciated at alarming rates, causing hardship on the Japanese exporters, the lifeblood of the economy. In an effort to stem the tide, the insurance industry has been permitted to increase their foreign securities holdings from 10 percent of total investment assets to 25 percent, thus creating demand for other currencies. In 1985, in response to pressures from foreign financial institutions, MOF permitted nine foreign banks to engage in the lucrative trust business, with the stipulation that they engage in an advisor agreement with one of the current Japanese trust institutions. Another topic for the future is a Tokyo Offshore Market. It has been recognized that Japan's deposit and short-term money markets lag behind those in other countries and that short-term funding markets remain limited. Therefore it is anticipated that a deposit market will be established for nonresidents that will subject them to as few financial and tax limitations as feasible. But, the biggest deregulatory question facing Japan today is the status of Article 65.

Article 65 of the Securities Transaction Law is the Japanese version of America's Glass-Steagall Act. While the Japanese financial structure is quite segmented, barriers are beginning to weaken, which could put this Act in jeopardy. The recent relationship between Goldman Sachs and Sumitomo Bank may be a precursor of things to come. The Japanese city banks have been suffering through the deregulatory process as loan spreads have narrowed and demand has decreased. Meanwhile, the brokerage industry has been experiencing rapidly rising profitability as transaction volume has soared and the number of products competitive with the banks has increased. As a result, the banking industry is anxious to invade the brokerage houses' domain of securities transactions. Should there be a substantial problem affecting the viability of the banking system, MOF may very well allow this extension of their activity. The effects would probably be a major consolidation of the system similar to what occurred in the United States following deregulation of interest rates.

A detailed discussion of deregulation in Japan could, no doubt, encompass an entire book. Therefore, suffice it to say that Japan is going through extensive deregulation that will inevitably result in Tokyo becoming the third major financial center in the world. Following is a summary of some of the major changes that have occurred over the last several years.

1980

January New Establishment of medium-term government bond fund.

April Abolition of "gensaki" ceiling on sales by city banks. (The "gensaki" market is a short-term repurchase market based on long-term government bonds.)

June Deregulation of interest rates on nonresident yen deposits.

November Loan position institutions and large securities companies permitted to take call money.

December Amended Foreign Exchange Law went into effect.

1981

January Creation of new financial instruments (lump-sum interest payment with limitations of the deposit amount).

March Widening of the difference between short-term prime rate and discount rate from .25% to .5%.

April City bank call loans permitted.
City bank gensaki purchases permitted.

May Selling began in treasury bill market.

1982

Loans at lower than long-term prime rate permitted

1983

Investments combining government bonds and others permitted in savings deposit market.

1984

January Reduction of minimum CD denomination from Y500 million to Y300 million.

April Enlargement of CD issues by foreign banks from 30% to 50% of annual assets.
Deregulation of yen-denominated lending to non-residents.
Relaxation of guidelines on Residents' Euroyen-bond issuance.
Sale of public bonds at banks permitted.

May Yen-Dollar Agreement signed by U.S. Treasury Secretary Donald Regan and Finance Minister Noburo Takeshita.

June Elimination of yen/dollar swap limitations.
Deregulation of short-term Euroyen lending.

July Abolition of designated-company rule became effective, foreign shareholding of designated companies no longer restricted.

October Approval of government bond dealings to three foreign banks.

November Tokyo Stock Exchange decision to allow unrestricted sales of memberships (number of seats held at eighty-three).

December Authorization for foreign brokerage houses to lead manage Euroyen bond issues.
Relaxation of guidelines on nonresidents' Euroyen bond issuance.
Plans for Yen Bankers' Acceptance market announced.
Criteria for foreign bank entry into the trust banking business announced.

1985

January Framework on Money Market Certificates announced.

March Money Market Certificate market began.

April Reduction of minimum CD denomination from 300 million to 100 million yen.
Reduction of minimum CD term from three months to one month.
Elimination of withholding tax on Euroyen bonds held by nonresidents.
Deregulation of medium- and long-term Euroyen loans to nonresidents.

May Approval of government bond dealing to five foreign banks.

June Yen Bankers Acceptance market began.
Nine foreign banks licensed to begin trust business.
July Noncollateral funding in the call market.
October Enlargement of CD and Money Market Certificate issuance to 150 percent of capital.
Deregulation of interest rates on time deposits exceeding one-billion yen.

1986

Creation of bond futures market.
Six foreign firms buy seats on TSE.

Future Deregulation

Establishment of a Treasury Bill market.
Reduction of minimum Money Market Certificate deposit account.
Deregulation of interest rates on interbank deposits.
Lifting the embargo on resident Euroyen-bond issues.
Deregulation of interest on small savings deposits.

UNITED KINGDOM

London has been, by consensus, the foremost financial center in the world. Although its size is exceeded by New York and Tokyo, in terms of domestic market turnover, it boasts a wide range of investment instruments and a degree of dealing sophistication that has evolved through centuries of tradition. Its domestic money market consists of a wide range of securities, including the recently initiated commercial paper market. Its domestic capital market is dominated by gilts (U.K. government bonds) in terms of value of turnover, while equities are dominant in terms of physical volume. In addition, London has been a major world center for gold bullion dealing as well as international transactions in Eurocurrencies and

Eurobonds. From a regulatory point of view, London is extremely open to foreign investment, with no distinction made between resident and nonresident borrowers or investors, with the exception of minor cost differences such as rates of stamp duty. With the abolition of all forms of exchange controls in October 1979, nonresidents are now free to enter the market and repatriate any proceeds without restriction. However, interest earnings are subject to withholding taxes (rates vary by treaty), and dividends are declared net of tax. On the surface, London seems to be conducting "business as usual," but in actuality, considerable uncertainty exists regarding the major deregulatory change that has been dubbed the "Big Bang."

On October 27, 1986, London's domestic equities and government securities markets were liberalized. This act of deregulation can be expected to have a significant impact on the traditional methods used to conduct securities transactions. It has already affected the participants, as various firms are attempting to position themselves to take advantage of the perceived opportunities afforded by the Big Bang. The advent of this change can be traced back to 1978, when the rules and regulations governing the Stock Exchanges' business practices were referred to the Restrictive Practices Court. Finally, after five years of litigation and legal fees in excess of seven figures, a compromise was struck between Sir Nicholas Goodison, the chairman of the Stock Exchange, and Cecil Parkinson, the Secretary of State for Trade and Industry. In effect, the government agreed to exempt the Exchange from the provisions of the Restrictive Practices Act, while the Stock Exchange agreed to abandon its traditional system of fixed commissions on deals in securities by the end of 1986. In addition to this action, other restrictions are being lifted through a series of measures which will include the following provisions:

- An outsider will be permitted to acquire 100 percent of a Stock Exchange member firm (previously the limit was 29.9 percent).
- Up to thirty firms will be permitted to deal in Government securities or gilts.

- The distinction between brokers and jobbers, or specialists, will be abolished, allowing all firms to act as principals.

This last provision, eliminating the distinction between brokers and jobbers, is a direct result of the move toward negotiated commissions, and, in turn, has caused massive turmoil within the securities industry. Prior to the Big Bang, the system known as "single capacity" was required. This meant that a broker could act only as an agent for a client by taking orders. These orders were then passed on to a jobber, who, much like a floor specialist in the United States, actually made a market by quoting two prices, a bid and ask. Thus brokers could not "make a book" in a security while a jobber could not deal with the public, therefore, each functioned in a "single capacity." After October 27, 1986, this barrier was eliminated and both participants are now forced to perform the functions of trading and sales in a competitive environment. Suddenly, risk positioning and arbitrage will be the driving force behind the securities markets, which will now demand a great deal more capital than heretofore.

These capital requirements have resulted in the turmoil alluded to earlier. Over the last few years, all of the leading jobbers and nineteen of the twenty largest bankers have sold their ownership interests, resulting in over eighty transactions valued at more than $2 billion. The purchasers were primarily major foreign banks and a number of British clearing banks and merchant banks (See Table 1). The underlying motivation for these acquisitions is the desire to evolve into a vertically integrated investment bank performing the functions of underwriting, jobbing, and brokering. Since there are no restrictions preventing banking entities from performing the underwriting function in Great Britain, this vertical integration is quite feasible. This revolutionary change in the London equity market should result in the survival of only few well managed and adequately capitalized firms which will be competitive with the large investment banking firms of the United States, the Universal Banks of continental Europe and the major securities houses of Japan.

The other major London capital market, the gilt market, is also

TABLE 1 ACQUISITIONS OF TOP TEN U.K. STOCKBROKERS

U.K. Firm	Purchaser
James Capel & Co.	Hong Kong Bank
Scrimgeour Vicker & Co.	Citibank (U.S.)
Hoare Govett Ltd.	Security Pacific (U.S.)
Wood Mackenzie & Co.	Hill Samuel (U.K.)
de Zoete & Bevan	Barclays (U.K.)
Phillips and Drew	Union Bank of Switzerland
Cazenove & Co.	None
Laing & Cruickshank	Mercantile House (U.K.)
Rowe & Pitman	S. G. Warburg (U.K.)
Greiveson, Grant & Co.	Kleinwort, Benson (U.K.)

undergoing dramatic structural change as a direct result of deregulation. Prior to the Big Bang, two firms dominated the dealing. At this writing, the Bank of England has approved a total of twenty-nine gilt market makers, including several foreign commercial and universal banks. This will result in an increase in invested capital from approximately $235 million (150 million pounds) to nearly $940 million (600 million pounds) and ensure a structure similar to the U.S. treasury market. Profitability for these firms will undoubtedly be a function of positioning skills, as commission rates are estimated to decrease by 25 to 35 percent. One hope is that increased volume will compensate for the reduction in margins. In any case, there will be winners and losers, and success may well depend upon the ability of the participants to integrate the origination, trading and distribution functions.

Acquisition activity in the gilt-edge security firms has also been quite aggressive, as many foreign financial institutions tried to gain entry into what was anticipated to be a very lucrative market (Table 2).

Another area of deregulation in the United Kingdom that is apart from the Big Bang is the British government's approval in 1985 of one to five year sterling corporate debt issues. This action was seen as a precursor to a British commercial paper market. Currently, corporate treasurers are forbidden to issue commercial paper directly in sterling since this would make them, according to the Banking Act, unlicensed deposit takers. However, it seems quite probable that in the near future regulatory authorities will follow the Netherlands and France in allowing the development of a domestic commercial paper market.

Deregulation is also having an effect on the domestic financial institutions as financial markets move toward more integration. During the 1970's the markets serviced by banks and building societies were segmented, primarily because the building societies had a substantial advantage in competing for most retail savings deposits. In addition, these institutions dominated mortgage lending because the Supplementary Special Deposits scheme, or "corset," limited interest-bearing bank deposits. Thus banks tended to lend only to their prime customers. However, in 1979, the lifting of exchange controls allowed for offshore centers, permitting banks to circumvent these restrictions. In 1980, the corset was abolished and banks entered the profitable mortgage market, forcing the building societies to press for a broadening of their lending powers. As the distinctions between the institutions began to erode, the government was forced to further relax regulations, until April 1985, when the authorities harmonized the tax treatment of interest paid on deposits in banks and building societies, effectively eliminating the advantage of the latter. The indication is that as the building societies

TABLE 2 ACQUISITIONS OF U.K. GILT MARKET FIRMS

U.K. Firm	Purchaser
Greenwell & Co.	Samual Montagu (Midland Bank) (U.K.)
Phillips & Drew	Union Bank of Switzerland
James Capel & Co.	Hong Kong Bank
Pember & Boyle	Morgan Grenfell (U.K.)
Mullens & Co.	S. G. Warburg
Buckmaste & Moore	Credit Suisse (Switzerland)
Hoare Govett Ltd.	Security Pacific (U.S.)
Fielding, Newson-Smith & Co.	National Westminster (U.K.)

develop, regulatory treatment of the two systems will become more similar. This will undoubtedly foster more competition and improve service to the consumer.

The various forms of deregulation in the United Kingdom are intended to solidify London's competitive position in the world's capital markets while improving the financial markets domestically. The geographic position of London places it in the center of the financial world; able to be in contact with the Tokyo markets in the morning, and with the New York markets in the afternoon. With the advent of 24-hour trading in the securities markets in the not too distant future, this advantage will provide the "City" with unique opportunities, as long as it is not burdened with unnecessary regulatory barriers. Deregulation is the key to building the modern, efficient marketplace required in this environment.

WEST GERMANY

Deregulation has been slower in evolving in West Germany than in the major financial centers. However, two interrelated issues have emerged to stimulate the regulatory authorities into various efforts to liberalize the German financial markets. The most important of these is a changed attitude by the Bundesbank regarding the role of the deutsche mark as a reserve currency. A few years ago, when the dollar was extremely weak, the central bank made every effort to resist the growth of the deutsche mark as a reserve asset. It feared that increasing capital inflows would force up the currency to export-damaging levels and in turn make the control of domestic money supply, and inflation, more difficult. But by 1984, the trend reversed, and the dollar strengthened, forcing the Bundesbank to attempt to stem the capital outflows. It seemed that the fundamentals of trade and current account surplus combined with a relatively low inflation rate were no longer enough to attract capital inflows and to support the deutsche mark. It was in this environment that the central bank was able to persuade the finance minister, Dr. Gerhard Stoltenberg, to abolish the 25 percent coupon, or withholding tax. Ironically, in 1986, the pendulum once again moved toward a stronger deutsche mark, and it should be interesting to observe the government's reaction in the next cycle.

The second issue stimulating deregulation is growing fears that Germany, in particular Frankfurt, could become an international financial backwater to London, New York, and Tokyo. This fear was reinforced in 1984 when Deutsche Bank decided to move its non-deutsche-mark Eurobond business to London. This action had a shock effect on German monetary authorities and accelerated further capital market liberalization. For example, the growth of international capital markets forced recent changes in regulations governing bonds denominated in deutsche marks. Under the new procedure, the committee of leading German banks that controlled the calendar for foreign bond issues has been disbanded and an informal arrangement has been established whereby issuing banks need only inform the Bundesbank of their intentions three days before the end of the month preceding the issue. The central bank has also agreed to allow foreign-owned banks based in Germany to lead-manage deutsche-mark denominated foreign bonds. It did, however, place a stipulation which specified that this privilege was open only to banks whose home countries offered similar freedoms to German banks. This effectively eliminated the Japanese banks who were eager to participate on the deutsche-mark market.

Deregulation in the bond market is also apparent by the approval of various new instruments in the spring of 1984. At that time the Bundesbank permitted the issuance of floating-rate notes, zero-coupon bonds and double-currency bonds, as well as bonds linked to interest rate swaps and currency swaps. Certificates of deposit have also recently been permitted. These vehicles provide residents and nonresidents with greater flexibility in meeting financial and investment needs. However, the secondary market in floating-rate notes has tended to move outside the country because of a 25 percent stamp tax on certain sales within Germany. The regulatory authorities are planning to eliminate this competitive disadvantage through repeal of the tax. The hope of the government is that these new instruments will stimulate the growth of Frankfurt as an international financial center.

West Germany's stock exchanges have also felt the need to reform in the face of growing foreign competition. In April 1986, the eight regional bourses unanimously agreed on a mini-reform to help improve their efficiency and coordination. Under the agreement, their current working group will be upgraded to an association with a permanent base and chairman. The new body will represent the interests of the exchanges abroad and handle major national stock market issues such as the introduction of new trading instruments. In addition, it will also issue an annual report and produce national statistical material, which up until now was nearly nonexistent. These efforts should improve the creditability of the exchange in the eyes of international investors.

Although the Germans have been slower than the other major financial centers in regard to liberalization, they have become aware of the need for deregulation, and, have taken some action. Should they continue to make their decisions based purely on nationalism, however, they may find themselves left behind in the movement toward internationalization.

FRANCE

France has been a late entrant in the deregulatory movement because of various political factors. The Socialist government of President Mitterrand was attempting to promote job creation with an outdated Keynsian demand stimulus in the late 1970's while the governments of Reagan, Thatcher and Nakasone were pursuing more conservative economic policies and deregulation. By 1982, however, French leaders began to recognize the effects of swimming against the current and rapidly joined the trend.

With the arrival of finance minister Beregovoy in July 1984, two important instruments were initiated which would substantially alter the French capital markets. Banks were permitted to issue negotiable certificates of deposit and companies were permitted to issue 10 to 180-day commercial paper. In effect, these instruments will allow the borrowing costs for companies to move closer to money market rates and in turn eliminate the monopoly that French banks held in corporate finance. As a result, bank profits will diminish, putting more pressure on capital ratios and accelerating the restructuring of the banking system. Thus, the initiation of CD's and commercial paper will go a long way toward giving France a more flexible capital market.

Other recent innovations should also have a positive impact. The introduction of financial futures contracts and laws permitting any investor, individual or institutional, to purchase Treasury Bills anonymously are two of these. The later will permit companies to invest in short-term securities without having to go through specialized investment funds. This will encourage a more liquid and efficient market while helping to lower interest rates.

The stock exchange is also undergoing change in an effort to compete internationally. In March 1986, a morning trading session began on an experimental basis, and in July 1986, a new computerized system allowed continuous trading in the major stocks from 9:30 A.M. to 5:00 P.M. In addition, the traditional monopoly of French stockbrokers is being eroded as a modern system of market makers and jobbers is implemented. Finally, negotiated commissions are scheduled for gradual implementation.

In May 1986, the government announced a new round of deregulatory measures intended to encourage investment and stimulate the economy. These provisions relax exchange controls for companies and individuals, dismantle credit controls by the end of 1986, lower government-regulated interest rates, reinforce the modernization of French financial markets, and boost competition in the banking industry. For example, the relaxation of exchange controls includes the elimination of the premium paid by French residents when purchasing foreign securities. Companies were granted more liberal funds management, including permission to hedge foreign currency risk. The elimination of credit controls will mean that the central bank will be forced to control money supply through interest rates rather than with a cumbersome system of credit controls that has impeded the banking system.

While the French were slow to begin deregulation, they have made up for lost time by taking an aggressive stance. The impact of this stance may have some adverse effects initially, particularly in the banking system, but the end result should be a stronger and more flexible financial structure capable of competing internationally. Denationalization of the banking system, insurance companies, and industrial groups should further this trend, although great care will be required with changes of this magnitude. On the whole, the strong nationalistic pride of the French should prevail, and France will emerge as a major participant in the world capital markets.

CANADA

The Canadian financial system is a mixture of both the U.S. and U.K. systems and has developed as a result of deliberate policy and encouragement by the Canadian government during the 1950's and 60's. The money market is very active, and due to the increased use of deficit financing, has seen a rapid expansion in the volume of issues over the last five years. The capital market, however, is relatively small when compared to the size of Canada's industry. This is a direct result of the high proportion of industry owned by U.S. companies. The bond market is dominated by Canadian Government bonds which, like all bonds, are traded in the over-the-counter market. The stock market, while comprising just about 3 percent of the total world market capitalization, is very active, having consistently produced the fourth or fifth highest turnover of all world stock markets. The primary reason for the level of activity and sophistication of the Canadian markets is directly linked to their proximity to the United States.

A high degree of economic interdependence exists between the two countries. For example, the United States accounts for 65 percent of Canada's foreign trade, 65 percent of indirect and portfolio investment, 70 percent of direct investment, and 80 percent of foreign-owned Canadian Government bonds. This interrelationship carries over to the regulatory environment. Like the United States, Canada has been very liberal in its relaxation of controls. For example, Canada has free foreign exchange markets and no restrictions on capital movements. In addition, nonresidents may freely open a deposit account with a domestic financial institution in either Canadian dollars or foreign currency and use that account to buy and sell domestic securities, foreign securities or real estate. Nonresidents may also repatriate proceeds of investments without restrictions. Although withholding taxes exist on interest and dividends, exemptions have been established for interest paid on many fixed income instruments, thus eliminating withholding taxes for those willing to investigate and purchase them. Financial innovation has also taken place in the area of derivative instruments. In 1976, options trading was introduced, and in mid-1980, financial futures were initiated. Thus, deregulation of the capital markets in Canada has taken place well in advance of that in many European and Asian Countries.

Another area that has been experiencing deregulatory change is the Canadian financial market. Stimulated by the familiar scenario of high nominal interest rates and technological advances, Canadian financial institutions have undergone a transformation similar to that of their U.K. counterparts. With no regulatory restrictions on bank deposit rates and an environment of double-digit inflation and interest rates, pressure was exerted on financial institutions to pay market rates on deposits in the late 1970s. At the same time, computer technology lowered the marginal costs of funds to banks, encouraging the expansion of certain deposit accounts. As a result, by 1981, daily interest checking accounts became widespread and use of ''sweep'' accounts by corporations increased. Sweep accounts moved deposits into a variety of short-maturity interest-bearing accounts and improved corporate cash management techniques while decreasing reserve requirements for the banks. This innovation would cause a major change in the Canadian banking industry.

The advent of interest-bearing demand deposits has blurred the distinction between savings and transaction balances and therefore forced banks and near-banks to offer such accounts to preserve competitiveness. Initially, chartered banks enjoyed an advantage in offering demand deposits because of their membership in the national payments system. However, in 1980, the Bank Act was amended to permit near-banks to join the Canadian Payments Association. Meanwhile, near-banks, such as trust companies, remained exempt from the Bank of Canada's reserve requirements, making them formidable competitors in the retail deposit market. Thus, an integration of the financial markets evolved, with the trust companies infringing upon the chartered banks' domain of consumer and business loans while the latter invaded the residential mortgage market.

The integration of the financial markets has also resulted in the rapid growth of financial conglomerates, which usually involved trust companies and life insurance firms. Many of these were chartered by the provinces, so they operated outside of federal controls. To combat this phenomenon, in April 1985, the government proposed a new form of federally incorporated holding company that could own trust banks, insurance companies, securities companies, and other financial institutions. This proposal would require any holding company owning two or more types of institutions to become federally incorporated, thus bringing the conglomerates under federal regulations. The result, however, should be the development of new large, broad-based institutions competing with the existing chartered banks, and improved efficiency in the financial system.

It has become quite apparent from this discussion that Canada is involved in the same cycle of consolidation and transformation seen in most financial systems in the industrialized world. We have seen the same type of competitive pressures and blurring of distinctions between institutions force change in the United States, the United Kingdom, and Japan. These factors will continue to fan the flames of deregulation and accelerate the evolution of a worldwide financial system.

OTHER NATIONS

Deregulatory changes in the major financial centers such as New York, London and Tokyo are obviously the most visible, however, almost all industrialized nations have become involved. The following are some brief examples.

The Netherlands

Since January 1986, the Dutch authorities have permitted the issuance of guilder denominated floating and variable rate notes, certificates of deposit, and commercial paper programs. Bond issues without sinking funds were also permitted, which should stimulate swap arrangements. In addition, foreign banks that are locally registered and whose home countries reciprocate can now lead-manage Dutch issues in the Netherlands.

On the Amsterdam stock exchange, further changes have occurred. In September 1985, official trading hours were expanded from two hours a day to 6.5 hours. Concurrently, the exchange began using a new electronic trading system that allows for continuous trading of the leading Dutch securities. The exchange has also lowered commission charges by allowing members to rebate up to 75 percent of the charge for large bond or stock transactions. They also plan to eliminate the "double commission" system which requires foreign purchasers of securities to deal with both a foreign and a Dutch broker.

Italy

In July 1986 a new Eurolira market was established. However, it is limited to non-Italian issuers.

Switzerland

Switzerland has traditionally been one of the most liberal capital markets in the world. Having adopted the concept of the "universal bank" many years ago, the financial institutions of this country have long been major competitors internationally. In Switzerland, deregulation involves the expansion of financial innovation rather than the liberalization of strict codes. In 1986, the initiation of zero-coupon bonds and perpetual floaters occurred. However, the authorities have yet to establish a CD or short-term money market. As other nations reach the plateau of deregulation existing in Switzerland, the authorities there will be forced to act to maintain their slowly eroding competitive position.

Sweden

In 1986, the Swedish central bank recommended the gradual relaxation of the country's stringent foreign-exchange regulations, which have existed since 1939. One area that should be affected is the requirement that forces Swedish corporations to finance direct investments abroad through loans in foreign currency over at least five years, a distinct competitive disadvantage.

In June 1985, authorities decided to permit the entry of foreign banks effective January 1986. This action was motivated by a desire to participate in Norwegian financial markets, which recently instituted a similar policy regarding foreign banks. Here is another example of a response to competitive pressures.

Australia

In Australia, deregulation has involved a lifting of exchange controls and most interest rate ceilings as well as the floating of the Australian dollar. In addition, the entry of foreign banks into the system has been eased.

REREGULATION

This chapter has concentrated on the major deregulatory wave that has been washing over the world's capital and financial markets. The strength of this trend has been considerable and, barring any unforeseen changes in the world's political environment, should continue for years to come. However, there is one caveat to this scenario—the new movement toward reregulation. As deregulation dismantles existing restrictions, there is a natural tendency to establish new limitations on the revaped system. For example, in December 1985, the U.K. government unveiled a plan for a major new regulatory agency for the deregulated financial markets. The new board will be responsible for virtually all investment business, with powers going far beyond those of any previous supervisory agency. In other countries, there is a fear that the new financial instruments being developed will be low-margin products which will eventually put pressure on financial institutions and threaten their profitability. The likelihood that risk is being reallocated in new patterns is also a threat. Hopefully, these concerns will be unfounded. However, should a change in the economic or political environment evolve that negatively impacts the stability of the world economic system or the viability of the financial structure of domestic economies, the current cycle of deregulation could rapidly subside and be replaced by a trend toward tighter controls or reregulation.

SUMMARY

The movement toward deregulation in the world's capital and financial markets has been initiated by a number of interrelated factors over the last fifteen years. High and variable interest rates combined with expanding government deficits were the result of inflationary pressures in the 1970's. Coinciding with this environment was the movement to floating exchange rates and the advent of technological change which enhanced the efficiency of transactions and dissemination of information. These factors facilitated massive capital mobility which, in turn, resulted in the introduction of new financial instruments designed to circumvent the regulatory authorities. Through financial innovation, financial institutions were able to participate in the competitive yet rapidly expanding capital markets. Government regulators saw the need to liberalize their markets to protect nationalistic interests and remain as functional participants in the world economic system. As regulatory barriers began to disappear, the process of deregulation accelerated, as each succeeding step caused new problems that had to be addressed. A review of the various countries examined in this chapter shows a repeating pattern of response to a changing environment.

One question remains: "What effect will deregulation have?" As with any change, there is uncertainty and confusion at first. In addition, there are also inefficiencies in the system that may be exploited. However, time is the key to answering this question. Only the passage of time and adjustment to the new environment can allow the benefits of deregulation to come to fruition. Although the inevitable consolidation of the financial industry and the resultant elimination of the undercapitalized and poorly managed firms will cause a temporary uproar, the survivors will emerge well equipped to manage efficiently in the transformed markets. Also, as the influence of government is reduced, the free market system will be permitted to operate, resulting in a free, efficient, and structurally sound world system that will benefit all participants.

BIBLIOGRAPHY

George, Abraham M. & Ian Giddy. *International Finance Handbook* (New York: John Wiley and Sons, 1983).

Kemp, Lynette J. *The Wardley Guide to World Money and Securities Markets* (London: Euromoney Publications Limited, 1984).

Koening, Peter. "Gearing up for Big Bang," *Institutional Investor* (March 1986).

Ricklefs, Roger and Thomas Kamm. "France Moves to Ease Trading in Stocks, Bonds," *The Wall Street Journal* (April 2, 1985).

Truell, Peter. "France Pushes to Liberalize Financial Markets," *The Wall Street Journal* (July 31, 1985).

Kamm, Thomas. "France Unveils Further Measures Meant to Encourage Investing, Boost Economy," *The Wall Street Journal* (May 16, 1986).

"Fair Stands the Wind for France," *The Economist* (February 8, 1986).

"City Regulation After Big Bang," *Bank of England Quarterly Bulletin* (March 1986).

Carr, Jonathan. "Financial Barriers Begin to Tumble," *Financial Times* (June 25, 1985).

Carr, Jonathan. "West German Bourses Agree to Reforms," *Financial Times* (April 22, 1986).

"The World Is Their Oyster," *The Economist* (March 16, 1985).

Horne, J. Paul. "Deregulation and Eurosclerosis : A Prognosis," Speech made to The Boston Economic Club (February 5, 1986).

Horne, J. Paul. "Deregulation Versus Dirigisme in France," Speech (January 20, 1986).

Nicoll, Alexander. "U.K. Commercial Papers Market on the Way," *Financial Times* (January 20, 1986).

Germany, J. David and John E. Morton. "Financial Innovation and Deregulation in Foreign Industrial Countries," *Federal Reserve Bulletin* (October 1985).

"Developments in International Banking and Capital Markets in 1985," *Bank of England Quarterly Bulletin* (March 1986).

Kirkland, Richard I. "The Stock Market," *Fortune* (October 14, 1985).

Rocco, Fiammetta. "A New Guide for Borrowers in Europe," *Institutional Investor* (March 1986).

CHAPTER EIGHT

TRAN Q. HUNG is a Vice President of Deutsche Bank Capital Markets since 1987. Previously he was with Merrill Lynch where he helped build Merrill's International Fixed Income Research Department. Prior to joining Merrill Lynch, Mr. Hung was a Vice President in the International Bond Market Research Group at Salomon Brothers where he worked for five years.

THE SECURITIZATION OF INTERNATIONAL FINANCE

Tran Q. Hung

Director
Fixed Income Research
Deutsche Bank
New York, New York

The securitization of international finance refers to the recent phenomenon by which lending and borrowing activities in the international financial markets have increasingly taken the form of marketable or securitized instruments at the expense of traditional international bank loans. Concretely, the new issue volume of Eurobonds and foreign bonds (including floating rate notes) has increased markedly in direct competition with medium- to long-term syndicated bank loans. Meanwhile, shorter-term revolving bank credits have been replaced by underwritten facilities such as Note Issuance Facilities (NIFs) or Revolving Underwritten Facilities (RUFs), and more recently, by non-underwritten facilities such as Euro-commercial paper programs or Euro-Medium-Term Note programs. NIFs/RUFs are medium-term facilities which let borrowers issue short-term notes to be placed by a syndicate of banks which also pledge to take the notes on their books if there are no final buyers for the notes. These facilities are very flexible because they guarantee the borrowers a medium-term source of short-term funds to be tapped only when needed. By contrast, Euro-Commercial paper or Euro-

Medium-Term Note programs carry no underwriting commitment from the banks which act merely as dealing agents for the borrowers.

THE FACTORS BEHIND THE SECURITIZATION PROCESS

Table 1 details the new issue volume of international bonds (Euro and foreign bonds), floating rate notes, NIFs/RUFs and other back-up facilities in comparison with syndicated bank loans in recent years. Chart 1 highlights the process of securitization by tracing the share of securitized forms of financing in the total borrowing. In the first half of 1986, securitized financing accounted for a whopping 85.5 percent of all international financing, up sharply from just 43.7 percent only four years ago.

A variety of factors, different in origin but interrelated in influences, has brought on and spurred the process of securitization. First and foremost has been the changing cast of borrowers and lenders in the international financial markets. During the 1970's, the explosive growth in international bank lending was associated with the recycling of petrodollars. From the early 70's to 1981, the OPEC countries had accumulated a current account surplus of about $400 billion, making them the major suppliers of funds to the international financial markets during that period. As investors, OPEC

TABLE 1 NEW ISSUE VOLUME OF INTERNATIONAL FINANCING (US$ BILLION)

	1982	1983	1984	1985	1986*
International Bonds					
Straights	60.2	57.6	73.3	109.3	191.1
FRNs	15.3	19.5	38.2	58.4	30.8
NIFs/RUFs	5.4	9.5	28.8	46.8	23.0
Syndicated Bank Loans	98.2	67.2	.0	42.0	37.0
TOTAL	179.1	153.8	197.3	256.5	281.9

Source: OECD
* Jan-May at annual rate

CHART 1 SECURITIZED FINANCING AS A PERCENTAGE OF TOTAL FINANCING

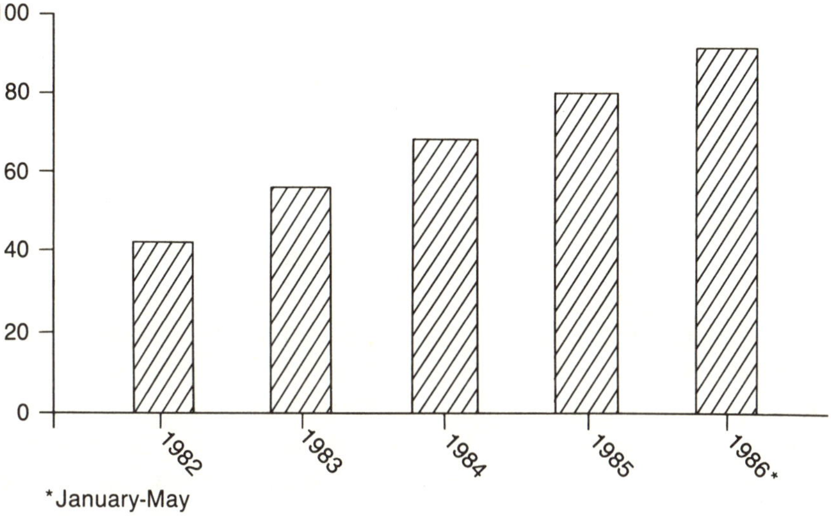

countries generally had a strong preference for liquid bank assets. Consequently, almost half of the cumulative surplus of OPEC was deposited with international banks. The banks then performed the traditional intermediation role by channeling the petrodollar deposits to the less developed countries and other countries to finance their balance of payment deficits and economic development programs. Since 1982, however, OPEC as a group has incurred an increasing current account deficit, causing member countries to withdraw funds, largely from the bank deposit market. U.S. banks have also changed from being net suppliers of funds to the international banking system, chiefly through the interbank market, to being net takers of funds since 1983. This resulted from the international debt crisis, which has prompted U.S. banks to reduce their international lending and has encouraged foreigners to shift their dollar deposits to the United States from the Eurodollar market. On the other hand, Japan and other western European countries such as West Germany and Switzerland have emerged as the major international suppliers of funds, having registered a cumulative current account surplus of almost $250 billion over the past five years. As investors, these countries, especially Japan, have shown a remarkable preference for securities, especially debt securities, which in the present period usually offer higher prospective returns and a better credit quality than bank deposits. In other words, while in the 1970's the recycling of petrodollars was carried out via the international banking system, in the present period, the recycling of Nippon-dollars is being accomplished through the international bond markets.

The second factor behind the securitization of international finance is the debt crisis, which exploded in the early years of this decade and has festered ever since. The debt crisis has had several effects. With regard to the banks, the quality of their assets has deteriorated, highlighted by the rising number of bank failures. The creditworthiness of many banks has suffered materially as a result. For example, only one U.S. bank currently enjoys a AAA rating by Moody's or Standard and Poor's, which compares with nine banks having such ratings in 1980. In response, banks have drastically reduced their international exposure both to non-banks and to the interbank market in order to improve their capital ratios and the quality of their balance sheets. This lending retrenchment has imposed supply constraints on the borrowing activities of less developed countries, who generally can only get access to a much smaller volume of credits through the painful process of debt restructuring. In addition, banks have been confronted with a rising cost of funds relative to other market participants, making the cost of bank intermediation non-competitive. Other prime-quality sovereign, supranational and corporate borrowers have taken this opportunity to borrow directly and more efficiently in the international capital markets (through bond issuance). This process, of course, will further complicate the banks' effort to upgrade their assets since they are being left to service the residual of less desirable borrowers who cannot issue bonds on economic terms.

The institutionalization of investment also has favored the securities markets over bank deposit markets. As the populations of the major industrialized countries have begun to age, social security and pension funds, both public and private, have accumulated huge pools of investible funds. (Total assets of privately sponsored pension funds in the major industrialized countries have already exceeded the $1 trillion mark.) Other financial institutions, such as insurance companies and mutual funds, also have grown in importance. Consequently, the investment decision has been shifted from individual households, who tend to rely on bank deposits, and concentrated in those institutions where funds are being managed by in-house or outside portfolio managers under rigorous performance standards. With the cost of information being reduced drastically by the revolution in communication technology, professional money managers can easily perform the evaluation of credit and investment opportunities, functions in which the banks once had a comparative advantage. Furthermore, they have every incentive to cut down on the cost of bank intermediation to improve their own performance.

Last, but not least, the increase in the volatility of interest rates in recent years has fueled the need for more marketable assets. Traditionally, during periods of stable interest rates banks perform their intermediation service by gathering short-term deposits and lending long, earning the spread between long- and short-term rates. In the new era of deregulated financial markets and basically anti-inflationary monetary policies, banks can no longer be certain of the profitability of mismatching maturities. One way out has been the popularity of spread banking, i.e., borrow and lend at variable rates of interest and lock in a spread between the cost of funds and the return on assets. In addition, there has been an increasing desire by banks to enhance the marketability of their assets so as to make it easier to manage their asset/liability exposures under rapidly changing circumstances. This desire is not only reflected in the acquisition of new assets in securitized form or making new loans transferable, but also in the effort to securitize assets already on their books. The phenomenal growth of Collateralized Mortgage Obligations (CMOs), which are bond-like securities with more definite maturity dates (except for the residual z-tranche) collateralized by a pool of existing mortgages, is the most eloquent example of this trend. Another is domestic and Euro bonds collateralized by car loans on the books of automobile financing companies in the United States.

More recently, many brokers have tried to build up a market for LDC loans, including direct swaps and debt-for-equity swaps.

THE FUTURE OF SECURITIZATION

Many of the factors mentioned above, such as the institutionalization of investment and the general preference for marketable assets, are structural in nature and hence, they are likely to underpin the securitization of international finance for many years to come. As well they should, because securitization on the whole has a beneficial impact on the international financial system. Financial assets, in marketable or securitized forms, are being widely distributed to different circles of investors, increasingly across national boundaries. The widespread distribution of risk is a good thing, in and of itself, because according to past experiences with financial crisis, it has always been the undue concentration of risks within a few institutions that created the most serious potential damage. Carrying out financial transactions in securitized form also subjects market participants to greater market discipline due to the automaticity of default. Failure to pay coupon interest on time constitutes default on a bond issue and, with cross-default clauses present in most bond indentures, will trigger default on all outstanding obligations, a severe penalty which is difficult to water down or paper over as is possible with bank loans. Moreover, since assets in securitized form are being traded in the marketplace, their values are being adjusted continuously by a multitude of participants. A realistic valuation of assets and a gradual adjustment in their values are desirable because they help reduce the risk and the severity of financial crisis. Furthermore, securitizing financial contracts increases the overall efficiency of the financial markets, particularly in the case of exchange-traded futures and options. On the one hand, it allows for the standardization of financial instruments, which greatly enhances the liquidity of the secondary market for these instruments. On the other hand, borrowers and investors alike can fine-tune their exposures on the asset or liability side to dovetail perfectly with their specific circumstances or expectations of future movements in interest rates or foreign exchange rates. In other words, participants can reap the best of both worlds with securitized financial markets. Finally, the securitization of financial transactions has greatly assisted the integration of the world's financial markets. Some securities, such as U.S. Treasury bonds, are already being traded on a 24-hour basis in New York, London and Tokyo. Shares of major corporations are also being cross-listed and traded in depository forms in stock exchanges outside their home countries. As more financial assets become available in securitized forms, they too can be traded internationally.

DOES SECURITIZATION INCREASE THE RISK IN THE FINANCIAL SYSTEM?

The recent concern about financial re-regulation, particularly with regard to off-balance-sheet risks, is not relevant nor detrimental to the securitization process. Off-balance-sheet risks refer to the measurement and adequate control of contingent liabilities, hence off-balance-sheet risks arise as banks engage in a variety of transactions such as NIFs/RUFs, interest rate and currency swaps, trading in interest rate and currency futures and options. These transactions have been favored by banks, as they generate income but do not boost banks' capital/asset ratios, which are being scrutinized by bank regulators and the markets alike. As a consequence, there is a perception that banks may be exposed to a heightened degree of risk, since in times of market difficulties such as a liquidity crisis, banks are most likely to be called upon to honor these contingent liabilities when it is least desirable for them to do so. However, it is important to recognize that even though some of the off-balance-sheet transactions increase with the trend to securitize assets, the two phenomena are conceptually different. Perhaps the most eloquent testimony to this distinction is the fact that as the major central banks express their concern over and start to impose capital adequacy controls on contingent underwritten liabilities of NIFs/RUFs, these types of facilities have been less used in favor of the non-underwritten facilities such as Euro-commercial paper programs, which are a truer form of securitized short-term instruments (see Table 2).

This does not mean that commercial banks are being disintermediated or reduced in importance. What has happened is that the meaning of "financial intermediation" has been changed, and banks have adjusted by becoming major participants in the securitization process. As borrowers, banks have raised significant amounts of funds in the international bond markets, mostly in the form of perpetual or long-dated subordinated floating rate notes (FRNs), which can count as primary capital for banks in many countries. For example, in 1985 banks issued almost $36 billion of international bonds (including FRNs), accounting for more than 21 percent of total international bond issuance. This volume of bond issuance by banks represents a 64 percent increase over the 1984 volume. As investors, banks have been major buyers of Eurodollar FRNs, Euronotes or Euro-commercial paper as well as international and domestic bonds (see Table 3). In addition, banks' trust and investment departments have cornered an ample share of the total funds managed by professional managers.

CONCLUSION

The securitization process, in the final analysis, cannot be viewed in isolation from financial deregulation and other economic develop-

TABLE 2 UNDERWRITTEN AND NON-UNDERWRITTEN FACILITIES (US$ BILLION)

	1982	1983	1984	1985	1986*
Underwritten (NIFs/RUFs)	5.4	9.5	28.8	46.8	23.0
Non-underwritten (Euro CP)	0.0	0.0	0.0	18.3	49.0

Source: OECD
* Jan-May at annual rate

TABLE 3 BANKS' HOLDINGS OF INTERNATIONAL BONDS (US$ BILLION, END OF YEAR)

	1981	1982	1983	1984	1985
Total Holding	46.7	59.2	76.7	99.5	157.7
Banks in the U.K.	16.8	22.9	32.4	41.7	64.6

Source: Bank of England

ments in recent years. As the financial systems of the major industrialized countries have become more liberalized and integrated, the nature of the problems and risks facing financial institutions have also changed. Since it enhances the flexibility and efficiency of borrowers and lenders in the saving and investment process on a global scale, securitization is likely to offer answers to many of the questions raised by the new financial environment.

SECTION II

Managing Risk in an International Portfolio

CHAPTER NINE

LAURENT JACQUE is on the faculty of the Management Department of the Wharton School, University of Pennsylvania, where he received his MA, MBA and Ph.D degrees. He is the author of *Management of Foreign Exchange Risk* (Lexington Books, 1978), now in its sixth printing, as well as several articles on International Financial Management, Multinational Control Systems, and International Risks and Insurance. He currently serves as an advisor and consultant to the Foreign Exchange Rate Forecasting service of Wharton Econometrics Forecasting Associates.

FOREIGN EXCHANGE RISK IN INTERNATIONAL PORTFOLIO INVESTMENT: WHEN TO HEDGE?

Laurent L. Jacque
The Wharton School, University of Pennsylvania,
Philadelphia, Pennsylvania

INTRODUCTION

The prime motivation for diversifying investment portfolios internationally is to improve the reward-to-risk tradeoff by taking advantage of the relatively low correlations among returns on securities traded on different national capital markets. However, such securities are typically denominated in foreign currencies whose nominal values have shown increasing volatility since the breakdown (in the early seventies) of the Bretton Wood world of quasi-pegged exchange rates. Thus international portfolio investment involves taking on additional risk in the form of currency risk, thereby begging the question of whether such exchange risk would not be so large as to offset the benefits of international diversification. A related question is what—if any—hedging strategies should be implemented to reduce the impact of foreign exchange risk on the performance of internationally diversified portfolios as measured in a home or numeraire currency.

This chapter will argue that *selective* hedging of currency risks in international portfolio management is always warranted based on empirical evidence that currency forecasters can beat the forward exchange market. This is covered in the next section on *Hedging Strategies in International Portfolio Management.* Accordingly, this chapter will consider the exchange rate forecasting conundrum both in the context of *floating* exchange rates (*Forecasting Floating Exchange Rates*)—which link well integrated capital markets (the case of most OECD countries)—and *controlled* exchange rates *(Forecasting Pegged Yet Adjustable Exchange Rates)*—characteristic of less-developed or newly industrialized countries (e.g., Mexico, Brazil, South Korea, India) whose segmented capital markets may offer abnormal returns. Typically the former question has received considerable attention from both scholars and forecasters whereas the latter has been to a large extent ignored.

At this juncture, one caveat should be spelled out: it is assumed that the currency hedging decision and the securities investment decision are *separable* and this chapter treats the first question independently from the second. Clearly this is only a working assumption as exchange rates and stock prices tend to be negatively correlated. Foreign bond prices, on the other hand, exhibit a very low degree of covariance with exchange rates.

HEDGING STRATEGIES IN INTERNATIONAL PORTFOLIO MANAGEMENT

Undoubtedly, exchange rate volatility has increased in recent years and is very significant when compared to the volatility of single national equity markets. Table 1 summarizes the volatility of equity returns in local currency terms, the volatility of exchange rate changes, and the volatility of returns in dollars for the major equity markets over the period 1970-1980. In almost all cases, the dollar returns are more volatile than the local currency returns, making clear the case for hedging currency risks in international portfolio investment.

TABLE 1 EQUITY AND CURRENCY VOLATILITY, 1970-80

Country	Return Volatility in Local Currency	Volatility of Exchange Rate	Return Volatility in US$
Australia	24.6	9.2	27.2
Belgium	13.3	11.0	18.8
Canada	18.9	4.2	20.3
France	22.0	10.2	25.8
Hong Kong	48.0	5.6	45.8
Italy	24.2	8.6	26.2
Japan	16.4	10.4	19.6
Singapore	35.8	6.5	36.0
Spain	16.7	9.1	20.3
Switzerland	16.8	14.7	21.4
The Netherlands	16.4	11.0	18.9
United Kingdom	28.9	8.9	31.6
United States	16.0	—	16.0
West Germany	13.9	11.9	18.4

Reprinted from Solnik, B.H. and B Noetzlin, "Optimal International Asset Allocation: Lessons from the Past," *Journal of Portfolio Management* (1981)

Hedging Strategies

There are three strategies for controlling foreign exchange risk available to the international portfolio manager.

Never Hedge This passive hedging strategy simply ignores currency risk. The advantages of such a strategy—beyond its naive simplicity—are the absence of transaction costs as well as the savings on costs associated with generating exchange rate forecasts either in-house or from commercial sources. This approach is intuitively aligned with the market efficiency hypothesis (see The Market Efficiency Hypothesis later in this chapter) according to which it is not possible "to beat the forward exchange market."

Always Hedge The active hedging strategy according to which the entire foreign portfolio should be covered against exchange risk all the time was shown empirically by Madura and Reiff [1984] to be always superior to a "never hedge" strategy. Practically, it may not be possible to hedge all foreign currency exposures all the time, as the local currency value of the portfolio will fluctuate with changing stock and bond prices thereby necessitating changes in the amount of the hedge.

Hedge Selectively By hedging some of the exposure some of the time the international portfolio manager should have the best of both worlds. Clearly it is based on the notion that currency forecasters can indeed "beat the forward exchange market" and that—depending upon the outcome—a forward or money market hedge is warranted (see Design of Composite Forecasts).

Hedging Tools

Foreign exchange risks can be hedged by entering into forward sale or foreign currency option contracts *(contractual hedge)* and by borrowing the local currency before investing it in the numeraire currency (*money market hedge)*.

For *convertible* currencies, the (expected) cost of hedging (money market hedge) is the difference between the interest rate differential of the two currencies and the expected percentage change in the exchange rate, whereas the expected cost of contractual hedging is the difference between the forward discount or premium and the expected percentage change in the exchange rate. Barring the risk of exchange controls on capital flows and/or access to forward exchange markets, the cost of both hedging policies should be close because of the robust interest rate parity relationship that exists.

By contrast, the cost of currency option contracts is known at the outset of the hedging horizon and equals the premium attached to the option: unlike a forward contract, a currency option bounds the downside currency risk faced by the international investor without limiting the upside potential resulting from an appreciating currency, since a currency option gives you the right without the obligation to sell the foreign currency at a predetermined rate called the strike price (see Table 2 for a recapitulation of various hedging instruments).

TABLE 2 HEDGING INSTRUMENTS

Instruments	Description	Pros	Cons
Forwards	An almost custom-made contract to buy or sell foreign-exchange in the future, at a presently specified price.	Maturity and size of contract can be determined individually to almost exactly hedge the desired position.	Use up bank credit lines even when two forward contracts exactly offset each other.
Futures	A ready-made contract to buy or sell foreign exchange in the future, at a presently specified price. Unlike forwards, futures have a few maturity dates per year. The most common contracts have maturity dates in March, June, September, or December. But, these contracts are almost continuously traded on organized exchanges. Contract sizes are fixed.	No credit lines required. Easy access for small accounts. Fairly low margin requirements. Contract's liquidity guaranteed by the exchange on which it is traded.	Margin requirements cause cash-flow uncertainty and use managerial resources.
Options	A contract that offers the right but not the obligation to buy or sell foreign exchange in the future, at a presently specified price. Unlike forwards and futures, options do not have to be exercised. Available on an almost custom-made basis from banks or in ready-made form on exchanges.	Allow hedging of contingent exposures and taking positions while limiting downside risk and retaining upside potential for profit. Also permit tradeoffs other than risk versus expected return.	Since an option is like insurance coupled with an investment opportunity, its benefits are not readily observable, leading some to conclude that it is "too expensive."
Swaps	An agreement to exchange one currency for another at specified dates and prices. Essentially, a swap is a series of forward contracts.	Versatile, allowing easy hedging of complex exposures.	Documentation requirement might be extensive.
Borrowing and lending	Creates a synthetic forward by borrowing and lending at home and abroad. For example, a long forward foreign-exchange position is equivalent to borrowing at home, converting the proceeds to foreign exchange and investing them abroad. The converse holds for a short forward foreign-exchange position.	Useful when forwards, futures or swaps markets are thin—particularly for long-dated maturities.	Utilizes costly managerial resources. May be prohibited by legal restrictions.

Reprinted from "The Nature and Management of Foreign Exchange Risk," N. Abuaf, *Midland Corporate Finance Journal* (Fall 1986) pp. 30-44

FORECASTING FLOATING EXCHANGE RATES

Exchange rate behavior under the floating rate system is characterized by relatively small exchange rate changes that occur continuously as new information is received. In the case of the U.S. dollar vs. foreign convertible currencies there is increasing evidence of prolonged periods of exchange rate "overshooting" which leaves economists somewhat perplexed.

This section opens by first questioning the general validity of generating exchange rate forecasts. This is based on confusing empirical evidence upholding the proposition that market exchange rates incorporate all currently available information and that, as a consequence, it might be futile to attempt forecasting exchange rates (*Market Efficiency* hypothesis) in the short term. Indeed, in an efficient market, portfolio managers would tend to favor *passive* investment strategies with respect to the foreign exchange dimension (i.e., no hedge policy) in order to minimize transaction costs and maximize diversification gains. Conversely, if the market is not fully efficient, a selective/pro-active hedging policy to exploit profit opportunities would be preferred.

The Market Efficiency Hypothesis

The return in early 1973 to floating exchange rates by a number of major currencies has generated considerable interest about the general question of whether foreign exchange markets do indeed constitute *efficient* markets. If clearly established, the *Market Efficiency* hypothesis would have far-ranging forecasting implications and could possibly establish the uselessness of building elaborate forecasting models, but, before this critical last point is further elaborated, a careful statement of the efficient markets hypothesis and review of available empirical evidence is in order.

A foreign exchange market in which exchange rates always fully reflect all available information is said to be *efficient.* Three degrees of Market Efficiency are customarily distinguished: (1) the *weakly* efficient market hypothesis holds that a series of historical exchange rates contain no information which can be used to forecast future spot exchange rates; (2) the *semi-strong* version of market efficiency holds that a large and competitive group of market participants has access to all publicly available information relevant to the formation of expectations about future rates. Finally, (3) if the set of available information also includes private or insiders' information, the market is said to be *strongly* efficient.

Clearly, in all of the above cases information itself is costly to collect and market participants in their own self-interest will never choose to be completely informed, meaning that market prices will never reflect *all* information at all times although it may reflect available information.

Failure to establish the weak form of Market Efficiency would lend credence to the *Price Dynamics/Currency Overshooting* view of exchange rate behavior. One version of this hypothesis (the so-called "bandwagon" theory) asserts that a subset of market participants (market leaders) are known or simply perceived by the rest of the market participants (market followers) to have earlier access to more timely and more accurate information concerning factors affecting future spot exchange rates and/or to have the use of more sophisticated forecasting models. Thus when the price of a currency begins to fall (to rise) market followers will "jump on the bandwagon,"—that is, join in the selling (buying) pressure as they attribute the price change to be a signal that market leaders (who know better) have themselves begun to sell (to buy). In so doing, market followers will be pushing the currency price down (up) further until it *"overshoots"* its equilibrium level and the trend eventually reverses itself. Clearly this view of exchange rate behavior supports the hypothesis that past exchange rates contain useful information in forecasting future exchange rates as information only disseminates itself slowly among market participants, thus disproving the Market Efficiency hypothesis. This also explains the existence of a successful technical forecasting industry which relies on momentum analysis.

The empirical evidence (Levich, 1978) for and against the efficiency of the foreign exchange market remains mixed at best, explaining the continued existence of a flourishing forecasting industry.

Forward Exchange Rates as Predictors of Future Spot Exchange Rates

Speculators who think that the forward rate $F_{\$,i}(d)$ is above their expectation of the future spot exchange rate $E[S_{\$,i}(t)]$ will sell the foreign currency forward, thus bidding down the forward rate until it equals the expected future spot rate. $F_{\$,i}(d)$ is the dollar price of one unit of currency i for delivery d days forward (at time t) as quoted at time 0; $E[S_{\$,i}(t)]$ is the mathematical expectation of the future dollar price of one unit of currency i to prevail at time t. Conversely, speculators who see the forward rate undervaluing the expected future spot rate will buy foreign currency thus bidding the forward rate up until both forward and expected future spot exchange rates becomes equal. If speculative demand for forward contracts were infinitely elastic and all speculators held homogeneous expectations with respect to the future spot exchange rate, the current forward exchange rate would be equal to the expected future spot exchange rate. In statistical terms, the current forward rate would be an unbiased predictor of the future spot exchange rate:

EQUATION 1

$$F_{\$,i}(d) = E[S_{\$,i}(t)]$$

However, it should be emphasized that this simple forecasting model doesn't claim to offer a point estimate of a future spot exchange rate; rather, it asserts that if the forecasting model is repeatedly used, on the average the forward exchange rate will be equal to the future spot exchange rate.

Empirical evidence for or against this simple hypothesis has been provided by several studies. All studies have the common weakness that they test an expectation theory (ex-ante concept) with historical (ex-post) data which is no more than second best from a methodological point of view.

In sum, however, it is generally possible to conclude that:

a. In earlier studies, the forward rate was generally found to be an *unbiased* predictor of the future spot exchange rate. However, in more recent studies, which rely on more sophisticated econometric testing methodologies, this result is being increasingly rejected. From a practical point of view, it is important to note that there is a close association between the level of the forward rate and the level of the future spot exchange rate as evidenced by the fact that variation in $F_{\$,i}(d)$ explains more than 90 percent of the variation in $S_{\$,i}(t+d)$.

b. In a similar vein, earlier studies tended to conclude that the forward premium/discount (F − S)/S was shown to be an unbiased predictor of the future exchange rate change

$$\frac{S_{\$,i}(t) - S_{\$,i}(0)}{S_{\$,i}(0)}$$

More recent empirical tests increasingly reject this result and in fact all studies agree that the forward premium or discount is a poor predictor of the actual exchange rate in the sense that variations in (F − S)/S explain less than 10 percent of the variations in

$$\frac{S_{\$,i}(t) - S_{\$,i}(0)}{S_{\$,i}(0)}$$

Econometric Modeling Approaches

After briefly sketching the nature of econometric forecasting, this section analyzes and assesses the type as well as the value of information and services that portfolio managers may purchase from econometric forecasting agencies and also provides a framework for assessing their track records.

Nature of Econometric Forecasting Exchange rate econometric forecasting models are a systematic effort to uncover a functional relationship between a set of explanatory (exogenous) variables, such as price level differentials, interest rate differentials, or differentials in the rate of growth in money supplies, and a dependent (endogenous) variable — namely, the exchange rate. The functional relationship may involve only the current period values of the exogenous variables or may be of a lagged nature, that is, incorporate past periods' values taken on by the exogenous variables. In this latter case econometric modeling is clearly inconsistent with the Market Efficiency hypothesis, whereas in the former case it is not necessarily so. As a matter of fact, one may be tempted to argue that econometric forecasting disregarding lagged functional relationships is assisting the market in correctly interpreting all currently available information, thus making it more efficient.

As an illustration, a simple forecasting model could express the percentage change in the U.S. dollar price of one Deutsche mark as a linear function of the expected differential in inflation rates and of the known differential in short-term interest rates:

EQUATION 2

$$\frac{S_{\$,DM}(t, t+1) - S_{\$,DM}(t)}{S_{\$,DM}(t)} = a[r_{us}(t, t+1) - r_{wg}(t, t+1)] + b[i_{us}(t, t+1) - i_{wg}(t, t+1)] + e(t)$$

where a and b are positive linear coefficients arrived at through multiregression analysis and $r_{us}(t, t+1)$, $r_{wg}(t, t+1)$, $i_{us}(t, t+1)$, $i_{wg}(t, t+1)$ are United States and West Germany inflation and interest rates respectively over the period [t, t + 1].

The specification of the model itself, that is, the nature of the functional relationship (not necessarily linear) as well as the choice of exogenous variables included, is generally a blend of economic theory (in this case a combination of the Purchasing Power Parity Theory and International Fisher effect) with the model builder's experience and intuition. In that sense, econometric building is as much an art as a science, thus the reader should expect the various forecasting services (reviewed below) to be idiosyncratic.

An in-depth discussion of the econometric methodology underlying multivariate regression analysis (that would, for instance, be used in deriving numerical values for coefficients a and b in equation 2) is beyond the scope of this chapter and will not be attempted here. Suffice it to say, at this point, that structural equations (usually one for each currency forcasted) are extracted from time series of exogenous or endogenous variables, that is, from past observations.

This means that if a drastic change in the structural relationship between independent and dependent variables were to occur and be disregarded in specifying functional relationships, the econometric model forecasting value would be adversely affected. Thus, if one accepts that the behavior of private and public market participants was markedly affected by the advent of floating exchange rates and two oil shocks, it is perhaps premature to forecast currency prices in the context of a floating exchange rates regime.

One last additional feature of econometric forecasting models worth commenting upon is the random error (e(t) in equation 2) that is always incorporated in this type of model. The inclusion of such a stochastic element allows probability statements to be made about the forecasted variable—for example, under a given set of conditions one might say that there is a 95 percent chance that the future (ninety days later) dollar price of one Deutsche mark will be bounded between .5112 and .5205. This is indeed an attractive feature compared with a point estimate (as provided, for instance, by forward exchange rates), especially when it is recalled that the information is to be used in a risk management context. However for econometric forecasting to be theoretically correct, several requirements must be met. The major flaw of current forecasting efforts is probably the normality assumption of exchange rates probability distribution which is generally made. That exchange rates are not normally distributed has been established beyond doubt.

Assessing Econometric Forecasting Models' Track Records

International portfolio managers decide, first, whether it is worth the subscription fee (as high as $25,000 per annum) to purchase such forecasting services and, second, which forecasting service to subscribe to. Before we attempt answering either question the reader should be reminded that at any single time the forward exchange market provides unconditional point estimates of future spot exchange rates (forecasting horizon is naturally given by maturities of forward exchange contracts — thirty, sixty, and ninety days) and that the forecasting service is free. Econometric forecasting services generally provide monthly, quarterly, semi-annual, and annual average exchange rates rather than end-of-period point estimates (see Table 3). Such point estimates come usually as unconditional forecasts but provisions for conditional forecasts can easily be made.

Traditionally, the performance of currency forecasting services is assessed against the forward exchange rate, i.e., whether the forecast surpasses the forward exchange rate in predicting the actual future spot exchange rate. Levich (1980) offers a methodological framework for conducting such performance analysis by focusing on the forecast error e defined as exchange rate forecast $\hat{S}_{\$,i}(t)$ minus the actual future spot exchange rate $S_{\$,i}(t)$. One obvious desirable property of such a forecast error is that it be small in absolute value; however, this simple criterion needs to be qualified according to the sign of the forecast error. Consider the example of the quarterly forward rate for the pound sterling $F_{\$,£}(90) = 1.50$ and two alternative forecasts—$\hat{S}_{\$,£}(90)^1 = 1.48$ and $\hat{S}_{\$,£}(90)^2 = 1.58$. If the actual spot exchange rate turns out to be $\hat{S}_{\$,£}(90) = 1.52$, the forecast error associated with the first forecast; $e_1 = -\$.04$ is smaller than the one associated with the second; $e_2 = +\$.06$. However, the second forecast; $\hat{S}_{\$,£}(90)^2$ is superior because it would lead investors to the correct decision, i.e., not to hedge any asset position in sterling resulting from holding stocks or bonds.

Thus if the magnitude of forecast errors is ignored, one can evaluate a forecaster's performance by calculating the fraction of periods where the forecast correctly predicts only the direction of exchange rate movements vis-a-vis the current forward exchange rate—the critical informational input for a selective hedging strategy in international portfolio management.

This *percentage-correct methodology* was used repeatedly by Levich in annual surveys in the Euromoney magazine. In a sample of twelve forecasting services and nine currencies' Levich concluded that there were too many forecasters with a high percentage (> 50%) of correct track records to be the result of chance. In this sense, currency forecasters appeared to demonstrate expertise relative to the forward rate. The most recent findings are summarized in Table 4.

TABLE 3 CURRENCY FORECASTERS: WHO DOES WHAT, AND HOW

Name	Sample dates	No of observations	Type of forecast	Horizons	Method	Price ($)
1) **Business International**	Mar 1978-Dec 1982	58	Quarterly average	6 quarters	Econometric	1,200
2) **Citibank-Economics Department**	Jan 1977-Dec 1982	59	Quarterly average	4 quarters	Judgmental	FREE
3) **Conti Currency**	Jan 1977-Dec 1982	67	End-of-quarter	4 quarters	Judgmental	5,000-25,000
4) **Data Resources Inc.**	Aug 1977-Dec 1982	52	Quarterly average	6 quarters	Econometric	4,700-8,700
5) **European American Bank**	Jan 1982-Dec 1982	12	End-of-quarter	4 quarters	Judgmental	5,000-15,000 (for forecasts only)
6) **Multinational Computer Models**	Oct 1979-Dec 1982	39	End-of-period	3, 6, 9, 12 months ahead	Real "PPP" model plus judgment	2,500+
7) **M. Murenbeeld and Associates**	Jan 1977-Dec 1982	67	End-of-period	3, and 12 months ahead	Econometric with judgment added	2,000
8) **Predex-Forecast**	Jan 1977-Dec 1982	72	Quarterly average	6 quarters	Econometric	15,000
9) **Predex-Technecon**	July 1978-Dec 1982	54	Monthly average	1, 2, 3 months ahead	Technical	14,000 (25,000 for both services)
10) **Wharton Econometric Forecasting**	Jan 1980-Dec 1982	35	Monthly average	24 months ahead	Econometric with technical added for 1 and 3 months ahead	8,000-12,000

Reprinted from "Currency Forecasters Lose Their Way." R. Levich, *Euromoney* (August 1983)

TABLE 4 PERFORMANCE OF CURRENCY FORECASTERS

Percentage correct forecasts, 1978-1982

Currency	BI	Citi	Conti	DRI	EAB	MCM	Murenbeeld	PF	PT	Wharton	
Can$	48.	51.	52.	53.	50.	49.	43.	53.	48.	54.	
Sterling	52.	23.	61.(C)	55.	58.	56.	33.	43.	46.	49.	
Bfr	57.(D)	33.	55.	NA	42.	38.	43.	50.	46.	49.	
Ffr	48.	35.	54.	NA	50.	51.	43.	53.	46.	54.	One-month horizon
DM	50.	26.	52.	51.	42.	44.	34.	52.	56.	40.	
Lire	45.	47.	54.	NA	42.	38.	43.	55.	52.	57.	
Dfl	47.	26.	43.	NA	50.	41.	36.	50.	52.	51.	
Swfr	45.	30.	57.	NA	58.	59.(D)	52.	45.	46.	63.(C)	
Yen	45.	40.	54.	45.	50.	59.(D)	41.	42.	52.	57.	
Can$	55.	42.	43.	55.	50.	44.	52.	57.	41.	66.(D)	
Sterling	45.	28.	45.	53.	25.	67.(D)	29.	43.	46.	69.(C)	
Bfr	50.	30.	43.	NA	33.	44.	43.	47.	44.	60.	
Ffr	50.	33.	45.	NA	33.	51.	48.	63.(D)	57.	66.(D)	Three-month horizon
DM	47.	28.	39.	45.	42.	54.	43.	50.	57.	57.	
Lire	47.	28.	46.	NA	42.	38.	45.	55.	54.	51.	
Dfl	48.	28.	46.	NA	33.	49.	40.	48.	52.	60.	
Swfr	48.	42.	43.	NA	50.	59.	60.	58.	69.(C)	69.(C)	
Yen	40.	35.	38.	59.	42.	51.	41.	32.	54.	54.	
Can$	67.(D)	40.	44.	50.	73.	34.	48.	53.	57.	62.	
Sterling	32.	14.	64.	60.	55.	76.(C)	25.	49.	49.	68.	
Bfr	47.	38.	45.	NA	55.	58.	46.	47.	57.	56.	
Ffr	49.	50.	45.	NA	27.	58.	55.	64.	70.(D)	65.	Six-month horizon
DM	42.	43.	47.	48.	64.	55.	50.	59.	57.	71.	
Lire	32.	26.	47.	NA	55.	45.	38.	53.	58.	50.	
Dfl	47.	40.	44.	NA	45.	42.	50.	42.	60.	53.	
Swfr	49.	43.	56.	NA	73.	61.	68.(D)	59.	70.(D)	71.	
Yen	25.	50.	38.	64.	64.	53.	54.	47.	55.	62.	
Can$	59.	32.	37.	33.	40.	16.	26.	60.	47.	61.	
Sterling	31.	37.	63.	58.	60.	94.(C)	48.	47.	55.	89.(D)	
Bfr	25.	16.	35.	NA	60.	31.	42.	36.	55.	75.	
Ffr	24.	39.	47.	NA	60.	25.	54.	77.(D)	68.	64.	12-month horizon
DM	24.	32.	47.	29.	60.	50.	48.	42.	64.	61.	
Lire	10.	11.	20.	NA	0.	9.	44.	51.	60.	79.	
Dfl	33.	21.	45.	NA	80.	34.	48.	38.	60.	71.	
Swfr	22.	45.	73.	NA	60.	56.	68.	74.	81.(D)	86.	
Yen	20.	47.	35.	67.	80.	56.	46.	51.	47.	75.	

Reprinted from "Currency Forecasters Lose Their Way," R. Levich, *Euromoney* (August 1983)

Design of Composite Forecasts

The above methodological framework—dubbed "the Right Side of the Market Approach" by Bilson (1983)—has clear limitations in the sense that it provides a currency-by-currency evaluation which compares each service against the forward rate but not against other services. Most importantly, there is no way of knowing whether some combination of two or more services would be superior to a single service—hence the idea of a *composite* forecast.

To correct the above deficiencies, Bilson (1983) proposed to construct a composite portfolio forecast by formulating an exchange rate forecasting equation as a weighted average of single forecasting services $\hat{S}_{\$,i}(t)^k$. For example, for maturity t and currency i the composite forecast $\hat{S}_{\$,i}(t)^c$ would be written as:

EQUATION 3

$$\hat{S}_{\$,i}(t)^C = (1 - w_i^1 - w_i^2)\, F_{\$,i}(t) + w_i^1\, \hat{S}_{\$,i}(t)^1 + w_i^2\, \hat{S}_{\$,i}(t)^2 + e_i\,(t)$$

where w_i^k is the estimate of the weight given to forecast $\hat{S}_{\$,i}(t)^k$ and derived through econometric techniques. Interestingly, a composite forecast could include (and weigh heavily) the forward exchange rate—as it does in equation 3—for a particular currency and maturity combination.

FORECASTING PEGGED YET ADJUSTABLE EXCHANGE RATES[1]

Emerging stock markets are increasingly perceived as the last truly high risk/high reward investment opportunities in the world economy. To some extent modern portfolio theory—which rests largely on efficient capital markets—becomes unstruck in the emerging stockmarkets of the newly industrialized countries such as South Korea, Taiwan, Mexico, Brazil, India, or Malaysia. These markets can be highly inefficient in pricing securities (one could argue the greater the scarcity of information, the greater the divergence in quoted prices from their true value), and their central banks are certainly not known for pricing their currencies realistically with exchange rates having gone, at times, through long periods of *overvaluation.*

The challenge faced here by the investment portfolio manager is different from the problem of forecasting floating exchange rates since he deals almost exclusively with currencies which are mispriced/overvalued, subjected to strict exchange controls, and for which the traditional hedging tools—readily available for convertible currencies—are generally absent except, perhaps, for the use of money market hedges. Although the threat of blocked funds can be circumvented through investment in closed-end country-specific funds listed on a major stock exchange (for example, the highly successful Korea Fund listed on the New York Stock Exchange since 1984) most portfolio investments in emerging stock markets will have to face a two-dimensional risk: (1) traditional exchange risk and (2) country risk in the sense of potential tightening of exchange controls which may turn a successful portfolio investment into a not so successful blocked funds portfolio.

This section develops a simple forecasting framework for pegged yet adjustable exchange rates distinguishing between a "stabilized" and a "controlled" exchange rate system. Valuation of securities themselves and how they relate to currency mispricing — although a key factor in the investment/divestment decision process is not attempted here.

The general forecasting procedure developed below is essentially a four-step sequence. First, through a review of selected economic indicators, the forecaster can identify which countries have a balance of payments that is in fundamental disequilibrium; second, for the currencies of such countries, the forecaster can measure the pressure that market forces exercise on prevailing exchange rates. Third, the level of central banks' foreign exchange reserves gives an indication of the future point in time at which the central bank will no longer be in a position to defend the prevailing exchange rate.[2] The fourth and crucial step is to predict the type of corrective policies that political decision-makers are likely to implement: will the country under pressure adjust through a manipulation of its exchange rate (devaluation or revaluation) or instead initiate, essentially for political reasons, deflationary or inflationary policies combined with exchange controls and extensive international borrowing?

Step One: Assessing Balance of Payments Outlook

This section develops an early warning system that will assist the international portfolio manager in pinpointing countries whose currencies are becoming potential candidates for adjustment. Like any early warning system, it should be carefully monitored for the early detection of meaningful variances from established patterns. The discussion now proceeds with the definitions of economic indicators that are critical in probing a country's balance of payments outlook. The definition of each indicator is followed by the design of indices that will enable the international portfolio manager to find out if the country's balance of payments is in fundamental equilibrium. Clearly this first step will be carried out repeatedly as new information on price levels, money supply, foreign trade, or international reserves becomes available. As long as the indicators introduced do not indicate any disequilibrium, the currency forecaster can disregard the subsequent steps.

The Case of Stabilized Exchange Rates

Evidence of a yawning deficit or surplus in a country's balance of payments will be provided by two "quick" and "dirty" indicators, respectively measuring the rate of depletion or growth in international reserves and the coverage of import spending by export earnings.

Rate of Change in International Reserves A country experiencing a widening deficit in its balance of payments, resulting from an overall imbalance in its current and capital account, must ultimately settle it by drawing down its central bank's liquid external assets of convertible foreign currencies (essentially U.S. dollars), gold, and Special Drawing Rights. These liquid assets, generally called *inter-*

national reserves, are analogous to the cash account of a firm's balance sheet and therefore disregard short-term liabilities that the country may have incurred through its public and/or private sector. Through depletion of its international reserves a country will be able to finance a deficit on its balance of payments. Conversely, a country experiencing a surplus in its balance of payments will accumulate international reserves. Formally an index, $\delta_i(t)$, measuring the rate of depletion or growth in country i's international reserves, over a time interval [t − 1, t] would be formulated as follows:

EQUATION 4

$$\delta_i(t) = \frac{R_i(t) - R_i(t-1)}{R_i(t-1)}$$

where $R_i(t-1)$ and $R_i(t)$ measure the total amount of international reserves available to country i at time (t − 1) and t respectively. This index, however, ignores country i's borrowing potential as measured by its quota with the International Monetary Fund, standby arrangements, and swap agreements with other central banks.

A rate of growth $\delta_i(t)$ significantly at variance from zero clearly points to a disturbance in country i's balance of payments equilibrium. It generally reflects systematic central bank intervention as the par value of its currency is being defended against downward (or upward) market pressures. A persisting trend away from zero will indicate that the disturbance is not of a random nature; that is, the disturbance is structural and likely to translate itself into fundamental disequilibrium.

Indicator of Trade Performance Evidence of a deteriorating balance of trade is signaled by a lower coverage of import expenditures by export earnings; instead of focusing on the absolute size of the ratio itself, the international portfolio manager should closely watch downward or upward trends in this indicator of trade performance. Formally, the following ratio should be computed for country i' at the end of period t:

EQUATION 5

$$\theta_i(t) = \frac{X_i(t)}{M_i(t)}$$

where $X_i(t)$ and $M_i(t)$ refer to the value of country i's exports and imports respectively during period t (year, quarter, or month), and $\theta_i(t)$ measures in percentage the coverage of country i's imports by its exports during period t.[3]

These indicators provide good ex-post evidence of a fully fledged disequilibrium in the balance of payments of the country under scrutiny. Of better forecasting value are indicators capturing underlying economic trends likely to reduce a lagged disequilibrium in the balance payments under study.

A deterioration in a country's balance of trade usually lags by as much as three to six months (depending on the nature of the country's foreign trade) a build-up of inflationary pressures, thus the international portfolio manager should refine his assessment of a country's balance of payments outlook by probing underlying trends in relative prices.

Higher domestic prices usually undermine the competitiveness of a country's export products in the world marketplace; more specifically, if domestic inflation entrenches itself at a rate exceeding that of the country's major trading partners and to the extent that higher domestic prices are indeed translated into higher export prices, foreign demand for domestically produced goods will seek lower-priced alternatives; conversely, domestic buyers will shift to the purchase of foreign (imported) goods. The resulting deterioration of the balance of trade (higher imports and lower exports) will put pressure on the prevailing exchange rate and devaluation will become necessary for the country to reestablish its trade position.

Indicator of Relative Prices The performance of a country's consumer price index (or preferably, wholesale price index where available) relative to its main trading partners provides a rough estimate of the competitiveness of the country's products on both the domestic and export markets. An index of comparative price performance, $\tau_i(t)$, can be formulated as the multilateralization of the Purchasing Power Parity hypothesis as:

EQUATION 6

$$\tau_i(t) = r_i(t) / \sum_{j=1}^{n} w(t)_i^j \cdot r_j(t)$$

where $r_i(t)$ and $r_j(t)$ measure countries i and j's respective rates of inflation over the last period that ended at time t, and $w(t)_i^j$ the percentage of its total foreign trade that country i does with country j. The index is computed to encompass each of the n countries with which country i trades.

As a general rule the further away from one the numerical value taken on by this index $\tau_i(t)$ goes, the more likely country i's balance of payments can be expected to move into fundamental disequilibrium. More specifically, whenever this index takes on a value larger than one ($\tau_i(t) > 1$), country i's rate of inflation is higher than the trade-weighted average of country i's major trading partners' rates of inflation, and the indicator points to a deterioration of country i's competitive position on world markets. Conversely, a value less than one for country i's index ($\tau_i(t) < 1$) means that country i is doing relatively better than its major trading partners as far as inflation rates are concerned. The international portfolio manager may find it helpful to compute this ratio using consumer price or, preferably, wholesale price indices.

Indicator of Real Trends in the Money Supply Growth in the money supply (defined as demand deposits plus money in circulation) that is not matched by a comparable growth in real GNP will also signal a build-up of inflationary pressures. Actually, increases in price indices—whether they are cost of living or wholesale price indices—often lag the indicator measuring real growth in the domestic money supply. As previously, such an indicator, $\lambda_i(t)$, should be defined on a comparative basis — that is, adjusted for the performance of the country's major trading partners. It could be formulated as follows:

EQUATION 7

$$\lambda_i(t) = \frac{\Delta M_i(t)}{\Delta GNP_1(t)} \Big/ \sum_{j=1}^{n} w(t)_i^j \frac{\Delta M_j(t)}{\Delta GNP_j(t)}$$

where $\Delta M_i(t)$ and $\Delta GNP_i(t)$ measure the percentage change in country i's *nominal* money supply and *real* gross national product. The trade weights $w(t)_i^j$ are as defined in equation 6.

Clearly, a significant deviation from one (country i is in fundamental equilibrium vis-a-vis its trading partners) should point to a fundamental disequilibrium, as an unchecked growth in the money supply ($\lambda_i(t) > 1$) will translate itself into higher prices and conversely.

Note on Foreign Trade Price-Elasticities The indicators of relative price changes developed so far assumed that different countries were characterized by identical price elasticities. It is clear enough that a country facing a relatively price-inelastic foreign demand for its exports will tend to be less affected by a relatively higher rate of inflation (as compared to the inflation rates of its major trading partners) than a country facing a relatively price-elastic foreign demand for its export goods. Similarly, a country characterized by a relatively price-inelastic domestic demand for imports-competing goods will see fewer of its domestic consumers switching to imports as the price of domestic imports-competing goods rises faster than the prices of imports as compared to a country characterized by a relatively price-elastic domestic demand for imports.

If such information on price elasticities were readily available, the currency analyst would compute an index of foreign trade price elasticities, $\varepsilon_i(P)$, defined as the sum of price elasticity for exports and price elasticity for imports:

EQUATION 8

$$\varepsilon_i(P) = e_i^M(P) + e_i^X(P)$$

where $e_i^M(P)$ measures the price elasticity of country i's demand for imported goods, defined as the increase (in percentage terms) of the quantity of imported goods for each 1 percent rise in the level of domestic price. If domestic demand is relatively price-inelastic, the increase in the quantity of imported goods will be less than 1 percent for a 1 percent rise in the level of domestic prices. Conversely, a price-elastic domestic demand means that for a 1 percent rise in the level of domestic prices the quantity of imported goods will increase by more than 1 percent.

Similarly, $e_i^X(P)$ measures the price elasticity of foreign demand for country i's exports, defined as the decrease (in percentage terms) in the quantity of country i's exports for each 1 percent rise in the level of country i's price level. If foreign demand is relatively price-inelastic, the percentage decrease in the quantity of country i's exports will be less than 1 percent for each 1 percent rise in the level of country i's domestic prices.

As a rule, a low index of foreign trade price elasticities ($\varepsilon_i(P) < 1$) will tend to dampen the negative impact of a relatively higher rate of inflation for country i (as compared to country i's major trading partners), and a high index of foreign trade price elasticities ($\varepsilon_i(P) > 1$) will operate in the opposite direction and tend to magnify the negative impact of a relatively higher rate of inflation for country i, resulting in an accelerated deterioration of country i's balance of trade.

The Case of Controlled Exchange Rates

So far the discussion has been primarily concerned with probing the balance of payments outlook of countries that maintain stabilized exchange rates. Such countries are, by and large, industrial countries or newly industrialized countries that are characterized by a well-diversified manufacturing base; therefore the design of economic indicators capturing movements in relative prices was emphasized because the exports of such countries are essentially manufactured products facing a relatively strong price and income-elastic demand.

By contrast, controlled exchange rates are usually maintained by developing countries characterized by export earnings heavily specialized into one or a very few staple commodities such as oil, coffee, rubber, or tin. Another distinctive feature of third-world countries is the heavy burden placed on their balance of payments by the servicing of foreign debt, both public and private. In such cases, the task of the international portfolio manager is clearly different: he is no longer concerned with identifying countries whose balance of payments is running into disequilibrium because, by definition, controlled exchange rates are maintained by countries whose balance of payments is already into disequilibrium. Rather, the task of the international portfolio manager is to anticipate the relative worsening (or in rare cases improvement) in the balance of payments disequilibrium of such countries, which may lead to the devaluation of the controlled exchange rate. This screening process, in the case of countries maintaining stabilized exchange rates, may be supplemented by the following economic indicators so the currency analyst can deal adequately with the case of less-developed countries maintaining controlled exchange rates.

Index of Exports Diversification The degree of export specialization is amazingly high for most less-developed countries. The index of export concentration, $\nu_i(t)^z$, measures the dependence of country i's export earnings on a strategic commodity z:

EQUATION 9

$$\nu_i(t)^z = X_i(t)^z \;/\; \sum_{z=1}^{n} X_i(t)^z$$

where $X_i(t)^z$ refers to country i's exchange earnings generated by commodity z during the period ending time t. Similarly, $\sum_{z=1}^{n} X_i(t)^z$ measures country i's total export earnings.

As a rule, the closer to unity this index of export concentration $\nu_i(t)^z$ is, the less diversified are country i's export earnings and, by implication, the more volatile country i's exchange rate can be expected to be. Qualifications, however, should be made depending on the nature of the export commodity z—for example, oil versus coffee. Certain primary commodities enjoy fairly stable prices on world markets because of cartel agreements among major exporting countries. Furthermore, some countries have committed a certain percentage of their production of their strategic export commodity z in long-term contract agreements.

The combination of a low degree of export diversification (index of export concentration is close to unity) with a crop failure and/or a slump in industrial countries' demand for that very strategic commodity z should point toward immediate devaluation pressure on country i's exchange rate. The ability of country i to weather such a random disturbance (crop failure, downward business cycle) will in turn depend on country i's level of international reserve assets.

Foreign Debt Service Ratio The amount of foreign indebtedness (that is, the amount of long-term financing granted by foreign public or private agencies such as the World Bank, the U.S. Agency for International Development, or multinational commercial banks), the severity of service obligations (that is, interest charges due on these foreign loans), and the maturity of principal repayments (that is, the amortization of the debt) will, of course, vary from country to country, but it is a generally safe assumption that for almost all less-developed countries, the management of the external debt will be of overriding concern.

The international portfolio manager should focus on the short- and medium-term relationship between the schedule of a country's external debt obligation relative to its payments capacity; an index of foreign debt servicing requirement $\sigma_i(t)$ for country i is defined as follows.

EQUATION 10

$$\sigma_i(t) = \frac{C_i(t) + A_i(t)}{X_i(t)}$$

where $C_i(t)$ refers to interest charges due by country i on its foreign debt during period t, $A_i(t)$ to the amortization of foreign debt (that is, repayment of principal due during period t), and $X_i(t)$ to the total export earnings of country i during period t.

Unless this elaborate early warning system produces clear signals of a country moving into disequilibrium (in the case of stabilized exchange rates) or evidence of a worsening trend in the existing disequilibrium (in the case of controlled exchange rates) the forecasting procedure should be discontinued once Step One has been implemented.

Step Two: Measuring Magnitude of Required Adjustment

Once a currency has been singled out for adjustment the currency forecaster should carry out the second step of the forecasting procedure—assessing the magnitude of the change in the exchange rate required to bring the balance of payments back into equilibrium. Essentially, this can be done in two ways.

Generalized Application of the Purchasing Power Parity Hypothesis The percentage change in the exchange rate between country i's currency and country j's currency is approximated by a trade-weighted average of inflation rate differentials:

EQUATION 11

$$\frac{S_{i,j}(t)^* - S_{i,j}(t)}{S_{i,j}(t)} = r_i(t) - \sum_{j=1}^{n} w(t)_i^j \cdot r_j(t)$$

where $S_{i,j}(t)$ is the currency i price of one unit of currency j before devaluation or revaluation (that is, in the disequilibrium situation), whereas $S_{i,j}(t)^*$ would similarly be the equilibrium exchange rate as predicted by the Purchasing Power Parity hypothesis; $r_i(t)$ and $r_j(t)$ measure the rate of inflation experienced by countries i and j over the period starting with the last parity adjustment up to time t and the $w(t)_i^j$ are the weights associated with each of the n trading partners of country i. This is in essence a trade-weighted generalization of the well-known Purchasing Power Parity formula.

Forward Rates of Exchange as Predictors of Future Spot Exchange Rate Under a system of stabilized exchange rates, the estimate of the equilibrium exchange rate $S_{i,j}(t)^*$ provided by a generalized application of the Purchasing Power Parity theorem will be usefully supplemented by the forward market anticipation of the future spot exchange rate. The earlier discussion of this forecasting model established that the forward premium (discount) provided a biased estimate of the future percentage revaluation (devaluation) of a currency, but that in most cases the forward exchange rate $F_{i,j}(d)$ underestimated the actual future value of the spot exchange rate; in absolute value terms this can be formulated as follows:

EQUATION 12

$$\frac{| F_{i,j}(d) - S_{i,j}(t) |}{S_{i,j}(t)} < \frac{| S_{i,j}(t)^* - S_{i,j}(t) |}{S_{i,j}(t)}$$

where $F_{i,j}(d)$ is the forward currency i price of one unit of currency j for delivery in d days, $S_{i,j}(t)$ is similarly the exchange rate at time t that has prevailed since the last parity change was made, and $S_{i,j}(t)^*$ refers to the equilibrium exchange rate. In the case of newly industrialized countries such as Korea or India, forward exchange rates may not be readily available from market sources; however, "home-made" forward exchange rates can always be computed with the help of the interest rate parity theorem: denoting by r_i and r_j the respective quarterly, semi-annual, or annual interest rates on short-term government securities the corresponding forward exchange rate $F_{i,j}(d)$ can be expressed as

EQUATION 13

$$F_{i,j}(d) = S_{i,j}(0) \frac{1 + r_i}{1 + r_j}$$

where d = 90, 180, or 360 days.

Free Market-Black Market Rates as an Indicator of the Future Spot Exchange Rate Under a system of controlled exchange rates (absence of a forward exchange market) a good proxy estimate of what the equilibrium exchange rate should be is provided by the exchange rate quoted by the free market and—in the absence of a free market—by the black market rate. Both, however, usually overestimate the extent of the needed devaluation to bring back the balance of payments into fundamental equilibrium and should be used in combination with the equilibrium rate provided by a trade-weighted application of the Purchasing Power Parity doctrine (see Figure 1 for an illustration of the black market rate in the case of Brazilian cruzerio).

Step Three: Timing of Adjustment Policies

Once the pressure on a given currency has been estimated as the discrepancy between the forecasted (equilibrium) rate $S_{i,j}(t)^*$ and the actual prevailing rate of exchange $S_{i,j}(t)$, the currency forecaster can probe the resistance capacity of the country under pressure to adjust. The ability to resist or to delay the implementation of corrective policies is very much dependent on the overall amount of international reserves that can be spent to finance the deficit resulting from the fundamental disequilibrium of the balance of payments. An index $\phi_i(t)$ measuring the "grace" period can be computed as follows:

EQUATION 14

$$\phi_i(t) = \frac{R_i(t) + R_i(t)^*}{D_i(t)}$$

where $\phi_i(t)$ measures the number of periods t (usually month or quarter) during which country i can afford to sustain a deficit of $D_i(t)$ per period, and $R_i(t)$ is the amount of total reserves (both owned and borrowed) available to country i. These are made up of owned

FIGURE 1 BLACK MARKET VERSUS OFFICIAL EXCHANGE RATES: BRAZILIAN CRUZEIRO

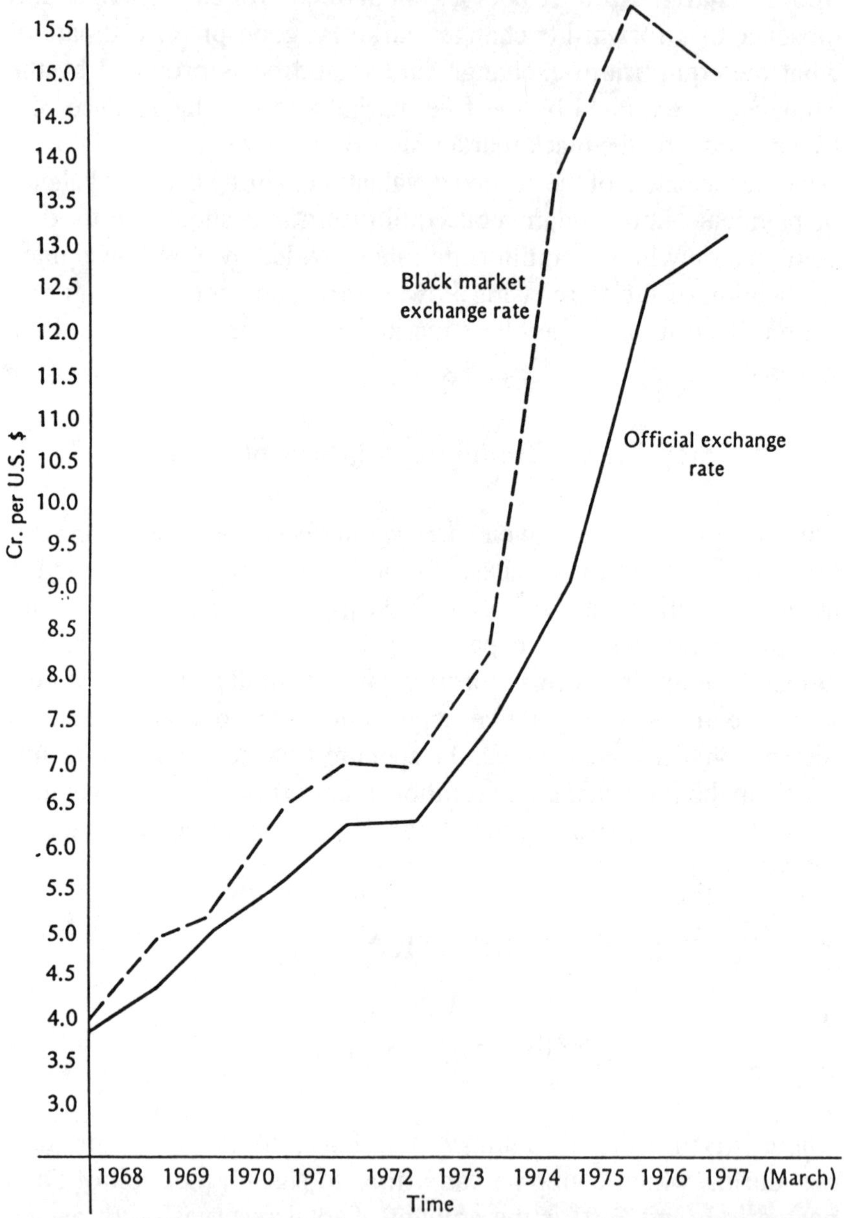

Reprinted from *Multinational Financial Management*, A.C. Shapiro (Allyn & Bacon, 2nd edition, 1986) p. 146

reserves of foreign exchange, gold, and Special Drawing Rights. $R_i(t)^*$ is the estimated amount of international liquidity that can be readily obtained from international sources (standby agreements), from other central banks (swap agreements), or simply borrowed from international money and capital markets such as the Eurobond market. As time runs out, the index $\phi_i(t)$ decreases and the "grace" period, by the end of which adjustment policies can no longer be postponed, shortens dangerously.

Step Four: Nature of Adjustment Policies

Whether a country whose balance of payments is in fundamental disequilibrium will actually devalue (revalue) its currency or let it float downward (or upward) to adjust is ultimately a political decision. No matter how necessary a devaluation (or revaluation) may be from an economic point of view, political factors have the final word in deciding between the implementation of inflationary (or deflationary) policies and/or the imposition of exchange controls versus a change in the par value of the currency. This discussion proceeds on the assumption that the nature of the balance of payments disequilibrium is of a deficit type; symmetrical results would be obtained in the case of a balance of payments surplus.

Deflating or Tightening Exchange Controls In the case of a structural balance of payments deficit, policy makers will first consider the implementation of a deflationary (contractionary) policy as a way of bringing the balance of payments back into fundamental equilibrium. An appropriate combination of restrictive fiscal and monetary policies (often dictated by the IMF when large foreign debt liabilities have to be refinanced) should presumably induce a reduction of aggregate domestic demand for both domestic and foreign-produced goods so that the demand for imports falls and the supply of exports rises. Such results may be easier to obtain if deflationary policies are combined with *internal* controls on wages and prices. Furthermore, external controls, essentially on capital account transactions, should further reinforce the improvement in the balance of trade that should follow a deflationary policy combined with internal controls.

Clearly, deflation will work best when the income elasticity of demand for imports is large, for example, if a cut of 1 percent in national income reduces the volume of imports by 3 percent (income elasticity is 3), only half as much deflation is needed to secure a given improvement in the balance of trade (lower imports resulting from lower national income) as when the income elasticity is 1½. The effect of domestic deflation on exports is less clear; much will depend on the modus operandi of deflationary policies and on the state of world trade. When world trade is buoyant, it is important to have supplies available and to be competitive in delivery dates; deflation will definitely help by making additional manufactured goods readily available for export. Conversely, when world trade slumps there is no shortage of supply and additional exports will be primarily achieved through reduced prices; deflation will prove of little help.

The cost of such remedial action for external disequilibrium (deficit in the balance of payments) is predictable enough: unemployment, which, to say the least, is unlikely to arouse popular enthusiasm. From the international portfolio manager's point of view, deflation combined with exchange controls will prove to be an expensive proposition if or when dividends or the proceeds from the sale of stocks become *blocked* funds.

Devaluation If a combination of deflation and controls does not work out the way it was intended, if the expected political cost of unemployment cannot be afforded by the decision makers in power, or if a policy of large-scale borrowing has reached its limits, the weapon of last resort will have to be used: devaluation.

At this point, political factors will have to be reviewed in a qualitative manner by the currency analyst. In so doing he should be able to determine how much longer a devaluation can be postponed for purely political reasons or even if devaluation is totally ruled out on a priori grounds by responsible decision makers. The following items are significant.

1. What are the personal philosophies and past activities of certain members of the incumbent or incoming administration and their major advisers regarding economic and financial matters? The personality of the head of the government should be given special consideration: some leaders are very stubborn and may perceive a devaluation ("amputation" in the value of national currency) as an unacceptable blow to national pride with which they do not want to be associated.
2. What are the economic philosophies of the party in power and its various supporting groups (such as labor unions or business associations) or the one (or those) likely to come into power soon? Some politicians and their parties are more adverse to exchange rate changes or the discipline of the marketplace than others.
3. Proximity of elections is a particularly favored timing for changing the par value of a currency: an incumbent government can be expected to devalue right after being sworn into office because the outgoing administration can be conveniently charged with "irresponsible economic management."

This forecasting procedure will be ineffectual in the case of countries whose currencies belong either formally or informally to such major currency areas as the dollar, sterling, or French franc. Under such circumstances a devaluation (or revaluation) of the major reserve currency often leads to *sequential* devaluations (or revaluations) by other countries that maintain close economic ties with it.

Implications of Forecasting Exchange Rates A general forecasting procedure for pegged yet adjustable exchange rates was developed in this section. No pretense was made to build a model that would be at once both so general and specific as to capture the idiosyncracies of each and every economy whose currency's price it is meant to forecast.

The mechanical implementation of this forecasting model should be accompanied by an in-depth analysis of relevant socio-political and socioeconomic indicators. In that sense, forecasting pegged yet adjustable exchange rates is as much an art as a science.

The pattern of discrete changes in the par values of "pegged yet adjustable" exchange rates compounds the task of the international portfolio manager. Not only is he responsible for the question of *how much* a foreign currency will devalue or revalue but he also must predict when the parity change will occur. The nature of his forecast is thus essentially *bidimensional.* A four-step forecasting procedure that should assist the currency forecaster in answering both questions was developed.

In Step One, by reviewing macroeconomic indicators the currency forecaster can pinpoint countries whose balance of payments is in fundamental disequilibrium. This *early warning system* should assist the currency forecaster in identifying currencies that are potential candidates for an exchange rate adjustment.

If this is indeed the case, the currency forecaster should measure the pressures that market forces are exercising upon the prevailing exchange rates, the output of Step Two is, therefore, the answer to the question of *how much* the currency will devalue or revalue.

Next, the level of the central bank's foreign exchange reserves (including borrowing facilities) should give a clue as to the future point in time at which the central bank will no longer be able to defend the current exchange rate, that is, it will be forced into a devaluation (revaluation) or an imposition (tightening) of exchange controls. Step Three thus provides the *timing* dimension of the remedial action to be taken by the central bank.

The last and operationally crucial step is to predict the type of corrective political action decision makers are likely to implement: will the country under pressure adjust through a parity change (devaluation or revaluation) or instead initiate, primarily for political reasons, deflationary or inflationary policies coupled with exchange controls and extensive international borrowing?

SUMMARY

International portfolio investment involves a complex tradeoff between the potential for reducing investment risk through geographical diversification and the unique costs/benefits of currency risks and blocked funds.

This chapter has argued in favor of a *selective* foreign exchange risk hedging strategy according to which some of the foreign portfolio exposure should be covered some of the time through appropriate forward and currency option contract or money market hedges. The case for a selective hedging strategy rests upon convincing evidence that exchange rate forecasts available from commercial sources are better than the forward rate or some easily available public forecast, or to use a popular expression, that it is possible "to beat the forward exchange market."

Thus, the specifics of forecasting floating exchange rates were first reviewed for floating exchange rates which link the well-integrated capital markets of major industrialized nations. Thereafter a four-step forecasting procedure was developed for pegged yet adjustable exchange rate currencies characteristic of newly industrialized countries' mildly segmented markets. Timing and magnitude of discrete changes in par values were earmarked as the forecasting output that would assist the international portfolio manager in exploiting a phase of currency overvaluation to divest and/or hedge a portfolio investment in such a country.

NOTES

[1]This section draws from Jacque [1978], chapter 4.

[2]The case of countries (primarily less-developed countries) maintaining *controlled* exchange rates is somewhat different; forecasting exchange rates under such conditions is a less perplexing proposition since such countries are already faced with a fundamental disequilibrium in their balance of payments and are merely suppressing it through controls. The critical warning signal is no longer the *absolute* magnitude of the fundamental disequilibrium but *rather* the relative trend in the magnitude of the fundamental disequilibrium over time (worsening/improvement). The forecasting procedure under such conditions would be essentially limited to Steps Two and Three of the sequence outlined.

[3]This ratio is traditionally low for countries enjoying a substantial surplus in their balance of invisibles. For example, Norway usually covers large deficit in its balance of visible trade by a large surplus in its balance of invisibles due to exports of shipping services; Spain balances its current account, traditionally in deficit from visible transactions (balance of trade) by large scale remittances from expatriate workers and earnings from tourism (invisibles). In such cases, this indicator should be redefined as the ratio of current account's exchange earnings to current account's exchange expenditures.

BIBLIOGRAPHY

Adler, Michael and David Simon. ''Exchange Risk Surprises in International Portfolios,'' *The Journal of Portfolio Management* (Winter 1986), pp. 44-53

Bilson, John F. O. ''The Evaluation and Use of Foreign Exchange Rate Forecasting Services,'' *Managing Foreign Exchange Risk,* ed. by R. J. Herring (Cambridge University Press 1983), pp. 149-180

Chollerton, Kenneth, Pierce Pieraerts, and Bruno-Solnick. ''Why Invest in Foreign Currency Bonds?'', *The Journal of Portfolio Management* (Summer 1986), pp. 4-8

Errunza, Vihang R. ''Emerging Markets: A New Opportunity for Improving Global Portfolio Performance,'' *Financial Analysts Journal* (September-October 1983), pp. 51-58

Jacque, Laurent L. *Management of Foreign Exchange Risk* (D. C. Heath: Lexington, 1978)

Levich, Richard M. ''Analyzing the Accuracy of Foreign Exchange Advisory Services: Theory and Evidence,'' *Exchange Risk and Exposure,* Levich R. and Wihlborg C. Eds. (D. C. Heath, Lexington, 1980)

______________, ''Further Results on the Efficiency of Markets for Foreign Exchange,'' *Managed Exchange-Rate Flexibility. The Recent Experience,* Federal Reserve Bank of Boston (Conference Series No. 20), (Boston, 1978)

Madura, Jeff and Wallace Reiff. ''A Hedge Strategy for International Portfolios,'' *The Journal of Portfolio Management* (Fall 1985), pp 7-74

Maldonado, R. and A. Saunders. ''International Portfolio Diversification and the Inter-Temporal Stability of International Stock Market Relationships, 1957-78'' *Financial Management* (Autumn 1981), pp. 54-63

Shaked, Israel. ''International Equity and the Investment Horizon,'' *The Journal of Portfolio Management* (Winter 1985), pp. 80-84

Solnik, Bruno H. and B. Noetzlin. ''Optimal International Asset Allocation: Lessons from the Past,'' *Journal of Portfolio Management* (June 1981)

CHAPTER TEN

CHRISTINE R. HEKMAN is Associate Professor of Business Administration at the Peter F. Drucker Graduate Management Center at The Claremont Graduate School. She received the Ph.D. degree from the University of Chicago and has served on the Business faculties at Harvard and Duke Universities. Dr. Hekman's fields of study include international corporate financial management with special emphasis on the relationship between foreign exchange and interest rates and the financial management of the firm. She has contributed to numerous academic and professional journals and magazines and consults with several major corporations and financial institutions.

EVALUATION OF RISK IN INTERNATIONAL PORTFOLIOS

Christine R. Hekman
Associate Professor
The Peter F. Drucker Graduate Management Center
The Claremont Graduate School
Claremont, California

INTRODUCTION

One of the most puzzling financial phenomena of recent decades has been the reluctance of investors and portfolio managers, U.S. and non-U.S. alike, to embrace international investment opportunities as fully and rapidly as might be expected. As a result, substantial gains through investing in international assets remain within reach of most investors.

The fundamental source of these extraordinary returns, as well as portfolio diversification, lies in the distinguishing characteristic of international, or foreign, investments, i.e., the "home base" of the business which generates the investment returns is different from that of the investor.[1] Incorporation of international investments into a portfolio whose objective is the protection of future purchasing power in the investor's economic environment directly exposes the investor to unforeseen events in foreign economies.

On the face of it, it would seem that such investments necessarily add risk to a portfolio and would be held only under expectation of sufficiently high returns. In fact, evidence suggests that expected returns to international investing substantially exceed returns which would represent sufficient compensation for the added risk. This phenomenon is partially explained by the diversification potential offered by most international investments. The diversification potential of international investments usually significantly exceeds the diversification potential of comparable domestic investments.

Further, the potential for diversification and relatively high expected returns to investing internationally have not disappeared as financial markets have globalized. Rather, they remain available to investors who have, until now, maintained a primarily domestic orientation.

This chapter explores both the attractive and negative aspects of international risk. It describes a method for evaluating the international risk of a particular investment and recommends a framework for assessing the effect of that investment on the risk of the entire investment portfolio.

THE ESSENTIALS OF RISK AND PORTFOLIO THEORY

At the aggregate level, the risk of a particular investment must be viewed in the context of the entire portfolio. In considering the addition of a foreign investment to a portfolio, the investor must evaluate the prospective contribution of that investment, on a marginal or incremental basis, to portfolio risk and return.

When evaluating the incremental effect of an investment in a particular security on a portfolio's risk, it is important to note that many security risks are diversifiable. This is because portfolio returns reflect the behavior of all the component securities and because the effects of unexpected events on individual securities often offset each other. For example, one event may reduce the value of one security while an independent but simultaneous event increases the value of another. When events affect security returns in this way an investor can immunize a portfolio from the risk of both events by selecting the appropriate investment mix.

In this example, the benefit of diversification is possible because the causal economic events were independent and had opposite effects on security values. In general, diversification potential exists when events which influence security returns occur independently.

Diversification potential is exercised when portfolio funds are allocated over a number of securities, so that the overall results depend on a relatively large number of independent events. In this case, the effects of a single event will be relatively small and will almost always be offset by an event with the opposite effect. Even securities which are highly risky, perhaps very sensitive to a particular event, add little to the overall risk of the portfolio if they account for a small share of total investment and if the event upon which the return depends is somewhat independent of the determinants of return for the rest of the portfolio.

In summary, the risks of particular securities are diversifiable when the events generating the risk are independent of the events affecting other security returns. Diversifiable security risks do not add to the risk of diverse portfolios, because in the aggregation of securities such risks are spread across securities and are usually offset by the effects of other independent events. For this reason, any component of the variability of a security's return which fails to move in tandem with the overall performance of the existing portfolio is potentially a noneffective risk.

Security risks are effective and add to the risk of a portfolio when all securities in the portfolio share a sensitivity to that particular risk. When all securities are affected by an event, the risk of that event cannot be reduced through diversification. Without the independence of events which characterizes diversifiable risks, there is no opportunity for events to offset each other.

Without diversification potential, the risk of the portfolio is increased incrementally as securities are added. Securities whose values are highly sensitive to commonly shared risks add substantially to the risk of host portfolios, because their addition reinforces or magnifies common risk.

Since an investor can diversify risk without sacrificing return by creating portfolios of securities whose returns move independently, such securities should be very attractive. In fact, one would expect to see the prices of such securities rising over time, and would be surprised to find many investors sacrificing return and carrying unrewarded risk by failing to diversify their portfolios fully.

THE APPLICATION OF PORTFOLIO THEORY TO INTERNATIONAL INVESTMENT

The possibility of changes in the returns to international or foreign investment exposes the investor to events in countries or economies other than his own. However, to the extent that these events move somewhat independently of events in the home economy, this risk is diversifiable and may actually reduce the volatility of the aggregate portfolio return.

In fact, the returns to portfolios of international or foreign investments do move independently from returns to domestic securities, and, for the most part, independently of each other. This independence of movement is implied by the cross-correlations of foreign equity and bond returns as computed by Ibbotson and Carr and shown in Exhibits 1 and 2.

This work, together with the work of several other authors, indicates sufficient independence between national markets for both equity and fixed-income investments to suggest that gains from diversification alone may be substantial. Obviously, investments with returns strongly influenced by these independent national economic behaviors are also independent from each other.

As reasoned above, one would expect the gains from diversification across national markets to diminish and then to disappear as investors increase the proportions of portfolios dedicated to international investments. This movement of funds should raise the prices and lower the returns on individual foreign securities to provide only adequate compensation for any incremental addition to the risk of a globally diverse portfolio. After this occurs, exceptional gains to an international investment strategy would disappear.

This complete movement of funds has not yet occurred, however.

EXHIBIT 1 WORLD EQUITY INVESTMENTS: CROSS-CORRELATIONS

World Equities: Cross-Correlations of Annual U.S.-Dollar-Adjusted Total Returns, 1960–1980

Series	*Austria*	*Belgium*	*Denmark*	*France*	*Germany*	*Italy*	*Nether-lands*	*Norway*
Austria	1.000							
Belgium	0.308	1.000						
Denmark	0.224	0.387	1.000					
France	0.155	0.559	0.259	1.000				
Germany	0.258	0.303	0.058	0.273	1.000			
Italy	0.180	-0.104	0.156	0.398	-0.004	1.000		
Netherlands	-0.012	0.567	0.342	0.484	0.537	0.031	1.000	
Norway	0.343	0.359	-0.100	0.188	-0.212	0.119	0.010	1.000
Spain	0.260	0.208	0.413	0.326	-0.075	0.338	-0.102	0.171
Sweden	-0.038	0.311	0.281	0.277	0.285	0.131	0.429	-0.100
Switzerland	0.454	0.465	0.134	0.444	0.700	0.129	0.658	-0.021
United Kingdom	-0.349	0.284	0.152	0.432	0.258	0.104	0.675	-0.136
Europe Total	-0.039	0.493	0.266	0.643	0.505	0.289	0.783	-0.039
Hong Kong	0.127	0.447	0.743	0.387	0.131	0.324	0.729	0.046
Japan	0.216	0.331	0.831	0.361	0.302	0.307	0.284	-0.257
Singapore	0.260	0.510	0.921	0.404	0.311	0.353	0.614	-0.157
Asia Total	0.211	0.337	0.845	0.365	0.281	0.314	0.308	-0.228
Australia	-0.241	0.281	0.213	0.504	0.321	0.420	0.766	0.089
Canada	0.239	0.623	0.341	0.441	-0.037	0.269	0.554	0.469
Other Total	0.029	0.544	0.329	0.528	0.157	0.363	0.743	0.358
Non-U.S. Total Equities	0.062	0.559	0.557	0.646	0.470	0.390	0.774	-0.114
U. S. Total Equities	-0.076	0.389	0.243	0.214	0.210	0.208	0.730	0.009
World Total Equities	-0.042	0.483	0.358	0.384	0.322	0.281	0.804	-0.045

Series	*Spain*	*Sweden*	*Switzer-land*	*United Kingdom*	*Europe Total*	*Hong Kong*	*Japan*	*Singa-pore*
Spain	1.000							
Sweden	0.313	1.000						
Switzerland	0.127	0.233	1.000					
United Kingdom	-0.039	0.301	0.454	1.000				
Europe Total	0.178	0.471	0.712	0.882	1.000			
Hong Kong	0.418	0.376	0.563	0.487	0.598	1.000		
Japan	0.337	0.340	0.240	0.171	0.374	0.707	1.000	
Singapore	0.585	0.439	0.584	0.338	0.547	0.898	0.927	1.000
Asia Total	0.338	0.337	0.244	0.198	0.391	0.759	0.997	0.952
Australia	0.090	0.282	0.432	0.674	0.731	0.667	0.184	0.512
Canada	0.260	0.312	0.350	0.360	0.505	0.791	0.231	0.598
Other Total	0.195	0.340	0.432	0.550	0.676	0.800	0.247	0.609
Non-U.S. Total Equities	0.242	0.522	0.643	0.716	0.905	0.785	0.688	0.826
U.S. Total Equities	-0.115	0.398	0.454	0.617	0.627	0.814	0.216	0.579
World Total Equities	-0.015	0.470	0.557	0.703	0.774	0.848	0.385	0.700

Series	*Asia Total*	*Aus-tralia*	*Canada*	*Other Total*	*Non-U.S. Total Equities*	*U.S. Total Equities*	*World Total Equities*
Asia Total	1.000						
Australia	0.224	1.000					
Canada	0.280	0.577	1.000				
Other Total	0.296	0.863	0.907	1.000			
Non-U.S. Total Equities	0.704	0.704	0.586	0.717	1.000		
U.S. Total Equities	0.260	0.699	0.710	0.787	0.667	1.000	
World Total Equities	0.422	0.753	0.716	0.818	0.831	0.967	1.000

Source: Ibbotson, Carr, and Robinson, "International Equity and Bond Returns," *Financial Analysts Journal,* July-August 1982.

EXHIBIT 2 WORLD BOND INVESTMENTS: CROSS-CORRELATONS

World Bonds: Cross-Correlations of Annual U.S.-Dollar-Adjusted Total Returns, 1960–1980

Series	*Austria*	*Belgium*	*Canada*	*Denmark*	*France*	*Germany*	*Italy*
Austria	1.000						
Belgium	0.853	1.000					
Canada	0.244	0.159	1.000				
Denmark	0.481	0.548	−0.010	1.000			
France	0.544	0.716	0.010	0.693	1.000		
Germany	0.823	0.771	0.179	0.217	0.427	1.000	
Italy	0.141	0.248	−0.225	0.426	0.530	−0.009	1.000
Japan	0.154	0.318	−0.172	0.358	0.276	0.265	0.239
Netherlands	0.884	0.928	0.211	0.448	0.644	0.862	0.036
Spain	0.344	0.309	−0.102	0.488	0.472	0.044	0.612
Sweden	0.586	0.630	0.264	0.418	0.281	0.338	−0.039
Switzerland	0.882	0.895	0.037	0.475	0.662	0.854	0.075
United Kingdom	−0.005	0.095	−0.147	0.121	0.099	0.125	0.288
United States	0.150	0.049	0.632	0.228	0.146	0.098	−0.132
Deutschemark Crossborder	0.853	0.810	0.215	0.342	0.546	0.938	0.018
Dutch Guilder Crossborder	0.935	0.980	0.289	0.463	0.665	0.872	0.233
Japanese Yen Crossborder	−0.060	0.274	−0.478	0.262	0.251	0.249	0.005
Swiss Franc Crossborder	0.749	0.842	0.105	0.421	0.673	0.905	0.286
U.S. Dollar Crossborder	0.172	0.154	0.250	0.442	0.169	0.157	0.083
Other Crossborder	0.194	0.434	−0.619	0.173	0.341	0.634	0.114

Series	*Japan*	*Nether-lands*	*Spain*	*Sweden*	*Switzer-land*	*United Kingdom*	*United States*
Japan	1.000						
Netherlands	0.244	1.000					
Spain	−0.158	0.235	1.000				
Sweden	−0.183	0.631	0.440	1.000			
Switzerland	0.383	0.944	0.174	0.463	1.000		
United Kingdom	0.500	0.033	−0.128	−0.238	0.134	1.000	
United States	0.095	0.166	0.072	0.059	0.104	0.076	1.000
Deutschemark Crossborder	0.293	0.903	0.158	0.400	0.901	0.025	0.242
Dutch Guilder Crossborder	0.360	0.996	0.274	0.462	0.968	−0.198	0.025
Japanese Yen Crossborder	0.982	0.242	−0.481	−0.355	0.408	0.400	−0.061
Swiss Franc Crossborder	0.594	0.858	−0.047	−0.032	0.949	0.104	0.115
U.S. Dollar Crossborder	0.325	0.178	0.117	0.036	0.167	0.168	0.715
Other Crossborder	0.944	0.443	−0.553	−0.554	0.610	0.666	0.160

Series	*Deutsche-mark Cross-Border*	*Dutch Guilder Cross-Border*	*Japanese Yen Cross-Border*	*Swiss Franc Cross-Border*	*U.S. Dollar Cross-Border*	*Other Cross-Border*
Deutschemark Crossborder	1.000					
Dutch Guilder Crossborder	0.931	1.000				
Japanese Yen Crossborder	0.281	0.273	1.000			
Swiss Franc Crossborder	0.933	0.868	0.550	1.000		
U.S. Dollar Crossborder	0.288	−0.113	0.215	0.132	1.000	
Other Crossborder	0.624	0.500	0.917	0.786	0.683	1.000

Source: Ibbotson, Carr, and Robinson, "International Equity and Bond Returns," *Financial Analysts Journal,* July-August 1982.

While one might expect the foreign component of most investors' portfolios to be close to the roughly 50 percent share of non-U.S. assets in global totals, few investors or investing institutions exhibit anywhere near such holding diversity. Rather, the portfolio composition of most foreign and U.S. investors and investing institutions exhibit strong biases toward holdings of domestic securities. The result of this apparent bias is that investment in international securities can still provide above average return and substantial diversification of domestic portfolio risk.

None of the various explanations for this apparent failure of financial market arbitrage is completely satisfactory. In the past, it was argued that restrictions related to currency, capital flow, taxation, and ownership had effectively prevented foreign investors from exploiting these potential advantages. Another explanation was that foreign financial markets were too small, undeveloped, and inefficient to provide a reasonable playing field for large U.S. investors.

However, effective capital market integration has expanded so dramatically that many of these obstacles should no longer be effective. Further, the probable gains to be made by including foreign securities in a portfolio are so large as to overwhelm many of these obstacles.

The most obvious and logical explanation for the failure of more investors to overcome home country biases is inexperience with the unique aspects of international investing, especially a lack of understanding of and facility for evaluating international risk. It is to this issue that the balance of this chapter is addressed.

INTERNATIONAL SECURITY RISK

At the danger of oversimplification, the evaluation of the risk of each foreign investment opportunity requires predicting the extent to which that particular investment's performance is influenced by the vagaries of various national economic and political events or by the national economic or cultural "filters" causing a differential response to changes in common global economies. As shown above, these independent or distinctive risks provide diversification potential. These uniquely international risks also are frequently seen as barriers to investment opportunities abroad.

Of course, both the diversifiable and non-diversifiable components of the risk of any investment must be evaluated. Even though the average international investment will provide substantial portfolio diversification, the total risk of any specific investment can be substantial. In fact, total risk is probably the main deterrent to potential investors in international securities.

For this reason, developing and implementing international investment strategies requires that the investor or investment manager fully understand the nature of the unique risks in this arena, and develop the ability to evaluate international risk.

THE SOURCE OF INTERNATIONAL RISK

International risk arises from the segregation of the underlying business activity into national components. This segregation may generate a *unique, specific*, response to changes in either specific national financial variables or global financial variables. Assessment of international risk is basically the characterization of heterogeneity in the performance of investment securities.

Foreign exchange risk is one example of a distinctly international risk. Foreign exchange risk is the risk that fluctuation in foreign exchange rates will alter the value of the investment in the firm or security. Methods used to evaluate this risk are easily transferable to the assessment of other international risks. For this reason, the character of foreign exchange risk and exposure will be explored here, and methods for its assessment described.

FOREIGN EXCHANGE EXPOSURE

The assessment of exposure—the sensitivity of the investment's value to changes in foreign exchange rates—is an essential step in the evaluation of foreign exchange risk. Total risk is the effect of changes in exchange rates operating on the particular investment's sensitivity to those changes. For example, a 10 percent loss in security value may be the combined result of a 20 percent depreciation of the "local" currency and a 50 percent sensitivity of investment value to that depreciation. Foreign exchange exposure is this 50 percent sensitivity, and translates a 20 percent fluctuation in the value of the currency into a 10 percent fluctuation in the security's value.

Foreign exchange exposure can be substantial when local currency prices and costs are not adjusted to offset changes in exchange rates. This inflexibility might be explained by local wage/price controls or specific competitive market conditions. In general, this exposure exists when the foreign business is segregated from the global economy and more heavily connected to events in the local economy.

Foreign exchange exposure is negligible or absent when fluctuations in currency values have no effect on a security's value. This behavior results when local returns are adjusted as exchange rates and exchange rate expectations change, so the returns and value in the investor's currency are protected. Protection is usually possible, or even natural, when the investment is in an industry or country closely linked to events in the global economy. In this case, returns are adjustable because all firms in that particular industry are affected by exchange rate changes; thus, returns are adjusted unilaterally.

Extreme examples of these investment types, plus two intermediate examples, are described in Exhibit 3. The companies described in the exhibits are hypothetical, with abstract characteristics emphasizing sources of foreign exchange risk. Considering the situation from the viewpoint of a U.S. investor, the investment returns are reported in both local currency and U.S. dollars. It is assumed that each company conducts its operations entirely within a single foreign country.

INTERNATIONAL METALS, LTD.
GLOBAL COSTS/GLOBAL REVENUES

The first company, International Metals, Ltd., imports sheet metal and fabricates and markets metal products entirely within the United

EXHIBIT 3 FOREIGN OPERATING EXPOSURE

	International Metals, Ltd.			Foodstuffs, Ltd.		
	Actual 1985	Budget 1986	Actual 1986	Actual 1985	Budget 1986	Actual 1986
Revenue	£7,619	£8,000	£8,347	£7,619	£8,000	£8,000
Costs of Goods Sold	4,571	4,800	5,029	4,571	4,800	5,029
Gross Margin	3,048	3,200	3,318	3,048	3,200	2,971
Operating Expenses	1,752	1,840	1,928	1,981	2,080	2,080
Other Expenses	686	720	720	457	480	480
Net Income Before Tax	610	640	670	610	640	411
Tax Expense	305	320	335	305	320	206
Net Income	£305	£320	£335	£305	£320	£206
Target Dollar Income		$442	$442		$442	$442
Exchange Rate ($/£)	$1.4500	$1.3810	$1.3182	$1.4500	$1.3810	$1.3182
Realized Dollar Income	$442		$442	$442		$271
Deviation from Budget						
(Actual less budget)			0.0			($171)
(Percent deviation)			0.0%			−38.6%

	English Antiques, Ltd.			White Horse Pubs, Ltd.		
	Actual 1985	Budget 1986	Actual 1986	Actual 1985	Budget 1986	Actual 1986
Revenue	£7,619	£8,000	£8,229	£7,619	£8,000	£8,000
Costs of Goods Sold	3,429	3,600	3,600	1,905	2,000	2,000
Gross Margin	4,190	4,400	4,629	5,714	6,000	6,000
Operating Expenses	1,143	1,200	1,200	3,429	3,600	3,600
Other Expenses	381	400	400	1,143	1,200	1,200
Net Income Before Tax	2,667	2,800	3,029	1,143	1,200	1,200
Tax Expense	1,333	1,400	1,514	571	600	600
Net Income	£1,333	£1,400	£1,514	£571	£600	£600
Target Dollar Income		$1,933	$1,933		$829	$829
Exchange Rate ($/£)	$1.4500	$1.3810	$1.3182	$1.4500	$1.3810	$1.3182
Realized Dollar Income	$1,933		$1,996	$829		$791
Deviation from Budget						
(Actual less budget)			$63			($38)
(Percent deviation)			3.2%			−4.5%

Kingdom. In appearance it is a British company and would seem, on the surface, exposed to changes in the dollar value of the pound sterling. In actuality it is effectively a global investment exposed to changes in metals prices, but almost totally insensitive to changes in the dollar/sterling exchange rate.[2] Thus, it adds no more risk to a portfolio of U.S. securities than would an investment in a similar firm operating entirely within the boundaries of the United States.

Because it imports a raw material which is traded on a global basis, International Metals' pound sterling cost is simply the U.S. dollar cost of the metals translated by the pound sterling rate plus transportation charges. Thus, the sterling cost of the imports increases in direct proportion to any decline in the value of sterling. Operating expenses are composed primarily of energy costs, because of the heavy use of capital equipment in production. These costs also increase in direct proportion to changes in sterling's value.

In contrast, remaining costs booked as "Other Expenses" reflect marketing and distribution activity and are composed primarily of wages and other local costs. These are relatively insensitive to changes in currency values, being determined instead by local economic conditions.

In budgeting for 1986, management assumed no real growth but forecast both inflation and sterling depreciation at 5 percent per annum. Budgeted profits, in sterling, increased in sympathy with the forecast 5 percent aggregate increase in British prices. This increase in pound sterling profits would merely offset the forecast 5 percent decline in the relative value of the pound sterling, thus dollar returns for U.S. investors are unchanged.

At the end of 1986, while the forecast for British inflation had proved accurate, the pound sterling had depreciated by 10 percent, in excess of the forecast by 4.5 percent. In the aggregate, this excessive depreciation implied an undervaluation of the British pound.[3]

The currency depreciation raised the sterling costs of energy and imported, unprocessed metal by 10 percent, exceeding budget by 4.5 percent. Other expenses demonstrated their relationship to local conditions by increasing along with local inflation at the forecast rate of 5 percent.

Target dollar income was achieved because management was able to adjust prices and revenue to protect expected dollar returns. This pricing flexibility existed because all competitors shared a similar cost structure and experienced the same currency-induced pressure to raise prices. Further, local competitors were all either subsidiaries of U.S. parent firms or were responding to dollar-based shareholders. As a result, industry prices increased naturally to provide a pricing umbrella under which local marketing management could offset cost increases.

These price increases produced local operating results which exceeded budget by 4.5 percent. Thus, the target dollar income was met even though the local results were translated to dollars at an unexpectedly weak exchange rate. Though apparently exposed to substantial international risk by virtue of location in the United Kingdom, the U.S. investor's position in International Metals, Ltd. was as free from the effects of currency depreciation as was a similar position in domestic securities.

This freedom from exchange risk resulted from the basic nature of International Metals' business and industry competition. At base, the success of International Metals and its competitors depends heavily on events in the global economy and is effectively independent of local economic events.

FOODSTUFFS, LTD. GLOBAL COSTS/LOCAL REVENUES

The second company, Foodstuffs, Ltd., also imports a commodity which is traded globally. However, in contrast to the insensitivity of International Metals to changes in foreign exchange rates, the impact of the pound's depreciation on Foodstuffs' income was substantially negative. Annual profits, in dollars, fell below budgeted dollar profits by 39 percent because of unexpected currency weakness.

The sensitivity of Foodstuff's operating results to changes in currency values arises because costs are determined globally and revenues are determined locally. Currency weakness increases import costs for Foodstuffs just as for International Metals. The effect on total costs is less for Foodstuffs, however, because currency changes don't affect the company's substantial operating expense component. Foodstuffs' heavy investment in local distribution capacity means that a relatively large share of its costs are locally determined and insulated from the global economy.

It is the competitive situation, however, that finally generates Foodstuffs' exposure. Where International Metals' competitors were commonly affected by currency depreciation and raised prices unilaterally, Foodstuffs' competitors did not. It appears that competitors' costs are different from Foodstuffs'. In particular, they source locally and local suppliers have not responded to the currency depreciation by raising prices.

Thus, an investment in Foodstuffs, Ltd. is struck twice by currency depreciation. Cost increases put them at a competitive disadvantage and depress local returns; lower pound sterling returns translate to dollars at a depressed exchange rate.

ENGLISH ANTIQUES, LTD.
LOCAL COSTS/GLOBAL REVENUES

English Antiques' business is distinguished by much higher operating and net profit margins than the other hypothetical companies. It is also unique in that all of its costs are locally determined.

This chain of stores serves major tourist centers and conducts a mail order business. Agents insure a supply of high quality antique furniture, jewelry, and chinaware through carefully maintained relationships with auction and estate managers. Because of the unique capabilities of its purchasing agents and staff of brokers, the business is in a very strong competitive position.

Most of the company's sales are for export, and its preeminent competitive position is preserved through the maintenance of its established reputation and sales channels. For this reason, management is able to increase pound sterling prices as the currency weakens even though costs are immune from exchange rate impact.

These cost and revenue linkages place English Antiques in an especially advantageous position as sterling weakens. The firm sources in the weak currency and sells in the strong currency. As a result, our hypothetical situation finds 1986 profits exceeding budget by 8 percent. After exchange translation, the dollar equivalent of these profits exceeded budget by 3.2 percent.

Thus, an investment in English Antiques is a play on the weakness of the pound sterling. Returns to a dollar-based investor rise when the British currency weakens unexpectedly.

WHITE HORSE PUBS, LTD. LOCAL COSTS/LOCAL REVENUES

The final example of investment exposure is a chain of small local pubs. From the perspective of a dollar-based investor, this investment is fully exposed to changes in the value of the pound sterling. In the example, the unexpected currency depreciation causes the dollar value of the operating profits to fall below budget by 4.5 percent.

The business' costs and revenues are all determined at the local level and show no sensitivity to changes in global economics. None of the inputs are imported, and customers' patterns of demand clearly depend on the British economic situation. (In fact, one could argue that the revenues are immune from or even counter-cyclical to changes in the British economy.)

For the potential U.S. investor, this security represents an investment in pound sterling. This company is the only one among these examples that provides a purely foreign investment.

THE AGGREGATE EXPOSURE COEFFICIENT AS A SINGLE-FACTOR MEASURE OF SENSITIVITY

These examples illustrate the direct and indirect effects of foreign exchange rate changes on the values of investment securities. They also illustrate the importance to investment analysis of more sophisticated understanding of foreign exchange rate risk and exposure. Such analysis must address the economics of the business and the competition. In particular, the analyst must characterize the important elements of the business as being either globally or locally determined, and must assess the net effects of these relationships.

Incorporating these lessons into a comprehensive system for investment evaluation requires capturing the extent of local/global economic determination in a single coefficient reflecting the degree of exposure to foreign exchange rate changes.

Estimation of this exposure coefficient begins with the segregation of the investment's total value into real and nominal components. This segregation reflects the fact that the foreign currency values of nominal assets and liabilities (such as Accounts Receivable and Long Term Debt) are not affected by fluctuations in the currency's value. From the U.S. investor's perspective these values are fully exposed to foreign exchange rate changes.

The remaining assets and liabilities reflect the values of cash flows whose values at maturity are, as yet, not fully determined. These flows may be altered by changes in the global economic environment. Inventories and fixed operating capital are included in this category.

The exposure of these assets depends on the extent to which underlying local currency values can be adjusted to offset changes in foreign exchange rates. When management is free, as in the case of International Metals, to adjust prices to offset foreign exchange rate changes, these assets may be naturally hedged. That is, their dollar values may be effectively insensitive to foreign exchange rate changes.

In measuring the extent to which pricing flexibility protects dollar values, is it useful to consider the length of time required for complete pricing adjustment. For example, if pricing adjustment requires half of the inventory turn period, one might consider half of that inventory's value exposed. That is, half of existing inventory will be sold (transformed to a financial asset) before price adjustment is fully effected. The price, and therefore the value, of the remaining half will adjust to offset foreign exchange rate changes.

The residual value, that unaccounted for by inventories and the net of financial assets, should be considered as the values of future productive capacity, and represents an option on the future opportunities of the firm. This value will usually be less exposed to changes in foreign exchange rates, because of the greater lead time before sale and pricing of future output of the firm. Longer lead time increases the potential for offsetting the effects of fluctuations in currency values by adjusting prices.

Exhibits 4 and 5 show the methodology by which these factors are summarized in an aggregate exposure coefficient. These exhibits display estimates of the aggregate exposure coefficients for International Metals and White Horse Pubs, Ltd., respectively.

EXHIBIT 4 FOREIGN EXCHANGE EXPOSURE INTERNATIONAL METALS, LTD. ($000,000 TRANSLATED FROM £)

	Market Value	Share in Total Market Value	Exposure Coefficient
FINANCIAL ASSETS AND LIABILITIES			
Cash	$2.0		
Marketable Securities	$3.0		
Accounts Receivable	$13.0		
LESS			
Acccounts Payable	$2.0		
Accrued Liabilities	$1.0		
Long Term Debt	$10.0		
NET FINANCIAL ASSETS	$5.0	0.1	1.0
REAL ASSETS			
Inventories	$15.0	0.3	0.0
Operating Capacity, and Option on Future Opportunities	$30.0	0.6	0.0
TOTAL MARKET VALUE	$50.0		
AGGREGATE EXPOSURE COEFFICIENT		10.0%	

The investment protection offered by International Metals' global competitive linkages is implied in the exposure coefficient of 10 percent. This coefficient implies that the value of the investment in this company will change by only 10 percent of the percentage change in the exchange rate. For example, if sterling declines unexpectedly by 20 percent, an investment in International Metals will lose only 2 percent of its value. This small percentage reflects the effect of the exchange rate change on the corporation's net financial investment in cash and receivables.

The absence of exchange risk protection for investment in White Horse Pubs is reflected in the exposure coefficient of 100 percent.

EXHIBIT 5 FOREIGN EXCHANGE EXPOSURE
WHITE HORSE PUBS, LTD.
($000,000 TRANSLATED FROM £)

	Market Value	Share in Total Market Value	Exposure Coefficient
FINANCIAL ASSETS AND LIABILITIES			
Cash	$2.0		
Marketable Securities	$3.0		
Accounts Receivable	$13.0		
LESS			
Acccounts Payable	$2.0		
Accrued Liabilities	$1.0		
Long Term Debt	$5.0		
NET FINANCIAL ASSETS	$10.0	0.2	1.0
REAL ASSETS			
Inventories	$15.0	0.3	1.0
Operating Capacity, and Option on Future Opportunities	$25.0	0.5	1.0
TOTAL MARKET VALUE	$50.0		
AGGREGATE EXPOSURE COEFFICIENT		100.0%	

The underlying assumption here is that local returns will never be adjusted to reflect exchange rate changes. Thus, fully 100 percent of any change in currency value will be reflected in the dollar value of the investment.

AGGREGATE EXPOSURE COEFFICIENTS AND INTERNATIONAL SECURITY RISK

In summary, the foreign exchange risk attached to each of these investments is the combined effect of their respective exposures and the variability of the dollar/pound exchange rate. One might think of the exchange rate fluctuations as the basic risk and the security exposure coefficient as the filter through which that risk is magnified or mitigated for each particular security.

The review of risk and portfolio theory which introduced this chapter concluded with several points. The most important of these, for the purposes of this chapter, is the following:

> The risk that an economic event will change the value of a particular security does not add to the risk of a portfolio's aggregate value when the occurrence of that event is not related to the occurrence of the other events which affect the portfolio's return.

In fact, the risks of unrelated or less than perfectly related events can actually reduce the portfolio's risk through diversification.

Other researchers have published data which show that, in the aggregate, the addition of international investments to portfolios composed primarily of domestic securities can reduce portfolio risk substantially. Further, this diversification potential is accompanied by the relatively high expected returns to investing internationally.

This chapter has described a method for evaluating the risk of particular securities. This assessment occurs in two stages?

1) Assess the character and magnitude of international risk or variability. This requires the evaluation of exposure to the risk

of changes in a basic economic or financial variable, and an assessment of the magnitude of likely fluctuation in that variable.

2) Assess the extent to which that variability enhances or mitigates the risk of the current portfolio. This will depend on whether the portfolio is already strongly influenced by changes in the basic economic or financial variable or whether changes in that variable are strongly correlated with other influencing variables.

In a practical sense, this assessment involves evaluating exposure in such a way as to capture both direct and indirect effects as well as short-run and long-run effects of changes in the variable. Capturing this assessment in an aggregate exposure coefficient facilitates its application to a measure of the variability of the underlying variable. In the examples described here the basic variable is the foreign exchange rate. The combination of underlying variability and exposure is foreign exchange risk.

The incremental effects of this risk on the overall risk of the current portfolio depend on the correlation between changes in portfolio returns due to changes in foreign exchange rates and changes due to other influences on portfolio returns.

If the exposure of a particular security is high and the occurrence of the event generating the foreign risk reinforces other risks in the portfolio, the investor should look for sufficiently high returns from that security. However, if the exposure is low or if the current portfolio returns seem unrelated to the risky foreign event, that risk is either noneffective or diversifying.

Most studies of foreign exchange exposure have suggested that aggregate exposure coefficients are much lower than commonly perceived. Studies of the behavior, in aggregate, of international investment returns have shown them to be relatively independent of returns to purely domestic portfolios. The implication of these findings is that substantial investment gains are still available for those willing to invest abroad.

NOTES

[1]Using location, or orientation, to determine whether an investment is foreign or international is adopted here to focus the discussion which follows. It should be noted, however, that a firm located in the United States, but with a strong U.K. orientation, should be considered a foreign firm. Likewise, a firm located in and managed from Japan, but with a strong orientation toward U.S. markets and competitors, may be effectively identical to a domestic U.S. firm.

[2]At this point in the discussion, the issue is the total insensitivity of International Metals' dollar operating profits to changes in foreign exchange rates. However, as shown later, the investment is somewhat sensitive to changes in the dollar/sterling rate by virtue of its net positive investment in financial assets.

[3]In more academic terms, Purchasing Power Parity was violated. This violation is implicit in the inequality between the decline in the internal value of the pound sterling (5 percent) and the depreciation in the external value (10 percent).

REFRENCES

Ehrlich, E.E. ''International Diversification by United States Pension Funds,'' *Federal Reserve Bank of New York Quarterly* (Autumn 1981)

Hekman, C.R. ''A Financial Model of Foreign Exchange Exposure,'' *Journal of International Business Studies* (Summer 1985)

Hekman, C.R. ''Foreign Exchange Exposure: Accounting Measures and Economic Reality,'' *Journal of Cash Management* (February/March 1983)

Hekman, C.R. ''Measuring Foreign Exchange Exposure: A Practical Theory and Its Application,'' *Financial Analysts Journal* (September/October 1983)

Ibbotson, R.C., R.C. Carr, and A.W. Robinson. ''International Equity and Bond Returns,'' *Financial Analysts Journal* (July-August 1982)

Lessard, D.R. ''Principles of International Portfolio Selection,'' *International Financial Handbook*, Giddy and George, eds. (1983)

Stulz, R.M. ''On the Effects of Barriers to International Investment,'' *Journal of Finance* (September, 1981)

CHAPTER ELEVEN

Dr. SAMUEL C. WEAVER earned a Ph.D. in finance and economics from Lehigh University in 1985. His current position combines the theoretical with the pragmatic and involves the analysis of many different facets of finance, including: merger and acquisition analysis, industry group comparisons, alternative financing evaluations, dividend policy, and cost of capital/capital expenditure analysis.

Prior to joining Hershey Foods as Manager of Corporate Financial Analysis, he was an Assistant Professor of Finance at Elizabethtown College and performed a consulting function at Hershey Foods. He currently is an adjunct professor in the MBA program at Lehigh University.

Additionally, he is a Certified Management Accountant.

INTEREST RATE RISK IN INTERNATIONAL PORTFOLIOS

Samuel C. Weaver
Manager, Corporate Financial Analysis
Hershey Foods Corporation
Hershey, Pennsylvania

The international bond market offers an investor many opportunities to add another dimension to his portfolio and enhance his total return. Along with these opportunities, the investor faces additional risk.

This chapter presents a theoretical framework for understanding the risks associated with international bond investment. These risks can be subdivided into:

- Interest Rate Risk
- Exchange Rate Risk

The theories of Interest Rate Expectations and Interest Rate Parity will be explored to develop a foundation for understanding the risks that an international bondholder faces. The year 1985 will serve as a focus for illustrating each of these risks. An integrated model combining both of these risks is presented at the conclusion of this chapter.

INTRODUCTION

A brief introduction to extraordinary domestic and international returns will provide the background from which a theoretical framework can be developed. An extraordinary return results when an investor earns a return greater than the yield anticipated when the security was purchased.

Extraordinary Domestic Returns

During 1985 an investor in domestic intermediate-term (seven- to ten-year) U.S. Government bonds experienced a 27 percent annual return. This extraordinary return resulted from a significant decline in interest rates. The seven-year U.S. Treasury bonds began 1985 with an interest rate of 11.57 percent, and through the year rates steadily declined to 8.87 percent at year-end. This 270-basis-point decline increased the value of the bond, accented the annual interest payments and provided the extraordinary return. Applying these market interest rates to an illustration of a bond with a 10 percent coupon segregates the return between capital appreciation and interest:

January 1, 1985	Bond Price	$914.96
(10% Coupon, 11.57% yield, 9 years)		
December 31, 1985	Bond price	$1,062.85
(10% Coupon, 8.87% yield, 8 years)		
	Capital Gain	$147.89
	($1,062.85 - $914.96)	
	Annual Interest	$100.00
	Total Return	$247.89
	Investment Amount	$914.96
	Annual Return	27%

Despite this extraordinary return, the domestic U.S. bond investor could have realized even higher yields provided by non-U.S. intermediate-term government securities.

Extraordinary International Returns

Table 1 summarizes the 1985 annual returns on seasoned intermediate-term governments expressed in local currency and U.S dollars. The ''Local'' return on Table 1 reflects the local currency rate of return due to the bond's price appreciation (related to the reduction of world-wide interest rates) plus the annual interest payment and is analogous to the U.S. domestic example presented above. The U.S. dollar return is further enhanced (in six of the nine cases) by the relative weakening of the U.S. dollar during 1985.

A ten-year West German Government Bond yielded 7.03 percent as of January 1, 1985, when the dollar was worth 3.164 Deutsch Marks (DM). By the end of the year the German government bond was trading to yield 6.35 percent, and the exchange rate was 2.462 DM per U.S. dollar. A 10,000 DM ten-year bond with an 8 percent coupon would have sold for 10,680 DM (or $3,375) on January 1, 1985. By the end of the year, the bond (now a nine-year instrument) would have been priced at 11,105 DM. This would have provided the German bondholder with a total value at the end of 1985 of 11,905 DM (including the interest) for a total return of 11 percent. However, in U.S. dollar terms these 11,905 DM were valued at $.4062 (2.462 DM/US$), or $4,835 total. This would result in a 43 percent U.S. dollar annual return on the $3,375 investment.

TABLE 1 1985 INTERMEDIATE-TERM BOND MARKET RATES OF RETURN

Government Issue	Local	U.S. $
French Franc	18.2%	52.8%
West German	10.9	43.4
Dutch Guilder	10.2	42.7
United Kingdom	12.5	40.6
Japanese	9.1	37.3
Swiss	5.8	34.3
United States	27.0	27.0
Canadian	24.8	17.5
Australian	6.4	(12.5)

The benefits of the exchange rate gain are a double-edged sword, as witnessed by the U.S. investment in a Canadian or Australian government bond. In the case of the Australian bond, the domestic return was 6.4 percent while the U.S. dollar return was a negative 12.5 percent, a result of a stengthening U.S. dollar relative to the Australian dollar.

The investor must understand the risks associated with an extraordinary return opportunity. The risks (volatility of returns) are easy to monitor on an historical basis and are presented in Table 2. Although a U.S. investor in French government bonds fared well in 1985, on average over this eight-year period the U.S. investor in a French government bond earned only an 8 percent U.S. return, while the domestic market averaged an 11 percent return.

The risks associated with a domestic bond investment are explained by the theory of Interest Rate Expectations, as discussed in the next section. The international bondholder also faces the compound risk depicted in the Interest Rate Parity theory, explored in the section following the discussion of interest rate risk.

INTEREST RATE RISK

Interest rate risk arises when actual interest rates differ from expected interest rates. Every yield curve or multi-period interest rate includes a prediction of what the next period or periods' interest rate will be. This market expectation, or implied interest rate, can be demonstrated within the following framework.

Long-Term Investment vs. Roll-Over Strategy

To place the concept of implied interest rates in context, suppose an investor wants to invest funds for two years and is faced with numerous investment alternatives. Specifically, suppose the investor has two alternatives: 1) to invest for two years in a zero-coupon instrument that returns an annual interest rate of 12 percent or, 2) to place his funds for one year in a 10 percent bank deposit and at

TABLE 2 ANNUAL U.S. DOLLAR RETURNS FROM INTERMEDIATE-TERM INTERNATIONAL INVESTMENT

Government	1978	1979	1980	1981	1982	1983	1984	1985	AVG
French	31%	0%	−8%	−16%	2%	−3%	2%	53%	8%
German	16	7	−11	−8	14	−8	−1	43	6
Dutch	22	7	−6	−9	16	−9	−3	43	8
U.K.	3	12	29	−19	26	1	−13	41	10
Japanese	32	−22	23	6	3	13	3	37	12
Swiss	35	−1	−10	−2	1	−5	−15	34	5
U.S.	1	5	0	5	33	5	14	27	11
Canadian	−6	−1	2	−2	36	10	9	18	8

the end of the first year to reinvest for the second year at the then prevailing one-year interest rate.

If the first alternative is accepted, so that \$1,000 is invested for two years at 12 percent, the investor will have \$1,254 at the end of the second year based on annual compounding as follows:

Equation 1

$$FV = PV\,(1 + i)^n$$

where:

FV = Future value at the end of period n

PV = Present value at the beginning

i = Stated interest rate

n = Number of years of investment

or, specifically:

$$\$1{,}254 = \$1000\,(1 + .12)^2$$

On the other hand, rolling the money over in sequential one-year investments assures the investor of nothing more than at the end of one year the amount will have increased by 10 percent to \$1,100 (in accordance with the above equation). The question facing the investor is: What will be the annual interest rate from the end of the first year to the end of the second year (denoted as i_{1-2})? To answer this question, Equation 1 must be rearranged to allow for differing annual interest rates:

Equation 2

$$FV = PV\ (1 + i_{0-1})\ (1 + i_{1-2})\ \ldots\ (1 + i_{(n-1)-n})$$

or, specifically:

$$FV = \$1{,}000\ (1 + .10)\ (1 + i_{1-2})$$

The following table presents the results of three different reinvestment rates (i_{1-2}) and the associated future values of the initial $1,000, assuming a 10 percent return in the first year of the two-year investment horizon:

Reinvestment Rate (i_{1-2})	Value at the End of Two Years
10%	$1,210
14%	$1,254
18%	$1,298

If the investment community thought the annual interest rate at the end of the first year would be only 10 percent, everyone with a two-year investment horizon would invest in a two-year investment rather than rolling over a one-year investment at an expected 10 percent reinvestment rate. This would put upward pressure on two-year security prices and downward pressure on one-year security prices, which would alter the stated interest rate relationship of 10 percent for a one-year investment and 12 percent for a two-year investment. Conversely, if the market expected the annual interest rates to increase next year to 18 percent, the roll-over strategy would appear to be more attractive. Again, the buying and selling pressure would alter the current stated interest rate relationships.

Interest Rate Expectations

Clearly, with the given structure of interest rates (one-year, 10 percent; two-year, 12 percent) in the example above, the investor would be indifferent regarding the choice between an investment of two years or an investment for one year at 10 percent that would be reinvested for the second year at 14 percent. Given the current stated rates, the market would be expecting the second year's one-year interest rate to be 14 percent. Furthermore, as illustrated in the previous example, the only point with no immediate market pressure to adjust interest rates was that where the long-term return was equal to the roll-over strategy, assuming reinvestment at the expected interest rate. This result—the market's expectation, or implied interest rate—can be derived by equating the future values of the two investment strategies as in Equation 3:

$$\text{Period n Investment} = \text{Roll-Over Strategy for n Periods}$$
$$PV\,(1 + i)^n = PV\,(1 + i_{0-1})(1 + i_{1-2})\ \ldots(1 + i_{(n-1)-n})$$

Equation 3

$$(1 + i)^n = (1 + i_{0-1})(1 + i_{1-2})\ \ldots(1 + i_{(n-1)-n})$$

or specifically, for the two-period investment noted above:

$$(1 + .12)^2 = (1 + .10)\,(1 + i_{1-2})$$
$$1.254 = 1.10\,(1 + i_{1-2})$$
$$1.14 = 1 + i_{1-2}$$
$$.14 = i_{1-2}$$

The example presented above suggests that by observing multiple period interest rates, it is possible to delineate the market's expectations for future single period interest rates. These expected future rates are described as implied rates. The risk the bondholder faces is that these expectations may not be realized. In the above example, if the actual one period interest rate (i_{1-2}) would have been only 10 percent, then the longer term strategy of investing for two years at 12 percent would have been more advantageous, providing a total terminal value of $1,254. On the other hand, if the actual one period interest rate (i_{1-2}) would have been 18 percent, then the roll-over strategy would have been more advantageous, providing a total terminal value of $1,298.

Table 3 presents the observed six-month and twelve-month segments of the yield curve for the first half of 1985 on a sequential weekly basis. From the listed six-month and twelve-month interest

TABLE 3 IMPLIED INTEREST RATES VS. REALIZED INTEREST RATES
(First Half of 1985 Expectations vs. Second Half Realizations)

ACTUAL OBSERVED PERIOD			IMPLIED PERIOD			
	6-Month	12-Month	6-Month Rate			
Week	Rate	Rate	Implied	Actual	Diff	Week
Jan 4	8.16%	8.46%	8.76%	6.78%	−1.98%	Jul 5
Jan 11	8.05	8.42	8.79	7.18	−1.61	Jul 12
Jan 18	7.94	8.30	8.66	7.27	−1.39	Jul 19
Jan 25	7.91	8.20	8.49	7.34	−1.15	Jul 26
Feb 1	8.32	8.52	8.72	7.49	−1.23	Aug 2
Feb 8	8.30	8.46	8.62	7.38	−1.24	Aug 9
Feb 15	8.26	8.45	8.64	7.30	−1.34	Aug 16
Feb 22	8.53	8.68	8.83	7.18	−1.65	Aug 23
Mar 1	8.92	9.05	9.18	7.32	−1.86	Aug 30
Mar 8	8.85	8.96	9.07	7.43	−1.64	Sep 6
Mar 15	8.99	9.17	9.35	7.38	−1.97	Sep 13
Mar 22	8.91	9.08	9.25	7.26	−1.99	Sep 20
Mar 29	8.53	8.73	8.93	6.93	−2.00	Sep 27
Apr 4	8.61	8.80	8.99	7.25	−1.74	Oct 4
Apr 11	8.26	8.45	8.64	7.36	−1.28	Oct 11
Apr 18	7.98	8.19	8.40	7.30	−1.10	Oct 18
Apr 25	8.03	8.25	8.47	7.42	−1.05	Oct 25
May 3	7.89	8.09	8.29	7.30	−.99	Nov 1
May 10	7.89	8.05	8.21	7.27	−.94	Nov 8
May 17	7.60	7.84	8.08	7.38	−.70	Nov 15
May 24	7.38	7.61	7.84	7.29	−.55	Nov 22
May 31	7.23	7.43	7.63	7.25	−.38	Nov 29
Jun 7	7.27	7.42	7.57	7.32	−.25	Dec 6
Jun 14	6.85	7.02	7.19	6.97	−.22	Dec 13
Jun 21	7.22	7.39	7.56	7.06	−.50	Dec 20
Jun 28	6.98	7.19	7.40	7.02	−.38	Dec 27

rates, the implied six-month interest rates for the last six-month roll-over period (i.e., months seven to twelve) were derived. These implied (or expected) interest rates were then compared to the actual realized six-month reinvestment rate. For instance, the yield curve on January 4, 1985, included a six-month rate of 8.16 percent and a twelve-month rate of 8.46 percent. By applying this information to Equation 3, it is possible to derive an implied six-month interest rate for the second six-month period (July 5, 1985, to January 4, 1986). On January 4, 1985, the market expected the July 5 six-month interest rate to be 8.76 percent. However, on July 5, the actual six-month interest rate was only 6.78 percent, a difference of 198 basis points. Table 3 highlights the vast differences from the implied or expected six-month interest rates that the U.S. short-term investment market experienced during 1985.

Table 4 illustrates the longer term changes in annual expected interest rates. At the end of January 1985, the intermediate yield curve consisted of an 8.21 percent return on a one-year investment, 9.72 percent on a two-year investment, etc. From this yield curve and the yield curves noted at the end of each month in 1985, the expected annual interest rates from the end of year one to the end of year two ($E(i_{1-2})$), the end of year two to the end of year three ($E(i_{2-3})$), etc., were developed. Table 4 documents the changes to annual interest rate expectations during 1985.

In concert with the short-term interest rate changes noted in Table 3 and presented in Table 4, all intermediate-term interest rates in the United States experienced a significant decline during 1985. Since these interest rates form the basis of determining expected future annual interest rates, this decline also is reflected in reduced expectations about future interest rates, as illustrated in the lower portion of Table 4.

Furthermore, the implied annual interest rate for January 1986 to December 1986 ($E(i_{1-2})$), as calculated in January 1985, was 11.25 percent. However, as seen in Table 4, the actual one-year interest rate in December 1985 was only 7.06 percent. Using this as a proxy for the January 1986 annual rate results in a difference of over 400 basis points from the early 1985 expectations.

TABLE 4 CHANGES IN INTERMEDIATE-TERM ANNUAL INTEREST RATE EXPECTATIONS (1985)

Month-End Yield Curve Components

End Of Month	One Year	Two Year	Three Year	Four Year	Five Year
Jan	8.21%	9.72%	10.15%	10.50%	10.65%
Feb	8.68	10.32	10.66	11.10	11.27
Mar	8.73	10.46	10.83	11.18	11.28
Apr	8.25	9.97	10.36	10.70	10.89
May	7.43	9.05	9.47	9.55	9.94
Jun	7.19	8.81	9.29	9.35	9.90
Jul	7.45	8.96	9.41	9.74	9.93
Aug	7.50	8.82	9.18	9.71	9.68
Sep	7.33	8.73	9.11	9.40	9.67
Oct	7.50	8.81	9.12	9.49	9.63
Nov	7.30	8.47	8.71	8.98	9.18
Dec	7.06	8.00	8.24	8.45	8.65

IMPLIED ANNUAL INTEREST RATES

		$E(i_{1\text{-}2})$	$E(i_{2\text{-}3})$	$E(i_{3\text{-}4})$	$E(i_{4\text{-}5})$
Jan	–	11.25%	11.02%	11.56%	11.25%
Feb	–	11.98	11.34	12.43	11.95
Mar	–	12.22	11.57	12.24	11.68
Apr	–	11.72	11.14	11.73	11.65
May	–	10.69	10.31	9.79	11.51
Jun	–	10.45	10.26	9.53	12.13
Jul	–	10.49	10.32	10.74	10.69
Aug	–	10.16	9.90	11.32	9.56
Sep	–	10.15	9.87	10.27	10.76
Oct	–	10.14	9.74	10.61	10.19
Nov	–	9.65	9.19	9.79	9.98
Dec	–	8.95	8.72	9.08	9.45

The realization of lower than previously expected interest rates and the changes to the underlying future interest rate expectations led to the tremendous "local" gains both in the United States and abroad. For example, a five-year bond issued at par in January 1985 provided a total return of 17.9 percent to the investor, as presented below:

1/31/85	Market Value of Five-Year 10.65% Bond Yielding 10.65%	$1,000.00
12/31/85	Market Value of Four-Year 10.65% Bond Yielding 8.45%	$1,072.14
12/31/85	Interest	106.50
	Total	$1,178.64

In the above case, the investor earned an additional $72, or 7 percent return, from the appreciation of the bond due to the lower interest rates. Remember, the returns from the appreciation of the bonds will be influenced and accented by the level of the coupon attached to the instrument.

On a broader frontier, the international investor is subject to the compounding effects of changing exchange rates. These opportunities (risks) are discussed in the next section.

EXCHANGE RATE RISK

This section illustrates exchange rate risk, discusses a theoretical framework to understand this risk (i.e., Interest Rate Parity), and develops a method of viewing expected future spot exchange rates.

Interest Rate Parity

The Interest Rate Parity theory addresses the potential exchange rate risk that exists with an international debt investment. The Interest Rate Parity theory states that national interest rates for securities of similiar risk and maturity should be the same except as reduced or enhanced by the forward premium or discount for the purchase or sale of foreign currency for delivery at the end of the investment period. The theory can be illustrated by a well-documented market equilibrium situation.

Assume a U.S. investor is looking to purchase a one-year government bond. His first choice is to invest in the United States and earn an 8 percent return. Accordingly, the investor would have a terminal value of $108 for every $100 of investment, assuming both interest and principal are paid at the end of the period. Another alternative would be to invest the funds abroad, perhaps earning a greater rate of return with no additional risk of default by a foreign government borrower. For instance, a Canadion one-year government instrument may pay 10 percent interest and offer the same guarantee of a default-free outcome. However, the investor must convert his U.S. dollars to Canadian dollars today to buy the bond. At the end of the year, the investor must sell his accumulated Canadian dollars to regain his original currency, U.S. dollars.

To continue the example, assuming that the Canadian dollar currently costs $.80, the investor can convert his $100 U.S. to $125 Canadian, which will be invested for one year at 10 percent. At the end of that year the investor will have a terminal value of CAN $137.50. The investor is now in a position for an enhanced or diminished return based upon the currency exchange rate at the end of the year. The following exhibit illustrates the results that would be obtained with alternative exchange rates at the end of this one-year investment period:

End of Year Exchange Rate US$ / CAN$	**U.S. Value of $137.50 CAN**
$.7500	$103.13
.7855	108.00
.8000	110.00
.8500	116.88

If the exchange rate does not change, the investor would indeed realize a 10 percent return and have a terminal value that would be \$2 U.S. greater with a Canadian investment than with the U.S. government bond. Notice, if the exchange rate is greater than \$.7855, the investor will make a return in excess of the 8 percent U.S. return.

At an exchange rate of \$.85 one year later, the investor would earn a total return of 16.88 percent. A portion of this is attributed to the foreign interest rate (i.e., 10 percent), the rest is a direct result of the 6.25 percent appreciation experienced in the value of the Canadian dollar (\$.80 to \$.85). In this case, the investor would buy Canadian dollars today to facilitate his foreign investment, and at the end of the year he would sell the Canadian dollars to return to his home currency. The total return would be:

Equation 4

$$\text{Return} = [(1 + i_{Can})(1 + i_X)] - 1$$

where: i_X = Foreign Currency Appreciation

or, specifically:

$$\begin{aligned}\text{Return} &= [(1 + .10)(1 + .0625)] - 1\\ &= 1.1688 - 1\\ &= 16.88\%\end{aligned}$$

If the exchange rate is less than \$.7855, the investor would have done better to maintain his investment in the United States. This includes the Canadian investor who, in this case, would receive a higher return with a U.S. investment than with a Canadian investment.

At the end of the period, an exchange rate of \$.7855/Canadian dollar represents an equilibrium where the investor makes an 8 percent rate of return with a domestic or international investment. Ultimately, in this international investment strategy, the investor is subject to the risk of changes in the spot exchange rate. This risk can effectively be managed via the forward or futures foreign exchange market.

Forward Foreign Exchange Market

By utilizing the one-year forward or futures foreign exchange market, the investor can "lock-in" immediately the exchange rate that will apply to the conversion of his investment to his home currency one year from now. The use of the forward, or the futures, foreign exchange market eliminates all risks associated with the exchange rate one year later. Interest Rate Parity theory contends that the equilibrium forward foreign exchange rate on the Canadian dollar should be $.7855. If the one-year forward rate were more than $.7855, investors would flock to Canada, as illustrated above. With many U.S. investors moving to Canada to take advantage of the price discrepancy, there would be an extraordinary amount of Canadian dollars sold on the forward exchange market. This forward selling (increased supply) would reduce the price of the forward Canadian dollar until all extraordinary investment incentive is removed and the forward rate becomes the equilibrium rate of $.7855 per Canadian dollar.

Conversely, if the forward Canadian dollar rate were at only $.75, Canadian investors would maximize their returns by investing in the United States. However, to do this in a "risk-free," or hedged, position the Canadian investor would want to buy forward Canadian dollars (i.e. sell forward U.S. dollars). As Canadians attempted to capture this abnormal return, the price of the forward Canadian dollar would be bid up to the point that all extraordinary investment incentive is removed, i.e., at $.7855 per Canadian dollar

This phenomenon would be further compounded by other investors (i.e., non-Canadian and non-American) entering into transactions to capture these extraordinary returns by buying and selling U.S. or Canadian dollar bonds in their portfolios in order to earn the abnormal returns resulting from the disequilibrium condition.

Interest Rate Parity highlights four variables within the above illustration:

- i_{US} = U.S. Interest Rate
- i_{CAN} = Canadian Interest Rate
- $X_{S,t}$ = Spot Exchange Rate (Time t)
- $X_{F,n}$ = Forward Exchange Rate (Time n)

Each of these four variables may be partially influenced as the investors in the above examples move in and out of various holdings to assume a more opportunistic position. However, as presented above, the forward exchange rate may be the single variable influenced the most by investors taking advantage of a profit producing strategy.

Interest Rate Parity is delineated as follows:

Domestic Return = Hedged International Return

Equation 5

$$A\ (1 + i_{US}) = (A/X_{S,t})\ (1 + i_{CAN})\ (X_{F,n})$$

In this equation "A" represents the investment amount.

Equilibrium can be illustrated by substituting the above national interest rate and exchange rate conditions into **EQUATION 5:**

$$\$100\ (1 + .08) = (\$100/\$.80)\ (1 + .10)\ (\$.7855)$$
$$\$108 = \$108$$

Interest Rate Parity further holds that the hedged investor, who contracts in the forward market, will obtain a return equivalent to the domestic risk-free rate of return. The forward market provides insight into expectations of future spot exchange rates.

Expected Future Spot Exchange Rate

From another perspective, it can be argued that the current forward exchange rate for period "n" approximates the expected future spot rate at period "n." If the forward rate were less (more) than the expected future spot rate, speculators would enter a forward contract to purchase (sell) the foreign exchange with the hopes of reaping a profit in the period "n" spot exchange rate market. Equilibrium is only found where expectations surrounding the future spot exchange rate equal the current forward exchange rate.

Given that the forward rate is equal to the expected future spot rate, a substitution can be made in the Interest Rate Parity model as follows:

Equation 6

$$A\ (1 + i_{US}) = (A/X_{S,t})\ (1 + i_{CAN})\ (E(X_{S,n}))$$

The exchange rate risk that the unhedged investor is subject to is that the currently expected future spot exchange rate is not realized.

The International Monetary Market in Chicago trades foreign currency future contracts, which are analogous to forward contracts. Table 5 contrasts the December 1985 future exchange rates, at each month-end during 1985, with the actual December exchange rates for the currencies that were traded at the International Monetary Market.

The top portion of Table 5 lists month-end December 1985 future contract prices of each currency, while the lower portion presents the percentage appreciation (depreciation) from each month-end's December 1985 future (or expected) exchange rate and the actual December 1985 spot exchange rate. At the end of January, the December future price (or expected future spot December rate) on West German Deutsch Marks was \$.3247/DM. The actual December spot price was \$.3964, representing a 22.1 percent strengthening over expectations for the Deutsch Mark. As demonstrated in the above example (Equation 4), this 22.1 percent appreciation directly enhances the return of the U.S. investor in a West German bond.

The appreciation of the Deutsch Mark may be contrasted with the January expectation for the December spot price for Canadian dollars. At the end of January 1985, the December future contract for Canadian dollars was priced at \$.7489 per Canadian dollar. The actual December spot exchange rate was \$.7192, representing a 4.0

TABLE 5 DECEMBER FUTURES CONTRACT PRICE FOR FOREIGN CURRENCY
(Month-End Value: $ per unit of Foreign Currency)

1985 Month	German DM	Swiss FR	Japanese Y	Canadian $	British L
Jan	$.3247	–	–	$.7489	$1.1050
Feb	.3084	$.3606	–	.7129	1.0575
Mar	.3355	.3970	$.004085	.7279	1.2265
Apr	.3266	.3911	.004029	.7264	1.2110
May	.3288	.3909	.004009	.7195	1.2510
Jun	.3337	.3995	.004057	.7309	1.2840
Jul	.3633	.4443	.004270	.7346	1.3950
Aug	.3637	.4436	.004241	.7313	1.3875
Sep	.3753	.4580	.004640	.7277	1.3850
Oct	.3839	.4680	.004738	.7303	1.4365
Nov	.3986	.4819	.004942	.7218	1.4885
Dec	.3964	.4744	.004932	.7192	1.4360
Actual Dec	.3964	.4744	.004932	.7192	1.4360

DECEMBER FUTURE CONTRACT PRICE FOR FOREIGN CURRENCY ACTUAL AS A % INCREASE FROM THE FUTURES PRICE AT MONTH-END ($X_{S,}$ Dec / $X_{F,n}$)

1985 Month	German DM	Swiss FR	Japanese Y	Canadian $	British L
Jan	22.1%	–	–	−4.0%	30.0%
Feb	28.5	31.6%	–	.9	35.8
Mar	18.2	19.5	20.7%	−1.2	17.1
Apr	21.4	21.3	22.4	−1.0	18.6
May	20.6	21.4	23.0	−.0	14.8
Jun	18.8	18.7	21.6	−1.6	11.8
Jul	9.1	6.8	15.5	−2.1	2.9
Aug	9.0	6.9	16.3	−1.7	3.5
Sep	5.6	3.6	6.3	−1.2	3.7
Oct	3.3	1.4	4.1	−1.5	−.0
Nov	−.6	−1.6	−.2	−.4	−3.5
Dec	0.0	0.0	0.0	0.0	0.0

percent weakening of the Canadian dollar from the January expectations. Note, also on Table 5, that the futures price tends toward the actual price as the time until maturity (December) diminishes.

The following section integrates the Interest Rate Expectation theory with the Interest Rate Parity theory. This integration provides a foundation for evaluating an international multiple period investment in fixed income securities.

INTEGRATED MODEL

Up to this point, two risks have been separately identified and illustrated. This section will integrate these components of risk into a single model allowing for examination of the combined risk that an international investor faces over a multi-period investment.

By combining the theories of Interest Rate Expectations and Interest Rate Parity, the following equation is derived for a two-period model:

Equation 7

$$A\ (1 + i_{US\ 0\text{-}1})\ (1 + E(i_{US\ 1\text{-}2}))$$
$$= (A/X_{S,t})\ (1 + i_{CAN\ 0\text{-}1})\ (1 + E(i_{CAN\ 1\text{-}2}))\ (E(X_{S,n}))$$

where: $i_{US\ 0\text{-}1}$ = One-period U.S. interest rate (time 0 to 1)

$E(i_{US\ 1\text{-}2})$ = Expected one-period U.S. interest rate (time 1 to 2)

$i_{CAN\ 0\text{-}1}$ = One-period Canadian interest rate (time 0 to 1)

$E(i_{CAN\ 1\text{-}2})$ = Expected one-period Canadian interest rate (time 1 to 2)

As defined, this equation consists of six variables, including three expected but uncertain variables:

- $E(i_{US\ 1\text{-}2})$
- $E(i_{CAN\ 1\text{-}2})$
- $E(X_{S,n})$

As discussed and illustrated above, unrealized expectations lead to enhanced or diminished returns. As the expectations are hedged, the returns approach the domestic risk-free returns. During 1985, expectations changed such as to benefit U.S. debt holders and investors of foreign securities. As interest rates and the expectations associated with the future interest rates fell, debt holders experienced extraordinary returns. Furthermore, as the dollar weakened (and other currencies appreciated), U.S. holders of non-U.S. fixed income securities benefitted. As illustrated by Equation 4, a non-U.S. debt holder received very attractive returns.

The extraordinary U.S. dollar gains presented in the introduction are segregated in Table 6 into the return that was associated with each risk: interest rate and exchange rate. This dichotomy segregates the total U.S. dollar return into its appropriate subcomponents. The "Interest Rate" column represents the in-country return, which was a function of the change in local expectations for future interest rates. The "Currency" column resulted from the strengthening of the foreign currencies during 1985. The theories of Interest Rate Expectations and Interest Rate Parity, respectively, provide the theoretical underpinning upon which these extraordinary 1985 results are delineated.

TABLE 6 COMPONENTS OF THE U.S. DOLLAR 1985 INTERMEDIATE-TERM BOND MARKET RATES OF RETURN

Government Issue	Total U.S. $	Interest Rate	Currency
French Franc	52.8%	18.2%	29.3%
West German	43.4	10.9	29.3
Dutch Guilder	42.7	10.2	29.5
United Kingdom	40.6	12.5	25.0
Japanese	37.3	9.1	25.8
Swiss	34.3	5.8	26.9
United States	27.0	27.0	N/A
Canadian	17.5	24.8	(5.8)
Australian	(12.5)	6.4	(17.8)

CONCLUSION

The analysis outlined in this chapter details a theoretical framework explaining the returns of the domestic and international bond market and the underlying risks associated with these returns. The year 1985 was used for illustrative purposes to provide a foundation for discussion. However, the concepts presented here can be applied to any currency and/or period of time.

Since each opportunity, or risk, was attributed to an expected variable—the expected domestic interest rates, the expected foreign interest rates and the expected future spot exchange rate—the investor with a definite opinion as to the future movement of either interest rates or exchange rates can use this analysis to select the best investment alternative. By determining the market's perception about future interest or exchange rates, comparing the market's view to his own and taking an appropriate investment position, the investor with strong viewpoints can take an investment position designed to capitalize on those opinions.

In the case of a domestic investment, the investor need have only an opinion of the next period's interest rate (Equation 3). If his opinion is that interest rates will be higher or lower than the market's expectation, then he can appropriately position his funds for a "rollover" short-term reinvestment strategy or a "locked in" long-term investment strategy, respectively.

If the investor is considering a single-period international investment, the investor must employ Equation 6, determine the market's expectation of the future spot exchange rate, compare this view to his personal expectations, and invest accordingly. If the investor holds an opinion that the future spot rate will be higher (lower) than the market's expectation, he will want to assume an international investing (borrowing) position.

The investor who wants to make extraordinary gains on a multiple-period international investment must have an opinion regarding the expected domestic interest rate, the expected international interest rate and the expected future spot exchange rate. By inserting into Equation 7 (the integrated model) his viewpoints along with the current spot exchange rate, the one-period domestic interest rate and the one-period international interest rate, the investor can select his best investment alternative.

Although this chapter has provided the theoretical framework for a retrospective or prospective analysis of investment positions, it has not attempted to prescribe a methodology for developing personal expectations. Extraordinary returns were provided to the international bond investor in 1985. However, as demonstrated in Table 2, these returns encountered numerous years of negative returns. In fact, on average over the past eight years, only the Japanese intermediate-term bond market provided higher U.S. dollar returns than the U.S. bond market (i.e., 12 percent vs. 11 percent). An international investor must fully appreciate the risks that he is accepting and, in accordance with Equation 7, must be aware of the sensitivity underlying his viewpoint on each expected variable.

BIBLIOGRAPHY

Dufey, Gunter and Ian H. Giddy. *The International Money Market,* (Prentice-Hall Inc., Englewood Cliffs, New Jersey, 1978, Chapter 2)

Eiteman, David K. and Arthur I. Stonehill. *Multinational Business Finance,* (Addison-Wesley Publishing Company, Reading, Massachusetts, Third Edition, 1982, Chapters 2-3)

Giddy, Ian H. ''An Integrated Theory of Exchange Rate Equilibrium,'' *Journal of Financial and Quantitative Analysis* (Dec. 1976), vol. 11, no. 6, pp. 883-892

Giddy, Ian H. and Gunter Duffy. ''The Random Behavior of Flexible Exchange Rates,'' *Journal of International Business Studies* (Spring 1975), vol. 6, no. 1, pp. 1-32

Hilley, J. L., C. R. Beidleman, and J. A. Greenleaf. ''Does Covered Interest Arbitrage Dominate in Foreign Exchange Markets?'', *The Columbia Journal of World Business.* (Winter 1979), pp. 99-107

Malkiel B. G. ''Expectations, Bond Prices, and the Term Structure of Interest Rates,'' *Quarterly Journal of Economics* (May 1962), pp. 197-218

McKinnon, Ronald I. *Money in International Exchange,* (Oxford Press, New York, 1979)

Rodriguez, Rita M. and E. Eugene Carter. *International Financial Management,* (Prentice-Hall Inc., Englewood Cliffs, New Jersey, 1979, Second Edition, Chapters 5 and 9)

Weston, J. Fred and Thomas E. Copeland. *Managerial Finance,* (The Dryden Press, New York, 1986, Eighth Edition, Chapter 7)

CHAPTER TWELVE

ADRIAN F. LEE, Vice President, is a member of the Client Services and Marketing Group and is responsible for capital market research and product development. Prior to joining Morgan in New York in 1980, Mr. Lee worked at Winklevoss and Associates in Philadelphia and at the University of Pennsylvania as a lecturer in statistics. A graduate of Trinity College, Dublin, and the holder of an MBA from the Wharton School, Mr. Lee joined the international Investment Group in 1984.

INTERNATIONAL ASSET AND CURRENCY ALLOCATION

Adrian Lee
Vice President
J. P. Morgan Investment Management Inc.
London, England

INTRODUCTION AND OVERVIEW

The focus of this chapter is on the long run international asset allocation issues that confront U.S. investors. These are:

(1) International assets versus domestic assets.
(2) International equities versus international fixed income securities.
(3) Foreign currency exposure versus foreign asset exposure.

We will show that, when an investor considers the full opportunity set of all the world's capital markets, both equities and fixed income, the risk reward preference as revealed by domestic asset allocation choices should also be reflected in international allocation choices. In other words, an investor with a balanced domestic portfolio is likely also to prefer a balanced international portfolio.

It will also be shown that, in international investment, it is appropriate to separate long run asset allocation decisions from long run currency allocation decisions. This suggests that investors will enhance their risk return opportunity set by making separately two forms of international allocation decisions, one concerning asset exposure and one concerning currency exposure. When these allocations differ, the use of continuously hedged international portfolios is implied.

We will use the results of the last 16 years to illustrate the effects of these choices. While the returns for various sub-periods differ and future returns will inevitably be different from past results, the arguments presented are quite general and should be expected to hold into the future.

INTERNATIONAL CAPITAL MARKET RETURNS AND RISKS

The world's investable capital markets excluding cash and real estate comprise some $10 trillion as of December 1985. This forms the universe for an institutional investor (See Exhibit 1). The world fixed income markets total some $6 trillion, while the world equity markets total $4 trillion. The U.S. markets comprise less than half the total of world markets in both the case of fixed income and equities.

The non-U.S. markets have offered significant opportunities for U.S. investors over the last 16 years. These opportunities can be seen in the form of return enhancement and risk reduction.

Return Enhancement:

Exhibits 2 and 3 show the returns in U.S. dollars from investing in international equity and fixed income markets over the last 16 years. Both for equities and fixed income securities, non-U.S. markets have yielded significantly higher returns than their U.S. equivalents. A market weighted average of all non-U.S. equity markets returned 13.4% p.a. compared with 8.7% p.a. from the U.S. equity market. Similarly non-U.S. fixed income markets returned 11.8% compared to the U.S. fixed income return of 9.4%.

EXHIBIT 1 WORLD CAPITAL MARKETS

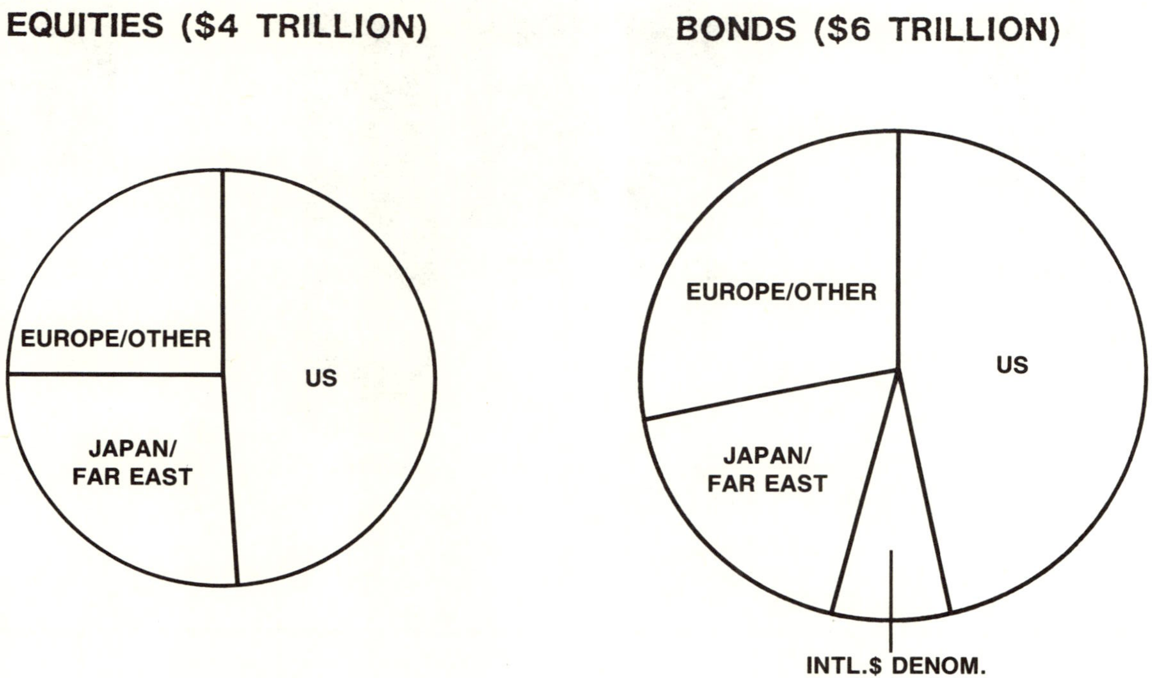

Sources: Morgan Stanley Capital International
Salomon Brothers Inc

EXHIBIT 2 INTERNATIONAL EQUITY MARKET RETURNS IN US DOLLARS 1970-1986

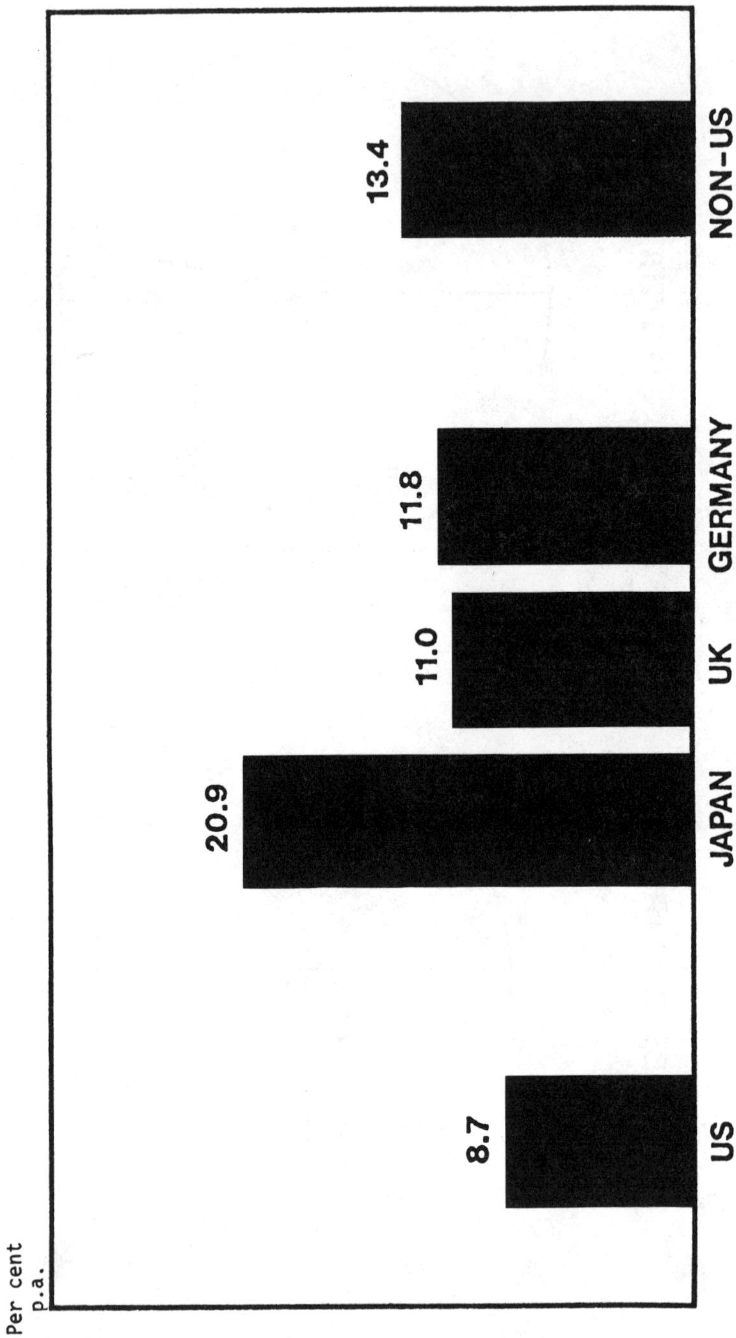

EXHIBIT 3 INTERNATIONAL FIXED INCOME MARKET RETURNS IN US DOLLARS 1970-1986

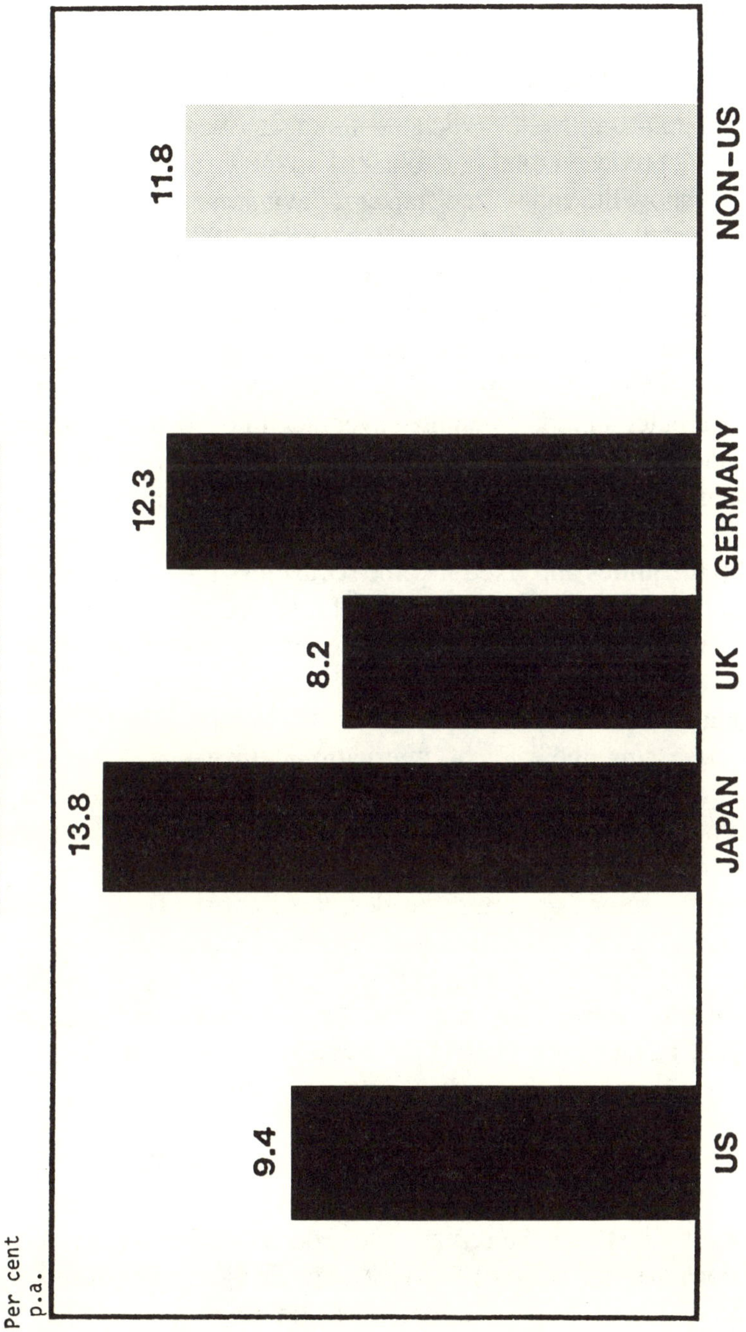

Risk Reduction:

While the non-U.S. capital markets offered a U.S. investor significant return opportunities, they did so without significantly increasing risk and in fact reduced total portfolio risk to the U.S. investor. Exhibits 4 and 5 show the annualized standard deviation of dollar return from the international markets over the period 1970-1986. While the individual international equity and fixed income markets are significantly more risky than their U.S. equivalent, a diversified portfolio of non-U.S. equities or non-U.S. fixed income securities is not significantly more risky than the equivalent domestic market. For example, a market weighted average of non-U.S. equity markets had an annual standard deviation of dollar return of 16.2% p.a., compared with 15.7% p.a. for the U.S. equity market.

This diversification *between* international markets is significant for both equities and fixed income securities. It is important to bear in mind that international investment for any investor, U.S., or otherwise, always offers two tiers of diversification — firstly diversification out of the domestic market and secondly diversification across the many markets outside the domestic market.

In assessing the risk of international investment the relevant measure is not total risk of the international markets, but their contribution to the risk of the investor's overall portfolio. From this perspective international investment offers risk *reduction* in addition to the return opportunities described above. Both for international equities and fixed income securities a capitalization weighted world portfolio of U.S. and non-U.S. markets is less risky than the U.S. market alone. This shows that diversification into international markets in fact reduces a U.S. investor's total portfolio risk.

INTERNATIONAL ASSET ALLOCATION

Exhibit 6 illustrates the returns and risks to various asset allocation decisions over the period 1970-1986. The line joining USS and NUSS shows that returns and risks to a portfolio ranging from 100% U.S.

EXHIBIT 4 INTERNATIONAL EQUITY MARKETS
STANDARD DEVIATION OF RETURNS IN US DOLLARS 1970-1986

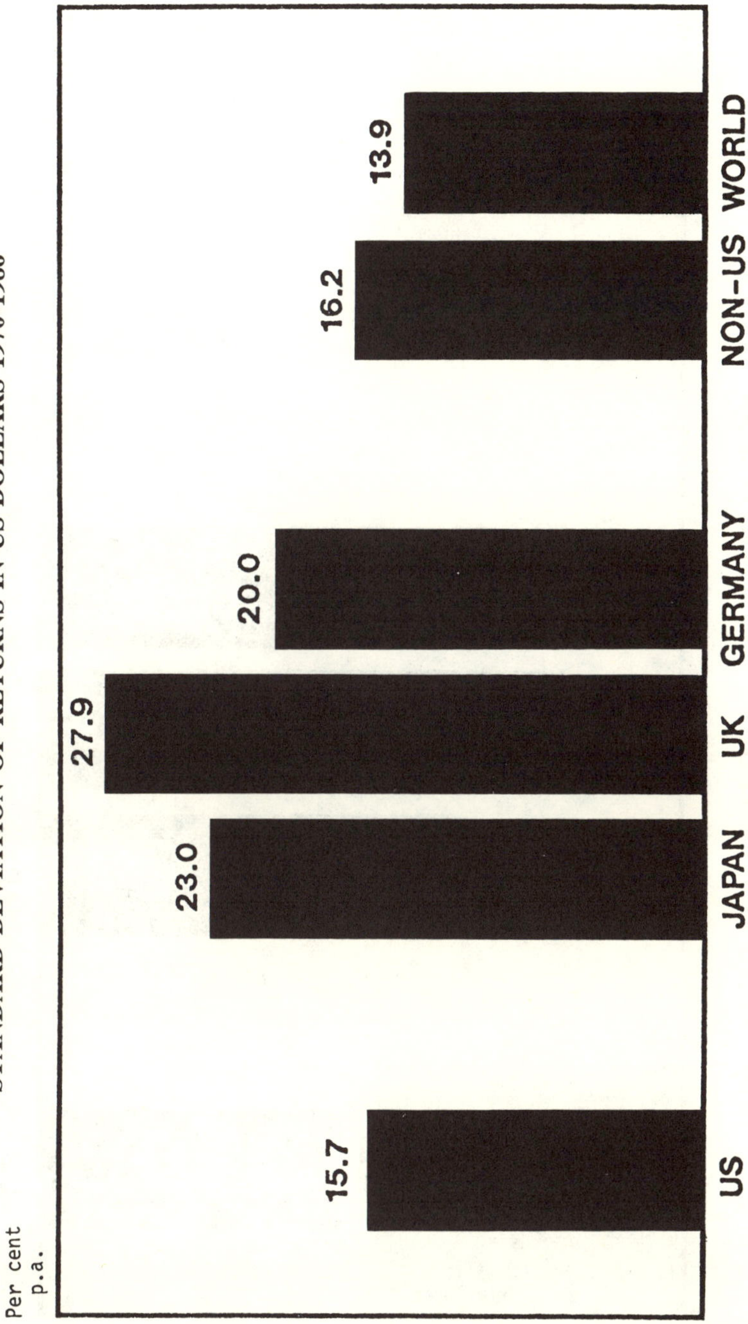

EXHIBIT 5 INTERNATIONAL FIXED INCOME MARKETS
STANDARD DEVIATION OF RETURNS IN US DOLLARS 1970-1986

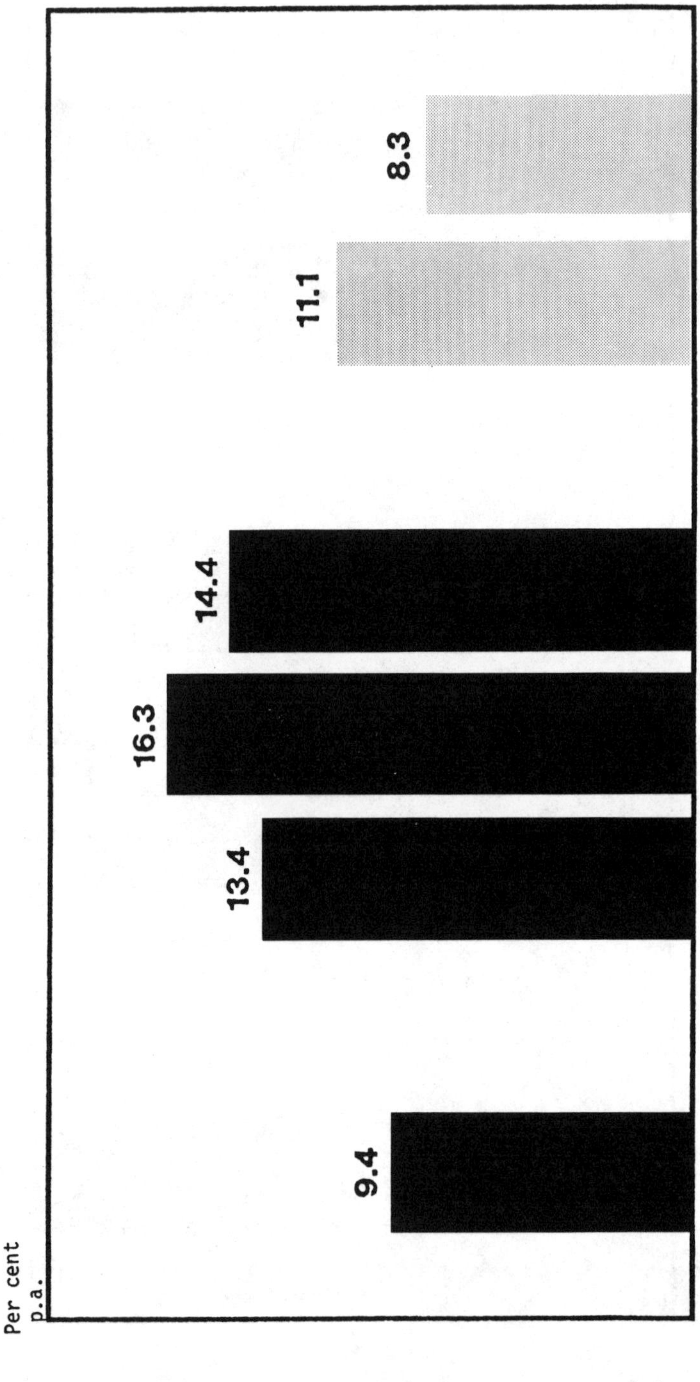

EXHIBIT 6 INTERNATIONAL EQUITY AND BOND MARKETS RETURNS AND RISK 1970-1986

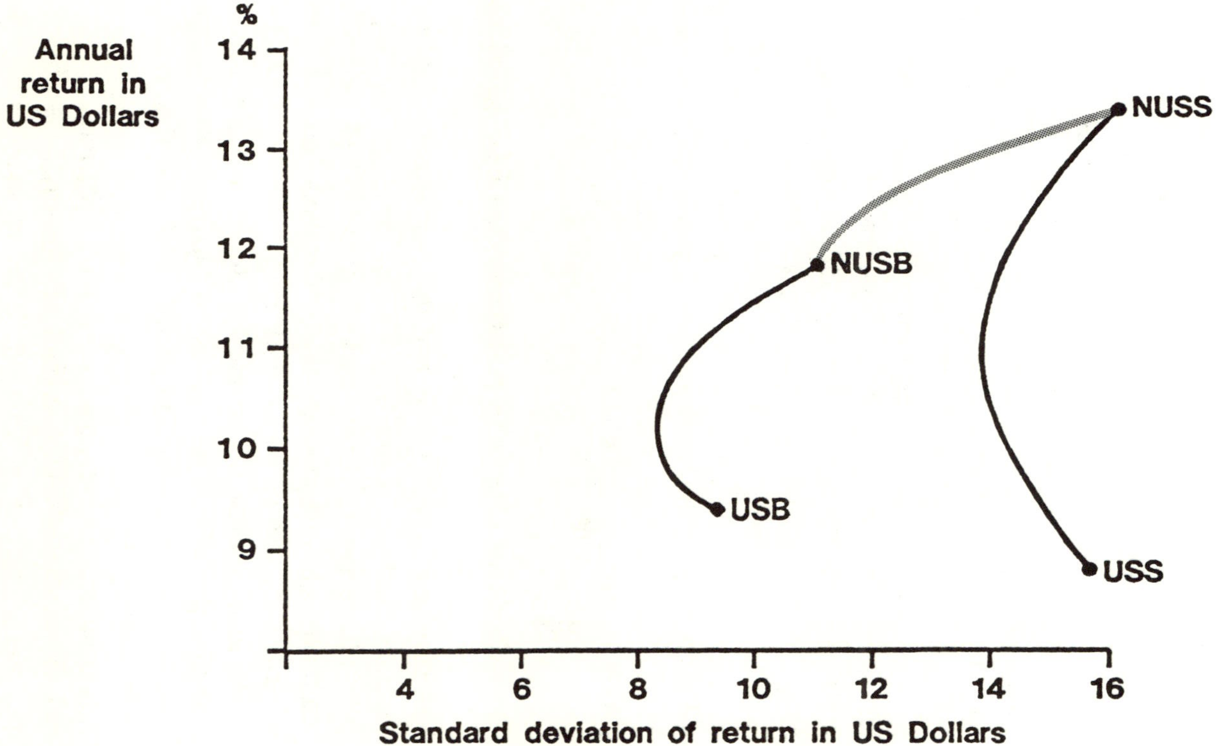

equities up to 100% non-U.S. equities. The line USB, NUSB shows portfolios ranging from 100% U.S. fixed income to 100% non-U.S. fixed income. The line NUSB, NUSS shows all combinations of international fixed income securities and international equities.

Exhibit 6 shows that not only do international equities and fixed income securities add value when compared with their domestic counterparts, but that they offer diversification among themselves, as illustrated by the opportunity sets offered by the line NUSB, NUSS. This is the third tier of international diversification, i.e. across international equity and fixed income.

From an asset allocation perspective it is appropriate to consider the full spectrum of all international assets simultaneously, when identifying an investor's portfolio risk/reward tradeoff. The frontier USB to NUSS represents the best combinations of allocations available. It is notable that this frontier everywhere dominates the USS, NUSS line. In other words, the more traditional domestic/international allocation question is more appropriately addressed in the context of simultaneous allocation across all four asset classes — U.S. equities, U.S. fixed income, international equities and international fixed income securities.

SEPARATION OF ASSETS AND CURRENCIES

Returns to a U.S. investor in international markets derive from two separate sources of return — local asset return and currency appreciation (depreciation) versus the U.S. dollar. The local and currency returns to U.S. investment in international equities and fixed income securities are shown in Exhibits 7 and 8.

The contribution of currency return to total return has been unsystematic; for some markets it has been positive and others negative and for diversified portfolios or non-U.S. markets it has been small.

In contrast, however, the contribution of currencies to investment risk is significant and systematically positive. Exhibits 9 and 10 decompose the total risk (standard deviation of return) of interna-

EXHIBIT 7 INTERNATIONAL EQUITY MARKETS
LOCAL AND CURRENCY RETURNS 1970-1986

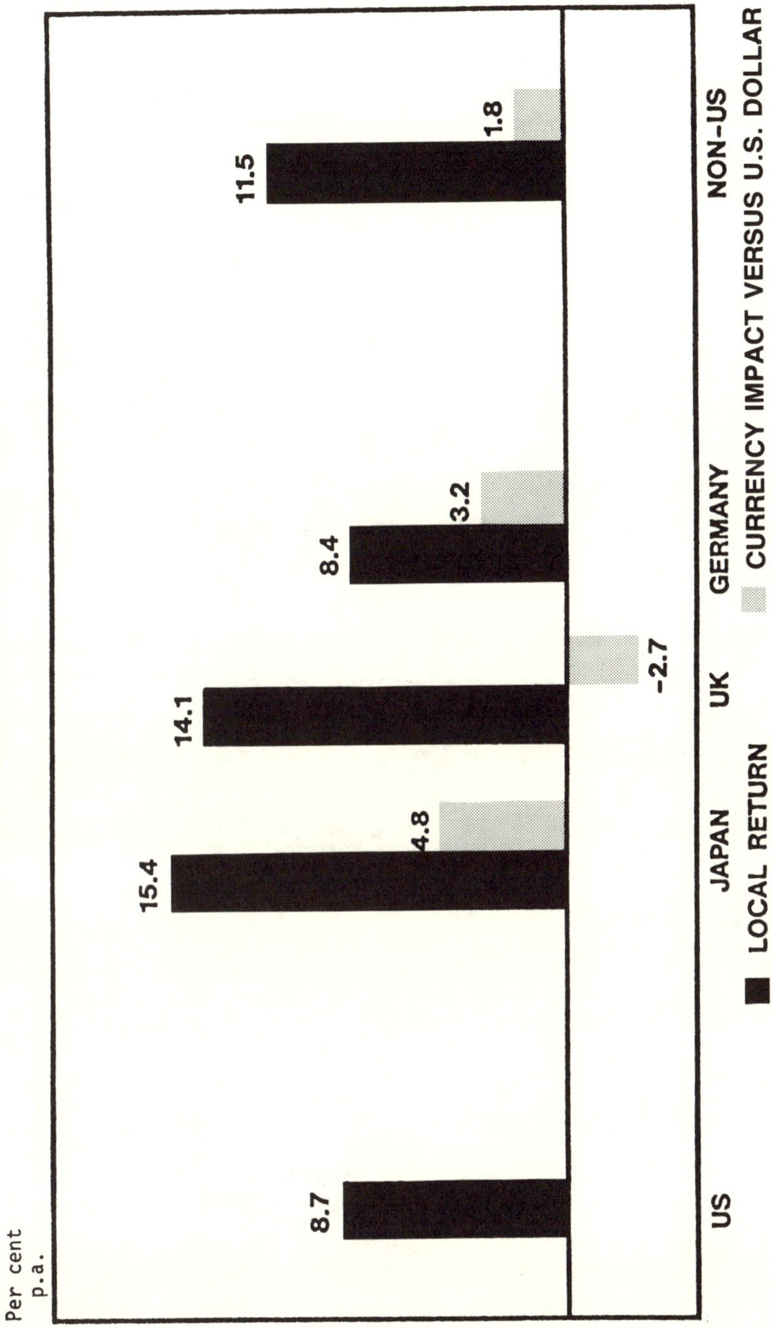

EXHIBIT 8 INTERNATIONAL FIXED INCOME MARKETS
LOCAL AND CURRENCY RETURNS 1970-1986

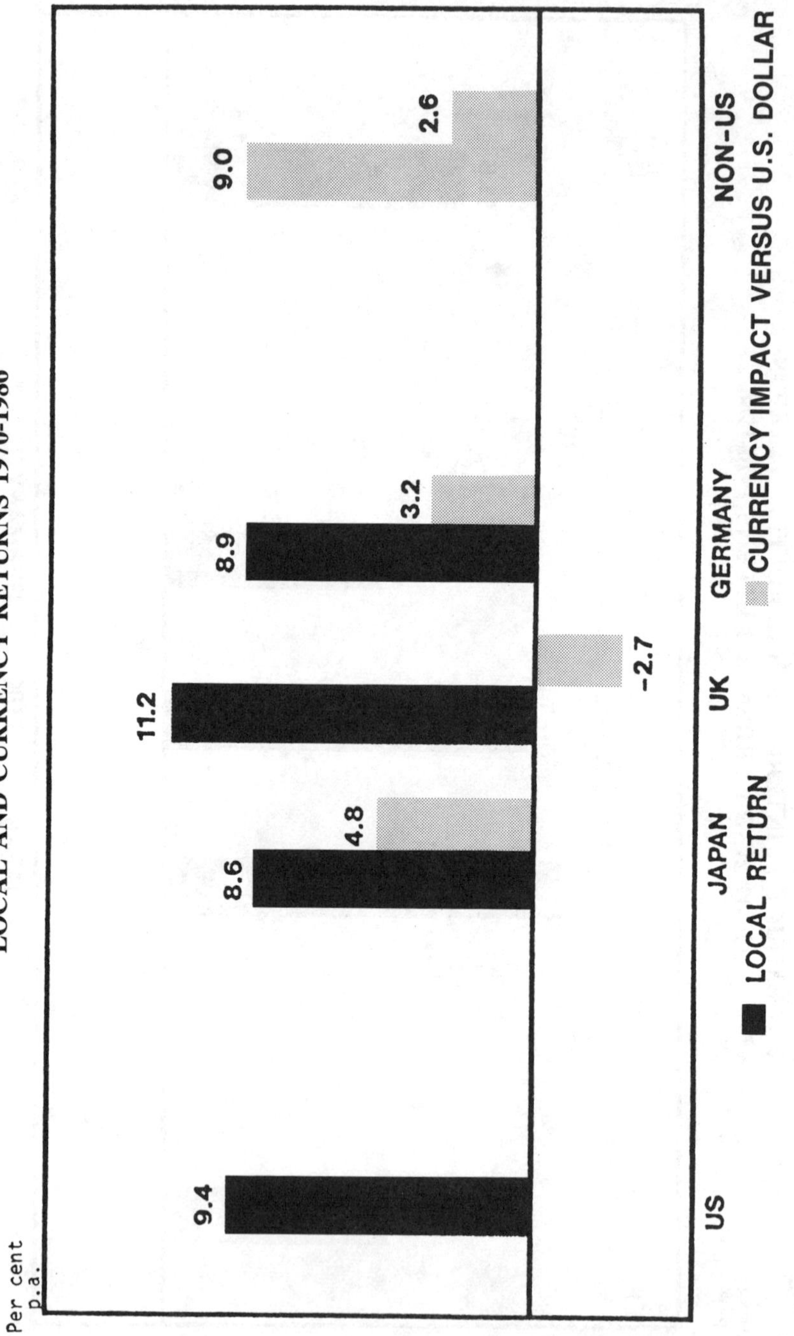

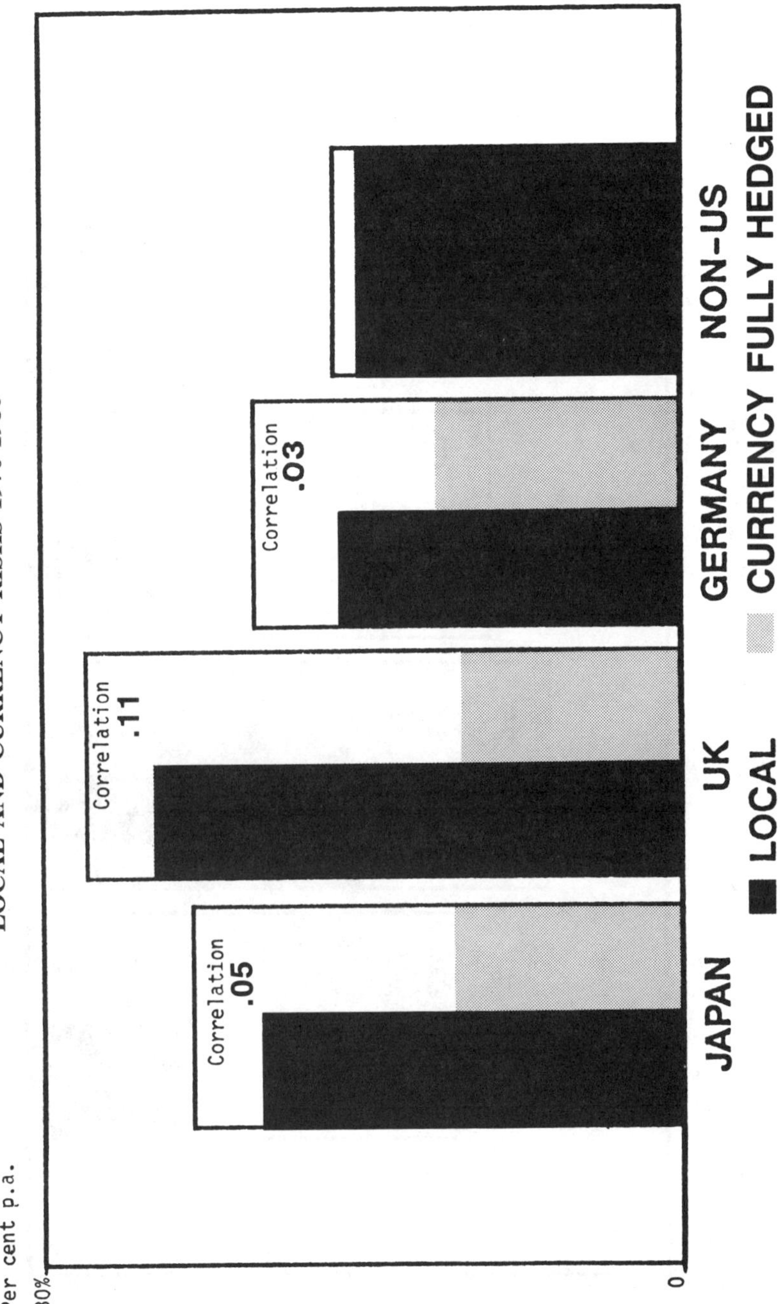

EXHIBIT 9 INTERNATIONAL EQUITY MARKETS
LOCAL AND CURRENCY RISKS 1970-1986

EXHIBIT 10 INTERNATIONAL FIXED INCOME MARKETS
LOCAL AND CURRENCY RISKS 1970-1986

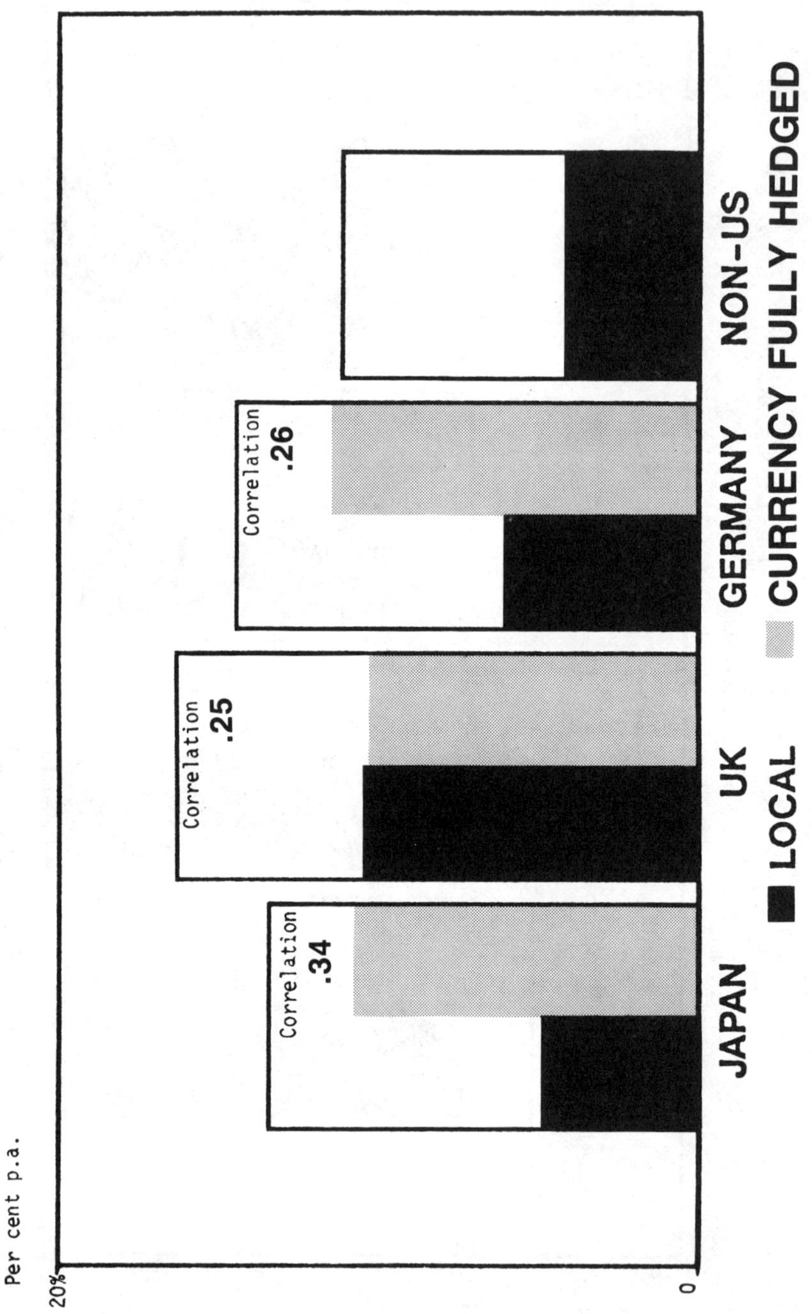

tional equities and fixed income markets into risk from local return volatility and currency volatility versus the dollar. Total risk is given by the outlined bar, and component risks are given by the inside bars. It can be seen that currency risk is approximately equal to 50% of the local risk of equity markets and more than 100% of the risk of local fixed income markets. It is worth pointing out that the total risk as indicated by the outlined bar is not equal to the addition of the two component risks, because standard deviations are not additive.

International portfolios that only have exposure to local asset return can be constructed by hedging the currency exposure of the underlying asset back into the dollar. The standard deviation of return of such hedged portfolios of all non-U.S. markets is also given in Exhibits 9 and 10. These risks show that hedged portfolios with only exposures to international assets and not currencies, can avoid the significant currency risks associated with international investment.

The correlations of local asset return and currency appreciation are also shown in Exhibits 9 and 10. These correlations are consistently small especially for international equities. This observation, combined with the fact that currency risk is a significant source of investment risk in international portfolios suggests:

(1) Currency risk should be managed and not simply assumed.
(2) Currency exposure decisions should be made separately from asset exposure decisions.

INTERNATIONAL ASSET ALLOCATION AND CURRENCY EXPOSURE

When an investor considers international asset allocation decisions separately from currency exposure, the risk reward opportunity set is greatly enhanced. This is illustrated in Exhibit 11 for the period 1970-1986.

By allowing hedged portfolios of international equities (NUSSH) and international fixed income securities (NUSBH), as an allocation

EXHIBIT 11 INTERNATIONAL EQUITY AND BOND MARKETS
RETURNS AND RISK 1970-1986

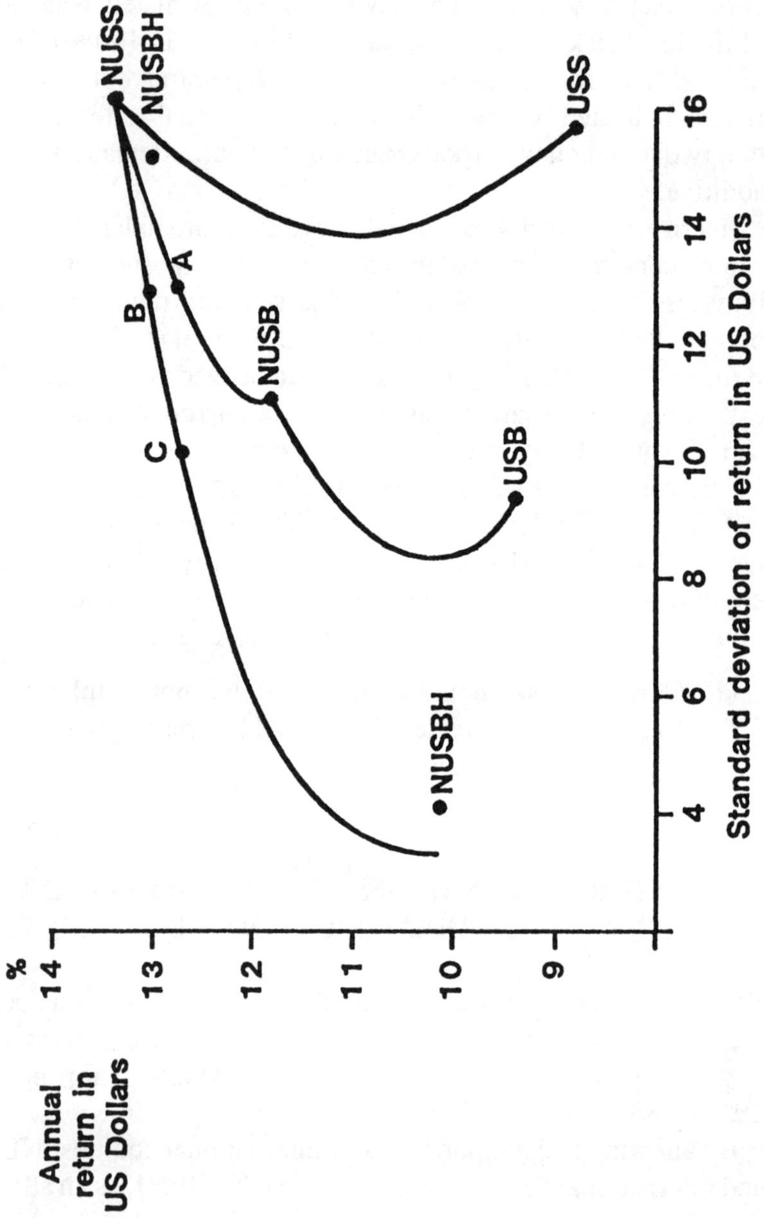

EXHIBIT 12 INTERNATIONAL EQUITY AND BOND MARKETS
RETURNS AND RISK 1970-1986
OPTIMAL ASSET AND CURRENCY ALLOCATION %

	A	B	C
International Equities Assets:	50	75	40
International Bonds Assets:	50	25	60
International Currencies:	100	75	60

to assets independent of currencies, into the investors opportunity set, the risk reward frontier is shifted up and to the left. This is illustrated by comparing portfolios A, B and C.

Portfolio A is a 50/50 portfolio of international equities and fixed income securities where currency exposure is equal to asset exposure.

Portfolio B has higher return but the same risk. This is achieved by a 75% allocation to international equity and 25% to international fixed income, but controlling risk by allowing a reduction in the currency exposure from 100% to 75% (see Exhibit 12). This reduction in currency exposure was achieved by continuously hedging 25% of the portfolio currency exposure back into the U.S. dollar.

Portfolio C has the same return as Portfolio A but less risk due to its 60% allocation to international fixed income securities and only 60% exposure to currencies.

SUMMARY

In considering international investment allocations a U.S. investor should address the question in the context of allocations across domestic equity, domestic fixed income, international equities and fixed income securities simultaneously. Domestic allocations may have inferences for international equity/fixed income allocations. In addition to the asset allocation question, the investor also faces a separate currency allocation decision. The identification of separate solutions to these questions greatly enhances the opportunity set of the U.S. investor.

CHAPTER THIRTEEN

LEE R. THOMAS, III is a Vice President and the Director of the Currency Strategies Group in the J. Aron Division of Goldman, Sachs & Co. The Currency Strategies group develops proprietory trading strategies, designs currency and commodity hedges for Goldman Sachs' own positions and those of its clients, and is also charged with new financial product development.

Mr. Thomas holds a Ph.D. in Economics from Tulane University. Most of his published research is in the areas of international finance, international monetary theory, and international financial markets.

MANAGING FOREIGN CURRENCY RISK USING FORWARDS AND OPTIONS

Lee R. Thomas
Currency and Commodity Strategies Group
Goldman, Sachs & Co.
New York, New York

INTRODUCTION

The sharp increase in the volatility of exchange rates that followed the breakdown of the Bretton Woods agreement created new risks and opportunities for international portfolio managers. In addition to those determinants of asset returns that domestic investors must consider when constructing their portfolios, international investors must also assess the likely course of exchange rates. Currency movements can substantially increase or reduce a portfolio's total return.[1]

In response to the increase in exchange rate risk that followed the collapse of the fixed rate system, old financial markets offering hedging instruments expanded, and new markets developed. Forwards and futures, contracts to buy or sell specific amounts of currency on particular dates at an agreed exchange rate, were the first hedging tools to be widely adopted. Currency options, representing the right (but not the obligation) to buy or sell foreign currency at specific prices for specific periods of time, were the second generation of hedging instruments to win acceptance.

Forwards, futures, and options each have unique advantages. Forwards and futures are easy to understand and use. Moreover, forward contracts have unusually low transactions costs; for example, a representative bid/offer spread on $1 million worth of a major currency is about $150. On the other hand, option users generally pay larger premiums; but options offer portfolio managers flexibility that forwards and futures cannot. However, because they are more flexible, options are more demanding of their users. Simply put, more choices must be made to design an option hedging strategy, because options expand the hedger's range of available positions.

This chapter describes basic hedging strategies using currency options and forward contracts. (With minor modifications to the hedge designs, futures contracts can be substituted for forwards.) In the case of forward contracts, we will consider the effects of covering a representative foreign currency exposure partially or completely. The option strategies treat the effect of partial and complete hedging, and also the effect of varying the option's strike price. In each case we will examine the probability distribution of the effective exchange rate (defined below), a hedge evaluation device that succinctly summarizes and illustrates the effect of options or forwards on the mean, the standard deviation, and the worst-case exchange rate associated with each strategy.

ON RISK

No foreign exchange strategy can promise a free lunch. An opportunity to earn profits from exchange rate fluctuations can only be secured by simultaneously bearing the risk of suffering losses if exchange rates move unfavorably. As a consequence, the mean-variance approach of modern portfolio theory, which provides a framework to evaluate the trade-off between expected return and risk, applies naturally to managing the foreign currency exposures that arise in the course of international investing. Once a portfolio manager has decided how much exchange rate risk he is willing to bear, the analytical techniques of modern portfolio theory can be used to find the position that produces the maximum expected return.

The international portfolio manager's task is to select from the menu of available hedging instruments those that produce the position that best conforms to his own exchange rate expectations and appetite for risk. Obviously, to choose this optimal position he must evaluate and compare the risks of alternative positions. To do so, he must be able to unambiguously define and measure risk.

There are at least two ways of thinking about exchange rate risk. Conventionally, applying the most popular version of modern portfolio theory to exchange rates, risk results from the uncertainty in an international transactor's forecast of future currency values, and can be measured by the standard deviation of the probability distribution of future exchange rates. If a transactor knows with certainty what the future exchange rate will be, his position is not risky, regardless of whether the prospective rate is favorable or unfavorable. On the other hand, if it is uncertain whether or not the exchange rate at the hedging horizon will be near its most likely value, the transactor's exchange rate exposures are risky. This view of exchange rate risk is symmetric in the sense that the transactor's forecast could either overestimate or underestimate the future exchange rate. (Of course, his concern will be focused on one or the other of these potential forecasting errors, depending on his position.)

This kind of risk can be controlled using forward (or futures) contracts. As we will see, an international portfolio manager with foreign currency exposure can adjust the standard deviation of his exchange rate distribution, without changing its basic shape, by using forward exchange contracts. If he is uncomfortable with the standard deviation implied by his unhedged currency position, he will ordinarily cover a portion (or all) of his exposure in the forward exchange market. This typically lowers the expected return to the portfolio. (If it does not, the portfolio manager should always hedge.)

The mean-variance approach to portfolio design or hedge construction, which implies that risk can be measured by the standard deviation of the exchange rate, is often criticized on theoretical grounds as being too restrictive.[2] More practically, for many portfolio managers another concept of risk may be as important, or even more important — the maximum possible loss on the position.

Usually it is assumed that the rates of return to assets, including foreign currencies, are normally distributed. If proportionate exchange rate changes are normally distributed, lowering the standard deviation of future exchange rates by hedging with forwards or futures — lower risk, measuring risk in the usual way — does not imply that a portfolio's maximum possible loss declines.[3] (It does imply that the *likelihood* of a large loss declines.) This is because the tails of the normal distribution, representing the likelihood of extreme outcomes, extend indefinitely in both directions, regardless of the distribution's standard deviation.[4] There is always some chance, even if it is a small one, of a very large loss. So, a hedger cannot reduce his worst-case loss by lowering the standard deviation of his hedged return, as long as his hedged position retains the shape of the normal distribution. Rather, to reduce this kind of risk requires changing the shape of the distribution of future possible exchange rate outcomes in a way that truncates the most unfavorable rates. Options can do this.

Assessing Risk Using the Probability Distribution of the Effective Exchange Rate

When both standard deviation and maximum possible loss are important to a portfolio manager, risk cannot be summarized or measured by a single number.[5] As a result, the conventional portfolio-theoretic approach to hedging, which characterizes a position by its expected profit and standard deviation of profits, is inadequate. In this case, hedge evaluation requires a more flexible tool.

Instead of assessing the risk of a position by measuring its standard deviation alone, in this chapter we wish to consider the effects of a hedge on the portfolio manager's entire probability distribution of outcomes, including the position's maximum possible loss. For a simple, representative international portfolio problem we will compare the probability distributions of the future effective exchange rate, considering both its dispersion (standard deviation) and shape (maximum possible loss), for a number of hedges using options or forward contracts. Examining the entire probability distribution of the effective exchange rate characteristic of each hedging strategy will permit us to evaluate the riskiness of the position in a more flexible and powerful way than would be the case if we used a simple statistical measure, such as the standard deviation.

The hedging strategy evaluations that follow focus on the distribution of the *effective* exchange rate. The effective exchange rate contains three components: the actual exchange rate at which the portfolio manager buys or sells foreign currency, at his (assumed) one-year hedging horizon; the ending values of any hedging instruments, such as forward contracts or options, that the transactor used; and the effective exchange rate adjusted to reflect any option premiums the hedger paid or received.

For a hedger who is buying currency, the effective exchange rate represents the "all in" cost of foreign currency. If the hedger is selling, the effective rate represents his net dollar realization per unit of foreign currency sold. In either case, hedging costs and the time value of money are explicitly considered.

In general our interest is not confined to the effective exchange rate that would result from a particular scenario. (Regrettably, hedgers often do evaluate strategies in this way.) Instead, we wish to ascertain what the range of possible ending effective exchange rates is, and how probable various values are. This information is contained in the effective exchange rate's probability distribution.

Figure 1 illustrates a representative probability distribution. For each range of ending effective exchange rates, tabulated at one-cent intervals, the figure shows the associated probability. For example, Figure 1 indicates that the probability of an ending rate lying between US$0.55 and US$0.56 is just under 5 percent.

BASIC STRATEGIES WHEN THE FORWARD RATE IS UNBIASED

As we will see, before designing a currency hedge a portfolio manager should first decide whether he believes the forward exchange

FIGURE 1 PROBABILITY DISTRIBUTION OF THE EFFECTIVE EXCHANGE RATE UNHEDGED POSITION

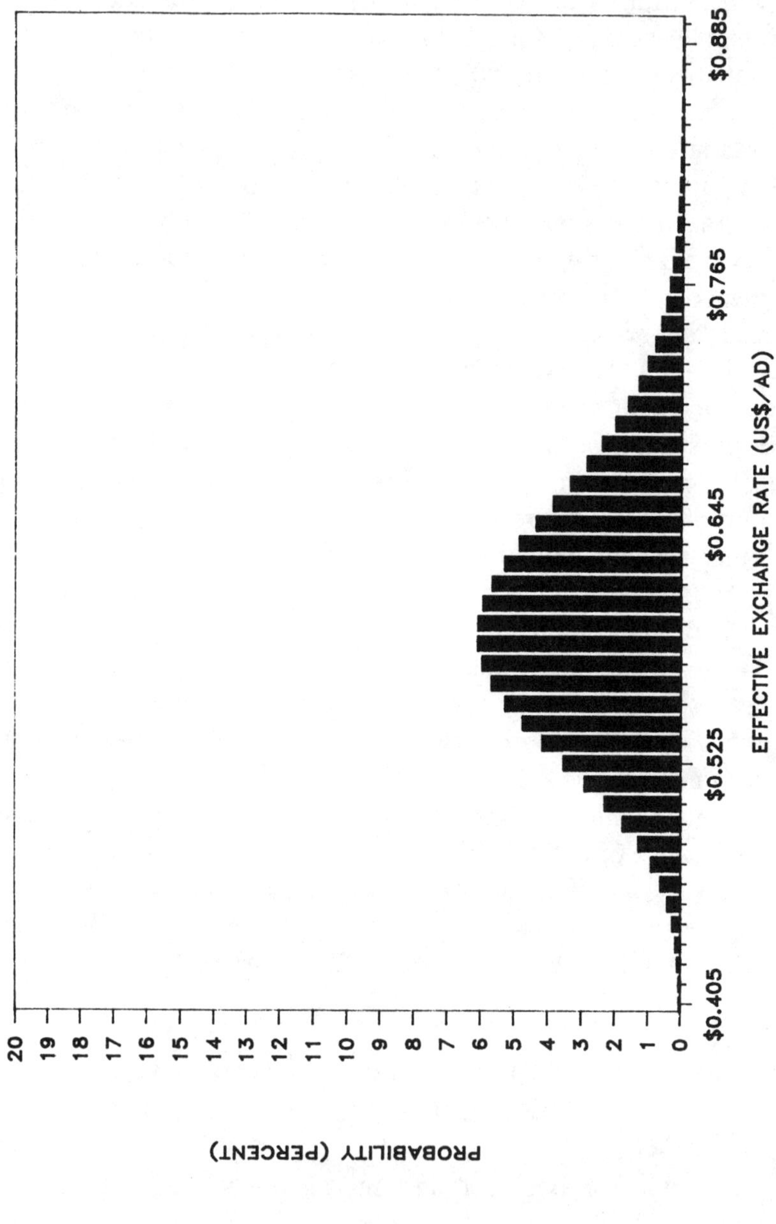

rate is an unbiased predictor of the future spot rate. "Unbiased" does not mean that the future spot rate will equal the current forward rate with probability one, or even with high probability. Rather, it means (roughly) that the spot rate is as likely to be above the forward as below it. This is not the portfolio manager's only decision; but, as we will see, it logically precedes the others he must make.

In this section we will examine the effects of forward and option hedging strategies in the case when the forward rate is unbiased.

Consider the case of an investor based in the United States who owns a portfolio of Australian dollar (AD) denominated bonds that he expects to sell in one year.[6] The prevailing spot and forward exchange rates are US$0.65/AD and US$0.60/AD, respectively. His choices are to remain unhedged, to hedge using a forward contract, or to hedge using an Australian dollar put option.

Strategy 1: Remain Unhedged

If a portfolio manager is clairvoyant, an optimist, or indifferent to bearing risk, he may decide not to hedge his currency exposure at all. The price at which he might sell his Australian dollars in a year is illustrated by the probability distribution of the future exchange rate (Figure 1).[7]

Figure 1 assumes that the return to an unhedged Australian dollar position conforms to the familiar bell-shaped curve of the normal distribution.[8] It further assumes that the most likely future exchange rate is the forward rate, US$ 0.60/A$, and that the annualized standard deviation of the return to an unhedged Australian dollar position is 11 percent.

These assumed values of the mean and standard deviation of the terminal Australian dollar exchange rate are only a convenience. Later we will see that the assumption that the mean of the probability distribution equals the forward rate has profound implications for hedging. In practice, a hedger might derive estimates of the mean and standard deviation of the future exchange rate from market data. For example, the market's expectation of the future mean exchange rate could be either the forward rate (the uncovered parity hypothesis) or the current spot rate (the random walk hypothesis).[9] The market's expectations of the standard deviations of major exchange rates could be deduced by observing option prices, and computing their implicit volatility using the appropriate variants of the Black-Scholes option pricing formula. Alternately, the hedge manager could substitute his own expectations of these parameters.

The horizontal axis of Figure 1 is the U.S. dollar per Australian dollar exchange rate prevailing in twelve months. In this example the hedger is assumed to own Australian dollars, so favorable Australian dollar exchange rates are to the right of center, while unfavorable rates are to the left. Along the vertical axis are plotted the probabilities associated with various ending exchange rates, at one-cent (US) intervals. The higher the bar at a given ending exchange rate, the more likely it is that the corresponding rate will prevail twelve months hence.

Since the distribution in Figure 1 represents an unhedged position, it constitutes a natural benchmark against which hedged positions can be compared. Basically, Figure 1 shows that an unhedged transactor is most likely to sell his Australian dollar near the expected future spot exchange rate, US$0.60/A$. For example, the odds are approximately 2/3 that the final Australian dollar rate will lie between US$0.67/AD and US$0.54/AD. But there is also some chance of selling at a much higher or a much lower rate. This is indicated by the significant probability located in the tails of the exchange rate distribution. In fact, with the (reasonable) volatility estimate used to construct Figure 1, there is a one-in-twenty chance that the ending rate in a year will exceed US$0.71/AD, and an equal chance that it will fall below US$0.41/AD.[10]

Strategy 2: Forward Exchange Contracts

If the portfolio manager is uncomfortable with bearing all of the exchange rate risk associated with an unhedged Australian dollar position, he may choose to eliminate all or part of his currency exposure by selling Australian dollars in the forward market. By hedging in this way the dollar-based investor eliminates all the chance of an unpleasant surprise — or of a pleasant one — on the portion of his exposure that he chooses to cover in the forward market.

Figure 2 illustrates the effect of the most extreme version of a forward market strategy. It represents the probability distribution of the effective exchange rate if the portfolio manager sells *all* of his Australian dollars forward for U.S. dollars.

The effect of covering any portion of the Australian dollar exposure in the forward market is to shrink the probability in the tails of the effective exchange rate distribution, and to increase the probability associated with the forward rate. For example, if the portfolio manager sells half of his foreign currency forward, the probability in the tails is reduced by 0.5, and the probability of an ending rate of US$0.60/AD is increased by 0.5. When the entire exposure is covered, as in Figure 2, the probability in the tails of the effective exchange rate distribution is completely eliminated. As a result, the probability distribution of the ending effective exchange rate collapses to a spike located above the forward exchange rate, US$0.60/AD.

Figure 2 shows that all of the portfolio manager's exchange rate uncertainty vanishes when he covers forward. Both kinds of risk, dispersion and maximum possible loss, were eliminated by the forward hedge. The portfolio manager's best case and worst case are now both US$0.60/A$, the forward exchange rate.

Figure 2 corresponds to a riskless position. Covering forward in this way is always the preferred strategy for a portfolio manager who is unwilling to bear any exchange rate risk. As we will see below, it is also always the preferred strategy for a portfolio manager who is willing to bear risk, but who does not believe that the forward exchange rate overestimates or underestimates the most likely future spot exchange rate.

Strategy 3: A Put Option Struck at the Forward

Unlike forward contracts, currency options permit hedgers to construct positions with asymmetric effective exchange rate distributions. A simple option strategy — buying a put option stuck at the

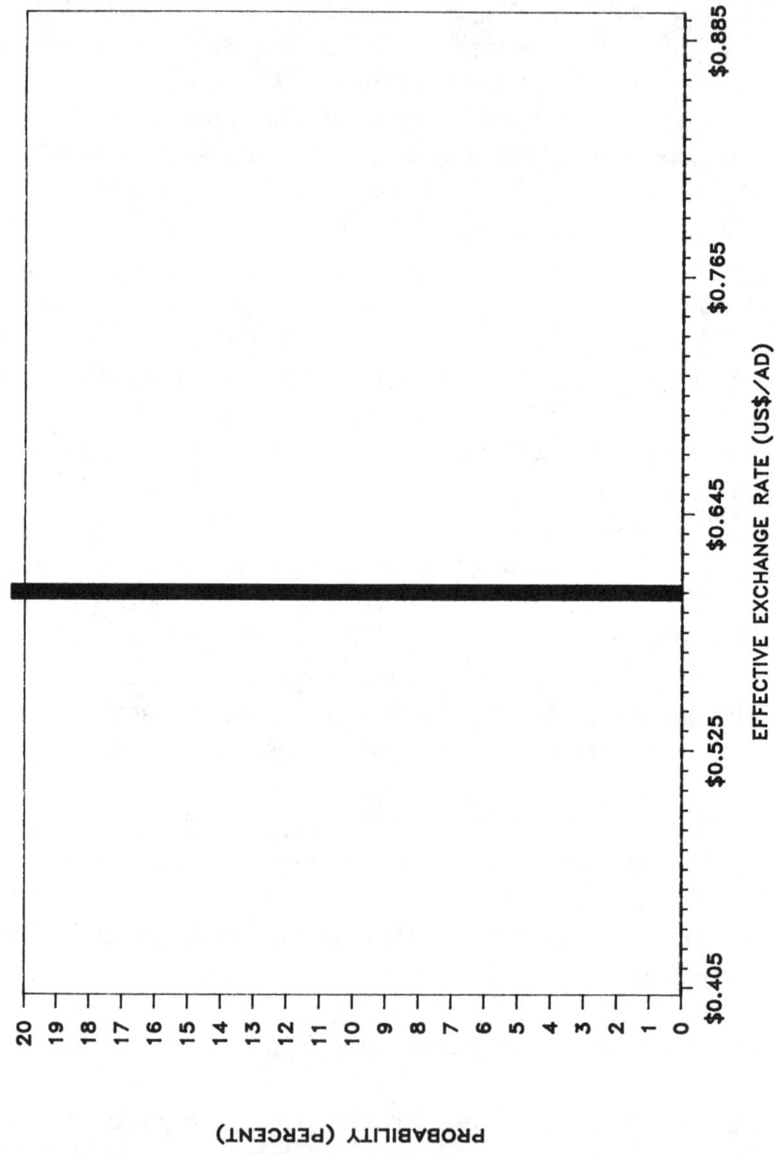

FIGURE 2 PROBABILITY DISTRIBUTION OF THE EFFECTIVE EXCHANGE RATE
FORWARD HEDGE

forward rate on the entire exposure — illustrates how an option strategy molds the ending effective exchange rate distribution in ways that static forward strategies cannot.

Recall that a put option gives the hedger the right, but not the obligation, to sell Australian dollars at the strike price. In this case the strike price is the forward exchange rate, US$0.60/AD. As a consequence, the portfolio manager's worst case becomes the forward rate, less an adjustment to reflect the option premium he paid.[11]

The major effect of buying Australian dollar put options is to limit the least favorable exchange rate outcomes, according to the option's strike price. Essentially, in terms of the effective ending exchange rate, a simple put option strategy truncates the left side of the unhedged probability distribution shown in Figure 1. At the same time, since the put buyer must pay a premium, the entire probability distribution shifts to the left to reflect the cost of the option. (Recall that the probability distribution we illustrate applies to the *effective* exchange rate, after factoring in any hedging fees the portfolio manager must pay.) The deeper in-the-money the put is, the greater the degree of truncation (favorable); but the greater also is the premium paid and the leftward shift of the entire distribution (unfavorable).

Figure 3 shows the probability distribution corresponding to a hedging strategy using a put option struck at the forward rate of US$0.60/AD, and written on the portfolio's entire exposure. The difference between the put's strike price, US$0.60/AD, and the worst case exchange rate shown in Figure 3, US$0.5740/AD, represents the premium of 2.48 cents (US) per Australian dollar, paid to the put writer, plus interest on this amount.

Simple option strategies limit the portfolio manager's worst-case effective exchange rate, while permitting him to participate in favorable exchange rate changes. In Figure 3 this option feature manifests itself as an asymmetric effective exchange rate distribution, truncated on the left, but not on the right. This asymmetrical distribution of favorable and unfavorable exchange rates cannot be accomplished using forward contracts, and represents the most attractive characteristic of options as a hedging instruments.

FIGURE 3 PROBABILITY DISTRIBUTION OF THE EFFECTIVE EXCHANGE RATE PUT AT .60 $/AD

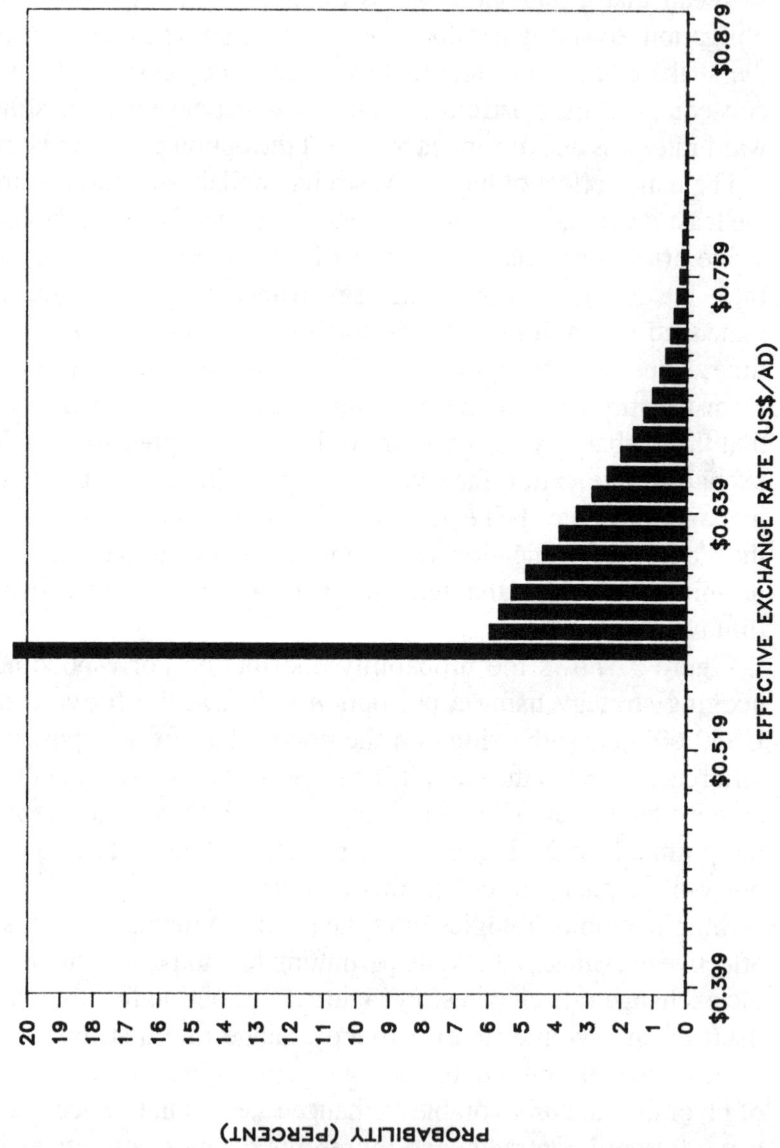

SIMPLE STRATEGIES COMPARED

So far we have evaluated three simple exchange rate risk management strategies: remaining unhedged (Figure 1), covering the entire exposure with forward contracts (Figure 2), and hedging with a put option written on the entire exposure and struck at the forward rate (Figure 3). Even though these are simple approaches, they allow us to reach some important conclusions.

The results of each of the three hedging strategies we have evaluated so far are summarized in Table 1 and Figure 4. They show that the expected effective exchange rate is identical for all three strategies. The portfolio manager cannot increase the expected return to his position by neglecting to hedge his exposure with a forward contract, or by using a put option to hedge. Hedging does change the risk of the position, measured either conventionally using the standard deviation (as in Figure 4), or by the position's maximum loss.

For this hypothetical hedger — under the assumption maintained in this section, that the forward rate is unbiased — choosing a hedging plan is simple. The forward market strategy produces a position that has the same expected exchange rate, but lower risk, than either alternative. This implies that the portfolio manager should always cover his currency exposure forward.[12] By doing so, he eliminates the position's uncertainty without sacrificing any expected return.

TABLE 1: THREE BASIC STRATEGIES SUMMARIZED

When the Expected Future Exchange Rate is $0.60

(All Figures in US$/AD, rounded to the nearest cent)

Strategy	Mean Effective Exchange Rate	Standard Deviation	Best Case	Worst Case
Unhedged	0.60	0.07	Unlimited	0.00
Forward	0.60	0.00	0.60	0.60
Put Struck at the Forward	0.60	0.04	Unlimited	0.57

FIGURE 4 HEDGING STRATEGIES SUMMARY

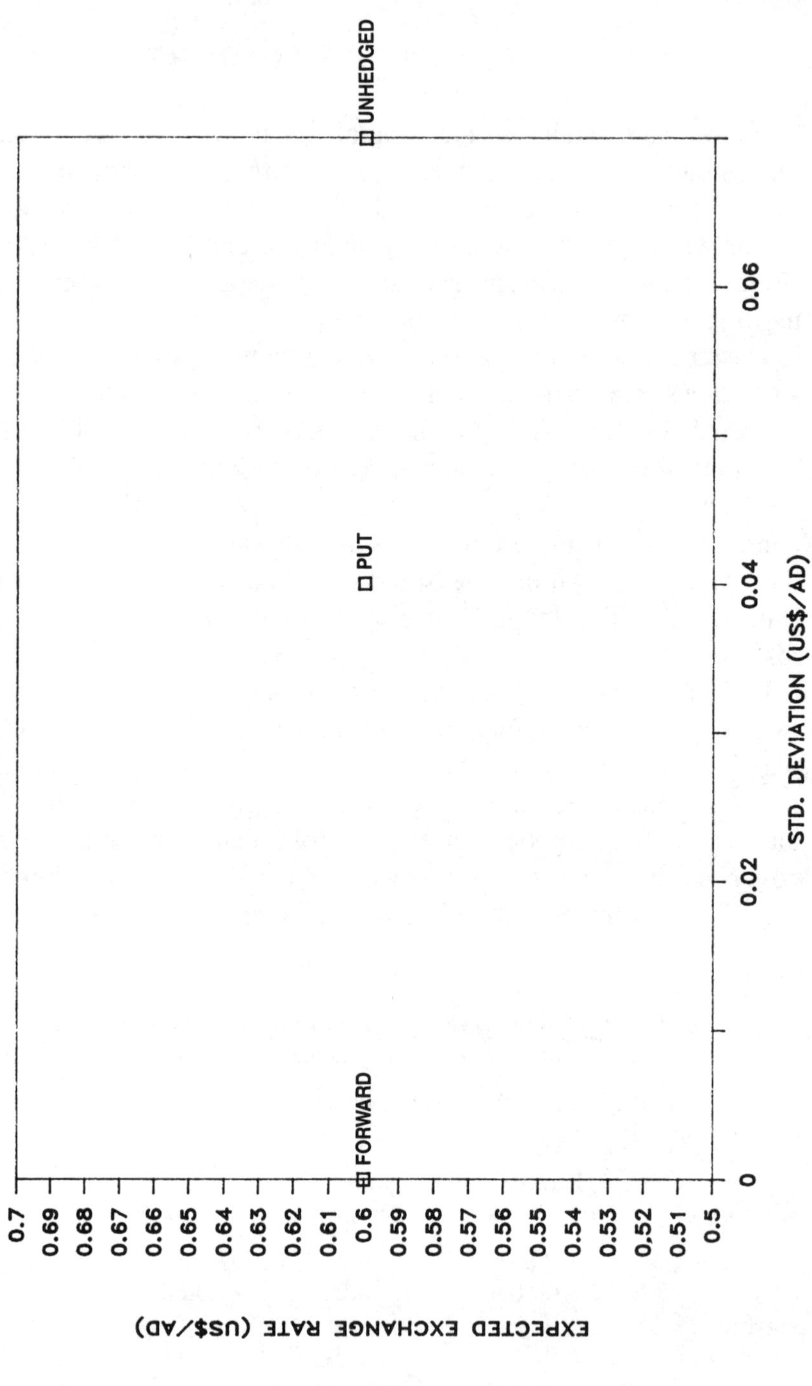

The portfolio manager should cover forward even if he is a risk-lover. (Normally, economic agents are assumed to be risk averse.) Since many financial markets offer a premium, in expected return terms, for assuming risk, even a risk-lover should refuse to bear risk gratuitously in the foreign exchange markets. Instead, he should hedge his currency exposures using forward contracts, and indulge his preference for excitement in markets that reward risk bearing.

The results derived in this section have two implications for portfolio managers with foreign currency exposures. First, any *hedging* strategy, other than covering in the forward market — including hedging using options or eschewing any hedge at all — is always a *speculation* that the forward exchange rate is biased.

Second, for any hedging strategy (other than covering the entire exposure forward) to *consistently* yield profits, the portfolio manager must *consistently* predict the evolution of exchange rates better than the forward rate does. If he is only right half the time, as the market efficiency hypothesis argues he will be, then the portfolio manager who does not cover forward merely increases the risk of his portfolio without improving its expected return. So choosing any strategy other than covering forward is an assertion that the forward exchange market is inefficient, and that the portfolio manager can "beat" it.

Only if the hedger believes that the expected future spot rate does not equal the forward rate, and that he can successfully forecast the direction of the bias, will partial forward market strategies or put option strategies be preferred to covering the entire exposure in the forward market. The next section considers the three basic hedging strategies in detail when the portfolio manager believes that the forward rate is biased.

BASIC HEDGING STRATEGIES WHEN THE FORWARD RATE IS BIASED

Since any hedging strategy (other than covering the entire exposure in the forward market) can only be justified if the forward rate and the expected future spot rate diverge, we will assume that they do.

For example, imagine that the portfolio manager believes that the current spot exchange rate, US$0.65/AD, rather than the forward rate of US$0.60/AD, is the better predictor of the future spot rate. That is, the portfolio manager favors the random walk hypothesis over the uncovered parity hypothesis.

Figures 5A–5C show the effective exchange rate distributions for the unhedged, forward, and put option strategies when the expected future spot exchange rate is US$0.65/AD. With this assumption, Figures 5A–5C replace Figures 1–3.

In Figure 5A, the expected effective exchange rate for the unhedged position (US$0.65/AD) exceeds the forward rate (US$0.60/AD). As a consequence, remaining unhedged, though riskier than taking forward cover, also promises a more advantageous exchange rate, *on average,* than covering forward. Apart from assuming different ending effective exchange rates, Figure 5A and Figure 1 are identical. (The volatility in both is 11 percent).

If the entire exposure is completely hedged in the forward market, the portfolio manager is not concerned with changes in the spot rate. So, in this case the expected future spot rate is irrelevant. Accordingly, Figure 5B is identical to Figure 2.

The distributions corresponding to option hedges, Figures 3 and 5C, are similar, but not identical. If the expected future spot rate is US$0.65/AD (rather than US$0.60/AD), the put option struck at US$0.60/AD is less likely to be exercised. In fact, the probability of exercise falls from 51.6 percent to 24.6 percent. As a result, the probability spike in Figure 5C is smaller than that in Figure 3.

Figure 6 and Table 2 replace Figure 4 and Table 1, under the new assumption that the expected future exchange rate is US$0.65/AD. Notice in Figure 6 that the put strategy does not *appear* to adequately compensate for its risk. That is, a straight line connecting the unhedged and forward hedged strategies passes above the put strategy. So, in a mean-variance framework, buying puts to hedge appears inefficient. However, as was argued above, a mean-variance framework may be inadequate for many hedgers.

The remainder of this section considers these three basic strategies in more detail.

FIGURE 5A PROBABILITY DENSITY OF THE EFFECTIVE EXCHANGE RATE UNHEDGED POSITION WITH DISTRIBUTION ABOUT .65 $/AD

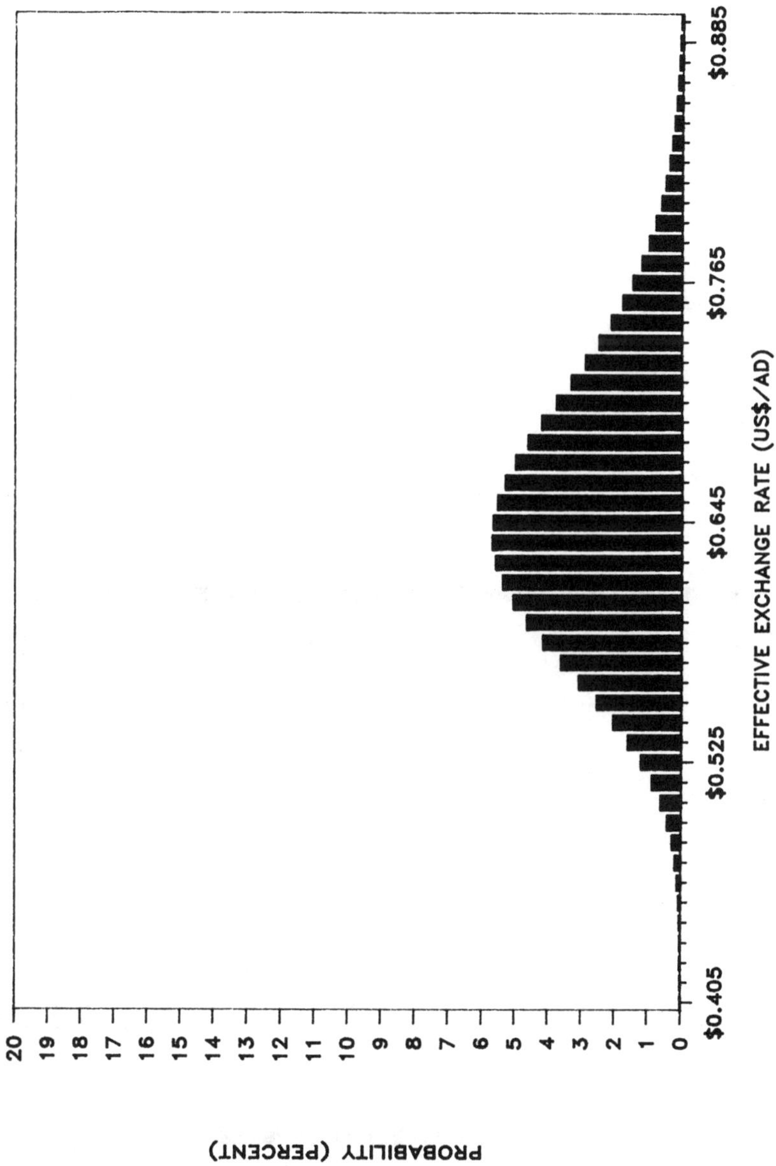

FIGURE 5B PROBABILITY DISTRIBUTION OF THE EFFECTIVE EXCHANGE RATE
FORWARD HEDGE

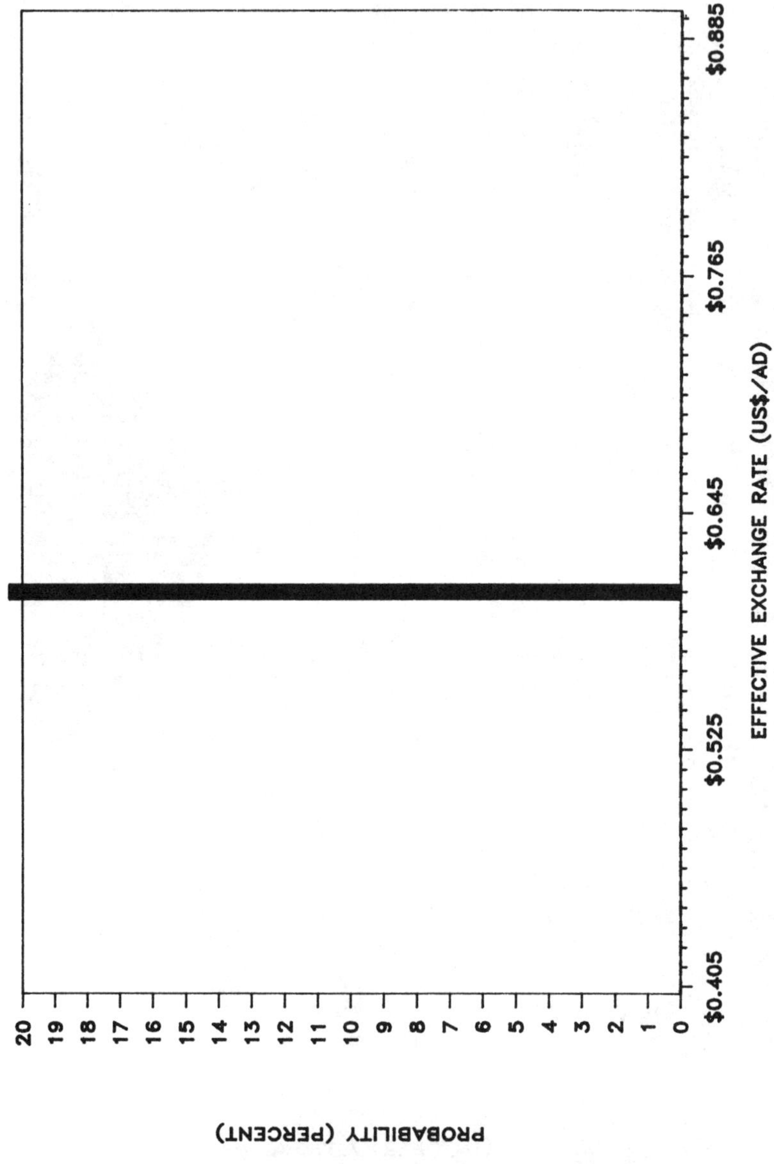

FIGURE 5C PROBABILITY DISTRIBUTION OF THE EFFECTIVE EXCHANGE RATE
Put at .60 $/AD with Distribution about .65 $/AD

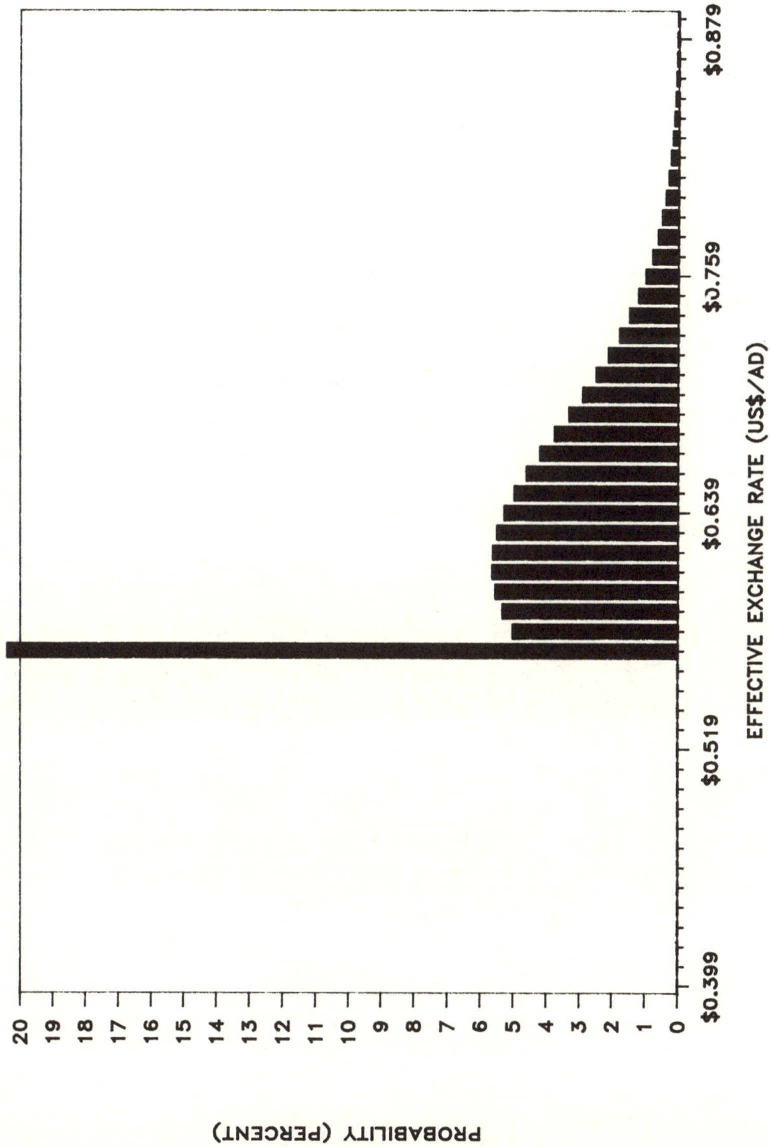

FORWARD MARKET STRATEGIES

Covering the entire exposure forward, the strategy represented in Figures 2 and 5B, is only one example of a hedging strategy that uses forward exchange contracts. If a portfolio manager wishes to reduce the standard deviation of his position, but not to eliminate his exchange rate exposure entirely, he may choose a partial forward strategy instead.

Figures 7A–7D show how the one-year, effective exchange rate distribution changes as a hedger progressively covers a percentage of his exposure, from 0 percent covered (Figure 7A) to 25 percent covered (Figure 7B), 75 percent covered (Figure 7C) and 100 percent covered (Figure 7D).

In Figures 7A–7D notice that the basic bell shape of the normal distribution is retained as the percentage hedged increases. But, as more of the exposure is covered forward, the probability associated with favorable and unfavorable exchange rate outcomes is reduced symmetrically. For example, consider the probability of receiving an exchange rate worse than US$0.55/AD when the Australian dollars are sold in one year. For the unhedged position this probability is approximately 8 percent; with a 25 percent hedge, it is 5 percent; with a 75 percent hedge it falls to 0.1 percent; and when the entire exposure is hedged, this probability is eliminated.

TABLE 2: THE BASIC STRATEGIES SUMMARIZED

When the Expected Future Exchange Rate is $0.65

(All Figures in US$/AD, rounded to the nearest cent)

Strategy	Mean Effective Exchange Rate	Standard Deviation	Best Case	Worst Case
Unhedged	0.65	0.07	Unlimited	0.00
Forward	0.60	0.00	0.60	0.60
Put Struck at the Forward	0.63	0.06	Unlimited	0.52

FIGURE 6 HEDGING STRATEGY SUMMARY

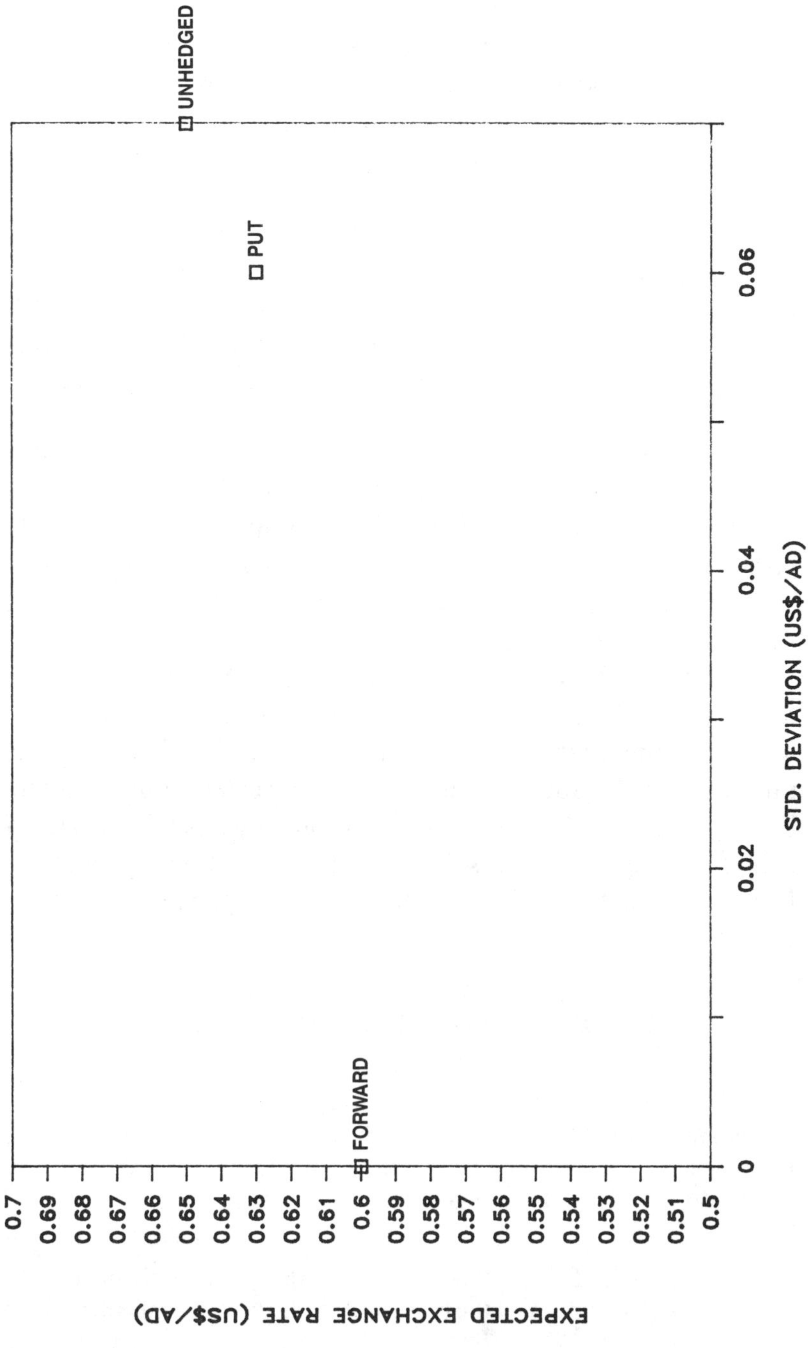

Table 3 summarizes the data illustrated in Figures 7A–7D.[13]

The risk (standard deviation) and expected return (given by the difference between the expected future spot rate and US$0.60/AD) of these forward market hedging strategies are illustrated in Figure 8. The relationship between risk and return is linear, and the slope, which shows how much additional expected return the hedger gains by bearing an additional unit of risk, is proportional to the difference between the forward rate and the expected future spot rate on the unhedged position (US$0.60/AD and US$0.65/AD, respectively). The slope also depends on the volatility of an exchange rate, in this case 11 percent (annualized).

Figure 8 shows that the more risk the hedger bears, the greater is his expected effective exchange rate. Furthermore, the increase in the expected effective rate is proportional to the additional risk borne. The price of securing an additional percent of expected return — how much additional risk must be born — depends on exchange rate volatility and the difference between the expected future exchange rate (here measured by the current spot rate) and the forward rate. When this difference is small, as when the portfolio manager believes that the forward rate is an approximately unbiased predictor of the future spot rate, the expected compensation for bearing exchange rate risk is low. Presumably this will lead the portfolio manager to cover a substantial fraction of his exposure in the forward market. If, however, the portfolio manager's expectation

TABLE 3: PARTIAL FORWARD STRATEGIES

(All in the US$/A$, rounded to the nearest cent)

Percentage of the Exposure Covered	Mean Effective Exchange Rate	Standard Deviation	Best Case	Worst Case
0%	0.65	0.07	Unlimited	0.00
25%	0.64	0.05	Unlimited	0.15
75%	0.61	0.02	Unlimited	0.45
100%	0.60	0.00	0.60	0.60

FIGURE 7A PROBABILITY DISTRIBUTION OF THE EFFECTIVE EXCHANGE RATE
0% Covered at Forward with Distribution about .65 $/AD

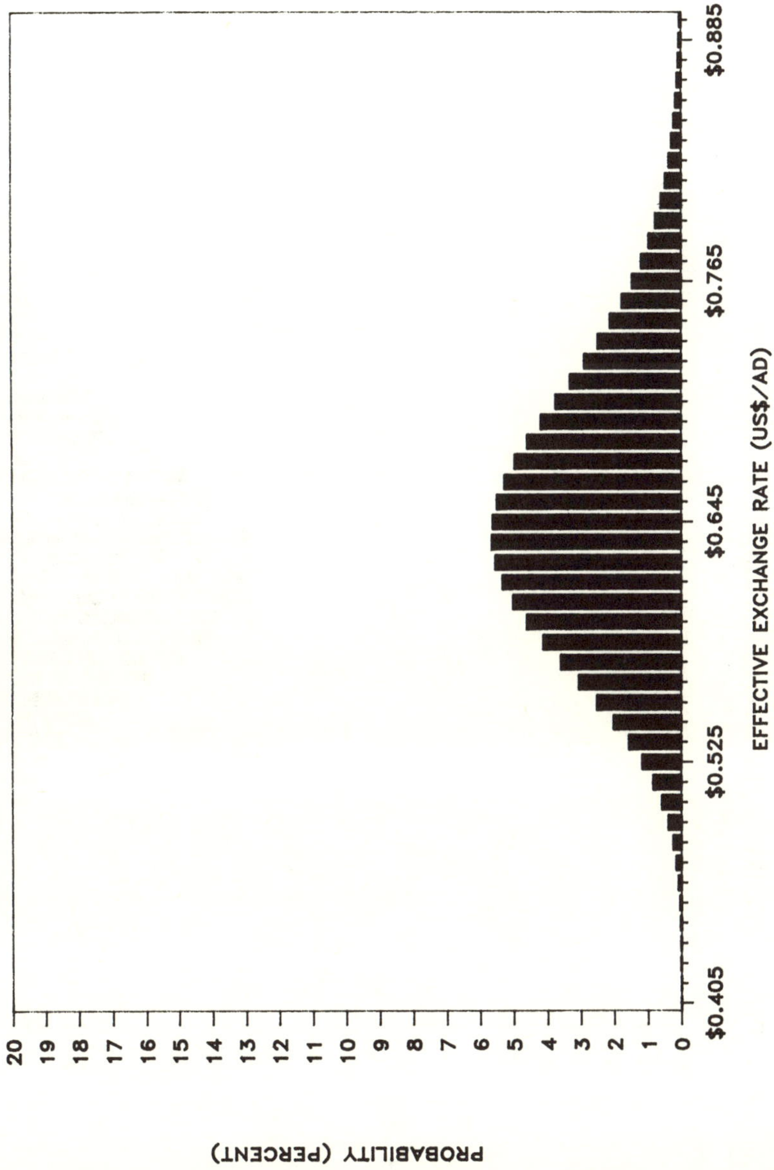

FIGURE 7B PROBABILITY DISTRIBUTION OF THE EFFECTIVE EXCHANGE RATE
25% Covered at Forward with Distribution about .65 $/AD

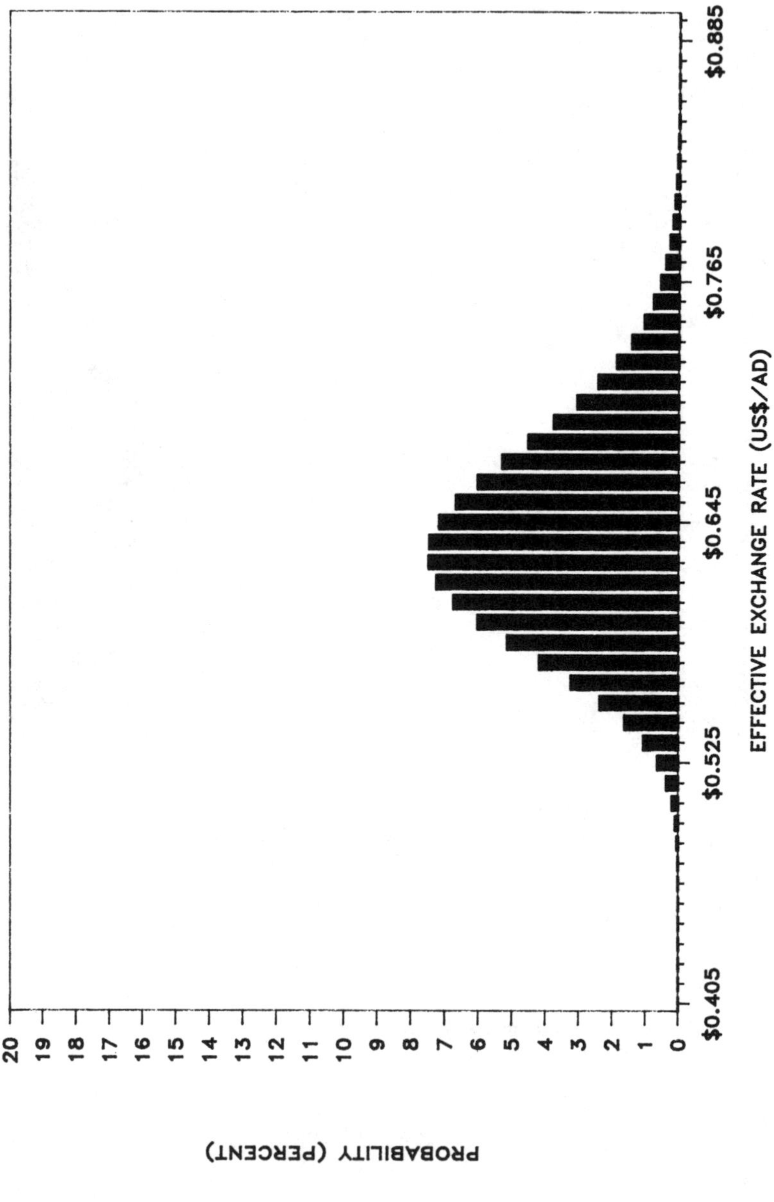

FIGURE 7C PROBABILITY DISTRIBUTION OF THE EFFECTIVE EXCHANGE RATE
75% Covered at Forward with Distribution about .65 $/AD

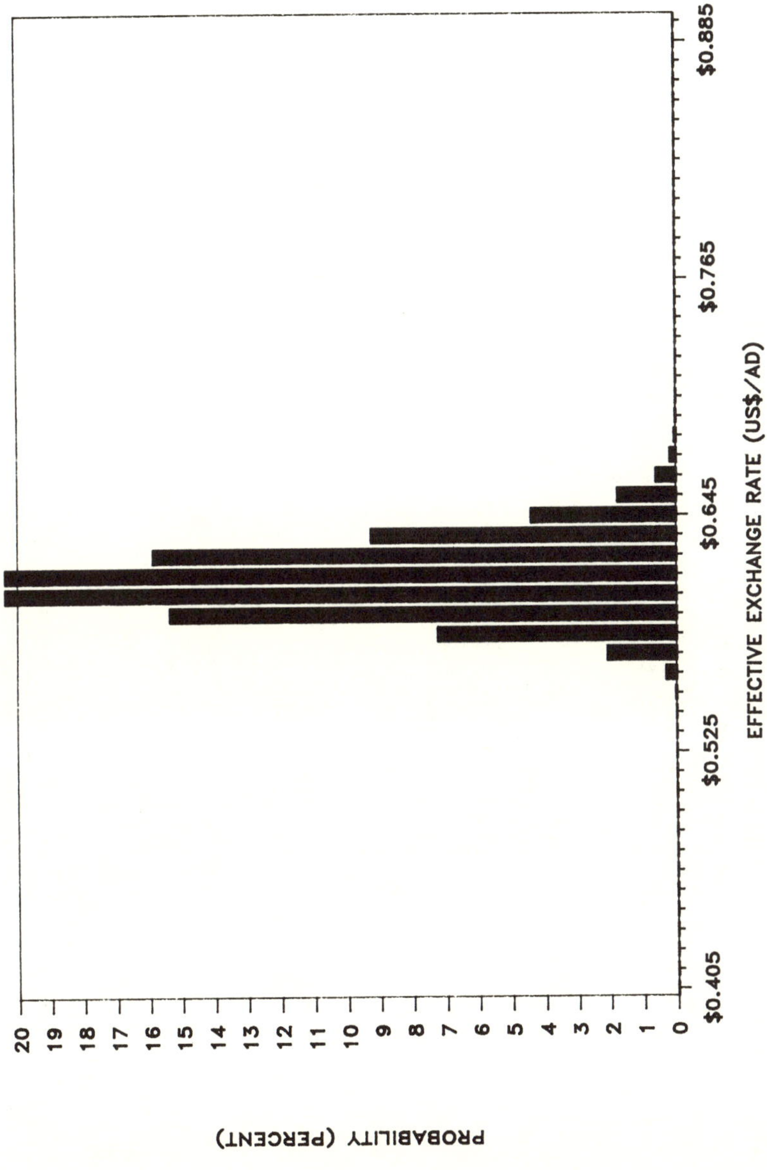

FIGURE 7D PROBABILITY DISTRIBUTION OF THE EFFECTIVE EXCHANGE RATE
100% Covered at Forward with Distribution about .65 $/AD

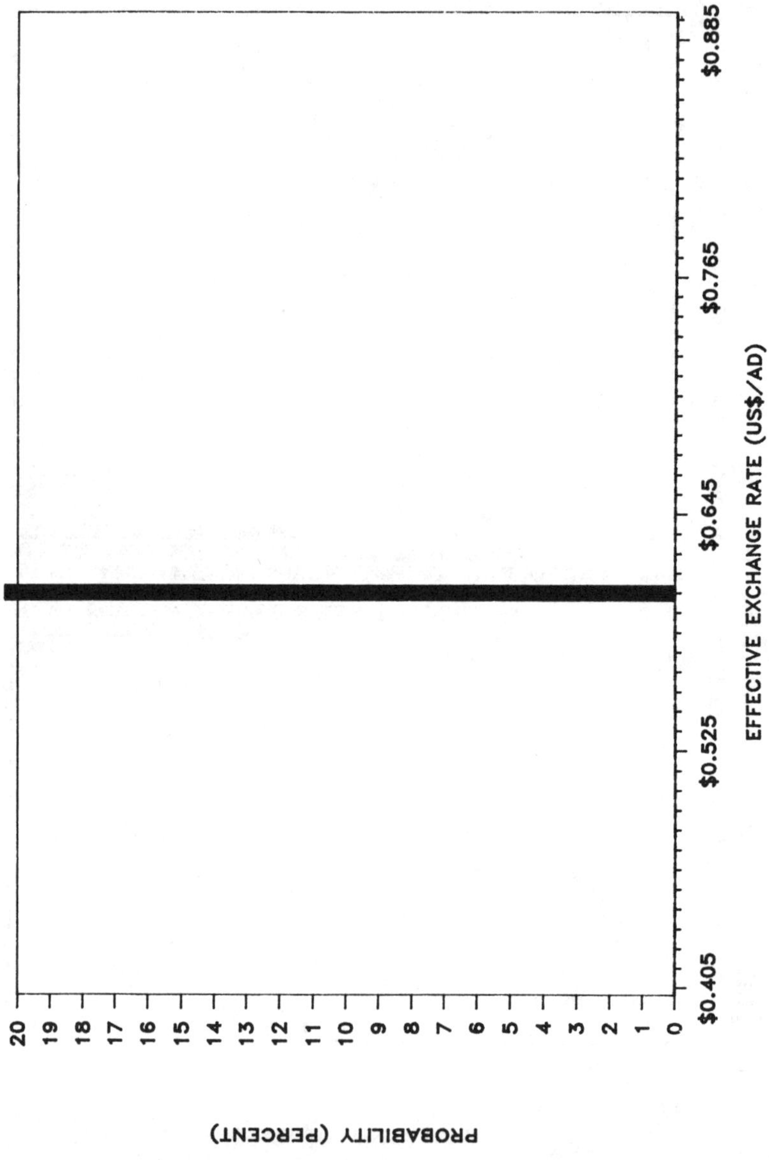

FIGURE 8 FORWARD HEDGES

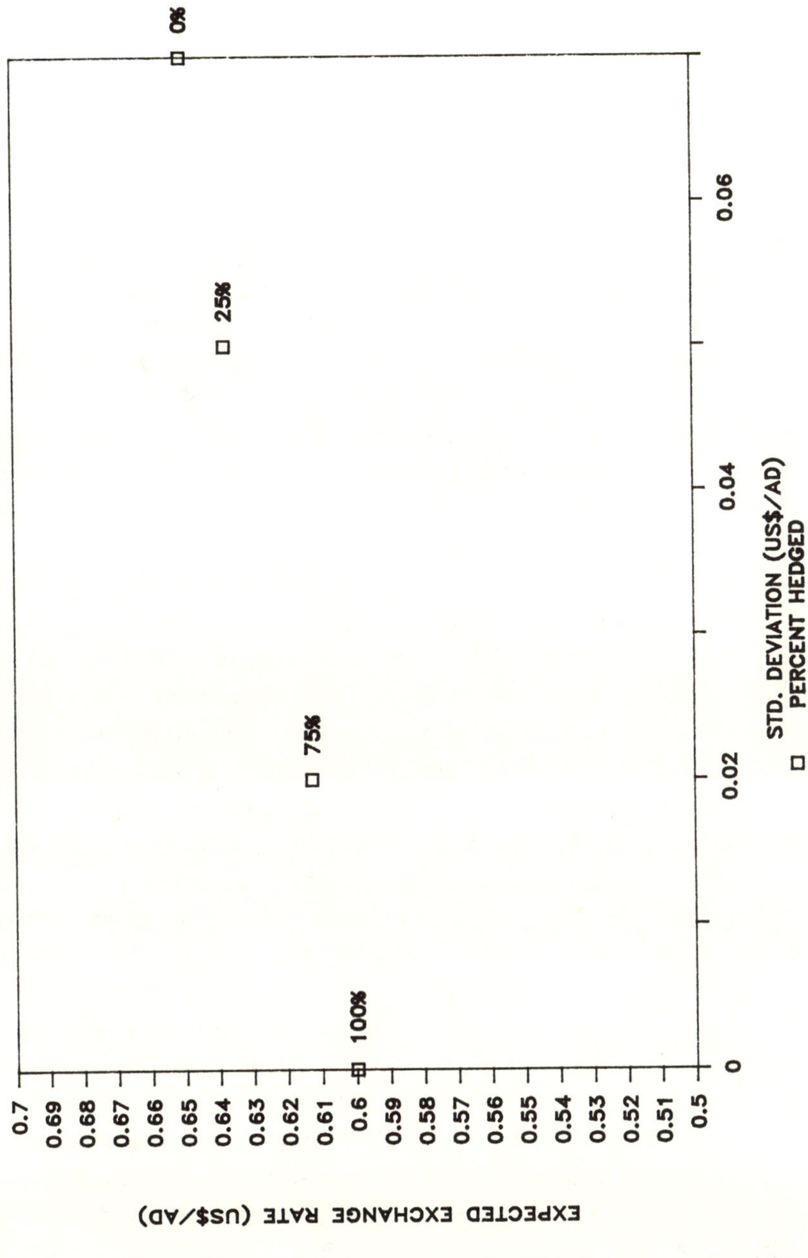

of the future spot rate diverges markedly from the forward rate, his apparent compensation for bearing exchange rate risk, in expected return terms, is substantial. Then the portfolio manager is likely to take a more aggressive position by leaving a larger percentage of his exposure unhedged, or by hedging with options rather than forwards.

Put Option Strategies

Hedgers who use forward contracts need only choose what percentage of their foreign currency exposure to cover. Put option strategies require selecting, at the very least, how much exposure to cover and what strike price to use to construct a hedge with the desired risk and return characteristics. We will complete our examination of simple hedging strategies by considering the effects of these two decisions on the probability distribution of the effective exchange rate.

Varying the Put's Strike Price

The wide range of hedging possibilities that can be secured by varying the strike price of the put option is illustrated in Figures 9A–9F.

Figures 9A–9C represent 25 percent, 10 percent and 5 percent out-of-the money put strategies, respectively. Figures 9D–9F illustrate 5 percent, 10 percent and 25 percent in-the-money put option hedging strategies. In all cases, sufficient options are purchased to enable the portfolio manager to sell his entire Australian dollar exposure at a known worst case exchange rate.

First, consider the effect of using relatively inexpensive, deep out-of-the-money puts.

Figure 9A shows that a deep out-of-the-money put option corresponds to an effective exchange rate probability distribution that resembles that of an unhedged position (Figure 5A). The probability distribution is almost symmetric, with equal chances of very large exchange rate profits or losses. This strategy requires paying only a small option premium, so that the entire probability distribution is simply the ending effective exchange rate shifted slightly to the left. But at the same time, it also affords little protection. As a result, only the extreme tail of the return distribution is truncated.

A deep out-of-the-money put is a minimalist — and aggressive — solution to the hedging problem. This strategy is like buying insurance with a large deductible. The premium is lower, but the insurance also offers less protection.

Figures 9B and 9C represent more conservative out-of-the-money put option strategies. In each case, the portfolio manager secures a significant absolute downside limit to his exposure, as is shown by the truncation of the left side of the probability distribution. As the option's strike price is shifted toward the forward rate, more of the unfavorable tail of the distribution of ending effective exchange rates is eliminated. Simultaneously, the entire distribution shifts to the left, reflecting the larger premium paid, and the probability peak at the unfavorable end of the distribution grows.

Figures 9D–9F continue the logical progression from out-of-the-money to in-the-money option hedges. As the strike price rises, the far left peak in the effective rate distribution begins to dominate the hedge. Eventually, the effective exchange rate distribution begins to resemble that of a forward hedge. Figure 9D — a deep in-the-money put option hedge — is virtually identical to Figure 5C.

Figure 9G compares the effective exchange rate distributions corresponding to a deep in-the-money put option strategy (Figure 9F) with complete forward cover (Figure 5C). Figure 9H compares a deep out-of-the-money put hedge (Figure 9A) with an unhedged position (Figure 5A). In either case the probability distributions are virtually identical.

In light of these similarities, the put option strategies illustrated in Figures 9B–9E can be seen to intermediate between a position that is effectively unhedged, and one that is completely hedged using a forward contract. That is, varying the strike price of the put option produces a continuum of effective exchange rate distributions, bounded on one side by a position that is effectively unhedged (Figure 9A), and bounded on the other side by a position that resembles one completely hedged with forward exchange contracts (Figure 9F).

Recall that varying the percentage of the exposure which was hedged with forward contracts (Figures 7A–7D) produced the same

FIGURE 9A PROBABILITY DISTRIBUTION OF THE EFFECTIVE EXCHANGE RATE
Put at .45 $/AD with Distribution about .65 $/AD

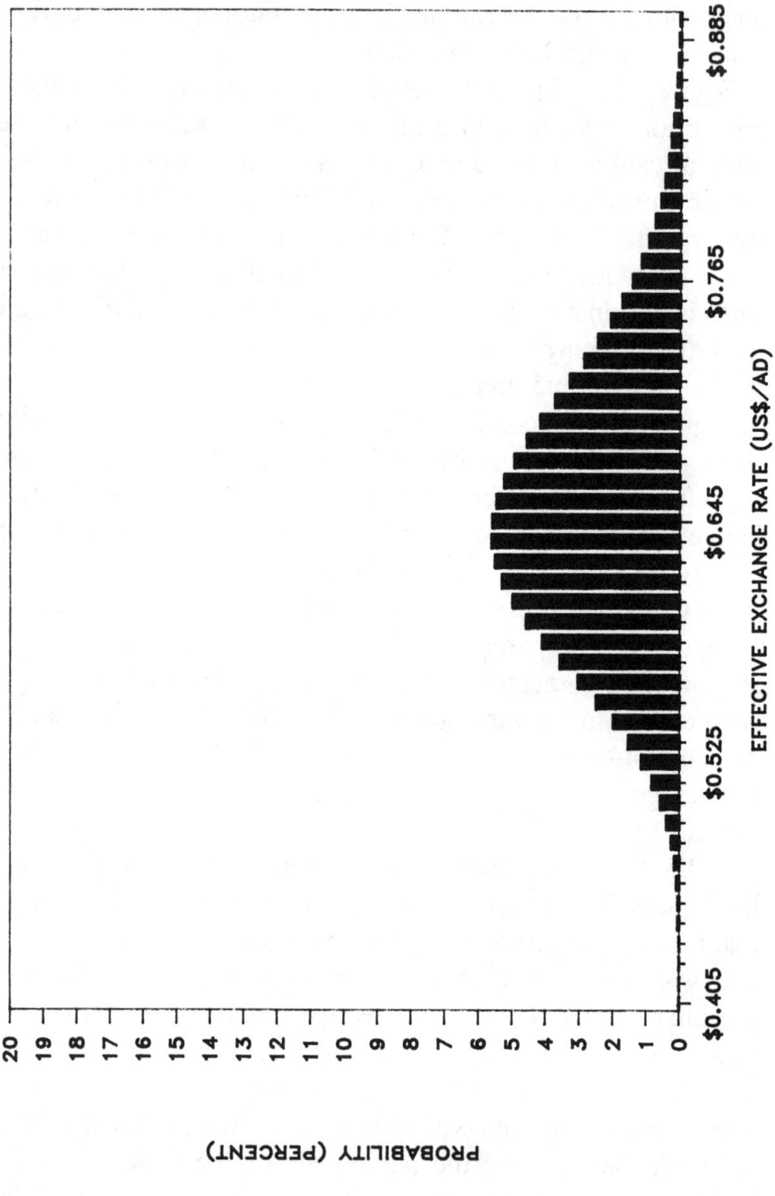

FIGURE 9B PROBABILITY DISTRIBUTION OF THE EFFECTIVE EXCHANGE RATE
Put at .54 $/AD with Distribution about .65 $/AD

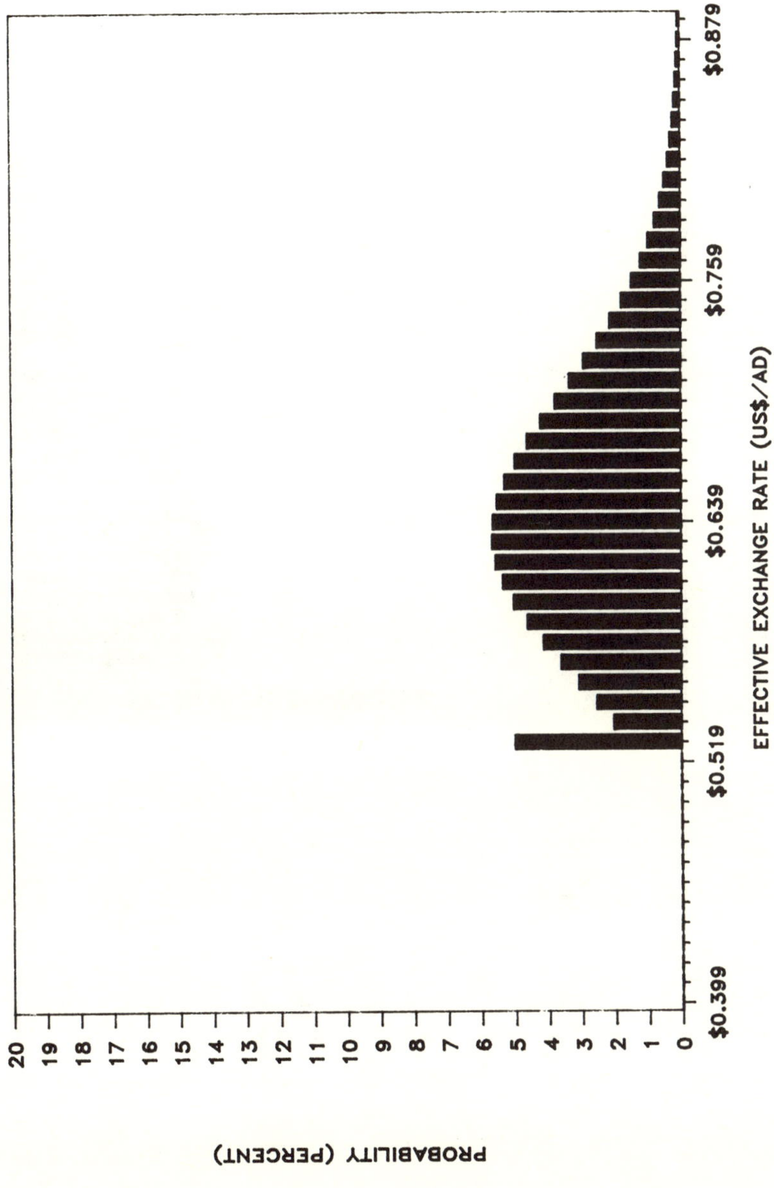

FIGURE 9C PROBABILITY DISTRIBUTION OF THE EFFECTIVE EXCHANGE RATE
Put at .57 $/AD with Distribution about .65 $/AD

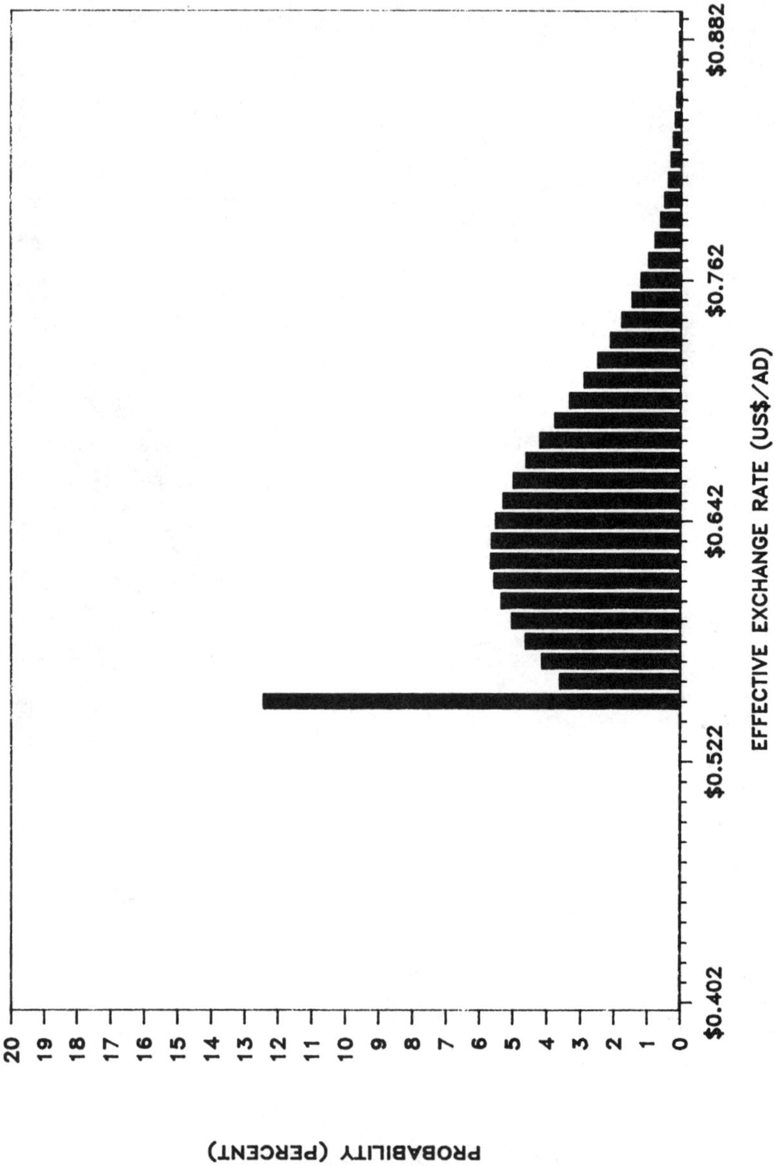

FIGURE 9D PROBABILITY DISTRIBUTION OF THE EFFECTIVE EXCHANGE RATE
Put at .63 $/AD with Distribution about .65 $/AD

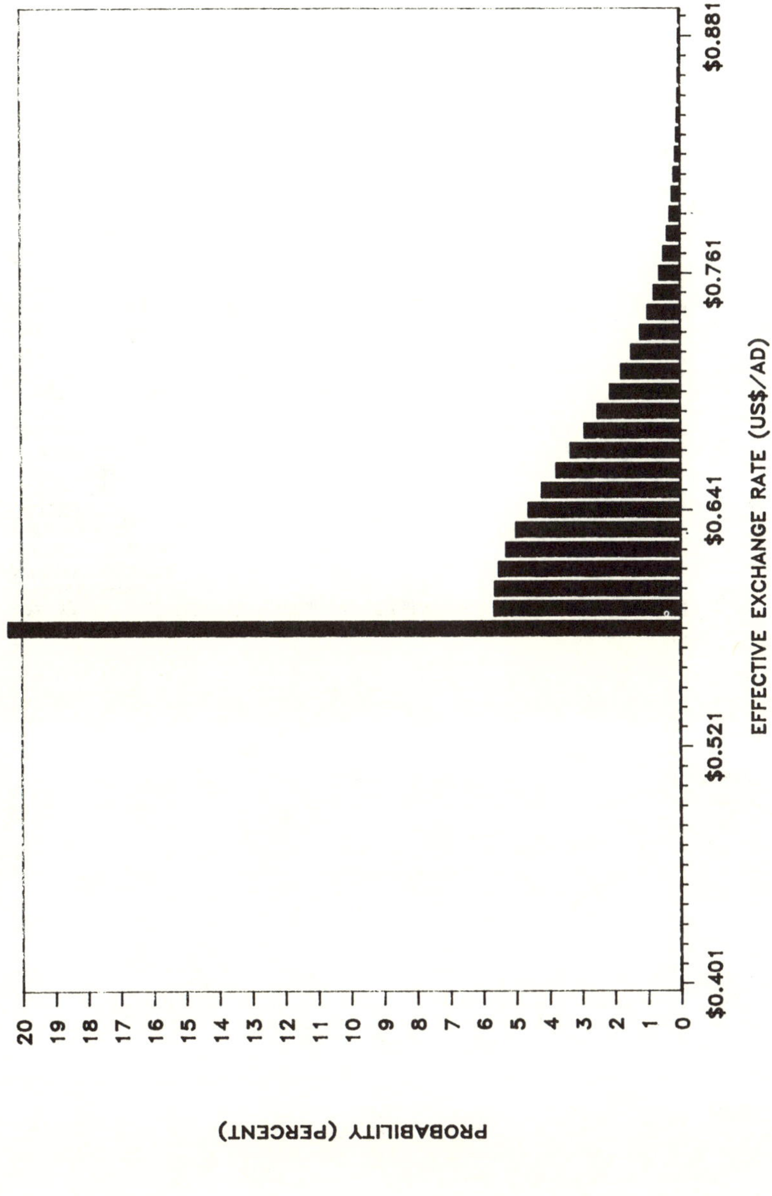

FIGURE 9E PROBABILITY DISTRIBUTION OF THE EFFECTIVE EXCHANGE RATE
Put at .66 $/AD with Distribution about .65 $/AD

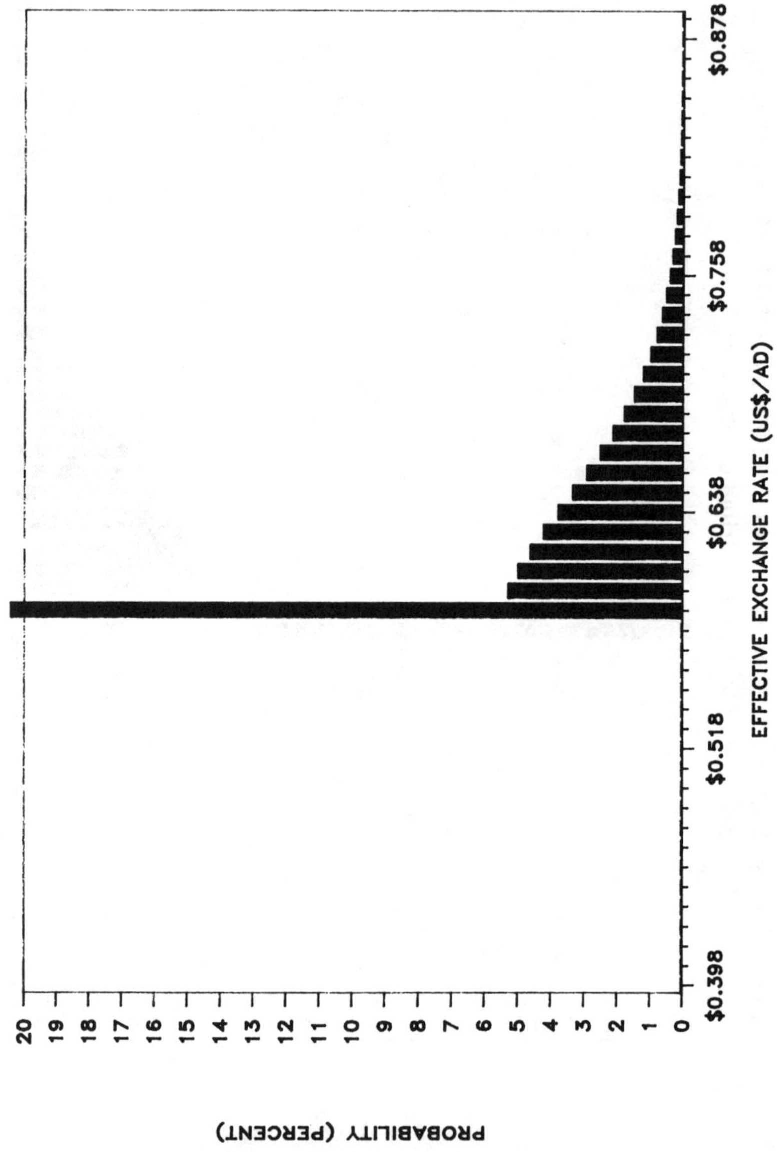

FIGURE 9F PROBABILITY DISTRIBUTION OF THE EFFECTIVE EXCHANGE RATE
Put at .75 $/AD with Distribution about .65 $/AD

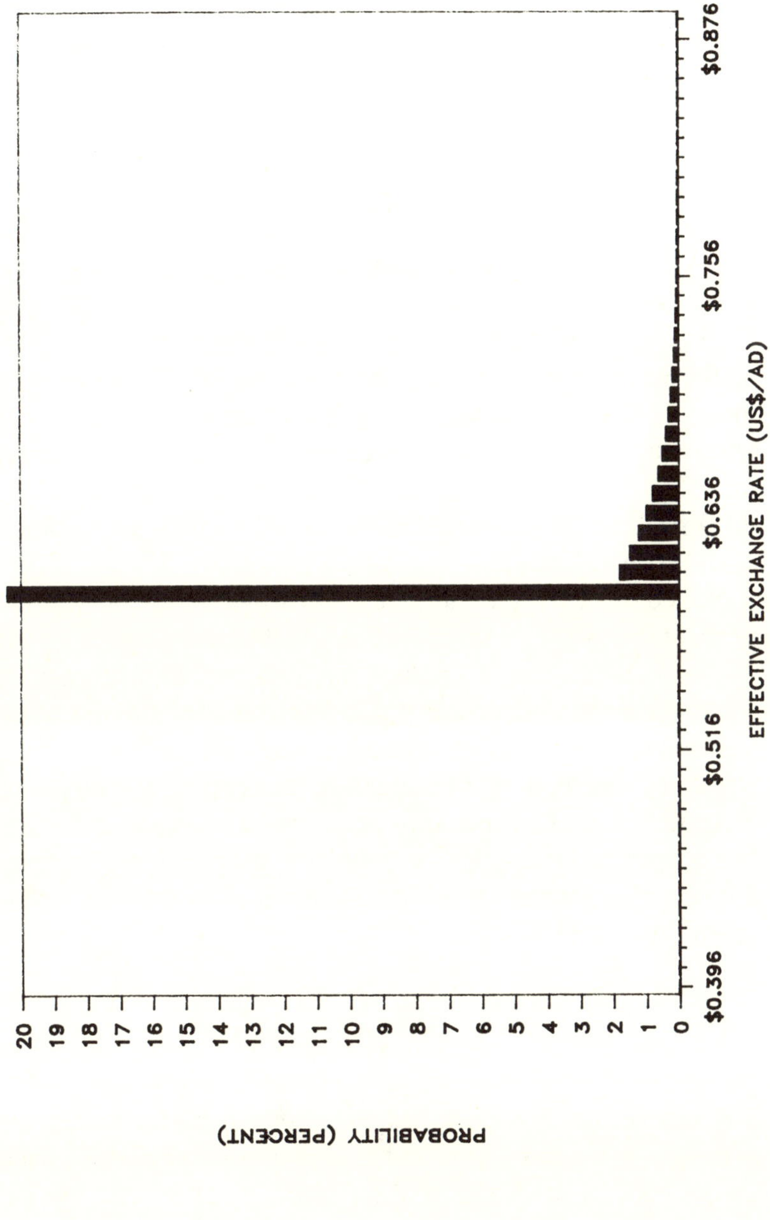

continuum of distributions, varying smoothly from a bell-shaped normal curve to a single spike located at the forward rate. Although forward rate strategies and put option strategies are bounded by the same limiting effective exchange rate distributions, the hedging strategies that intermediate between an unhedged and a completely hedged position are different. Forward strategies produce symmetric effective rate distributions, shown in Figures 7A–7D; the corresponding put option strategies, Figures 9B–9E, are asymmetric.

Varying the Number of Put Options Bought

Figure 5C illustrated the effect of hedging by buying a put option on the entire foreign currency exposure. As an alternative, a portfolio manager could employ a put option strategy which covers only a portion of his foreign exchange exposure. Figures 10A–10F illustrate the effect of covering 0 percent, 20 percent, 40 percent, 60 percent, 80 percent and 100 percent of the exposure with put options struck at the forward rate.

Notice that even though partial put strategies do not eliminate the probability in the unfavorable tail of the distribution of effective exchange rates, they do reduce the unfavorable outcomes, without a corresponding reduction in the likelihood of the most favorable outcomes. The effective exchange rate distribution of partial put strategies, like that of covering the entire exposure with put options, is asymmetric. The resulting positions are similar to bond portfolios constructed with positive convexity: the position gains more from a favorable exchange rate change than it loses from an unfavorable change of equal magnitude.

CONCLUSION

This chapter has examined hedging a representative foreign currency exposure using basic forward and option strategies. In each case, the probability distribution of the effective exchange rate was used

FIGURE 9G IN-THE-MONEY PUT AND FORWARD STRATEGIES COMPARED

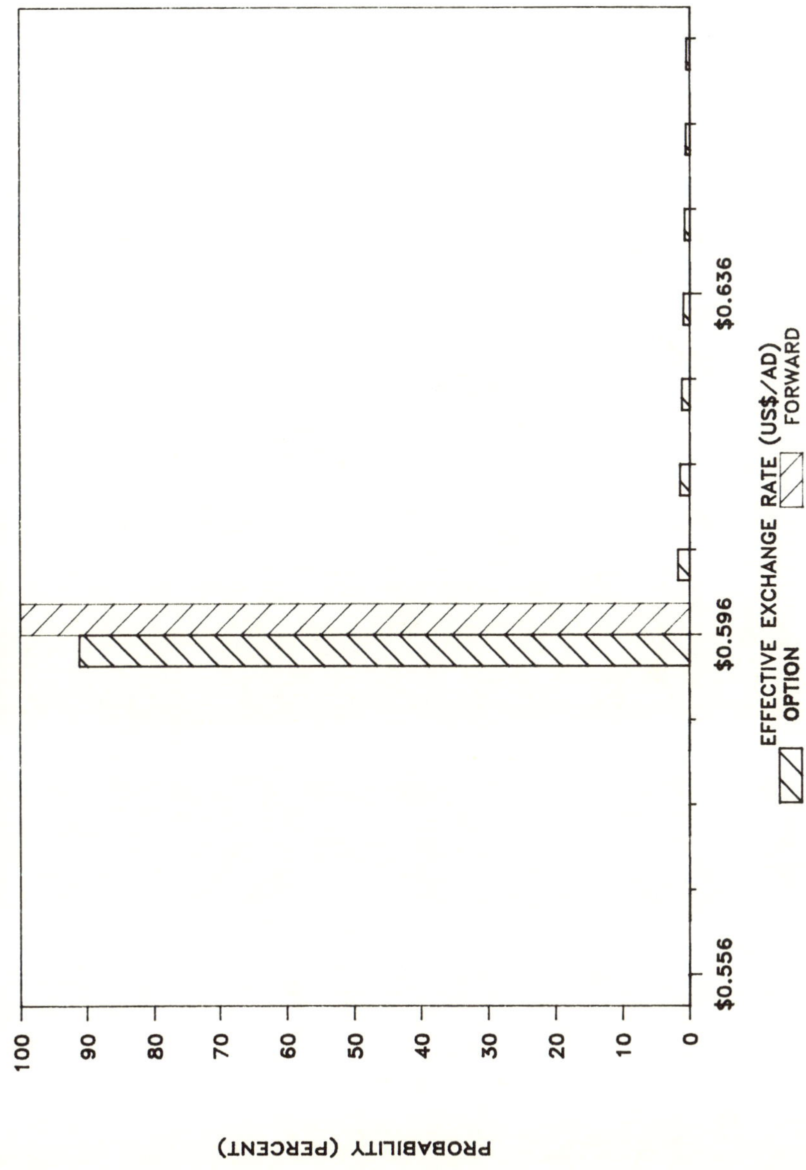

FIGURE 9H OUT-OF-THE-MONEY PUT AND UNHEDGED STRATEGIES COMPARED

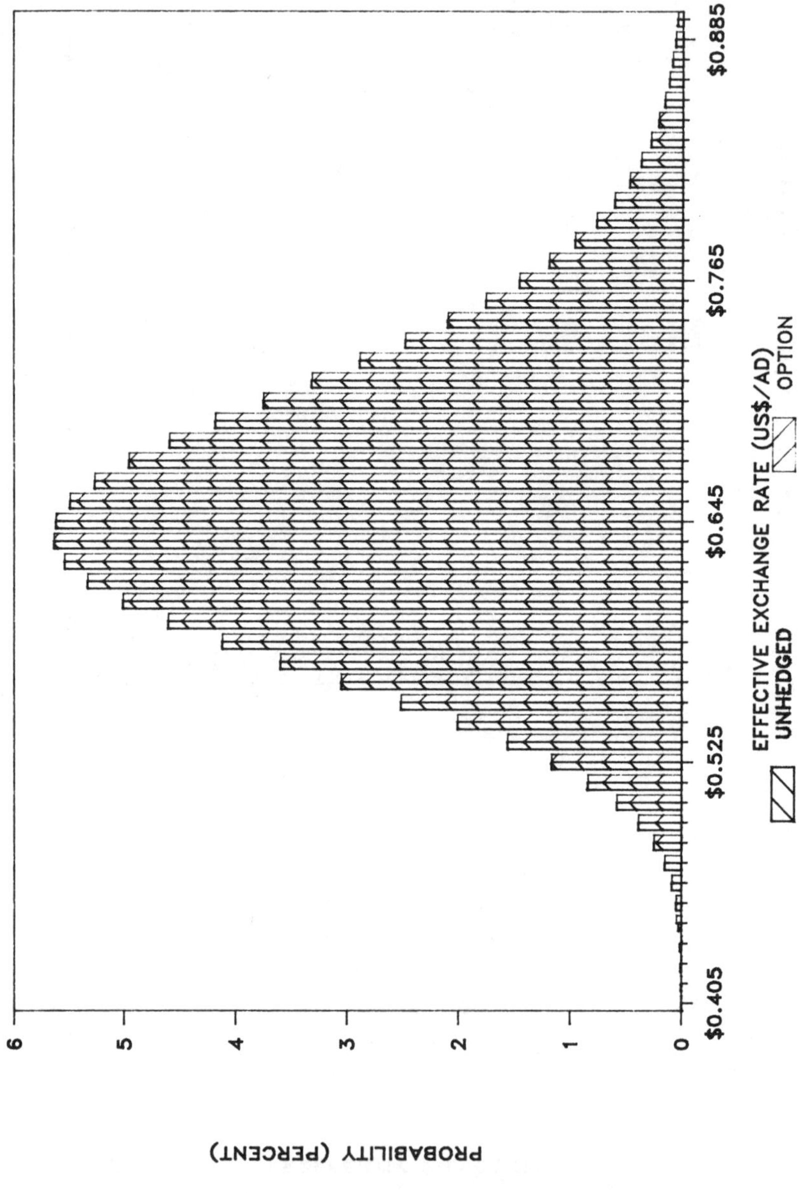

FIGURE 10A PROBABILITY DISTRIBUTION OF THE EFFECTIVE EXCHANGE RATE
0% Put Protection at .60 $/AD with Distribution about .65 $/AD

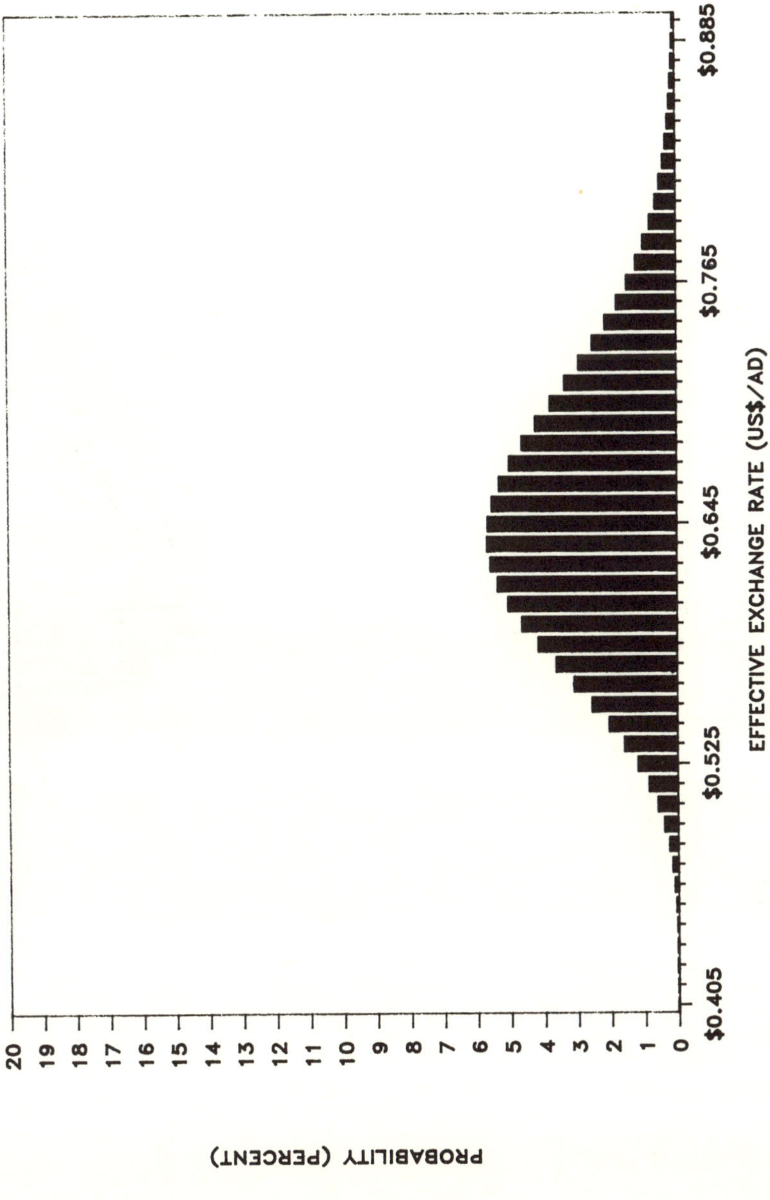

FIGURE 10B PROBABILITY DISTRIBUTION OF THE EFFECTIVE EXCHANGE RATE
20% Put Protection at .60 $/AD with Distribution about .65 $/AD

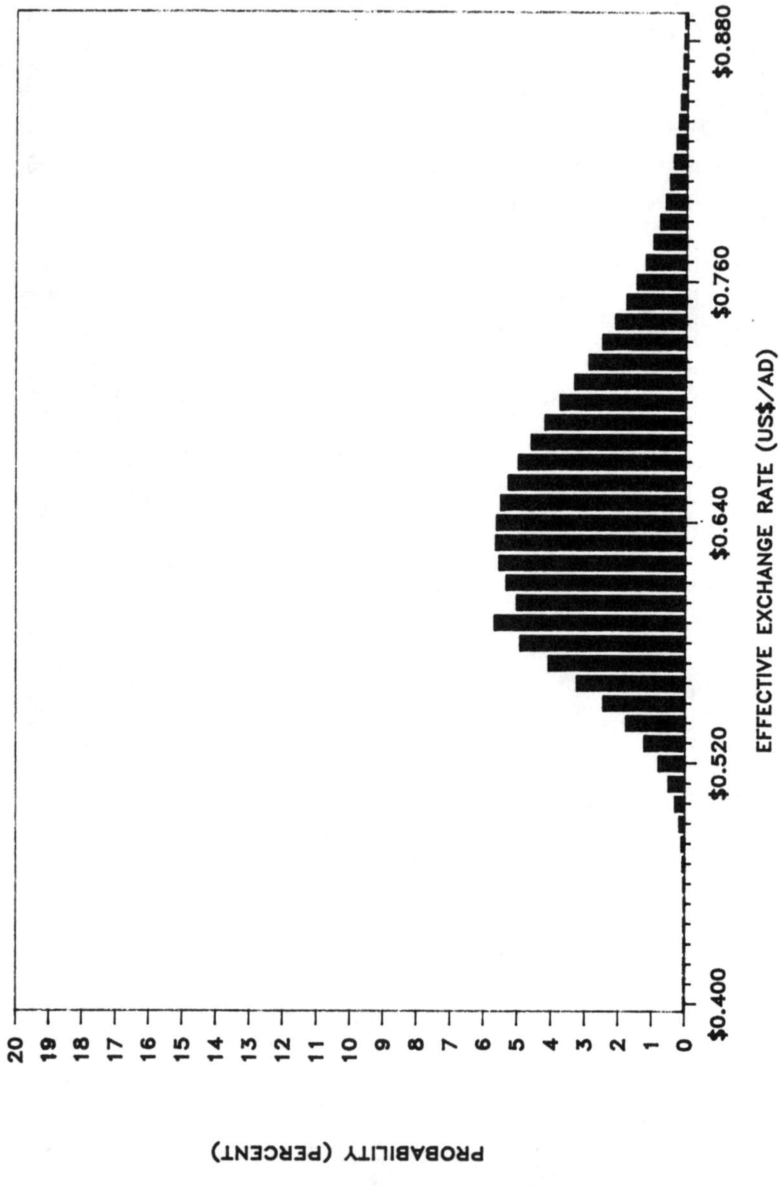

FIGURE 10C PROBABILITY DISTRIBUTION OF THE EFFECTIVE EXCHANGE RATE
40% Put Protection at .60 $/AD with Distribution about .65 $/AD

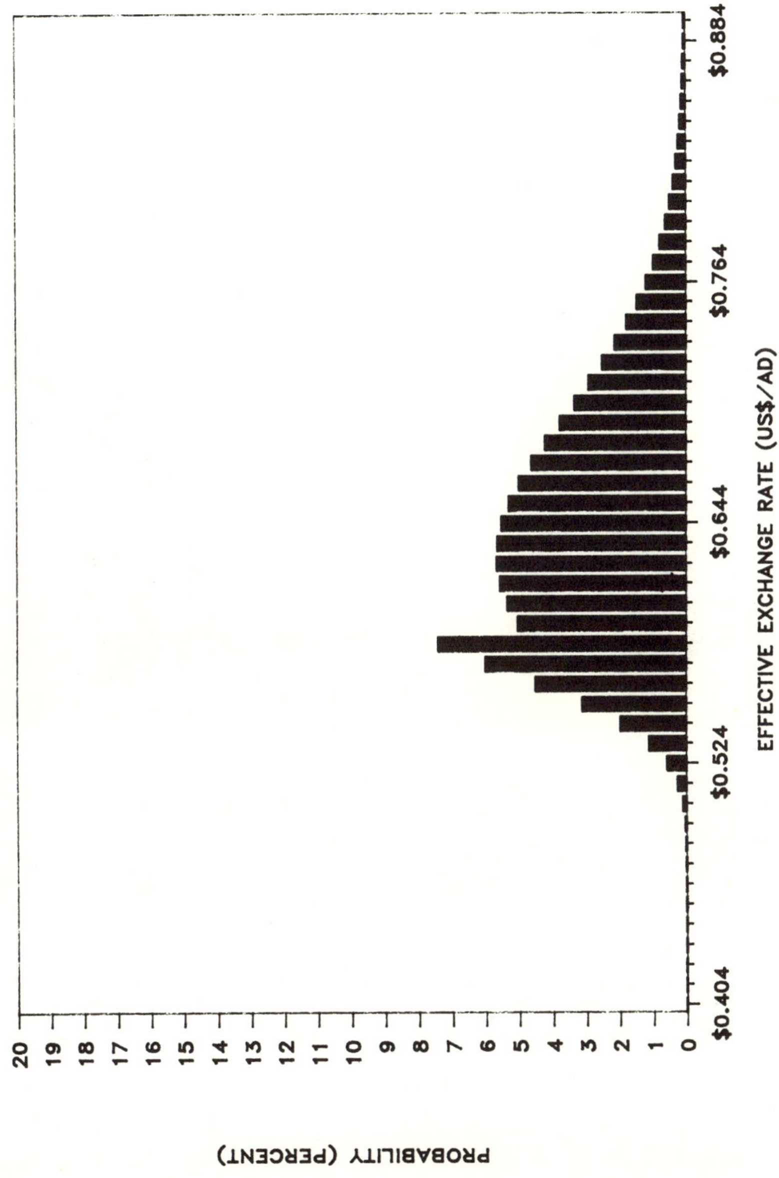

FIGURE 10D PROBABILITY DISTRIBUTION OF THE EFFECTIVE EXCHANGE RATE
60% Put Protection at .60 $/AD with Distribution about .65 $/AD

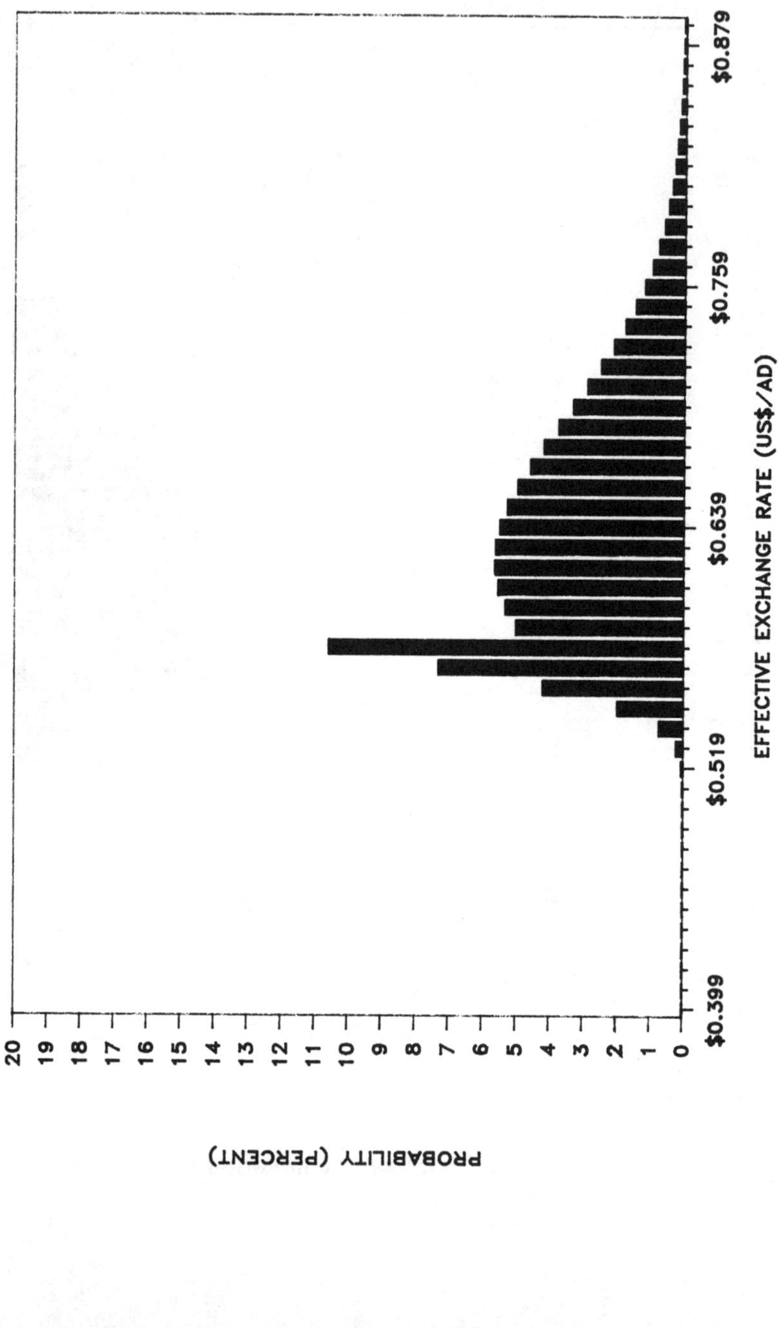

FIGURE 10E PROBABILITY DISTRIBUTION OF THE EFFECTIVE EXCHANGE RATE
80% Put Protection at .60 $/AD with Distribution about .65 $/AD

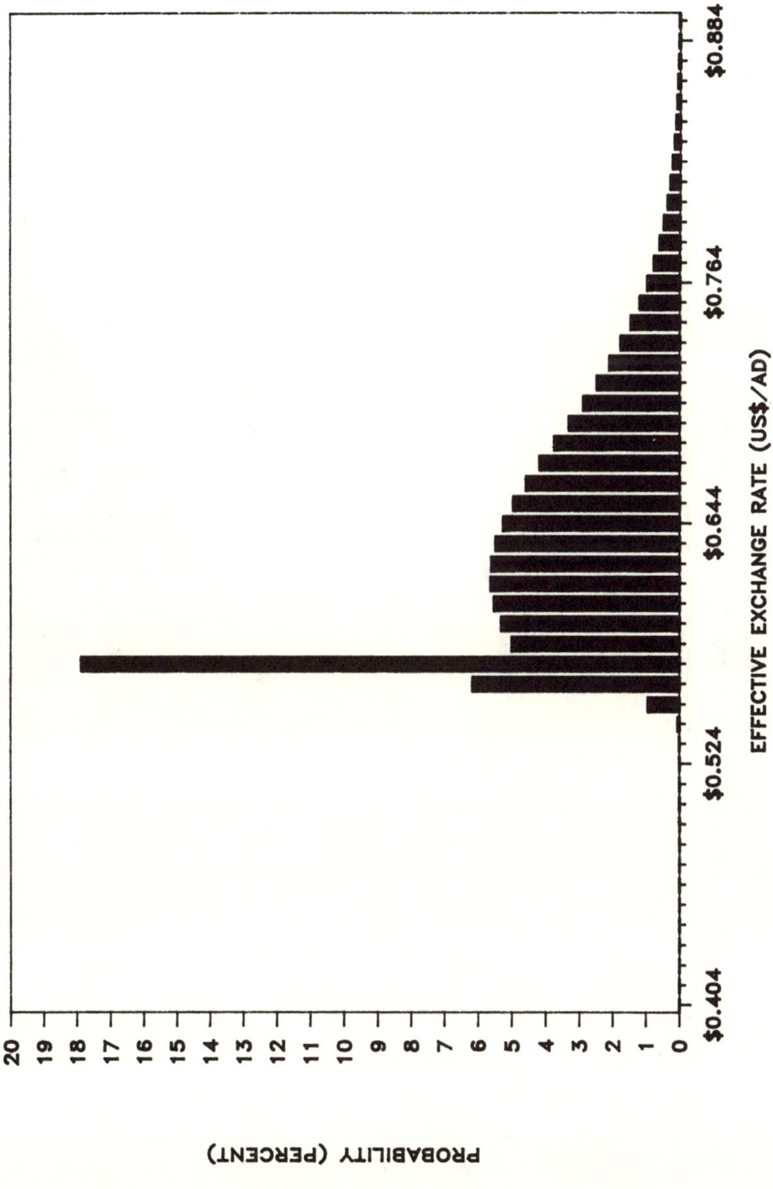

FIGURE 10F PROBABILITY DISTRIBUTION OF THE EFFECTIVE EXCHANGE RATE
100% Put Protection at .60 $/AD with Distribution about .65 $/AD

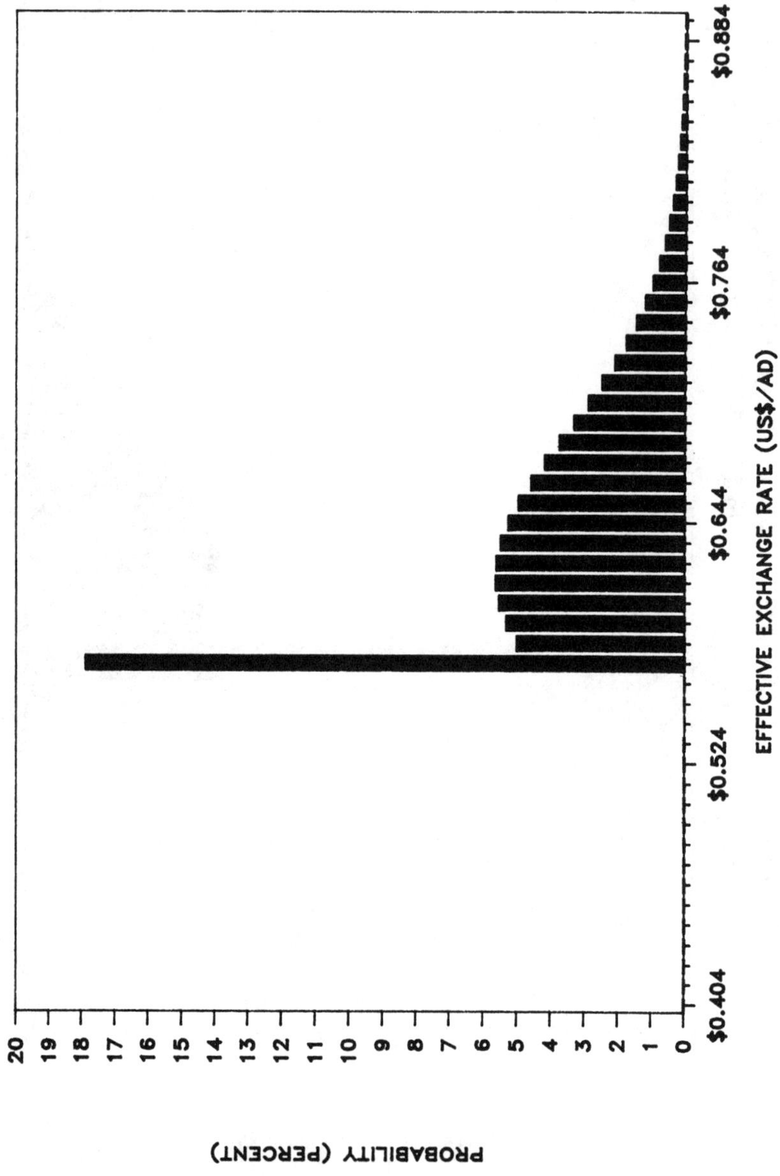

to illustrate the most important features of the hedged position: the mean, or expected effective rate, its dispersion, and the best or worst case outcome. The major conclusions are:

(i) A portfolio manager who believes that the forward rate is an unbiased predictor of the future spot rate should always hedge his exposures entirely in the forward exchange market.

(ii) The unhedged distribution, Figure 5A, and the forward hedge, Figure 5B, are limiting cases of forward market strategies. As we have shown in Figures 9A and 9F, they are also the limiting cases of put option strategies. The intermediate hedges, however, differ: forward hedges produce symmetric probability distributions, while option hedges characteristically produce a skewed distribution.

BIBLIOGRAPHY

Arditti, F. and K. John. ''Spanning the State Space with Options,'' *Journal of Financial and Quantitative Analysis* 15 (March 1980), pp. 1-9

Bilson, John. ''The Speculative Efficiency Hypothesis,'' *Journal of Business* 54 (July 1981), pp. 435-54

Black, Fischer. ''Fact and Fantasy in the Use of Options,'' *Financial Analysts Journal* 31 (July 1975), pp. 36-41

Black, Fischer and Myron Scholes. ''The Pricing of Options and Corporate Liabilities,'' *Journal of Political Economy* 81 (May 1973), pp. 637-54

Bookstabler, Richard M. and Roger C. Clarke. *Option Strategies for Institutional Investment Management* (Addison-Wesley 1983)

Thomas, Lee. ''Currency Risk in International Equity Portfolios'' (Goldman, Sachs & Co. 1986)

Thomas, Lee. ''A Winning Strategy for Currency Futures Speculation,'' *Journal of Portfolio Management* (Fall 1985), pp. 65-69

Thomas, Lee. ''Random Walk Profits in Currency Futures Trading,'' *Journal of Futures Markets* 6 (No. 1 1986), pp. 109-25

NOTES

[1]For example, over the 1980-1985 period, exchange rate changes accounted for an average of one-quarter of the total variability of foreign equity prices, as measured by a dollar-based investor. See Thomas (1986).

[2]Particularly, mean-variance portfolio construction is applicable only to the class of quadratic utility functions.

[3]Except in the extreme case when the standard deviation is reduced to zero.

[4]In the case of assets with limited liability, such as currencies, a portfolio manager's maximum possible loss on an unhedged exposure is 100 percent.

[5]We could, of course, extend mean variance portfolio theory by maximizing a utility function with three arguments: expected return, standard deviation of return, and skewness.

[6]This example illustrates hedging a long currency position. It could as easily illustrate hedging a short position — for instance, that of an investor who anticipates purchasing Australian securities one year hence. A parallel set of diagrams could be drawn and analogous strategies constructed. Also, the Australian dollar proceeds of the bond sale are taken to be given, and known in advance. This is a heroic assumption, but consideration of an integrated framework for interest rate and exchange rate risk management is beyond the scope of this chapter.

For formal discussion of options' usefulness in expanding investors' opportunity set, see Arditti and John (1980). Bookstabler and Clarke offer empirical evidence.

[7]The conventional assumption is that the logarithm of the future exchange rate, rather than the level of the exchange rate, is normally distributed. For example, the probability that the logarithm of the future exchange rate will lie 0.05 above its mean equals the probability that it will lie 0.05 below its mean. This implies that the chances the exchange rate will be US$0.6307/AD (+3.07¢) is the same as the chance it will be US$0.5707/AD (−2.93¢). As a consequence, the probability distribution of the level of the future exchange rate, shown in Figure 1, is slightly asymmetric.

[8]In this simple case, the effective exchange rate equals the ending rate, since no option premiums are paid or received. So, the ending exchange rate probability distribution and the ending effective exchange rate distribution are identical.

[9]Bilson (1981 and Thomas (1985, 1986) compare the forecasting efficacy of the uncovered parity and random walk hypotheses.

[10]Option replication trading rules, also called dynamic forward market strategies, can approximate the return distributions of options. They are discussed in the next chapter.

[11]The options are assumed to be priced at their theoretical value, given the assumed volatility of 11 percent (annualized) and the interest rate differential implied by the forward discount of US$0.05/AD on Australian dollars.

[12]Strictly, this is only true if exchange rate risk is systematic (or if the market prices nonsystematic risk). If it is not, hedging yields no advantage and may raise transactions costs. The subject of diversifying exchange rate risk is beyond the scope of this chapter.

[13]The worst case selling price for Australian dollars, shown in Table 3, is computed as follows. With, for example, 25 percent covered, the portfolio manager is assured of receiving US$0.60/AD on a quarter of his exposure; in the worst case, he receives nothing for the remainder. His worse average effective exchange rate is then 0.25(0.60)+0.75(0.00).

CHAPTER FOURTEEN

LEE R. THOMAS, III is a Vice President and the Director of the Currency Strategies Group in the J. Aron Division of Goldman, Sachs & Co. The Currency Strategies group develops proprietory trading strategies, designs currency and commodity hedges for Goldman Sachs' own positions and those of its clients, and is also charged with new financial product development.

Mr. Thomas holds a Ph.D. in Economics from Tulane University. Most of his published research is in the areas of international finance, international monetary theory, and international financial markets.

OPTION REPLICATION STRATEGIES FOR MANAGING FOREIGN CURRENCY EXPOSURES

Lee R. Thomas, Director
Currency and Commodity Strategies Group,
Goldman, Sachs & Co.
New York, New York

The purpose of this chapter is to describe dynamic hedging techniques for managing foreign currency exposures. Before proceeding, it will be helpful to consider some hypothetical examples illustrating the kinds of hedging problems that frequently arise in international trade or investment.

Example 1. A U.S. pension fund manager who bought Japanese stocks in early 1984 enjoyed a substantial profit over two years. Part of that appreciation came from the local currency change in Japanese share prices. The remainder resulted from the decline of the U.S. dollar against the yen.

The manager still wishes to hold Japanese equities, but, observing that the dollar has fallen substantially, he wants to insure against foreign exchange losses in the event of a reversal. At the same time, he does not want to sacrifice his potential return in its entirety if the yen appreciates further. The manager is not permitted by the pension plan sponsors to hedge using options.

Example 2. A U.S. investor who owns a large portfolio of high-yielding bonds denominated in Australian dollars is concerned about his exchange exposure. He could cover interest and principal in the long-dated forward exchange market, but by so doing he would concede all of his yield advantage. Buying dollar call options, which would guarantee his receiving at least the current U.S. dollar/Australian dollar exchange rate when he sells his foreign currency, would cost even more than using forward contracts.

Example 3. A U.S. firm has won a major contract to supply computerized control equipment to an Austrian chemical plant. To win the bid, the company's treasurer agreed to take payment in local currency, and his schilling exposure extends over the next two years. Company policy generally prohibits hedging with options. But this is irrelevant in this case, since there is no market for two-year Austrian schilling options.

Any of these hypothetical hedging problems can be solved using "portfolio insurance," a strategy that is executed in the forward or spot exchange market, but which produces a return profile like an option's. Portfolio insurance can also be called dynamic hedging, or synthetic option replication. Its foundations lie in the option pricing literature.

THE BLACK-SCHOLES MODEL

The Black-Scholes option valuation formula, published in 1973, was the first theory to satisfactorily explain the pricing of contingent claims. Its arbitrage argument is based on the following thought experiment.

Imagine that an investor sold an option, and simultaneously bought just enough of the underlying security, foreign currency, or commodity so that his overall position was perfectly hedged. Then the return to his portfolio—short an option, and long the underlying asset—would be immunized against small changes, up or down, in the underlying asset's price. Because this portfolio is riskless, the market would have to price it to produce a yield equal to that offered by short-term, default-free debt.

To execute this strategy, option writers must determine how much of the underlying asset to buy to be perfectly hedged. Black and Scholes derived the necessary hedge ratio under one set of assumptions; others subsequently developed the correct option pricing and hedging formulas under different assumptions.[1] These problems and their solutions stimulated an interest in portfolio insurance.

Portfolio insurance strategies follow easily from the logic of the Black-Scholes option pricing model. If a position in the underlying asset can perfectly hedge an option, then that position must exactly duplicate the option's payoff (but in reverse). That is, whenever the option rises in value, then the position in the underlying asset must fall by an equal amount. So holding the appropriate position in the underlying asset—in fact, the same position an option writer would use to hedge his exposure—must yield identical results (under ideal conditions) to holding the option itself. If the option *writer* can *hedge* himself by synthesizing the option's payoff in another market, then the option *buyer* can also synthesize the option's payoff in that market, and so secure option-like hedging protection without actually buying options.

In short, option pricing theory is based on insights concerning option hedging; option hedging is a way to duplicate an option's payoff by buying and selling the underlying asset. Portfolio insurance is a strategy that substitutes an option-replicating position in the underlying stock, commodity or currency for the option itself. This is why we call "portfolio insurance" a "synthetic option" or an "option-replicating" strategy. To see why it could also be called a "dynamic hedging strategy," we must consider how an option is hedged, or replicated, by trading the underlying asset.

DELTA HEDGING

The quantity of the underlying asset that an option writer must buy to optimally hedge an option, expressed as a fraction, is called the option's "delta." Delta depends on the characteristics of the option, asset volatility, interest rates and the current price of the underlying currency, equity, or commodity. As the price of the underlying asset rises, the delta for a call option will also rise. When the call is deeply in the money, delta approaches one. As the price of the underlying asset falls, the value of delta approaches zero.

As the value of the underlying asset rises, so does the delta of a call on that asset. To maintain a hedge, an option writer would have to buy more of the underlying asset whenever it appreciated. As the value of the underlying asset fell, the call writer would adjust this hedge by reducing his position in the underlying asset. As the price of the underlying asset rises and falls, the hedger systematically "buys high" and "sells low," losing money on each completed trade.

Black and Scholes proved that an option is worth the present value of the losses a writer expects to sustain by following this hedging strategy over the option's life, discounted at the riskless interest rate. That is why volatility is so important in determining the value of an option—the more volatile the underlying asset's price, the more of these losing hedging transactions the writer should expect over the option's life.

SIMPLIFYING PORTFOLIO INSURANCE

Unfortunately, portfolio insurance that uses delta hedging to replicate an option requires prodigious calculations. The complicated option formulas make it hard to evaluate and compare competing strategies. However, effective option-like return profiles with a floor or ceiling can be constructed using simple and easy-to-understand trading rules.[2]

Consider the portfolio manager described in the introduction who holds yen-denominated financial assets.[3] Suppose he decided to place a floor of 80 percent under the dollar value of his yen holdings; that is, he is unwilling to lose more than 20 percent of the dollar value of his yen.

The manager could accomplish this by partitioning his portfolio into two parts, i.e., a hedged and an unhedged component. The hedged yen are then covered by a forward contract that obligates the portfolio manager to sell them on a set day at a set dollar price. As a consequence, the hedged yen holding is equivalent to a dollar holding. Because of covered interest parity, it yields the same interest rate as a dollar holding, and its dollar value is free of any exchange risk.

In contrast, the portfolio manager's unhedged yen earn the yen rate of interest, and yield capital gains if the yen appreciates against the dollar. Of course, if the yen falls, the manager suffers a capital loss on the unhedged position. The unhedged yen define his exchange rate exposure.

A simple way to ensure that the manager could lose no more than 20 percent of his portfolio's value would be for him to hold only 20 percent of the starting value of his yen unhedged at all times. That is, he could sell 80 percent of his yen forward. Then, even if the yen became worthless, he would lose only 20 percent of his initial stake.

Unfortunately, with this position the manager would not benefit much if the yen appreciates. Fortunately, he can secure more exchange rate exposure while still maintaining an 80 percent *floor* on the value of his yen. The following explains how to create this option-like exchange risk hedge without using option pricing models.

The first step is to define the investor's cushion, which is the difference between the current dollar value of the portfolio manager's yen holdings and the floor. Recall that the floor is the portion of the portfolio that is protected by a forward currency contract. Obviously, the cushion represents the most a manager can lose without violating his floor. The cushion changes whenever the yen appreciates or depreciates. For example, if the yen portfolio is originally worth \$5MM, and the floor is set at 80 percent of this, or \$4MM, then the cushion starts at \$1MM. If the value of the portfolio subsequently falls to \$4.8MM as a result of a decline in the yen, then the cushion drops to \$0.8MM.

Since the portfolio manager can never let his cushion fall below zero, he must trade conservatively when it becomes low. But if the yen appreciates his cushion will rise, and he can become more aggressive and increase his yen exposure. The manager's trading strategy will be to cover more yen as the exchange rate moves unfavorably, and to hold more yen uncovered as the yen appreciates.[4]

This strategy can be illustrated as follows: First, the portfolio manager should choose his initial exposure at a level greater than his cushion. For example, with the yen portfolio worth \$5MM and the floor fixed at \$4MM (cushion = \$1MM), he might set his exposure equal to \$2MM, or twice his cushion. The amount of exposure that he assumes divided by his cushion is called his multiple.

Each day the portfolio manager must recompute his cushion by comparing the dollar value of his hedged and unhedged yen holdings (and his forward contracts) to \$4MM. Then he buys or sells enough forward contracts to bring his exposure back to twice his cushion. This simple trading rule will ensure that he never violates his floor, while permitting him to participate in any favorable exchange rate changes.

Of course, a hedger could set his initial exposure at some other multiple—say, three rather than two times his cushion. Higher multiples are more aggressive. The hedger enjoys larger gains if the yen appreciates, but if the yen falls, he approaches his floor more quickly. As a consequence, there is a greater chance that in any given period a hedger using a higher multiple will reach his floor. In this event, he must stop trading in forward currency contracts.

In brief, to use "portfolio insurance" in the currency markets a hedger need only follow this strategy:

(i) Choose a *floor*. The difference between the floor and the dollar value of the foreign currency holdings is the *cushion.*
(ii) Choose a *multiple* of the cushion. This gives the initial exchange rate exposure.
(iii) Each day buy or sell forward foreign currency until the exposure equals the cushion times the multiple.

SUMMARY

Dynamic currency risk hedging permits international traders or investors to participate in favorable exchange rate changes, while simultaneously placing an absolute floor on their exposure. The original designs for dynamic hedging strategies were based on formulas derived from the option pricing literature. They used option pricing formulas, which many hedgers may find complex and difficult to use. Recently, new and conceptually simpler approaches have been developed.

One approach described in this chapter depends on buying and selling forward contracts on a fraction of the exposure. The fraction of the portfolio that is unhedged ("the exposure") approaches zero (asymptotically) as the value of the portfolio approaches the floor, or minimum portfolio value, specified when the hedge was initiated. The trajectory of the exposure is controlled by a parameter ("the multiple") which can be varied so that aggressive or conservative hedging schemes can be implemented.

This dynamic hedging approach is simple and easy to implement. It does not require understanding option pricing theory, even though it offers option-like hedging performance.

BIBLIOGRAPHY

Black, Fischer and Jones, Robert. ''Simplifying Portfolio Insurance'' (Goldman, Sachs and Co.) (August 1986).

Black, Fischer and Scholes, Myron. ''The Pricing of Options and Corporate Liabilities,'' *Journal of Political Economy* 81 (1973): 637-59.

Brennan, Michael and Solanki, R. ''Optimal Portfolio Insurance,'' *Journal of Financial and Quantitative Analysis* 16 (September 1981): 279-300.

Cox, John and Ross, Stephen. ''The Valuation of Options for Alternate Stochastic Processes,'' *Journal of Financial Economics* 3 (1976): 145-66.

Leland, Hayne. ''Option Pricing and Replication with Transaction Costs,'' *Journal of Finance* 60 (1986): 1283-1301.

Perold, Andre. ''Constant Proportion Portfolio Insurance,'' unpublished manuscript, Harvard Business School.

Tilley, James and Latamer, Gary. ''A Synthetic Option Framework for Asset Allocation,'' *Financial Analysts Journal* (May-June 1985): 32-43.

NOTES

[1]Particularly, see Cox and Ross (1976).

[2]The following section relies heavily on Black and Jones (1986). Also, see Perold (1986). Ironically, Fischer Black, who along with Myron Scholes developed the first successful option pricing formula, has also been prominent in devising portfolio insurance strategies that eschew these formulas.

[3]What follows treats the yen value of the portfolio as a constant. Implicitly, we assume that the portfolio manager does not wish to hedge his yen-measured equity price risk. By suitably modifying the trading rules, the portfolio manager could manage his exchange rate risk and equity risk simultaneously.

[4]This is the trading strategy followed by someone who has sold a yen call and is hedging his exposure. It is also the trading style of a speculator who believes that exchange rates follow trends.

SECTION III

Instruments Available to International Investors

CHAPTER FIFTEEN

EDWARD R. HART is a Vice President of Bache Securities, responsible for International Fixed Income. He has some ten years' experience of world capital markets, gained in both broking and international fixed income portfolio management.

Prior to his current appointment he was manager of the London branch of Julius Baer Investment Management Inc, an SEC registered investment advisor specialising in institutional money management.

Edward Hart received a Master's degree in Economics from the London School of Enonomics.

THE ROLE OF FIXED RATE INSTRUMENTS IN INTERNATIONAL PORTFOLIOS

Edward R. Hart
Vice President, Bache Securities
Geneva, Switzerland

INTRODUCTION

International investment, rigorously interpreted, is no more than fifteen years old. The gradual collapse of fixed exchange rates in the early 'seventies provided the impetus for a closer examination of the investment opportunities available, though practical difficulties were considerable. Initial difficulties included a general ignorance regarding the theory of international investment and the instruments of foreign markets; and practical problems—settlement and clearance procedures, tax liabilities, etc.—were poorly documented. In terms of fixed income markets, the dollar Eurobond market was, perhaps, the primary exception. This market was also the closest to the U.S. domestic capital market due to the absence of exchange rate risk and the fact that its behavior most closely mirrored that of domestic dollar interest rates.

It is not surprising, therefore, that the bulk of U.S. institutional investment abroad (for which the most accurate data are available) has been in the shape of equities rather than fixed income. Indeed, only in the last few years—with the increasingly available knowledge of foreign capital markets, together with the gradual dismantling of withholding taxes worldwide—has the concept of a program of investment in international bond markets begun to receive a small following in the U.S. institutional market.

Data compiled by InterSec Research Corp., Stamford, CT. show that by the end of 1985 some $3 billion of U.S. pension fund money was invested in foreign fixed income compared with about $24 billion in overseas equities. Indeed, total investment abroad by U.S. pension funds has risen from only $7 billion at the end of 1982. In view of the size of the U.S. ERISA market (currently $1.5 trillion), this demonstrates how little diversification into foreign assets has actually occurred, irrespective of the split between stocks and bonds.

The fact that foreign stocks should have attracted more attention than foreign bonds cannot be ascribed to any real difference in the sizes of these markets nor in their suitability for large-scale institutional investment (see Figure 1). Both bond and stock markets, taken as a whole, have shown similar rates of growth in recent years. The

FIGURE 1 PRINCIPAL WORLD BOND AND EQUITY MARKETS
U.S. Dollar Billions

	Bonds	Equities
1977	2,100	1,387
1978	2,490	1,632
1979	2,880	1,835
1980	2,860	2,321
1981	3,050	2,230
1982	3,380	2,352
1983	3,870	2,858
1984	4,679	2,945
1985	5,850	4,039
Compound annual rate of growth	13.7 %	14.2 %

Source: Morgan Stanley Capital International Perspective/Salomon Brothers

apparent neglect of foreign bonds is probably the consequence of other factors, to be examined later in this chapter.

CHARACTERISTICS OF WORLD DEBT MARKETS

Although the U.S. is easily the largest single bond market in the world (measured by market capitalization), it nevertheless accounts for just over half of a universe consisting of the world's major fixed income markets. Japan's market is roughly one-third the size of the U.S. market; the remaining markets are significantly smaller (see figure 2).

As shown in Figure 3, foreign bond markets tend to have a higher preponderance of government and government-related issues relative to corporate issues than is the case in the United States. This most likely reflects different tax structures abroad and, until recently, the fact that other major Western economies have tended to run larger fiscal deficits (when measured as a proportion of gross national product). Foreign bond markets, therefore, need not necessarily involve the investor in an appraisal of specific credit risk, given that some

FIGURE 2 RELATIVE BOND MARKET SIZE
$ Billions

	Market Capitalization	% Total	% Non-$U.S.
Japan	$ 1110	19	40
Germany	414	7	15
Italy	272	5	10
U.K.	206	4	7
France	163	3	6
Canada	131	2	5
Switzerland	82	1	3
Other Major Markets	422	7	14
U.S.	3,050	52	-
Total Markets	**$5,850**	**100%**	**100%**

Source: Salomon Brothers

FIGURE 3 QUALITY OF WORLD DEBT MARKETS

	Central Govt/Agency	Bank Mortgage	Corporate	*Other
Japan	68%	16%	5%	11%
Germany	21	66	–	13
Italy	74	12	14	–
U.K.	87	–	6	7
Canada	41	–	23	36
France	78	–	18	4
Australia	75	–	20	5
Other European	48	27	12	13
Total Non-U.S.	**59%**	**25%**	**7%**	**9%**
U.S.	53	–	23	24
Total Markets	**56%**	**11%**	**12%**	**21%**

*Includes Municipals and International Bonds

Source: Salomon Brothers

59% of foreign markets constitute government and government agency borrowers, compared with 53% in the United States. Of equal note is that foreign markets have, to a large extent, a second tier of high quality bank mortgage paper (accounting for some 25% of non-U.S. markets) which has not yet been featured as a bond market vehicle in the U.S.

Over the last decade or so an impressive degree of sophistication has been added to world bond markets. This has occurred principally in the U.S. dollar market, but recently has spread to other markets most notably, Sterling, the Swiss franc and the German mark. Within the U.S. dollar sector a major stimulus has been the volatility of interest rates. In the context of a very competitive and unregulated Euro-market, this volatility has fostered a range of fixed income innovations. Consequently, discerning investors have been provided with instruments which embrace any of their interest rate and currency projections, while borrowers have been able to reduce their cost of capital. The so-called current coupon ''plain vanilla'' bond has become much less frequently used while zero coupon bonds, extendibles, put and call features and warrant deals, to name but a few, have become quite common. The increased securitization of debt of all kinds also has provided the markets with very different kinds of credit risk on which a view may be taken.

Of key importance to the growth of world bond markets and the pace of innovation within them has been the gradual dismantling of capital market and foreign exchange controls, both in the United States and elsewhere. This dismantling has been as significant to the process of widening and deepening markets as was the initial move to flexible exchange rates in 1973. More recently, the abolition of withholding tax in all the principal markets has fostered a further major move toward a global and increasingly interdependent market in multi-currency debt. Among the markets of the United States, Canada, Japan, France, the United Kingdom, West Germany, the Netherlands and Switzerland, only Japan, the United Kingdom and Switzerland now withhold tax on income.

The United States, the United Kingdom and Canada traditionally have displayed the longest debt markets, all with a maximum maturity of some thirty years. With the gradual breakdown of barriers to capital mobility, other markets are beginning to extend their maximum maturity beyond the more normal ten years that have obtained to date. Thus, both the German and Swiss markets now offer maturities of thirty years; and with the advent of zero coupon bonds in these markets, the maximum available duration has been stretched from some seven years out to thirty years (see also Figure 10 below).

RATIONALE FOR FIXED INCOME INVESTMENT ABROAD

The conceptual case for including non-dollar fixed income securities in U.S. institutional portfolios has been much slower to gain acceptance than the case for international equities. This has stemmed in part from a concern that the underlying theory is not as clear-cut as in the case of equities. Also relevant has been the rather arbitrary question of into which asset class international bonds should be placed—do they belong with international equities as "international securities,'' or should they be considered the counterpart to domestic fixed income?

From the point-of-view of the private investor, both of these questions are perhaps of less importance than the more mundane observation that exposure to several markets gives access to the continual changes occurring in foreign exchange and interest rate relationships world-wide. Since different economies can find themselves at various stages of their respective economic and interest rate cycles, international portfolio management can capitalize on these non-synchronous relationships in ways not possible were funds to be restricted to a single market. As Figure 4 shows, such an opportunistic approach—seeking out the most attractive markets from a global perspective—would have offered the possibility of very different rates of return over recent years. Indeed, in the ten years prior to 1985 the U.S. dollar market was either the best or the worst performer 60 percent of the time—when a comparison is made of returns among the six principal markets of the world, all expressed in dollar terms.

By using the forward foreign exchange markets, the investor can segregate a bond market strategy from a foreign exchange strategy in order to maximize returns from a U.S. dollar base. If a currency is deemed to be weak but its bond market attractive, then it will be appropriate to buy the bond market but sell the currency forward against your base currency. In mapping out a currency strategy, the investor will need to construct his own total return projections and relate these to the cost of forward cover. Nineteen-eighty-five provided a good example: while domestic U.S. dollar and Eurodollar bond markets showed the highest returns in local currency terms, when all markets were measured in U.S. dollars, the U.S. performance was at the bottom of the rankings. An effective strategy would, therefore, have been to own the dollar bond market but sell dollars forward into the strongest currency for that year.

It also can be shown that a strategy of active switching would have yielded higher returns than would have been obtained from purely domestic investment. Figure 5 describes the trend in exchange rates that has held over the last ten years. Clearly, this time span divides itself into two distinct periods of dollar weakness followed by dol-

FIGURE 4 WORLD BOND MARKETS: TOTAL RETURN RANKINGS

U.S. DOLLAR TERMS

1976		1977		1978		1979		1980		1981		1982		1983		1984		1985	
DM	26.06	L	51.78	SF	31.23	L	17.17	L	25.14	$D	4.95	$D	35.05	Y	13.03	$D	17.08	DM	42.16
SF	24.04	Y	46.51	Y	30.48	FL	7.23	Y	24.96	$E	3.40	$E	28.25	$E	12.12	$E	15.28	L	41.54
FL	20.21	SF	35.27	FL	23.41	DM	6.40	$E	4.96	Y	3.24	L	20.89	$D	5.71	Y	1.87	FL	41.47
Y	15.36	DM	30.06	DM	17.34	$D	2.21	$D	0.49	SF	−0.97	FL	20.45	L	2.06	DM	−0.47	Y	38.21
$D	14.25	FL	16.49	$E	2.87	SF	1.15	FL	−6.44	FL	−7.87	DM	13.43	SF	−3.66	FL	−2.57	SF	34.74
$E	12.60	$E	6.70	L	−0.58	$E	−1.02	SF	−8.90	DM	−8.11	SF	2.47	DM	−7.66	SF	−9.83	$D	25.23
L	−10.62	$D	2.27	$D	−0.77	Y	−20.05	DM	−11.02	L	−19.70	Y	1.97	FL	−8.60	L	−11.80	$E	21.33

LOCAL CURRENCY TERMS

1976		1977		1978		1979		1980		1981		1982		1983		1984		1985	
SF	16.05	L	35.54	FL	6.64	L	4.15	L	16.88	Y	11.49	L	42.49	L	13.74	$D	17.08	$D	25.23
$D	14.25	Y	20.02	Y	5.63	FL	3.47	Y	6.22	FL	6.52	$D	35.05	$E	12.12	$E	15.28	$E	21.33
DM	13.54	DM	16.28	SF	4.62	$D	2.21	FL	5.23	$D	4.95	FL	28.30	Y	11.43	DM	15.02	L	13.97
$E	12.60	SF	10.64	$E	2.87	DM	0.68	$E	4.96	DM	4.76	$E	28.25	FL	6.29	FL	13.18	DM	11.15
Y	10.79	FL	7.96	DM	1.21	SF	0.19	DM	1.76	$E	3.40	DM	20.33	$D	5.71	Y	10.51	Y	10.51
FL	9.91	$E	6.70	$D	−0.77	$E	−1.02	SF	1.09	L	1.05	SF	13.59	DM	5.66	L	10.27	FL	10.35
L	6.23	$D	2.27	L	−4.56	Y	−1.33	$D	0.49	SF	0.70	Y	8.94	SF	5.28	SF	7.38	SF	7.61

Definitions: $D = Dollar (domestic) $E = Eurodollar Y = Japanese yen L = Pound sterling
DM = West German mark FL = Dutch guilder SF = Swiss franc

Source: InterSec Research Corp., Stamford, CT.

FIGURE 5 FOREIGN EXCHANGE MOVEMENTS

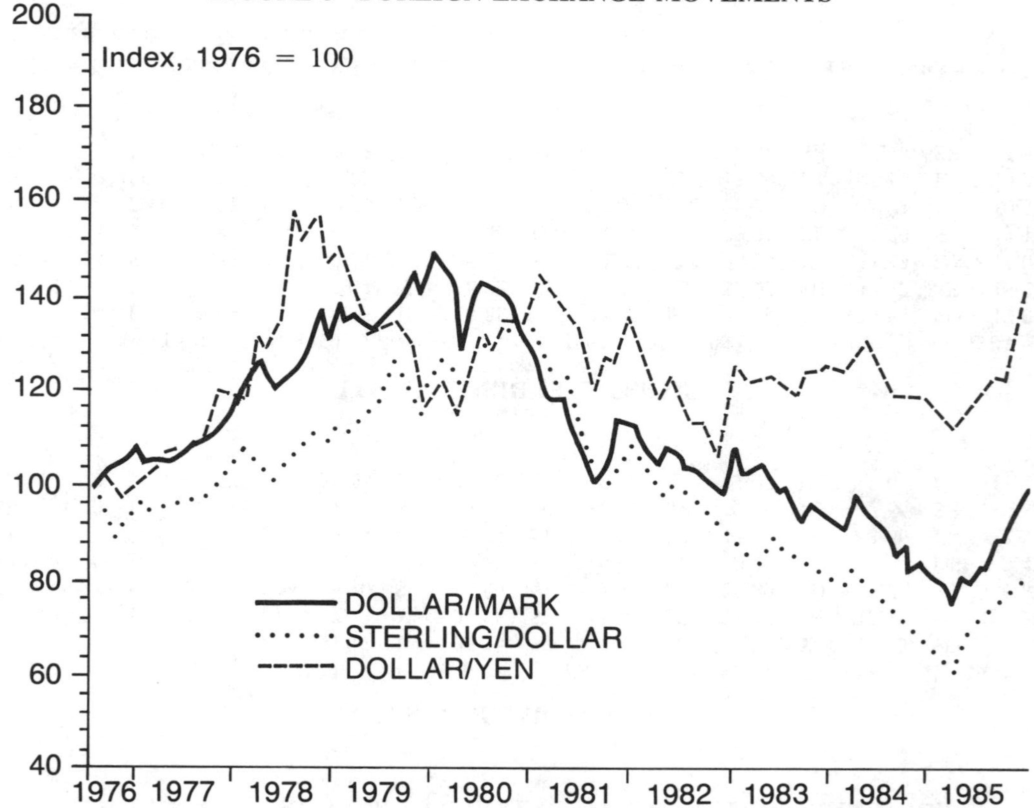

Source: Datastream

lar strength; so much so that it would have been sufficient merely to identify periods of relative dollar strength or weakness on an ad hoc basis in order to secure rates of return above that available from domestic instruments. Figure 4 reflects this difference in the dollar's performance between the late 'seventies and early 'eighties: prior to 1980, the dollar bond market was consistently in the bottom half of the rankings while in the 'eighties it moved back to the upper half.

The case for an international exposure in equities follows the argument that some economies abroad are likely to grow faster than the U.S. This in turn will be reflected in the pace of earnings growth and thus the appreciation of stock prices, leading to a better overall performance than could have been achieved by investing only in the U.S. market. The equivalent argument on the fixed income side can be couched in terms of selecting markets where expected real long-term rates of interest are higher than in the United States. As a result such foreign bonds will offer the prospect of a higher rate of return reflected in income, capital performance and exchange rate appreciation.

Modern portfolio theory suggests that on the basis of expected returns and estimates of standard deviations an efficient portfolio can be constructed from a (larger) universe of risky securities. In this context an efficient portfolio is defined as a subset of the total universe which will provide the highest expected return for a given degree of risk or, equivalently, the least risk for a given expected return. As Figure 6 shows, when the universe of risky assets is constrained to a single market, the efficient set of portfolios must lie to the right of that which obtains when the universe is extended. Points along the frontier represent the different efficient portfolios within the defined universe. As the universe is enlarged, the leftward movement of the efficient set implies a decline in portfolio risk for a given expected return. From the point of the U.S. investor it entails an improvement in his opportunity set.

In other words, it can be said that the addition of carefully selected foreign bonds to a portfolio exposed uniquely to U.S. fixed income instruments will reduce the risk or volatility of the entire portfolio.

FIGURE 6 EFFICIENT SETS WITH AND WITHOUT FOREIGN BONDS

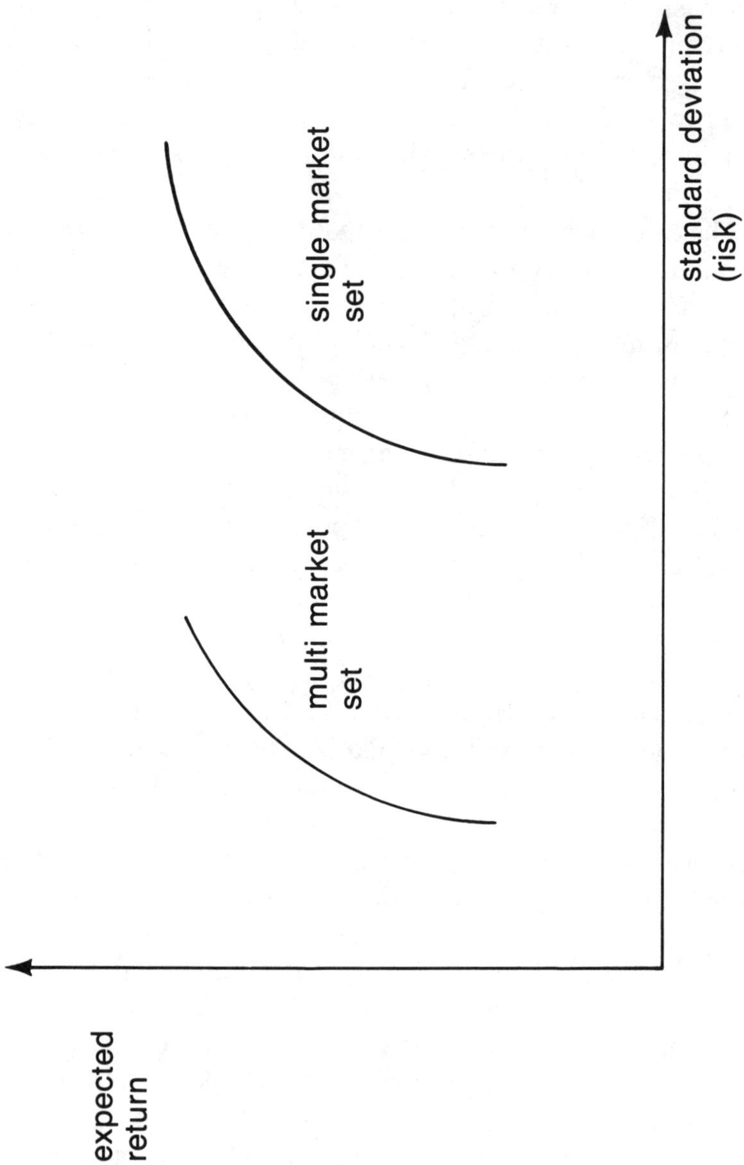

Source: Julius Baer Investment Management Inc.

On a market-by-market comparison the inclusion of foreign markets will, however, raise volatility compared with that of the domestic market by virtue of the foreign currency component that will not be present in a single market portfolio. That exchange rate movements raise market volatility follows from the economic observation that foreign currency rates and bond prices must tend in the long run in the same direction. Thus, relatively tighter monetary policy than elsewhere will raise the exchange rate and bond prices via lower inflation and lower yields.

Figure 7 demonstrates that all major foreign markets have had a higher standard deviation of total returns (defined as total bond market return measured in U.S. dollars) than the United States for the ten years through 1985. Such a time period encompasses the bulk of the world's relevant experience with international fixed income investment given that exchange rates only began to float from 1973 and initially experienced a "catchup" from the Bretton Woods days as rates moved to market determined levels.

The less than perfect (and varying) correlation between individual markets makes it clear why a distinction must be made between increased individual market volatility and the reduced volatility of an internationally diversified portfolio. Precisely because individual markets are not correlated with the U.S. market, the inclusion of more risky markets (taken on their own) to a purely domestic port-

FIGURE 7 VOLATILITY OF RETURNS IN THE UNITED STATES AND ABROAD
10 Years Through 1985

	Total Returns	Standard Deviation
Japan	14.0%	14.0%
Germany	9.5%	15.1%
U.K.	9.4%	17.3%
Switzerland	9.2%	16.2%
Holland	9.3%	14.6%
Non-U.S. Bonds	11.4%	12.0%
U.S.	10.1%	10.0%

Source: Julius Baer Investment Management Inc.

folio will lower the riskiness or volatility of the total portfolio (considered as a whole). The lack of correlation will stem not only from economic causes—the relative stage of the economic cycle, the varying balance of monetary forces, etc.—but also from non-economic factors such as market structures, specific barriers to free markets and political practices, to name but a few. Countries sharing far reaching ties will have a higher degree of correlation between their respective bond markets, as in the case of the Deutschmark bloc (West Germany, the Netherlands and Switzerland). These economies not only share a degree of political interdependence, but also have significant trading links and maintain exchange rate ties, explicitly expressed in the case of West Germany and the Netherlands through the European Monetary System of exchange rate zones.

A decision rule for an institutional fund might, therefore, be to undertake international diversification insofar as it reduces overall fund volatility and raises returns from those respective levels that would be achievable from investment in the domestic market alone. In general, the lower the correlations and the higher the respective volatilities, the stronger the case for a strategy of diversification internationally as compared to single market specialization. As Figure 7 shows, returns over the past ten years have been higher abroad, but then so was volatility. A fund might, therefore, attempt to reach the optimum distribution between domestic and foreign debt as is compatible with reducing risk for a given return (or, equivalently, raising return for a given risk level) and its own internal objectives. The latter will vary from fund to fund, so that foreign bonds will play a different role in various kinds of portfolios as their dissimilar objectives accord differing relative weights to potentially higher returns and the reduction of risk through diversification.

By running a simulation over the last ten years, Julius Baer Investment Management has demonstrated that a U.S. portfolio would have benefitted on both these key criteria by implementing a global investment program. On the basis of an investment universe comprising the major six bond markets (United States, Japan, United Kingdom, West Germany, the Netherlands and Switzerland), portfolio performance and volatility were measured with varying proportions of for-

FIGURE 8 CORRELATION OF GLOBAL FIXED INCOME RETURNS 1976-1985 Returns in U.S. Dollars

	U.S	U.S. Euro	Japan	U.K.	Germany	Nether-lands	Switzer-land
U.S.	1.00						
U.S. Euro	.83	1.00					
Japan	.05	.07	1.00				
U.K.	.08	.12	.11	1.00			
Germany	.14	.12	.27	.18	1.00		
Netherlands	.17	.15	.26	.20	.90	1.00	
Switzerland	.13	.12	.28	.18	.71	.68	1.00

Source: Julius Baer Investment Management Inc.

eign bonds. The two extremes, as set out in Figure 9, corresponded to either an entirely domestic portfolio or an entirely foreign portfolio. The most important finding is that successive increments of non-dollar debt to a dollar portfolio would have achieved these twin aims of reducing volatility and raising return. The experience of the period 1976-1985 suggests that an "optimal" allocation of 70% dollar/30% non-dollar would have reduced the standard deviation of returns by one percent with a somewhat smaller improvement in portfolio performance.

ACTIVE AND PASSIVE MANAGEMENT

As Figure 4 has shown, the accurate forecasting of exchange and interest rate trends at home and abroad can yield returns far in excess of those available from the dollar market alone. In practice, this is equivalent to asking whether or not an actively managed account will outperform a passively managed one, without increasing standard deviation risk. The proposition that active management will

FIGURE 9 THE TRADE OFF BETWEEN RISK AND RETURN FROM FOREIGN MARKETS

(0-100% international bonds, 10 years ended December, 1985)

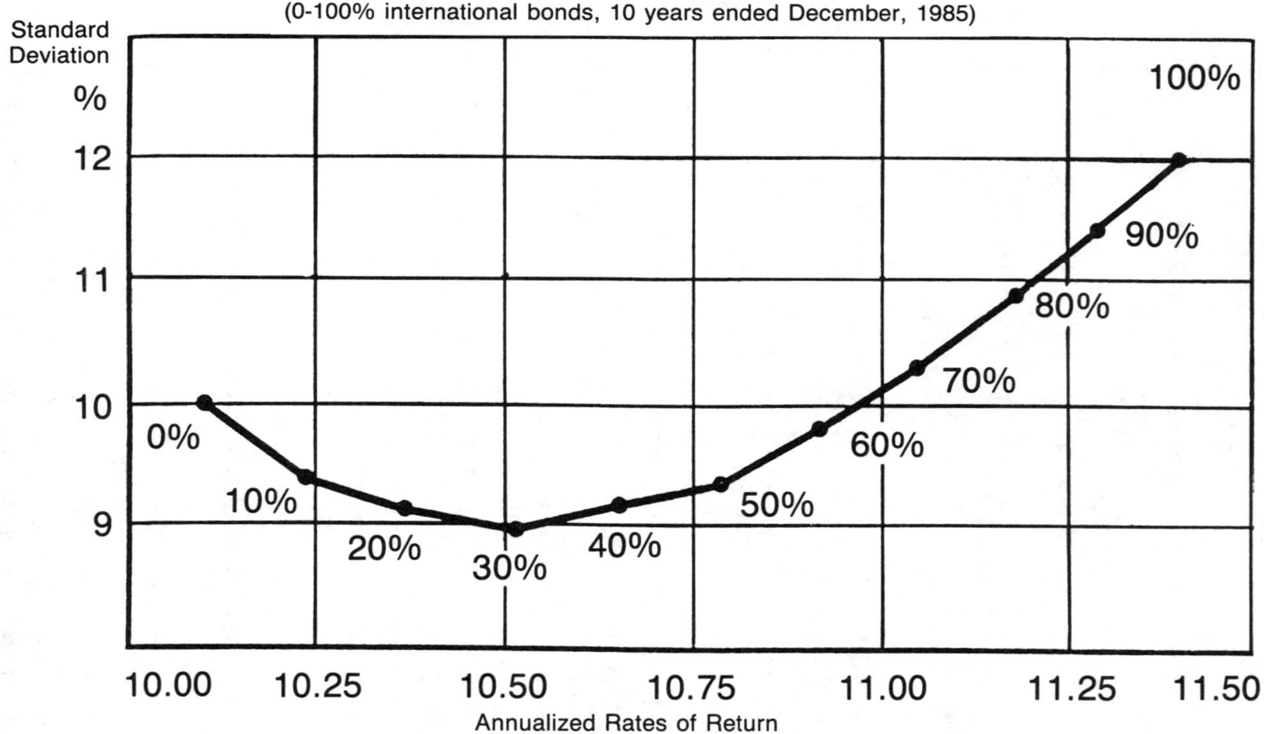

Source: Julius Baer Investment Management Inc.

add value to internationally diversified portfolios depends on the assumption that fixed income markets are imperfect, thereby providing opportunities for the specialized and knowledgable investor. By the same token, the basic premise of the passive investment approach is that world markets are efficient in the sense of free mobility of capital, fully flexible asset prices, perfect information, etc.—as a result, there is no possiblity to earn above-market returns because current prices discount all available information.

While this argument has gained some acceptance in the U.S. domestic capital markets, it nevertheless is the case that passively managed portfolios are much less prevalent than actively managed ones. The growth of a very prosperous investment advisory industry confirms this. That the efficient market case can be argued on an international level is, however, more doubtful. Markets are rarely comparable one to another; many are relatively immature with differing trading characteristics and, in some cases, barriers exist to totally free markets. Indeed, foreign exchange forward rates—whether short or long term, have failed to prove effective predictors of future spot rates, bearing witness to the imperfection of world foreign exchange markets. The latter is often held out as one of the most perfect markets currently in existence. Set against this market, foreign capital markets look quite inefficient, such that the active investor should be able to add value. Thus, passive investing has to date gained few followers in either international equity or debt investment by U.S. institutional investors.

Within the U.S. capital market, programs such as immunization and dedication are often used by institutional investors to generate regular income and minimize long term risk. Matching income with the actuarial liabilities of the fund can insulate the fund from expected return and risk considerations. Dividing fund strategies into two components also has been popular: one portion will be immunized or dedicated according to actuarial requirements, while another will be actively managed on the basis of some projected risk adjusted return. It is doubtful whether this degree of sophistication can be achieved in a multi-currency environment as opposed to within a single currency. To immunize or dedicate internationally would require the existence of long term forward markets that are currently to a large extent underdeveloped, and thus illiquid. And in addition, active and passive management techniques are difficult concepts in the case of bonds. Fixed income instruments, as opposed to equities, have distinct maturities, so there is no passive strategy that is as truly passive as in the case of stocks. When bonds mature they must be reinvested and a range of new maturities and instruments presents itself.

THE INTERNATIONAL DEBT MARKETS IN PRACTICE

In terms of tradeable securities, foreign capital markets include essentially three components: the Eurobond markets, the foreign bond markets, and their domestic counterparts. The Eurobond is an entirely international vehicle in the sense that the Euromarket is used by international syndicates for international borrowers, with issues being distributed worldwide. A Eurocurrency is a pool of money that exists outside of its country of origin. By contrast, a foreign bond is issued for a foreign borrower within one country by a local syndicate. It is denominated in the currency of the country within which it has been issued. Thus a foreign borrower registered in the domestic U.S. capital market, selling bonds in that market, will be creating Yankee-bonds (foreign bonds) issued in dollars. Various other characteristics distinguish foreign bonds from Eurobonds, of which the most important are set out in Figure 10. Apart from individual government debt markets, foreign debt markets have not been extensively used by U.S. investors, because of tax constraints, inadequate liquidity and lack of information.

International, as opposed to domestic, markets are post-World War II developments. Two events in the United States were key to their birth and subsequent growth. The first took place in 1963 in response to a sizable capital account deficit in the United States. Following World War II, foreign governments, in particular, had looked to the U.S. domestic capital market as a prime source of raising capital in large amounts in an acceptable currency. Many of these issues then returned abroad rather than remaining in the United States, thereby creating a capital account deficit in the United States. The Kennedy Administration imposed the Interest Equilization Tax, reducing the after-tax yield on such foreign bonds and creating the impetus for a move of the market to Europe. As a result, internationally held dollars could be tapped directly by borrowers of any nationality with syndicates made up of non-U.S. as well as U.S. banks. The market's growth was then spurred in 1968 by the establishment of the Office of Foreign Direct Investments, which sought to encourage U.S. companies financing foreign commitments to do so abroad rather than at home. After 1968 this was compulsory, thereby providing the Euromarket with prime credits and a steady flow of borrowers.

Due to the lack of an official regulatory body governing the Euromarkets, they have in general grown faster than other foreign counterparts. There is no central trading floor but market participants are all linked by telephone for trading purposes. Nevertheless, most Euro issues are listed on a recognized stock exchange, usually Luxembourg, in order for them to be available for purchase by institutional investors. In the earlier years, when the bulk of the Eurobond market was dollar denominated, the market was quite long term as maturities were generally in the ten to fifteen year range. With the world-wide rise in long rates and inflation from 1974, the market shortened up and the majority of issues fell into the five to ten year area. Only since long rates have fallen from the highs of the early Eighties has the dollar market again lengthened, with issues up to thirty years maturity now more common. The last few years also have witnessed the lengthening of other markets with perhaps the Japanese yen remaining the prime exception (see Figure 10).

The growth rate of the Euromarkets would have been impossible without internationally effective clearing systems capable of accepting the range of instruments and currencies now being traded. There are two depository and trade clearing systems in the form of Euroclear (Euro-clear Clearance Systems Limited) and CEDEL (Centrale de Livraison de Valeurs Mobilières), located in Brussels and

FIGURE 10 KEY FEATURES OF INTERNATIONAL SECURITIES

Market	Secondary market liquidity/ $ millions	Form	Day basis/ Interest payment schedule	Max. maturity of issues	With-holding tax	Clearing system
US dollar						
Govt. (Treasury Notes & Bonds)	50-100	registered	actual/365 semi-annual	30 years	no	Federal Reserve book entry
Foreign (Yankee)	1-5	bearer or registered	30 day month/360 semi-annual	30 years	no	New York custodian Euroclear, Cedel
Euro	1-5	bearer	30 day month/360 annual	30 years	no	Euroclear, Cedel
Canadian dollar						
Govt.	10-20	bearer or registered	30 day month/360 semi-annual	25 years	no	Custodian bank
Euro	1-5	bearer	30 day month/360 annual	20 years	no	Euroclear, Cedel
Japanese Yen						
Govt.	5-10	bearer or registered	actual/365 semi-annual	10 years	yes	Custodian banks
Foreign (Samurai)	1-2	bearer or registered	actual/360 semi-annual	10 years	no	Custodian banks
Euro	1-2	bearer	30 day month/360 annual	15 years	no	Euroclear, Cedel

FIGURE 10 KEY FEATURES OF INTERNATIONAL SECURITIES (continued)

Market	Secondary market liquidity/ $ millions	Form	Day basis/ Interest payment schedule	Max. maturity of issues	With-holding tax	Clearing system
Sterling						
Govt. (Gilts)	10-20	registered	actual/365 semi-annual	30 years	yes	Custodian banks
Euro	0-1	bearer	30 day month/360 annual	20 years	no	Euroclear, Cedel
Deutschmark						
Govt.	0-10	bearer	30 day month/360 annual	30 years	no	Custodian banks
Euro	0-5	bearer	30 day month/360 annual	30 years	no	Euroclear, Cedel
Dutch Guilder						
Govt.	0-20	bearer	30 day month/360 annual	11 years	no	KAS Associate
Euro	0-5	bearer	30 day month/360 annual	7 years	no	KAS Associate
Swiss franc						
Govt.	0-1	bearer	30 day month/360 annual	15 years	no	SEGA
Foreign	0-1	bearer	30 day month/360 annual	30 years	no	SEGA

Luxembourg, respectively. On the basis of matching instructions from both parties to a trade, delivery of securities and the payment for them is made by centralized bookkeeping entries. Euro-clear/CEDEL transfers "via the bridge" are straightforward, with each party using the opposite clearing system. By virtue of Eurobonds being bearer securities, Euro-clear and CEDEL are fungible depository systems. Account holders own a nominal amount of a given bond without those bonds being specifically identifiable on the basis of serial numbers. Within CEDEL it is, however, possible to operate a non-fungible account—though this facility is not widely used.

Generally, spreads between bid and offer are smallest in the respective domestic government market and widest in its Euro or foreign counterpart. This suggests that the government market will, as a rule, be the prime bond market in that currency, given that government debt will typically be the finest credit and receive regular support from central bank operations. As a result, liquidity will be greatest in that market and the actual number of bonds will be relatively smaller. The Euromarkets will enjoy a range of credits and greater variety of instruments available so that market making will be on a more ad hoc basis in accordance with lead management priorities. Liquidity per bond will be on average much less, so that typical spreads in either the major foreign or Euromarkets will be greater than in the domestic government market. A usual Euromarket spread will be one half of one percent, although this can extend to one percent for less frequently traded bonds, while rarely traded bonds may have no active market at all.

Although Eurobonds and foreign bonds have always been free of withholding tax, the abolition of withholding tax in the United States, West Germany and France in the last few years has gone a long way towards creating a global market in debt and, moreover, a 24-hour trading environment for some debt instruments. The U.S. "long bond" is perhaps the world's most widely traded fixed interest instrument, boasting very fine spreads, and being actively bought and sold through all time zones. It is doubtful whether this would have occurred in the absence of the abolition of withholding tax.

For bonds that have not been registered with the SEC, i.e., all foreign securities including Eurodollar bonds, a so-called "seasoning" restriction applies. Such non-exempt securities may not be sold to U.S. residents until they are deemed to be "seasoned," which has generally been interpreted as being 90 to 180 days since payment date. Certain borrowers have been exempted from this restriction—specifically, the World Bank and various other prominent international organizations.

THE ROLE OF INTERNATIONAL BONDS FOR THE U.S. INVESTOR[1]

It has been suggested that the failure of international bonds to command as wide a following in the U.S. institutional market as that of foreign equities has been due to their being neither "fish nor fowl." Institutional investors have been increasingly willing to view international equities as the logical counterpart to their domestic stock portfolios, but have disagreed as to whether foreign bonds should fall in with the overall bond component or form part of a separate asset class called "international," in which foreign equities also would be placed. Certainly the main characteristic that foreign bonds share with foreign equities is the role of the dollar's foreign exchange rate. International managers running either bond or equity programs will develop exchange rate projections, and these must be based on a world macroeconomic scenario that will encompass interest rates, real growth, etc. In this sense, by virtue of their common macroeconomic linkage, equities and foreign bonds fall very much into the same category. Nevertheless, it also may be argued that the main reason why bonds and stocks have been separated domestically is that bonds guarantee a fixed income stream and are, therefore, intrinsically different instruments from equities. On this criterion, international bonds and domestic bonds are logical bedfellows. Thus, if a sufficient time period is taken, preferably including an "up" and "down" cycle for the dollar, currency effects tend to wash out and principal and interest returns dominate. Figure 11 sets out the

FIGURE 11 RETURN COMPONENTS FOR GOVERNMENT BONDS FOR LAST 10 YEARS

(10 years annualised through 1985)	Local Principal + Interest	Currency Effect	Total Return
Japan	9.3%	4.7%	14.0%
Germany	8.8%	0.7%	9.5%
U.K.	13.2%	−3.8%	9.4%
Switzerland	6.6%	2.6%	9.2%
Holland	9.6%	−0.3%	9.3%
Non-U.S. Bonds	9.5%	1.9%	11.4%
U.S.	10.1%	–	10.1%

Source: InterSec Research/Julius Baer Investment Management Inc.

comparison of returns on alternative government bonds for the ten years through 1985 which, broadly speaking, comprised one weak dollar and one strong dollar period.

If a shorter time period is taken, currency changes can be very significant (see Figure 5), so that principal and interest returns are more than offset by exchange rate changes. In that context, international bonds clearly have more in common with foreign stocks, and the difference in characteristics relates more to the time period examined than to intrinsic dissimilarities as between domestic and foreign bonds. Nevertheless, international bonds will represent a purer currency play than stocks. Hard currencies tend, in the long run, to have strong bond markets because both follow from an absolutely and relatively tighter balance of monetary forces than elsewhere. Stock markets are likely, however, to suffer from strong currencies as the export sector experiences a lack of competitiveness and thus GNP growth is depressed. Ultimately, therefore, it may be that the precise role of international bonds for the U.S. investor may be defined by a range of factors including the kind of investor, his objectives, his time horizon and his currency forecast for the dollar. In the case of a passive investment approach, these complications need not apply as such a strategy must, by definition, sidestep the key question of the investor's objectives.

CONCLUSION

That international investment as a discipline has attracted only a small proportion of institutional assets in the United States is increasingly less defensible. This is true in the case of equities or bonds, given the well-documented evidence on the potential benefits of risk reduction through diversification. Irrespective of the kind of investor and his objectives, the appropriate strategy in the face of economic and political uncertainty is global diversification. While it can be shown, with the benefit of hindsight, that a given market will have produced the highest return, such an ex-ante approach favoring single market specialization may not be the "best" one in view of the riskiness of that return. Indeed, such an approach is suspect because it presupposes perfect foresight. To the extent that uncertainty exists, some degree of international diversification is always optimal.

For international equities to have received more attention than bonds is no doubt a reflection of practical constraints. Chief among these was the relative underdevelopment of foreign bond markets and the apparently greater simplicity of an equity as opposed to a bond program given the greater homogeneity of foreign equity instruments. In most recent years this has become increasingly less the case as withholding taxes have been abolished, capital markets the world over have been freed up and the concept of a global capital market has become quite realistic. In this context, a global bond investment program is appropriate as a source of diversification along with equities, especially as both universes are equally large and suitable for institutional funds. On the practical side, settlement and clearing procedures have become more efficient, centralized and well documented.

With the now parallel development of international bond markets to equity markets, there is perhaps less justification for the practice of placing international bonds and equities in a hybrid asset class labelled "international." Rather, a more valid case can be made for both being run separately as counterparts to domestic bond and equity programmes, though the precise implementation of such an approach will depend on the nature of the end investor and his objectives. Given the intricacies of international investment as compared to domestic investment, there is potentially a greater possibility for active portfolio management to achieve higher returns than passive management. Indeed, were it not for the complexities of such foreign investments, there would be no chance of achieving incremental return and reduced portfolio risk.

NOTES

[1]This section has drawn from C. M. Small and M. D. Hadzima, "*International Portfolio Management,*" The Handbook of Fixed Income Securities (Dow Jones-Irwin 1983) p. 888.

CHAPTER SIXTEEN

GIOIA M. PARENTE is an Analyst in the International Bond Market Research Group at Salomon Brothers Inc in New York. She studies both dollar and nondollar international floating-rate markets and has written numerous publications describing the market and assessing relative value. Ms. Parente holds a Bachelor of Science Degree in Journalism and a Masters of Business Administration in Finance.

RECENT DEVELOPMENTS IN FLOATING-RATE MARKETS*

Gioia M. Parente
Salomon Brothers Inc
New York, New York

INTRODUCTION

In 1970, the floating-rate concept was first incorporated into the debt structure—the inaugural Eurodollar issue by Ente Nazionale per L'Energia Elettrica (ENEL), the Italian railway, marked the commencement of a new financial instrument that would grow dramatically in importance in the international marketplace. Issue volume statistics highlight this tremendous growth: In 1980, close to $5 billion was issued in the Eurodollar floating-rate note (FRN) market; in 1985, almost $48 billion of new securities was brought to this market—an increase of 900 percent in just five years.

CHARACTERISTICS

A FRN is a medium- or long-term debt instrument with a coupon

*Revised from "An Anatomy of The Floating-Rate Markets: 1986 Update," Salomon Brothers Inc, 1986.

that resets periodically at some spread above or below a short-term reference rate. The lion's share of outstandings is denominated in U.S. dollars. However, securities have also been structured in other currencies, including the Deutschemark, Japanese yen, British pound and European currency unit. In the Eurodollar market, the reference rate usually applied is LIBOR — the London Interbank Offered Rate for U.S. dollars. LIBOR has typically been the highest yielding, dollar-denominated money market rate in the world. Interbank rates have been the most widely used reference rate in both the dollar and nondollar markets reflecting the development of this market as an alternative to bank loans. Treasury bill, certificate of deposit and prime rates also have been utilized as reference rates.

Traditionally, coupons in this market reset and pay on a quarterly or semiannual basis over three- or six-month LIBOR, respectively. In addition, weekly, monthly and annual coupon reset/payment features also are available. Recently, many innovations to the coupon reset mechanism have been engineered. During 1985, the "mismatch" FRN became popular. Mismatch FRNs possess coupons that reset and pay at different intervals. Generally, the reference rate is equivalent to the payment frequency, while the coupon refixes at shorter intervals. The most common variety are issues with coupons that reset monthly at a six-month rate, with payment occurring every six-months. The coupon payment is an average of the previous six monthly coupon fixes. Mismatch FRNs also have been structured with weekly resets and quarterly payments; quarterly resets and semiannual payments, among others. In a positively-shaped yield curve environment where, for instance, the six-month rate is substantially above the one-month rate, the funded investor may borrow at a *low* one-month rate and receive a coupon based off of the higher six-month rate.

Coupon reset margins also have changed in recent years. In the early 1980s, most high-quality issues possessed coupons that reset about 25 basis points above LIBOR. Since that time, margins have shrunk dramatically: The most typical reset formulas now available on traditionally-structured FRNs are flat or one-eighth of a percentage point over LIBOR.

ATTRACTIONS

Many factors help explain the success of this market. Issuers—in particular, sovereign entities—increasingly recognized the substantial flexibility and cost savings that these instruments provided in comparison with syndicated loans—the chief form of floating-rate finance utilized in the 1970s. Investors, on the other hand, were attracted to the superior yield offered by these securities: Eurodollar FRNs have consistently outperformed alternative money market investments. In addition, during periods of rising interest rates, these instruments—with coupons linked to short-term interest rates—also outperformed the bond markets. Furthermore, because the coupon level is adjusted to current market levels on a regular basis, FRNs generally offer a high degree of principal protection. Barring a significant change in the credit quality of the issuer, the prices of these securities will return to a stable level at the coupon reset date. Thus, an FRN investment—which very often has a maturity of at least ten years—can be considered analogous to purchasing a stream of short-term certificates of deposit (CDs). The FRN market also provides an investor with a variety of names to choose from. The large volume of high-quality sovereign issuers—including both government and government-guaranteed entities—allows for diversification away from strictly bank credits. The availability of several types of reset mechanisms also permits the investor to actively manage an FRN portfolio given certain interest rate forecasts. In addition to choosing FRNs that fit certain credit specifications, an investor may discriminate among a wide variety of reference rates, coupon formulas, coupon-reset and payment frequencies. Lastly, large issue amounts and tight dealing spreads typically provide the investor with substantial liquidity.

This chapter discusses the profound changes that have taken place in recent years in the floating-rate markets. A detailed description of the composition of U.S. dollar and nondollar floating-rate outstandings, including nationality, maturity, industry, credit and issue size profiles is also provided. In addition, the current characteristics of the market are contrasted with those of 1983 outstandings in an attempt to identify major trends that have evolved in the past few years.

RECENT CHANGES

The floating-rate markets have undergone dramatic change in the past few years. The securitization of international finance, which began in the early 1980s, accelerated during this period, drawing an increasing number of sovereign borrowers away from syndicated loan financing and toward the cheaper and more flexible Eurodollar FRN market. International banks—eager to improve their capital standings—also sought greater financing opportunities in the long-term Eurodollar FRN market. In 1983, the volume of international bank loans outnumbered that of Eurodollar FRN issues by more than four to one: Only $14.1 billion in Eurodollar FRNs was issued, compared with $60.2 billion in bank loans. By year-end 1985 this differential had almost disappeared: $47.7 billion in new Eurodollar FRNs was launched in that year, compared with $53.5 billion in bank loans (see Figure 1). However, the spectacular bond market rally, as well as increased competition from new floating-rate structures, caused issue volume of Eurodollar FRNs to decline dramatically in the first quarter of 1986: Just over $6 billion was offered in this period, compared with a $12-billion quarterly average in 1985.

Concurrent with this explosive growth, issuer costs relative to LIBOR decreased dramatically. The increased appetite for floating-rate assets—particularly among commercial banks—allowed prime sovereign borrowers to issue jumbo securities bearing coupon reset margins below LIBOR. Lower-profile borrowers—such as second-tier sovereign names, U.S. thrift institutions and U.S. regional banks—also achieved attractive borrowing terms. During 1985, the FRN market attempted to adjust to the conflicting interests of issuers and investors: Issuers introduced innovative coupon reset mechanisms that substantially lowered their costs, while providing investors with above-market coupon reset formulas. However, many of

FIGURE 1 ISSUE VOLUME IN THE FLOATING-RATE MARKETS, 1982-85
(U.S. Dollars in Millions or Equivalent)

Market	1985	1984	1983	1982
Eurodollar FRNs	$47,668	$29,224	$14,080	$11,160
Domestic LIBOR FRNs	7,568	4,000	1,160	800
Domestic Treasury Bill FRNs	2,638	1,595	4,100	1,000
Nondollar FRNs[a]	7,874	2,769	966	147
Euronote/Eurocommercial Paper Facilities	57,392	19,828	3,145	2,706
International Bank Loans[b]	53,461	53,219	60,209	90,756

[a] Euro and foreign FRNs. Does not include domestic FRNs issued in Italy and France, for example.
[b] As published by the Organization for Economic Cooperation and Development (OECD).

these issues—most notably the coupon-cap FRN—performed poorly in the market as investors were not initially compensated for the interest rate risk they were assuming. Coupon cap FRNs have generous coupon spreads by today's standards—usually one quarter of a percentage point — but the coupon is restricted from exceeding a prescribed level, usually around 13 percent. The increased flexibility of the market for issuers, coupled with narrow coupon reset margins, caused a flood of issuance during 1985, despite sustained interest rate declines. Furthermore, the implementation of liberalization measures in a number of countries triggered healthy growth of the nondollar FRN market: Authorities in West Germany, France and Japan expanded their capital markets to include a number of financial innovations such as FRNs.

Ironically, the trend towards increased securitization—originally the impetus behind the spectacular popularity of the Eurodollar FRN—is creating new competition for this market. In particular, the note issuance facility (NIF) has emerged as a more flexible, and possibly cheaper, financing vehicle for sovereign borrowers. In addition, corporations—long absent from the Eurodollar FRN market—have become a dominant force in the NIF market, arranging medium-term facilities to obtain short-maturity, floating-rate funds. A number of these NIFs have been put into place by U.S. corporations seeking to replace high-cost bank lines as backups to their U.S. commercial paper programs. The interest rate swap market has also proven to be viable competition; high-quality sovereign borrowers have been able to create far cheaper floating-rate finance through swap agreements.

Thus, the Eurodollar FRN market is currently at a significant turning point in its development: Following several years of unprecedented popularity, the market must now compete with structures offering numerous attractions to both issuers and investors. The distinctions between FRNs and NIFs have already become blurred: Some Eurodollar FRNs now carry an obligation for the investor to purchase Euronotes at a future date, while the concept of yield curve notes evolved in 1986 as an attempt to merge FRNs into the interest rate swap market.

MARKET SIZE

The outstanding volume of Eurodollar FRNs increased to $99.3 billion at the close of 1985, a spectacular 146 percent increase over the year-end 1983 level. This dramatic increase occurred despite rampant early redemptions of high-coupon obligations by borrowers during the past two years. (Many of the issues that were redeemed, however, subsequently reentered the market at more favorable terms.) In 1985, for the first time, issuance of FRNs outpaced fixed-rate debt in the Eurodollar market. As illustrated in Figure 2, FRNs claimed 51 percent of the market, compared with just 40 percent in 1983. The nondollar FRN has also increased its presence in the international markets — as of December 31, 1985, $12.2 billion was outstanding in this market (see Figure 3). This volume includes Euro-Deutschemark, Euroyen and Euro-French franc issues—newcomers to the FRN market during 1985. Also during 1985, the Dutch Government announced the details of a capital market liberalization plan, which includes FRNs. This plan came to fruition in early 1986 with the issuance of the first foreign Dutch guilder-denominated FRN for Security Pacific Bank. In addition, Australian and New Zealand dollar FRNs were introduced to the U.S. domestic market in Janaury 1986. (Because they have 1986 issue dates, these FRNs are not included in 1985 outstandings.) FRNs claim 12 percent of total nondollar bond outstandings, a respectable share when compared with the 3 percent level posted in 1983. Among the nondollar FRN sectors, Eurosterling FRNs are the most dominant, making up one half of total nondollar FRN outstandings, followed by Deutschemark FRNs, which represent about one quarter of this market.

Other floating-rate markets also experienced sizable growth. Outstandings in the domestic LIBOR market reached close to $11 billion at the end of 1985, following a period of heavy issuance the prior year. Arrangements of NIFs ballooned during 1985, reaching $57.4 billion. The secondary market for Euronotes and Eurocommercial paper—by-products of the note issuance facility—climbed

FIGURE 2 FIXED VERSUS FLOATING-RATE FINANCE IN THE INTERNATIONAL BOND MARKETS, 1981-85 (U.S. Dollars in Millions or Equivalent)

		Eurodollar		Nondollar	
		Fixed[a]	Floating-Rate	Fixed[a]	Floating-Rate
1981	Amount	$14,486	$7,017	$18,017	$502
	Pct. of Total	67.4%	32.6%	97.3%	2.7%
1982	Amount	$27,888	$11,160	$25,580	$147
	Pct. of Total	71.4%	28.6%	99.4%	0.6%
1983	Amount	$20,933	$14,080	$31,729	$966
	Pct. of Total	59.8%	40.2%	97.0%	3.0%
1984	Amount	$32,390	$29,224	$36,726	$2,769
	Pct. of Total	52.6%	47.4%	93.0%	7.0%
1985	**Amount**	**$45,347**	**$47,668**	**$56,918**	**$7,874**
	Pct. of Total	**48.8%**	**51.2%**	**87.8%**	**12.2%**

[a] Includes straight and convertible bonds.

FIGURE3 A PROFILE OF THE MAJOR NONDOLLAR FLOATING-RATE NOTE MARKETS, BASED ON PAR VALUE OUTSTANDING, 31 DEC 85 (Units in Millions)

Market	No. of Issues	Amount Outstanding	Equivalent U.S. Dollar Amount[a]
Euro-Deutschemark	18	DM8,025	$3,205
Eurosterling	47	£4,398	6,281
European Currency Unit: Euro	15	ECU1,420	1,238
European Currency Unit: U.S. Domestic Issues	2	ECU300	262
Euroyen	1	¥30,000	148
Euro-French Franc	1	Ffr350	46
Swiss Franc	41	Sfr2,219	1,054
Total	**125**	—	**$12,234**

[a] Exchange rates effective 31 Dec 85 used for conversion from local currency terms.

to $15 billion. We envision further developments of this secondary market, given the huge volume of arrangements already in place.

INNOVATIONS

A number of innovations that were introduced to the Eurodollar FRN market, particularly during 1985, boosted the total volume outstanding of nontraditional securities. Many of the new coupon reset mechanisms developed were an attempt to reconcile the trend towards increasingly lower margins with the desire of funded investors for a current pickup in spread. These coupon reset mechanisms allow investors to assume certain interest rate risks in return for a higher margin on assets. As Figure 4 illustrates, mismatch FRNs became a prominent financing vehicle in 1985. During this year, forty such FRNs were issued, totaling almost $10 billion—roughly 20 percent of the new issue market. Most of these issues were launched during the winter of 1985, a period characterized by record steepness in the short end of the yield curve. The concept was enhanced further with the introduction of the protected mismatch FRN. Almost half of the mismatch FRNs carried insurance, by being set at the higher of two short-term rates, against the chance of a significant change in the shape of the yield curve.

The capped FRN—the second type of coupon innovation that carried some interest rate risk—made its debut in 1985. Approximately 10 percent of the 1985 new issue market was composed of these high-margin FRNs. Once again, the FRN market refined the structure of the innvoation shortly after it was introduced; seven of the thirty-five capped FRNs launched in 1985 possessed a delayed cap feature. (In most cases, the cap limitation could become effective only after five years.) Perpetual FRNs also provide investors with above-market coupon reset formulas. In this case, rather than an interest rate risk, the investor obtains a relatively high margin for the willingness to accept an issue with no final maturity date. Over 16 percent of the issues launched in 1985, and 12 percent in 1984, were of this variety. As shown later on Figure 13, the heavy issue volume of perpetual FRNs in these years boosted the *outstanding*

FIGURE 4 INNOVATIONS IN THE EURODOLLAR FLOATING-RATE NOTE MARKET, BASED ON ISSUE VOLUME, 1984-85 (U.S. Dollars in Millions)

	Number of Issues		Amount Issued		Percentage of Total Volume	
Type of FRN	**1984**	**1985**	**1984**	**1985**	**1984**	**1985**
Total Mismatch	14	40	$2,110	$9,795	7.2%	20.5%
• Protected mismatch[a]	2	17	600	4,445	2.1	9.3
Total Capped	—	35	—	4,700	—	9.9
• Delayed cap[b]	—	7	—	775	—	1.6
• Mini/max[c]	—	5	—	700	—	1.5
Total Perpetual	12	20	3,500	7,685	12.0	16.1
• U.K. issuers	4	13	1,275	6,100	4.4	12.8
Total with Warrants	4	7	800	1,295	2.7	2.7

[a] Coupon resets at the higher of a short- or long-maturity money market rate.

[b] The cap rate limitation is delayed, generally for five years.

[c] Coupon floor and ceiling present.

market share of these issues to close to 11 percent by year-end 1985. Only one $200-million perpetual issue was among outstandings at the end of 1983. Figure 4 demonstrates the significant share of the perpetual market represented by British banks: In 1985, almost 80 percent of the perpetual issue volume belonged to these institutions.

DOMINANT ISSUERS

Figure 5 shows the largest single issues of Eurodollar FRNs outstanding at the close of 1985. As illustrated, fifteen jumbo FRNs, brought to the market by ten different borrowers, were among 1985 outstandings. These issues range in size from a $2.5-billion deal for the United Kingdom to several $600-million securities. At the close of 1983, only four jumbo issues, ranging in size from $650 million to $1.8 billion, were in the universe of outstanding securities. Interestingly, in 1985 a number of U.K. banks were among these large-scale borrowers, evincing the trend toward the issuance of jumbo perpetual securities by these institutions. Also noteworthy is the presence of second-tier sovereign borrowers. Both the Republic of Italy and the Federation of Malaysia launched jumbo FRNs of $1.0 billion and $850 million, respectively. Both issues were larger than any currently outstanding for the Kingdom of Sweden—a traditional high-profile borrower in this market.

The nationality profile of issuers also has changed in the past two years. U.S. entities currently dominate the market, claiming almost 17 percent, followed closely by Great Britain and France with 14.6 percent and 13.9 percent, respectively (see Figure 6). This was not the case at the close of 1983, when French banks and government-guaranteed entities were clearly the most prolific borrowers, stacking up 23 percent of the outstandings. Sweden was in second place at that time, claiming only 9.0 percent of the market, and U.S. institutions took the fourth-place slot with just 7.0 percent.

Overall, the nationality profile of nondollar FRN issuers is similar to the Eurodollar FRN market (see Figure 7). However, on a currency-by-currency basis, certain differences are evident. Eurosterling FRNs—the largest sector of this market—is overwhelmingly composed of U.K. issuers. Of the $6.3 billion currently outstanding, $2.8 billion of nondollar FRNs was brought to the market by British entities. Building societies launched the bulk of these securities in anticipation of certain tax law changes. U.S. and French borrowers ranked second, each issuing close to $700 million. In the Deutschemark sector, Swedish, West German and Malaysian entities are the dominant borrowers, representing half of the outstandings, while in the ECU sector, French and Italian borrowers claim the largest share—roughly 66 percent of the market. In contrast, a wider cross-section of borrowers is represented in the foreign Swiss franc sector, which is made up of a large proportion of private-placement transactions.

Certain individual issuers still dominated the Eurodollar FRN market in 1985, but the concentration was not as great as it was at the close of 1983. Figure 8 shows twenty-four individual borrowers, all with $1 billion or more outstanding in 1985. In 1983, one third of the market was represented by only ten borrowers. As in 1983, the Kingdom of Sweden was the leading issuer, claiming 3.7 percent of total 1985 outstandings, although this was considerably lower than Sweden's 8.2 percent share of the market in 1983. In 1985, the Federation of Malaysia was at Sweden's heels, with 3.3 percent of total outstandings. In 1983, the second-place borrower—the European Economic Community—claimed 4.5 percent of the market, much less than Sweden's share that year. Among the largest individual issuers at the end of 1985 were the Federation of Malaysia, Credit Lyonnais, Banque Nationale de Paris, and Midland Bank—which were all present on the 1983 list. In contrast, Citicorp—with nine issues totaling $2.6 billion in 1985—was a newcomer to the top borrower list, a reflection of the recent predominance of U.S. issuers in this market.

The industry profile of outstandings in 1985 is similar to the composition of the 1983 market. Banks continue to be the most prolific issuers, with a 55 percent market share in 1985 compared to 51 percent in 1983. Activities of other financial institutions increased by 4 percent over 1983 levels. Government financing in the Eurodol-

FIGURE 5 LARGEST SINGLE ISSUES OF EURODOLLAR FLOATING-RATE NOTES, BASED ON PAR VALUE OUTSTANDING,[a] 31 DEC 85 (U.S. Dollars in Millions)

Issuer	Amount	Maturity Date	Issue Date
United Kingdom	$2,500	Oct 92	Oct 85
European Economic Community	1,800	Jul 90	Jul 85
Republic of Italy	1,000	Nov 94	Nov 84
Federation of Malaysia	850	Aug 93	Aug 83
Lloyds Bank	750	Perpetual	Jun 85
Kingdom of Sweden	750	Jun 00	Jun 85
Midland Bank	750	Perpetual	Jun 85
Kingdom of Sweden[b]	750	Perpetual	Jul 84
Kingdom of Sweden	700	Jan 05	Jan 85
Federation of Malaysia	650	Oct 05	Oct 85
Federation of Malaysia	600	Apr 15	Apr 85
Barclays Bank	600	Perpetual	Jul 85
Banque Francaise du Commerce Exterieur	600	Sep 99	Sep 84
Federation of Malaysia	600	Dec 09	Dec 84
Barclays Bank	600	Perpetual	Nov 84

[a] Includes all issues of $600 million or more outstanding.
[b] This issue was redeemed by the issuer effective 9 Jan 86.

FIGURE 6 PROFILE OF THE EURODOLLAR FLOATING-RATE NOTE MARKET—NATIONALITY OF THE ISSUER, BASED ON PAR VALUE OUTSTANDING, 31 DEC 85
(U.S. Dollars in Millions)

	No. of Issues	Amount	Pct. of Total Outstanding
United States	106	$16,545	16.8%
Great Britain	64	14,513	14.6
France	75	13,763	13.9
Italy	35	7,750	7.8
Sweden	14	4,240	4.3
Canada	25	3,650	3.7
Belgium	12	3,075	3.1
Malaysia	7	3,290	3.3
Spain	22	2,994	3.0
Japan	31	2,856	2.9
Denmark	19	2,797	2.8
Supranational	6	2,714	2.7
Ireland	14	2,071	2.1
Total	**430**	**$80,258**	**81%**

FIGURE 7 PROFILE OF THE NONDOLLAR FLOATING-RATE NOTE MARKET—NATIONALITY OF THE ISSUER, BASED ON PAR VALUE OUTSTANDING, 31 DEC 85
(U.S. Dollar in Millions[a])

Nationality	DM	£	ECU[b]	¥	Ffr	Sfr	Total
Algeria	—	—	—	—	—	$62	$62
Australia	—	$111	—	—	—	—	111
Belgium	$200	143	—	—	—	—	343
Brazil	—	—	—	—	—	14	14
Canada	279	286	—	—	—	—	565
Costa Rica	—	—	—	—	—	9	9
Denmark	40	321	$131	—	—	24	516
France	100	693	563	$148	—	185	1,689
Great Britain	—	2,849	35	—	—	—	2,884
Greece	200	—	—	—	—	—	200
Ireland	200	214	131	—	—	—	545
Italy	—	286	424	—	—	187	897
Ivory Coast	—	—	—	—	—	11	11
Japan	100	114	—	—	—	209	423
Korea	—	214	44	—	—	—	258
Malaysia	479	—	—	—	—	—	479
Morocco	—	—	—	—	—	14	14
Multinational	—	—	87	—	—	—	87
Netherlands	40	—	—	—	—	—	40
New Zealand	—	286	—	—	—	—	286
Poland	—	—	—	—	—	20	20
South Africa	—	71	44	—	—	—	115
Spain	—	—	41	—	—	203	244
Supranational	50	—	—	—	—	47	97
Sweden	599	—	—	—	—	36	635
Trinidad & Tobago	—	—	—	—	—	24	24
United States	399	693	—	—	$46	—	1,138
West Germany	519	—	—	—	—	—	519
Yugoslavia	—	—	—	—	—	9	9
Total	**$3,205**	**$6,281**	**$1,500**	**$148**	**$46**	**$1,054**	**$12,234**

[a] Exchange rates effective 31 Dec 85 used for conversion from local currency terms.
[b] Includes FRNs issued in both the Euro and U.S. domestic markets.

FIGURE 8 LARGEST INDIVIDUAL ISSUERS OF EURODOLLAR FLOATING-RATE NOTES, BASED ON PAR VALUE OUTSTANDING,[a] 31 DEC 85 (U.S. Dollars in Millions)

Issuer	No. of Issues	Amount	Pct. of Total Outstanding
Kingdom of Sweden	6	$3,700	3.7%
Federation of Malaysia	6	3,250	3.3
Credit Lyonnais	13	2,855	2.9
Republic of Italy	5	2,800	2.8
National Westminster	8	2,775	2.8
Kingdom of Belgium	7	2,600	2.6
Citicorp	9	2,550	2.6
United Kingdom	1	2,500	2.5
Banque Nationale de Paris	9	2,450	2.5
Midland Bank	6	1,875	1.9
European Economic Community	1	1,800	1.8
Lloyds Bank	5	1,800	1.8
Barclays Bank	4	1,750	1.8
Kingdom of Denmark	5	1,700	1.7
Ferrovie dello Stato	5	1,480	1.5
Standard Chartered Bank	6	1,475	1.5
Republic of Ireland	8	1,471	1.5
Spain	5	1,425	1.4
Banque Francaise du Commerce Exterieur	3	1,270	1.3
Societe Generale	6	1,250	1.3
Chemical New York	5	1,150	1.2
ENEL	6	1,030	1.0
Dresdner Finance	3	1,000	1.0
Wells Fargo	7	1,000	1.0
Total	**139**	**$46,956**	**47.4%**

[a] Includes all borrowers with $1 billion or more outstanding. Early redemptions by the borrower effective in early 1986 are not considered.

lar FRN market increased marginally as well, to 21.6 percent of 1985 outstandings from 20.5 percent in 1983. However, the market share represented by government-guaranteed entities decreased in 1985 to 11 percent, 8 percent less than in 1983 (see Figure 9).

The types of U.S. issuers to tap the Eurodollar FRN market has changed significantly in the past few years. Figure 10 breaks down the U.S. portion of the Eurodollar FRN market into borrowing by corporations, multinational banks, regional banks, thrift institutions, and other financial entities. Currently, multinational banks—the traditional U.S. borrower in this market—represent only about 59 percent of total U.S. outstandings. Commencing in 1984, regional banks began to tap the Eurodollar FRN market, accelerating their borrowing activities in 1985. This heavy issuance in 1985 brought total regional bank outstandings at year-end 1985 to $3.6 billion, just under one quarter of the total U.S. market. Thrift institutions also began experimenting with the Eurodollar FRN market in 1984; by the close of 1985, these issuers had brought $2.2 billion of AAA-rated, collateralized obligations to the market—13.3 percent of total U.S. outstandings. This reflects the opening up of the Eurodollar FRN market to less well-known institutions. In the domestic LIBOR market, regional banks claim 22 percent of the borrowings by U.S. issuers. These issuers have launched twenty-nine securities totaling $2.3 billion. Multinational banks have tapped the market less frequently but still represent 20 percent of the U.S. portion. Thrift institutions also have tested the domestic LIBOR market (see Figure 11).

OTHER CHARACTERISTICS

Issue Size. Similar to the 1983 breakdown, the most prevalent issue size amount is in the $100-199 million range. Figure 12 highlights this concentration: 216 issues, representing roughly 25 percent of the total dollar amount outstanding, fell within this range. In addition, as in 1983, only three issues of $1.0 billion or more are currently outstanding. The $500-999 million issue size grouping has experienced the greatest growth over the past two years:

FIGURE 9 ISSUERS OF EURODOLLAR FLOATING-RATE NOTES BY INDUSTRY, BASED ON PAR VALUE OUTSTANDING, 31 DEC 85 (U.S. Dollars in Millions)

	No. of Issues	Amount	Pct. of Total Outstanding
Banking and Finance			
Commercial Banks	420	$54,721	55.1%
Other Financial Institutions	43	5,055	5.1
Sovereign			
Government	60	$21,441	21.6%
Government Guaranteed	61	10,971	11.0
Supranational	6	$2,715	2.7%
Corporate	68	$4,409	4.5%
Total	**658**	**$99,312**	**100%**

FIGURE 10 EURODOLLAR FLOATING-RATE NOTES ISSUED BY U.S. ENTITIES, BASED ON PAR VALUE OUTSTANDING, 31 DEC 85 (U.S. Dollars in Millions)

Type of Institution	No. of Issues	Amount	Pct. of Total Outstanding
Multinational Bank[a]	45	$9,675	58.5%
Regional Bank	31	3,635	22.0
Thrift	16	2,200	13.3
Corporate	4	235	1.4
Other Financial	10	800	4.8
Total	**106**	**$16,545**	**100%**

[a] Included in this category are issues by BankAmerica, Bankers Trust, Bank of Boston, Chase Manhattan, Chemical, Citicorp, Continental Illinois, First Chicago, Irving Trust, Manufacturers Hanover, Republic New York, and Security Pacific.

FIGURE 11 DOMESTIC LIBOR FLOATING-RATE NOTES ISSUED BY U.S. ENTITIES, BASED ON PAR VALUE OUTSTANDING, 31 DEC 85 (U.S. Dollars in Millions)

Type of Institution	No. of Issues	Amount	Pct. of Total Outstanding
Multinational Bank[a]	11	$2,050	19.8%
Regional Bank	29	2,255	21.8
Thrift	4	500	4.8
Corporate	8	2,683	25.9
Other Financial	16	2,875	27.7
Total	**68**	**$10,363**	**100%**

[a] Included in this category are issues by BankAmerica, Bankers Trust, Bank of Boston, Chase Manhattan, Chemical, Citicorp, Continental Illinois, First Chicago, Irving Trust, Manufacturers Hanover, Republic New York, and Security Pacific.

FIGURE 12 OUTSTANDING AMOUNTS IN THE EURODOLLAR FLOATING-RATE NOTE MARKET, BASED ON PAR VALUE OUTSTANDING, 31 DEC 85
(U.S. Dollars in Millions)

Issue Size	No. of Issues	Pct. of Total Number Outstanding	Amount	Pct. of Total Volume Outstanding
$1,000 or More	3	0.5%	$5,300	5.3%
$500 - 999	31	4.7	17,700	17.8
$200 - 499	138	21.0	38,583	38.9
$100 - 199	216	32.8	25,243	25.4
$50 - 99	154	23.4	9,438	9.5
$49 or Less	116	17.6	3,048	3.1

thirty-one FRNs totaling $17.7 billion fell within this range at year-end 1985, compared with only four such issues in 1983.

Maturity. The trend toward issuing floating-rate securities with longer maturities accelerated during the past two years. Based on final maturity, almost half of the outstanding Eurodollar FRNs will come due in eleven or more years (see Figure 13); this includes thirty-one perpetual-maturity securities. The greatest volume of securities will mature in eleven years. Interestingly, the perpetual structure is the second-most prevalent maturity based on total dollar volume outstanding. Based on 1983 outstandings, the largest proportion of FRNs would mature in just six years. As in 1983, the put option feature has a noticeable effect on the maturity structure of outstandings: More than 40 percent of these securities will mature in 1986-93 based on the first put date. In contrast, based on the final maturity date, only 30 percent of these issues will come due during this same time span.

Credit Quality. Over the past two years, a greater volume of FRNs have been rated by both Standard & Poor's and Moody's. Currently, 136 outstanding issues totaling $35.4 billion are rated by Standard & Poor's, representing approximately 36 percent of the total market (see Figure 14). Similar to the 1983 profile, high-quality borrowers still dominate the market. In fact, 86 percent of the rated issues have received AA− or better designations. However, a smattering of lower-rated borrowers is evident. In the BBB+ category, for example, eight issues, representing 7 percent of the market, are present. These borrowers include recently downgraded U.S. multinational and regional banks.

SUMMARY

Floating-rate instruments remain an attractive investment in the international fixed-income marketplace. As the preceeding discussion indicates, diversity is one of the dominant features of this marketplace. Once the investor is comfortable with the floating-rate concept—its inherent price stability and superior money market

FIGURE 13 MATURITY PROFILE OF THE EURODOLLAR FLOATING-RATE NOTE MARKET—FIRST PUT DATE VERSUS FINAL MATURITY, BASED ON PAR VALUE OUTSTANDING, 31 DEC 85 (U.S. Dollars in Millions)

	Based on Final Maturity				Based on First Put			
	No. of Issues	Amount	Pct. of Total Outstanding	Cumulative	No. of Issues	Amount	Pct. of Total Outstanding	Cumulative
1986	24	$1,112	1.1%	1.1%	39	$2,125	2.1%	2.1%
1987	25	1,853	1.9	3.0	38	2,748	2.8	4.9
1988	37	1,715	1.7	4.7	58	5,048	5.1	10.0
1989	43	2,931	3.0	7.7	65	7,364	7.4	17.4
1990	38	4,707	4.7	12.4	43	8,932	9.0	26.4
1991	48	4,230	4.3	16.7	43	3,985	4.0	30.4
1992	61	8,687	8.8	25.5	63	7,473	7.5	37.9
1993	29	4,039	4.1	29.6	22	3,034	3.1	41.0
1994	61	7,755	7.8	37.4	44	6,095	6.1	47.1
1995	51	6,731	6.8	44.2	43	5,236	5.3	52.4
1996	41	6,893	7.0	51.2	31	5,313	5.4	57.8
1997	69	11,982	11.8	63.0	67	11,042	11.0	68.8
1998	2	172	0.2	63.2	1	47	0.1	68.9
1999	24	5,625	5.7	68.9	19	5,725	5.8	74.7
2000	32	7,040	7.1	76.0	26	7,510	7.6	82.3
2001	—	—	—	76.0	—	—	—	82.3
2002	1	200	0.2	76.2	1	200	0.2	82.5
2003	—	—	—	76.2	—	—	—	82.5
2004	9	2,650	2.7	78.9	2	600	0.6	83.1
2005	20	6,725	6.8	85.7	14	4,170	4.2	87.3
2006-2008	—	—	—	85.7	—	—	—	87.3
2009	4	1,300	1.3	87.0	3	700	0.7	88.0
2010	2	300	0.3	87.3	1	100	0.1	88.1
2011-2084	6	1,925	1.9	89.2	5	1,325	1.3	89.4
Perpetual	31	10,740	10.8	100.0	30	10,540	10.6	100.0

FIGURE 14 CREDIT QUALITY OF THE EURODOLLAR FLOATING-RATE NOTE MARKET, [a] BASED ON PAR VALUE OUTSTANDING, 31 DEC 85
(U.S. Dollars in Millions)

Rating	Number of Issues	Amount	Pct. of Total Rated Issues	Cumulative	Pct. of Total Market	Cumulative
AAA	36	$13,275	37.5%	37.5%	13.4%	13.4%
AA+	26	6,850	19.4	56.9	6.9	20.3
AA	19	2,690	7.6	64.5	2.7	23.0
AA-	27	7,625	21.5	86.0	7.7	30.7
A+	8	1,100	3.1	89.1	1.1	31.8
A	7	975	2.8	91.9	1.0	32.8
A-	1	100	0.3	92.2	0.1	32.9
BBB+	8	2,400	6.7	98.9	2.4	35.3
BBB-	1	100	0.3	99.2	0.1	35.4
BB+	1	200	0.6	99.8	0.2	35.6
BB-	1	50	0.1	99.9	—	35.6
D	1	30	0.1	100.0	—	35.6
Total	**136**	**$35,395**	**100%**		**35.6%**	

[a] Includes only issues rated by Standard & Poor's.

return—he can then choose between a number of market sectors according to his investment requirements or interest rate forecast. High-quality issues are available in various currencies, with different reset benchmarks and payment frequencies, among other characteristics. Mismatch and coupon cap FRNs—recent market innovations—allow the investor to make a bet on the future shape of the yield curve and level of interest rates. As in the past, the floating-rate markets will continue to innovate, developing new structures that will attract various types of investors.

CHAPTER SEVENTEEN

RICHARD SEGAL is currently a research analyst in the International Bond Market Research group at Salomon Brothers Inc in London, where he concentrates mainly on the Eurodollar and the Japanese, Canadian, and Dutch Government bond markets. He has also collaborated in the development of trading strategies for the above markets. Prior to his arrival at Salomon Brothers in 1983, Mr. Segal worked at the Gillette Company in Boston, Massachusetts. Mr. Segal received a degree in economics from the Massachusetts Institute of Technology in 1982. His major focus of study was international macroeconomic policy.

AN ANALYSIS OF THE EURODOLLAR VERSUS DOMESTIC DOLLAR BOND YIELD DIFFERENTIAL, 1981-86

Richard Segal

Salomon Brothers Inc
London, England

INTRODUCTION

In the past several years, fixed-income investors have become more oriented toward international diversification, as both academic and financial industry research have demonstrated that global portfolios often provide performances superior to strictly domestic portfolios while at the same time providing lower volatility of the total returns. Although many investors are still wary of currency exposure, one may nevertheless diversify internationally by investing in the Eurodollar market. The first section of this chapter will explain some of the major differences between the Eurodollar market and the U.S. domestic market. Subsequent sections will examine the determinants of the yield differential between these two markets.

EURODOLLAR AND DOMESTIC BOND MARKETS CONTRASTED

Although the market for international trade is centuries old, the market for international finance, and more specifically, that of international fixed-income securities, is fairly new. This chapter focuses on the largest of the international bond markets: the Eurodollar bond market. The determination of whether an issue is categorized as a domestic or as a Eurodollar bond mainly concerns the location of the bond underwriters. Generally, domestic bonds are issued in New York, mostly by U.S. entities. The major issuers include the U.S. Government, U.S. Government agencies, states and municipalities, and U.S. financial and nonfinancial corporations. Foreign entities occasionally issue bonds on the U.S. domestic credit markets; these bonds are known as "Yankee" bonds. Meanwhile, any U.S. dollar-denominated bond issued outside of the United States is categorized as a Eurodollar bond. Most Eurobond underwriters are based in London, and many Eurobonds are listed and traded on the Luxembourg Stock Exchange. Popular types of Eurobonds include Eurodollar straights, floating-rate notes and convertibles, although this study focuses on the Eurodollar straight issues.

By definition, anyone may issue a Eurodollar bond. Major issuers of Eurodollar bonds include sovereign nations, supranational organizations, and U.S. and foreign financial and nonfinancial corporations. Major investors in the Eurodollar bond market include globally oriented pension funds, insurance companies and investment managers, as well as private individual European investors.

Those who invest in the Eurodollar bond market normally consider the U.S. Treasury market as the principal alternative investment. Therefore, when making a statement about Eurodollar/domestic differences, the words "domestic," "Treasuries," and "U.S. Governments" are typically used interchangeably. When analyzing the relative yields available in the two markets, bonds with ten years remaining maturity are generally compared, as Eurodollar straight bonds are infrequently issued with original maturities of greater than ten years. The term "spread" refers to the yield differential over the yield on the benchmark instrument, expressed in basis points, or hundredths of a percent. In this case, the spread refers to the yield of ten-year Eurodollar straight bonds minus the yield of ten-year U.S. Treasuries.

One of the most important spurs to the development of the Eurobond market has been its freedom from regulations. Although the worldwide trend in regulation has been toward relaxation, both relaxation and restriction have marked the U.S. domestic credit markets and have indirectly affected the Eurobond market. On January 1, 1983, the U.S. Treasury began to require that all domestic securities be issued in registered, rather than bearer, form. This move facilitated bookkeeping for the Treasury, but it also served to eliminate tax avoidance by U.S. citizens. On the other side, the 20 percent withholding tax on foreign holdings of domestic bonds was abolished in July 1984. Although this act reduced the relative attractiveness of Eurodollar bonds to investors, it did not lead to the demise of the Eurobond market, as many predicted. The market continued to thrive, partly because the bearer bond advantage still existed, and partly because of substantial promotion by Eurobond underwriters.

In Eurobond market lore, the typical investor is commonly referred to as the small private investor, whether from Switzerland or from one of the Benelux countries. While this categorization is somewhat exaggerated, the Eurobond market does retain a retail flavor. In contrast, large institutional investors have dominated trading activity in the U.S. Treasury market. Also, because of its location and because of primary market distribution regulations, the Eurobond market comprises a larger percentage of nondollar-based investors, who are subject to currency, as well as capital, risk. Although these distinctions have been fading, they are unlikely to disappear completely.

In the past few years, Eurobond underwriters have increased their use of the U.S. Treasury market as a pricing benchmark in the primary market. This trend, along with the increases in size and liquidity in the Eurobond market, has facilitated arbitrage in the secondary market between the Eurodollar and Treasury markets. Those that have become active in playing the Eurodollar versus U.S. Treasury yield differential must understand, both qualitatively and quantitatively, the factors which determine this yield differential. Historical yield differentials are presented in Figure 1. The following sections examine the determinants of this yield differential and their stability.

EURODOLLAR AND DOMESTIC BOND YIELD DIFFERENTIALS

At about the time when the dollar was at its peak, a proposition was put forth that due to increased U.S. institutional investor involvement in the Eurodollar market, it was unlikely that Eurodollar versus U.S. Treasury yield differentials would approach the wide levels of the late 1970's and early 1980's.[1] According to the theory, currency factors were no longer a major determinant of Eurodollar versus domestic yield differentials. It was felt that U.S. institutional investors had become so prominent in both markets that nondollar-based investors' currency-based Eurobond transactions would no longer exert a heavy influence on this yield differential. Recently, the dollar has dropped by about 25 percent on a trade-weighted basis, and by 30-35 percent versus the German mark and the Japanese yen. Meanwhile, the yield differential between Eurodollar bonds and Treasuries has reached its widest point in the past few years. Therefore, it is an appropriate time to ask two key questions: 1) Is the widening of the Eurodollar versus Treasury yield differential related, in a statistically verifiable manner, to the plunge of the dollar? and 2) Has this spread behaved in a predictable manner thus far in the 1980's? This study attempts to answer these questions in a quantitative form, and also to examine qualitatively some of the intricacies of the Eurodollar market which occasionally cause erratic and even contrarian behavior in certain sectors. The following section describes the various factors which may influence the Eurodollar versus Treasury yield differential and discusses the idiosyncratic behavior of the Eurodollar market. Subsequent sections describe the samples for the yield series and present the model, the results, the

FIGURE 1. EURODOLLAR VERSUS U.S. TREASURIES, TEN-YEAR MATURITY

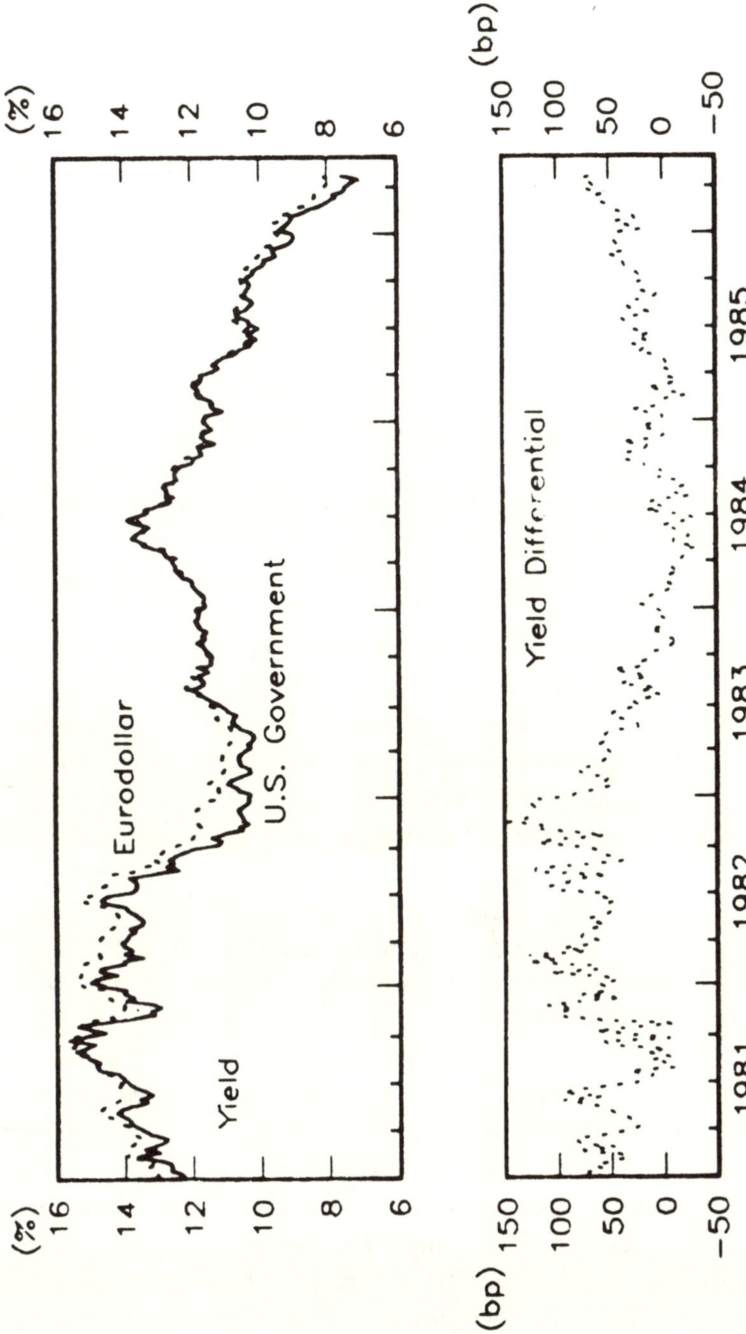

conclusions, and the forecasting usefulness of the model, with particular attention to the post-G5 period.

DETERMINANTS OF THE EURODOLLAR VERSUS DOMESTIC YIELD DIFFERENTIAL

Of the factors which have influenced Eurodollar versus domestic spreads, the following are most often cited:

a) The general level of interest rates. The concept of quality spreads suggests that yield differentials versus risk-free Government bonds should fall most rapidly when yields approach cyclical lows, and should be highest when yields approach cyclical peaks. However, spreads of Eurodollar versus Government bonds have been extraordinarily high in periods of low interest rates (mid-1979, late 1982 to early 1983), and sharply negative at cyclical highs in rates (late 1980, mid-1984).
b) Changes in the level of rates. It is noticeable, generally through anecdotal evidence, that changes in yield levels in the Eurodollar market lag those in the U.S. Government market, on both the upside and the downside.
c) Currency effect. The proportion of investors for whom the dollar is a foreign currency is likely to be much higher in the Eurodollar market than in the U.S. Treasury market, at any given time. Depreciations in the dollar reduce the value of their principal, and may cause them to sell dollar bonds to limit potential losses.
d) Relative supply. The financing needs of the U.S. Treasury have increased dramatically over the past several years. Meanwhile, Eurodollar primary market activity has risen substantially, although at a more sporadic pace. This oversupply may affect relative yield levels either through a time trend, or through a specific relative supply variable.
e) Tax legislation. The removal of the 20 percent withholding tax on foreign holdings of domestic bonds became effective

in July 1984. Since Eurobonds had always been free of withholding tax, this new regulation removed a major attraction of the Eurobond market. As a result, Eurodollar versus Treasury spreads appear to have shifted upwards, following an initial adjustment period (see Figure 2).

EURODOLLAR MARKET IDIOSYNCRACIES

In addition, certain other factors exist which may influence specific issues or sectors, but which are unlikely to affect the Eurodollar market overall. For example, Eurodollar bonds cannot legally be sold in the United States until various distribution criteria are met, amounting to a minimum of three months after the issue date. It is a common occurrence that issues of certain names, which are well-regarded in the United States but are poorly known in Europe, will outperform the rest of the Eurodollar market, when this legal buying, or "seasoning" date, approaches. A prime example of the seasoning factor as a determinant of spreads in the Eurodollar market is illustrated in Figure 3. As the bottom panel of the chart shows, the Boise Cascade 12 percent 1992 Eurodollar issue was trading as much as 90 basis points above the overall Eurodollar curve before the issue was legally purchasable in the United States. However, in the three weeks after the seasoning date, it traded an average of just 50 basis points above other Eurodollar bonds.

Instead of increasing liquidity, heavy primary market activity may cause "indigestion," affecting specific sector groups. For example, when an issue is moving slowly through its primary market distribution phase solely because of oversupply, other issues of the same borrower with similar coupon and maturity may cheapen as a result, until primary market distribution is complete. Also, certain classes of investors have historically been partial to the securities of specific high-quality borrowers. This locking-away of bonds causes these issues to trade at a much lower yield than would be typical in the home market of the same issuer.

Differentials in tax laws across nations have also altered normal

FIGURE 2. YIELD DIFFERENTIAL:
AA- AND AAA-RATED U.S. CORPORATE EURODOLLAR VERSUS U.S. TREASURY BONDS

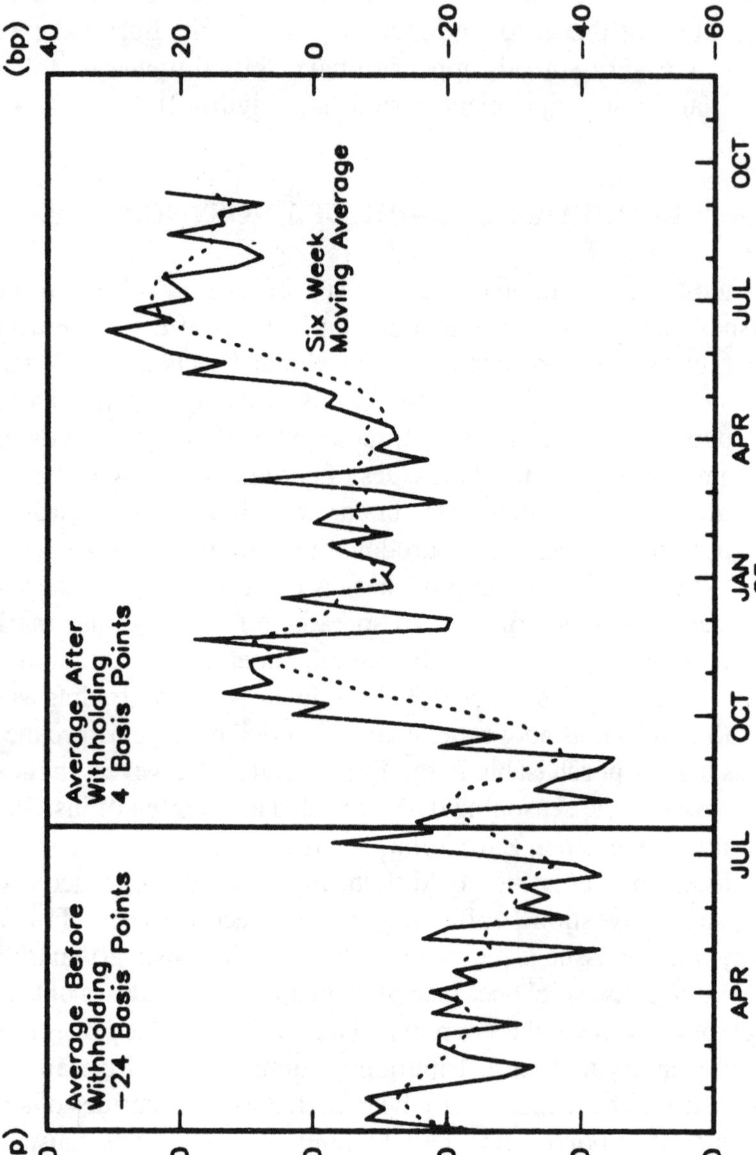

FIGURE 3. THE "SEASONING FACTOR" AS A DETERMINANT OF SPREADS IN THE EURODOLLAR MARKET

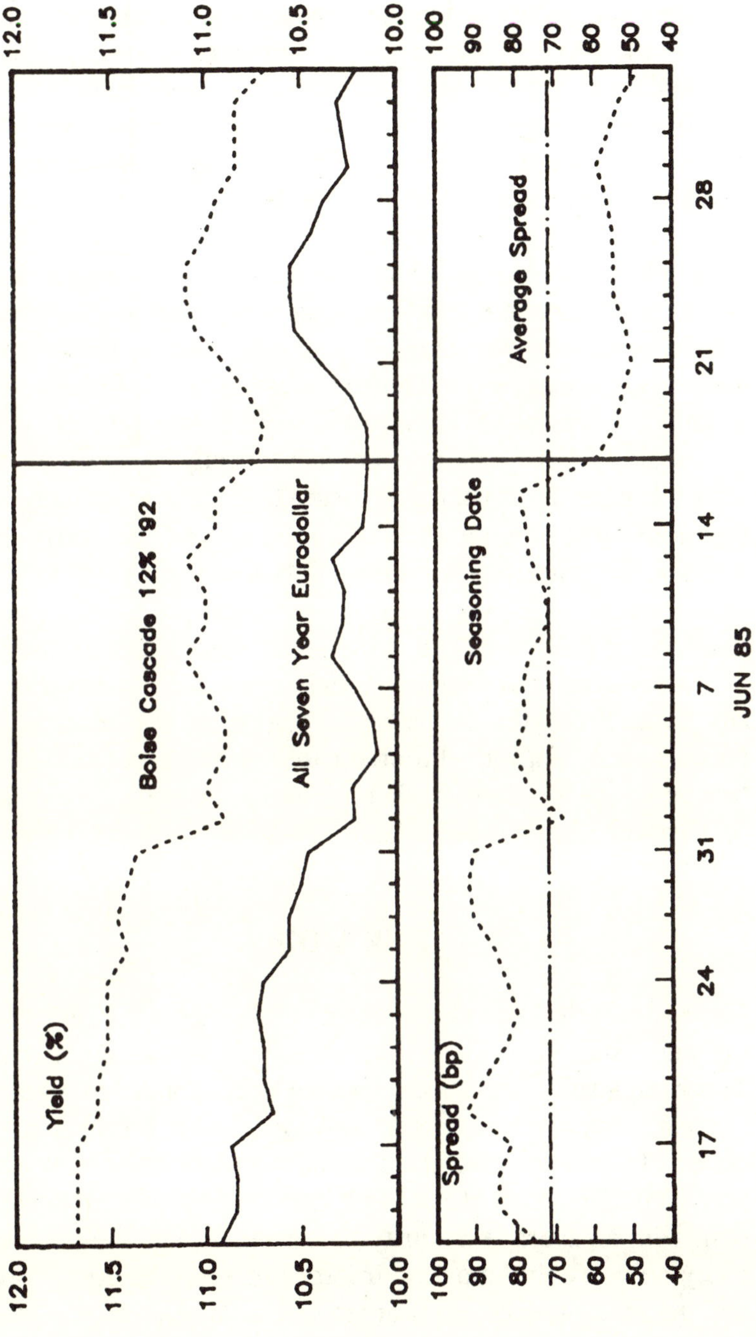

trading relationships within narrow sectors. Japanese tax laws provide an incentive to hold zero-coupon bonds, at the expense of full-coupon bonds. Meanwhile, Japanese citizens were for a long while precluded by regulation from purchasing zero-coupon "receipt products," such as CATS and TIGRs. This created a tremendous demand for Eurodollar zero-coupon bonds among Japanese investors, prior to July 1985,[2] despite a yield to maturity which was often well below that of equivalent U.S. Treasury zero-coupon bonds.

The latest example of idiosyncratic behavior is due to a factor which has been categorized as "event risk." Recent leveraged buyout and merger activity in the United States has resulted in severe downgradings in the credit rating of the securities of several large U.S. corporations. European investors subsequently became wary of U.S. names in general, causing their issues to trade at a much higher yield than those of foreign entities. Although investors clearly did have a reason for concern (see Figure 4), there is some evidence that they overreacted. As Figure 5 shows, the Sears 11⅝ 1991 Eurodollar issue traded about even with U.S. Treasuries throughout 1985. However, this event-risk factor suddenly caused European investors to shy away from the Sears issue beginning in December 1985. Nevertheless, with a solid credit rating, and an equity capitalization of about $17 billion, Sears is unlikely to become a takeover or leveraged buyout candidate.

THE MODEL

The basis for the U.S. Government yield series is the current coupon ten-year issue, as this issue is the most actively traded ten-year issue. This benchmark issue is rotated every three months, in order to keep the maturity constant at about ten years, and to create a continuous series. The sample for the Eurodollar yield series consists of a representative group of AA- and AAA-rated issues, of current coupon, with an average maturity of ten years. The sample is revised every six to twelve months, in order to keep the coupons current and the maturities constant at ten years. Whenever possible, non-

FIGURE 4. MAJOR CORPORATE DOWNGRADINGS, 1985-86

Company	S&P Rating Change		Date of Change	Major Event
	From	To		
Chesebrough-Ponds	AA-	BBB	Feb 85	Acquisition of Stauffer Chemical
Phillips Petroleum	AA	BBB	Mar 85	Takeover battle with Mesa Petroleum
Unocal	AA+	BBB	May 85	Takeover battle with Mesa Petroleum
RJ Reynolds	AA	A	Jun 85	Acquisition of Nabisco Brands
Levi Strauss	A	B+	Aug 85	Leveraged buyout[a]
Texaco	A+	B	Dec 85	$11.1-billion jury verdict favoring Pennzoil
Union Carbide	A	B-	Jan 86	Takeover battle with GAF Corporation, plus industrial accident-related lawsuits
Revlon	A+	B	Jan 86	Acquisition by Pantry Pride

[a] Eurodollar 11% 1990 bond was defeased in January 1986.

FIGURE 5. THE EFFECT OF LEVERAGED BUYOUT ACTIVITY ON EURODOLLAR VERSUS DOMESTIC YIELD DIFFERENTIALS

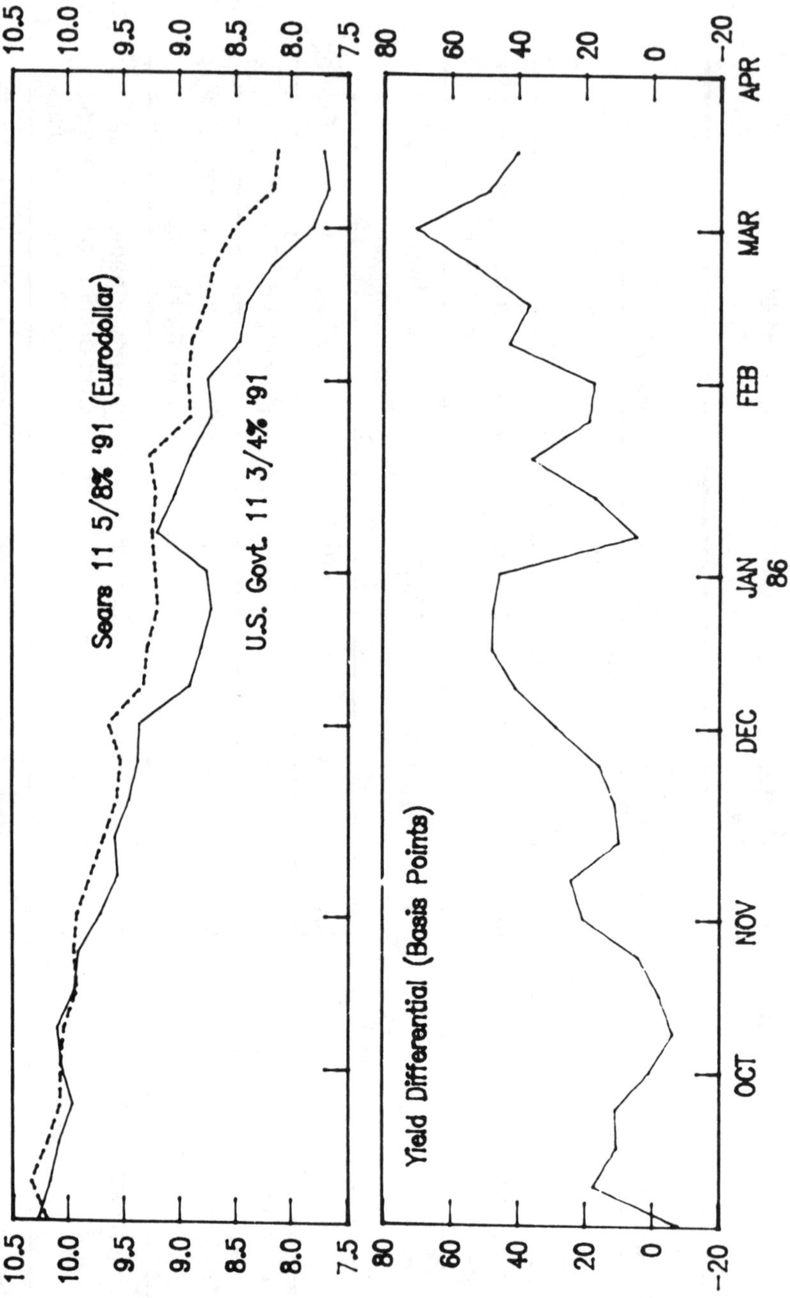

callable issues are used. The yield is then calculated by taking the simple average of the yields of those issues in the basket. Using this method, a homogeneous series is created.

In this way this study compares the effect of investing in a portfolio of Eurobonds, rather than in a single benchmark issue. A study which simulates the holding of a ten-year benchmark Eurodollar issue, and rotating the issues to create a long time series, would probably produce different results. However, such results would not necessarily be consistent with the overall market trend, as a Eurodollar series constructed in this way would be non-homogeneous, and may be biased due to the market idiosyncracies illustrated above. Despite the fact that the results of this study may be sample-dependent, due to data difficulties and inconsistencies, any other sufficiently diversified portfolio would likely arrive at the same conclusions. Moreover, this method should provide a fair and efficient method for discerning the overall market behavior.

Drawing on the theory of the determinants of the Eurodollar versus domestic yield differential, the following model was developed and tested:

1) $SP = a + b_1US + b_2\Delta US + b_3\Delta DM + b_4DUM + b_5TIME + e$

where,

SP = Eurodollar versus U.S. Treasury spread or yield differential, ten-year maturity (basis points)

US = Ten-year U.S. Government bond yield (percent)

ΔUS = One-month change in ten-year U.S. Government bond yield (basis points)

ΔDM = One-month change in DM/US$ exchange rate (pfennigs $\times$ 100)

DUM = Dummy variable 0 prior to July 1984 withholding tax removal
1 after July 1984 withholding tax removal

TIME = January 1981 = 1, February 1981 = 2, . . ., April 1986 = 64

e = random error term

The data set begins in January 1981, and goes through April 1986. The rate of change variables are calculated as the monthly average of the day-to-day change. For the other variables, the individual data points are calculated as the monthly average of the daily observations.

The following result was obtained:

$$1)\ SP = 322.38 - \underset{(5.41)}{18.66US} - \underset{(3.76)}{2.03\Delta US} - \underset{(1.68)}{4.38\Delta DM} - \underset{(3.90)}{1.95TIME}$$

t-statistics are in parentheses, $R^2 = 0.85$, D.W. = 1.82

Note: To correct for the presence of strong first order serial correlation, an autoregressive error model (AR1) was used to estimate the coefficients.[3] Also, the dummy variable was dropped from the equation, on the basis of a very low t-statistic.

Overall, the results confirm the major hypotheses set forth earlier. In answer to the first question posed, the currency effect appears to be moderate, though not statistically significant. In answer to the second question, reference to Figure 6 shows that the Eurodollar versus Treasury spread relationship, as modeled above, has behaved in a very predictable manner over the 1981-1986 period. An interpretation of the results follows.

THE INTEREST RATE VARIABLE

One may consider the large constant term and the Government bond yield variable as tandem variables. A nominal interest rate on bonds of close to zero would result from a prolonged period of deflation. Deflation, however, might force corporate borrowers to repay long-term debt with more expensive dollars. Such a circumstance would negatively affect corporate balance sheets, and lead to increased default risk, thereby increasing yield differentials versus risk-free

FIGURE 6. EURODOLLAR VERSUS U.S. TREASURIES—ACTUAL VERSUS FITTED SPREADS (SAMPLE PERIOD: JAN 81 TO APR 86)

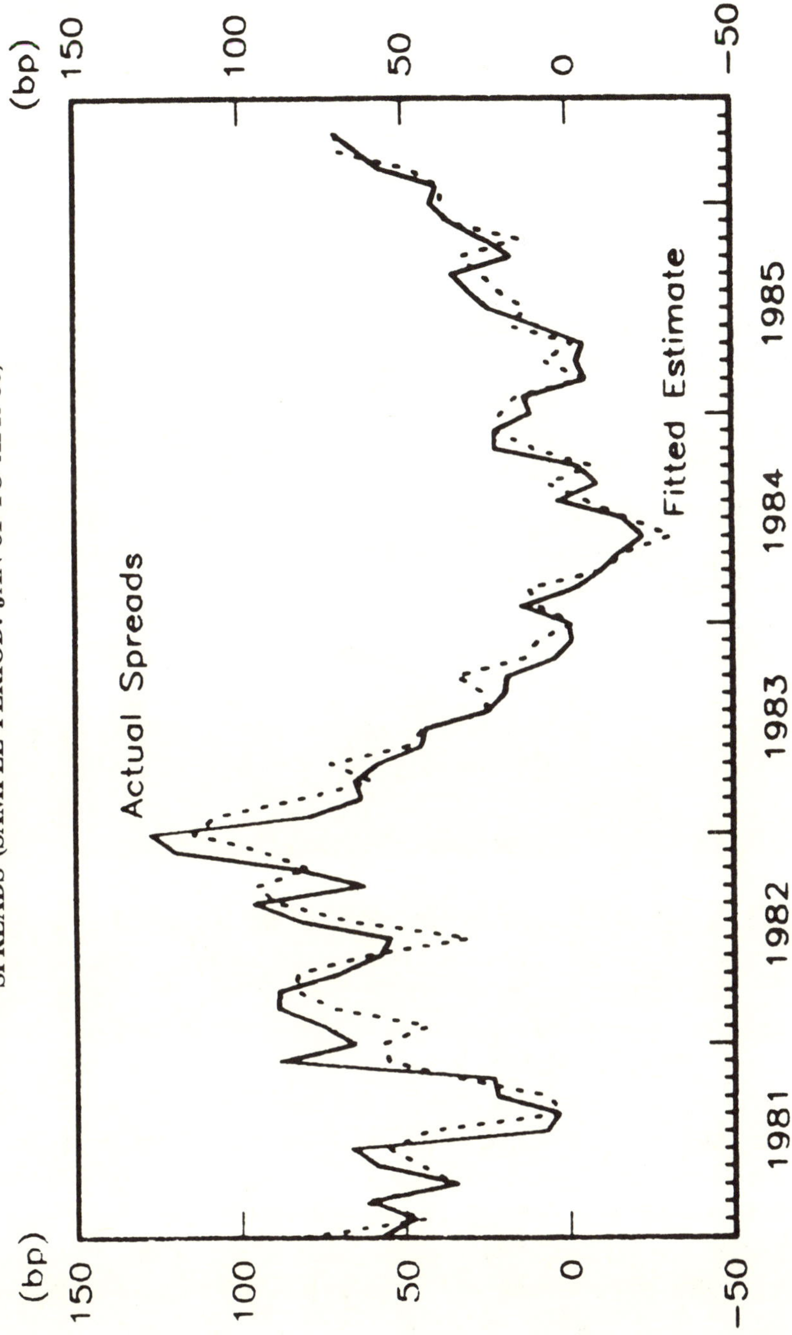

Government bonds. Indeed, in a very low interest rate scenario, the model predicts a very wide spread versus Treasuries. Conversely, the model predicts a negative spread versus Treasuries when interest rates are very high. As pointed out earlier, Eurodollar versus Treasury differentials turned negative during the 1981 and 1984 peaks in the interest rate cycle. This suggests that the behavior of spreads is inversely related to the behavior of interest rates, in contradiction to the concept of quality spreads.

Also, the Government bond yield variable is the dominant variable of the equation, indicating that movements in the Treasury market precipitate changes in the Eurodollar versus domestic yield differential. This confirms the anecdotal evidence that movements in the Eurodollar market consistently lag movements in the U.S. Government market. In quantitative terms, the model predicts that, *ceteris paribus,* a 100 basis point decrease in the ten-year U.S. Government bond yield will cause the spread to increase by 18.6 basis points. The bond yield change variable exerts a minor influence on the yield differential, as its coefficient value is rather small. Also, the mean value of the bond yield change variable is only −0.25 basis points, and its maximum absolute value only 6.82 basis points.

RELATIVE SUPPLY

While different specifications were attempted in order to capture the relative supply effect, it appears that the time trend variable is the most appropriate proxy to model the relative supply of Eurodollar and Treasury issues in the credit markets.[4] Since Treasury auctions are regularly scheduled throughout the year, the impact of a higher level of Government borrowing on yield spreads would likely be gradual but steady. Indeed, equation 1) indicates a significant gradual narrowing of Eurodollar versus Treasury spreads since 1981 at the rate of two basis points per month. Although Eurodollar primary market issuance has increased exponentially in the past few years, it is still well below that of U.S. Treasury bond issuance. Also, the impact of increased Eurodollar issuance, which most frequently appears in bursts, is likely to be a short-lived widening of spreads. Unless specifically designed, the statistical tests performed above would not pick up such a blip in spreads.

Taking these variables into account, the model predicts that yields of high-quality Eurodollar bonds will move 83 percent as much as yields in the Treasury market during a rally, and 79 percent as much during a market setback. This predictably low volatility makes Eurodollar bonds attractive as defensive instruments, while the negative time trend causes prices of Eurobonds to match those of Treasuries more closely during a rally than during a setback.

CURRENCY EFFECT

Despite an intuitive link between the strength of the dollar and the spread, the statistical link is not as strong. (The model uses the Deutschemark to test the currency effect, because the Deutschemark is the main sparring partner of the dollar in the foreign exchange markets, and because the Deutschemark is the major reserve currency in Europe.) Although various specifications were tested, only the rate of change variable (ΔDM/US$) proved even moderately significant, and then only at the 90 percent confidence level.

There are no statistics available concerning investors' transactions of Eurodollar bonds. However, it is well-accepted that the participation of U.S. institutional investors in the Euromarkets has increased substantially in the past few years, as this group has become more diversification-oriented, and as U.S. corporate issuance in the Eurodollar market has increased sharply. If U.S. investors are more likely than European investors to arbitrage any widening Eurodollar versus domestic yield differential, it is reasonable to assume that the growing presence of the former group in the Eurodollar market (as they are not exposed to currency risk) would cause the currency effect to diminish over time.

In order to test for a change over time in the influence of the dollar strength variable, the regression was broken up into two time periods.[5] In the 1981-1982 period, the currency strength variable was found to be a significant determinant of the Eurodollar versus domestic dollar yield differential, while in the latter period,[6] it was very insignificant. Barring sophistocated statistical tests, the weakening of the currency effect appears to be confirmed. Also, it may be that any seeming significance of the currency effect is spurious, as the currencies generally move in the same direction as interest rates, and because currency strengths have tended to follow long time trends.[7]

TAX LEGISLATION EFFECT

While the tax effect variable is not significant for the entire sample period, it is important to note that relevant tax legislation was also enacted in 1982. Therefore, it may be invalid to construct a dummy variable to measure the tax effect, using the 1984 withholding tax removal as the sole proxy. This other piece of legislation is the Tax Equity and Fiscal Responsibility Act, which required that all domestic bonds be issued in registered or book-entry form, as opposed to bearer form, beginning January 1, 1983. The bearer/registered effect is likely to be different from the withholding tax removal effect, because the former should have a greater effect on the tax evader, whereas the latter should have a greater effect on the tax avoider. In order to isolate the effect of the withholding tax removal, the regression was rerun for the post-bearer bond period, from January 1983 to April 1986.[8] In this regression, the tax effect variable was found to be significant, with a value of 23 basis points. Although the sample for this test differs from the sample used in Figure 2, it is comforting nevertheless that the difference in pre- and post-withholding average differential (28 basis points) is very close to the value we have calculated for the effect of the removal of the withholding tax (23 basis points). The combined effect of this tax change and the time trend, when considered from the beginning of 1983, can be interpreted as in Figure 7.

FIGURE 7. THE COMBINED EFFECT OF TAX LEGISLATION AND THE TIME TREND ON EURODOLLAR VERSUS DOMESTIC YIELD SPREADS

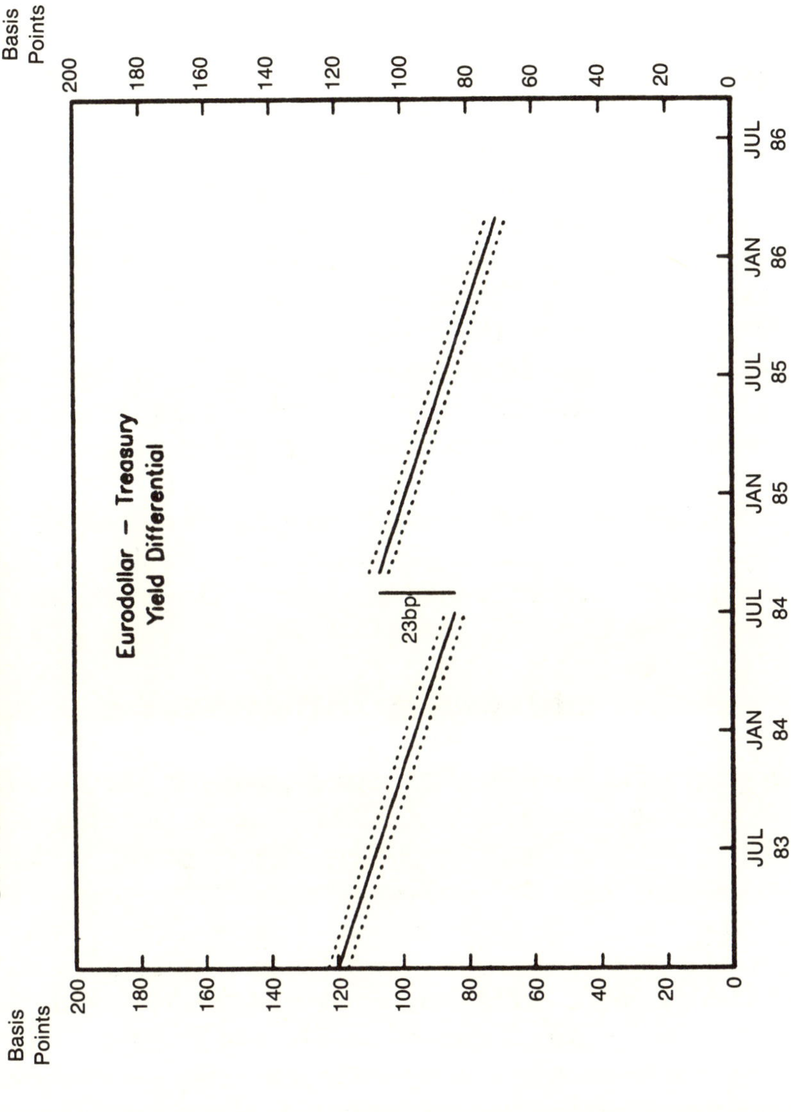

SUMMARY AND CONCLUSIONS

To recap, the yield spread between high-quality Eurodollar bonds and U.S. Treasuries, between 1981 and 1986, behaved in a very predictable manner. In addition, the Treasury bond yield variable appears to be the most important determinant of the Eurodollar versus domestic yield differential. While other factors clearly influence the relation, one can easily forecast the level of the Eurodollar versus Treasury spread, once one knows the direction of the Treasury market. Also, various technical factors, such as "seasoning," investor affinity and event risk, from time-to-time affect certain sector groups, but exert no overall effect on the performance of a broad-based basket of Eurodollar bonds. The currency effect appears to have subsided for the time being. Still, it would be unwise for a dollar-based investor to ignore the potential effect of a rapidly-declining dollar on Eurodollar bond prices. It is most likely that these factors should remain influential over the medium term, and with roughly the same magnitude. However, the necessary ingredient for forecasting the Eurodollar versus Treasury yield spread is the ability to forecast the level of interest rates, which is clearly another matter.

OUTLOOK FOR THE FUTURE

A major drawback of econometric models is the uncertainty surrounding the usefulness of estimates, in the face of significant structural change, or in the case of a severe external shock to the model. While equation 1 has been successful in pinpointing the major determinants of the Eurodollar versus Treasury yield spread, the model's forecasting prowess has yet to be tested. Also, while the overall currency effect has been termed moderate, most of the sample period can be characterized as one of dollar strength. Therefore, we would hope to be able to test the forecasting usefulness of the model by measuring the performance of the model during a period of severe dollar weakness. Conveniently, a major structural change to a major variable in the model occurred in September 1985, with the meeting of the Group of Five finance ministers. Subsequent to their accord, a severe drop in the value of the dollar ensued. As a test for the model, the coefficients have been reestimated from January 1981 through August 1985, and the spread has been forecasted out of sample through April 1986.[9] Surprisingly, the coefficient estimate of the dollar strength variable is moderately higher for the shorter sample period. Despite the sudden change to the trend behavior of the dollar strength variable, the other coefficient estimates change little when the sample period is shortened. As Figure 8 shows, the out of sample forecasts are accurate, further indicating the statistical appropriateness of the model, at least for the time being.

FIGURE 8. EURODOLLAR VERSUS U.S. TREASURIES—TEN-YEAR MATURITY, ACTUAL VERSUS FITTED SPREADS (SAMPLE PERIOD: JAN 81 TO AUG 85)

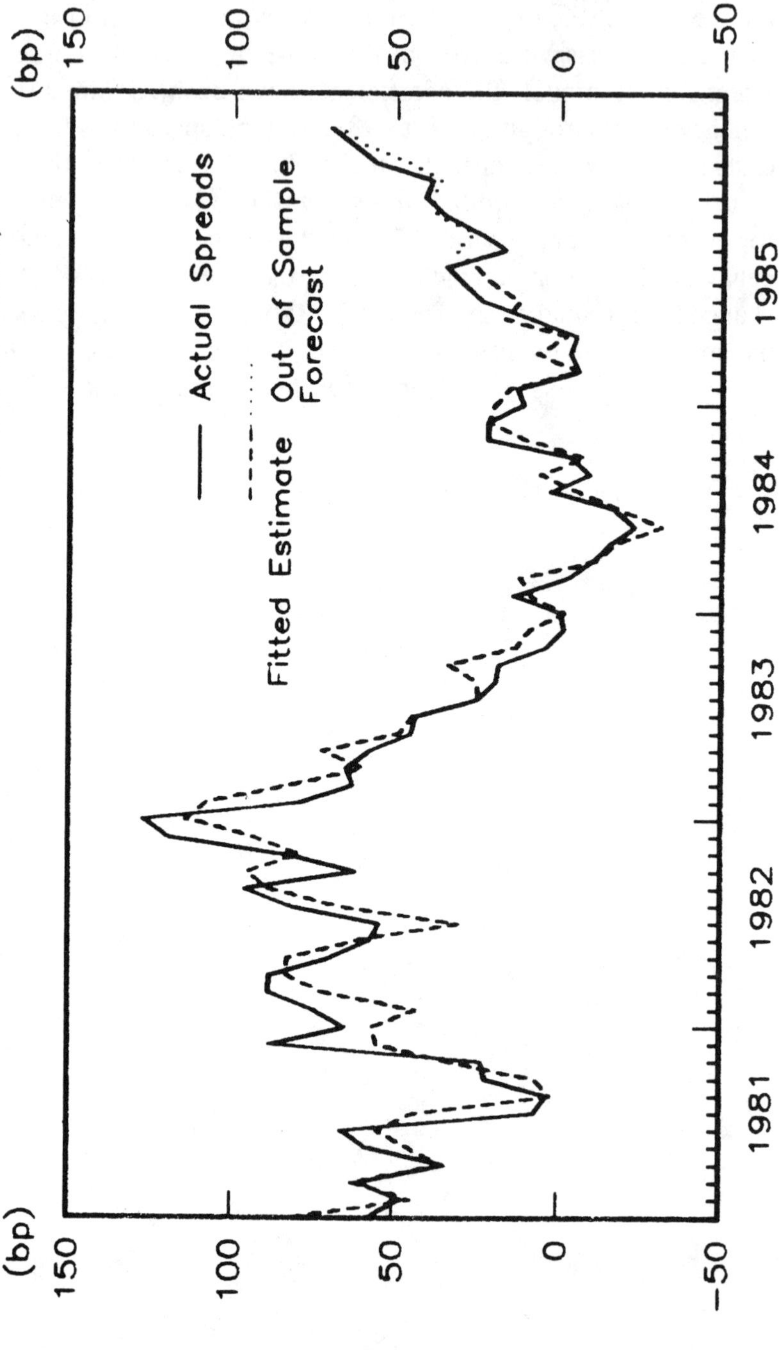

NOTES

[1]See "Eurodollar versus domestic bond yield spreads—Why a weaker dollar will not cause them to widen significantly," Salomon Brothers Inc., August 9, 1985.

[2]Japanese investors were allowed to purchase certain stripped zero-coupon bonds, known as "corpus STRIPS," shortly after the U.S. Treasury began to officially sponsor these securities.

[3]The original specification is as follows:

$$SP = \underset{}{331.10} - \underset{(4.58)}{12.55US} - \underset{(4.11)}{4.26\Delta US} + \underset{(2.60)}{36.03\Delta DM} - \underset{(4.78)}{1.76TIME} + \underset{(2.07)}{20.07DUM}$$

$R^2 = 0.65$ D.W. = 0.66

At first glance, the equation appears satisfactory in terms of the significance of coefficients at the R^2 term. However, the low Durbin-Watson statistic (0.66) suggests the presence of serial correlation, leaving little confidence in the validity of the other statistics. Reference to Figure 9 demonstrates the high serial correlation of the error variable. This equation overpredicts the actual values of the spread for most of 1981, and 1983 through the first half of 1984, while it underpredicts wildly for most of 1982. The respecification with the error model, as in equation 1, improves the R^2 from 0.65 to 0.85, and the dummy variable drops out of the equation. Although a low Durbin-Watson statistic initially suggests an omitted variable, no additional variable is readily apparent to the author. The final test of a model is its predictive powers. From reference to Figure 6, it is clear that the model based on equation 1 has passed this test.

[4]The time trend and the relative supply variables each appeared to be significant when included in the model separately. However, the relative supply variable dropped out when both variables were included, indicating a degree of collinearity between the two series.

[5]For the 1981-82 period, the specification is:

$$SP = 362.84 - \underset{(2.82)}{10.48US} - \underset{(0.87)}{1.20\Delta US} - \underset{(1.82)}{83.40\Delta DM} - \underset{(2.71)}{2.98TIME}$$

$R^2 = 0.63$ D.W. = 1.49

For the 1983-86 period, the specification is:

$$SP = 295.58 - \underset{(7.42)}{19.17US} - \underset{(2.88)}{1.51\Delta US} - \underset{(0.65)}{1.26\Delta DM} - \underset{(3.67)}{1.03TIME}$$

$R^2 = 0.91$ D.W. = 1.80

An error model (AR1) was used to estimate the equation.

[6]The beginning of the latter period coincides with the elimination of bearer bonds in the U.S. domestic market. A dummy variable was introduced into the model

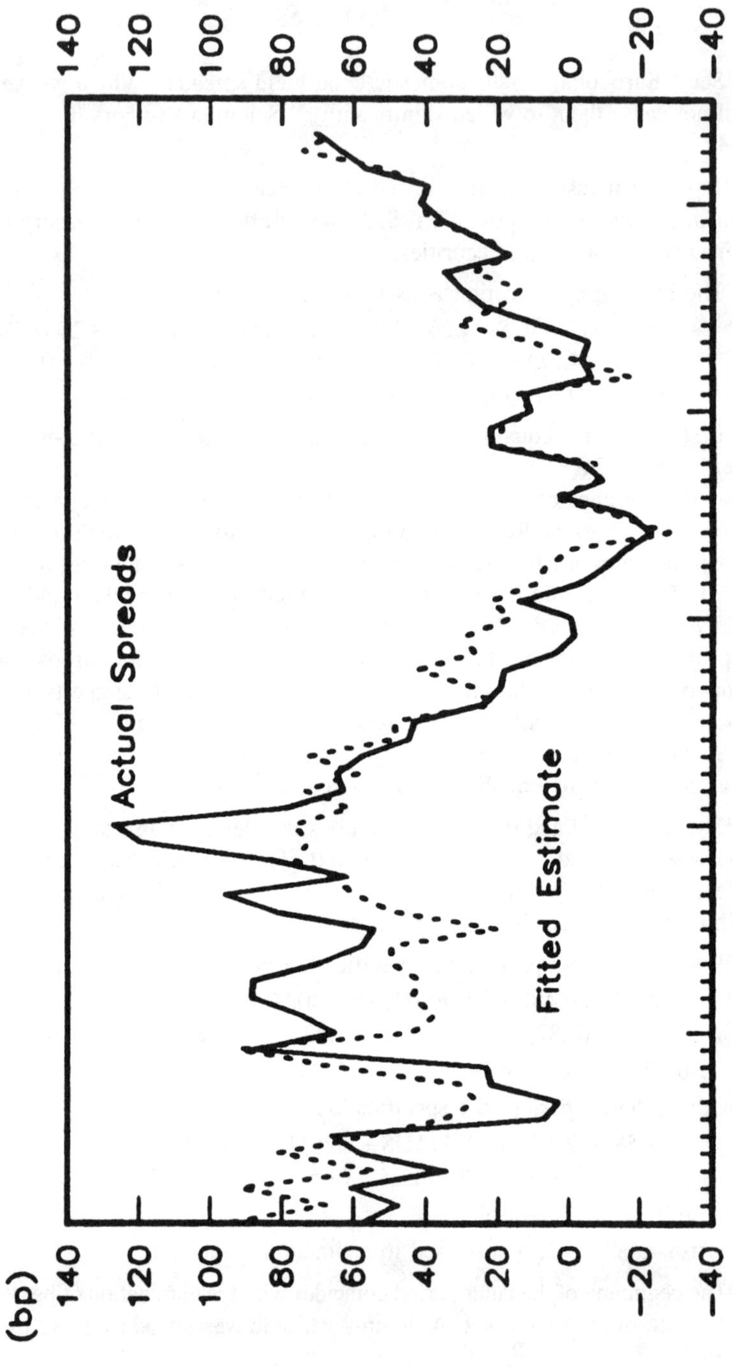

FIGURE 9. EURODOLLAR VERSUS U.S. TREASURIES—TEN-YEAR MATURITY, ACTUAL VERSUS FITTED SPREADS (SAMPLE PERIOD: JAN 81 TO APR 86)

to measure the effect of this restriction on the Eurodollar versus Treasury spread. However, the amount of structural changes taking place in the Eurodollar market at the same time make it unlikely that this dummy variable picked up exclusively the bearer bond advantage.

[7]The following regression was run in order to test this possibility. The specification is as follows:

$$DM = 1.58 + \underset{(1.83)}{0.04US} + \underset{(4.67)}{0.016TIME}$$

$R^2 = 0.93$ D.W. $= 1.67$

An error model (AR1) was used to estimate the coefficients. Since both variables are significant at at least the 93 percent confidence level, one may safely accept the hypothesis that the DM/U.S. dollar exchange rate has been correlated with the level of U.S interest rates, as well as with the time trend. This may help to explain the lack of significance of the currency effect variable in equation 1. Note: The above regression was run through November 1985 only, due to the break between the dollar strength and the time trend. However, the main purpose of this regression is to establish a link between the interest rate and the currency strength variables. Also, a regression which tests the recent weak dollar period would not have sufficient degrees of freedom to produce meaningful results.

[8]The specification is as follows:

$$SP = 173.71 - \underset{(4.54)}{14.35US} - \underset{(3.14)}{1.55\Delta US} + \underset{(1.91)}{2.03(\Delta DM)} - \underset{(4.39)}{1.77TIME} + \underset{(2.66)}{23.15DUM}$$

$R^2 = 0.93$ D.W. $= 1.80$

[9]The specification for the January 1981 to August 1985 period is as follows:

$$SP = 322.16 - \underset{(4.68)}{18.61US} - \underset{(3.49)}{2.02\ \ US} - \underset{(1.63)}{4.92\Delta DM} - \underset{(3.40)}{1.97TIME}$$

$R^2 = 0.85$ D.W. $= 1.77$

An error model (ARI) was employed to estimate the coefficients.

CHAPTER EIGHTEEN

GIOIA M. PARENTE is an Analyst in the International Bond Market Research Group at Salomon Brothers Inc in New York. She studies both dollar and nondollar international floating-rate markets and has written numerous publications describing the market and assessing relative value. Ms. Parente holds a Bachelor of Science Degree in Journalism and a Masters of Business Administration in Finance.

DEVELOPMENTS IN THE EURONOTE AND EUROCOMMERCIAL PAPER MARKET*

Gioia M. Parente
Salomon Brothers Inc
New York, New York

INTRODUCTION

Euronotes and Eurocommercial paper are short-term unsecured promissory notes that are issued in discount or interest-bearing form. Euronotes are distributed through facilities that guarantee a prescribed amount of funds for a stated number of years. These facilities are underwritten by banks committed to purchase notes at predetermined rates if they are not placed by tender panel members. These banks may also make advances. Borrowers tap the facilities through dealer placement or competitive tender panels. Euronotes are generally issued in one-, three- and six-month maturities. In contrast, Eurocommercial paper is distributed through dealership-sponsored programs that provide for distribution of securities through nominated dealers on a best-effort basis. The amounts and maturities that are issued are flexible and many be matched to investors' cash flow requirements.

Amid heightened interest in the international short-term markets, Euronotes and Eurocommercial paper (ECP) have experienced

*This chapter is extracted from *Critical Issues in the Euronote and Eurocommercial Paper Market,* Salomon Brothers Inc, June 1986.

unprecedented growth in recent years: Since the beginning of 1984, an estimated $95.7 billion of these facilities was arranged—greater than the issue volume of Eurodollar floating-rate notes (FRNs) for the same period (see Figure 1). Actual utilization of these facilities also has increased, albeit at a slower pace: Approximately $20 billion of these short-term promissory notes is currently outstanding, compared with $4 billion just over one year ago. This rapid expansion has created a plethora of new financing structures, resulting in general confusion among investors and issuers over the general nature of the market and its potential. In this chapter, we describe the dynamics of the market and analyze its potential as a viable international short-term investment and an alternative funding vehicle. We also discuss critical issues that affect the market's development, including structural, regulatory and secondary-market considerations.

KEY TRENDS

Recently, some key trends have emerged in the Euronote and ECP market, including the following:

Widening Investor Base. The note issuance facility market, in which Euronotes are issued, was first conceived as a cheaper and more flexible financing alternative to medium-term syndicated loans. Thus, the *initial* emphasis was on the underwriting commitment guaranteed by the banks in the arrangement, rather than on the potential for the future issuance of securities. That focus has changed in the past several months: Now, the development of a large, committed investor base has become increasingly important for the future of this market. The structuring of a large number of facilities in which the standby (or underwriting commitment) is separated from the issuance facility—creating uncommitted Euronotes or ECP—is also indicative of this trend.

This action was also spurred by recent Bank of England regulations regarding the potential risk of underwriting commitments amassed by the British banking community. (The U.S. authorities have considered similar actions.) In an effort to replace dwindling

FIGURE 1 THE EURONOTE AND EUROCOMMERCIAL PAPER MARKET VERSUS OTHER FLOATING-RATE MARKETS, 1982-FIRST QUARTER 1986
(U.S. DOLLARS IN MILLIONS OR EQUIVALENT)[a]

	1Q 86 (Annualized)	1985	1984	1983	1982
Euronote/Eurocommercial Paper Facilities	**$73,812**	**$57,392**	**$19,828**	**$3,145**	**$2,706**
Eurodollar FRNs	24,064	47,668	29,224	14,080	11,160
Domestic LIBOR FRNs	3,000	7,568	4,000	1,160	800
Domestic Treasury Bill FRNs	—	2,638	1,595	4,100	1,000
Nondollar FRNs[b]	11,808	7,874	2,769	966	147
International Bank Loans[c]	42,884	53,461	53,219	60,209	90,756

[a] The volume of Euronotes/Eurocommercial paper facilities represented here is arrangements, not actual drawdowns. Issue volume is presented for other markets.

[b] Euro and foreign FRNs. Does not include domestic FRNs issued in Italy and France, for example.

[c] As published by the Organization for Economic Cooperation and Development (OECD).

syndicated loan business, commercial banks have entered into agreements whereby they guarantee to purchase any Euronotes tendered and subsequently not sold. In return for this contingent liability, a commitment fee is paid to the banks by the issuer. However, competition among underwriting banks to gain a presence in the Euronote market has driven these fees to thin levels, causing the regulatory agencies further concern.

Various types of investors have demonstrated interest in Euronotes and Eurocommercial paper, both on the institutional and retail level. These types include: banks, bank trust departments, central banks, corporations, insurance companies, and money and pension funds. The superior return of these instruments versus alternative money market investments is the primary attraction: In many cases, an investor may purchase a top-quality sovereign credit—such as the Kingdom of Sweden—and obtain a hefty spread over U.S. Treasury bills, which is a comparable credit. Traditional money market investors also may diversify away from strictly bank credits—such as certificates of deposit—into securities issued by government, government-guaranteed or corporate entities.

Distribution Methods. Concurrent with the emergence of the uncommitted facility, the *dealership* distribution method has gained popularity. Interestingly, the trend has come full circle. At the market's inception, the sole dealership was the primary distribution method incorporated into the structure of the note issuance facility. As the market expanded, the tender panel—boasting attractive rate levels and high visibility for issuers, because of its competitive bidding process—became more popular. Now the dealership method has made a comeback. Critics of the tender panel contend that it does not allow for orderly placement, and that tender panelists cannot guarantee Euronotes to potential investors until after the bidding is completed and they are awarded securities.

The development of uncommitted ECP has also been fashioned, in part, after U.S. commercial paper (CP), a market that has thrived in the sole- or multiple-dealership arrangement. As the U.S. CP experience demonstrates, the dealership method lends itself to the development of an established investor base—a primary goal of the

Euronote/ECP market. The distribution mechanism utilized in the future will depend on the credit quality of the institution as well as on the purpose of the financing.

Credit Quality. The credit quality of borrowers in the Euronote/ECP market also has changed in the past year. At its inception, the market was largely comprised of traditional syndicated loan borrowers, certainly low-profile issuers in the securities markets. In the past year, however, a spate of top-quality U.S. corporations—many of which are prolific borrowers in their domestic CP market—has arranged programs (see Figure 2). Currently, Euronotes—where the underwriting commitment is embedded in the structure—have replaced bank lines for these borrowers, serving as low-cost standbys to support active U.S. CP programs. On the other hand, many borrowers also have structured ECP programs—for the purpose of issuing securities—hoping to capitalize on any future cost advantages in the Euromarket versus the U.S. market, as well as to gain name recognition in the European market. Consequently, many market participants speculate that a *global commercial paper market,* where borrowers can simultaneously access either market depending on cost considerations, will emerge.

Prospects for a Global Commercial Paper Market. Whether the ECP market will mature into the European counterpart of the large and highly successful U.S. CP market remains a key question. Indeed, several characteristics of the U.S. market—notably, flexible-issue amounts, odd-date maturities and dealership placement—have been incorporated into the structure of many ECP programs in recent months. Moreover, the large volume of arrangements already in place in Europe portends hefty outstanding volume of paper, and the ECP market may eventually emerge as a significant complement to the U.S. market. Certain fundamental differences—particularly the stimuli behind their development—remain between the markets, however. U.S. CP emerged as a means for large corporate entities to exchange excess liquidity, while ECP grew out of the international loan market. Certain regulatory restrictions, as well as time zone differences, also may prohibit the total merging of the two markets; for example, the ECP market—unlike

FIGURE 2 REPRESENTATIVE U.S. ISSUERS IN THE EURONOTE AND EUROCOMMERCIAL MARKET
(U.S. DOLLARS IN MILLIONS)[a]

	Amount	Term (Years)
Deere & Co.	$1,300	5
Beatrice Co.	1,200	3
Unilever Capital Corp.	1,000	7
IBM Credit Corporation	500	5
Chrysler Financial Services	500	—
Houston Natural Gas Corp.	450	7
Arco	400	5
EBS Finance	1,030	5
Borden, Inc.	300	5
Cigna	300	3
Weyerhaeuser Corp.	300	5
CBS, Inc.	200	5
Colgate-Palmolive	200	5
Occidental Petroleum	200	5
Fleet Financial Group	150	5
Republic New York Corp.	150	5
Goodyear Tire & Rubber Co.	100	—
U.S. Bancorp	75	3
PepsiCo, Inc.	Unspecified	—
General Electric	Unspecified	—
First Interstate Bancorp	Unspecified	—

[a] These are single facilities recently arranged by U.S. entities. Volume represented is arrangements, not drawdowns.

its U.S. counterpart—operates in a regulatory-free environment without rating and backup line requirements.

COMPOSITION OF THE MARKET

In general, the Euronote/ECP market comprises a large diversity of nationality and industry types. In fact, in 1985 the composition of the market changed dramatically in terms of nationality of arrangements. U.S. entities were the top borrowers by far in 1985, stacking up over 30 percent of the market that year, compared with shares of 14.5 percent and 7.9 percent in 1984 and 1983, respectively (see Figure 3). The majority of last year's U.S. facilities was for corporate borrowers, with a smattering of bank- and utility-type issuers. British corporations have also increased their presence: In 1985, British institutions claimed just over 10 percent of the market, compared with 4.4 percent in 1984 and nothing at all in 1983. Scandinavian countries also are important borrowers: Sweden, Finland and Norway all ranked among the top borrowers for 1985. The Swedish borrowers' share declined by almost 15 percent this past year, however, after finishing first in 1984. Australia and France remained in the second- and fifth-place slots, respectively, in 1985.

The industry profile of arrangements also has shifted in the past three years. Sovereign borrowers' growing significance is particularly apparent: In 1985, they represented 62 percent of the market, more than twice the 1982 share. In contrast, banks' portion of the market dwindled below 8 percent in 1985 from 34 percent in 1982.

CRITICAL ISSUES: STRUCTURAL CONSIDERATIONS

The homogeneity of the Euronote/ECP product is a primary concern for both issuers and investors. As Figure 4 shows, there are fundamental differences among the key primary- and secondary-market conventions operating in the Euronote, ECP and U.S. CP markets. In general, the Euronote/ECP market is in flux, which has

FIGURE 3 TOP BORROWERS IN THE EURONOTE/EUROCOMMERCIAL PAPER MARKET BY NATIONALITY, 1983-85
(U.S. DOLLARS IN MILLIONS)[a]

	1985			1984			1983	
	Total	Pct. of Market		Total	Pct. of Market		Total	Pct. of Market
United States	$16,770	30.4%	Sweden	$4,535	22.9%	Japan	$1,150	36.6%
Australia	10,571	19.2	Australia	3,068	15.5	France	1,005	32.0
Britain	5,611	10.2	United States	2,855	14.5	Australia	300	9.5
Sweden	4,501	8.2	New Zealand	1,575	7.9	United States	250	7.9
France	2,711	4.9	France	1,233	6.2	Malaysia	100	4.8
Italy	2,203	4.0	Denmark	1,200	6.1	Spain	100	3.2
Netherlands	1,550	2.8	Switzerland	1,100	5.5	Norway	70	2.2
Finland	1,175	2.1	Britain	877	4.4	Sweden	70	2.2
Norway	1,123	2.0	Spain	500	2.5	Kuwait	50	1.6
Canada	922	1.7	Turkey	500	2.5			
			Supranational	500	2.5			

[a] Volume represented is arrangements, not actual drawdowns.

resulted in many of the current structural differences relative to its U.S. counterpart. Attempts are underway, however, to standardize some of these characteristics. In particular, an industry association—composed of the dominant market participants—has recently been formed to address the great disparity in market practices.

Naming Conventions. A host of different acronyms that, ironically, *differentiate similar*—or even *identical*—financing structures has sprung up with the development of the Euronote market, which has created widespread confusion among both investors and issuers. Structures classified as NIFs, RUFs, TRUFs, PUFs, SNIFs, SNCFs, GRUFs, BONUSES, among others, are existing simultaneously. Despite these differentiations, the market is straightforward. From a financing standpoint, all of these facilities provide a borrower with access to medium-term funds that can be utilized as a standby or mechanism to issue securities. To the investor, there is no practical difference among the byproducts of these facilities; each produces identical short-term, unsecured promissory notes in either discount or interest-bearing format.

Within this maze of acronyms, certain financing vehicles are distinctive, demonstrating important trends in the market. In particular, the *multiple option facility* allows issuers to immediately adapt to rapidly changing conditions—which have become a hallmark of this market—without having to restructure. The multiple option facility offers borrowers several different funding options in a number of different markets and currencies. For example, an issuer may choose to tap the Euronote, or the U.S. or Dutch guilder commercial paper markets (or any other currency that may subsequently become eligible). Short-term advances in various currencies also can be obtained through these facilities. (It is important to note, however, that the documentation for a mulitple option facility is complex and often cumbersome.) The *global note issuance facility,* another structure indicative of the market's development, allows borrowers to access the Euronote and U.S. CP markets simultaneously.

Ratings. Market participants are currently debating the necessity of U.S. commercial paper-type ratings in this market. (Unlike the U.S. market, ratings are not required on Euronotes or ECP.)

FIGURE 4 EURONOTE, EUROCOMMERCIAL PAPER AND U.S. COMMERCIAL PAPER MARKETS PART A: EURONOTES

	Euronote
Outstandings	$20 billion including Euronotes and ECP.
Arrangements	Over $100 billion including Euronotes and ECP.
Issuer Types	Sovereign, quasi-sovereign, banks, corporations.
Investor Types	Both institutional and retail, including banks, bank trust departments, central banks, corporates, insurance companies, money and pension funds.
Issuer's Motivation	Standby or note issuance.
Buyer's Motivation	Investment or arbitrage. Primarily a traded instrument; paper is positioned.
Underwriting Commitment	Group of banks commit to purchase any unsold paper.
Setup Cost	Typically higher than U.S. CP and Euro CP.
Eligible Currencies	U.S. dollar, ECU, Dutch guilder, French franc, sterling.
Size of Facilities	Wide range, from $20 million to $4 billion.
Maturity of Paper	Standard, one, three or six month; other maturities possible.
Distribution Mechanism	Primarily through tender panel; sole or multiple dealer also operate.
Rating Requirement	Not required.
Backup Requirement	Underwriting commitment integral part of structure.
Settlement Facilities	Euroclear, Cedel, First Chicago, Chase Manhattan.
Settlement Procedures	Generally two days; same-day settlement has been introduced.
Delivery	Physical or book entry.
Eligibility for Sale in U.S.	Generally not eligible, except by offshore subsidiary of U.S. entity.[a]
Minimum Denominations	Large, generally ranging from $100,000-$1 million; smaller sizes have been done.
Quoting Convention	Currently in terms of LIBOR/LIBID; moving toward absolute yield basis.
Interest Calculation	Discount or interest-bearing basis.
Secondary Market Liquidity	Liquidity growing; trading tends to be somewhat erratic, however.
Dealers	Ten major dealers; approximately 40 other fringe dealers.

[a] May be eligible for sale under the private-placement exemption of the Securities Act of 1933.
ECP Eurocommercial paper. ECU European currency unit. NA Not applicable. NIF Note issuance facility.

FIGURE 4 EURONOTE, EUROCOMMERCIAL PAPER AND U.S. COMMERICAL PAPER MARKETS
PART B: EUROCOMMERCIAL PAPER AND U.S. COMMERCIAL PAPER

	Eurocommercial Paper	U.S. Commercial Paper
Outstandings	$20 billion including Euronotes and ECP.	$300 billion.
Arrangements	Over $100 billion including Euronotes and ECP.	NA
Issuer Types	Primarily large multinational corporations and banks.	Mix of financial and nonfinancial entities. Foreign borrowers also present.
Investor Types	Both institutional and retail, including banks, bank trust departments, central banks, corporates, insurance companies, money and pension funds.	Deep institutional demand, including money and pension funds, insurance companies, corporates, bank trust departments.
Issuer's Motivation	Note issuance.	Exchange of excess liquidity through placement of paper.
Buyer's Motivation	Investment or arbitrage.	Investment; most paper placed directly with end buyers.
Underwriting Commitment	None. Generally distributed on best-effort basis. Separate NIF may be set up in conjunction.	None. Distributed on best-effort basis.
Setup Cost	Overall costs cheaper than U.S. CP because of absence of rating and backup requirements.	Lower than most other short-term funding sources.
Eligible Currencies	U.S. dollar, ECU, Dutch guilder, French franc, sterling.	U.S. dollar.
Size of Facilities	Wide range from $20 million to an unlimited amount.	Generally not specified.
Maturity of Paper	Odd-dates: 7-365 days for international issuers; 7-183 for U.S. issuers.	14-45 days most common; all odd-dates up to 270 days possible.
Distribution Mechanism	Multiple dealers obliged to make markets.	Sole or multiple dealers obliged to make markets.
Rating Requirement	Not required.	Customary. (There are a few unrated programs.)
Backup Requirement	Not required, but advisable because of changing nature of market conditions.	100% backup, usually in the form of bank lines, generally required.
Settlement Facilities	Euroclear, Cedel, First Chicago, Chase Manhattan.	Various commercial banks.
Settlement Procedures	Generally two days; same-day settlement has been introduced.	Same-day settlement.
Delivery	Physical or book entry.	Physical.
Eligibility for Sale in U.S.	Generally not eligible, except by offshore subsidiary of U.S. entity.[a]	No restriction.
Minimum Denominations	Large, generally ranging from $100,000-$1 million ($500,000 minimum for U.S. issuers); smaller sizes have been done.	Large; $100,000 or more, with any denomination over this possible. (Round lot is usually $1 million).
Quoting Convention	Currently in terms of LIBOR/LIBID; moving toward absolute yield basis.	Absolute yield basis.
Interest Calculation	Discount or interest-bearing basis.	Generally discount basis, can be on an interest-bearing basis.
Secondary Market Liquidity	Liquidity growing; trading tends to be somewhat erratic, however.	Excellent, primarily a placement market.
Dealers	Ten major dealers; approximately 40 other fringe dealers.	Five primary dealers.

[a] May be eligible for sale under the private-placement exemption of the Securities Act of 1933.

NA Not applicable. NIF Note issuance facility.

Proponents of the rating system maintain that the designations will facilitate the development of a broader investor base, in particular with nonbank buyers. In addition, short-term investors tend to be more risk averse than longer-term buyers, and may find comfort in an established rating system. Ratings would also promote a more orderly trading pattern for these securities; there is currently no established tiering of credits in the market. High-quality borrowers will also enjoy more attractive terms after their credit has been qualified. Opponents assert, however, that the Euromarket—unlike its U.S. counterpart—is not accustomed to ratings; rather, "name" recognition and perceived credit quality play the dominant role in investment selection.

Both Moody's and Standard & Poor's (S&P) rate Euronote and ECP programs, although their methodologies are quite different. At S&P, each individual program is evaluated upon the issuer's request, just as they are in the U.S. market. Despite the absence of required swinglines, S&P is concerned that adequate sources of liquidity exist to support each ECP program. Moreover, the same rating designations utilized in the Unitied States are applied in this market. S&P currently rates twenty-four Euronote/ECP programs, including the Commonwealth Bank of Australia—the first rated facility in this market (see Figure 5). Seventeen of these programs were awarded an "A-1+" rating—the highest S&P short-term designation.

In contrast, Moody's assigns short-term ratings that do not apply to specific programs, as do S&P's, but rather to the issuer's general capacity to repay any promissory obligations with an original maturity of under one year. ECP and Euronote issuers who currently have a Moody's CP rating in the U.S. market, therefore, have a *global* CP rating; they can utilize that rating for issuance in any market. Approximately 110 Euronote/ECP borrowers have a Moody's short-term rating. In addition, non-U.S. issuers may apply for a Moody's short-term rating, which can subsequently be utilized in any short-term market.

Maturity, Quotation. The origin of Euronote programs as bank facilities has shaped the market in many respects. For example,

FIGURE 5 EURONOTE AND EUROCOMMERCIAL PAPER PROGRAMS RATED BY STANDARD & POOR'S[a]

	Rating		Rating
British Petroleum Capital (PG)	A-1+	Northern Indiana Public Services Co.	A-1
Banco Internacional SNC	A-1+	PacifiCorp	A-2
Commonwealth Bank of Australia (PG)	A-1+/AAA[b]	PKbanken	A-1+
CSR Finance Ltd. (PG)	A-1	Prudential Funding Corp.	A-1+
Christiania Bank	A-1+	Reckitt & Colman Finance	A-1
Den norske Creditbank	A-1+	Redland Credit Corp.	A-1
EBS Finance	A-1+	Skandia Int'l. Capital	A-1+
Equitable Life Assurance Society	A-1+	State Bank of New South Wales	A-1+
Gotabanken	A-1	Svenska Handelsbanken	A-1+
City of Gothenburg, Sweden	A-1+	The Washington Post Co.	A-1
Merrill Lynch & Co.	A-1+	Volvo	A-1+
National Australia Bank	A-1+		
Kingdom of Spain	A-1+		

[a] Ratings as of 30 May 86.

[b] Intermediate-term Euronotes with maturities beyond 365 days receive bond designations.

PG Parent guaranteed.

Euronotes are usually structured in standard, monthly maturities, illustrating the market's development as a substitute for bank investments such as certificates of deposit. In addition, secondary-market quotations are in terms of LIBOR or LIBID, which, being bank rates, are particularly appropriate for bank investors. In an attempt to broaden the nonbank investor base, there has been a move toward quotation on an absolute rate basis, as is currently the case in the U.S. CP market. To encourage broad investor appeal, a consistent pricing strategy must be maintained relative to overall market conditions, not just LIBOR.

The development of odd-date-maturity Eurocommercial paper, which mimics the U.S. market, will also enhance the product's appeal. In return for allowing investors to choose maturities to fit cash flow requirements, an issuer is guaranteed a loyal investor following that will consistently purchase securities, resulting in a stable cost of funds over time.

Settlement. Settlement procedures have not been standardized in the short-term Euromarket, although the process has been refined substantially in the past year: Euronotes and ECP commonly settle on a two-day basis, while U.S. CP is on a same-day schedule. Same-day settlement is also technically possible in the Euromarket. Euroclear, Cedel, First Chicago, and Chase Manhattan have all set up facilities to clear these securities; at this point, however, transfers are usually not accomplished smoothly. This largely results from different practices: At Euroclear, no definitive notes are issued; securities are represented by a single, global note. First Chicago offers definitive notes in limited circumstances, while Cedel offers same-day settlement with definitive securities. To complicate matters further, each of the settlement houses has a different cutoff time after which same-day settlement is no longer possible.

In another variation, grid notes which represent beneficial ownership in securities held by a trustee on behalf of residual owners have been introduced to the Euronote/ECP market to facilitate the same-day settlement process. As with global notes, physical notes do not exist in the grid note system; rather, securities are held in the form of a *single* document and transfers of ownership are made in book entry form by a central registrar. Borrowers are spared the expense of printing, authenticating and issuing definitive notes. This minimizes the possibility of loss, theft or forgery of the securities.

Denominations. Euronote and ECP minimum denominations tend to be large, usually $500,000. However, in a landmark ECP arrangement, Export Development Corporation of Canada (EDC)—as a non-U.S. issuer—reduced minimum denominations dramatically—to $10,000—in order to broaden its investor base to include the retail purchaser.

Sales Restrictions. Under current regulations, a standard Euronote or ECP offering cannot be sold into the United States, because these instruments are not registered under the Securities Act of 1933. In certain limited circumstances, however, these instruments may be sold to sophisticated institutional investors in accordance with the Act's private-placement exemption. This requires that the securities be issued in registered form (bearer format is the norm) and that an agent be assigned to control and monitor the distribution process carefully. A small percentage of the facilities arranged to date accommodates such procedures. Offshore subsidiaries of U.S. corporations, on the other hand, can freely purchase these securities.

Nondollar Short-Term Market. The growth of the Euronote/ECP market has been tied, in part, to the piqued interest in the international short-term market. These instruments offer alternatives to such traditional dollar-denominated investments as Eurodeposits and certificates of deposit. However, the development of similar nondollar products has been slow. Only the European currency unit (ECU) and the U.S. dollar were utilized under the traditional underwritten note issuance facility. Now, the Dutch guilder, French franc and British pound are also eligible currencies. Due to the lack of nondollar products, borrowers have raised nondollar funds through other means; most commonly, U.S. commercial paper programs have been established, with the liabilities then converted into the desired currencies through the foreign exchange markets. (Along the same lines, U.S. dealers will often quote U.S. CP in terms of several different currencies.) In the Euromarket, the concept of a *currency play* *tender panel* was introduced. In this arrangement, two tender panels are put into place: One group acts as a conventional distributor of dollar-denominated Euronotes, while the second offers spot and forward foreign exchange rates that allow the borrower to transform liabilities into other currencies.

The recent institution of liberalization measures in a number of countries portends further growth of the nondollar short-term markets. Recently, authorities in France and the Netherlands authorized the issuance of commercial paper in their respective currencies, and the Japanese are expected to follow suit. In a major move, the Bank of England revised the Banking Act to allow for the issuance of sterling-denominated commercial paper by British and foreign entities. Issuers have already begun to arrange programs in this market. In fact, several U.S. institutions have been given permission to become dealers in this market. The market will be fashioned, in part, after the U.S. CP market. As in the United States, paper will be distributed through dealers and may carry flexible, odd-date maturities, but ratings will not be required. To provide for investor protection, initial access is restricted to companies with listed British stock and net assets of at least £50 million.

CRITICAL ISSUES

Regulatory Restrictions

Authorities in several countries have been concerned about the underwriting responsibilities that banks are assuming in Euronote programs. The Bank of England was the first to act to regulate the market: In April 1985, it announced that it would include a weighting of 0.5 percent for note issuance facilities in the risk/asset ratio calculation, to ensure that British underwriting banks are not amassing large amounts of contingent liabilities without adequate capital backing. Recently, the Federal Reserve followed suit, announcing that it was considering the imposition of a risk/asset ratio of 0.3 percent of U.S. banks involved in underwriting activities in the note issuance facility market. The Bank of Japan also has announced guidelines to control off-balance-sheet risks.

These regulatory issues have affected the structure of the Euronote/ECP market markedly. For instance, in the wake of the Bank of England ruling, the *transferable underwriting facility* was devised, permitting banks to transfer their underwriting commitments. Other deals protected banks from additional costs that might arise from the tightening of capital adequacy ratios in their countries. The most important development, however, is the advent of ECP programs, which are uncommitted facilities. These financings are becoming more popular as underwriting banks reconsider their involvement in these transactions. Borrowing costs also are lower, because there are no underwriting fees. However, many ECP borrowers also have set up separate backup facilities, which still qualify as contingent liabilities.

Development of the Secondary Market

The secondary market for Euronotes and ECP has expanded considerably in 1985. About $20 billion—encompassing a wide range of issuers—is currently outstanding. Figure 6 shows a sampling of the types of credits now available in the secondary market; as illustrated, possible investments include banks, corporates, sovereign states, and government-related entities. The narrowing spread between LIBOR—the benchmark for the Euronote/ECP market—and U.S. CP is one factor that has contributed to the enhanced liquidity of the secondary market. The spread between prime one-month commercial paper and LIBOR, on a CD-equivalent basis, is currently about 28 basis points—37 basis points less than the average spread of the past five years. Furthermore, many borrowers in the Euronote/ECP market—in particular, top-tier sovereign and corporate issuers such as the Kingdom of Sweden and Unilever—achieve terms well below LIBOR, and their securities are quoted in terms of LIBID.

Certain immaturities still exist in the secondary market, however. For example, tender panelists attempting to impress issuers bid for

FIGURE 6 THE ACTIVE MARKET FOR EURONOTES AND EUROCOMMERCIAL PAPER[a]

Sovereign, Gov't. Guaranteed Entities	Gov't. Owned, Partly Owned Entities	Banks	Corporates
Commonwealth Bank of Australia	Australian Wheat Board	Fleet Financial	EBS Finance
Credit National	Norsk Hydro	Korean Exchange Bank	Elders IXL
ENEL	Statoil	Security Pacific Australia	Grand Metropolitan
New Zealand		Union Bank of Finland	PepsiCo
Portugal			Unilever
Spain			United Biscuits
State Bank of New South Wales			United Technologies
Statoil			
Sweden			

[a] These borrowers have drawn down on their facilities.

paper at unrealistic levels. In addition, weak tender panel members, without adequate placing power, may sell newly issued securities to the professional market after failing to find other buyers.

OUTLOOK

Standardization of market conventions—including distribution and settlement procedures, quoting conventions and rating requirements, among others—will undoubtedly broaden the investor base for Euronotes and ECP. In addition, the institution of liberalization measures in several countries will expand the variety of nondollar short-term securities, which includes foreign-denominated Euronotes and ECP. These developments will further enhance the opportunities for issuers and investors in this market.

CHAPTER NINETEEN

EDWARD J. RAPPA is a member of Bear Stearn's Management Committee and chairman of the Advertising and Marketing Committee.

He joined Bear Stearns in 1977 as an institutional salesman of fixed-income securities and was admitted to the partnership in 1979. Prior to joining Bear Stearns, Mr. Rappa served as executive vice president, R.W. Pressprich from 1971 to 1977, and from 1961 to 1971 was an associate with The Chase Manhattan Bank.

Mr. Rappa attended Bernard Baruch College.

CLIVE BERGEL is a member of Bear Stearn's Credit Committee and the Advertising and Marketing Committee.

Mr. Bergel joined Bear Stearns in 1979 as an institutional salesman of fixed-income securities and was admitted to the partnership in 1980. Prior to joining Bear Stearns, he served as Vice President, Merrill, Lynch, Pierce Fenner & Smith from 1968-1979, and from 1964-1968 was a director of David S. Bergel & Son.

He attended Leicester University, England.

RICHARD E. SCOFIELD joined Bear Stearns's Corporate Finance Department in 1977 and was made a limited partner of Bear, Stearns & Co. in 1985. Currently he is an Associate Director of Bear, Stearns & Co. Inc. Prior to joining Bear Stearns, Mr. Scofield worked with Manufacturer's Hanover Trust's Commercial lending department and the Money Market Division of Citicorp's Merchant Banking Group.

Mr. Scofield holds a B.A. from Lawrence University, and an MBA from Amos Tuck School at Dartmouth College.

THE ECU: THE ALTERNATIVE EUROPEAN CURRENCY*

Edward J. Rappa
Managing Director, Bear, Stearns & Co. Inc.
Clive Bergel
Managing Director, Bear, Stearns & Co. Inc.
Richard E. Scofield
Associate Director, Bear, Stearns & Co. Inc.
New York, New York

INTRODUCTION

The European Currency Unit (ECU) is just like any other currency except that you cannot hold it in your hand. You can have ECU bank accounts, write insurance policies in ECU, transfer ECU funds over the wire, denominate bond issues in ECU, invoice in ECU and even get ECU traveler's checks at Heathrow or Charles de Gaulle airports.

The ECU is a "composite currency" consisting of specified amounts of currencies of the "Member States" of the "European Communities", excluding Spain and Portugal. The European Communities are three similar supranational organizations: the European Economic Community (EEC or the Community), European Coal and Steel, and EURATOM. The Member States of the European Communities are Germany, France, the United Kingdom, Italy, the Netherlands, Belgium, Luxembourg, Denmark, Ireland, Greece,

*The authors appreciate the editorial and statistical assistance of Elizabeth Monaco and Robert Fisher of Bear, Stearns & Co. Inc.

Spain and Portugal. Although Spain and Portugal entered the European Communities in January 1986, inclusion of the currencies of those two countries in the ECU is not expected to occur before 1989.

The ECU has great appeal to both issuers—governments, supranationals and multinationals—as a way to hedge currency exposure, and to institutional and retail investors, as a way to diversify currency holdings. In fact, the ECU is now the fifth most common currency for denominating international bond issues. (See Table 1.)

From a base of only five ECU-denominated issues in 1981, the growth in ECU usage has been dramatic. As of June 30, 1986, there were approximately 20 billion par amount of public ECU-denominated securities issued in the Eurobond markets. (See Table 2.)

The first publicly offered non-dollar issue registered with the Securities and Exchange Commission (SEC) in the United States was denominated in ECU, signaling a new phase in the integration and expansion of the world's capital markets and indicating the ECU's appeal to investors seeking currency diversification. There is now ECU 800 million principal amount outstanding in the U.S. market, making ECU-denominated securities the second largest sector of the non-dollar market in the United States.

TABLE 1 INTERNATIONAL ISSUES OF BONDS NEW ISSUE VOLUME
(Millions of U.S. Dollars)

	1981	**1982**	**1983**	**1984**	**1985**	**June 30, 1986**
1. U.S. $	25,761	42,228	39,205	65,334	96,482	52,988
2. DM	1,396	3,253	4,042	4,324	9,491	8,592
3. YEN	410	598	233	1,190	6,539	7,338
4. U.K. Sterling	535	846	2,153	3,965	5,766	5,965
5. **ECU**	153	823	2,191	2,938	7,038	3,995
6. C $	688	1,200	1,067	2,147	2,822	2,140
7. Dutch Guilder	417	618	747	986	682	281
TOTALS	29,360	49,566	49,638	80,884	128,820	81,299

Source: OECD Financial Statistics Monthly.

TABLE 2 PUBLIC ISSUES OF ECU-DENOMINATED DEBT PAR AMOUNT

	1981	1982	1983	1984	1985	June 30, 1986
Public ECU-denominated bond issues in the Eurobond market (in millions of ECU)	190	722	1,930	3,444	9,419	4,488
Number of issues	5	18	44	63	131	51

Source: European Economic Community.

The ECU has met specific needs in the market. Put simply, if there had not been a broad base need for the ECU, it would have fared as did the Special Drawing Right (SDR), now rarely used outside of Central Banking activities. This chapter briefly explores the nature of the ECU, the political and economic reasons for the incredible success of the ECU, its role in the European Monetary System, its role as an instrument for the currency diversification for investors and its effectiveness as a currency hedge for issuers.

WHY THE ECU?—A HISTORICAL PERSPECTIVE

The factors that spawned the political need for the European Monetary System (the EMS will be discussed shortly) and the ECU are similar to those that created the impetus for the great commercial success of the ECU. Put simply, the ECU created a hedge against currency uncertainty.

This need has existed since intra-European trade began centuries ago. That is, fluctuations in the values of the different European currencies tend to impede trade. These fluctuations create uncertainty as to the ultimate value of the currency of payment against one's home currency. Because of the significant interdependence of European countries, there has historically been a need to reduce, or manage, this uncertainty to enhance trade.

The simplest way to deal with this uncertainty would be to create a "Common European Currency." It is, however, politically unfeasible to create a denovo currency which supercedes or replaces all local European currencies. The genius of the ECU was that it created a common currency "comprised" of European currencies, giving the Member States of the European Communities a vested interest in its success. The ECU became an "exclusively" European currency, as opposed to predecessor composites, such as the SDR, which contains the U.S. dollar.

The need for stability of currency exchange rates among the EEC member states was addressed in the Treaty of Rome in 1957, which established the Community. The treaty recognized the need for exchange rate stability and each Member State was to treat currency exchange rates as a matter of common interest. The Commission of the European Communities—equivalent to the Executive Branch of government in the United States—was given the authority to take necessary measures for a limited period of time to counter the consequences of an exchange rate policy which seriously distorted conditions of European competition.

However, the comfort created by the Bretton Woods Agreement of 1944, which established fixed exchange rates among the U.S. dollar and European currencies, limited the need for a formal currency exchange rate mechanism among the EEC Member States.

Even though Bretton Woods was operating effectively, the concept of a "Common European Currency" was not extinguished and was discussed at the Hague summit of the European Communities in 1969. More initiative towards a common currency was made in the Werner Plan. However, these discussions were primarily theoretical.

In 1971, this perspective changed. President Nixon officially freed the dollar from gold and launched floating exchange rates. Currency exchange rate uncertainty again became a major political and commercial issue. It also became apparent that the Community was dependent on a non-European currency over whose value it had no control.

The stability of Bretton Woods had been breached, and in an

attempt to alleviate this currency uncertainty in Europe, the European Snake was adopted in 1973. The goal of the Snake was to reestablish a Bretton Woods type system on a regional basis. The Snake was designed to limit fluctuations of participating European currencies against each other by 2 1/4 percent and each currency against the U.S. dollar by 4 1/2 percent. If one drew a tunnel of 4 1/2 percent on each side of the dollar and them superimposed the 2 1/4 percent limits within this tunnel, a squiggly line resulted which resembled a Snake.

Although the Snake ultimately failed because there were no formal procedures to deal with adjustments in cross-central rates and no integrated initiatives for closer cooperation among economies, important lessons were learned which would lead to a much more efficient and disciplined EMS. In addition, the European Monetary Cooperation Fund (EMCF) was established during this period and continues to operate and assist Member States to finance any necessary currency intervention.

The concept of a Common European Currency again came to the forefront on October 27, 1977, when the President of the European Commission the Rt. Hon. Roy Jenkins called for a renewal of the debate on European monetary integration. German Chancellor Helmut Schmidt set forth his ideas for a ''European Zone of Monetary Stability'' on April 7-8, 1978, and the Bremen Summit in July set forth the broad outlines of the EMS. On December 5, 1978, the European Monetary System and role of the ECU in the European Monetary System were approved by the Community.

WHAT IS THE ECU?

The ECU is the pillar of the European Monetary System (EMS). Neither the ECU nor the EMS can be understood without reference to the other. But first, we shall examine several key concepts which are intertwined throughout any description of the ECU, and define the ECU; then, we can examine why the ECU is an integral part of the EMS's harmonization effort.

Key Concepts in Understanding the ECU

Several concepts are crucial to understanding the definition of the ECU and the use of the ECU within the EMS. Table 3 illustrates the key concepts discussed below with reference to the appropriate columns in the table.

1) ''Quantity'' of each Member State's currency in the ECU (Column 1)—There is a fixed Quantity of each currency within the ECU. For example, as Table 3 indicates, 1 ECU has a value equal to the sum of the values of the specified Quantity of each currency in the ECU. That is, as of September 17, 1984, 1 ECU = .719 German marks + 1.310 French francs + .256 Dutch guilders + 140 Italian lira + 3.71 Belgian francs + .219 Danish kroner + .00871 Irish pounds + .0878 United Kingdom pounds + 1.15 Greek drachmas.

2) ''Central Rates'' (Column 2)—Central Rates are established by the Community and the Member States and are defined as the amount of each local currency which is the equivalent of 1 ECU: for example, 2.11083 DM = 1 ECU.

3) ''Bilateral Exchange Rates'' (Coumn 3)—Bilateral Exchange Rates are determined by dividing the Central Rates of two selected currencies. Column 3 indicates the Bilateral Exchange Rates for the Deutsche mark to the other currencies. These calculations are done for each other currency to determine the ''Parity Grid'' of Bilateral Exchange Rates. Currencies are allowed to fluctuate within 2 1/4 percent on either side of the Bilateral Exchange Rates (except the Italian lira, which can fluctuate within 6 percent on either side of its Bilateral Exchange Rates). Therefore, the Bilateral Exchange Rate of 1DM = 3.2561FF should not vary outside the range of + or − 2.25% or DM1 = FF3.18284 and DM1 = FF3.32936 (see footnote 3 of Table 3).

4) ''Central Weights''—Central Weights for each currency are computed as the ratio of each currency's Quantity to its Central Rate. Central Weights are stable as long as the Central Rates are not changed by the EMS; (i.e. Central Weights change when either Revisions and/or Realignments are made).

TABLE 3 ILLUSTRATION OF KEY ISSUES REGARDING THE ECU

Currency	Column 1 Quantity	Column 2 Central Rates	Column 3 Bilateral Exchange Rates of 1 DM to Other Currencies	Column 4 Central Weights %	Column 5 Market Rates (Oct 1/86) Units/ECU	Column 6 Relative Weights (Oct 1/86)	Column 7 Maximum Limits of Diversion	Column 8 Effective Limits of Diversion	Column 9 Threshold of Divergence
Deutsche Mark	0.719	1ECU = DM 2.11083	1 DM = 1 DM	34.06	2.09022	34.40%	+ or − 2.25%	+ or − 1.48%	+ or − 1.11%
French franc	1.310	1ECU = FF 6.87316	1 DM = 3.2561 FF	19.06	6.84430	19.14%	+ or − 2.25%	+ or − 1.82%	+ or − 1.36%
Dutch guilder	0.256	1ECU = DF 2.37833	1 DM = 1.1267 DG	10.76	2.36146	9.22%	+ or − 2.25%	+ or − 2.00%	+ or − 1.50%
Italian lira	140.000	1ECU = ItL 1,476.95	1 DM = 699.70 ItL	9.48	1444.90	10.32%	+ or − 6.0%	+ or − 5.12%	+ or − 4.07%
Belgian franc	3.71	1ECU = BFr 43.5149	1 DM = 20.615 BFr	8.53	43.3417	8.56%	+ or − 2.25%	+ or − 1.54%	+ or − 1.54%
Luxembourg franc	0.14	1ECU = LFr 43.5149	1 DM = 20.615 LFr	0.30	43.3417	0.32%	+ or − 2.25%	+ or − 2.06%	+ or − 1.54%
Danish kroner	.219	1ECU = DKr 7.81701	1 DM = 3.703 DKr	2.80	7.88477	2.78%	+ or − 2.25%	+ or − 2.19%	+ or − 1.64%
Irish pound	.00871	1ECU = IrL .764976	1 DM = 0.362 IrP	1.14	.762246	1.14%	+ or − 2.25%	+ or − 2.22%	+ or − 1.66%
United Kingdom Pound	.0878	1ECU = UKL .679256*	1 DM = 0.322 UKP*	12.93*	.713486	12.31%	*	*	*
Greek Drachma	1.15	1ECU = Dra 137.049*	1 DM = 64.93 GD*	0.84*	139.754	0.82%	*	*	*

*The United Kingdom pound and the Greek drachma do not participate in the EMS so they do not have divergence limits. However, they do have notional Central Rates which are included above.

(1) Quantities effective as of September 17, 1984.

(2) Established by the Community and the Member States.

(3) Bilateral Exchange Rates for the DM to other currencies, for illustration purposes. For example, the DM/FF Bilateral Exchange Rate is determined as the ratio of the Central Rate for the FF divided by the Central Rate for the DM (i.e. 6.87316/2.11083 = 3.2561).

(4) Central Weights are computed as the ratio of each currency's quantity and its Central Rate.

(5) Official Exchange Rates for official use by the European Communities as of October 1, 1986. For purposes herein we have assumed the official exchange rates are the same as the market rates.

(6) Relative Weights are computed as the ratio of each currency's quantity of its market rate as of October 1, 1986, with the ECU.

(7) Maximum Limits of Divergence as established by the EMS.

(8) Effective Maximum Divergence Limits are calculated to illustrate that Divergence Limits vary according to the Weight of a currency in the ECU. These Effective Maximum Divergence Limits are calculated as follows:

2.25% or 6% × (1 − Central Weight of Currency for which Divergence Limit is being Calculated).

(9) Effective Threshold of Divergence is computed as follows:

(0.75 × 2.25% or 6%) × (1 − The Central Weight of Each Currency).

The Quantities of each currency in the ECU are selected so that the Central Weight of each component roughly reflects the relative size and importance of each Member States' economy relative to the total Gross Domestic Product of the Community and the relative importance of each Member States' economy in intra-EEC trade. Therefore, because Germany has the largest economy in the EEC, the Deutsche mark accounts for approximately 34 percent of the ECU's value.

5) "Market Rates" (Column 5)—Because currencies are allowed to fluctuate within a band around the Central Rate, the Market Rates for each Member State currency to the ECU fluctuates on a daily basis. Column 5 includes the exchange rates, as calculated by the Commission of the European Communities for official use, as of October 1, 1986. These official rates are calculated on a daily basis at 2:30 P.M. Brussels time and are available on Reuters screen FXEZ.

6) "Relative Weights" (Column 6)—Relative Weights are calculated in a manner similar to the Central Weights except that they are based on prevailing market rates. Relative weights fluctuate when either Revisions and/or Realignments are made, or on a daily basis depending on market exchange rates. (See below.)

7) "Maximum Divergence Limit" (Column 7)—In addition to maintaining a band around Bilateral Central Rates, each currency must also maintain a value of + or − 2.25 percent (6 percent for the Italian lira) of its Central Rate with the ECU.

8) "Effective Divergence Limits" (Column 8)—Because each currency is also a composite of the ECU, and a currency cannot fluctuate against itself, the Effective Divergence Limits of any particular currency are dependent on its Weight within the ECU. That is, because Germany has the largest Central Weight within the ECU, its Effective Divergence Limit is less than that of the French franc, which has a smaller Weight within the ECU.

9) "Threshold of Divergence"(Column 9)—When a Member State's currency pierces the Threshold of Divergence, which is 75 percent of the Maximum Divergence Limit, it is presumed that the Central Bank of the Member State concerned will take cor-

rective action. The fact that each currency is also a composite in the ECU also alters the Effective Threshold of Divergence because a currency cannot fluctuate against itself.

ECU Defined

The ECU was defined in 1978 as the sum of specified amounts of the currencies of the Member States. The ECU's composition, and thus its value, was identical to that of the European Unit of Account (EUA) which had been used in the EEC's accounts since 1975. The ECU has replaced the EUA in all EEC uses.

The 1978 Council Resolution requires that the Relative Weights, at then prevailing exchange rates, of the ECU's component currencies be examined every five years and, if necessary, the specified amounts of the component currencies be revised (Revision). This resulted in the September 1984 Revision discussed below. In addition, any Member State may request a reexamination if the Relative Weight of a currency in the ECU has changed by at least 25 percent since the previous Revision.

Since 1978, the specified amounts of the currencies that make up the ECU have only been changed once. In September 1984, following the reexamination required every five years, the Council changed the composition of the ECU and incorporated the Greek drachma as required by the treaty of accession of Greece to the EEC and the other European Communities. In addition to the inclusion of the Greek drachma, the principal Revisions were to decrease the amounts of German marks and Dutch guilders included in the ECU and increase the amounts of Italian lira and French francs. These changes were made mainly to bring the Central Weights of the component currencies in line with underlylng economic criteria and had the effect of compensating for the appreciation of the German mark and Dutch guilder and the depreciation of the French franc and Italian lira over the previous five-year period. Table 4 below indicates the Quantities effective March 13, 1979, and those that have been in effect since the since the September 17, 1984, Revision.

Importantly, a Revision can occur only by unanimous decision

TABLE 4 ORIGINAL AND CURRENT ECU COMPOSITION

	Quantities Effective from March 13, 1979* to September 16, 1984	Quantities in Effect Since the September 17, 1984 Revision
German marks	0.828	0.719
United Kingdom pounds	0.0885	0.0878
French francs	1.1500	1.31
Italian lira	109.00	140.00
Dutch guilders	0.2860	0.256
Belgian francs	3.6600	3.71
Luxembourg francs	0.14	0.14
Danish kroner	0.217	0.219
Irish pounds	0.00759	0.00871
Greek drachma	—	1.15

*The ECU went into ''force'' in the EMS on March 13, 1979.

of the Council of Ministers (comprised of the Heads of State of the Member States), and must be made in line with underlying economic criteria, including the relative gross domestic products and trade among the Member States. Indicative of the careful treatment the ECU receives, when a Revision is considered, a computer program examines 20,000 separate variables and takes approximately twenty-four hours to run.

It is required that any Revision not, in and of itself, modify the exchange rate of the ECU. This is accomplished by choosing a set of specified amounts of the component currencies which ensures that, on the day of calculation, the exchange rate of the ECU under its revised composition is identical to its exchange rate under the superseded composition. For example, the exchange rate of the ECU against the U.S. dollar as of the day of calculation for the September 1984 revision remained at 1 ECU = U.S. $.742589 under both the revised and the superseded compositions. Because of the revised composition, however, the exchange rate will differ over time from what it would have been under the superseded composition.

The ECU, the EMS and Economic Harmonization

The EMS, as stated in its founding Resolution, was to be "a fundamental component of a more comprehensive strategy aimed at lasting growth with stability, a progressive return to full employment, the harmonization of living standards and the lessening of regional disparities in the Community" and was "to have a stabilizing effect on international economic and monetary relations."

With the EMS, the ECU serves four primary functions aimed at enhancing European economic harmonization:

(1) The ECU is the Denominator (Numeraire) for the parity grid that establishes the Bilateral Exchange Rates for each Member State currency. While the United Kingdom pound sterling and the Greek drachma are included in the ECU, they do not participate in the EMS. The Central Rate for each Member State currency in ECUs (Participating Currencies) and a "notional" rate for sterling and the drachma (Non-Participating Currencies), is fixed by the EMS and used to establish Bilateral Exchange Rates.

Bilateral Exchange Rates are determined using the Central Rates as illustrated in Column 3 in Table 3. The participating currencies are allowed to fluctuate 2 1/4 percent (6 percent for the Italian lira) on either side of their bilateral exchange rate.

By using the ECU as the Numeraire, no single Member State currency (or the U.S. dollar) is the Numeraire. This is consistent with the Community's approach toward monetary integration previously discussed in the "Historical Perspective" section.

The most important aspect of this parity grid is that each Central Rate becomes a Community concern, with any adjustments to the Central Rate decided by the Community rather than by individual Member States.

(2) The ECU is the "Indicator of Divergence" within the EMS. Fluctuation margins of + or − 2.25 percent (+ or − 6 percent for the Italian lira) are allowed on either side of the Central Rates. However, when a currency exceeds 75 percent of the allowed Indicator of Divergence (Threshold of Divergence), it is presumed

that the Member State will take appropriate action to bring its currency back within the prescribed band. Essentially, the ECU acts as an early warning system identifying currencies that are straying markedly from their central rates.

Because each Participating Currency is a composite of the ECU, and because a currency cannot fluctuate against itself, the degree of divergence from ECU Central Rates is not the same for each currency. The maximum divergence for a currency with a heavy weight in the ECU basket will be less than that of a currency with a smaller weight. Thus, the more heavily a currency is represented in the ECU, the less it can diverge from its ECU Central Rate. Calculations of Divergence Limits and the Threshold of Divergence are illustrated in Columns 7, 8 and 9 in Table 3.

(3) The ECU is the currency that the Central Banks of the Member States use to intervene. The central bank of the strong currency buys the weak currency and the central bank of the weak currency sells the strong currency. This action is financed either from reserves or by borrowing from the European Monetary Cooperation Fund (EMCF)

(4) The ECU serves as a means of settlement between monetary authorities.

As #1 and #2 above illustrate, there are two constraints which may require central bank intervention in the currency markets: (1) deviation outside of the defined bands around the Bilateral Exchange Rates; and (2) deviation from a currency's Central Rate with the ECU. The London *Financial Times* publishes two charts indicating these two constraints on the EMS exchange rates every Monday. The following charts are taken from the September 29, 1986, *Financial Times* for currency exchange rates as of September 26, 1986. Chart 1 shows the deviations from bilateral exchange rates against the weakest currency in the EMS, the Danish Kroner of 9/26/86, and Chart 2 indicates ECU Divergence.

As indicated above, if a currency crosses the Threshold of Divergence, it is presumed that the central bank of the Member State concerned will intervene in the currency markets to bring the currency back into line. If this currency intervention fails and the currency

CHART 1 EMS BILATERAL EXCHANGE RATES VS. WEAKEST CURRENCY

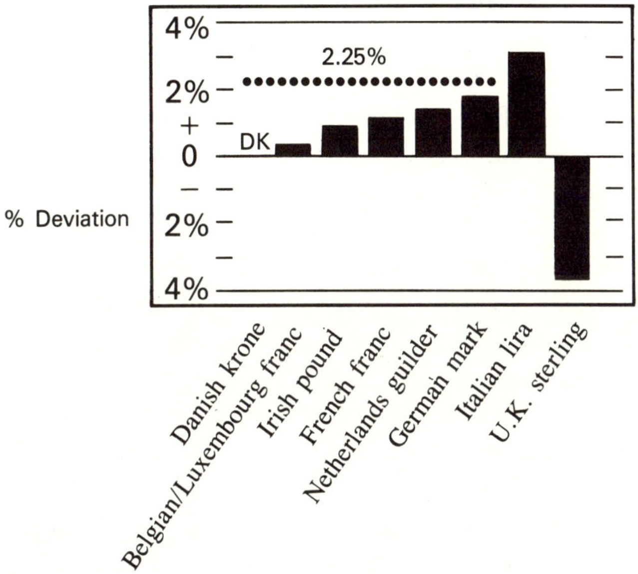

CHART 2 CENTRAL RATE DIVERGENCE VS. ECU

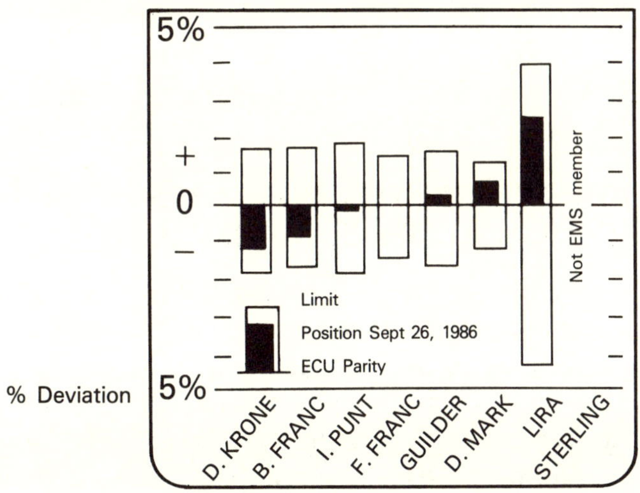

strays beyond the Divergence Limit, then the government concerned must begin appropriate monetary or fiscal policies to mitigate the fundamental problem affecting the currency.

Ultimately, if these two actions do not bring the currency back into line with its central rate, there is a realignment (Realignment) mechanism which allows for modifications (revaluation/evaluation) in the Bilateral Central Rates for each Member State currency. This allows the ECU to be fluid and adapt to changes in the economies and currency exchange rates of the Member States.

There have been nine realignments since the EMS agreement came into effect. (The May 21, 1983, realignment was a technical adjustment induced by a variation in the pound sterling "notional" central parity.) While realignments do not affect the fixed composition of the ECU, the exchange rate of the ECU in subsequent trading may change because of the increased or reduced exchange rates of its components. Table 5 shows the ECU central rates since the EMS came into effect.

The overall effect of the ECU's role within the EMS is to create a managed float of the Community's currencies with the EMS acting as the guardian of the ECU's composition and value. This procedure creates discipline among the Member States toward effecting policies acceptable to the Community, rather than solely to an individual Member State's interest.

ADVANTAGES FOR INVESTORS SEEKING CURRENCY DIVERSIFICATION

The ECU is an ideal instrument for investors seeking currency diversification. The easiest way to illustrate the benefits of investing in ECU-denominated securities is through an example. In November of 1984 Bear, Stearns & Co. Inc. managed the first SEC-registered non-U.S. dollar offering for the European Economic Community

TABLE 5 EMS ECU CENTRAL RATES (1)

	Mar. 13 1979	Sept. 24 1979	Nov. 30 1979	Mar. 23 1981	Oct. 5 1981	Feb. 22 1982	June 14 1982	May 21 1983	May 21 (2) 1983	July 22 1985	Apr. 7 1986	Aug. 27 1986
Belgian/Luxembourg franc												
Units of national currency per ECU	39.4582	39.8456	39.7897	40.7985	40.7572	44.6963	44.9704	44.3662	44.9008	44.832	43.6761	43.5149
Percentage change from previous central rate		0.98	−0.14	2.54	−0.10	9.66	0.61	−1.34	1.20	−0.15	−2.58	− .37
Percentage change from initial central rate		0.98	0.84	3.40	3.29	13.28	13.97	12.44	13.79	13.62	10.69	10.28
Danish krone												
Units of national currency per ECU	7.08592	7.36594	7.72336	7.91917	7.91117	8.18382	8.2340	8.04412	8.14104	8.12857	7.91896	7.81701
Percentage change from previous central rate		3.95	4.85	2.54	−0.10	3.45	0.61	−2.31	1.20	−0.15	−2.58	−1.29
Percentage change from initital central rate		3.95	9.00	11.76	11.65	15.49	16.20	13.52	14.89	14.71	12.75	10.32
Deutsche mark												
Units of national currency per ECU	2.51064	2.48557	2.48208	2.54502	2.40989	2.41815	2.33379	2.21515	2.24184	2.2384	2.13834	2.11083
Percentage change from previous central rate		−1.00	−0.1	2.54	−5.31	0.34	−3.48	−5.08	1.20	−0.15	−4.47	−1.29
Percentage change from initial central rate		−1.00	−0.1	1.37	−4.01	3.68	−7.04	−11.77	−10.71	−10.84	−14.83	−15.92
French franc												
Units of national currency per ECU	5.79831	5.85522	5.84700	5.99526	6.17443	6.19564	6.61387	6.79271	6.87456	6.86402	6.9628	6.87316
Percentage of change from previous central rate		0.98	−0.14	2.54	2.99	0.34	6.75	2.70	1.20	−0.15	1.44	−1.29
Percentage change from initial central rate		0.98	0.84	3.40	6.49	6.85	14.07	17.15	18.56	18.38	20.08	18.54
Italian lira												
Units of national currency per ECU	1,148.15	1,159.42	1,157.79	1,262.92	1,300.67	1,305.13	1,350.27	1,386.78	1,403.49	1,520.6	1,496.21	1,476.95
Percentage change from previous central rate		0.98	−0.14	9.1	2.99	0.34	3.46	2.70	1.20	8.34	−1.60	−1.29
Percentage change from initial change rate		0.98	0.84	10.00	13.28	13.67	17.60	20.78	22.24	32.44	30.31	28.64
Irish pound												
Units of national currency per ECU	0.662638	0.669141	0.668201	0.685145	0.684452	0.686799	0.691011	0.71705	0.725690	0.724578	0.712956	.76497
Percentage change from previous central rate		0.98	−0.14	2.54	−0.10	0.34	0.61	3.77	1.20	−0.15	−1.60	7.30
Percentage change from initial central rate		0.98	0.84	3.40	3.29	3.65	4.28	8.21	9.52	9.35	7.59	15.44
Netherlands guilder												
Units of national currency per ECU	2.72077	2.74748	2.74362	2.81318	2.66382	2.67296	2.57971	2.49587	2.52595	2.52208	2.40935	2.37833
Percentage change from previous central rate		0.98	−0.14	2.54	−5.31	0.34	−3.49	−3.25	1.20	−0.15	−4.47	−1.29
Percentage change from initial central rate		0.98	0.84	3.40	−2.09	−1.76	−5.18	−8.27	−7.16	−7.30	−11.45	−12.59

(1) Positive sign indicates depreciation relative to the ECU.
(2) Technical adjustment induced by a variation in the Pound Sterling ''notional'' central parity.

Source: EEC Commission.

in the United States. Bear Stearns began working with the EEC in the early summer of 1983 to explore the feasibility of completing an ECU offering in the United States. It took eighteen months of interaction with certain institutional investors to ensure that the offering would be successful and with regulatory and legal bodies to ensure that there were no legal impediments (i.e. securities or banking restrictions) to such an offering.

An offering for ECU 150 million was filed in October 1984 with the Securities and Exchange Commission. At the time of pricing, the investor book was approaching ECU 400 million and the offering was increased to ECU 200 million, which at that time became the largest single tranche ECU-denominated offering ever completed. The offering was priced five basis points through the Euro-ECU market and its twelve-year maturity was the longest ECU-denominated offering ever completed. The offering was an overwhelming success.

The Marketing

In marketing this ECU-denominated offering to U.S. based investors, we heard the same question over and again: Why invest in a currency other than dollars? We knew we first had to educate U.S. investors about the benefits of currency diversification; then we could sell the attributes of the ECU-denominated security.

Since World War II, the U.S. economy had been predominant among the world's economies and had the deepest and most liquid capital market in the world. The U.S. investor had so many investment opportunities close to home that there was little need to look overseas for more.

This is no longer the case. The U.S. fixed-income capital market now makes up only about one-half of the world's debt market. Therefore, an investor investing only in the United States is missing half the available opportunities, and now needs to look overseas for incremental investment opportunities.

Moreover, the benefits of currency diversification have been well documented: it allows investors to increase total returns over time while decreasing the portfolio risk (as measured by the standard deviation of the total returns from that portfolio).

Chart 3 shows the "efficient frontier" for diversifying foreign-pay bonds for the 1975-1985 period. As a U.S. investor allocated a portion of his assets into a diversified pool of non-dollar fixed income securities for the 1975-1985 period, the return increased and the standard deviation decreased. Diversifying even a small portion of one's portfolio internationally made economic sense.

Even perceptions about fiduciary responsibility in international investing were changing. Five or ten years ago, money managers argued that investing overseas could be construed as a breach of their fiduciary responsibilities. They didn't want to be the first to invest overseas and the first to be sued. However, in the fall of 1984 money managers began to realize that if they didn't look overseas for opportunities they could be perceived as violating fiduciary responsibilities. The bottom line in today's internationalized capital markets is that U.S. investors simply have to adopt global investment strategies.

Why the ECU?

Once we convinced U.S. investors of the need for currency diversification, we turned our discussions to the benefits of investing in ECU and why the ECU is integral to any global strategy. A diversified pool of non-dollar fixed income investments should, to some degree over time, mirror the respective levels of the Gross Domestic Products (GDP) of the world's economies. Therefore, the European component of a global pool of investments should have a significant European mix because it represents such a significant portion of the world's gross domestic product. Table 6 indicates that the EEC accounted for 43 percent of the combined 1985 GDPs of the United States, Japan and the EEC.

Because the ECU is composed of ten different EEC currencies weighted by their respective GDPs, it is already diversified. Therefore, the ECU investment decision was easy. An investor needs diver-

CHART 3 U.S. AND FOREIGN PAY BONDS* RISK AND RETURN

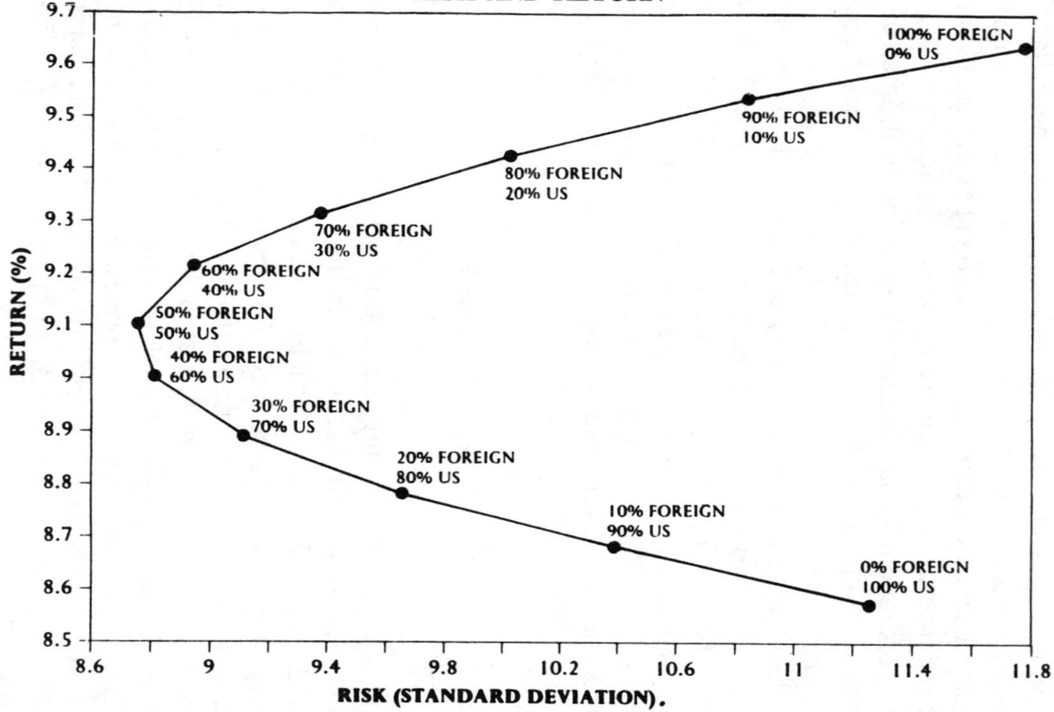

*Bear Stearns Foreign Pay Bond Index is based on the major European and Asian economies and the returns and the standard deviations of these returns from investment in these countries' government securities, denominated in the respective local currencies, from 1975-1985. These returns are converted into U.S. dollar returns and weighted by the respective GNP. Total returns are comprised of coupon income, price appreciation/depreciation and gain or loss on the currency.
Source: Bear Stearns and Co., Inc.

TABLE 6 1985 GROSS DOMESTIC PRODUCTS OF ECC, U.S. AND JAPAN

	EEC	U.S.	Japan
Population (millions)	320	234	120
Gross Domestic Product (1) (billions of U.S. $)	3,236	2,949	1,282
Imports (2) (monthly averages in millions of U.S. $)	54,713	30,136	10,856
Exports (3) (monthly averages in millions of U.S. $)	53,756	17,762	14,652

Source: OECD Main Economic Indicators, September, 1986.
(1) Expressed in 1980 prices and 1980 exchange rates
(2) C.I.F.
(3) F.O.B.

sified European currency exposure and the ECU is the easiest way to obtain it.

It is often pointed out that the time to start a global strategy is when the dollar appears to be getting overvalued because one will stand to make a substantial return over a short time. Given huge budget and current account deficits in the United States, declining interest rates and a growing protectionist trend in Congress, the continually rising dollar was not consistent with the economic and political facts. At some point, the dollar had to begin to reflect economic reality and depreciate against other currencies. The offering was completed three months prior to the turn in the ECU/dollar exchange rate.

Total Returns

Chart 4 implicitly depicts another critical point in global investing: that investors must look at total return in assessing non-dollar investments. Total return here means coupon income, price appreciation/depreciation and gain or loss on the currency.

CHART 4 U.S., $/ECU VS. U.S. $/DM EXCHANGE RATES

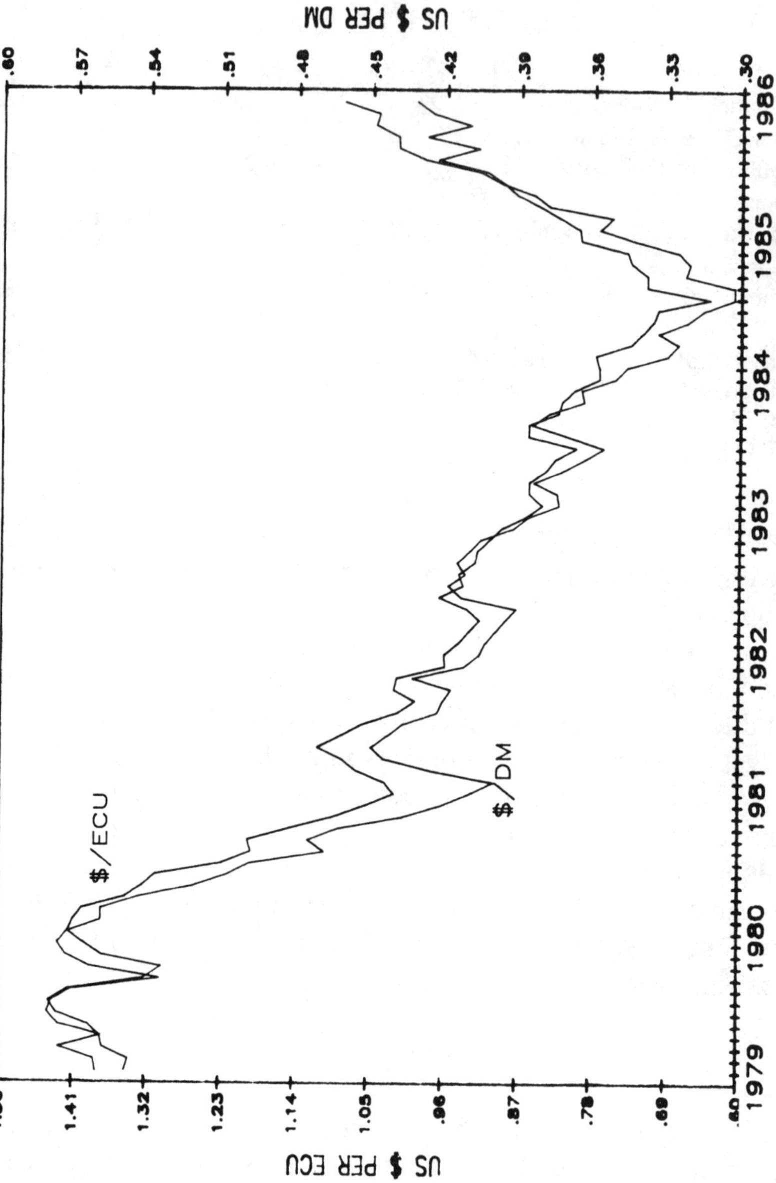

Source: Data Resources Inc.; Bear, Stearns & Co., Inc. Month End Exchange Rates.

In explaining this facet of an ECU-denominated bond to U.S. investors we described the benefits of ECU-denominated bonds as analogous to those of a convertible bond. One must first look at the underlying currency (''equity'') and then compare the interest rate attributable to this underlying equity. Just as various convertible issues have different coupons, different currencies have different interest rates attributable to their currencies. Therefore we had to explain both the equity and income characteristics of ECU-denominated bonds.

Historically, U.S. investors seeking currency diversification have chosen the DM because of Germany's economic presence in Europe and the world. Also, there exists the perception that the Bundesbank is very protective of the DM's intrinsic value. An example of this historical preference is that when the dollar was very weak in 1979 lines of people waited to buy DM-denominated traveler's checks from American Express offices.

The ECU, therefore, was particularly attractive to U.S. investors because of the heavy Deutsche mark and Dutch guilder (the guilder historically trades with the DM and acts as a DM proxy) weighting. At the time of the offering, the DM and the guilder comprised approximately 42 percent of the ECU's value. In fact, the correlation coefficient of the DM to the ECU from 1979 to July 1986 was 98.9 percent.

The yield give-up relative to U.S. Treasuries (or comparable credits denominated in U.S. dollars) on straight DM-denominated bonds can be significant. The yield give-up on ECU-denominated bonds relative to U.S. Treasuries is not as significant due to the participation of some of the weaker currencies in the ECU. Chart 5 indicates the historical yield give-up of both DM-denominated and ECU-denominated bonds relative to U.S. Treasuries. Money managers were particularly conscious of yield levels at the time of the EEC's offering; they wanted currency diversification, but were not willing to give up 300 basis points to obtain it.

Specifically, at the time the EEC's ECU offering was completed, the ten-year U.S. Treasury market was at 11.25 percent; the EEC's offering was priced with a yield to maturity of 9.95 percent. U.S.

CHART 5 DM VS. ECU VS. U.S. $ BOND YIELDS

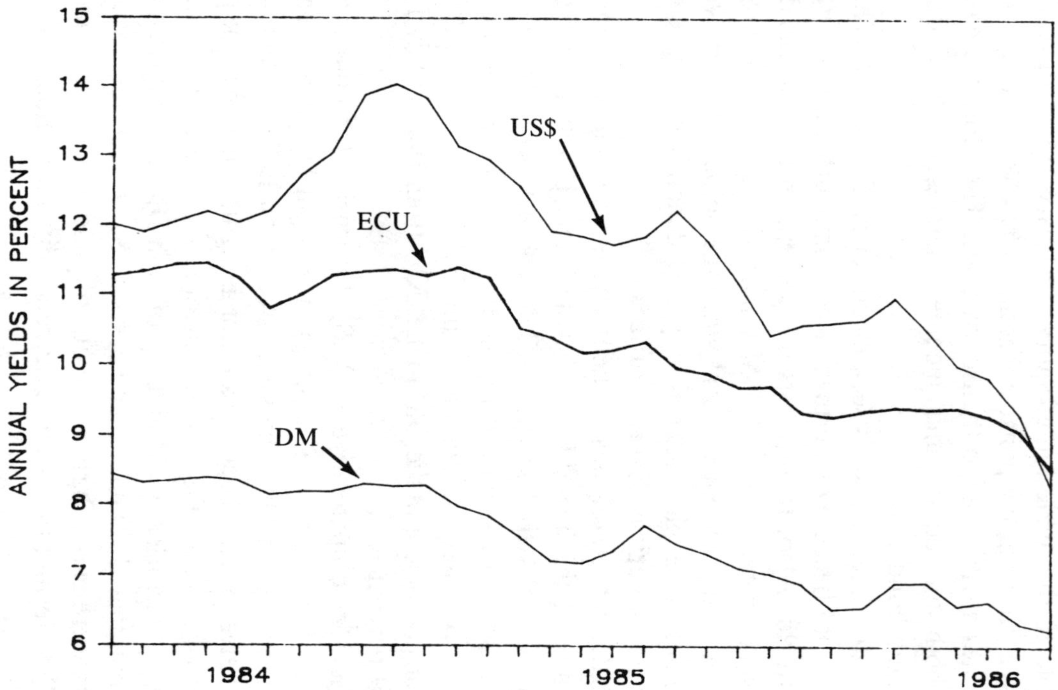

Source: Morgan Guaranty Trust Company of New York, "World Financial Markets" for U.S. and Germany; Istituto Bancario San Paolo di Torino—San Paolo Bank, "ECU Newsletter" for ECU.

investors therefore gave up approximately 130 basis points in current yield relative to U.S. Treasuries.

At a give-up of 130 basis points, investors felt comfortable that the ECU would appreciate by 1.3 percent per year relative to the dollar, at which level they would be "made whole" relative to their U.S. Treasury alternative.

The ECU was attractive because it had a 98.9 percent correlation to that of the DM, but offered a yield closer to that of U.S. Treasuries. In fact, at the time of the EEC's ECU offering a number of major sophisticated European institutions were swapping out of DM denominated bonds into ECU denominated bonds to benefit from higher yields.

Another major question dealt with was how efficiently ECU-denominated obligations are priced relative to the underlying government securities of the Member States. In essence, was it more economic for a money manager to create a synthetic ECU portfolio than to buy an ECU-denominated bond? Practically, however, transaction costs, lack of liquidity in some local markets, and withholding taxes levied by some of the Member States of the EEC would make this an almost impossible operation, especially for a money manager based in the United States.

Chart 6 compares the actual long-term yields on ECU-denominated securities with those which are synthetically derived by multiplying the yield on long-term government or high quality corporate domestic bonds denominated in the ECU's component currencies by the weight of each currency in the ECU and then summing the results.

As Chart 6 indicates, the ECU market has increasingly become more efficient relative to the underlying EEC government securities markets. In September 1983 actual ECU yields were higher than the underlying EEC theoretical yield by about twenty-five basis points. This was primarily due to the novelty of ECU-denominated bonds and somewhat due to the initial lack of liquidity until the market matured. During the initial phases of marketing the concept of ECU, we emphasized the fact that there was a yield pick-up relative to this underlying theoretical rate and that as the market in ECU became more liquid, this gap would close, creating a larger capital gain poten-

CHART 6 ACTUAL VS. SYNTHETIC ECU YIELDS

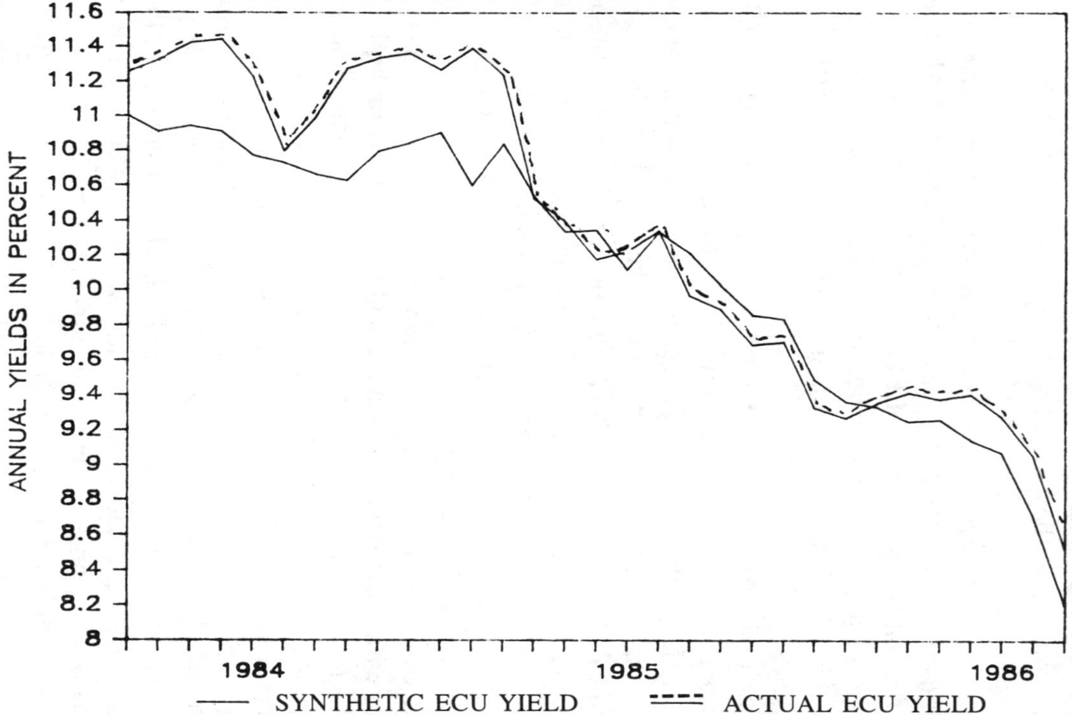

Source: Istituto Bancario San Paolo di Torino-San Paolo Bank, "ECU Newsletter," for synthetic ECU yields; Morgan Guaranty Trust Company, "World Financial Markets," for actual yields. Yields were derived by multiplying each country's interest rate by its weighting within the ECU and then summing those products.

tial. This gap had closed by November 1984, the time of the offering by the EEC.

After coming out of an inflationary period in the 1970's, investors also were interested in hedging against inflation. Chart 7 (page 28) indicates that from an investor's perspective, ECU-denominated debt has historically acted as an attractive hedge against U.S. inflation. The chart illustrates the historical ECU/U.S. dollar exchange rates and inflation as measured by the quarterly percent change in the personal consumption deflator. As the personal consumption deflator rose (i.e, U.S. inflation rose), the dollar tended to depreciate against the ECU. A regression analysis based upon the historical data indicates that as inflation increased 1, percent the U.S. dollar depreciated 3.04 cents relative to the ECU. This correlation was statistically significant and while it is not designed to forecast the value of the ECU, it did explain 79.8 percent of the variation in ECU/U.S. dollar exchange rates since 1976.

In summary, the ECU offers investors seeking currency diversification a simple means to execute a program of European currency diversification and should be an integral part of a global fixed income portfolio. As indicated by Table 7, the numbers speak for themselves.

TABLE 7 RATES OF RETURN: U.S. TREASURY VS EEC ECU

	U.S. Treasuries 11 5/8% of 11/15/1996	**EEC 9 7/8% due 12/1/86**
Total Rates of Return from November 1984 to July 31, 1986	39.1%	69.8%

YANKEE ECU AND EURO-ECU: A GLOBAL PARTNERSHIP

Traditionally, a Yankee bond issue was one in which a non-U.S. entity raised capital denominated in U.S. dollars in the U.S. capital markets. For example, the EEC's first dollar-denominated issue reg-

CHART 7 U.S. CENTS/ECU VS. PERSONAL CONSUMPTION DEFLATOR

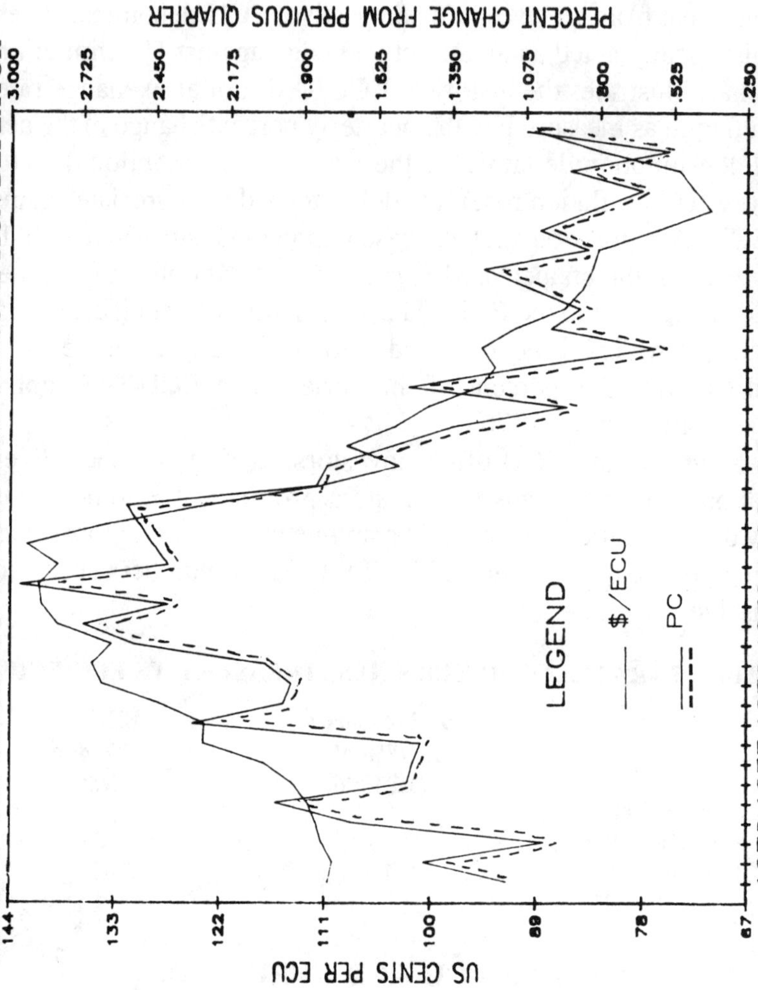

Source: Data Resources Inc.: U.S. Personal Consumption Deflator; Bear, Stearns & Co. Inc. for month-end exchange rates.

istered with the SEC in 1977 was a Yankee bond issue. Also, the EEC ECU issue in November 1984, because it was for a non-U.S. issuer in a currency other than dollars, was also referred to as a Yankee ECU issue. As the U.S. market for ECU-denominated securities continued to develop any ECU-denominated issue, irrespective of the issuer's domicile, was referred to as a Yankee ECU. Therefore, although three of the ECU issues in the U.S. market have been completed by U.S. institutions, the offerings are referred to as Yankee ECUs. Table 8 lists the ECU-denominated issues which have been completed in the United States through mid 1986.

TABLE 8 YANKEE ECU ISSUES

Issuer	Date Offered	Principal Amount Offered	Coupon	Maturity	Lead Managers
EEC	11/29/84	ECU 200,000,000	9 7/8%	12/1/96	Bear Stearns, First Boston Morgan Stanley
Hercules Corp.	3/15/85	ECU 50,000,000	10 1/8%	3/15/92	First Boston
Credit Foncier	3/29/85	ECU 150,000,000	9 3/4%	1/1/95	Bear Stearns First Boston Morgan Stanley
Kingdom of Denmark, Inc.	5/8/85	ECU 150,000,000	Current 7.043%	5/15/90	Salomon Brothers
Banque National de Paris[1]	10/3/85	ECU 150,000,000	Current 7.0567%	10/15/95	Salomon Brothers
Credit National[2]	11/21/85	$150,000,000	Current 6.597%	12/01/95	Salomon Brothers
Federal Home Loan Banks	2/6/86	ECU 100,000,000	8 3/4%	2/15/96	Bear Stearns
J.P. Morgan	7/24/86	ECU 100,000,000	6 3/4%	12/15/91	Bear Stearns

[1]The offering by Banque National de Paris was not registered with the SEC, but was issued as a Certificate of Deposit (under the 3 (a) 2 exemption to the Securities Act of 1933). This offering had the effect of creating a non-dollar deposit in the United States and was in effect a violation of the Federal Reserve's prohibition against non-dollar accounts in the United States. The Federal Reserve has, through moral suasion, effectively eliminated this means of raising ECU-denominated capital in the United States.

[2]Convertible at the option of the holder into Floating Rate Notes due 1995 denominated in ECU, on any Interest Payment Date falling in or before December 1987 at the conversion rate of $0.85265 per ECU.

With the globalization of the world's capital markets, it is becoming common to have bond and equity offerings distributed simultaneously in Europe and in the United States. Although ECU-denominated offerings were originally a European phenomenon, Yankee ECU issues have bridged a significant deficiency of Euro-ECU, namely, the current "seasoning" constraints of U.S. securities laws that preclude the sale of Euro-ECU offerings into the U.S. markets until ninety days have elapsed from the date of final distribution. Since Yankee ECU's are registered with the SEC, initial distributions can be made immediately both into the United States and Europe simultaneously.

Secondly, certain U.S. institutions want to make payment against physical delivery of the securities. With Euro bearer securities, custodian accounts need to be set up in Europe and the securities may never physically enter the United States. When a U.S. institution holds bearer bonds, they must disclose their holdings to the U.S. government or face penalties. Filing such forms is cumbersome and it is easier for U.S. institutions to buy registered securities.

Yankee ECU issues offer some specific advantages over Euro-ECU for certain U.S. institutional investors and represent a significant step forward in globalizing the capital markets.

ECU AS A CURRENCY HEDGE FOR ISSUERS

Issuers of debt also need currency hedges. There are three major categories of ECU issuers: sovereign, supernational and multinational.

Sovereigns

Many sovereigns are unable to finance themselves completely in their own domestic capital markets. Denmark, Sweden, Australia, and France, as well as other European countries, have capital markets which are too small to absorb all their capital needs. Therefore, they turn to the Euro and U.S. debt markets to raise capital.

Whenever a sovereign borrows in a currency other than its domestic currency, it assumes currency risk. To minimize the currency risk of borrowing in other currencies, many sovereigns want to borrow in different currencies, thus creating a diversified pool of liabilities. The ECU is ideal for this purpose because, by definition, it is already a diversified currency. Borrowers that are Community Member States are attracted to the ECU because their currencies are included in the basket, thus mitigating some of the currency risk.

Sovereigns are often borrowers of such significant magnitude that they need to tap various markets. The development of the Yankee ECU market provided another market for sovereigns to access.

Supranationals

Supernationals have the same funding problem as sovereigns, but to an even greater degree. Although they are often owned or sponsored by sovereigns, supernationals operate outside the bounds of any particular country and, by charter, generally have significant funding needs (i.e., the EEC, the European Investment Bank, the World Bank, Asian Development Bank, and other institutions of this type). Therefore, they don't have captive domestic capital markets which can provide a portion of their funding requirements, and they need access to different capital markets.

Multinationals

Multinationals, by their very nature, need to finance their global operations in the currency of the country in which the subsidiary is located or they will be in an unhedged position and expose themselves to currency fluctuations. (The very large currency translation losses and gains over the last several years have been due to this very situation—funding an operation in a given country in another currency.) To the extent that a multinational has operations throughout the EEC, the ECU can be an attractive currency for its debt issues.

For example, Hercules, a U.S. chemical company, completed an ECU 50 million offering in early 1985. Hercules broke the ECU into its component currencies and used these liabilities as hedges against their operations in various EEC Member States.

Swap-Driven Financings

Swap-driven ECU offerings have been utilized by many sovereigns, supranationals and multinationals. For example, Bear Stearns lead managed a Yankee ECU offering for the Federal Home Loan Banks (FHLB), an agency of the U.S. government. The FHLB was able to raise ECUs more advantageously in the United States than the EEC was able to do in Europe. Correspondingly, the EEC was able to raise dollars in Europe more advantageously than the FHLB could do in the United States. The proceeds from the simultaneous offerings in the United States and Europe were swapped and each party received the desired proceeds (and the corresponding liability) at an advantageous rate.

The major counterparties for such ECU swap-driven offerings have been French and Italian institutions. As further counterparties are identified, this aspect of the ECU market will continue to grow.

THE ECU AS AN INVOICING CURRENCY

A particularly attractive use of the ECU is for invoicing. A large portion of intra-EEC trade has typically used the dollar as an invoicing currency. Since there can be a significant amount of exchange rate volatility between the dollar and the currency of the European country in which the exporter is based, companies are increasingly attracted to the ECU because it lessens currency exchange-rate risk.

As an invoicing currency, the ECU offers the advantage of stability. Companies that had been previously invoicing in dollars and hedging these revenues to avoid losses on sales or purchases in dollars no longer have to hedge. Such hedging techniques can be particularly expensive when hedging the weaker currencies (i.e., the Italian lira).

The best example of a multinational using the ECU to invoice is Saint-Gobain of France. Saint-Gobain began denominating its internal intergroup billings in ECUs in 1981, began being paid in ECUs by its subsidiaries in 1983 and is planning to start denominating commercial operations in ECUs.

For trade between the United States and the EEC, one party will still have to bear currency exposure, so that the need to hedge will continue. The recent introduction of ECU futures and options, which allow for the possibility of shifting the exchange rate risk from the dollar to the ECU or vice-versa, makes invoicing U.S./EEC trade in ECUs attractive.

WHERE DOES THE ECU GO FROM HERE?

The ECU has been an overwhelming success in its short lifespan. This chapter has explored many of the reasons why it has been so attractive to a number of sectors of the financial, political and business communities. These reasons are the following:

- The ECU provides an ideal vehicle for investors seeking currency diversification because it is a solely European, diversified currency with the EMS guarding its stability;
- The ECU has been especially attractive to U.S. investors because it has a 98.9 percent correlation with the DM but a relatively higher yield;
- The ECU has historically acted as a hedge against U.S. inflation;
- Multinationals find it attractive because it can hedge diversified European revenue flows or asset bases;
- The ECU can be used by sovereigns and supranationals because it easily allows them to diversify liabilities;
- The ECU is especially attractive to the Member States of the Community because their currencies are included in the ECU, thus minimizing currency risk;
- The development of the Yankee ECU market has opened another source of capital for issuers;

- In swap-driven financings, the ECU can allow issuers to raise capital more economically in one capital market, and then swap into a desired currency;
- The ECU is ideal for invoicing European trade because of its stability vis-a-vis the Member State component currencies;
- European/U.S. trade can use the ECU, as the introduction of ECU futures and options now allows for the transfer of exchange risk.

The fact that there is no ECU script or currency has not, and will not, significantly hamper its growth. The economist Wicksell concluded nearly 100 years ago that physical money does not need to exist. In a "credit economy," all that is needed to originate money transactions is simply the will to take and to make payments in the "credit currency." The ECU has become Wicksell's European "credit currency."

Several steps will ensure the ECU's further growth as an alternative currency. The United Kingdom still does not participate in the EMS. As one of the major EEC Member States, the ECU warrants full U.K. sponsorship in the future. The Italians should narrow the band for lira fluctuations, and Germany must officially recognize the ECU as an international currency.

Significant improvements have recently been made in ECU clearance to allow for a better means of moving a major international currency. The Society for Worldwide Interbank Financial Telecommunications (SWIFT) will complete the netting function and will act as the technical agent of the clearing mechanism. The Bank for International Settlements will play the role of banking agent in the clearing system.

Essentially, the ECU and the EMS created a regional Bretton Woods type agreement that remains the best model from which to draw ideas and concepts for a global exchange rate management system. A structure similar to the EMS could be created with three major currencies participating: the dollar, the ECU and the yen. Such a model could enhance worldwide economic stability by managing exchange rate variability, thus harmonizing economic policies and international trade.

CHAPTER TWENTY

LIZABETH L. PALUMBO is a Vice President of Merrill Lynch Asset Management where she is an associate portfolio manager. Previous to this, she worked in the London and New York offices in the Fixed Income Research Department of the Global Securities Research and Economic Group where she was responsible for the analysis and recommendations of international securities and markets.

She began her career in 1971 as an equity analyst at the Home Insurance Company and then as a fixed income analyst at the Bowery Savings Bank. Ms. Palumbo received a B.B.A. in finance from the University of Georgia, an M.B.A. from New York University and is a Certified Financial Analyst.

SUPRANATIONAL INSTRUMENTS FOR WORLD PORTFOLIOS

Lizabeth L. Palumbo, CFA
Merrill Lynch Asset Management, Inc.
Princeton, New Jersey

INTRODUCTION

Supranational institutions are organizations formed by sovereign nations through international treaties for the purpose of promoting economic development of the member countries. Ownership of the institution lies with the member countries as set out in the respective agreements and/or charters.

The objective of these institutions — raising the standard of living in the developing member countries — is accomplished by channeling funds through them, first as a borrower on the international markets, and then as a lender to the respective member countries. In this way supranational organizations act as intermediaries transferring financial resources from industrialized countries to developing regions of the world.

As conduits, these international development banks typically provide long-term fixed-rate funds from the public capital markets to countries that are unable to attract this type of capital directly on favorable terms. Supranationals have been able to do this successfully because their operational and financial structures have provided a type of security to bondholders not otherwise obtainable from the countries directly.

SUPRANATIONAL INSTITUTIONS

The International Bank for Reconstruction and Development (IBRD) and its affiliate, the International Development Association (IDA), are commonly referred to as the World Bank. The Bank was established after the second world war and has been operating since 1946. Of the two organizations, the IBRD is the larger entity and the only one to borrow on the public bond markets. Presently it has 148 member countries. The largest subscribers to capital are the United States (accounting for approximately 21 percent), Japan (7 percent), the United Kingdom (6 percent), France (6 percent), Germany (6 percent), China (4 percent), and Canada (4 percent).

In general, the broad objective of the Bank is to improve the efficiency of the international financial and trading markets. Its principal activity is providing loans for specific projects, related technical assistance and, more recently, for structural adjustments. In this latter regard, the purpose is to bring about reform in underlying economic policies through its lending programs. The World Bank is the largest of the supranationals, with over $80 billion in total assets.

While the World Bank was the first multinational bank to be established, several institutions have since followed. The later banks generally replicate the form and structure first utilized by the World Bank. However, they differ in two important respects — in terms of the specific member countries and the region in which each bank lends.

For example, the Inter-American Development Bank (IADB) promotes economic growth in the developing countries of the Americas. Subscribers to capital are the United States (35 percent), Canada (4 percent), twenty-seven regional members (48 percent) (including Argentina, Brazil, and Mexico, with subscribed capital of the former two countries of approximately 12 percent and the latter of 8 percent), and other non-regional members (13 percent).

This is in contrast to the Asian Development Bank (ADB), where the Pacific basin and Asia account for its lending sphere. The largest subscribers to capital include the United States (17 percent), Japan (17 percent), India (8 percent), Australia (7 percent), Korea (6 percent), and Germany (5 percent), with other regional (24 percent), and non-regional (16 percent) members holding the balance.

Another example is the Nordic Investment Bank (NIB). The purpose of this supranational, as the name implies, is to promote economic growth in the Nordic countries. Members include Sweden (43 percent), Denmark (22 percent), Norway (18 percent), Finland (16 percent), and Iceland (1 percent).

Another type of supranational is exemplified by the European Investment Bank (EIB). The Bank was established by members of the European Economic Community (EEC) under a separate agreement to promote balanced regional development, serve the common interest of the member states, and further industrial modernization and conversion. Member countries and their approximate percentage of subscribed capital are as follows: Germany (19 percent), France (19 percent), Italy (19 percent), United Kingdom (19 percent), Spain (7 percent), Belgium (5 percent), Netherlands (5 percent), Denmark (3 percent), Greece (2 percent), Portugal (1 percent), Ireland (1 percent), and Luxembourg (<1 percent).

In addition to the European Investment Bank, members of the EEC established institutions for specific purposes, in contrast to the former's broader directive. For example, the European Coal and Steel Community (ECSC), the first institution established by the member states, has as its purpose the development and integration of the Community's coal and steel industries. Similarly, the European Atomic Energy Community (Euratom) is responsible for the development of their operations on the international capital markets with the backing of the members of the EEC, as set down in the respective charters. Furthermore, the EEC borrows to finance programs which it directly implements but which are typically administered by the European Investment Bank. These supranational institutions are less frequent issuers on the capital markets than the larger European Investment Bank.

SOURCES OF FUNDS

Supranational organizations fund their lending programs by borrowing across the world's capital markets. In aggregate they constitute a major sector of the public bond markets. As shown in Table 1, the amounts borrowed by this sector increased from $7.4 billion in 1980 to a $19.4 billion annual rate through May 1986.

The traditional currency sectors in which supranationals issue securities are the U.S. dollar, the German mark, the Swiss franc, and the Japanese yen. In general, this reflects the size and importance of these sectors in the world capital markets. Additional markets to which the supranationals have access include U.K. sterling, the Dutch guilder, the French franc, the Belgian franc, and the Italian lira. The largest currency sector, the U.S. dollar, is by far the most frequented market, accounting for close to 40 percent of the total bond offerings by supranationals over the 1980-1986 period. The larger Eurodollar bond market has been the primary source of funds, accounting for over 70 percent of financings, with the remaining amount coming from the smaller foreign market, the Yankee market.[1]

However, when measured as a percentage of total gross borrowings, the supranational sector has decreased in importance across the major currencies' bond markets. Their share of total gross borrowings declined from 20 percent in 1980 to 8 percent through May 1986. Two factors account for this. First, as previously mentioned, the international capital markets in general have experienced rapid growth. Accordingly, offerings by the supranational sector account for a smaller portion of the larger pie. Second, and relatedly, has been the emergence of the currency and interest rate swap markets. As described in the chapter on financial swaps, these markets enable an issuer to change, i.e., to swap, the original borrowed currency and/or set interest rate into an alternative currency and/or rate.

[1]Borrowings on domestic markets by non-residents are referred to as foreign markets. The foreign market denominated in the U.S. dollar is known as the Yankee market; in U.K. sterling as the Bulldog market; and in Japanese yen as the Samurai market.

TABLE 1 SUPRANATIONAL INSTITUTIONS GROSS BORROWINGS BY CURRENCY
(US$ millions equivalent)

Fixed Rate	**1980**	**1981**	**1982**	**1983**	**1984**	**1985**	**1986***
U.S. Dollar	1,906.0	3,075.9	4,535.0	5,798.7	2,802.6	7,209.8	5,892.0
German Mark	2,638.3	1,015.6	1,611.7	2,215.6	2,185.7	2,323.9	3,614.2
Japanese Yen	662.1	1,180.1	1,071.3	1,459.5	1,786.7	2,837.0	2,248.8
Swiss Franc	1,280.7	1,026.3	1,633.7	1,367.4	1,375.4	1,861.1	2,745.4
Dutch Guilder	182.2	452.6	658.0	778.3	689.1	723.0	1,359.1
U.K. Sterling	155.2	217.8	556.8	375.6	1,241.2	476.3	261.4
ECU	—	88.4	216.7	670.1	1,023.9	1,146.9	1,592.6
French Franc	363.0	88.6	221.3	265.2	—	511.0	972.0
Canadian Dollar	—	—	—	125.1	385.8	55.4	173.0
Other	236.4	371.1	236.4	288.1	307.4	883.1	509.0
Total	7,423.9	7,516.4	10,740.9	13,343.6	11,797.8	18,026.9	19,367.5
Floating Rate							
Amount	57.5	—	—	1,800.0	600.0	2,737.4	1,226.2
Percent of Total	0.77	—	—	13.49	5.09	15.19	6.33

*January-May annualized

Source: OECD

The World Bank has been instrumental in the development of the currency and interest rate swap markets from their inception. The Bank's large funding needs required it to look for financings outside its traditional sources. By using swaps the World Bank was able to change the currency denomination of its borrowings to preferred currencies on more favorable terms. During fiscal year 1985 the Bank executed $1.4 billion (equivalent) in currency swaps, reducing its cost on these borrowings by 5.38 percent.

With the growth of the swap market, supranational organizations were able to swap borrowings in minor currency sectors, such as the Canadian dollar, the Australian dollar, the New Zealand dollar, and the Norwegian kroner markets, to alternative currencies. Of particular importance to EEC-related institutions has been the emergence of the European Currency Unit (ECU) bond market; the currency of account for these institutions is described more completely in the chapter on ECUs. Consequently, the percentage of gross borrowings by supranationals in the public markets of the major currency sectors has declined of late, as shown in Table 2, with the minor currency sectors taking on greater importance. However, as previously noted, when swap activity is considered, tabulations on gross borrowings do not correctly indicate the effective currencies borrowed.

TYPES OF INSTRUMENTS EMPLOYED

Fixed Rate Securities

Typically, supranational offerings take the form of intermediate to long-term fixed-rate debt (in keeping with the usual nature of their lending programs) with fine rates (reflecting their high credit standing). Because supranational institutions borrow extensively across the world's markets there is a considerable diversity of their fixed income securities available.

In addition to the numerous currencies, there is a broad range of coupons reflecting the disparity of the interest rate levels between

TABLE 2 SUPRANATIONAL INSTITUTIONS GROSS BORROWINGS BY CURRENCY AND AS A PERCENT OF TOTAL MARKET
(billions)

		1982	1983	1984	1985	1986*
U.S. Dollar						
Euro and Yankee Markets						
Intl Dev Org	(US$)	3.7	2.4	2	3.8	0.9
EEC Related	(US$)	0.8	3.4	0.8	3.3	0.9
Total	(US$)	4.5	5.8	2.8	7.1	1.8
% of Market		9.3	13.2	4.0	7.0	3.8
Swiss Franc						
Foreign Market						
Intl Dev Org	(SF)	0.8	2.8	3.4	3.7	0.9
EEC Related	(SF)	2.5	0.8	1.0	0.7	0.6
Total	(SF)	3.3	3.6	4.4	4.4	1.5
% of Market		14.3	12.8	14.5	12.3	7.9
Japanese Yen						
Euro and Samaurai Markets						
Intl Dev Org	(Yen)	165	265	365	543	110
EEC Related	(Yen)	70	95	60	90	55
Total	(Yen)	235	360	425	633	165
% of Market		24.3	37.1	29.4	21.4	9.5
German Mark						
Euro and Foreign Markets						
Intl Dev Org	(DM)	1.8	2.7	4.1	4.8	2.1
EEC Related	(DM)	2.1	2.6	3.0	1.7	1.4
Total	(DM)	3.9	5.3	7.1	6.5	3.5
% of Market		30.0	31.5	36.8	20.3	20.1

*January-May
Source: OECD

international money and capital markets. Further differences occur with regard to maturity. For example, on the foreign U.K. sterling (Bulldog) and U.S. dollar (Yankee) markets maturities extend out twenty years or more. This is in contrast to the larger Euro counterparts where, except for the World Bank in the dollar market, maturities usually are no longer than fifteen years at issue and typically shorter. Another example is the Dutch guilder market where, until recently, regulations required redemptions through sinking funds. Consequently, fixed income securities issued by supranationals on the guilder market are typically subject to redemption prior to maturity.

While in aggregate there is an extensive diversity of outstanding debt reflecting the various characteristics of the respective markets, fixed-income securities issued by supranationals are similar across the markets in several important respects. Typically, they are very liquid, high quality instruments which enjoy ready acceptance by market participants. World Bank securities most clearly exemplify these characteristics in that they form the nucleus of the international fixed-income markets.

Floating Rate Notes

Floating-rate notes are less frequently issued, as shown in Table 1. There are several reasons for this. Typically, financing is sought for long-term projects and a mismatch in funding is, in most instances, imprudent (interest payments on floating rate notes are adjusted to short-term rates). Furthermore, developing member country borrowers generally do not have direct access to fixed-rate debt due to their perceived low credit quality (subjective or objective) by the public markets. This is in contrast to floating-rate debt, where they do have access to adjustable rate loans from banks. In addition, for some supranationals their charters do not permit lending at floating rates while for others their borrowing structures were put into effect prior to the development of the floating-rate market.

Nevertheless, supranationals have on occassion made use of this market. Specifically, the World Bank has borrowed on such a basis with the rate adjusted to the U.S. Treasury bill market, in contrast to the more common benchmark, the interbank dollar deposit market. The EEC has also been an issuer of floating rate notes, with a $1.8 billion offering in 1983 (which has since been redeemed).

Other Instruments

Further finding vehicles includes a medium-term note program and a discount note program, both implemented by the World Bank in the U.S. domestic market. Under the former, the Bank from time to time issues securities with maturities and on terms determined by market conditions at the time of sale. Securities issued under this program differ from traditional offerings in the U.S. market in the method of distribution. The securities may be sold to dealers and underwriters, as with traditional offerings, or they may be sold directly by the Bank or through agents. Under the discount note program, the Bank offers on a discount from par, i.e., bearing no coupon, through dealers.

CREDIT QUALITY OF SUPRANATIONAL ORGANIZATIONS

Credit ratings on borrowings by supranational institutions typically carry triple A ratings from the U.S. public rating agencies. The high quality ratings assigned to supranational borrowers reflect the following conservative financial policies and strong capital structures.

Callable Capital

Member governments subscribe to two types of capital in supranational institutions, paid-in capital and callable capital. The former is actually paid to the supranational institution to be used for general purposes. The latter and larger amount, however, is available only to meet obligations on borrowings in the unlikely event that these liabilities cannot be paid. The commitment of governments to make capital payments are independent and not joint and several. Each government is required to make payments until either the liability or their capital obligation is discharged. Consequently, borrowings by supranationals are in essence guaranteed by its member governments.

Particular attention is given to the extent to which capital is callable from members that are also borrowers from the institution. This is important, in that if a borrower is unable to make payments on its loans to the bank it is unlikely that their callable capital commitment could be met, if needed. Accordingly, it is financially prudent, if the industrialized member countries are not borrowers of the bank. Typically this is the case. Furthermore, as most borrowings are financed on the capital markets of the industrialized countries, there is an inherent interest for these governments to ensure prompt and timely payments of debt obligations by supranationals to investors.

Loan Limitations

In general, the amount of guarantees and loans which the development banks may advance is restricted to their capital, surplus and reserves. This in effect protects against erosion of the banks' capital base.

Liquidity Policies

The development banks tend to have conservative liquidity policies. Adequate liquidity is important in ensuring prompt payments to their borrowers as well as their creditors. Furthermore, it provides a necessary cushion for the timely scheduling of offerings on favorable terms in the world's capital markets.

Borrowing Limitations

For some institutions there are specific limits regarding total borrowings. Typically the amount may not exceed total callable capital. For others there is an implied limit based on lending restrictions and liquidity policies.

Quality of the Loan Portfolio

Loans are usually tied to a specific project, with the bank taking steps to ensure that the project is technically feasible and economically sound. Furthermore, if the advance is not a direct government loan, a government guarantee is usually attached. Finally, the banks have a policy of not participating in the rescheduling of debt. This policy is honored by indebted nations for two important reasons. First, there is usually an ongoing lending program, making it economically advisable for debtors to keep current on their payments and, second, the banks have a special relationship with their borrowers, i.e., their governments are, in most instances, member countries of the supranational.

Reserve Policies

In general, the banks maintain reserves to mitigate against future loan losses.

Avoidance of Exchange Rate Risk

The banks have a policy of not bearing exchange rate risks in their activities. Proceeds from borrowings are placed in securities denominated in the same currency until disbursed. The banks also require that borrowers bear any exchange risk by requiring loan repayments in the same currency in which disbursed.

Pricing of Assets

The banks lend at rates to cover the cost of funding and to provide a limited return on assets. The rate and method of determination differs between institutions. Some lend at a fixed rate against a specific borrowing, i.e., back-to-back. Others lend at a variable rate, adjusted over set periods, based on the composite interest costs that they bear, i.e., a basket rate.

ATTRACTIVE OPPORTUNITIES FOR INVESTORS

Investors in securities issued by supranationals include both individuals and institutions seeking high quality, intermediate to long-term fixed-rate debt investments. The majority of offerings are tailored for investors desiring bonds with these characteristics, particularly since they best match the needs of the supranationals. However, there are securities incorporating alternative features, creating a market of diverse instruments for investors, e.g., floating rate notes and discount notes. Furthermore, many of the securities in the supranational sector are non-callable, a feature of particular importance in declining interest rate environments. In addition, frequent accessing of the primary market together with large size has led to an active secondary market.

The high credit quality of supranational institutions and the good liquidity of their securities are reflected in secondary market yields. Yields on supranational securities in various currencies compared to respective government securities are generally narrow, as indicated in Figures 1-4. A comparison against high quality private borrowers and sovereigns would generate similar results.

The extent of the yield difference against treasuries is dynamic and dependent on respective market conditions at the time. This is also indicated in Figures 1-4, which show yield comparisons of World Bank securities (typically the richest issuer in the sector) against various treasuries across four markets. While spreads tend to favor supranational issues, e.g., in the Yankee and Eurodollar markets, for some markets yield relationships may favor treasuries, e.g., in the Eurosterling and Deustche mark markets. These differences reflect the supply and demand conditions operating in the respective markets at the time. In the U.S. domestic market, spreads have widened with the onslaught of new issue volume. While the supply in the Yankee market has been moderate, spreads have

FIGURE 1 YIELDS AND SPREADS IN THE EURODOLLAR BOND MARKET
(Monthly data)

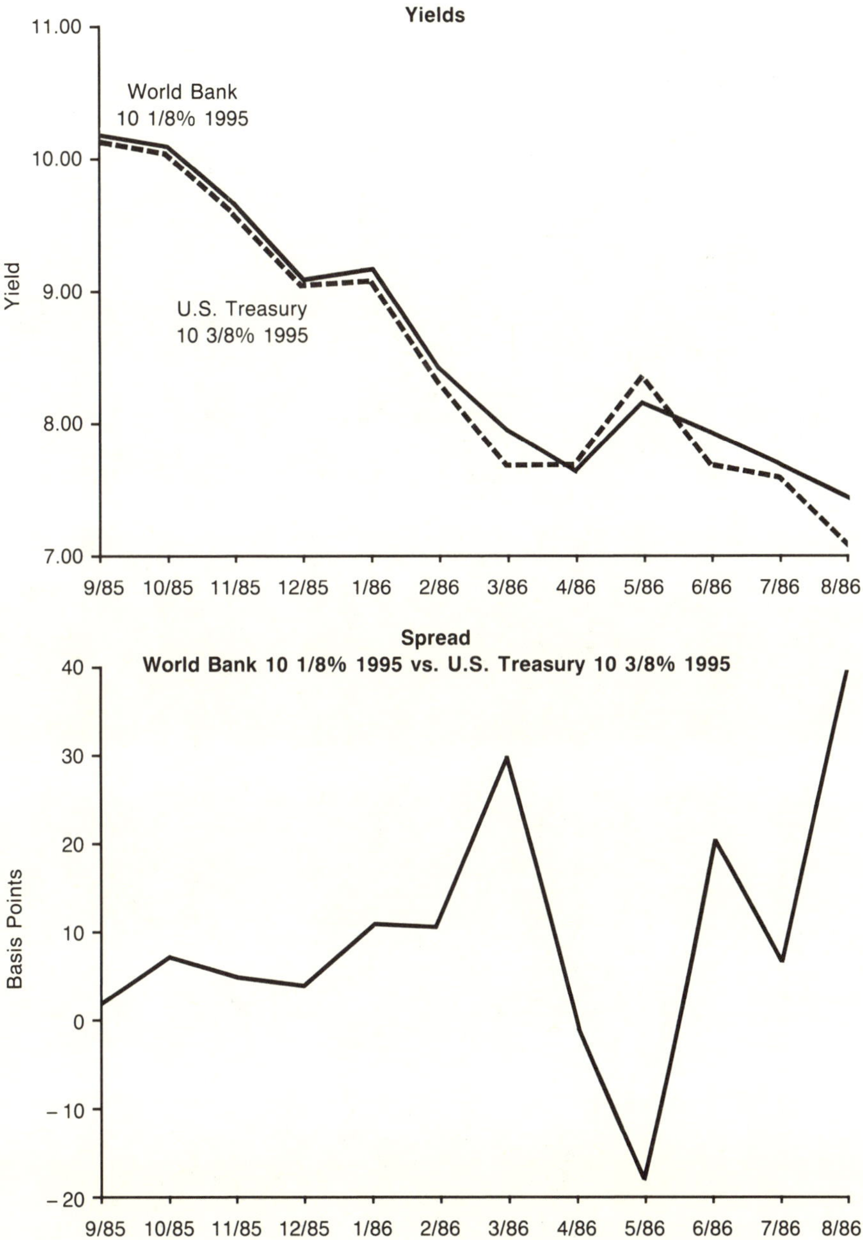

FIGURE 2 YIELDS AND SPREADS IN THE YANKEE BOND MARKET
(Monthly data)

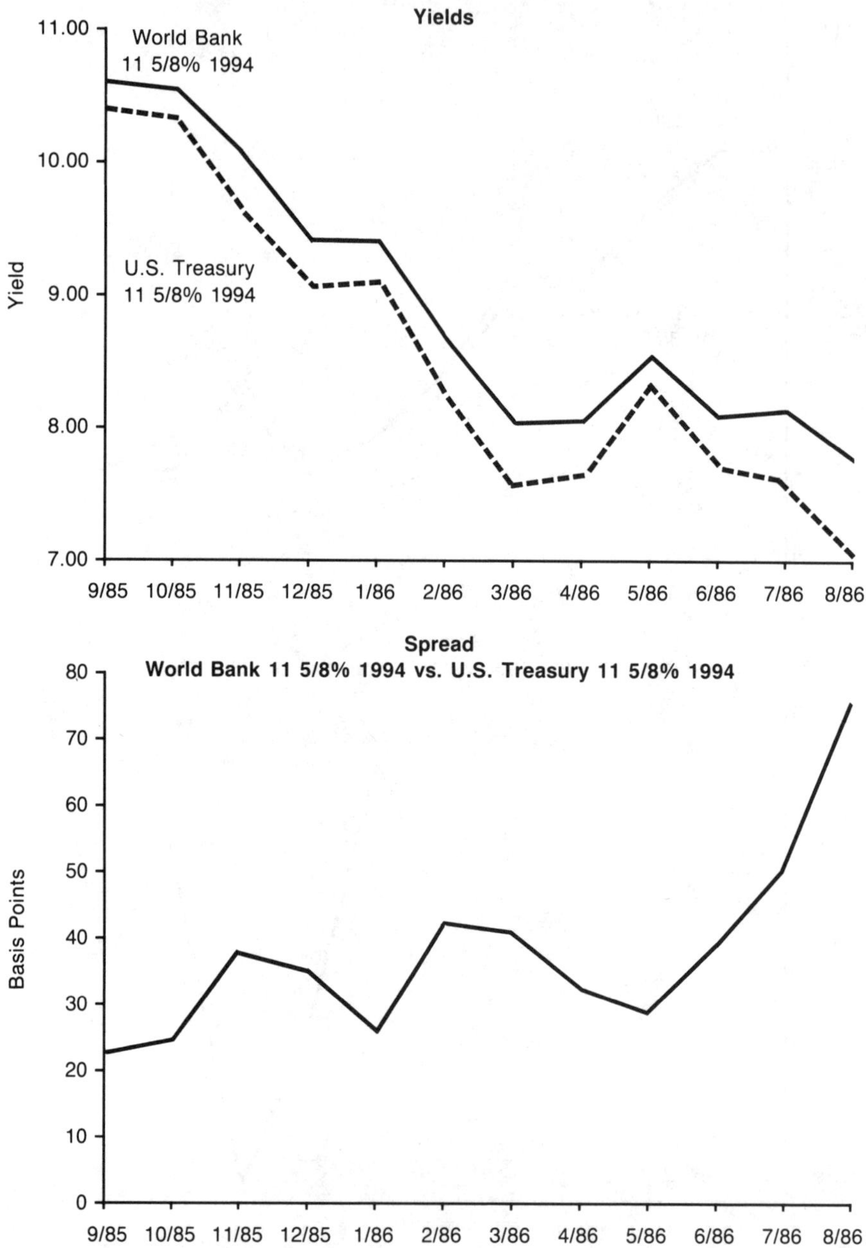

FIGURE 3 YIELDS AND SPREADS IN THE EURO STERLING BOND MARKET
(Monthly data)

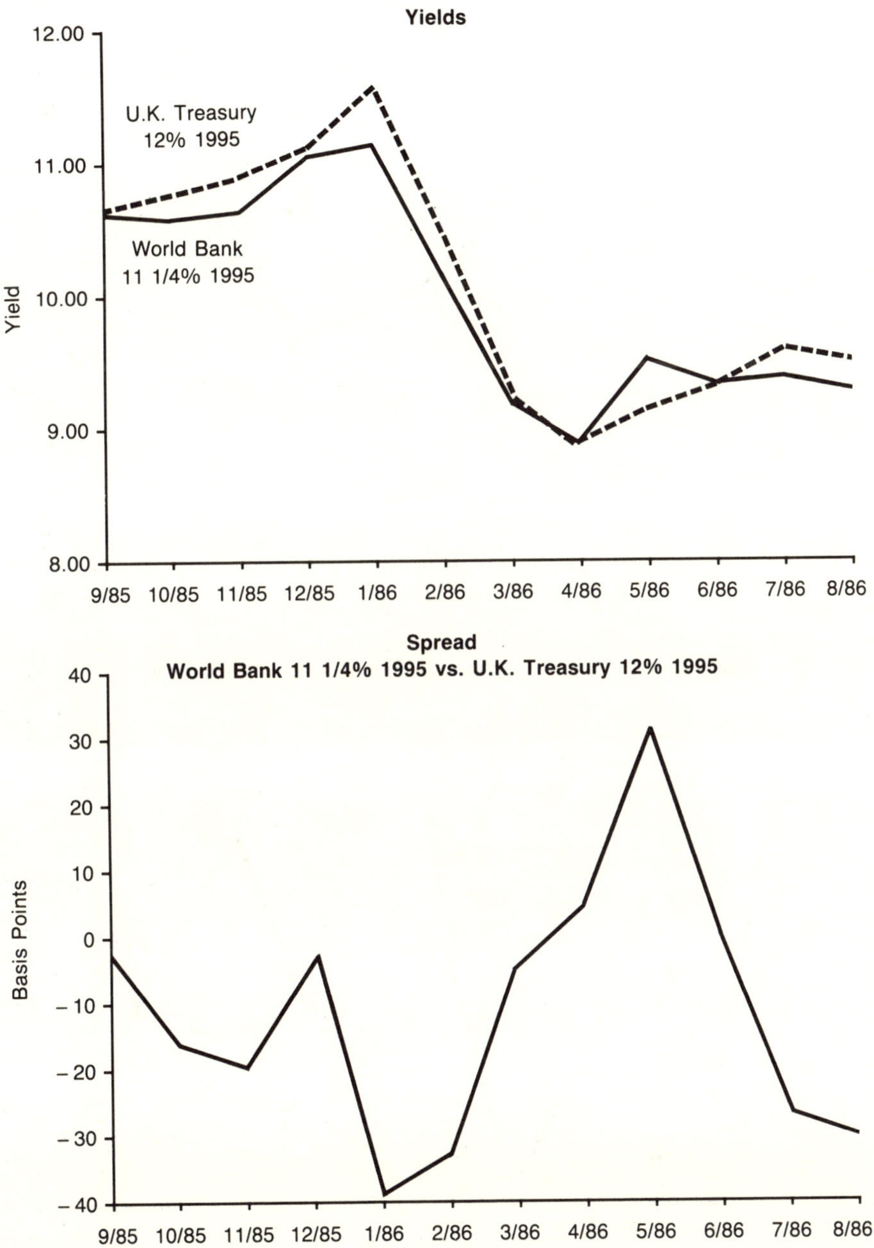

FIGURE 4 YIELDS AND SPREADS IN THE FOREIGN DEUTSCHE MARK BOND MARKET
(Monthly data)

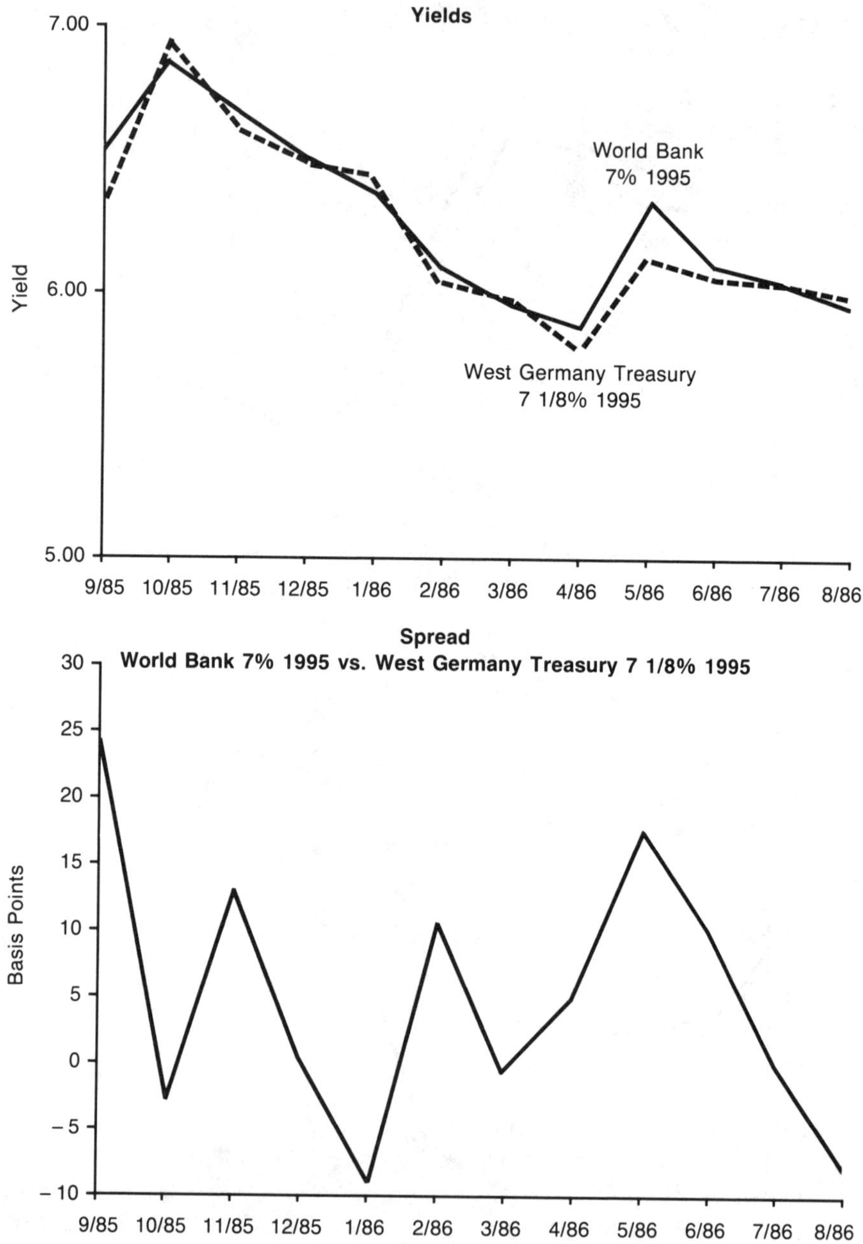

widened against treasuries following this general widening trend in the U.S. corporate market. In contrast, foreign investor demand for assets denominated in Deutsche marks has led to narrow spreads which, at times, have even been negative. Nevertheless, securities issued by supranational organizations tend to offer investors attractive alternatives in the high quality sectors of their investment portfolios.

Figures 5-8 show the proximity of secondary market yields among like securities of different supranational borrowers in four selected markets. Apparent in the charts are the favorable rates commanded by World Bank securities. Less apparent are the regional preferences of markets. For example, securities issued by the Inter-American Development Bank tend to be favored by investors in the U.S. domestic market, compared to its Eurodollar counterpart. Similarly, securities issued by organizations of the EEC enjoy ready acceptance by European investors in their domestic and Euro markets, compared to offerings on the U.S. domestic market. The same can be said of the Asian Development Bank, i.e., Japanese investors favor securities by this borrower. While yields tend to be similar, regional preferences of investors are disclosed in the secondary market, creating attractive opportunities across the international markets.

SUMMARY

Securities issued by supranational institutions are typically accorded an AAA rating by the agencies. This high credit standing is backed by the strong capital commitment of the industrialized member countries. Further strengths of these organizations are apparent when examining their asset quality, capital adequacy, funding and liquidity parameters, and profitability. In addition, they compare very favorably to other types of financial institutions.

Their high credit quality also gives them access to the world's financial markets. This enables them to create and open markets more readily than other borrowing sectors. For example, the establishment of the ECU market and the currency and interest rate swap

FIGURE 5 YIELDS IN THE EURODOLLAR BOND MARKET
(Monthly data)

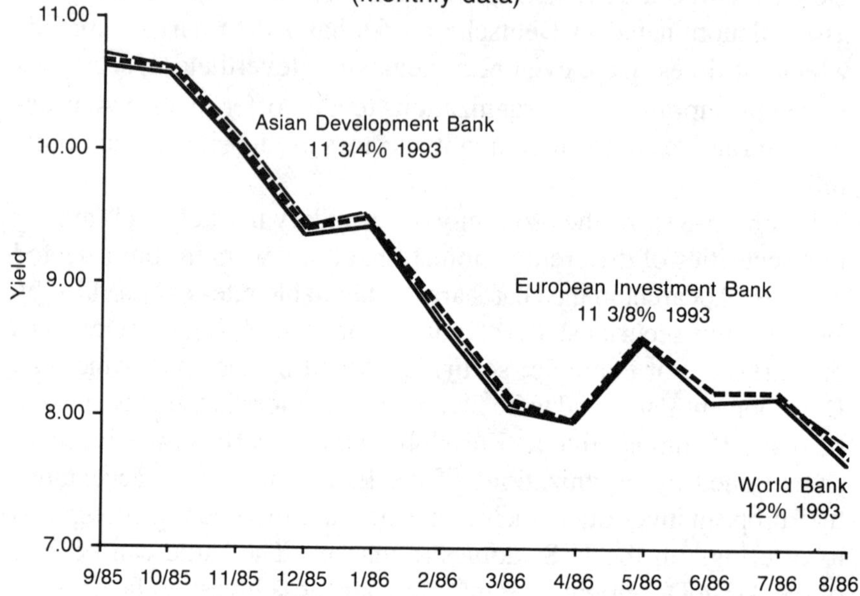

FIGURE 6 YIELDS IN THE YANKEE BOND MARKET
(Monthly data)

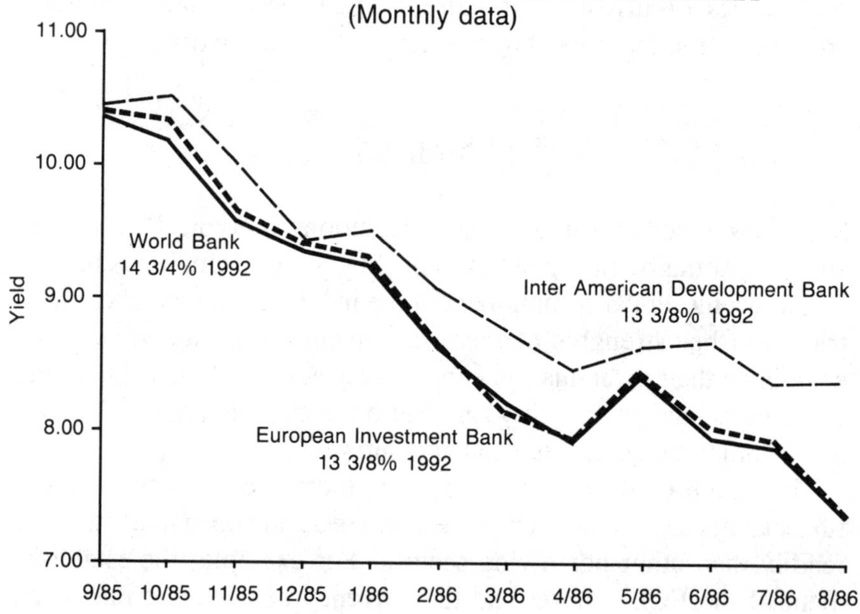

FIGURE 7 YIELDS IN THE EURO STERLING BOND MARKET
(Monthly data)

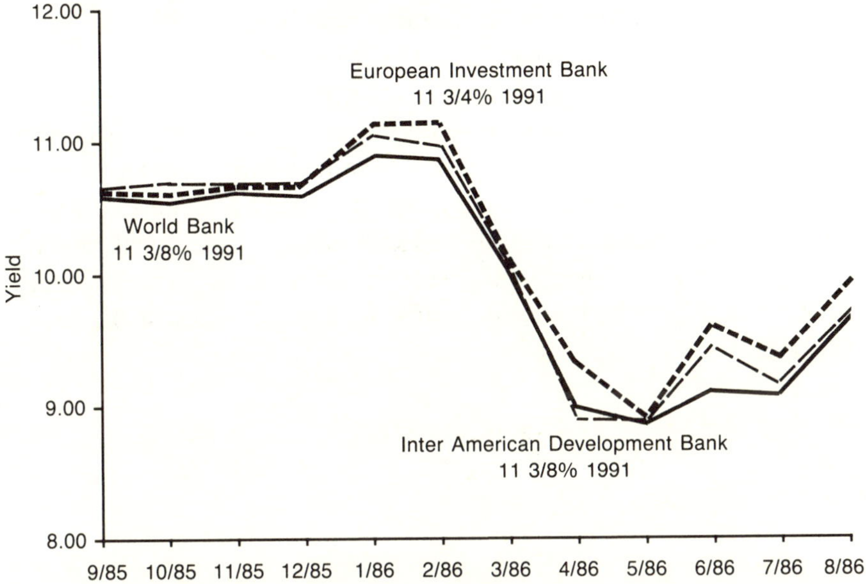

FIGURE 8 YIELDS IN THE FOREIGN DEUTSCHE MARK BOND MARKET
(Monthly data)

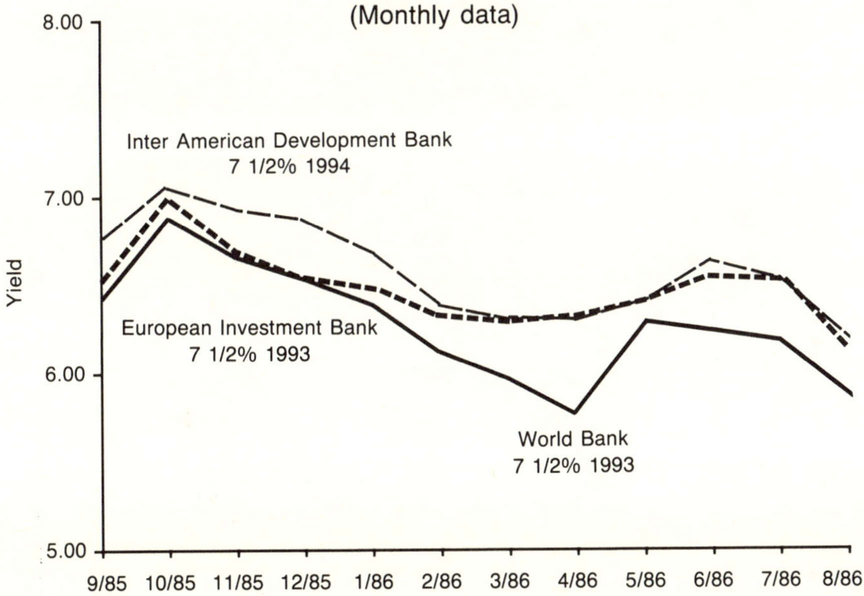

markets were in large part due to the efforts of supranational institutions. Furthermore, in many primary markets it is not unusual for record volumes to be set by a supranational borrower. At the forefront of these activities has been the World Bank.

In general, the high credit quality and good liquidity of these securities have made them attractive investments. In part this is due to the desire of supranational institutions to maintain their high credit ratings. This is a particularly important objective given that funding in the international capital markets is such an intregal part of their operations. Consequently, securities issued by supranationals should continue to be rewarding investment vehicles across the international bond markets.

CHAPTER TWENTY-ONE

MICHAEL KATZ born in 1952 in Melbourne, Australia, Michael Katz graduated from the University of New South Wales in 1973. After some years work experience in the Australian Credit Card Industry he moved to the University of Geneva, Switzerland, to undertake post-graduate studies. This led to a faculty position with the International Management Institute (IMI), the international business school associated with the University of Geneva, in 1978. In 1981, he joined Citicorp's Merchant Banking unit in Geneva. Working for Citicorp for five years, he was directly associated with some of the more interesting innovations in the Swiss capital market during that time. Michael Katz is now a Vice President of Morgan Stanley S.A. in Zurich.

AN INTRODUCTION TO INTERNATIONAL EQUITY LINKED SECURITIES

Michael Katz
Morgan Stanley S.A.
Zurich, Switzerland

INTRODUCTION

This chapter is concerned with the markets for international equity linked securities. It is written from Switzerland where equity related securities have a long and distinguished history. This Swiss franc foreign bond market raised approximately Sfr36 billion in new funds for non-Swiss entities in 1985. Of this amount almost 40 percent consisted of equity related securities.

This chapter will deal with the two basic forms of equity linked securities; convertibles and warrants. After a brief review of the instruments themselves and the reasons for companies issuing them, a more detailed discussion of the advantages for the investor is provided. This is followed by a section on "Traps for the Unwary." The terms "share" and "stock" have been used interchangeably to refer to the commonly traded equity capital of a public corporation or company. The terms "bonds" and "notes" are also used interchangeably to refer to traded, bearer fixed income securities as commonly issued in the international capital markets.

DESCRIPTION OF THE INSTRUMENTS

Convertibles

The convertible bond is probably the oldest and most common form of equity linked instrument. The international capital markets in the late 1970s saw Japanese corporations begin to issue significant numbers of convertible bonds and notes as a substitute for the issuance of additional equity capital in the Japanese domestic market. These issues have had an enviable record of success in parallel with the general growth in the Japanese stock market.

A convertible bond or note is typically a debt security which can be exchanged for equity stock in the issuing company. The convertible bond is a hybrid structure on a scale somewhere between an issue of pure equity and an issue of straight debt. The most important variable is the relationship between the coupon and the conversion premium. The coupon is the interest rate payable on the debt. The conversion premium is the percentage difference between the conversion price and the market price of the stock at the time of the issue. The conversion price is the price at which the holder of the convertible bond may convert par value of debt into the common shares of the issuing company.

The length of time during which investors have the right to exchange or convert their bonds into shares of the issuer is also of importance. This is known as the conversion period. The conversion period for a Japanese issue normally begins as soon as possible after the launch of the underlying debt and runs until just prior to the final maturity of the bonds. In some domestic markets there are significant restrictions on the conversion period. These restrictions are almost unknown in the international markets.

The convertible debt instrument is traditionally exchanged for the common shares of the issuer. The investor who converts debt for a nominal amount, say Sfr50,000, receives common shares in the issuing company for a value equal to Sfr50,000 at the predetermined conversion price set at the time of the issue of the debt. Example

1 sets out the exact calculation of conversion price and explains the operation of the fixed exchange rate.

EXAMPLE 1

Scenario Aoki Corporation of Japan issued Sfr150 million in convertible five year notes starting in 1987. The following are the key terms and conditions:

Market Price of Stock (S)	: Yen 781 at the time of issue
Fixed Exchange rate (X)	: Sfr 1 = Yen 91.00 (spot rate at time of issue)
Conversion Premium (P)	: 5%
Denominations (FV)	: Each note is issued with a nominal or face value of Sfr50,000.

Calculation

Conversion Price (CP) = Market Price of Stock × Conversion Premium

= S × (P + 100)/100

= 781 × (5 + 100)

= Yen 820

Stock Issued on Conversion = Nominal Value of Note

Conversion Price × Exchange rate

= FV/(CP) × X

= Sfr50,000/820 × 91.00

= 5,549 shares issued on conversion

The fixed exchange rate remains constant throughout the life of the bond or note. This ensures that the investor will always receive a fixed number of shares in the issuing company on conversion. It also implies that the investor has a continued interest in the base currency of the issuer as well as the stock itself. Even if the stock price does not move, the value in Swiss francs of the shares to be received on exercise of the conversion right will fluctuate with movements in the spot exchange rate over the life of the note.

Variations on the basic structure outlined above include:

- Convertibles which can be converted only on specific dates
- Conversion periods which begin only after a considerable period has elapsed since the issue date
- Convertibles which are exercised into the equity of a third company
- Convertibles with very high conversion premiums and high coupons
- Convertibles which are exercisable into gold or other commodities rather than equity

Undoubtedly, many other variations on the basic concept of the convertible security will be developed as the international financial markets continue to demonstrate their capacity for innovation.

Warrants

Warrants are a more sophisticated version of the basic equity linked convertible security outlined above. The key difference is that the warrant is a separate security only initially attached to the underlying debt instrument. It is essentially similar to a call option with an extended maturity. When the warrant is attached to the underlying debt instrument the security is known as a "bond cum warrant." The investor in a bond cum warrant purchases a debt instrument with a right to participate in the long-term success of the issuer through an attached equity option. The investor also has the right to separate the debt obligation from the warrant and sell either part. Once again, the primary source of international equity warrants has been issues by Japanese corporations. As of mid-1986 the market capitalization of outstanding international Japanese equity warrants was equivalent to approximately U.S. $7 billion.

In the case of the warrant, the first key variable is the total warrant premium. This premium is the amount per share which the investor pays for the right to buy the share at any time over the life of the warrant. The total warrant premium is calculated by assuming that the investor must begin by purchasing a bond cum warrant. The bond alone, "ex warrant," is then assumed to be sold into the market at a discount price to generate the normal yield to maturity on a straight bond of similar quality and duration, "the ex-warrant price." The difference between the issue price and the ex-warrant price is the cost of the warrant. The total warrant premium is calculated as the cost of the warrant plus the cost of exercising the warrant divided by the cost of purchasing the shares directly. Other key variables are:

- the gearing or leverage on the warrant, being the amount by which movements in the underlying share price are magnified in movements in the price of the warrant
- the exercise period during which the warrant can be exercised
- the exercise price at which the warrant is exercised
- the warrant coverage, being the value of the warrants when exercised divided by the nominal value of the bonds

Example 2 sets out the basic calculations for an issue of bonds cum warrants in the Swiss market. The analysis of the warrant premium is based on the assumption that the investor actually detaches the warrant from the bond as soon as possible after issue.

EXAMPLE 2

Scenario Aoki Corporation issued Sfr150 million in five-year 1.25 percent bonds guaranteed by a prime Japanese City Bank with equity warrants attached. There are eleven warrants attached to each bond with a nominal face value of Sfr50,000. Each warrant gives the holder the right to purchase 500 shares in Aoki at a price of Yen 800 per share. It is assumed that if Aoki Corporation were to issue straight bonds with the same maturity and guarantee the coupon would be 5.25 percent. The following are the key terms and conditions:

E	=	Warrant exercise price = Yen 800
S	=	Market price of stock = Yen 781
B	=	Number of warrants per bond = 11
N	=	Number of shares per warrant = 500
FV	=	Face value of the bond = Sfr50,000
X	=	Initial exchange rate = 91.00 yen/Sfr
EW	=	Price of ex-warrant bond = 82.8% to yield 5.25% to redemption.

Calculation

Exercise Premium : Warrant exercise price/market price

$= (E/S - 1) \times 100$

$= (\text{Yen } 800/\text{Yen } 781) - 1 = 2.4\%$

Warrant coverage : Number of warrants × Shares per warrant × Exercise price

(Face value of the bond × Exchange rate)

$= (B \times N \times E/FV \times X) \times 100$

$= 11 \times 500 \times \text{Yen } 800/(\text{Sfr}50{,}000 \times 91.00 \text{ Yen/Sfr}) \times 100$

$= 96.70\%$

Cost of warrant : $= (FV - EW \times FV)/B$

$= [\text{Sfr}50{,}000 - 82.8\%(\text{Sfr}50{,}000)]/11$

$= \text{Sfr}781.8$

In order to calculate the total warrant premium one must determine the exact opportunity cost of purchasing the equity through the warrant versus the cost of purchasing the stock directly over the stock exchange. For the purposes of comparability broker commissions are normally ignored.

Cost of purchasing
stock direct : = N × Market price
= 500 × 781 Yen = Yen 390,500

Cost of Purchasing shares
through the warrant = Cost of warrant + Cost of exercise
= Sfr781.8 × 91.00 Yen/Sfr +
500 × Yen 800
= Yen 71,144 + 400,000
= Yen 471,144

Total premium = Cost of purchase through warrant/Cost of direct purchase
= (471,144/390,500 − 1) 100
= 20.65%

A short form of this calculation which is used by many investors is as follows:

Premium = Issue price − Price to yield straight coupon + Exercise premium
= 100% − 82.8% + 2.4%
= 19.6%

The premium as calculated above does not fully reflect the true value of the warrant because the coverage is less than 100 percent. In recent years the importance of the coverage, or warrantability, of a new issue has grown, as issuers, particularly non-Japanese, issue bonds with warrants attached for only a relatively small fraction of the nominal value of the bonds.

The example as calculated above differs somewhat from normal practice in the dollar market. Japanese warrants issued in London are normally issued on the basis of a single warrant per $5,000 bond. This reduces the importance of the concept of warrant coverage and at the same time tends to make the warrant "heavier" in the sense that the price of each warrant is considerably higher. Warrants are traded in the dollar market on the basis of a price expressed as a percentage of \$5,000. In Switzerland, Warrants are traded on the basis of the absolute Swiss Franc cost of the Warrant.

The final key variable used to define a warrant is the leverage or gearing. The leverage of a warrant is defined as the value of shares to which the investor has exposure divided by the cost of the warrant. This gives an approximate idea of how much the warrant price will move in response to a corresponding change in the underlying share price. The leverage on the Aoki warrants can be calculated as follows:

EXAMPLE 3

Leverage = Value of shares/Cost of warrant
= S × N/(cost of warrant)
= (781 × 500) ÷ (Sfr 781.8 × 91 Yen/Sfr)
= 390,500/71,144
= 5.49

For every 1 percent movement in the share price of Aoki the warrant price should move 5.49 percent. As the price of the warrant rises in accordance with a rise in the underlying share price the leverage on the warrant tends to decline.

In more theoretical terms the investor in an equity linked security, whether a convertible or a warrant, purchases a right but not the obligation to obtain an equity interest in the issuing company. This right has two principal components which determine its value, the price at which the right may be exercised and the time over which it may be exercised.

ADVANTAGES TO THE ISSUER

Before analyzing the advantages of equity linked securities for the investor it is important to understand the motivation behind the issuance of these instruments. It has already been noted that Japanese corporations use international equity linked instruments as a substitute for direct placements of equity in the domestic market. In addition, issuers are attracted by the possibility of expanding the investor base for their shares. The issuer of international equity linked securities normally assumes that at least a portion of the quasi-equity so issued will remain in the hands of international investors. This typically forms part of the generally accepted financial strategy of maximizing the diversity of sources of capital in order to avoid dependence on any single source of funds. In the case of Swiss franc instruments the investor base is particularly highly valued because of the perception of Swiss investors as being of "high quality." High quality in this context is a synonym for loyal.

A second reason for issuing equity linked securities is that the securities, whether warrants or convertibles, provide for equity to be issued at a premium. Alternative forms of equity placement require the equity to be issued either at the market price or at a discount to market price. This is particularly important for companies which are sensitive to dilution of existing shareholder interest.

Convertibles

The issuer of convertibles is typically attracted by the extremely low coupons which are possible with this kind of instrument. Recent issues of Swiss franc convertibles have had coupons of less than 1 percent. This is attractive in its own right and may be particularly attractive for issuers unable to avoid domestic withholding tax on the issue of offshore debt.

The convertible is intrinsically attractive in that it allows the elimination of the foreign exchange risk normally associated with foreign currency borrowing. This is achieved on conversion of the bonds or notes. When a Swiss franc convertible security is converted by the investor the Swiss franc debt outstanding on the balance sheet of the issuer is converted into equity denominated in the base currency of the issuer. Conversion may eliminate foreign exchange risk. This is not a full hedge of the foreign exchange risk associated with foreign currency borrowing, since the convertible bonds may never be converted, in which case the foreign currency risk of repayment of the liability will remain.

Warrants

Warrants are attractive to issuers for a number of reasons. Firstly, the warrant potentially raises a multiple of the volume of funds raised with either a straight or a convertible issue. The additional funds are raised with only a very marginal additional fee being paid to the underwriters. This is a result of the warrant structure whereby funds are first raised through issuance of the bonds cum warrants. Then, upon exercise of the warrants, additional funds are raised since the investor must subscribe additional capital at the exercise price. Under the original conception of the warrant, the additional funds raised on exercise were used to repay the underlying debt.

Warrants also provide issuers with attractive coupons. Recent issues in the Swiss market have been made with coupons of between 1 and 2 percent and exercise premiums of 2½ percent. This provides the issuer with opportunity to swap the proceeds of the debt issue back into the currency of his choice. The swap transaction eliminates the entire foreign exchange risk on the transaction.

In summary, equity linked instruments provide many advantages to the issuer. These advantages are low cost, risk avoidance, and improved investor relations. The advantages to the issuer are important in ensuring a steady supply of new issues to the market, providing investors with a good selection of investment opportunities.

ADVANTAGES TO INVESTORS

Having discussed the advantages for the issuer it is now possible to turn to the advantages for the investor. Once again these will be analyzed in terms of both the general advantages of equity linked securities and the specific relative merits of convertibles and warrants.

Advantages of Equity Linked Securities

Equity linked securities provide the investor with access to equity positions in stocks which would otherwise be unavailable, difficult to access, or unacceptably risky to fixed-income investors. An investor who prefers to invest only in instruments listed on the European stock exchanges will have relatively little access to stocks from outside Europe or those blue chip stocks from the United States which may be listed on one or more of the European exchanges. There are only approximately 450 stocks worldwide which are listed outside their home country. A listed equity linked security for a foreign company will provide the investor with a "play" in the shares of that company without the need to deal outside the normal channels which he is accustomed to use for domestic securities.

In order for a typical Swiss investor, Hans Gantenbein, to purchase an equity interest in a Japanese company such as Aoki Corporation he would normally have to proceed as follows. Hans would first place an order with his bank for the purchase of Aoki shares. The bank would execute the order through the Swiss office of one of the Japanese broker. The Japanese broker would purchase the shares in Tokyo. The bank would purchase the yen necessary to pay for the stock and charge Hans for the cost of the transaction, including their spread on the foreign exchange transaction, their commission, and the commission charged by the Japanese broker. Hans would receive the shares at some future date and would immediately be subject to the foreign exchange risk on the yen cost of the shares.

If Hans were to select the convertible bonds issued by Aoki Corporation as outlined in Example 1 above, the transaction would be much simpler. Hans would merely instruct his bank to purchase the convertibles. The bank would buy the convertibles for the account of Hans and charge him for them in Swiss francs. There would be a small commission payable to the bank for the securities transaction. There is no commission payable in Japan and no foreign exchange spread against the investor. At the same time Hans would have established an effective equity interest in Aoki through the convertibles.

In other cases the investor may be attracted to the prospect of an equity investment in a small foreign company. The lack of information on the company or the exceptionally risky nature of the business of the company may, however, discourage a direct investment. In this situation the equity linked debt instrument provides the investor with the comfort that the principal value of this investment is relatively secure. Even if the stock price of the company does not perform as hoped, the investor would expect to receive his payments of interest through the coupon together with repayment of principal on maturity of the underlying debt. The only exception is the situation when the company is totally bankrupt and cannot repay its debt obligations.

SPECIFIC ADVANTAGES OF CONVERTIBLES FOR INVESTORS

The technical advantages of the convertibles as an investment vehicle have been described above. In this section we examine how the typical investor, Hans Gantenbein, can actually profit from his investment in Aoki Corporation convertibles. The analysis shows how a convertible provides a "triple play" on the share price, the exchange rate, and interest rates.

As a traded security the convertible bond or note has a secondary market price. This is the price at which the security can be brought and sold at any time after it has been issued and prior to final maturity. We will assume that Hans purchased his Aoki convertibles in the primary market, at issue price. In the secondary market, equity linked securities are expected to trade at a premium to "parity." Parity can be defined as the secondary market price for an equity linked bond which eliminates the premium or discount for the purchase of the underlying equity. In Example 4 we look at how the parity of the convertible is determined.

EXAMPLE 4

Rate Scenario It is assumed that the market price of Aoki Corporation stock has risen in the first year since Hans purchased his Sfr50,000 convertible bond. The current spot rate Sfr/Yen has, however, declined.

M = Market price of stock : Yen 878
Xc = Current exchange rate : Yen 96.4 = Sfr 1
X = Fixed exchange rate : Yen 91.00 = Sfr 1
CP = Conversion price : Yen 820

Parity is calculated as follows:

$$\text{Parity} = \frac{\text{Current market price} \times \text{Fixed exchange rate}}{\text{Conversion price} \times \text{Current exchange rate}} = \frac{M \times X}{CP \times X} \times 100$$

$$= (878 \times 91.00)/(820 \times 96.4) \times 100$$
$$= 101.1\%$$

A parity of 101.1 percent indicates that at this price the purchase of the bond is no more expensive than purchasing the equity directly. In the example, a rise in the share price of Aoki has been offset in part by a decline in the value of the yen. In a normal market Hans would expect his convertible to trade at a premium to parity, reflecting the additional advantages of the convertible over the direct purchase of the shares and in particular the remaining time value of the right to purchase the stock of the issuer. In the example above the exchange rate "play" has counteracted the gain on the equity "play." In recent years the yen has tended to rise against the Swiss franc while the Tokyo stock exchange has seen annual average growth of the order of 30 percent for the Nikkei Index. Historically, the two markets have tended to reinforce each other. This benefit has been further compounded by the decline in interest rates over recent years which has added further value to the debt portion of the convertible.

The secondary market price of a fixed interest rate security will normally rise as the general level of interest rates falls. This is the third "play" available to the investor in international convertible bonds. Over recent years the worldwide decline in interest rates has given additional support to the price of convertible bonds in the secondary markets.

Specific Advantages of Warrants for Investors

In this section we will examine the potential benefits which might accrue to Hans' brother Rudi, who invests in Aoki Corporation Sfr bonds with equity warrants attached. He purchases Sfr50,000 in bonds cum warrants at an issue price of 100 percent. Rudi is convinced that the share price of Aoki will rise substantially and therefore he sells the underlying bonds and retains the warrants. Example 5 sets out the net result of Rudi's investment assuming the same rate scenario as in Example 4.

EXAMPLE 5

Rudi sells the bonds at a discount price to yield 5.25 percent. Given the coupon of 1.25 percent per annum, the price required to obtain the desired yield is 82.8 percent. The cost of the warrants is therefore 17.2 percent (issue price less market price of the bonds ex-warrant). The total investment in Aoki equity is now Sfr50,000 × 17.2% = Sfr8,600 for eleven warrants or Sfr781.82 per warrant. As noted in Example 2, this is a total premium of 20.56 percent.

As in the case of the convertibles, the secondary market price of the warrants will reflect the movements in the share price of Aoki Corporation. The following calculation demonstrates the impact of the rise in the share price of Aoki on the value of Rudi's investment.

E = Warrant exercise price = Yen 800
B = Warrants per bond = 11

Each warrant gives the holder the right to purchase 500 Aoki shares at Yen 800 each. The market price for Aoki shares is now Yen 878. The warrant is therefore "in the money" by the difference between the market price and the exercise price. When Rudi purchased his warrants he paid a total premium of 20.56 percent. This premium represents the appreciation in the share price which the market expects over the full five-year life of the warrant together with the value of the leverage included in the warrant. After only one year we would normally expect the warrants to continue to trade at a significant premium to parity on the basis of the continued value as an option and the time value of the remaining four years of the warrant life.

If we make an assumption that the premium should decline in a linear fashion the premium after one year of a five-year warrant would be

$$20.56 \times 4/5 = 16.45\%$$

If the warrants trade with this premium, the warrant price could be calculated as follows:

$$\begin{aligned} \text{Cost per share plus premium} = C &= M(1+16.45\%) \\ &= 878(1.1645) \\ &= \text{Yen } 1022 \\ \text{Price of the warrant} &= (C-E)N/X_c \\ \text{Price of the warrant} &= (1022 - 800)500/96.4 \\ &= \text{Sfr}1151.4 \end{aligned}$$

Clearly Rudi has made an extremely attractive investment. On a per warrant basis the value of his investment has grown by 47 percent in one year. The leverage on the warrant after one year has, however, declined to only 3.6 times. Figure 1 shows an example for Mitsubishi Corporation Warrants in dollars. This demonstrates the typical price behaviour of a warrant in the international market as the price of the underlying shares fluctuate in value. Note especially that, as with almost all dollar warrants, the price is expressed as a percentage of the nominal value of the origianl bond ($5,000). Also of interest is the impact or the leverage implicit in the warrant as the share price began to increase in mid-May 1984.

An additional advantage of the warrant is that if the share price declines, the maximum loss is limited to the cost of the warrant. Unfortunately, warrant premiums are much more volatile than indicated here. Although the time value of the warrant is important, most warrant investors appear to be more concerned with the immediate

FIGURE 1 ONE-YEAR PRICE HISTORY OF MITSUBISHI CORPORATION U.S. DOLLAR WARRANTS ON A WEEKLY BASIS. PERCENTAGE CHANGE IN WARRANT PRICE AGAINST PERCENTAGE CHANGE IN SHARE PRICE.

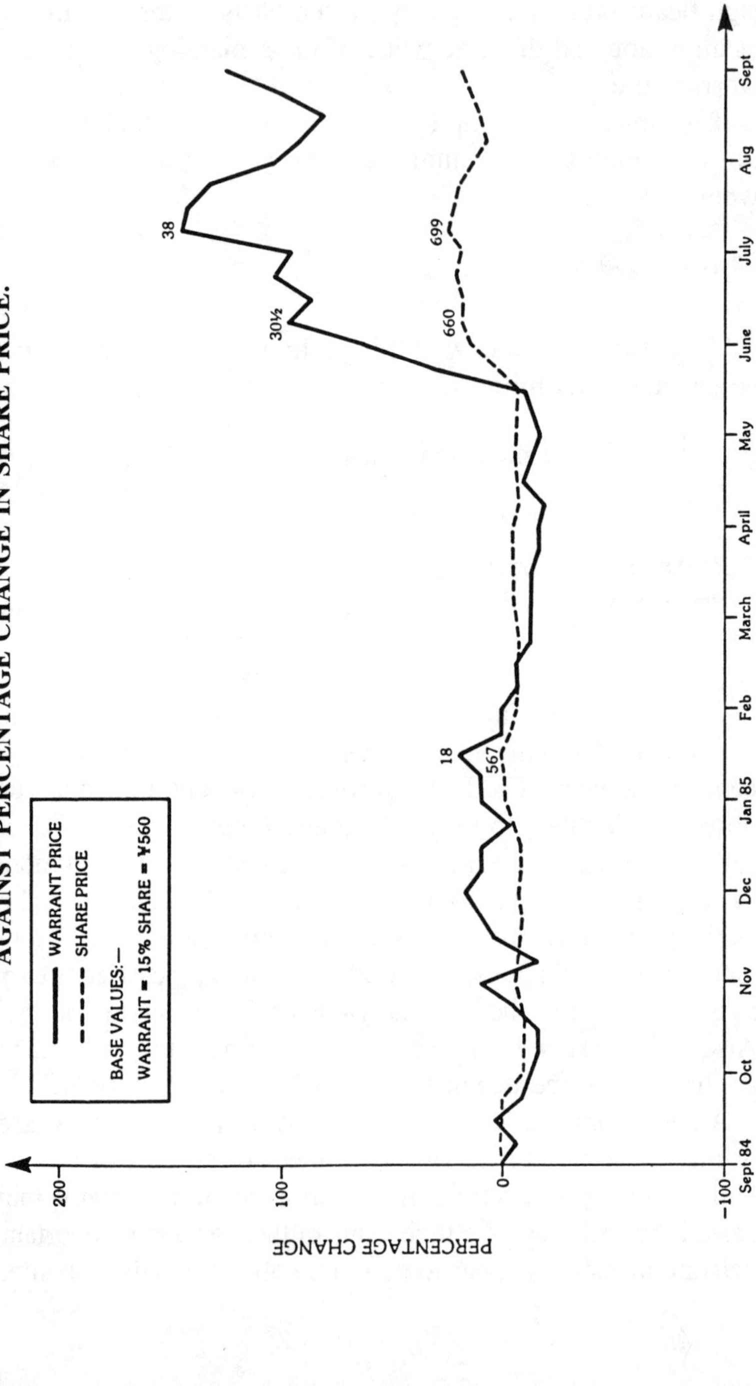

Source: Daiura Securities Ltd.

performance of the underlying equity. Total warrant premiums are therefore relatively volatile. Warrant investors would appear to have relatively high rate of return hurdles, which cause expectations of future performance of the underlying equity to be heavily discounted.

TRAPS FOR THE UNWARY

Despite the many advantages of equity linked instruments, they are not without risk. The most significant problem with many convertibles and warrants is that the liquidity in the issue may be less than satisfactory. In this sense liquidity refers to the ability of an investor to buy or sell the securities at the current market level without unduly moving the price. Liquidity is a function of:

- the size of the initial issue
- the number of professional firms willing to make a market in the security
- the age of the issue
- the success of the initial placement of the issue
- the liquidity of the underlying shares

All these factors can significantly impact the investor's ability to buy and sell the securities. The underlying equity market provides some natural support to the liquidity of the issue. Particularly in the case of a convertible issue, an investor wishing to sell a convertible note may find that even if no buyers exist for the convertible there will almost always be buyers for the underlying shares at a price. In this situation the investor can convert his bonds into shares at approximately parity and sell the shares back into the domestic exchange. In most cases banks will intermediate in this type of situation in order to simplify the individual investor's task. They will purchase the bond at just below parity and undertake the conversion for their own account. This eliminates the somewhat difficult administrative tasks otherwise associated with actual conversion of a foreign security into a domestic yen-based instrument for investors.

The principal disadvantage of converting an equity linked security into the underlying share and selling the shares is the loss of entire value of the equity link. The investor loses both the remaining time value of the option and the value of the right to exercise or convert. In the case of a warrant it is relatively rare for a warrant to trade at a discount to parity, which would allow the warrant to be exercised for an immediate gain.

The problem of liquidity has been gradually diminishing as increasingly large numbers of market makers and investors become active in the international equity linked securities markets. Declines in the Tokyo stock market in late 1986 did, however, cause a number of investors to pull back from these markets as they realized that there is no such thing as a one-way street in the financial markets.

SUMMARY

Equity linked securities provide added dimensions to the flexibility now available to international investors. They allow investors to straddle pure debt or pure equity positions with a hybrid security. They provide an opportunity for increased leverage in equity positions and they provide investors with an opportunity to obtain foreign currency positions indirectly without the cost and inconvenience associated with direct investments in foreign markets.

SECTION IV

Opportunities for Yield Enhancement in International Markets

CHAPTER TWENTY-TWO

RICHARD H. PETTWAY is Walter J. Matherly Professor of Finance at the Graduate School of Business, University of Florida, Gainesville. He received his BAA, MBA, and PhD from the University of Texas at Austin. He has published extensively and is currently Associate Editor of two academic journals in the finance field. He was Fulbright Research Scholar to Japan and China in 1982, and received a Special Fulbright Research Grant to Japan, where he was a Visiting Professor at Keio University, Tokyo for the summers of 1984 and 1985.

T. CRAIG TAPLEY is Assistant Professor of Finance at the Graduate School of Business, University of Florida, Gainesville. He has also taught at Indiana University and in Executive Development programs for IBM and Harris Corporation. He received his BS from Trinity College (Hartford), his MBA from The Amos Tuck School of Dartmouth College, and his DBA from Indiana University. His research interests are business finance, investments, and the futures markets and he has published in these areas.

EFFICIENCY OF WORLD CAPITAL MARKETS: THE CASE OF JAPAN AND THE UNITED STATES

Richard H. Pettway
T. Craig Tapley
University of Florida
Gainesville, Florida

Major cultural, governmental, and economic differences exist between Japanese and U.S. capital markets. Much has been written about the many Japanese restrictions which allegedly keep their markets segmented and not open to the full impact of world-integrated economic activities. The purpose of this chapter is to determine if the apparent restrictions and cultural differences are significant enough to cause the market for equities in Japan to be segmented from the U.S. market.

Past studies of equity prices listed on various stock exchanges of the world have been concerned with their efficiency, comovements, returns and the merits of international diversification. Market efficiency of various world stock exchanges has been tested by Hong, Jennergren-Korsuold, D'Ambrosio and others. The specific market efficiency of the shares listed on the Tokyo Stock Exchange (TSE) has been examined by Jaffe-Westerfield, Kato-Schallheim, Komine, Lau-Quay-Ramsey and Pettway-Tapley. Agmon, Hilliard, Panton-Lessig-Joy, Ripley and Robichek-Cohn-Pringle have studied the comovements of world exchange indexes and stocks. Returns and wealth of international shares have been explored by Ibbotson-Carr-

Robinson and Ibbotson-Siegel. Grubel, Levy-Sarnat and Solnik, as well as others, have investigated international diversification. Thus, there is extensive and rich research literature on the important stock exchanges of the world.

In addition to the studies of stock exchanges, Adler-Dumas, Adler-Horesh, Lessard and Stehle have considered the related issue of segmented versus world-integrated capital markets. Protopapadakis-Stoll studied the integration of commodities traded on international futures markets. Their study is unique in that it implicitly tests for integration of world markets by determining how well the Law of One Price (LOP) holds for real assets. Generally, their research found that the lower the transportation costs and the regulatory constraints, the more valid LOP becomes. Nevertheless, some commodities remained where large riskless arbitrage returns were possible.

Basically, the LOP states that the same asset, valued in a common currency and trading in two different markets, cannot trade at different prices, except for differences in transportation and transaction costs. If the LOP is violated, this indicates that asset prices are reacting individually to factors specific to only one of the relevant markets. Thus, in markets where the LOP does not hold for the same assets, these markets are said to be segmented because of institutional, cultural or regulatory constraints.

This study continues the research on segmented versus world-integrated stock markets. It differs from previous studies that used cross-sectional regressions of various world stock exchange indexes which have either weak or no control for security risk differences. This study examines the comovements of the *same* financial assets traded in two different markets and tests the validity of the LOP applied to these individual stocks. Consequently, there are no differences in the underlying security risk between the markets. To determine precisely if the Japanese stock market is segmented or subject to world-integrated economic conditions, we examine the returns on seventeen stocks which are dually listed on both the NYSE and the TSE.[1] Through careful analysis of price and return movements of the *same assets* on different markets we are able to measure the effects of institutional, cultural or regulatory restrictions. If the prices and returns of the same financial assets in two dissimilar markets react differently over time and violate the LOP, then it can be concluded that these markets are segmented.[2]

Given well-known institutional, cultural and regulatory constraints, there is reason to believe that securities traded simultaneously on the TSE and NYSE might violate the LOP. Japan has been very successful in isolating its domestic markets from the equalizing effects of world flows of goods, capital and services, as indicated by its continued balance of trade with the world, its continued lower domestic interest rates, as well as its performance in other markets. The Japanese government, especially the Ministry of Finance and the Ministry of International Trade and Industry, also has been accused of restricting and protecting the Japanese industrial and financial systems from the competitive pressures of world economic factors.

Many unique features of the Japanese equity market may cause differences in investors' expectations of returns. One crucial difference of the Japanese market is that profits made on the trading of shares listed on the TSE are exempt from Japanese capital-gains tax. Another is that the Japanese financial system is much more "indirect" than the American financial system in the way in which money flows occur. A larger proportion of savings in Japan first flow into the 86 Japanese banks, then flow into bank investments. Additionally, there is an extensive amount of reciprocal equity ownership among Japanese businesses (especially between old *zaibatsus* and *keiretsus*, or large groups of companies); reciprocal ownership also includes banks that own stock in the companies to whom they lend. Still another important factor is that Japanese individuals generally do not view the purchase of equity shares as a form of saving or investing, many individuals consider it similar to gambling. And further, there are a large number of institutional differences in the way the two markets operate that could restrict the free flow of capital and information.[3]

Recent research points to some significant differences between the returns on Japanese versus American indexes and finds some anomalies in Japanese stock returns. Using daily returns on two popular indexes of Japanese stocks and the S&P 500, Jaffe-Westerfield find significant differences between Japanese and American stock returns in terms of the day of the week patterns. Using daily returns of specific individual listed securities and portfolios, Pettway-Tapley also report different day of the week patterns between the TSE and the NYSE. Using monthly returns, Kato-Schallheim describe seasonal and size anomalies in Japanese equity returns, especially the possibility of a January as well as a June seasonal effect. Thus, there is evidence that equity returns on the TSE are not completely similar to American stock returns. This dissimilarity may be an indication that the TSE is segmented from the U.S. market.

The purpose here is to determine more rigorously if Japanese restrictions, constraints and cultural differences are significant enough to cause the prices and returns of dually listed securities to violate the LOP, which, in turn, would indicate that the Japanese markets are segmented.

I. METHODOLOGY AND DATA

The patterns of prices and returns on the TSE and the NYSE, for the same security, are critical for determining if the LOP is valid and, consequently, whether one or both of the markets are segmented. If the patterns of prices on the TSE are not similar to the patterns of prices on the NYSE for the same security, then the LOP would be violated and restrictions exist which curtail the free flow of capital and information. The ability to arbitrage is important if the LOP is to hold. In essence, if there appears to be arbitrage possibilities, but investors are unable to remove them, then the two markets would be segmented or artificially isolated from each other.

Protopapadakis-Stoll (PS) state that if markets are efficient and the ability to arbitrage exists, then the prices of a single asset, traded in two different markets expressed in a common currency, must be related as follows:

Equation 1

$$P = P^*\pi U$$

where P and P* are the domestic and foreign price for the same asset; π is the relative exchange rate factor between domestic/foreign currency; and U is a random variable representing differential transportation, information and transaction costs. Analyzing prices of *real assets,* PS were concerned with the export-import point transportation costs represented by U. For *financial assets* (equity) the transportation costs associated with their trading should be small or zero; therefore, for the LOP to hold for our seventeen dually listed stocks, we should have

Equation 2

$$P = P^*\pi$$

The LOP will be tested using share prices, but it also will be tested using holding period returns, since to be valid the LOP should hold for both. For instance, if the LOP is valid, then Equation 2 can be stated in terms of returns by taking the natural log of both sides:

Equation 3

$$p = p^* + CE,$$

which implies

Equation 4

$$p - p^* = CE$$

where p and p* are domestic and foreign price changes or returns and CE is the change to the exchange rate. Equations 3 and 4 simply state that if the LOP is valid, then the return on the security in the domestic market must be equal to the return on the security in the foreign market, plus any additional return that arises from changes in the relative exchange rates.

Equations 2 and 4 will be tested, but their validity does not guarantee that the LOP holds—since their validity is one necessary, but alone insufficient, condition to confirm LOP. Therefore, we must perform an additional test for integration versus segmentation. Specifically, we wish to determine if

Equation 5

$$p = f(V_1, V_2 \ldots, V_n) = f^*(V_1, V_2 \ldots, V_n) = p^*,$$

where $f(V_1, V_2 \ldots, V_n)$ and $f^*(V_1, V_2 \ldots, V_n)$ represent functional *sets* of explanatory factors that determine returns for a particular stock in the domestic and foreign markets. These functional sets represent the factors which explain the underlying return generating process of these security returns. If these functional sets are not equal, even if Equations 2 and 4 appear to hold, it indicates that the two markets are segmented.

The original data consist of daily prices and dividends for the seventeen dually listed stocks which are traded on both the TSE and the NYSE over the period June 2, 1980 through October 31, 1983.[4] The daily yen and dollar prices for each of the seventeen dually listed stocks are first matched by date, and, after adjusting for relative exchange rates, they are then used to test equation 2. These matched yen and dollar prices, with dividends per share added, are also converted into matched pairs of holding period return vectors for each of the companies (that is, TSE versus NYSE).[5] The first half of the matched pairs is the spot price (or holding period return) in the domestic market of primary location of the company. The second half of the matched pairs is the equivalent spot price (or holding period return) in the foreign market or country of secondary location.

The holding period return of the stock in the primary market is matched against the return over an equivalent holding period in the secondary market. Since there may be infrequent trading in the secondary market, the secondary market defines the length of the holding period for both the secondary and primary market comparisons.[6]

Five separate minimum holding period lengths of 1, 7, 14, 28 and 56 days have been established for testing.

The study of these matched pairs of returns based on closing prices was begun after the proper "matching" of returns of the same security on the NYSE and TSE. Since the closing time of the two exchanges was not identical and the time interval between closings was not always constant over the period, various leads and lags of the matched pairs of holding period returns were used to determine the best matching with regard to "economic time."[7]

After finding the best matching of returns in terms of calendar leads and lags, the first test determined whether there were statistically significant differences in the matched pairs of returns for the same security over the various holding periods and whether this difference was equal to changes in the exchange rates described in Equation 4. If the LOP was valid and if both markets were responding to a similar set of economic information, then the differences between the matched pairs of returns should be equal to changes in the exchange rate for the same time period.

In the second phase of the study, the pattern of differences in matched pairs of returns was compared with returns on the Japanese stock index, the United States stock index, and the World stock index.[8] This is a test of Equation 5 and determines the primary underlying factors which help to explain the returns to the security in each capital market. If the underlying factors were the same for the two markets, for a given security, this would support the validity of the LOP and would support the argument that the two markets are integrated.

The final phase of the study consisted of an indirect test of Equation 5. It involved a macro-test of world integration using cluster analysis to determine whether the returns on the dually listed securities clustered differently. If there was no discernable difference in the pattern of clustering, then this would be another indication that the Japanese equity market was not segmented. That is, even though there were real differences between the characteristics of Japanese and American firms, their returns still may have been based on world-integrated factors.[9]

II. RESULTS

Test of LOP with Prices

Equation 2 describes the relationship that should exist between the prices of the same financial asset traded in two different markets. To test this relationship, the yen prices of the ten American companies traded on the TSE were converted into dollar prices using the daily exchange rate. They were then subtracted from the corresponding dollar price of the same firm on the NYSE. These sets of differences between matched prices in a common currency for each company were then analyzed. The average differences over the test period ranged from −\$0.74 for Chase Manhattan to −\$0.11 for General Motors. Similarly, the dollar prices of the seven Japanese companies traded on the NYSE were converted to yen prices and matched against the corresponding yen prices of the same company on the TSE. For the Japanese firms, the average differences ranged from −37 yen for Pioneer to +45 yen for TDK. None of the seventeen individual company differences were significantly different from zero.[10] Thus, the LOP appeared to be valid for the seventeen dually listed companies, when applied to prices which had been converted to a common currency. Yet, because these currency corrected prices were not perfectly correlated for any of the dually listed companies, the matched holding period returns may have had more volatility or lower correlation. Therefore, it was also important to test the LOP using matched pairs of returns for various holding periods as an alternative to the comparison of prices.

Test of the LOP with Returns

To test the differences in returns with various holding periods required, first, solving the problem of calendar time versus economic time period matching of returns. As stated previously, the closing prices on the NYSE and TSE are not always separated by a constant time period in real time.[11] To examine matched pairs of returns for the dually listed stocks traded in two markets, this nonsynchronous trading time must be addressed. To solve this problem, we began with the *a priori* belief that the matching of holding period returns should be based on some rational concept of "economic" time, not on some "calendar" time construction that involved an arbitrary delineation of an international dateline.

Unless a firm were a true multinational, it would seem logical that any fundamental change in the firm's value would first arise from factors within its domestic, or primary, market. Given that the NYSE and TSE are not in operation at the same time, these factors should first be recognized and acted upon by the dominant investors within that primary market.[12] Adjustments could not take place on the secondary exchange until that exchange once again opened for trading. The data support our conclusion that the major "play" for a stock normally takes place in the firm's primary market, since this market has the most frequent trades and the highest volume of trading. Thus, there should be a lead/lag relationship between calendar dates so that changes in stock prices follow the natural flow of information between the two markets in real economic time.[13] Note that this does not imply any inefficiency or market restrictions in terms of the dissemination of information or investor reactions to this information. However, because of the difference in trading hours it is impossible for both markets to simultaneously react to the arrival of relevant information.

To test the validity of using "economic" time matching, holding period returns on the NYSE were correlated against the equivalent holding period returns on the TSE for each of the seventeen companies. This was done first with no lag (that is, using calendar time matching), and second with a one calendar day lag. The correlation coefficients between the TSE and NYSE returns, using five different investment holding period horizons, are shown in Table 1. The results confirm our hypothesis that the domestic market is also the primary, or leading, market for stock price changes. The returns on the NYSE, for the ten American companies, have a higher correlation for each holding period when the returns on the TSE have been lagged one calendar day. On the other hand, the returns on the NYSE, for the seven Japanese companies, have a higher correlation for each holding

TABLE 1 CORRELATION COEFFICIENTS BETWEEN THE MATCHED HOLDING PERIOD RETURNS OF DUALLY LISTED STOCKS ON THE NYSE AND TSE, WHERE THE RETURNS OF THE TSE STOCKS ARE EITHER LAGGED OR NOT LAGGED

AGGREGATE OF TEN AMERICAN COMPANIES

Minimum Holding Period (Days)	1	7	14	28	56
Not Lagged	.43790	.68899	.80949	.84298	.90718
Lagged	.76246	.81881	.83724	.86289	.91656

AGGREGATE OF SEVEN JAPANESE COMPANIES

Minimum Holding Period (Days)	1	7	14	28	56
Not Lagged	.67577	.87829	.90265	.90237	.94662
Lagged	.41789	.78907	.84878	.87928	.93351

period when the returns on the TSE have not been lagged in calendar time.[14]

Also notice that the correlations between the NYSE and TSE returns, for both the American and Japanese firms, increase as the length of the holding period lengthens. One would expect this relationship since any real operating time differential would have less total impact as the length of the holding period increases.[15]

Average Returns of Major Variables

Mean returns over the five different holding periods and significance levels were calculated for the seventeen companies in each of the two markets, as well as for the market indexes and for the yen/dollar exchange rate.[16] These results are reported in Table 2. Since the

TABLE 2 MEAN VALUES FOR IMPORTANT VARIABLES

AMERICAN COMPANIES

Holding Period (Days)	1	7	14	28	56
Returns (TSE)	.002697*	.006797*	.011282*	.020383*	.042088*
Returns (NYSE)	.002271*	.005900*	.009800*	.017474*	.034160*
Returns (JAPAN)	.001510*	004108*	.006906*	.012597*	.021179*
Returns (USA)	.001362*	.003780*	.006330*	.011484*	.021179*
Returns (WORLD)	.000910*	.002536*	.004259*	.007759*	.013966*
Change (Y/D)	.000307	.000888	.001507	.002643	.007039*
TSE minus NYSE	.000426	.000898	.001482	.002909	.007928*
Number of Days	4.01	10.90	18.24	32.45	60.94
Number of Observations	2,968	1,089	650	364	190

JAPANESE COMPANIES

Holding Period (Days)	1	7	14	28	56
Returns (TSE)	.001287*	.005426*	.010870*	.021690*	.045027*
Returns (NYSE)	.001215*	.005430*	.010710*	.021233*	.043380*
Returns (JAPAN)	.000627*	.002756*	.005470*	.011099*	.021994*
Returns (USA)	.000641*	.003056*	.005934*	.011717*	.023852*
Returns (WORLD)	.000469*	.002248*	.004390*	.008700*	.017480*
Change (Y/D)	.000050	.000188	.000492	.000890	.002348
TSE minus NYSE	.000072	−.000004	.000160	.000456	.001647
Number of Days	1.62	7.27	14.25	28.34	56.24
Number of Observations	4,490	997	507	255	127

*Significant at .05 level (two-tailed test).

returns were generally similar for the individual American and Japanese companies, the results are reported for these two groups as aggregates.[17] Finally, the difference between the holding period returns calculated for each company on the TSE and the NYSE (TSE minus NYSE) are reported in aggregate for each of the five holding periods.

The average number of days for each holding period classification and the number of return observations are provided at the bottom of Table 2. Note that the length of the holding period (1, 7, 14, 28, 56 days) is a minimum number of days allowed in the match. Due to the lack of continuous trading of the shares in the secondary market, the number of average days in each holding period was larger than the minimum required for each classification. For example, for those American companies with a specified minimum holding period of 1 day, the average holding period was actually 4.01 days over 2,968 observations of returns. This result was obtained because the American companies were infrequently traded on the TSE and only actual trading dates were used in this study. Also notice that the Japanese companies have an average holding period much closer to the specified minimum in each of the categories. This is because the Japanese companies were traded more frequently on the NYSE than the American companies were traded on the TSE.

Several other results found in Table 2 are noteworthy. The first five categories of returns, all categories except for the changes in the yen/dollar exchange rate and the difference between the returns on the TSE and the NYSE, are positive, significantly different from zero, and become larger as the holding period increases. However, the fact that the changes in the yen/dollar exchange rate, with one exception, were insignificantly different from zero is not surprising. One would not expect *consistent* positive (negative) changes in the yen/dollar exchange rate over time.

Perhaps the most important result in terms of the question of market segmentation versus integration is that the difference between the holding period returns on the TSE and the NYSE, with one exception, are not significantly different from zero. This evidence supports the previous tests using prices; it suggests that the LOP holds and that the dually listed stocks are reacting to international or integrated factors, rather than to local or segmented factors. Only at the longest holding period in the study are there opportunities to earn a significant nonzero return by purchasing the ten American firms on the TSE versus the same ten firms on the NYSE. However, this nonzero difference appears to be closely related to the returns arising from changes in the yen/dollar exchange rate, which also is significant for this same holding period. In fact, for the American firms, there appears to be almost a one-to-one relationship between the differences of the returns in the two markets and the returns arising from changes in the relative exchange rates (Y/D). This result is exactly what one would expect from Equation 4 if the LOP is valid. However, the same relationship for the Japanese companies is much less exact and indicates that the study should be continued to examine the nature of the underlying return generating process of these stock returns as suggested by Equation 5.

An Examination of the Differences Between the TSE and NYSE Returns

The average differences between the returns on the TSE and NYSE are not, with one exception, significantly different from zero. For the American companies, the differences that exist seem to correspond to changes in exchange rates. However, this degree of correspondence is not as great for the Japanese firms. One possible explanation for this is that security-specific segmentation exists. That is, the returns on dually listed Japanese firms may be responding to underlying factors that differ between the two markets, whereas the dually listed American firms are not. To test this possibility, step-wise regressions were run, where the dependent variables were the differences between the returns on the TSE and the NYSE. The independent variables employed were the returns over the same holding periods on the JAPAN index, the USA index, and the WORLD index, and the percentage change in the Yen/Dollar exchange rate. In nine cases out of ten, the percentage change in the exchange rate was the first explanatory variable to enter the regression. Again, this is a confirmation of the relationship posited by Equation 4.

The second variable to enter the step-wise regression was different for the American and the Japanese firms. In general, the second most important variable to explain the differences in returns for Japanese companies on both the NYSE and TSE exchanges was the returns on the JAPAN index. For the differences in returns of the American companies on the two exchanges, the returns on the USA index was the second most important variable.

The correlation coefficients found in Table 3 confirm the results of the step-wise regression analysis. Sections D for both American and Japanese companies show that the differences in returns between the two markets (T-NY) had the highest single-variable correlation

TABLE 3 CORRELATION COEFFICIENTS BETWEEN VARIOUS RETURNS

AMERICAN COMPANIES

Holding Period (Days)	1	7	14	28	56
A. TSE vs. NYSE	.76246	.81881	.83724	.85289	.91656
B. TSE vs. JAPAN	.06418	.11958	.10458	.12493	.16396
TSE vs. USA	.41610	.42723	.43226	.43240	.47154
TSE vs. WORLD	.29458	.30992	.31186	.31502	.34194
TSE vs. Y/D	.11950	.14120	.14058	.23852	.33110
C. NYSE vs. JAPAN	.19024	.26527	.24522	.20914	.23273
NYSE vs. USA	.53815	.53919	.54500	.50106	.54643
NYSE vs. WORLD	.49008	.50868	.51335	.47469	.50808
NYSE vs. Y/D	−.16363	−.20008	−.20952	−.09179	−.03137
D. T-NY vs. JAPAN	−.16518	−.23339	−.24173	−.14287	−.13770
T-NY vs. USA	−.11435	−.16471	−.18442	−.08258	−.34057
T-NY vs. WORLD	−.23104	−.31199	−.34198	−.26290	−.34057
T-NY vs. Y/D	.4092	.56515	.61250	.63521	.90006

JAPANESE COMPANIES

Holding Period (Days)	1	7	14	28	56
A. TSE vs. NYSE	.67566	.87829	.90265	.90237	.94662
B. TSE vs. JAPAN	.61169	.60496	.60244	.59353	.60766
TSE vs. USA	.05827	.24113	.28427	.27745	.22450
TSE vs. WORLD	.24644	.34683	.33900	.34114	.30952
TSE vs. Y/D	−.14600	−.16246	−.05333	−.01497	.03470
C. NYSE vs. JAPAN	.48580	.61463	.65479	.64149	.62453
NYSE vs. USA	.27261	.32067	.36330	.31925	.30332
NYSE vs. WORLD	.40660	.45331	.48152	.46364	.42546
NYSE vs. Y/D	−.30098	−.39092	−.34935	−.34310	.23593
D. T-NY vs. JAPAN	.13782	−.13232	−.21816	−.18569	−.09016
T-NY vs. USA	−.27120	−.21065	−.22891	−.13156	−.25732
T-NY vs. WORLD	−.20899	−.28645	−.38490	−.32592	−.37717
T-NY vs. Y/D	.19934	.50679	.69495	.75955	.83299

with the returns arising from changes in the relative exchange rates (Y/D). In fact, these correlations reached a high of .90006 for American companies and the 56 day holding period. Again, given Equation 4, this result is consistent with the validity of the LOP for these dually listed securities.

Table 3 also provides further support for the LOP in terms of the relationship specified in Equation 5. According to 5, returns in the two markets should respond to the same underlying factors, and this is exactly what is observed. For American companies, the returns calculated on either the TSE or NYSE have the highest correlation with the returns on the USA index over all holding periods. For the Japanese companies, the calculated returns on both the TSE and the NYSE have the highest correlation with the JAPAN index. Further, the next highest correlation for *both* the American and Japanese companies, and for *both* exchanges was the WORLD index. The WORLD index always had a higher correlation than the JAPAN index for American companies. For Japanese companies, the WORLD index, even though it is composed of a high proportion of American companies, also had a higher correlation than the USA index. The presence of this relationship is a clear indication that returns on the dually listed securities react primarily to factors in their primary market, but that both markets are strongly integrated in a world context. If the Japanese market were truly segmented, then one would expect that returns on all securities traded on the segmented market should react primarily to factors that affect that market. Since this was not the case, we have further evidence that the LOP is valid and that the Japanese equity market is not segmented.

Cluster Analysis

As a final test of segmentation versus integration in the spirit of Equation 5, cluster analysis was performed. Cluster analysis allows the grouping of observations into sets that demonstrate similar characteristics. Three variables were analyzed: (1) returns on the TSE, (2) returns on the NYSE, and (3) the differences between the returns on the TSE and the NYSE. It is hypothesized that if segmentation exists on a macro scale, due to differences in the characteristics between Japanese and American firms, then the return observations of the Japanese companies should all be assigned to one cluster, while the returns for the American companies should be assigned to an alternative cluster.

The results of the cluster analysis for the three variables are found in Table 4, which provides the percentage of total return observations in each cluster, for the aggregate of the American and Japanese firms. The data illustrate that the clustering patterns for the American and Japanese firms were similar. For example, when observations were clustered in terms of the holding period returns on the TSE (Section A of Table 4), the percentages in the two clusters are similar for both the Japanese and American firms. If the TSE was segmented on a macro scale due to differential firm characteristics, then one would expect all American observations to be assigned to one of the clusters and all of the Japanese observations to be

TABLE 4 CLUSTER ANALYSIS FOR THE AGGREGATE OF AMERICAN AND JAPANESE FIRMS (Percentages of total in each cluster)

A. VARIABLE: RETURNS (TSE)

Holding Period (Days)	1		7		14		28		56	
Cluster	A	B	A	B	A	B	A	B	A	B
American Firms	18%	82%	49%	51%	50%	50%	38%	62%	31%	69%
Japanese Firms	13	87	43	57	45	55	39	61	32	68

B. VARIABLE: RETURNS (NYSE)

Holding Period (Days)	1		7		14		28		56	
Cluster	A	B	A	B	A	B	A	B	A	B
American Firms	35%	65%	50%	50%	31%	69%	35%	65%	29%	71%
Japanese Firms	38	62	48	52	38	62	39	61	32	68

C. VARIABLE: RETURNS (TSE-NYSE)

Holding Period (Days)	1		7		14		28		56	
Cluster	A	B	A	B	A	B	A	B	A	B
American Firms	23%	77%	37%	63%	44%	56%	35%	65%	32%	68%
Japanese Firms	24	76	33	67	47	53	36	64	31	69

assigned to the other cluster. These results were not observed for any of the three different measures of returns. In fact, the pattern of the percentages, for each of the five holding periods analyzed, is remarkably similar for both the American and the Japanese companies. These results are a further indication that, at least on a macro scale, the dually listed security returns analyzed in this study are world integrated, not segmented.[18]

IV. SUMMARY

There are major cultural and other economic differences between Japanese and American capital markets. It has often been argued that many Japanese markets, unlike American markets, are segmented and do not respond to changes in world-economic factors in an integrated fashion. The purpose of this chapter is to determine if the apparent Japanese restrictions and cultural differences are significant enough to cause the market for equity securities in Japan to be segmented from the U.S. equity market, and therefore to violate the Law of One Price (LOP), or whether the national markets represent a fully integrated world capital market. In addition to testing whether the LOP holds for dually listed securities, both in terms of price and returns, the study also tests whether the underlying explanatory factors or the return generating process differs between the Japanese and American stock markets. Finally, there is a test for macro segmentation in returns due to differences in the financial characteristics of Japanese and American firms.

The data employed are the spot prices and realized holding period returns for seventeen stocks which are dually listed on the TSE and the NYSE. These data and the particular methodologies employed are unique, as most previous research on international equity market integration only analyzed the differences in market indexes. Since market indexes, or portfolios, employed in prior studies do not include the same stocks and differ in perceived risk and expectations of return, and since these studies have great difficulty controlling for comparative risks, their results are subject to a wide range of interpretations. On the other hand, our data set of dually listed stocks represents equivalent ownership in the *same* underlying assets and, thus, all investment risks are the same in both markets. Therefore, the use of these prices and realized returns allow superior tests for the segmentation versus integration of the markets and the validity of LOP for these stocks. Further, since any Japanese cultural or economic restrictions would apply equally to all securities traded on the TSE, not only to the dually listed stocks, the results of this study provide evidence that the TSE is not segmented.

The findings of this study are as follows:

1. The matched prices in a common currency of each of the seventeen dually listed stocks over the time period were very highly correlated and their differences were not significantly different from zero. This indicates that the law of one price is supported.
2. The returns of all seventeen companies on both exchanges were positive, significantly different from zero, and increased directly with the length of the holding period. The difference between the matched holding period returns of the same shares on the two markets generally were not significantly different from zero. Thus, there is a high degree of similarity between the two sets of returns over the five holding periods studied. The results indicated that the LOP is not violated, and thus suggests the world-integration as opposed to segmentation of the Japanese market.
3. The most significant variable in explaining the differences in the returns for the same stock on the two exchanges was the percentage change in the exchange rate. This result is to be expected if the LOP is valid. The second most important variable was the returns in the primary market for each of the particular firms. If the markets were segmented, the returns of both the Japanese and American companies traded on the TSE should be primarily affected by movements in the Japanese capital market. Since this relationship was not found, the results

indicate the integration, rather than the segmentation, of the Japanese market.

4. A cluster analysis of the returns of Japanese versus American companies indicates a similarity of clustering patterns, suggesting that no segmentation exists due to differences in the financial characteristics between Japanese and American dually listed firms.

There are major differences between the Japanese and American equity markets, such as: taxation, requirements for foreign purchasers, investor attitudes toward savings and equity investments, and the protective nature and actions of government officials. However, even with all the apparent cultural, institutional and regulatory restrictions, the results of our analysis indicate that the prices and returns for stocks dually listed on the Tokyo and the New York Stock exchanges exhibit patterns of returns which are well integrated in terms of world market conditions, and which are not indicative of segmented markets. Thus, it is concluded that the Tokyo Stock Exchange is not a segmented market.

NOTES

[1]During the study period, the dually listed Japanese companies are: Hitachi, Honda, Kyocera, Matsushita Electric Industrial Co., Pioneer Electric, Sony and TDK. The American companies are Bank of America, Chase Manhattan, Citicorp, Dow Chemical, 1st Chicago, General Motors, I.T.T. Electric, I.U. International, IBM and Sperry Corporation. The Japanese firms may be generally classified as growth companies as they tend to pay low dividends and have high retention ratios. The American firms are predominately either banks or large and well known companies. The dividend payout ratios of these American companies tend to be higher than for the Japanese firms. Three of the Japanese companies listed on the NYSE (Hitachi, Honda and Matsushita) are traded in ADR units which are equivalent to ten regular shares of the same company on the TSE. The ADR unit of Kyocera, Pioneer and TDK traded on the NYSE is equivalent to two shares of the same company traded on the TSE. Sony on NYSE has a one-to-one equivalence with its shares on the TSE.

[2]It should be noted that a rejection of the law of one price (LOP) for dually listed securities would be a clear indication of market segmentation, but an acceptance of the LOP is not necessarily proof that markets are integrated.

[3]For instance, before 1982 non-Japanese brokers were prohibited from being fully-participating members of the TSE, whereas Nomura and Daiwa Securities were full members of the NYSE. In early 1982, the 83 members of the TSE removed their prohibition against non-Japanese broker members. However, as of November 1983, the end of the study period, no foreign security firm was a full member of the TSE, although there were six non-Japanese brokerage firms operating in Japan under license by the Ministry of Finance: four American, one British and one from Hong Kong. On February 1, 1986, well after the end of this study period, six foreign brokers were allowed full membership on the TSE. There were three American brokers (Merrill Lynch, Goldman, Sachs & Co. and Morgan Stanley & Co.); two British firms (Vickers de Costa, Ltd. and S.G. Warburg & Co.); and one from Hong Kong (Jardine Fleming Securities, Ltd.). Further, a foreign investor who purchases stock on the TSE must appoint either a Japanese resident or a resident corporation as his/her proxy. This is a costly requirement. Additionally, the minimum number of shares required to constitute a unit of trading also differs between the NYSE and TSE. See *How to Invest in Japanese Stocks*. Also, the trading hours and operating days of the week differ for the TSE and for the NYSE. On the TSE, there are generally two trading sessions Monday through Friday and one morning session on each Saturday, except for the third Saturday of each month. Because daylight-savings time is observed seasonally on the NYSE and because of the third Saturday closings of the TSE each month, there is no entirely consistent difference in hours between the daily closing times on the two exchanges.

[4]Daily dollar prices and dividends for the NYSE listed shares were obtained from the Center for Research into Security Prices at the University of Chicago. Daily yen prices and dividends for the TSE listed shares were obtained by personal correspondence. These are closing prices on both exchanges and are the only data that is available during a trading day. Much assistance for this research was provided by the New York and Tokyo offices of Daiwa Securities Research Institute.

[5]The returns in each market are adjusted for dividends on the "ex-dividend" date. This is a normal practice in calculating holding period returns, but the international comparison of the dually listed stocks adds at least two significant problems. First, the international dateline separates New York and Tokyo. Further, the TSE shares go ex-dividend four full business days before the date of record, whereas the NYSE requires five full business days prior to the date of record. Therefore, the ex-dividend dates for the same shares traded on the two exchanges are different. Second, the dividends are paid in the national currency of the corporation and any conversion to another currency will be made at the actual payment date, which is after the ex-dividend date. Therefore, the actual amount of the adjustment for the dividend payment is more complicated than is usually the case on the ex-dividend date.

The procedure employed in this paper is to adjust for dividends on the ex-dividend date in each of the specific markets. All TSE shares, both American and Japanese, will use the ex-dividend dates in Tokyo, and all NYSE shares will use the ex-dividend dates in New York. To aid understanding we call the NYSE the primary national market for American firms. The TSE is the secondary national market for these same dually listed shares. The actual amount of the dividend of a company on the secondary market (in local currency) is determined by adjusting the company's dividend in the primary market by the exchange rate on the secondary market's ex-dividend date. For example, Honda shares went ex-dividend 8/25/80 in New York and 8/27/80 in Tokyo. The first date will be used to determine the ex-dividend price on the NYSE and the second date will be used to determine the ex-dividend price on the TSE. Further, the five yen dividend per share declared by Honda in Tokyo was converted to dollars using the yen/dollar exchange rate of 8/25/80 (i.e., the ex-dividend date on the NYSE). Because our adjustment for dividends was only one of many possible methods which could have been used, it may have introduced a disturbance into the calculation of the return data on ex-dividend dates. Therefore, all analyses were performed both with and without the inclusions of dividends. Since the conclusions of all analyses were shown not to be dependent upon the inclusion of dividends, we reported only those results where dividends have been included in the calculation of returns.

[6]To provide a specific example for understanding, take the case of Citicorp. Citicorp is traded daily on the NYSE, the primary market, but was not traded

every day on the TSE, the secondary market. Therefore, the first price and subsequent holding period return in the matched pairs was determined as the price and holding period return of Citicorp on the TSE. The first closing price for Citicorp traded on the TSE, after the beginning date of the study, was chosen as the beginning price and called Po. Po was 4,830 yen on June 9, 1980. The next closing price for Citicorp on the TSE after June 9, 1980, was selected as P1, and was 4,900 yen on June 11, 1980. The stock did not trade on Tuesday, June 10 on the TSE. The holding period return was then calculated as [P1 + D1 − Po)/Po] where D1 represents any dividend paid during the holding period. Since there was no dividend paid between these dates, the holding period return for this period was .014492754. A similar procedure was used to calculate the equivalent holding period return in the primary national market (NYSE) for Citicorp. The second and all other sets of matched pairs of holding period returns for Citicorp were then determined in the same way. Generally, this procedure was required because the stocks in the secondary market were less frequently traded than in the primary market. Note that the length of the holding period will be the same for the returns of matched pairs, but that the holding period length of each matched pair might differ over time.

[7]Economic time is used here to describe the time period that a single piece of new information is acted upon in the two markets. This may be different from calendar time. Time matching and the resolution of this problem will be discussed at length in Section II.

[8]In order to reduce the introduction of bias, we have chosen to select all the indexes and the exchange rates from the same source. Capital International S.A., Geneva, is recognized throughout the world for publication of the *Capital International Perspective*. Daily returns indexes on the performance of the stocks on the United States, the Japanese, and on all the major stock markets of the world, called the World Index, were obtained from Capital International. The daily yen/dollar exchange rates also were obtained from this same source.

[9]There are numerous illustrations of differences between firms listed on the two exchanges. For example, the shares listed on the TSE generally have much lower dividend payout ratios than the shares of NYSE listed firms. Since there is no capital gains tax on profits made from trading equity shares in Japan, Japanese firms tend to favor high growth, high retention, and low payout of dividends. The payout ratios of the following companies listed on the TSE illustrate the low payout of Japanese firms in 1981: Sony (18.6%), Matsushita Elec. Ind. (17.7%), TDK (14.7%), Honda (24.4%), Toyota (18.6%) and Nissan (24.2%). See *Japan Company Handbook*. Further, dividend payments in Japan are paid only twice per year compared to quarterly in the U.S. Yet, this low payout policy is not easy to understand when one realizes that dividends are taxed at the corporate level at lower rates than are earnings that are retained. For large companies, the current

tax rate on income distributed as dividends is 32%, while it is 42% on income not distributed as dividends. Also, Japanese firms tend to have significantly higher degrees of financial leverage than American firms in similar industries. Japanese industrial firms typically have about 75% to 84% debt in their capital structure; whereas, American industrial firms typically have only 35% to 48% debt. Hodder-Tschoegi report total liabilities to total assets of 77.9% for nonfinancial firms listed on the TSE in 1983. These higher debt ratios for Japanese firms, along with historically lower nominal interest rates, have provided the Japanese firms generally with lower costs of capital than their American counterparts.

[10]Additionally, for each of the seventeen companies, the matched pairs of prices in the currency of the parent company were very highly correlated. Both the American and Japanese companies had aggregate correlations of prices of greater than 0.99 over the test period.

[11]On page 266 Jaffe-Westerfield state that "Tokyo is fourteen hours ahead of New York." Applied to the closing prices on the TSE and the NYSE, this statement is only true if you do not consider daylight-savings time of the NYSE in the summer and if you do not consider the Saturday closing time of the TSE. Please see note number 2 for the details of the operating characteristics of the two exchanges and the time interval between closing prices.

[12]It is also logical to assume that specific companies will be followed by more security analysts and portfolio managers in their primary market than in their secondary market, and that these individuals will trade in the primary market.

[13]To better illustrate this point, consider the closing of the NYSE price of an American company, on say June 13. Because of the difference in calendar time, the next possible closing price on the TSE occurs on June 14. This next calendar day closing price is the closest "economic" time for American companies traded on the TSE. Therefore, the returns on the TSE are lagged one day for all American companies in order to have the best economic match with the returns on the NYSE for the same company. On the other hand, the best "economic" time match for the closing price for a Japanese company on the TSE on June 13 is the closing price for the same calendar day on the NYSE. This occurs because the closing of the TSE on June 13 will precede the opening of the NYSE on June 13. Thus, for returns of Japanese firms, using the same calendar time on the TSE and NYSE provides the best economic match. To summarize, the returns for Japanese companies on the TSE are matched in calendar time with the returns for the same Japanese firms on the NYSE, whereas the returns for American companies on the TSE are lagged one calendar day to be matched against their returns on the NYSE.

[14]The correlation coefficients reported in Table 1 which show the proper information/time relationship are quite different from the leads and lags provided by

Jaffe-Westerfield (JW), but these differences are easily explained. First, and most importantly, the correlations in Table 1 are for the same assets and therefore related to the same fundamental information, whereas the coefficients reported by JW are on indexes of different securities (S&P 500 versus Nikkei-Dow and TSE index). Second, because the returns correlated in Table 1 are based on the same financial asset, it is more likely that they will be related in some time-dependent way to changes in information, whereas there are few *a priori* reasons to believe that indexes of different stocks in Japan and the U.S. would be related in any time-dependent way. Finally, the correlations in Table 1 are highly significant, whereas those of JW are quite low and may not be statistically different from one another.

[15]All tests were initially performed with and without dividends included in the returns. Since the payment of dividends and the necessary dividend adjustment did not affect the results nor our conclusions, we report only the results which included the payment of dividends as part of the holding period returns. Finally, since an "economic" matching approach has been supported by the results of this correlation study, all subsequent tests will maintain these economically-matched relationships.

[16]Remember that the holding period length is established by the secondary national market for a particular stock and that it will vary for each firm. Therefore, the average returns reported in Table 2 for the JAPAN, USA and WORLD indexes, as well as the Yen/Dollar exchange rate, have been calculated over holding periods which match those for each of the individual firms. This difference in holding period length accounts for the differences among the average values for JAPAN, USA, WORLD and Y/D in the aggregate in Table 2.

[17]The returns of the seventeen firms were calculated from prices denominated both in yen (TSE) and dollars (NYSE). Thus, the returns for each exchange do not include adjustments for changes in the relative exchange rate between the dollar and the yen. The JAPAN and USA index values are denominated in their local currency. The WORLD index, on the other hand, is in dollars. Therefore, the holding period returns listed as JAPAN and as USA have not been adjusted for currency movements, whereas the WORLD index includes currency movements relative to the dollar.

[18]The results in Table 4 indicate that there is no macro-segmentation of American versus Japanese firms in terms of their returns on the TSE, the NYSE, or the differences between the returns for companies on the two exchanges. This similarity of clustering patterns for returns is somewhat surprising, since the Japanese and American companies differ in many "industrial" respects, and one might expect their returns to differ significantly from each other. However, it might be argued that what is really happening is that all of the observations for

some of the companies (both American and Japanese) are being assigned to the other cluster. To demonstrate that this is not the case, a cluster analysis was performed on each individual company. The variable which was tested was the difference in returns on the TSE and the NYSE. For the seventeen dually listed stocks, the results of the cluster analysis for each holding period exhibit a very similar clustering pattern. No company has observations assigned to only one particular cluster. The similarity of clustering of returns for the individual companies confirms that the dually listed security returns analyzed in this study are world integrated, not segmented.

Bibliography

Adler, M. and B. Dumas. "Optimal International Acquisitions," *Journal of Finance* (March 1975), pp. 1-19

Adler, M. and R. Horesh. "The Relationship Among Equity Markets: Comment," *Journal of Finance* (September 1974), pp. 1311-1317

Agmon, T. "The Relations Among Equity Markets in the United States, United Kingdom, Germany and Japan," *Journal of Finance* (September 1972), pp. 839-855

D'Ambrosio, C.A. "Random Walk and the Stock Exchange of Singapore," *The Financial Review* (Spring 1980), pp. 1-12

Grubel, H. "Internationally Diversified Portfolios: Welfare Gains and Capital Flows," *American Economic Review* (December 1968)

Hilliard, J.E. "The Relationship Between Equity Indices on World Exchanges," *Journal of Finance* (March 1979), pp. 103-114

Hodder, J.E. and A.E. Tschoegi. "Some Aspects of Japanese Corporate Finance," *Journal of Financial and Quantitative Analysis* (June 1985), pp. 173-191

Hong, H. "Predictability of Price Trends on Stock Exchanges. A Study of Some Far Eastern Countries," *The Review of Economics and Statistics* (November 1978), pp. 619-621

How to Invest in Japanese Stocks (Tokyo: Nomura Securities Co., Ltd., January 1982)

Ibbotson, R., R.C. Carr, and A.W. Robinson. "Internationally Equity and Bond Returns," *Financial Analysts Journal* (July-August 1982), pp. 61-83

Ibbotson, R. and L.B. Siegel. "The World Market Wealth Portfolio," *Journal of Portfolio Management* (Winter 1983)

Jaffe, J. and R. Westerfield. "Patterns in Japanese Common Stock Returns: Day of the Week and Turn of the Year Effects," *Journal of Financial and Quantitative Analysis* (June 1985), pp. 261-272

Japan Company Handbook, 1st Half 1982 (Tokyo: Toyo Keizai Shinposha, Ltd., 1982)

Jennergren, L.P. and P.E. Korsuold. "The Non-Random Character of Norweigan and Swedish Stock Market Prices," *International Capital Markets,* Edited by E.J. Elton and M.J. Gruber (Amsterdam: North Holland Publishing Co., 1975)

Kato, K. and J.S. Schallheim. "Seasonal and Size Anomalies in the Japanese Stock Market," *Journal of Financial and Quantitative Analysis* (June 1985), pp. 243-260

Komine, M. *Test of Stock Market Efficiency with Fair Game Model: An Empirical Analysis of the Tokyo Stock Exchange,* Technical Paper No. 35 (Tokyo: Japan Securities Research Institute, July 1975), In Japanese

———. *Rates of Return in Relation to Risk: An Empirical Analysis of the Tokyo Stock Exchange,* Technical Paper No. 40 (Tokyo: Japan Securities Research Institute, January 1977), In Japanese

Lau, S.C., S.R. Quay, and C.M. Ramsey. "The Tokyo Stock Exchange and the Capital Asset Pricing Model," *Journal of Finance* (May 1974), pp. 507-514

Lessard, D.R. "World, National and Industry Factors in Equity Returns," *Journal of Finance* (May 1974), pp. 379-391

———. "World, Country, and Industry Relationships in Equity Returns," *Financial Analysts Journal* (January-February 1976)

Levy, H. and M. Sarnat. "International Diversification of Investment Portfolios," *American Economic Review* (September 1970), pp. 668-675

Panton, D., V. Lessig, and M. Joy. "Comovement of International Equity Markets: A Taxonomic Approach," *Journal of Financial and Quantitative Analysis* (September 1976), pp. 415-432

Pettway, R.H. and T.C. Tapley. "The Tokyo Stock Exchange: An Analysis of Stock Market Prices," *Keio Business Review,* Vol. 21, No. 4 (Tokyo: Keio University, March 1984), pp. 75-93

Protopapadakis, A. and H.R. Stoll. "Spot and Futures Prices and the Law of One Price," *Journal of Finance* (December 1983), pp. 1431-1455

Ripley, D. "Systematic Elements in the Linkage of National Stock Market Indices," *Review of Economics and Statistics* (August 1973)

Robicheck, A., R. Cohn, and J. Pringle. "Returns on Alternative Investment Media and Implications for Portfolio Construction," *Journal of Business* (July 1972)

Solnik, B. "Why Not Diversify Internationally Rather than Domestically?" *Financial Analysts Journal* (July-August 1974), pp. 48-54

Stehle, R. "An Empirical Test of the Alternative Hypotheses of National and International Pricing of Risky Assets," *Journal of Finance* (May 1977), pp. 493-502

CHAPTER TWENTY-THREE

Dr. CARL R. BEIDLEMAN joined the Lehigh University faculty in 1967, was promoted to associate professor of finance in 1972, and was awarded the Allen C. DuBois Distinguished Professorship in Finance in 1975. He was named chairman of the Department of Management and Finance in 1975, a position which he held until 1978. In 1983 he was appointed the first chairman of the newly organized Department of Finance.

A native of Wilkes-Barre, PA, and a graduate of Lafayette College, Dr. Beidleman earned the M.B.A. degree at Drexel University and the Ph.D. at the Wharton School, University of Pennsylvania.

He is currently engaged in several research projects at Lehigh University, including business and economic studies related to the new Engineering Research Center for Advanced Technology for Large Structural Systems.

Dr. Beidleman has had articles published in the *Columbia Journal of World Business, Sloan Management Review, Euromoney, National Tax Journal, Journal of Business Finance, Financial Analysts Journal, Journal of Business Education, Managerial Planning, The Accounting Review,* and *Accounting and Business Research.*

He is a member of the boards of directors of the Martin Guitar Corp., Independence Bancorp Inc. and Bucks County Bank and Trust Co., and has served as a consultant to commercial banks, legal counsel and industrial firms.

YIELD ENHANCEMENT USING FINANCIAL SWAPS

Carl R. Beidleman
DuBois Professor of Finance
Lehigh University
Bethlehem, Pennsylvania

INTRODUCTION

Innovation in finance has proceeded at a varying pace since the inception of finance as a field of endeavor. Like most other professions, improvements and new developments have occurred in fits and starts, with the most significant advances being the result of attempts to find solutions to former impediments to the smooth flow of investment or financing. It has been said that the period since 1980 has been a golden age of financial inventiveness, as evidenced by the promulgation of new products and concepts such as original issue discount bonds, zero coupon bonds, stripping of coupon from principal, defeasance, partly paid bonds, options on almost anything, currency swaps, coupon or interest-rate swaps, dual currency issues and adjustable rate preferred stocks, to name some of the more popular innovative products.

Many of these innovative concepts have been in response to the problems imposed on financial managers by the high level and variability of both inflation and interest rates in recent years. The high and volatile rates of inflation in many countries have caused wide fluctuations in interest rates, and together, high and fluctuating inflation and interest rates have contributed to significant movements in exchange rates. These modulations have been facilitated by the movement from fixed to floating exchange rates in many of the developed countries in 1973 and, in the United States at least, by the change in fixation of the monetary authority from an emphasis on interest rates to monetary aggregates as targets of monetary policy.

This chapter focuses on two of these innovative financial products—currency swaps and coupon or interest-rate swaps—and examines how they can be helpful in improving the all-in yield to fixed income portfolios. Above market returns can now be obtained by separating the currency or coupon basis of an individual financial asset from the currency or coupon basis of its portfolio. The potential for obtaining above market yields is due to the presence of market anomalies. The transition from one currency or coupon to another is accomplished through the use of financial swaps.

First, this chapter offers a brief review of financial swaps. This is followed by a rudimentary examination of some underlying market anomalies that allow the magic of swaps to occur. A number of case illustrations and examples are then presented to illustrate how yield enhancement can be achieved without incurring undesirable currency or principal risk.

FINANCIAL SWAPS

Financial swaps entail an exchange of one set of cash-flows for another, presumably more desirable, set of cash flows. Currently popular versions of coupon swaps call for the exchange of one coupon configuration for another, say a fixed-rate coupon for a floating-rate coupon or the exchange of a coupon pegged to one floating-rate basis for a coupon keyed to another floating-rate basis. Currency swaps provide for exchange of all interest and principal payments in one national currency for another currency at a predetermined currency exchange rate. Other forms of cash-flow exchanges could be arranged and may become popular in the future, but current strategies tend to be limited to the exchange of currency and coupon flows.[1]

Coupon Swaps A coupon or interest-rate swap provides a convenient means of altering the coupon cash flows on a debt instrument. Its primary objective is to exchange fixed-rate interest payments for floating-rate payments or vice versa. During previous periods of interest rate stability, contractual coupon payments tended to be fixed over the life of a debt security. In recent years, with the increased volatility of rates, debt issues that call for coupon payments that float or are reset every three or six months have abounded. The basis for these revisions is some well-documented market rate such as the London interbank offer rate (Libor), some short-term Treasury bill rate, commercial paper or certificate of deposit composite rate or other index of rates.

The quality or certainty of the level of coupon cash payments or receipts on floating-rate instruments is lower (more uncertain) than on fixed-rate instruments. This difference in certainty of the coupon flows may provide either an attraction or an aversion for various types of market participants. That is, some players prefer to receive floating-rate payments over fixed-rate payments, or vice versa. On the financing side, certain borrowers prefer to pay a fixed rate of interest while others, because of their asset structures, are more inclined to pay floating rates.[2] Despite these preferences, it frequently works out that players find it less burdensome and costly to access debt markets that require coupon flows that conflict with their natural preferences. A solution to this financial dilemma rests in the use of a coupon swap.

A coupon swap may be defined as an exchange of a coupon or interest payment stream of one configuration for another coupon stream with a different configuration on the same notional principal amount. Coupon swaps in which payments are based on one floating-rate index or basis in exchange for a different floating-rate index or basis are also available, i.e., a floating-rate versus floating-rate swap in which Libor flows are exchanged for prime flows less some negotiated spread. These swaps would be carried out to alter the quality or configuration of the coupon cash flows and to make them more compatible with the preferences of investors or issuers of debt instruments.

Note that, in a coupon swap, the principal is only notional to the transaction. While the principal determines the size of the coupon flows, it is not swapped, and, hence, not at risk. This significantly reduces the risk to the parties and to the market intermediaries. All that is at risk is the interest differential between the fixed- and floating-rate coupon determinants. Because of the financial characteristics of the parties, this difference generally satisfies their underlying preferences.

Currency Swaps The currency in which cash flows are denominated is important because it may significantly alter the ultimate cash flows to an investor after conversion to his home currency. If the currency of the cash flow is other than the home currency of the investor, and if that foreign currency may be expected to fluctuate in terms of the home currency, the home currency value of the residual cash flow may be seriously altered. This condition may be more onerous the further away the expected foreign currency flows are from the present. It can be particularly serious for flows with a time horizon of up to ten to fifteen years. Given all the forces that influence exchange rates, to project them that far out in time, with any degree of confidence, is extremely difficult. Nevertheless, it is still necessary to make long-term financial commitments where cash flows are denominated in foreign currencies over many years.

As in the case of coupon exchanges, instruments have been developed that enable participants to cover long-date foreign exchange risk. In this context, "long-date" means beyond one year and, in many cases, implies periods of up to ten years. The menu of instruments is somewhat broader than in coupon swaps, but the substance of the arrangement is essentially the same. In a currency swap, each party simply exchanges cash flows in one currency for cash flows in another on day one, with an agreement to reverse the exchange at some specified future point in time at a specified exchange rate. Currency exchange agreements may consist of a stream of currency in each period, such as one year, as may be necessary to service the interest payments or receipts on an obligation in foreign currency, or they may provide for a simple one-shot or bullet transfer of funds at the maturity of the agreement.

Many applications exist for currency exchanges and various instruments have been devised to accommodate the intricacies of alternative applications. Those applications that involve cross-currency investments to obtain above-market yields tend to rely on currency swaps whereby the cash flows generated in the undesired currency of an investment are swapped for the home cash flows of the investor or portfolio manager. The possibility of all-in market yields greater than those available in the domestic market derives from anomalies that persist across markets. A number of the major intermarket anomalies that facilitate yield enhancement are examined in the next section.

MARKET ANOMALIES

Hedged investing draws on market imperfections to increase the all-in rate of return. It employs instruments denominated in unattractive currency or coupon configurations. In capital markets where the supply of funds exceeds local demand, returns tend to be bid down. With efficient world communication and funds transfer, it is a relatively simple matter to transfer funds to another currency or coupon configuration where risk-adjusted returns are higher. Such a strategy not only can produce superior risk-adjusted returns but it can also improve the allocation efficiency of *the* world capital market. Avoidance of the concomitant exchange risk or interest-rate risk requires long-date currency or coupon cover. Despite the cost of cover, it has been possible for investors to increase their all-in rate of return by shifting some of their investments to fully hedged instruments in unattractive currencies or coupons.

There are numerous market anomalies or inefficiencies to which arbitrage investment strategies can be employed to seize the opportunity for improved risk adjusted yields.[3] To illustrate the prevalence and depth of market anomalies, three of the major anomalies that underlie many of the opportunities to enhance the yields on fixed-income securities will be presented: (1) differential credit risk perception across national capital markets, (2) differential market depth and derivative attractiveness accorded high-grade securities between national markets, and (3) differential risk premiums demanded in fixed-rate and floating-rate markets in the same currency.

International Credit Risk Differentials

Differences in the ways in which default risk is perceived and monitored can affect the risk premiums required by investors in national capital markets. In markets such as the United States, a gradation of risk is assessed by security analysts of rating firms and a prospective borrower is given a relative qualitative rating, e.g., AAA, AA, A. . .CCC, CC, C, by, say, Standard and Poor's or Moody's. This rating process ranks the creditworthiness of issuers along a more or less continuous scale of quality rating, using plus and minus qualifications to shade intermediate ratings. The risk premium component of the yield that investors require to invest in a rated security bears a direct relationship to the quality rating. To illustrate, a BBB-rated credit at times commands a yield of 150 to 200 basis points, i.e., 1.5 to 2.0 percent, greater than a higher quality AAA-rated credit for term financing. The yield spread may vary somewhat based on conditions in the credit markets and the stage of the business cycle, but a significant yield spread is generally required for the lower credit issues.

In contrast, continental European capital markets such as Switzerland and West Germany tend to be more liquid and require that a lower-quality acceptable credit pay a yield spread of only 40 to 60 basis points higher than the very best credits. This lower-risk premium requirement is possibly related to the higher savings rates or liquidity extant in the continental countries or to their reduced concern over gradations in the credit rating process. They are more inclined to view a credit as either sound or unsound and act accordingly without serious attempts to fathom intermediate creditworthiness.

This intermarket anomaly has been called "spread compression," since the risk premium spread is lower in the continental countries than in the United States. Its effect is augmented by the fact that continental investors are very much attuned to the *name* of a borrower and its implications regarding the borrower's creditworthiness. If a lower-rated credit who has a broad international presence because it is the producer of a well known product comes to market for capital, the everyday usage and acceptance of its name tends to be a major advantage in its ability to access continental debt markets. A similar enhancement is not available in the United States, where name means far less in the credit evaluation and rating of a firm's securities. As a result, "name" borrowers with a BBB or even lower rating in New York can obtain funds in Zurich or Frankfurt at significantly lower risk premiums than would be available in New York.

The ability to arbitrage market inefficiences of this nature can produce increased yields for investors in countries such as Germany or Switzerland who are willing to invest in, say, dollar instruments of name firms at the lower end of the investment grade quality rating range. This strategy leads, of course, to an asset exposure in a foreign currency, which, unless covered, could cause subsequent exchange losses that exceed the yield advantage. The solution is to hedge the foreign currency (U.S. or Canadian dollar) asset by swapping it for a home currency asset. In this way the rather permanent market anomaly of spread compression or name arbitrage can lead to an improved all-in yield to qualified investors.

International Valuation Differences Differences in supply and demand for similar types of instruments offered in alternative national markets also has provided an opportunity for yield enhancement using financial swaps. A major case in point can be found in the U.K. Treasury or gilt market for two- to three-year maturities. When compared with off-shore issues of Eurosterling bonds we observe that the risk premium or spread between Eurosterling bonds and gilts of the same maturity has tended to be slightly negative to zero over the last few years. Under equilibrium conditions one would expect that the obligations of a sovereign issuer as stable as the U.K. Treasury would sell at a price premium or a yield discount to more risky bonds offered in off-shore sterling markets by private or other issuers. The fact that the spread between Eurosterling bonds and gilts was seldom positive in 1985 suggests that the supply and demand activity surrounding these instruments may be dissimilar to that in other national capital markets.

Perhaps this phenomenon can be explained by the relative glut of gilts and dearth of private sterling issues coupled with the fact that shorter-term gilts tend to be purchased primarily by the clearing banks and other institutional investors rather than by individuals, as in other countries. U.K. institutional investors, who frequently have to fund their purchases in the interbank market, must have a higher yield on gilts to cover their cost of carry. In contrast, Treasury securities in other countries, such as the United States, are attractive to individuals as well as to institutions. In mid-1985 an 8¾ percent yield on a three-year U.S. Treasury bond compared quite well with an approximately similar yield on a three-year certificate of deposit of a money market bank that carried the risk of a sizable portfolio of loans to Third World countries. Hence the widening of demand for intermediate-term Treasury issues in the United States has caused them to sell at a yield discount from the more risky Eurodollar bonds of the same maturity floated by private sector and other issuers. This risk premium has exceeded 100 basis points on three-year U.S. Treasury bonds and has averaged 36 basis points in the year ending in mid-1985. Somewhat lower, but sharply positive, risk premiums could be found at the same time on Deutschemark bonds and still higher premiums persist on Canadian dollar bonds. These spreads suggest that the anomaly is one that has centralized in the gilt market. As a result, yield enhancement could have been arranged in each of these currencies using financial swaps.

What we have here is a case of Eurosterling bonds persistently selling through the U.K. government yield curve and other Eurocurrency issues selling at a premium to their respective government issue yield curves. This intermarket anomaly could be arbitraged by non-sterling investors in government securities by converting their currency to sterling, investing in the relatively higher yielding gilts, and then swapping the sterling interest and principal for their home currency. The pricing of the sterling-non-sterling currency swap depends upon interest differentials in the term interbank deposit market.[4] Term interbank deposit markets in sterling and other currencies are not affected by the intermarket anomaly of Eurosterling bonds selling through gilts. Hence the swap exchange rate pricing will enable the yield advantage available to investors in gilts to be transferred to investors in government securities denominated in other currencies. All of this could be accomplished without incurring the exchange-rate risk inherent in a gilt investment by non-sterling investors. The key to this arbitrage is the use of a currency swap. The power of swaps would enable international investors in other countries to enjoy much of the yield advantages implicit in gilts that had been selling cheap to other market alternatives.

Domestic Credit Risk Differentials The single driving force behind virtually all coupon swaps in the early stages of their application was the differential risk premium attached to credit risk in the floating and fixed-rate debt markets. This market anomaly is due to the demand by term bond investors such as insurance companies, pension funds and other institutional investors for an increasing risk premium for increasingly large credit risk. In some sense this premium is related to their protracted commitment of funds at fixed rates of interest. In contrast, weaker credits can borrow floating-rate money from banks at only a modest risk premium over top quality credits. Perhaps the continuous repricing of interest payments and closer surveillance on the part of lenders accounts for their willingness to accept lower-risk premiums on variable-rate loans, or, perhaps, lenders' desire for floating-rate assets contributes to a greater tolerance for credit risk than found in fixed-rate lenders. A characteristic upward sloping yield curve may also provide some explanation of this practice. In any event, this differential pricing of incremental credit risk between the fixed-rate and floating-rate term debt markets has produced a momentous market anomaly which the deployment of coupon swaps can readily arbitrage. The persistence of this anomaly has enabled investors to execute coupon swaps to commit fixed-rate, medium-term funds at significant yield improvement relative to fixed-rate financing alternatives. A coupon swap opportunity is created by the fact that the fixed-rate market generally requires a larger premium for credit risk than does the floating-rate market.

Two parties are needed to complete the necessary transaction: an investor, who is a natural fixed-rate receiver; and a weaker credit (typically a corporate borrower), who is a natural fixed-rate payer. The key is for the investor to purchase term floating-rate instruments from a high quality issuer, say a money-market bank, and for the weaker, say BBB, corporate borrower to borrow floating-rate funds. Because of the market anomaly, the BBB firm typically would be assessed a risk premium of, say, 1.5 percent over what an AAA firm would pay for fixed-rate finance and only a 0.5 percent risk premium in the floating-rate market. A portion of this differential risk premium can be obtained by an investor who enters into a fixed-for floating-rate coupon swap with the BBB borrower. Since principal is not at risk, the investor winds up with an improved yield associated with a weaker credit but with the principal risk of an AAA money-market bank.

An examination of examples and case studies of each type of swap application will clarify the mechanics of hedged investing. However, before looking at specific applications, it is necessary to review some of the opportunities that swaps make available to investors, as well as certain concerns investors should consider before engaging in swap transactions.

HEDGED INVESTING

Professional investors may have a very positive view on a country and its investment performance but may not want to take a currency exposure in that country. A preference for a country's securities may be for political, geographical or economic reasons. Hedged investment began when U.K. and Dutch life insurance companies and unit trusts developed an interest in U.S., Canadian and Australian dollar instruments. The Dutch also were interested in U.K. securities. In other applications, Japanese investors wanted to diversify out of Japan with dollars available from U.S. trade deficits because of their fear of the potentially devastating effects of natural disasters on investments in Japan. Although much of the flow has been to U.S. dollar instruments because of the country's political stability, U.S. institutional investors often prefer a foreign stock market because of its prospects for capital gain. Frequently, these investors don't want to assume the concomitant currency risk. The long-date currency cover permits investors to unbundle the choice of issuer from the currency of the investment.

A deterrent to the process of covered investing is the perceived or actual need for liquidity; i.e., the ability to exit the swap or sell out the forward contract. This does not tend to be a problem for most private placement type investors, but, at times, it may be a serious consideration for other types of investors. Nevertheless, liquidity can usually be managed by alternative means of liability management such as gap management, lines of credit and maintaining alternative sources of purchased funds. Moreover, exit from long-date currency agreements in major currencies can be rather readily accomplished and the market in coupon swaps has been sufficiently productized to facilitate trading in swaps as needed.

Documentation ease has reached the point that, if you know the other side, forward contracts can be handled on foreign exchange tickets. Ease of exit is also illustrated by the fact that if the hedge runs well and a sizable unrealized gain is evident, it is not unusual for the investor to reverse the hedge and take the gain. This practice represents a speculative action based on the view that the direction of the exchange rate or interest rate move will reverse and the hedge can be reinstituted when rates have moved back to their former level. Policies of this type are similar to those applied in the trading activities of banks and other financial institutions, and have contributed to the increase in volume of long-date currency and coupon swap activity. These policies illustrate that entry and exit to long-date currency and coupon swap deals are no longer formidable obstacles.

CURRENCY SWAP APPLICATIONS

An intriguing application of hedged investing to exploit market inefficiencies lies in two alternative currency liabilities of a captive finance company of a major U.S. multinational. In this example, a U.S. investor in mid-1981 converted to Canadian dollars and bought the five-year Candollar obligations of the finance company on a fully hedged basis to yield an all-in rate of return of 17 percent. At the same time the U.S. dollar five-year obligations of the same finance company were yielding only 15 percent. In this case we have the same issuer, maturity and terms but a 200 basis point higher yield. Such opportunities resulted from the huge natural supply, at the time, of forward U.S. dollars from Canadian firms who received cash flows denominated in U.S. dollars.

An illustration of a typical investment hedge is a U.K. Investment Trust who in mid-1983 wanted to invest L20 million in U.S. equities. The U.K. Trust liked the investment prospects of the year-old bull market in dollar equities. However, they wanted to separate the currency risk from the equity risk because they believed that the dollar would weaken against sterling. They accomplished these objectives by swapping the L20 million sterling for dollars for five years. The other side was a U.S. multinational firm who employed an asset hedge to cover its investment in plant and equipment in the United Kingdom.

Market practices and mechanisms may also evoke an improvement in yields using long-date currency cover. One of these is the way in which long-date currency agreements are priced. Most banks price their forward contracts off the interbank term deposit market. Because of the low volume of interbank term deposit transactions, these quoted rates can become sluggish or nonresponsive to market forces, thereby prompting an opportunity for profitable arbitrage. To exploit such an opportunity, an investor may seek a compound investment strategy which would require building a position in the long-date currency market, i.e., a strategy in which a long-date currency contract is one side of a multilateral deal. Two examples will be used to illustrate the way in which price sluggishness may augment valuation differentials between national capital markets.

In the first example we begin with a yen investor who in July 1983 was seeking to improve his return on 2½-year money over the 6.9 percent available on Japanese government bonds. To implement an improved yield he converted the yen to spot dollars, invested in 2½-year U.S. government notes and sold the dollar interest cash flows forward for yen at each coupon date and the principal for yen at maturity. The result was an all-in yield of 8.2 percent; a return equivalent to Japanese prime but in an investment with U.S. government credit quality.

In a second illustration a U.S. investor sold spot dollars for sterling and invested in a three-year U.K. gilt (Treasury obligation) at ⅛ percent over the offer rate. At the same time he sold the sterling interest cash flows forward for dollars at each coupon date and the principal cash flow at maturity. The result was an investment with U.S. government credit quality at a yield pickup of up to 60 basis points over the Treasury yield curve. It is notable that when these deals are assembled, investors may be able to operate within the quoted bid-ask spreads and thereby further improve their investment outcome.

ASSET COUPON SWAPS

A representative portfolio coupon swap can be used to highlight the limited risk features of a coupon swap. In this case a U.S. life insurance company purchased a five-year floating-rate CD in mid-1983 at six-month Libor plus 0.25 percent. The life insurance firm preferred term fixed-rate assets whose cash flows more nearly coincided with its expected disbursements and whose fixed-rate returns could be relied upon to produce required returns for policyholders. Thus the life firm sought to swap its floating-rate CD interest income with a weak (BBB) corporate credit. It could have considered even weaker credits without undue fear of loss, because the principal in the transaction was not at risk. Other logical counterparties would be thrift institutions or small banks. The BBB-rated firm in this case utilized existing floating-rate or short-term debt. It could also have sourced its funds from a bank, relying on the floating-rate interest payments from the life firm to service its floating-rate debt.

The BBB firm was interested in fixed-rate debt and was willing to pay a spread of 300 basis points over five-year Treasuries. Five-year Treasuries were yielding 10.5 percent making the fixed-rate payment to the life firm 13.5 percent. In exchange, the life firm paid over to the BBB firm its floating-rate interest receipts of 0.25 percent over the six-month London Interbank Offer Rate (Libor) (10 percent at the time) or 10.25 percent in the first interest period. Of course, the six-month Libor rate would be reset every six months.

The advantage to the life firm was that it received fixed-rate income at a yield reflecting a BBB-rated credit as if it lent the funds to a BBB-rated firm rather than investing them in a bank issued floating-rate CD. The BBB firm also enjoyed the benefits of obtaining fixed-rate finance at a time when fixed-rate funds were not otherwise available and at a cost which reflected no increase in its cost of debt capital.

The risk profile faced by the life firm in this example is of interest. First, the risk of principal was limited to that of the issuer of the CD, a bank in this case, since principal is not swapped in a coupon swap. Thus, the only risk that the insurance company was exposed to was the uncertainty that the BBB firm may not remit the required fixed-rate interest flows. Even then the level of exposure was only the difference between the 13.5 percent fixed-rate and the 10.25 percent and subsequent floating-rate payments. Moreover, this risk is really an opportunity type of risk, i.e., the risk that the insurance firm may have to reinvest its principal at a lower fixed rate.

In a diametrically opposite application, another life insurance company at another time used a coupon swap to exchange some of its illiquid, private placement, fixed-rate assets for floating assets. In this case the counterparty was a bank. Evidently the life company, for asset management reasons, preferred to move into floating-rate assets; or perhaps it engaged in the swap because its view on total floating-rate interest receipts exceeded the fixed-rate receipts which it gave up. In any event, its position regarding the illiquidity of its assets remained unchanged because the portfolio of the life company still carried the illiquid assets. That is, only the interest payments and not the principal were swapped.

These examples serve to illustrate typical applications for fixed versus floating-rate coupon swaps. They also illustrate that different firms often have opposite asset or liability management motives, each for a good reason.

SUMMARY

Financial swaps were originally intended to enable financial managers to manage exchange rate risk and interest rate risk. Their initial applications primarily consisted of altering the currency or interest configuration of future cash flows to a form that was more nearly consistent with that preferred by the financial officer. When the swap mechanism became understood and accepted, its uses multiplied. The ability to arrange and rearrange the currency and form of interest flows made financial swaps a natural choice to arbitrage market anomolies across international and domestic markets. Capital market applications of swaps were quickly seized upon by borrowers seeking to reduce their all-in cost of finance.

Intermarket anomalies also appeal to investors seeking to improve their all-in yields. The use of financial swaps enables astute investors to enhance their investment performance over that available on alternative investment strategies. Our discussion of market inefficiencies considered just a few major intermarket anomalies. There are numerous others, some of which are short-lived or even reverse in direction. Each of the anomalies that have been highlighted is rooted in the concept of compression of a risk premium or spread from one market to another. The individual anomalies have been discussed separately for ease in analysis and presentation but each represents an opportunity to purchase a relatively cheap asset vis-a-vis a rich alternative in another market. As in all financial arbitrage, the appropriate policy is to buy or hold the cheap and sell or avoid the rich (to the market) instrument. Financial swaps enable investors to implement such arbitrage policies without having to bear undesired exchange rate or interest rate risk. Competitive pressure to improve investment performance suggests that adoption and acceptance of financial swaps will continue to grow rapidly. And in the process, the efficiency of world capital markets will continue to improve.

NOTES

[1]See Beidleman, C.R., *Financial Swaps: New Strategies in Currency and Coupon Risk Management,* Chapter 15 (Dow Jones-Irwin, 1985) for a more complete discussion of innovative applications for financial swaps.

[2]For an extended discussion of the preferences of coupon payers and receivers, see Beidleman, op cit., pp. 203-209.

[3]See Beidleman, op. cit., Chapter 4 for a more complete discussion of the major imperfections currently prevalent in the fixed-income markets of the world.

[4]For a fuller discussion of the pricing of currency swaps, see Beidleman, op. cit., Chapter 3.

CHAPTER TWENTY-FOUR

ADRIAN F. LEE, Vice President, is a member of the Client Services and Marketing Group and is responsible for capital market research and product development. Prior to joining Morgan in New York in 1980, Mr. Lee worked at Winklevoss and Associates in Philadelphia and at the University of Pennsylvania as a lecturer in statistics. A graduate of Trinity College, Dublin, and the holder of an MBA from the Wharton School, Mr. Lee joined the international Investment Group in 1984.

OPTIMAL CURRENCY HEDGING STRATEGIES

Adrian F. Lee
Vice President,
J.P. Morgan Investment Management Inc.
London, England

INTRODUCTION AND OVERVIEW

This chapter discusses the strategies available to investors in international fixed income markets. Specifically, we concentrate on one important aspect of the management of multicurrency portfolios: the separation of the portfolio building process into (1) the optimal construction of an asset portfolio and (2) a separate optimal currency portfolio. The difference between the optimal asset exposure and the optimal currency exposure is termed the optimal hedge. We show that portfolios constructed on the basis of this separation will always be expected to outperform portfolios that do not explicitly separate the asset and currency decision.

In reviewing historical returns and risk to international fixed income investment for the period 1971-1985, we note that currencies are a systematic source of risk and return in international portfolios. We also observe that currencies move relatively independently of local asset return, suggesting a need to separate the asset investment decision from the currency exposure decision.

We then describe how the optimal portfolio structure for a multicurrency portfolio is defined by an optimal asset weight and an optimal currency exposure—when they differ for any one market this implies a currency hedge or forward position. The optimal portfolio structure is then solved for and identified by expectations for local return, currency return, forward currency premia and all related variances and covariances.

We then investigate whether or not it is necessary to have any currency forecasting insight in order for the separation of asset and currency decisions to provide any value added to the active management of assets. In other words, if exchange rates cannot be forecasted, does it make any sense to consider currency exposure and risk management separately from the asset decision?

Through simulation of the historical use of such optimal portfolio building techniques over the period 1971-85, it is shown that this separation provides considerable value added and that this result is independent of the level of currency forecasting ability. The important implication of this analysis is that if multicurrency portfolios are managed according to this separation approach, then they will inevitably outperform portfolios not invested in this way. Index portfolios are the most obvious example of portfolios whose asset and currency exposure are always equal.

HISTORICAL RETURNS AND RISKS OF INTERNATIONAL BOND MARKETS

Reviewing the performance of international bonds of the major economies over the last fifteen years (see Figure 1), we note that different markets have offered sizeably different opportunities for return. In each case we used ten-year government bonds, or the longest available maturity. These differences are not just short-term differences but have persisted for periods as long as five years. This differential between one market and another can be viewed as an opportunity for an investor to invest outside his home market and earn a better return. Alternatively, if the differential is negative, then this

FIGURE 1 RETURNS FROM INTERNATIONAL FIXED INCOME MARKETS 1971–1985

Percent annual return in dollars

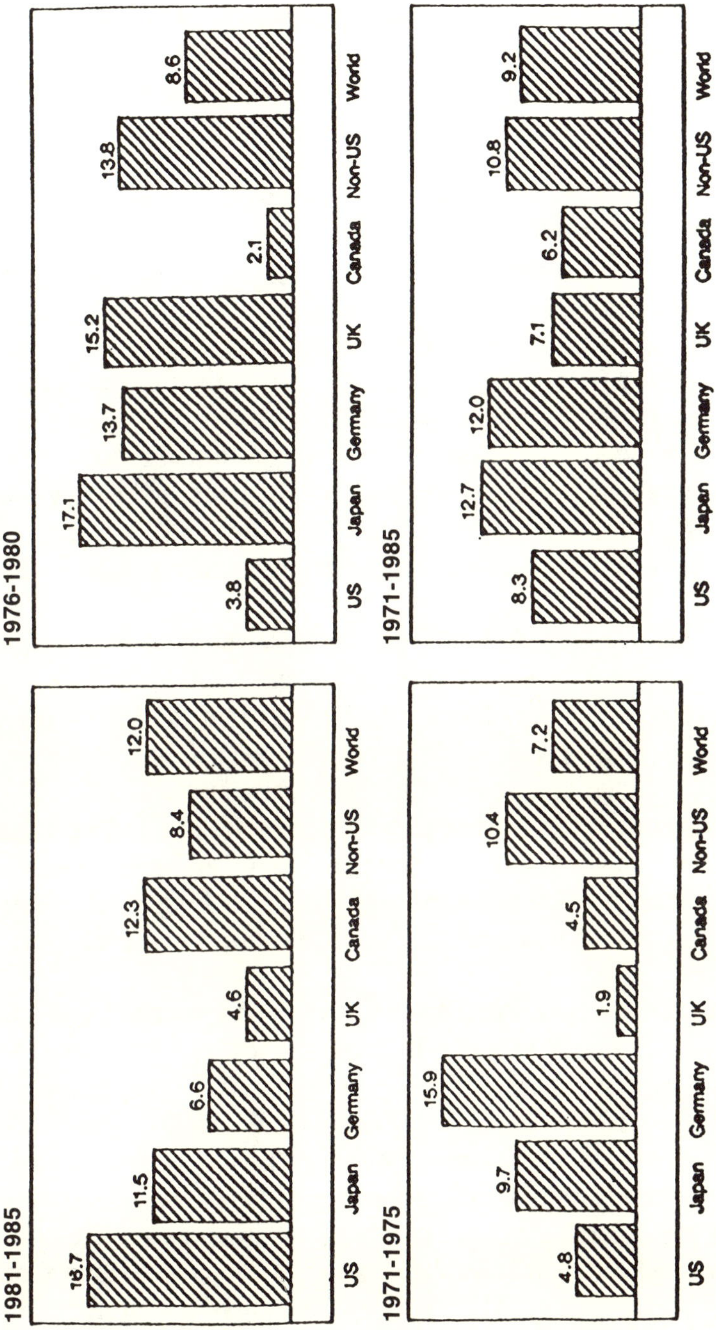

Source: J. P. Morgan Investment and Salomon Brothers Inc

condition should be viewed as a risk. For example, a U.S. bond investor investing outside his home market in proportion to the market capitalization of non-US markets over the period 1981–1985 would have lost return compared to what he would have achieved in his domestic market. However, a similar strategy over the previous five years, 1976–1980, would have paid off handsomely.

Over the total fifteen-year period a U.S. investor would have earned 10.8 percent p.a. from a market capitalization weighted portfolio of non-U.S. bonds compared to 8.3 percent from simply investing in the U.S. bond market alone.

These differentials in return to international investment are more appropriately viewed as the result of two separate sources of return—local bond market return and currency return. Figure 2 decomposes the total dollar returns to a U.S. investor in international bond markets into the local bond market return and associated currency movement versus the U.S. dollar. For example, over the period 1981–1985 the poor performance of the foreign markets from a U.S. perspective, noted above, can be traced to moderate underperformance of the local markets coupled with weakness of the associated foreign currencies. It can also be seen that the outperformance of the foreign markets in the period 1976–1980 was due to local outperformance and strong foreign currencies.

Figure 2 clearly indicates that currencies are a significant source of return in international bond portfolios and that they can add to or detract from return even over periods as long as five years. Also, currency return appears to be rather independent of local market return.

In other words, currencies do not appear to move together in any systematic way, nor is a strong currency uniquely associated with a strong bond market. This apparent relative independence of bond markets and currencies is borne out by an analysis of the correlations of local bond market returns and currency returns (see Figure 3).

The correlations of a local bond return and its own currency (versus the dollar in this case), while positive in all cases, are quite small. The highest is 0.34 in the case of the Japanese bond market and the Yen versus the U.S. dollar. The equivalent numbers from Ger-

FIGURE 2 RETURNS FROM INTERNATIONAL FIXED INCOME MARKETS: 1971–1985

Annual bond market return in local currency and currency movement versus dollar

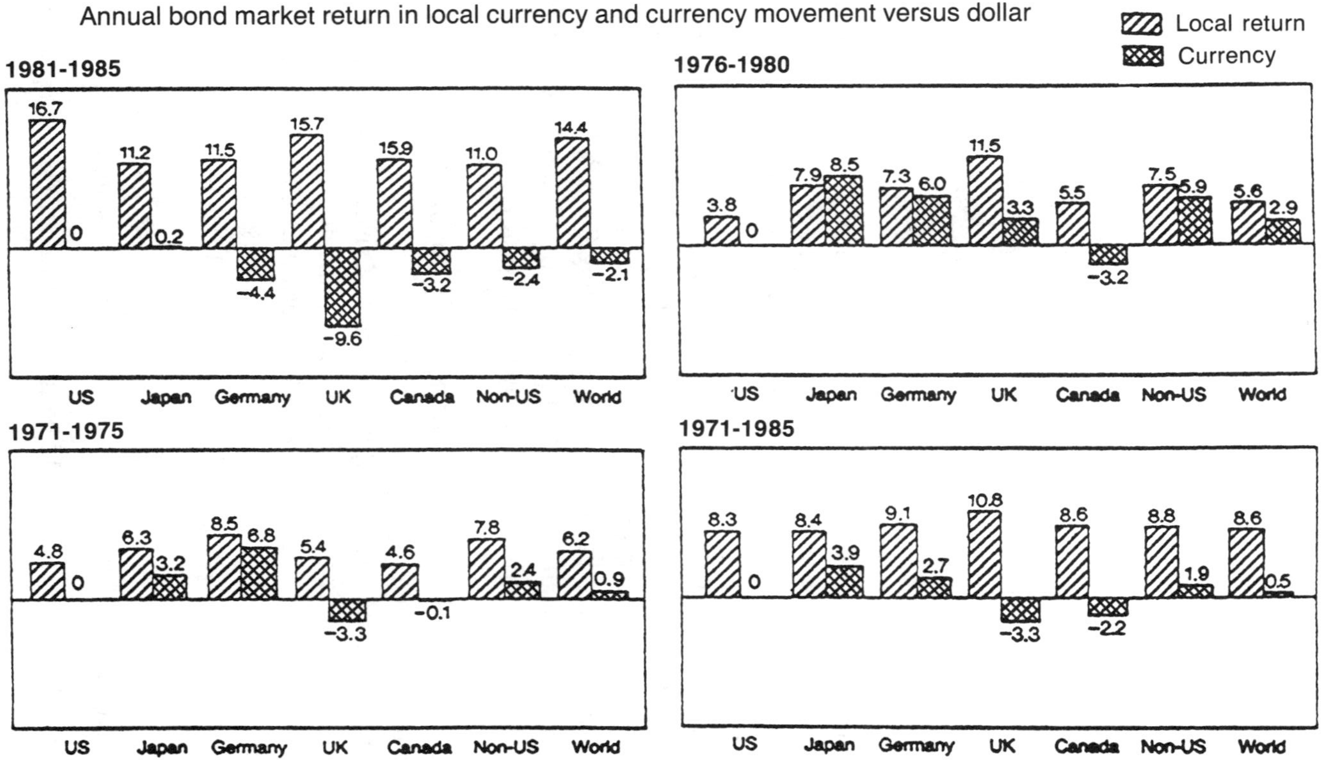

Source: J. P. Morgan Investment and Salomon Brothers Inc

FIGURE 3 CORRELATIONS OF RETURNS FROM LOCAL BOND MARKETS AND CURRENCY 1971–1985

U.S.	1						
Japan	.20	1					
Germany	.37	.37	1				
U.K.	.23	.19	.21	1			
Yen	.13	.34	.15	.14	1		
DM	.11	.23	.25	.01	.54	1	
Sterling	.16	.14	.20	.25	.46	.54	1

Source: J. P. Morgan Investment

many and the United Kingdom are 0.25 and 0.25 in their respective currencies. Therefore, the bond investment and the underlying exposure to that currency clearly cannot be viewed as one and the same investment.

While currency movements have been a rather uncertain source of return over the last fifteen years (they can be positive or negative), they have been a constant source of risk. This constant risk can be observed in Figure 4 by comparing the risk (standard deviation of return) of a diversified portfolio of all non-U.S. bonds and a hypothetical portfolio made up of the local returns from the same markets. Consistently, in each of the five-year periods, the effect of currencies has been to approximately double the risk of the portfolio of the underlying local markets.

In summary, a review of the returns and risks of international bond investment over the last fifteen years indicates that (1) local market and currency returns (the two key variables affecting returns) are separate sources of return and (2) currencies, while not a systematic source of return, are a systematic source of risk in international bond portfolios.

These observations have two significant implications for the management of international bond portfolios on an ongoing basis:

1) Currency risk should be managed rather than simply ignored or assumed.

FIGURE 4 CURRENCY RISK ASSOCIATED WITH INTERNATIONAL FIXED INCOME INVESTMENT

Annual standard deviation of monthly return

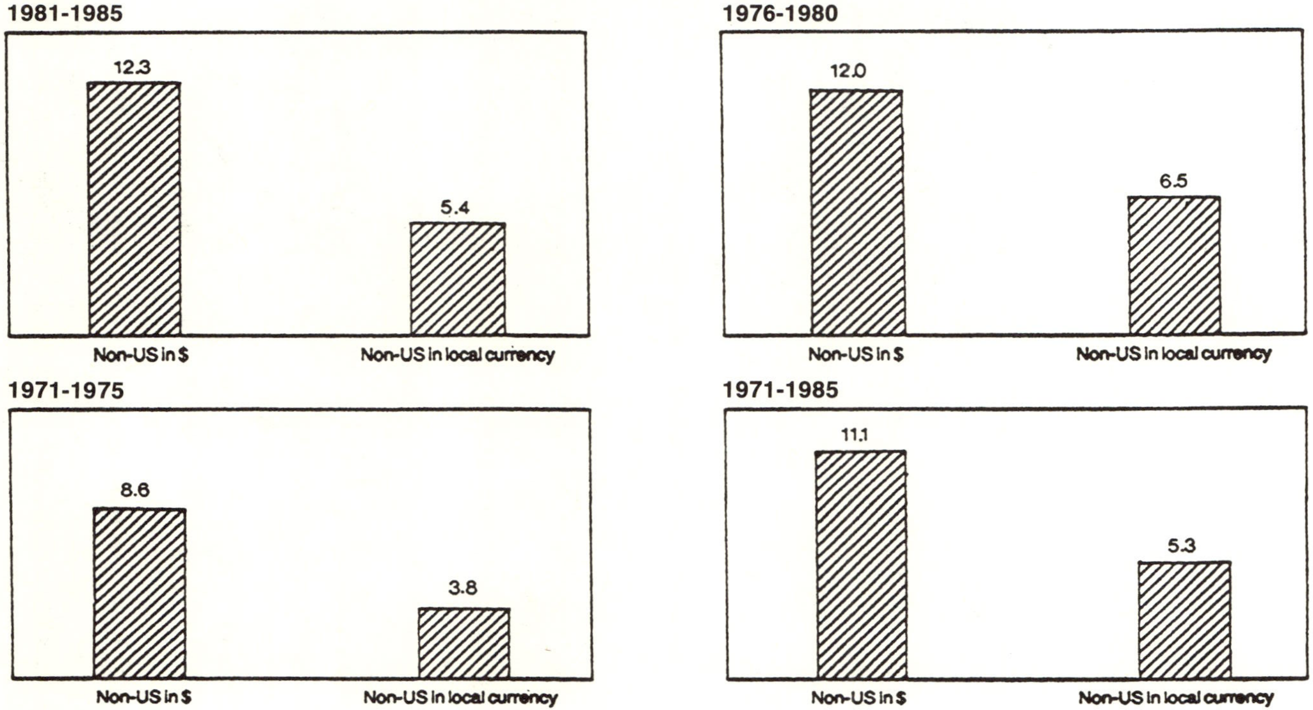

Source: J. P. Morgan Investment

2) The management of an international bond portfolio should be based on the separation of the process into the management of local bond market exposure and currency exposure.

THE SEPARATION OF ASSETS AND CURRENCIES—OPTIMAL PORTFOLIO CONSTRUCTION

Mathematically, the return on a multicurrency bond portfolio is the product of the returns from two separate portfolios—the local asset portfolio and a currency portfolio. An investor seeking to maximize total return on his own currency and minimize risk in his own currency must maximize the sum of the returns from the local asset portfolio and the currency portfolio while minimizing the sum of their risks. The analytical solution to this optimization problem is readily identified through quadratic optimization techniques.

In practice, the solution to this problem involves the separation of the economic outlook into the outlook for local asset returns, interest rates and currency returns. The identification of local risks, currency risks and the estimation of interdependencies of currencies and assets are important inputs. Figure 5 provides an example of such forecasts for local bond market returns, currency returns and risks in the case of the bond markets in the United States, Japan, Germany and the United Kingdom. These numbers would normally reflect investment management expectations and not past or historical results.

From these inputs optimal portfolios can be identified using quadratic optimization techniques. The resulting optimal portfolios are characterized by an optimal asset exposure and a uniquely associated optimal currency exposure. Where these exposures are different for a given market, then a currency hedge is required to alter the currency exposure from that of the local asset exposure. The term "hedge" is a little misleading in this context, in the sense that the hedge is used to *alter* the exposure from one currency to another and does not necessarily imply hedging foreign currency back into base currency. Figure 6 illustrates this optimal procedure using as

FIGURE 5 PORTFOLIO CONSTRUCTION—AN ILLUSTRATION

Bond Market	Expected Local Return	Standard Deviation
U.S.	9.3	9.2
Japan	9.2	6.5
Germany	10.0	7.0
U.K.	11.9	10.8
Currency	**Expected Appreciation vs. Dollar**	
Yen	8.4	15.7
Deutschemark	9.0	11.8
Sterling	5.2	16.9

input the expectations from Figure 5. A range of optimal portfolios for differing levels of risk are shown. For example, at higher levels of risk, Portfolio No. 5 is optimal, and suggests a 100 percent exposure to the German bond market, but only a 12 percent exposure to the DM, implying hedging 88 percent of the DM exposure into the other currencies, including the U.S. dollar.

These six portfolios represent the maximum expected dollar return for each level of risk in U.S. dollars. The actual level of risk chosen is a function of the investor's risk preferences and total return objectives.

In order to highlight the importance of the separation of assets and currencies in this whole optimization process, these portfolios can be contrasted with portfolios built on the basis of an investment process that simply adds together local asset and currency return into one composite measure of attractiveness. In other words, portfolios constructed in a way that does not allow for hedging of currency positions.

Figure 7 details the results of these two contrasting methods of portfolio construction, charting the return and risk opportunity set of portfolios ranging from low risk and return on the bottom left

FIGURE 6 EFFICIENT INTERNATIONAL FIXED INCOME PORTFOLIOS

Portfolio No.	Bond Market Exposure %				Currency Exposure %				Expected Return in dollars	Standard Deviation in dollars
	US	Japan	Germany	UK	Yen	DM	Sterling	Dollar		
1	15	48	28	9	0	0	0	100	11.7	5.5
2	5	43	48	4	0	0	2	98	12.5	5.7
3	0	19	81	0	5	0	11	84	14.5	7.4
4	0	6	94	0	9	2	15	74	15.5	8.6
5	0	0	100	0	15	12	23	50	17.0	15.8
6	0	0	100	0	25	20	55	0	20.5	16.8

Source: J. P. Morgan Investment

FIGURE 7 EFFICIENT INTERNATIONAL FIXED INCOME PORTFOLIOS

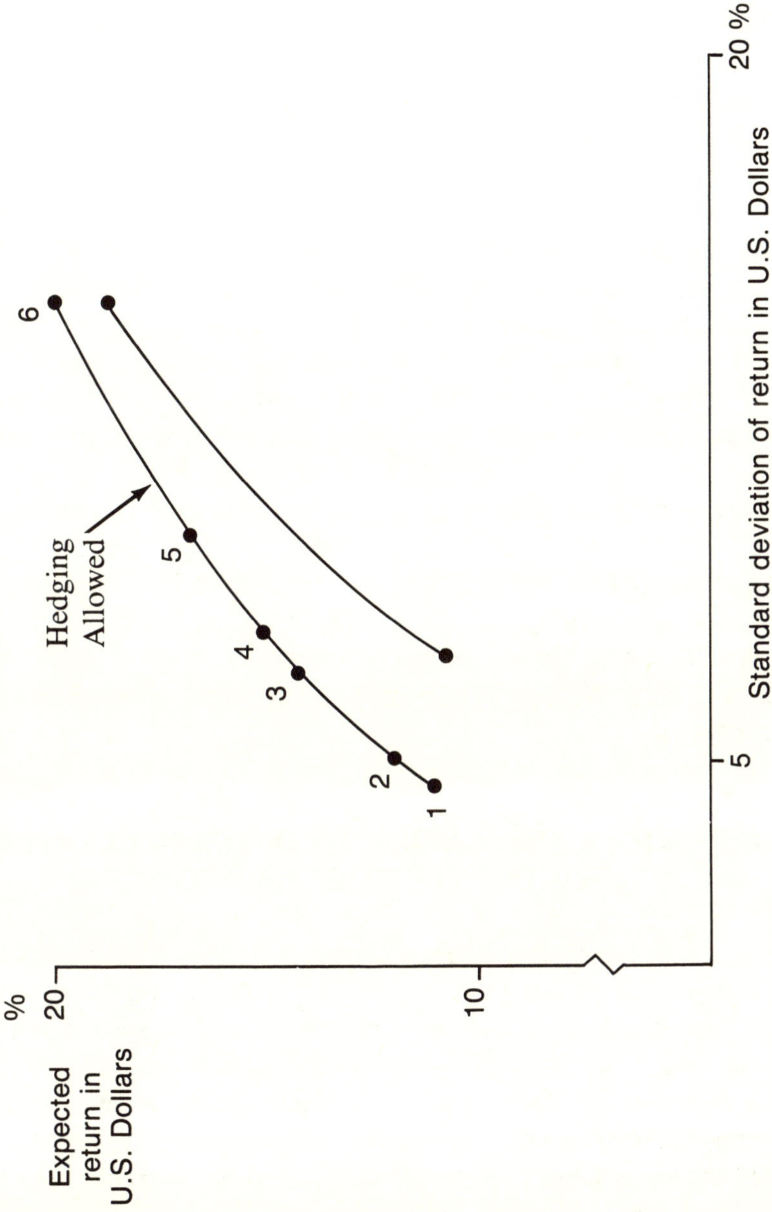

Source: J. P. Morgan Investment

to high risk and return on the top right. Obviously, for any given level of risk, portfolios based on the separation of assets and currency (the higher line) always are expected to return more than portfolios not taking this separation into account and not allowing for hedging.

This consistent value added to explicit separation of assets and currencies is important. These optimally separated—or optimally hedged—portfolios will always be expected to outperform portfolios that do not allow hedging. This result is independent of the inputs used, i.e., expected returns, risks and covariances, although the value added from separation will vary according to the inputs.

The critical question remains whether or not this expected outperformance of the optimally hedged portfolios can be realized in practice. In other words, how much of the expected outperformance is contingent on the ability to forecast currency returns?

The simulation results in the next section will show that even under the most pessimistic assumptions about currency forecasting ability, international bond portfolios constructed emphasizing quadratic optimization techniques and explicity separating assets and currencies will consistently outperform portfolios not allowing for this separation, i.e., portfolios that constantly assume equal asset and currency exposures.

HISTORICAL SIMULATION OF OPTIMAL CURRENCY HEDGING TECHNIQUES 1971–1985

In order to test whether or not the expected excess returns associated with using the optimal hedging techniques of the previous section can be realized in practice, we simulated the use of such techniques in the major international bonds markets over the last fifteen years. We compared two basic types of portfolios: one that held asset and currency exposure equal versus the optimally hedged portfolio that held the same asset exposure, but allowed the currency exposure to alter according to what the optimization techniques suggested for currency exposure.

Each quarter the optimally hedged portfolio was constructed using naive estimates of risk and correlation from historical data up to that point and alternative assumptions with respect to actual currency return forecast. The currency forecast was of the general form:

Currency Forecast = Actual Currency Return + Forecast Bias + Random Error

Forecast bias is defined as a consistent error of forecasting currency return, around the actual return. Random error is a random term with a mean of zero and standard deviation equal to volatility of the forecast.

Each quarter the optimally hedged portfolio was derived on the basis of those purely historical inputs and the return calculated. The return was then compared to that of a portfolio that held the same asset mix and a currency exposure equal to asset exposure, i.e., no hedging was allowed.

The results over the period 1971–1985 for the U.S., Japanese, German and U.K. bond markets are portrayed in Figure 8. An unhedged balanced portfolio consisting of 25 percent in dollar, yen, deutschmark and sterling assets had a return of 12.2 percent per annum (p.a.) and an annual standard deviation of 11.1 percent p.a. On the other hand, a continuously, fully hedged portfolio had a return of 9.8 percent p.a. and a standard deviation of 7.3 percent p.a.

In contrast, various optimally hedged portfolios at alternative levels of risk and under differing assumptions, as represented by the four lines on Figure 8, consistently outperformed the unhedged portfolio and the continuously hedged portfolio, both in terms of return and risk.

The line S = 0 represents the performance of the optimally hedged portfolio at various levels of risk, assuming no bias in currency forecasting and no error, i.e., perfect forecasting ability. This portfolio outperformed the passively unhedged portfolio by 12 percent p.a. with the same level of risk.

The lines S = 1 and S = 2 represent the results of an optimally

FIGURE 8 SIMULATED OPTIMAL HEDGING STRATEGIES US, JA, GE, UK BOND MARKETS 1971-1985

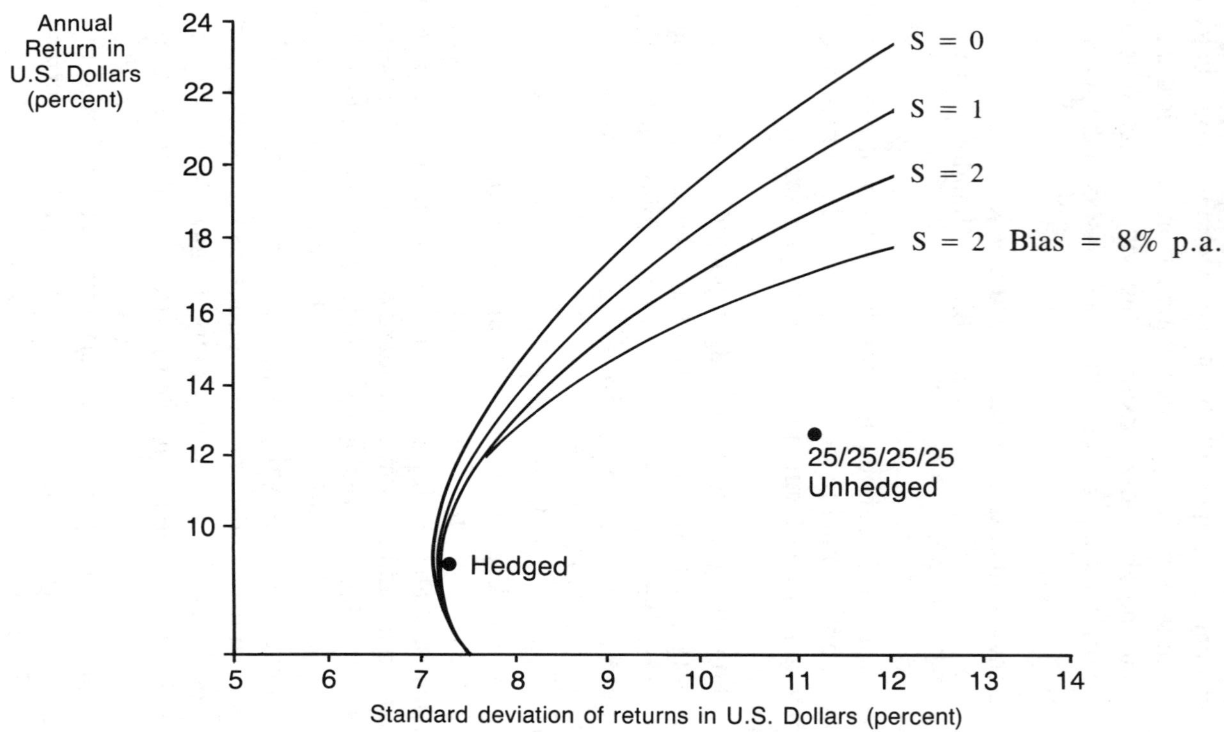

Source: J. P. Morgan Investment

hedged portfolio, assuming no forecasting bias but that the currency forecasting error is equal to one time and two times the actual currency volatility. Currency forecasting error equal to currency volatility represents a situation of no insight. Error greater than actual volatility represents a distorted situation by which the forecasting process actually adds error beyond that which is inherent risk in the system. The line S = 2 and bias = 8 percent p.a. represents extremely pessimistic assumptions about currency forecasting ability, possibly even unrealistically pessimistic.

Under all these sets of assumptions the optimally hedged portfolio outperforms the others in terms of return and risk. Under the most pessimistic case this outperformance is of the order of 4 percent p.a.

No allowance for transaction costs has been made in these simulations. The turnover observed in the portfolio and transaction costs in exchange markets are such that significant excess returns are still likely to remain after adjustment for transaction costs.

In summary, the results of these historical simulations using naive forecasting methodologies strongly suggest that by explicitly taking into account the potential differences between local asset return and currency return, and by identifying optimal asset and currency exposure, the resulting portfolios will inevitably outperform portfolios that do not explicitly separate the asset decision from the currency decision.

The intuitive rationale for this outperformance is the simple value added to (1) separating decisions and (2) balancing the currency exposure across countries in relationship to the relative risks of the currencies. The risks and interdependencies of the currencies amongst themselves have been *relatively* stable historically, so that optimization using historical values as inputs provides value added.

In practice, it is reasonable to assume that active investment management of assets and currencies must inevitably provide greater value added than the naive forecasting techniques used above; therefore, the potential for outperformance should be considerably greater than shown.

CHAPTER TWENTY-FIVE

DENNIS T. OFFICER, Ph.D., has been an Associate Professor of Finance at the University of Kentucky since 1985. His principle research and teaching interests, in addition to international securities and investing, include option pricing, public utility regulation, and corporate financing issues. He has published extensively in a wide variety of scholarly and professional journals and serves as an active financial consultant to corporations, financial institutions, and governments.

J. RONALD HOFFMEISTER is an Associate Professor of Finance at Arizona State University. He has over 15 years of teaching and research experience in the areas of Financial Management and Investments. He earned his M.S. and Ph.D. in Finance at the University of Illinois. Dr. Hoffmeister is the author of numerous articles in professional journals including the *Financial Analysts Journal, Journal of Portfolio Management, Financial Executive, Journal of Finance, Journal of Bank Research,* and *Financial Management.* He is a member of the American Finance Association, Financial Management Association, and the Western Finance Association.

AMERICAN DEPOSITARY RECEIPTS:
A DOMESTIC ALTERNATIVE FOR INTERNATIONAL DIVERSIFICATION*

Dennis T. Officer
Associate Professor of Finance
University of Kentucky
Lexington, Kentucky
and
J. Ronald Hoffmeister
Associate Professor of Finance
Arizona State University
Tempe, Arizona

INTRODUCTION

Portfolio theory suggests that the degree to which diversification can reduce risk depends upon the correlation among security returns. If security returns are not correlated, diversification can eliminate risk. On the other hand, if security returns are perfectly correlated, no amount of diversification can reduce risk.

Within the domestic economy there is a strong tendency for economic activity among most industries to be positively correlated. Investors can reduce their portfolio risk but not eliminate it completely through diversification. For example, Grubel (1968) found the correlation coefficient between the U.S. equity market and the Canadian market to be +0.7, while correlation with the European

*Reprinted from the Winter 1987 issue of *The Journal of Portfolio Management*.
The authors would like to thank Pat Sarwal and Jill Forsyth for their data collection and computational assistance.

and Japanese markets was only in the +0.1 to +0.3 range. Additional risk reduction could have been achieved by diversifying an equity portfolio internationally.

Direct international diversification is difficult due to a number of factors. However, a convenient way for U.S. investors to achieve international diversification of their equity portfolios is to invest in American Depositary Receipts (ADRs). ADRs enable U.S. investors to buy or sell foreign securities with U.S. dollars without any of the administrative problems associated with taking physical possession of foreign securities.

The purpose of this chapter is to examine the investment characteristics of ADRs, as they provide such a convenient way for U.S. investors to invest in foreign securities. The question as to whether a significant portfolio advantage has existed when ADRs were combined into portfolios with U.S. securities will be explored. The remainder of the chapter is organized as follows: Section I describes direct foreign equity investment; Section II examines in detail the nature of ADRs; Section III develops the sample of ADRs and methodology utilized, and Section IV presents the diversification results from various portfolio combinations. An analysis of the significance and implications of this study is provided in Section V.

I. POTENTIAL PROBLEMS WITH DIRECT FOREIGN EQUITY INVESTMENT

Solnik (1974) and Levy and Sarnat (1970) have found that combining U.S. stocks with stocks of foreign countries produces portfolios that have about half the risk of a well-diversified domestic stock portfolio (with the same number of securities in the portfolio). The potential advantages of international diversification are often reduced by institutional, political, and economic factors. Fluctuations in prices of securities on foreign exchanges are not the only consideration in a foreign investment. The transfer of stock certificates and the collection of dividends in foreign currencies can be difficult. In Japan, for example, an investor must present the certificates of ownership to the firm or its agent before dividends can be paid. The sale of shares of stock and settlement is often tedious due to the bearer nature of most foreign securities. In addition, investors must convert dollars into another currency when buying foreign securities, and then convert back into dollars when selling the securities. Exchange rate risk can impact on the risk and return associated with investing in foreign securities. Since 1971, the world has been on a system of managed floating exchange rates. With foreign currency investments, U.S. investors run the risk that a currency may decline in value relative to the U.S. dollar, causing the return realized in U.S. dollars to be reduced by the amount of the currency decline.

II. THE NATURE OF ADRs

ADRs are usually issued by U.S. banks called depositaries that certify that a specific number of foreign shares have been deposited with the bank's overseas branch or custodian and will be held on deposit as long as the ADRs remain outstanding. Through their foreign correspondent banks these depositaries take physical possession of foreign securities and then issue receipts on them (ADRs). The bank or its correspondent receives dividends on these stocks, pays any foreign withholding taxes, converts the proceeds into U.S. dollars, and passes the dividends to the receipt holders. These receipts are listed on a national stock exchange or the over-the-counter market. This enables investors to buy and sell them as easily as any other U.S. security. The holder of ADRs may, at any time, obtain the underlying shares. Similarly, individuals owning foreign securities can exchange them for ADRs. The depositary bank collects a fee for services they perform.

American Depositary Receipts were introduced in 1927 by the old Guaranty Trust Co. of New York. It began this function by acting as transfer agent, notifying investors of dividends, and distributing them in dollars. Currently, overseas banks and their agents help U.S. depositary banks keep informed as to subscription rights, recapitalization plans, exchange offers, annual meeting notices, and the like for the foreign companies underlying ADRs. The depositary bank performs all the functions that average holders of foreign securities would find difficult or impossible to do on their own.

The decision to issue an ADR is made by the depositary bank, provided that the corporation has no objections. Listing of ADRs requires that the ADR and the underlying foreign company comply with all exchange and SEC regulations. There are two types of ADRs, sponsored and unsponsored. Sponsored ADRs involve foreign companies that have fully registered with the SEC and whose stock could be listed on either the NYSE or the ASE. Unsponsored ADRs are issued for foreign companies who have not fully registered with the SEC. They are traded in the OTC market. The number of ADRs has grown rapidly in recent years. In 1961 only 150 ADRs were available for investors, this number growing to 390 in 1978 and 550 in 1984. A possible drawback to ADRs today is that only twenty-five are sponsored, eighteen traded on NYSE and seven traded on ASE, while 525 unsponsored ADRs are traded in the OTC market.[1]

A typical ADR represents a single share of stock. However, if the price of a foreign company's stock in U.S. dollars would be either very low or relatively high compared with its U.S. counterpart, the ADRs will be issued in units that represent either a fraction or multiple shares of stock.

III. SAMPLE AND METHODOLOGY

The ADR sample chosen for this study consisted of twenty securities that were continuously traded on the NYSE and the ASE as well as twenty-five actively traded in the OTC market during the period 1973 through 1983. This provided a sample of forty-five ADRs, all of which were traded continuously during the 1973-1983 study period, a period of floating exchange rates. In order to investigate the relative advantage of using ADRs to improve portfolio diversification, we also selected a random sample of forty-five common stocks continuously traded on the NYSE and ASE during 1973-1983.

TABLE 1 DESCRIPTION OF ADRs BY COUNTRY OF ORIGIN AND MARKET WHERE THE ADRs WERE TRADED

COUNTRY	NYSE/ASE	OTC	TOTAL
Australia	0	2	2
Japan	5	6	11
Netherlands	3	0	3
South Africa	1	12	13
United Kingdom	11	5	16
TOTAL	20	25	45

A description of the ADRs by country of origin and the market in which they were traded appears in Table 1.

Monthly rates of return were calculated for all domestic stocks, ADRs, and for an equal-value weighted index for the NYSE and ASE taken from the Center for Research in Security Prices (CRSP) file. Since all securities are traded in U.S. dollars, the returns can be calculated in the usual manner (without dividends) without any exchange rate adjustments as:

$$R_{i,t} = \frac{P_{i,t} - P_{i,t-1}}{P_{i,t-1}}$$

$P_{i,t}$ = the dollar value of the ith common stock at the end of month t.

$R_{i,t}$ = the rate of return in month t.

The omission of dividends from these security return calculations will reduce the magnitude of the returns, but will not preclude comparisons between securities, as all returns are computed similarly.

Systematic Risk

The first part of the investigation centers on an evaluation of the systematic risk of ADRs. The familiar single-index market model was utilized to estimate systematic risk of the sample securities.

Assuming bivariate normal returns, the return-generating process can be described as:

$$R_{i,t} = \alpha + \beta R_{m,t} + e_{i,t}$$

where $R_{i,t}$ and $R_{m,t}$ are the rates of return on security i and the CRSP equal-weighted market index respectively, α and β are the intercept and slope of the regression, and $e_{i,t}$ is an error term assumed to satisfy the usual OLS assumptions. The model in Equation (2) was estimated in portfolio form across time and securities by country of origin.

Portfolio Formation

The second part of the analysis is concerned with the extent and ease of diversification that can be achieved from purely domestic portfolios and ADR portfolios. Using the technique developed by Evans and Archer (1968) random portfolios of various sizes were constructed from the sample of ADRs and domestic securities. For example, twenty one-stock portfolios were constructed from our sample of domestic firms, then twenty two-stock portfolios through twenty twenty-five stock portfolios. Average rates of return were calculated for each stock over the 1973-1983 sample period. The portfolio average mean rate of return was calculated such that:

$$R_p = \frac{1}{N} \sum_{t=1}^{N} R_i$$

Finally, the average portfolio standard deviation was calculated for each portfolio constructed as follows:

$$\sigma_p = \left[\frac{1}{N} \sum_{t=1}^{N} (R_p - R_i)^2 \right]^{1/2}$$

Portfolios formed were either 1) purely domestic securities; 2) purely ADRs; or 3) combinations of domestic and ADR securities.

IV. RESULTS

Beta Estimates

Table 2 shows the systematic risk for all ADRs in our sample from a particular country and for the entire sample of ADRs. There appears to be only a small degree of co-movement in prices of ADRs compared to prices in the domestic stock market. The beta estimates range from .423 for ADRs from Japan to .067 for the Netherlands. The portfolio beta for the sample ADRs across all countries of origin is .264, in contrast to the portfolio beta of the domestic securities of 1.010. A *t*-test of equality of means between the ADRs and domestic securities' systematic risk is rejected, suggesting that the systematic risk of the ADRs is significantly lower than that of the market as a whole. These betas are low enough to suggest that a significant reduction in standard deviation will occur if portfolios are made up of domestic stocks and the stocks of one or more of these foreign ADRs.[2]

TABLE 2 ESTIMATES OF SYSTEMATIC RISK (β_P) OF ADRs BY COUNTRY (1973-1983)

Country	β_P	R^2
Australia	.291	.14
Japan	.423	.21
Netherlands	.067	.07
South Africa	.213	.10
United Kingdom	.211	.10

ESTIMATES OF SYSTEMATIC RISK (β_P) OF ADRs AND DOMESTIC SECURITIES (1973-1983)

	β_P	R^2
ADRs	.264 (21.03)*	.11
Domestic stocks	1.010 (48.37)*	.29

*Significant t-statistics at the .01 level

Diversification Effects

Purely domestic portfolios were first constructed to determine how portfolio standard deviations decreased as the number of securities in the portfolio increased. The results of this analysis appear in Table 3

TABLE 3 MEAN PORTFOLIO STANDARD DEVIATION OF RANDOMLY SELECTED DOMESTIC SECURITIES AND ADRs IN PORTFOLIOS 1973-1983

	Domestic Stock Portfolio (N=45)		ADR Portfolios (N=45)	
Portfolio Size	Standard Deviation	% of Total Risk	Standard Deviation	% of Total Risk
1	0.0856	100.00	0.0998	100.00
2	0.0661	77.2	0.0933	93.4
3	0.0631	73.7	0.0799	80.0
4	0.0623	72.8	0.0703	70.4
5	0.0582	68.0	0.0680	68.1
6	0.0571	66.7	0.0652	65.3
7	0.0572	66.8	0.0622	62.3
8	0.0555	64.8	0.0623	63.1
9	0.0551	64.3	0.0621	62.2
10	0.0550	64.2	0.0623	63.1
11	0.0549	64.1	0.0626	62.7
12	0.0555	64.8	0.0626	62.7
13	0.0545	63.6	0.0623	62.4
14	0.0542	63.3	0.0620	62.1
15	0.0528	61.7	0.0612	61.9
16	0.0531	62.1	0.0579	58.0
17	0.0530	61.9	0.0573	57.4
18	0.0529	61.8	0.0570	57.1
19	0.0529	61.8	0.0567	57.4
20	0.0527	61.6	0.0571	57.2
21	0.0526	61.4	0.0572	57.9
22	0.0528	61.6	0.0565	56.6
23	0.0527	61.6	0.0563	57.0
24	0.0527	61.6	0.0550	55.1
25	0.0521	60.9	0.0550	55.1

in tabular form and graphically in Figure 1. Most of the unsystematic variation for domestic securities is eliminated by the time a portfolio of eight securities is reached, a finding similar to that of Evans and Archer (1968). The average eight-stock domestic portfolio had a monthly standard deviation of 0.0555 compared to a slightly lower standard deviation of 0.0521 for a portfolio made up of twenty-five domestic stocks. The average monthly rate of return on the domestic portfolio was .0111, equivalent to an annualized rate of .1332.

FIGURE 1 MEAN PORTFOLIO STANDARD DEVIATION

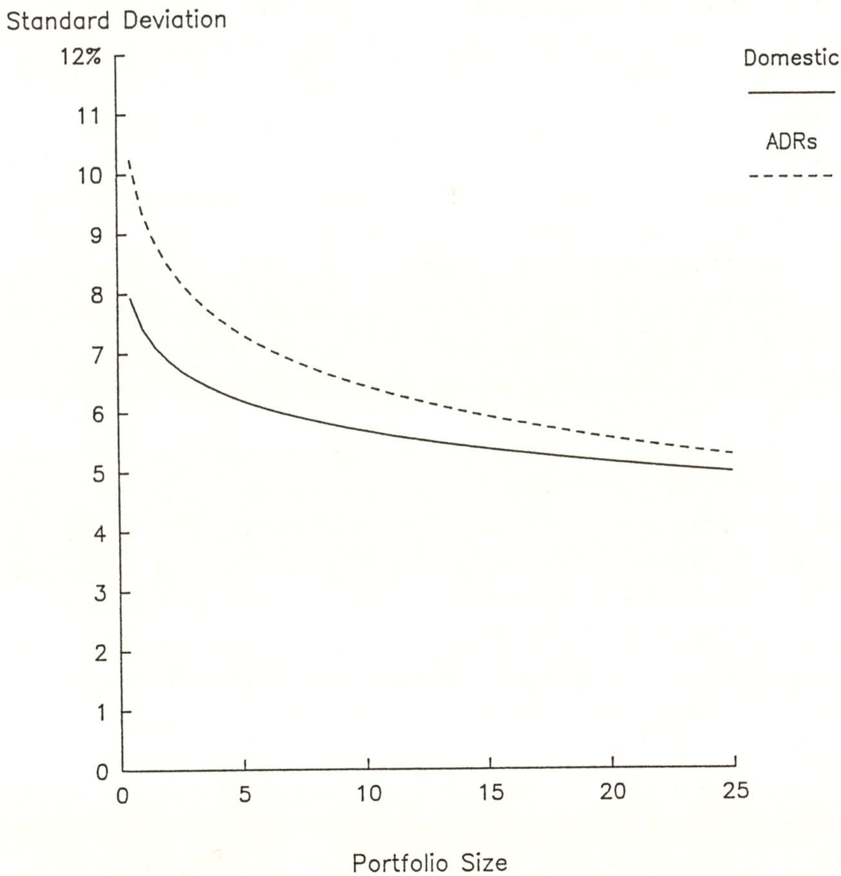

Portfolios of ADRs were selected from our sample of 45 ADRs. The average standard deviation for each of the different portfolios is reported under ADRs in Table 3. Standard deviations for the ADR portfolios are higher than for domestic portfolios, but again most of the unsystematic variation in the ADR portfolios is eliminated by the time portfolios of eight stocks are constructed. The average eight-stock ADR portfolio had a standard deviation of 0.0623 compared to the slightly lower standard deviation of 0.0550 for the average of the portfolios made up of twenty-five domestic stocks. The annualized rate of return of the ADR portfolio is equal to .1296, slightly lower than the purely domestic portfolio. However, a *t*-test of equal means between the mean rates of return cannot be rejected at the .05 level, suggesting that annual rates of return for these ADRs were not significantly different from a portfolio of domestic stocks.

If some independence among foreign economies and the U.S. economy exists then it is possible for investors to capture some additional benefit from holding a portfolio that is internationally diversified. A lack of perfect co-movement of returns between the stocks of any one country and domestic securities suggests that U.S. investors could reduce the standard deviation of portfolio returns by making use of equities traded in both countries. Evidence by Grubel (1968), Lessard (1976), Solnik (1974), and Bergstrom, Koeneman, and Siegel (1982) suggests that substantial benefits may be provided by international diversification.

The last step was to develop internationally diversified, or "combination," portfolios. These portfolios were constructed using the same technique as that used for constructing the other portfolios, except the selection of securities alternated between the two groups — ADRs and domestic securities. The selection within each group was made randomly and an equal investment was assumed to be made in each security. Domestic securities were combined with ADRs, with the matching done randomly. Table 4 shows the standard deviations for the "combination" portfolios. The undiversifiable risk is much lower than for either the domestic or ADR portfolios across all portfolio sizes. With an average eight-stock portfolio most of the unsystematic risk has been eliminated. The standard deviation of an eight-stock "combination" portfolio is 0.0435, 20 to 25 percent lower than the purely domestic or ADR portfolios. Diversification using domestic stocks and ADRs appears to be a superior method of producing diversified portfolios. Although the standard deviation of ADRs is greater than for domestic securities, the port-

TABLE 4 PORTFOLIO STANDARD DEVIATION OF RANDOMLY SELECTED INTERNATIONAL PORTFOLIO COMPOSED OF DOMESTIC SECURITIES AND ADRs

1973 - 1983

Combination (ADR & Domestic Stock) Portfolios

Portfolio Size	Standard Deviation	% of Total Risk
1	0.0677	100.0
2	0.0592	87.4
3	0.0514	76.0
4	0.0490	72.3
5	0.0477	70.4
6	0.0458	67.7
7	0.0443	65.4
8	0.0435	64.2
9	0.0433	64.0
10	0.0441	65.1
11	0.0443	65.4
12	0.0442	65.3
13	0.0432	63.8
14	0.0436	64.4
15	0.0434	64.1
16	0.0425	62.7
17	0.0423	62.5
18	0.0421	62.1
19	0.0423	62.5
20	0.0436	64.4
21	0.0420	62.0
22	0.0413	61.0
23	0.0416	61.4
24	0.0401	59.2
25	0.0400	59.2

folios have lower total risk when combined with domestic securities. The annual rate of return of the ADR-domestic portfolio is 0.1308, similar to the average rates of return on the domestic and ADR portfolios. The international portfolio produces lower levels of risk without a proportional reduction in return.

V. SUMMARY AND CONCLUSION

Previous studies of international diversification have made unrealistic assumptions about the foreign investment process and have failed

FIGURE 2 MEAN PORTFOLIO STANDARD DEVIATION

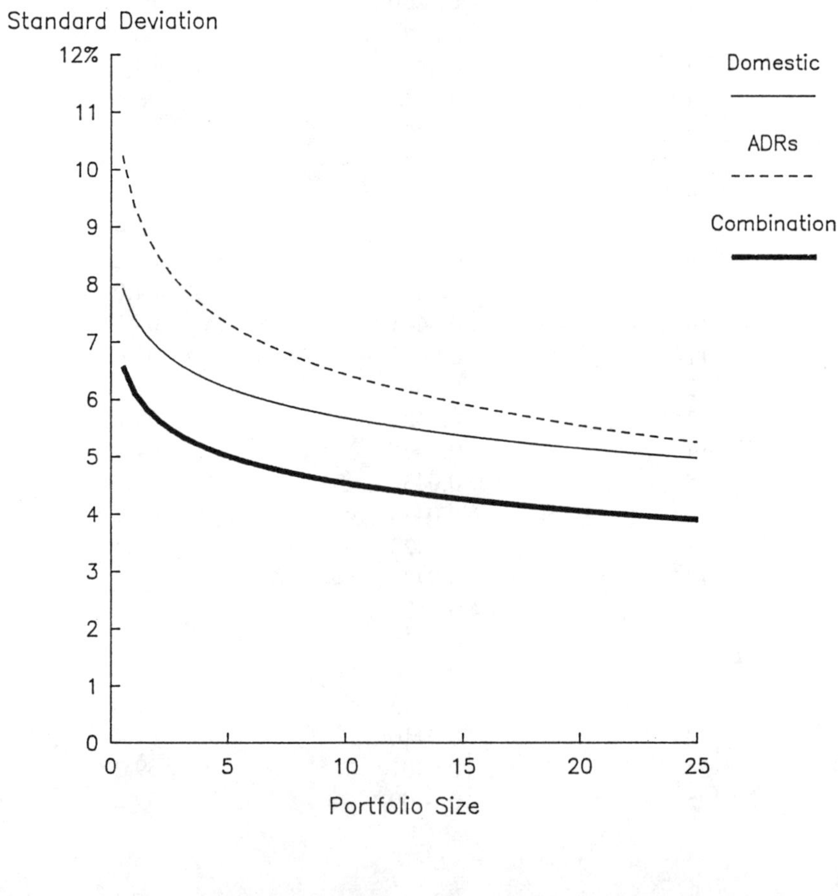

to account for the costs involved in dealing with the practical difficulties of investing in foreign countries.

By combining ADRs with domestic securities, U.S. investors can overcome many of the problems of international investing. There are no direct exchange rate problems, no difficulty in collecting dividends, and no lack of marketability associated with owning ADRs. The favorable risk-return results from portfolios of ADRs and domestic securities found in this study are available to the typical U.S. investor. Most studies of international diversification assume that investors are able to hold large portfolios of securities in each country in which they might invest. When as few as four ADRs are combined with four domestic securities into portfolios, investors can reduce their risk exposure by 20 to 25 percent without any reduction in expected returns. These results were obtained from a limited number of ADRs representing only five foreign countries.[3]

While our results are not directly comparable to other studies that advocate direct foreign investment, it appears that "combination" ADR-domestic stock portfolios have provided a realistic and useful alternative for U.S. investors. ADRs allow investors to avoid many of the practical and costly problems associated with investing in foreign equities while receiving the major benefits of international diversification.

NOTES

[1]A good description of the nature and history of ADRs can be found in Merjos (1978).

[2]A world-market portfolio could be constructed and the beta of these ADRs calculated relating their returns with the returns on the world-market index. Since U.S. investors typically invest primarily in U.S. securities, then returns are only relevant in U.S. dollars. Thus, the risk of foreign securities is determined by relating their returns with the returns of a U.S. Market Index.

[3]ADRs are now available from France, Germany, Hong Kong, Israel, Jamaica, Malaysia, Mexico, New Guinea, Singapore, Spain, and Sweden.

BIBLIOGRAPHY

Agmon, T. "The Relations Among Equity Markets: A Study of Share Price Co-movements in the United States, United Kingdom, Germany and Japan," *Journal of Finance* (September, 1972), pp. 839-856

Bergstrom, Gary L., Koeneman, John K., and Siegel, Martin J. "International Securities Markets," *Readings in Investment Management,* Frank Fabozzi (Ed.), (Homewood, Ill.: Richard D. Irwin, 1982)

Cornell, Bradford. "Spot Rates, Forward Rates, and Market Efficiency," *Journal of Financial Economics* (August, 1977), pp. 55-65

Cornell, W. Bradford and Dietrich, J. Kimball. "The Efficiency of the Market for Foreign Exchange Under Floating Exchange Rates," *Review of Economics and Statistics* (February, 1978), pp. 111-120

Evans, J. and S. Archer. "Diversification and the Reduction of Dispersion: An Empirical Study," *Journal of Finance* (March, 1978), pp. 761-767

Grubel, H. G. "Internationally Diversified Portfolios: Welfare Gains and Capital Flows," *American Economic Review* (December, 1968), pp. 1299-1314

Jacquillat, Bertrand and Solnik, Gruno H. "Multinationals Are Poor Tools for Diversification," *Journal of Portfolio Management* (Winter, 1978), pp. 8-12

Lessard, Donald R. "International Portfolio Diversification: A Multivariate Analysis for a Group of Latin American Countries," *Journal of Finance* (June, 1976), pp. 619-633

Levy, H. and Sarnat, M. "International Diversification of Investment Portfolios," *American Economic Review* (September, 1970), pp. 668-675

Merjos, Anna. "How to Invest Abroad, American Depositary Receipts Help Simplify Matters," *Barron's* (July 24, 1978), p. 9

Rosenthal, Leonard. "An Empirical Test of the Efficiency of the ADR Market," *Journal of Banking and Finance* (March, 1983), pp. 17-29

Senchack, A. and W. Beedles. "Is Indirect Diversification Desirable?", *Journal of Portfolio Management* (May, 1980), pp. 49-57

Solnik, Bruno H. "Why Not Diversify Internationally?", *Financial Analysts Journal* (July-August, 1974), pp. 48-54.

SECTION V

Investors in International Portfolios

CHAPTER TWENTY-SIX

GAVIN DOBSON attended Gordonstown School in Scotland, followed by Dundee University where he gained an M.A. specializing in economics, and Edinburgh University, where he gained an LL.B. He qualified as a solicitor in Edinburgh in 1976, then moved to London to work in the International Corporate Finance department of Kleinwort Benson. In 1980, he joined Murray Johnstone and moved to Chicago to start a joint venture with Kemper Financial Services. He has been Vice President of Kemper-Murray Johnstone International since its inception in 1980 and he is involved in investing over $500 million of international assets for its U.S. clients, including pension funds, a foundation, insurance companies, and the Kemper International Fund.

INTERNATIONAL INVESTING BY INDIVIDUAL INVESTORS

Gavin Dobson
Vice President
Kemper-Murrary Johnstone International
Chicago, Illinois

INTRODUCTION

This chapter develops the proposition that the principles behind General Motors' need to invest their pension assets overseas apply in equal measure to a personal portfolio.

The chapter is divided into four major sections. It begins with the discussion of the case for international investing, focusing on currency factors, the power of international diversification and fixed income investments versus equity shares. The impediments to direct investment abroad by individual investors are covered in the treatment of direct investing overseas. Topics include market dealing procedures, taxation, transaction costs, information costs and lot sizes. Next, examination of American Depository Receipts (ADRs) indicates how ADRs can be employed by international investors and lists their advantages and disadvantages. Finally, the discussion of Mutual Funds and Investment Trusts examines the role of pooled funds and assesses the distinctions between global and international mutual funds. Regionally-targeted funds and single country funds also are described and evaluated as to their prospective interest to individual investors.

SECTION I

The Case for International Investing

The reasons for investing overseas are the same as for investing anywhere—to make money, to diversify, to beat your chosen U.S. benchmark and to discover new opportunities.

Perhaps the most remarkable thing is how few individuals in the United States invest in foreign markets despite a coral reef of evidence, accruing year after year, showing that you can make more money, diversify effectively, regularly beat your chosen U.S. benchmark and continually discover new pastures, all by investing overseas. Clearly, international investing is a completely valid asset class, alongside U.S. real estate, U.S. equities, U.S. bonds and U.S. cash. A well-rounded portfolio *must* include foreign securities to achieve superior long-term performance and diversification.

Table 1 shows the stock market capitalizations of the seventeen major stockmarkets around the world in June 1986. The left column lists the total market capitalizations in billions of U.S. dollars. The middle column contains the percentage that each market represents of the total in mid-1986, and the right column shows what those percentages were in December 1970.

Table 2 lists annualized returns for various nations' equity markets. In the 1960's, it was mainly the "resource" markets, such as Australia, Canada, Switzerland and Norway, that did well. In the 1970's, the United States only managed to beat Spain, Italy and Australia. Throughout the period, Japan was climbing to dominance as a global economy, as reflected in strong stockmarket performance.

In the 1980-85 period, Europe's markets did well, due to economic recovery and the political shift to center-right policies.

CURRENCY

Currency is an oft-cited reason for not investing overseas. One of the most common questions that investors ask is, "What about cur-

TABLE 1 STOCK MARKET CAPITALIZATIONS JUNE 1986

	U.S.$ BILLION	% OF TOTAL	1970 %
USA	2291	44.7	66.3
JAPAN	1429	27.9	4.6
UK	426	8.3	8.2
GERMANY	201	3.9	3.0
CANADA	158	3.1	6.1
FRANCE	119	2.3	2.5
ITALY	101	2.0	1.1
SWITZERLAND	98	1.9	1.0
AUSTRALIA	64	1.3	2.8
NETHERLANDS	62	1.2	1.2
SWEDEN	45	0.9	0.5
HONG KONG	38	0.7	0.2
SINGAPORE/ MALAYSIA	29	0.6	0.2
BELGIUM	29	0.6	0.7
DENMARK	15	0.3	0.1
NORWAY	10	0.2	0.1
AUSTRIA	5	0.1	0.1
TOTAL	5120	100.0%	100.0%

Source: Morgan Stanley—Capital International

rency risk?'' The reply should always be: ''Every risk has a corresponding opportunity.'' Table 3 demonstrates that clearly. In the December 1980-84 period, the dollar rose against every key currency. International investing was an uphill struggle, though overseas investors would still have come out on top. In 1985, the dollar fell sharply and U.S. investors with assets in foreign currencies captured a terrific windfall.

International investors should realize there is also currency risk throughout the S&P 500. A look at any company in the United States that manufactures tradeable goods, imports commodities or provides a competitive service will show a currency vulnerability/sensitivity in its results. When the dollar was very strong in 1984, Boeing found

TABLE 2 ANNUALIZED COUNTRY INDEX TOTAL RETURNS
Equity Markets—US Dollars
Percent per year

	1960-70	1970-80	1980-85	1985
UNITED STATES	3.99	8.02	14.9	32.7
CANADA	4.97	11.90	5.5	15.9
UNITED KINGDOM	2.50	11.02	13.0	52.9
GERMANY	1.25	8.79	24.5	139.2
FRANCE	(0.65)	9.17	13.1	85.5
SWITZERLAND	5.34	10.81	15.5	107.4
HOLLAND	2.09	11.54	NA	NA
BELGIUM	0.56	13.03	22.6	84.1
ITALY	(1.59)	0.32	14.1	133.7
SWEDEN	2.43	8.09	26.4	58.3
NORWAY	5.43	14.43	13.4	69.9
DENMARK	(0.17)	12.13	17.8	61.3
SPAIN	11.11	(0.14)	10.2	56.5
AUSTRIA	3.84	11.89	13.3	177.4
JAPAN	5.55	18.42	19.3	43.4
HONG KONG	28.64	0.1	51.6	
SINGAPORE	22.84	(5.9)	(22.2)	
AUSTRALIA	6.45	7.93	(0.6)	20.9
EAFE*	2.63	11.30	15.7	56.9
CAPITAL INT'L WORLD INDEX	3.87	8.68	14.8	41.8
RELATIVE POSITION OF U.S.A.	7/18	15/18	8/18	15/18

*Europe, Australia & Far East Index (EAFE)
Source: Frank Russell

the European Airbus to be tough competition. By mid-1986, the European currencies had risen over 30% against the dollar and Boeing could sell more competitively again in world markets. To single out foreign investing as too dangerous because of currency risk is unrealistic, since currency risk and opportunity lie everywhere. There are also ways of hedging foreign stock portfolios against a rise in the dollar. Investors can hedge forward in the interbank

TABLE 3 EXCHANGE RATE CHANGES AGAINST THE U.S. DOLLAR

	12/1980–12/1984 4 YR. % CHANGE	1985 ANNUAL CHANGE %
CANADA	(2.6)	(5.6)
MEXICO	(43.5)	(54.3)
UNITED KINGDOM	(16.5)	24.4
GERMANY	(11.1)	27.9
FRANCE	(17.1)	27.6
SWITZERLAND	(9.1)	25.3
BELGIUM	(15.9)	26.0
ITALY	(16.7)	15.0
SWEDEN	(16.4)	18.3
NORWAY	(13.1)	19.8
DENMARK	(14.5)	25.7
AUSTRIA	(10.9)	27.8
NETHERLANDS	(11.9)	28.3
JAPAN	(5.1)	25.1
HONG KONG	(10.1)	0.2
SINGAPORE	(1.1)	3.5
AUSTRALIA	(8.5)	(17.4)

Source: Frank Russell

market, buy futures or write options on the major currencies. There are many strategies available to protect a portfolio from negative currency swings. For example, many foreign companies do well when the dollar is strong, so an equity investor can buy shares in Japanese and German exporters to profit from a weakening of the dollar against these currencies.

DIVERSIFICATION

The Beta coefficients of the key markets against the S&P 500 in the ten years to December 31, 1985, provide a measure of the diversification power of foreign investing. Table 4 reveals that most of

TABLE 4 WORLD EQUITY MARKETS VS. S&P 500
The Beta of Foreign Stock Indices Relative to the S&P 500

TEN YEARS ENDING DECEMBER 31, 1985

	Beta Coefficients 10 Yrs. Based on quarterly observations
CANADA	1.123
MEXICO	0.608
UNITED KINGDOM	0.572
GERMANY	0.686
FRANCE	0.628
SWITZERLAND	0.900
BELGIUM	0.710
ITALY	0.735
SWEDEN	0.796
NORWAY	0.869
DENMARK	0.662
SPAIN	0.271
AUSTRIA	0.746
NETHERLANDS	0.886
JAPAN	0.541
HONG KONG	1.176
SINGAPORE	0.725
AUSTRALIA	0.687
SOUTH AFRICAN GOLD MINES	1.000
EUROPE, AUSTRALIA & FAR EAST INDEX (EAFE)	0.624

Source: Frank Russell

the key foreign markets have a low Beta coefficient, meaning that a slice of foreign stocks in a U.S. portfolio would have significantly reduced the volatility of that portfolio over a ten-year period.

FIXED INCOME INVESTING

Investing in foreign bonds also can be a lucrative way of obtaining an overseas position. As with equities, there are times when foreign bond markets can offer superior total returns. Currency has a more direct impact on these returns than with equities, since both the instruments and the yield are strongly governed by the foreign currency. Some foreign equities, on the other hand, will actually benefit from a strong dollar. For example, German or French exporting companies will have increased earnings from their U.S. sales, so margins will tend to improve. Foreign currency bonds belonging to U.S. holders will fall rapidly as the dollar rises.

Table 5 shows the dollar-adjusted performance of various bond markets around the world. During the period of dollar ascendancy (1982-1984), it was generally preferable to remain in dollar bonds. However, even in those years there were some competitve alternatives to U.S. bonds. In 1982, Canadian Governments showed superior total returns, as did Japanese Governments, Eurobonds and Samurai bonds in 1983. Only in 1984 were U.S. bonds unequivocally superior to other bond markets.

The impact of the falling dollar in 1985 and 1986 led to some highly competitive returns in foreign markets. All categories of bonds in Germany, Japan, the United Kingdom, Switzerland, France and the Netherlands outperformed the U.S. bond indices (see Table 5).

SECTION 2

INVESTING DIRECTLY IN FOREIGN SECURITIES

It is possible for well-organized U.S. individuals to trade directly on foreign markets, but it is an efficient proposition only for the very rich, who have the necessary economies of scale. This is true for many reasons, including:

1. The cost of intercontinental communications
2. Keeping a float position with foreign brokers
3. Foreign exchange transactions
4. Transaction costs
5. The difficulty of keeping up-to-date with each company

TABLE 5 BONDS
COMPOUND ANNUAL TOTAL RATES OF RETURN
United States Dollar Terms

	1980-84	1980	1981	1982	1983	1984	1985	6 mon. 1/81-6/86
UNITED STATES DOLLAR								
Domestic Bonds Govt.	9.99	-0.78	3.88	31.33	4.06	14.29	28.5	15.8
Eurobonds	12.70	4.59	4.45	30.47	11.20	14.71	20.5	8.9
Yankee Bonds	12.16	-1.28	0.63	40.10	10.07	15.89	27.9	10.1
GERMAN MARK								
Domestic Bonds Govt.	-3.19	-10.58	-8.40	14.09	-8.06	-1.03	43.4	17.3
Eurobonds	-3.49	-11.58	-7.01	12.54	-6.75	-2.99	42.3	15.8
JAPANESE YEN								
Domestic Bonds Govt.	9.13	22.92	5.47	3.28	12.55	2.69	37.3	31.8
Eurobonds	8.83	23.33	3.59	5.30	11.26	2.02	35.4	30.0
Samurai Bonds	8.78	26.42	-0.98	4.86	14.44	1.65	35.5	27.1
BRITISH POUND								
Domestic Bonds Govt.	3.01	28.90	-19.00	26.51	1.04	-13.11	40.6	21.5
Eurobonds	1.25	16.27	-13.43	11.77	4.09	-9.13	38.2	19.9
SWISS FRANC								
Domestic Bonds Govt.	-6.09	-9.61	-1.70	1.18	-4.82	-14.66	34.4	17.8
Foreign Bonds	-4.53	-9.17	-0.62	2.78	-3.80	-11.15	36.0	17.7
FRENCH FRANC								
Domestic Bonds Govt.	-4.95	-8.10	-16.06	1.88	-2.81	1.60	52.7	24.4
Eurobonds	-3.73	-6.66	-16.17	3.94	-0.09	1.76	46.0	18.6
CANADIAN DOLLAR								
Domestic Bonds Govt.	9.93	1.70	-2.43	35.73	9.57	8.80	17.5	10.0
Eurobonds	11.04	4.19	11.69	15.30	15.26	9.13	10.6	7.8
DUTCH GUILDER								
Domestic Bonds Govt.	-2.34	-5.78	-8.56	15.85	-8.61	-2.61	42.7	16.7
Eurobonds	-1.37	-4.35	-6.87	15.34	-6.17	-3.17	42.3	14.9
Foreign Bonds	-1.39	-5.83	-7.95	17.18	-7.14	-1.13	42.7	17.6

Source: Frank Russell

6. The inadequacy of on-line screen services and the cost of the services which do exist

Market Dealing Procedures

Market dealing procedures for equity transactions also differ widely from country to country. The following table describes the settlement procedures, commissions and taxes for dealing in some of the key markets. An individual would have to be familiar with these procedures, and be prepared to wire money to his broker, as the mails obviously could not be relied upon to deliver a check to Germany in two days, for example.

Market Dealing Procedures for Equity Transactions

USA

Settlement:	Five working days
Commission:	In general, commission varies with the share price and the size of the transaction. Typically, institutions will pay 0.3-0.6 percent and small investors 0.9-1.1 percent. However, all commissions are negotiable.

CANADA

Settlement:	Five working days
Commission:	In general, commission varies with the share price and size of the transaction. Typically, institutions will pay 0.3-0.6 percent and small investors 0.9-1.1 percent. However, all commissions are negotiable.

JAPAN

Settlement:	Four working days, excluding Saturdays.
Commission:	On a sliding scale from 1.25 percent on considerations up to one million Yen to 0.25 percent over one billion Yen plus a flat fee. Banks and brokers pay 80 percent of the basic rates.
Taxation:	0.55 percent on sales.

HONG KONG

Settlement:	Officially cash; two days in practice.
Commission:	1 percent
Taxation:	0.3 percent stamp duty; HK$5 transfer duty on sales, per board lot (usually 1,000 or 2,000 shares)

SOUTH AFRICA

Settlement:	Officially on each Tuesday, in practice against delivery or payment.
Commission:	0.85 percent plus 1/2¢ per share.

UK

Settlement:	On the Monday, 10 days after the end of

	the fortnightly account.
Commission:	1.65 percent on the first 17,000 pounds sterling consideration; 0.55 percent on the next 18,000; 0.5 percent on the next 115,000; 0.4 percent on the next 170,000; 0.3 percent on the next 600,000; 0.2 percent on the next 1.1m; * 0.125 percent thereafter.
Taxation:	1 percent stamp duty on purchases; VAT at 15 percent on commission (UK investors only). NOTE: In October 1986, *all* commissions became negotiable.

GERMANY

Settlement:	Two days; five working days can be arranged.
Commission:	Generally 0.5 percent for institutional clients.
Taxation:	0.08 percent courtage (stock exchange fee)

SINGAPORE

Settlement:	On the Tuesday of the week after that in which the transaction is executed.
Commission:	Officially 1 percent, often as low as 0.5 percent in practice.
Taxation:	0.1 percent contract stamp; 0.2 percent transfer stamp on purchases.

AUSTRALIA

Settlement:	Officially payment against delivery; usually two to five days.
Commission:	Commission rates are negotiable depending on the size of the bargain. On transactions up to A$150,000 investors pay around 1 percent; on larger transactions anything down to 0.5 percent
Taxation:	0.3 percent contract stamp.

NETHERLANDS

Settlement:	Normally two days, but flexible.
Commission:	1.5 percent on the first Dfl 5,000; 1.0 percent on the next Dfl 15,000; 0.7 percent thereafter.
Taxation:	Dfl 7.50 contract stamp duty.

FRANCE

Settlement:	For the end of the monthly account, or, for certain stocks for cash settlement, two days forward.
Commission:	0.65 percent on the first Ffr600,000 consideration; 0.43 percent on the next Ffr500,000; 0.325 percent on the next Ffr1,100,000: 0.215 percent on the excess.
Taxation:	Stamp duty of 0.3 percent on the first

	Ffr1,000,000, 0.15 percent thereafter.
SWITZERLAND	
Settlement:	Two days.
Commission:	0.8 percent on the first Swfr50,000 consideration; 0.7 percent on the next Swfr50,000; 0.6 percent on the next Swfr50,000; 0.5 percent on the next Swfr150,000; 0.4 percent on the next Swfr300,000 0.3 percent on the next Swfr400,000; 0.2 percent on the next Swfr1,000,000* NOTE: negotiable above SF2,000,000.
Taxation:	0.075 percent Federal tax; 0.015 percent state tax.

The fact that a significant percentage of U.S. institutional money invested abroad by U.S.-based money managers is not invested directly overseas, but through ADRs, should tell the individual investor that he should not risk this route as a way of foreign investing. Lastly, the individual will find that he is dealing with different languages and business cultures which are fraught with danger for the unsuspecting American.

TAXATION

Taxation is another consideration to be dealt with by individual investors. Table 6 shows the effective rates of withholding tax deducted from dividends paid to U.S. shareholders by companies domiciled in various countries.

The rates shown are the effective rates of withholding tax. In many cases, higher rates of tax are deducted in the first instance, but the difference can then be reclaimed under the terms of the appropriate double tax agreement. The total tax which the shareholder ultimately suffers on the dividend depends upon the tax laws in his own country.

TABLE 6 RATES OF WITHHOLDING TAX ON DIVIDENDS

Company's domicile	Withholding Tax % U.S. Shareholders
Canada	15
UK	15
Germany	15
France	15
Netherlands	15
Switzerland	15
Ireland	—
Australia	15
Japan	15
Singapore	—
Hong Kong	—
South Africa	—

FIXED INCOME

Individuals can buy bonds overseas on a low-denomination basis, but they will encounter problems similar to those faced by investors in foreign equities. The cost of communications, currency transactions, credit analysis and the inadequacy of on-line screen services in the United States for foreign bonds all militate against smaller investors buying overseas bonds. Denominations vary from country to country, and anything under $10,000 (equivalent) has expensive transaction costs. Although it is possible (for example) to buy a Belgian Franc 1000 bond, it is hardly worthwhile due to transaction costs. Although Eurobonds have no withholding taxes, many Eurobond prospectuses prohibit U.S. investors. Locally-issued bonds elsewhere generally suffer withholding taxes. In Japan, 20 percent is normally withheld at source for non-resident holders. In the United Kingdom, some categories of government bonds are exempted from withholding taxes for non-residents, and, following a U.S.-German tax treaty, non-resident Americans need not pay German withholding taxes. In other cases, withholdings on interest payments range from 15 percent to 30 percent.

SECTION 3

AMERICAN DEPOSITORY RECEIPTS (ADRs)

The ADR is a more satisfactory way for the individual American to buy foreign equities. There are over 500 foreign companies listed in ADR form, representing many of the major international blue chips.

WHAT IS AN ADR? An ADR is a certificate issued by a U.S. depository (generally a bank) which evidences the ownership of a foreign security held by the bank on behalf of the ADR holder. They are negotiable receipts traded on the NYSE, American Stock Exchange or Over-The-Counter markets certifying that a stated number of shares of a foreign company have been deposited with the U.S. depository's overseas branch or a designated sub-custodian. ADRs are interchangeable with such shares and serve as a receipt of ownership.

ADRs can either represent the underlying shares on a one-for-one basis (for example, one Allied Lyons (United Kingdom) share equals one ADR). Or they can represent a multiple or fraction of underlying shares, such as South Pacific Petroleum (Australia), where two underlying shares make up one ADR.

The advantages of ADRs are:

- The time involved in buying and selling the security is shortened, since the transfer of the ADR on the depository's books is all that is necessary. When the ADR owner sells, he merely delivers the endorsed ADR to the depository, which telexes the foreign custodian to release the shares to the transferee.
- Dividends are paid in U.S. dollars and the depository takes care of the foreign exchange transactions.

- Certificates are in English and subject to U.S. transfer regulations. A holder does not need to worry about settlement procedures overseas—these are dealt with by the depository.
- The depository must keep ADR holders informed of recapitalization plans, stock exchange offers and noting issues pertaining to the underlying shares.
- Liquidity—it is fairly common to see companies like Jaguar or Batus with high daily trading volume alongside leading U.S. stocks. The institutional and private following of foreign stocks by Americans is creating a large, liquid market in the United States.

There are also some disadvantages, such as:

- Cost—an investor pays a brokerage fee to his own broker, a fee to the depository and sometimes a fee to the foreign custodian. Each issuing bank has its own fee schedule, but the table below is quite typical of the cost of buying ADRs:

    1. The \$2—\$3—\$4 basis:
       \$2 per 100 when selling at \$5.00 or less
       \$3 per 100 when selling between \$5.01 and \$10.00
       \$4 per 100 when selling over \$10.00.

    2. The \$3—\$4—\$5 basis: as above, but scaled up to provide a higher return to the bank and a higher cost to the investor.

    There are often other charges, such as telex costs, stamp duties, and transfer and stock splitting fees which may be appropriate.

- Many foreign companies with ADRs tend to be the large international blue chips whose rapid growth phase has already passed. A listing on a U.S. exchange is often done to give the company access to U.S. capital markets rathar than to give shareholders the benefit of a superior investment.

SECTION 4

POOLED FUNDS

Foreign pooled funds are arguably the best and most efficient way for individual U.S. investors to go overseas. They take care of all the administration, currency, country allocations, withholding tax and the extra dimensions involved in foreign investing. A significant number of buyers of these funds are sophisticated people who would not normally use mutual funds, but who recognize that this is the most efficient access to foreign markets.

There are three broad categories of pooled funds that an individual investor can buy for international investment purposes: Global Mutual Funds, International Mutual Funds and Regionally Targeted Funds.

GLOBAL MUTUAL FUNDS

A global fund is one which can invest anywhere in the world, including the United States. In mid-1986, there were twenty registered mutual funds with a global objective. Table 7 shows many of the fund groups now offering global funds.

Perhaps the doyen of global funds is the Templeton Growth Fund. It was launched in 1954 and has always had the objective of finding bargains anywhere in the world. From November 29, 1954, to April 30, 1986, the fund produced a total return of 4,586 percent, compared with a Dow Jones Index return of 359 percent over the same period. As an illustration of how Templeton manages its assets actively, Table 8 shows two random allocations in 1981 and 1986.

The main advantage of a global fund is that its managers do all the country allocating for its shareholders, making it relatively safe for an investor to put a higher percentage of his assets into such a fund—providing, of course, that the fund's managers are allocating assets effectively. Some funds have a front-end commission that

TABLE 7 GLOBAL MUTUAL FUNDS

Below $100 Million	6/30/86 Size $ Millions	Commission	12 Month Performance to July 31, 1986
Alliance Global	$3	Yes	*
First Investors Int'l	$33	Yes	22.57%
GAM Global	$10	No	*
J. Hancock Global	$53	Yes	46.16
Principal World	$5	Yes	33.80
World Trends	$43	Yes	*

Above $100 Million	6/30/86 Size $ Millions	Commission	12 Month Performance to July 31, 1986
Dean Witter World Wide	$326	No	53.26%
Mass. Financial Int'l Bonds	$118	Yes	$40.25
Merrill Lynch Int'l Holdings	$282	Yes	46.59
New Perspective Fund	$865	Yes	31.27
Oppenheimer AIM	$379	Yes	70.97
Paine Webber Atlas	$218	Yes	66.54
Prudential-Bache Global	$300	No	64.41
Putnam International	$322	Yes	67.31
Shearson Global	$295	Yes	50.16
Templeton Global I	$321	Yes	24.13
Templeton Global II	$521	Yes	18.28
Templeton Growth	$1781	Yes	17.71
Templeton World	$3208	Yes	20.71
United Int'l Growth	$189	Yes	45.17

* - Funds not existing for a full twelve months.

Source: Lipper Analytical Services

Note: The growth of assets in the global category has been strong. Between 3/31/85 and 3/31/86, assets in global funds rose from $4986 billion to $8298 billion.

investors must pay. Templeton Growth, for instance, has a commission scale with a maximum of 8½ percent for investments under $10,000. GAM Global, Prudential-Bache Global and Dean Witter Worldwide, on the other hand, do not charge a front-end commission.

TABLE 8
ASSET ALLOCATIONS OF TEMPLETON GROWTH FUND

	1981	**1986**
Japanese Stocks	7%	15%
Misc. Bonds and Governments	10%	31%
U.S. Stocks	65%	27%
Canadian Stocks	11%	11%
Japanese Stocks	4%	2%
Australian Stocks	3%	14%

Source: Securities Fund Investors, Inc.

For longer-term investors, a front-end commission should not be a deterrent, but a full 8½ percent commission is arguably a lot of money to pay if the investor only plans to be in the fund for a short time.

Since the load funds are sold mainly through stockbrokers or financial planners, potential investors can contact their brokers to get prospectuses and performance history. Prospectuses for the broker-run funds, such as Prudential-Bache Global or Paine Webber Atlas, can be obtained directly from the relevant brokers.

INTERNATIONAL MUTUAL FUNDS

This group of funds invests exclusively outside the United States, and can invest in all of the non-U.S. markets. The leading international funds are shown in Table 9.

International funds also experienced strong asset growth in the twelve months from March 31, 1985 to March 31, 1986, and as a group they grew from $1320 billion to $4442 billion under management. As with global funds, the style of management of international funds varies from manager to manager. The portfolio weightings of the Transatlantic Fund and Kemper International Fund at December 31, 1985, are given in Table 10.

In this instance, the Kemper International Fund concentrated holdings in fewer countries than the Transatlantic Fund. At other times

TABLE 9 INTERNATIONAL MUTUAL FUNDS

Below $100 Million	$ Millions	Commission	12 Month Performance to July 31, 1986
FT International	$89	No	93.48
GAM International	$23	No	76.13
Keystone	$67	No	55.97
Transatlantic Fund	$84	No	91.39
Above $100 Million	**$ Millions**	**Commission**	**12 Month Performance to July 31, 1986**
Alliance Int'l	$139	Yes	80.88
Fidelity Overseas	$1826	Yes	119.75
IDS Int'l	$183	Yes	79.82
Kemper Int'l	$152	Yes	76.06
Scudder Int'l	$639	No	66.32
T. Rowe Price Int'l	$625	No	77.87
Templeton Foreign	$179	Yes	28.28
Trustees Commingled	$650	No	45.90
Vanguard World	$353	No	*

* - Fund not existing for a full twelve months.

TABLE 10 PORTFOLIO WEIGHTINGS OF INTERNATIONAL MUTUAL FUNDS
December 31, 1985

	Transatlantic Fund	Kemper International Fund
Australia	1.6%	—
Canada	—	1.5%
France	11.7%	20.9%
Germany	8.9%	23.5%
Hong Kong	3.7%	4.9%
Italy	4.2%	0.3%
Japan	25.9%	18.6%
Mexico	3.7%	—
Netherlands	10.8%	8.5%
Sweden	2.7%	—
Switzerland	10.2%	13.4%
U.K.	15.4%	4.6%
Cash	1.2%	3.8%

the Kemper International Fund has had a wider distribution of assets, but the managers decided to significantly overweight fewer countries in 1985.

An exceptional international fund is the Massachusetts Financial International Trust Bond Fund. This $130 million fund currently is the only major mutual fund investing purely in international bonds. It is a total return fund that has shown an annualized 17.01 percent in performance from inception in 1981 to July 31, 1986. As with equities, international bond markets now represent an increasing percentage of the total capitalization (47.4 percent non-U.S.), and this fund aims to invest in those markets. The managers have a policy of investing only in Government Guaranteed bonds, supranationals, or U.S. corporate bonds issued in foreign currencies. At end-July 1986, the fund's assets were invested as shown in Table 11.

The biggest advantage of these international funds is that the investor knows that at all times his assets are invested outside the U.S. As discussed earlier, investors can significantly reduce the Beta of their portfolios by investing overseas. Investing in global funds may not provide adequate diversification, as investors might discover that half or more of their portfolios are invested in the United States. International funds, with a broad mix of assets in many countries, are a safe way of taking advantage of foreign markets and ensuring

TABLE 11 CURRENCY ALLOCATION OF MASSACHUSETTS FINANCIAL INTERNATIONAL TRUST BOND FUND
July 31, 1986

Deutschmark Bonds	50%	
Yen Bonds	20%	
Sterling Bonds	5%	(Hedged into Deutschmark)
Australian Bonds	5%	
New Zealand Bonds	5%	
ECU Bonds	2%	
French Franc Bonds	2%	
U.S. Currency & Bonds	11%	
TOTAL	100%	

This fund has a maximum front-end commission of 7.25 percent and can take minimum subscriptions of $250.

diversification. Typically, an investor might invest 15-20 percent of his assets in this way.

REGIONALLY TARGETED FUNDS

These are funds which invest in a single country or region. There are two categories: open-ended mutual funds and closed-end investment trusts. The open-ended mutual funds have a bid price that reflects the net asset value per share. The closed-end investment trusts are investment companies in which the investor buys shares. These shares can be at a premium of discount to asset value, but rarely reflect exact values (see Table 12).

Except for the Canadian fund, these mutual funds are well diversified within a region. For example, Table 13 shows the allocations of the Nomura Pacific Basic Fund on March 31, 1986.

TABLE 12 REGIONAL MUTUAL FUNDS

Open-ended Funds	6/30/86 Size $ Millions	Commission	12 Month Performance to July 31, 1986
Canadian Fund	$24.9	Yes	3.01%
GT Europe Growth	$6.4	No	66.33
GT Pacific Growth	$48.5	No	76.67
Merrill Lynch Pacific	$333.2	Yes	93.47
Nomura Pacific Basin	$44.9	No	93.49

(Note: Funds under $5 million have been omitted.)

TABLE 13 NORMURA PACIFIC BASIN FUND MARCH 31, 1986 PORTFOLIO

	% in Fund	% of Pacific Basin
Japan	85.8%	90.6%
Australia	5.6	4.7
Hong Kong	3.2	2.5
Singapore	1.1	1.7
South Korea	0.1	0.5
Other Assets	4.2	

Similarly, the G.T. Europe Growth Fund's portfolio of investments on December 31, 1985, had the allocations shown in Table 14.

These open-ended regional funds are inherently more risky to U.S. investors than an international fund, since they are less diversified. However, there are times when particular groups of markets do well relative to others, in which case, taking the regional route can be more lucrative. The main problem is that few U.S. investors know enough about international markets to make that judgement. Total assets in this group of funds were $343 million in March 1986.

SINGLE-COUNTRY INVESTMENT TRUSTS

Single-country investment trusts have had an uncanny knack of being launched near the top of a particular country's market cycle, when both the stock market and currencies looked their rosiest. This represents the highest risk category of overseas fund investing, since the investor is staking everything on a single economy and market.

This should be the last category of funds that people invest in overseas, since they do not provide the same degree of diversification as global or international funds. In the United Kingdom, this type of fund has been more widespread, as investors there traditionally have had to go overseas for investment opportunities, and the level of general awareness tends to be higher.

TABLE 14 G.T. EUROPE GROWTH FUND PORTFOLIO DECEMBER 31, 1985

West Germany	25.2%
France	10.0
Italy	6.6
Norway	9.8
Sweden	7.8
Switzerland	8.9
Netherlands	10.5
Fixed Income	4.1
Other Assets	17.1

However, there are some special cases worth considering. The Korea Fund is the only access that U.S. investors have to that market, although it sometimes trades at a premium of 40 percent above Net Asset Value. Similarly, an India Fund will shortly be available. Other single-market funds include those investing in Mexico, Italy, France, Japan and Australia.

CONCLUSION

There are numerous ways in which individual investors can participate in foreign stock markets. The complexities of direct investing can be overcome, but at this point, it remains an expensive and time-consuming proposition. The use of ADRs is relatively easy, since a foreign company that is quoted on one of the U.S. exchanges has to conform to U.S. accounting standards. But perhaps the most efficient way for U.S. individuals to participate in foreign markets is to buy a well-diversified international mutual fund, managed by a team of professionals experienced in the vagaries of foreign investing.

CHAPTER TWENTY-SEVEN

TIMOTHY P. PRINCE, is Chairman of the Board of Warner Prince Incorporated. He was educated in Australia and the United States in economics and geography. Between 1979 and 1986, Mr. Prince was responsible for the management of the $5.6 billion United Nations Joint Staff Pension Fund which is invested globally in stocks, bonds, and real estate. Prior to that he headed the investment departments of Capel Court Corporation (Melbourne), from 1974 to 1978, and Schroder, Darling & Co. (Sydney), from 1967 to 1974. Earlier, he was Senior Research Officer, Australian Consulate-General (New York); and Personnel Officer, Department of Foreign Affairs (Canberra).

AN INSTITUTIONAL INVESTOR'S APPROACH TO INTERNATIONAL INVESTMENT

Timothy Prince
Warner Prince Incorporated
Collinsville, Connecticut

INTRODUCTION

International portfolio investing is a new and fearsome concept for many American institutional investors. This is so despite the fact that many American corporations have been making substantial direct investments abroad for a large part of the century, particularly since the 1950's. Moreover, a sound theoretical justification for international portfolio diversification has been developed over the last three decades by people such as Markowitz, Sharpe, Tobin, Lessard and Solnik, and the actual experience of those few who have ventured into international markets has been generally favorable.

This chapter is intended to take much of the mystery out of international portfolio management and to provide guidance to institutional investors who are entering international markets. It deals with the subject pragmatically, based on the author's experience, particularly as Chief of Investment Management at the United Nations. This responsibility included the holdings of the United Nations Joint Staff Pension Fund (UNJSPF) of over $5 billion invested in a global portfolio of stocks, bonds, currencies and real estate. Since the mid-1960's the UNJSPF has followed a strategy of global investment, a strategy which was largely responsible for the fund obtaining above average rates of return, after conversion into U.S. dollars, with below average rates of market risk. The fund has also followed a strategy, supplemental to the main theme of global diversification, of investing in emerging markets. It has thus moved beyond the confines of the markets of the United States and the other OECD countries.

In attempting to provide a clear guide to international portfolio investment this chapter reviews the major advantages of a strategy which includes increased opportunities for return and reduction of market risk through international diversification and improved perspectives. It also examines the major disadvantages of such a strategy, including the perception of higher risk, limited marketability and dealing problems, shortages of information, foreign exchange risk, accounting differences, political risks and taxation. An attempt is made to put these disadvantages into perspective, recognizing that the perception of the disadvantages of international investment is often greater than the reality. A philosophical approach to international investment is outlined and the use of a combination of fundamental and technical analysis in decision making is described. Finally, a brief comment on the use of outside resources is useful in developing a unique approach to decision making.

THE ADVANTAGES OF INTERNATIONAL INVESTMENT

Many of the chapters in this book have examined in some detail the advantages of international investment. In addition, a very sound theoretical groundwork has been laid which demonstrates quite clearly that over time international diversification can provide higher rates of return at lower risk than investment in a single market. The question may linger, however, as to why this should be the case.

Increased Opportunity

A major part of the answer is that international investment provides a much broader range of opportunities than investment in a single market. This is true even in a market as large as the United States, which accounts for nearly half of the world market. An investor restricted to the United States is cut off, in effect, from more than half the available investment opportunities. It is useful to remember that even though the British capital market was the world's largest in the mid-nineteenth century, the British were avid international investors. They played a large part in financing the growth of the United States, the former British Empire countries and Latin America. They were well aware of the benefits of international diversification, even when Britain was experiencing significant domestic growth, but they were also well aware of the risks. Losses were suffered from time to time, of course, but on balance the gains from international investment outweighed the losses.

A broad range of opportunities exists for international investors because of the varying "comparative advantage" between countries. The concept of comparative advantage is simple: one country is more efficient at producing a particular type of good or service than another country. The reasons range from more abundant natural resources (e.g., Australia and Canada) to a more skilled and productive workforce (e.g., Japan and the United States). The country with a comparative advantage produces a particular good or service more cheaply than competitor countries and is therefore able to attract more customers. For the investor, it is important to identify those countries, and the companies within those countries, that produce particular goods most efficiently. Over the medium to longer term those investments should provide superior rates of return.

It is important to understand not only the concept of comparative advantage, but particularly that the advantage is not static. The United States, for example, is currently suffering from shifts in global competitiveness which have enabled the Japanese to achieve a significant position in the U.S. automobile market and to dominate the consumer electronics industry. The American investor would have been significantly better off investing in Japanese automobile companies rather than U.S. automobile companies over the last ten years.

More Market Inefficiencies to Exploit

Another benefit available to the international investor is a significantly enhanced ability to take advantage of market inefficiencies. These are found mainly in national securities markets that are not as well developed as those of the United States in terms of availability, quality and timeliness of information. While the case for strong efficiency of the U.S. market is not well established beyond the top two or three hundred companies, market efficiency is even less in most other world markets. Even though some countries have well developed individual markets that may be relatively efficient, there is no evidence that the world market as a whole is efficient. The wide differences in the quality and quantity of information provided in most of the world's markets, together with the fact that these markets are affected independently by various legal, cultural and structural factors, suggests that efficiency of the world capital market is low. Market inefficiencies provide the diligent researcher with significant opportunities.

Access to Fast Growth Economies

Increased opportunities also come to the international investor from investing in faster growing economies. In the United States the trend rate of GNP growth in real terms is a fraction over 3 percent per annum. In contrast, trend rate of growth in the Japanese economy over the last ten years has been 4.5 percent per annum and the trend for the OECD has been 2.8 percent per annum.[1]

Poor Correlation Between Markets

The benefits of diversification provide other advantages to the international investor. It has been well demonstrated both theoretically and empirically that over time international diversification will reduce risk and enhance return over that obtainable in a single market. The reason is that there is an imperfect correlation both between various economies and between various markets. In other words, when the U.S. economy is doing poorly there is a high probability that there will be other economies which will be doing well. This is due to a number of factors, including the substantial leads and lags within the global economy due to varying patterns of world trade. Also, governments do not all follow similar fiscal and monetary policies at the same time. The international investor has the opportunity to shift assets from a market that is approaching the limits of reasonable valuation to other markets which have been neglected.

The poor correlation between markets is shown in Table 1. The Canadian market has by far the closest correlation with the United States at 0.77, largely because the Canadian economy is dependent

TABLE 1 CORRELATION BETWEEN U.S MARKET AND OTHERS IN U.S. DOLLARS

	United States
Hong Kong	0.16
Singapore	0.38
Japan	0.31
Australia	0.53
U.K.	0.53
Canada	0.77
Switzerland	0.56
Netherlands	0.58
Germany	0.45
France	0.36
Belgium	0.33
Norway	0.47
Denmark	0.40
Sweden	0.37
Italy	0.17
Spain	−0.02

Source: Abstracted from Quantec *World Market Research Quarterly—First Quarter 1985*, as cited by Morgan Stanley *Investing Internationally*, undated.

on the United States to a considerable degree. The Netherlands has the next closest correlation with the United States at 0.55, which indicates that significant divergences in performance have occurred.

Improved Perspectives

Finally, there is the perhaps intangible advantage of improved perspective through the ability to compare and contrast developments in different economies and markets. This is especially valuable in an institutional setting. There is a danger, however, of taking this argument to an extreme by expecting that a particular development in one economy will necessarily be paralleled in another. Nevertheless, there are often broad similarities between developments in one economy and those in another which can be a useful guide to the international investor.

Furthermore, a reading of economic history suggests that an understanding of broad secular trends is an important aid to more accurately estimating future developments. Although the past is not a precisely accurate guide to the future, the observation that "those who do not remember the past are condemned to relive it"[2] is apposite. To use a somewhat different formulation, those who study only one economy in the context of the immediate present restrict themselves to a very narrow range of experience and therefore have limited guideposts to the future.

THE PERCEIVED DISADVANTAGES OF INTERNATIONAL INVESTMENT

It is not difficult to find arguments to support the *status quo* or to identify reasons to avoid venturing into new territory. There is a general reluctance, by institutions in particular, to undertake new ventures, and considerable ingenuity is displayed by those who would avoid risk at all costs. It would be foolish to argue that there are no risks in international investment. When the rhetoric is stripped away, however, investment management is risk management, *not* risk avoidance. The investor who obtains better than average returns is the one who takes sensible, well-appraised risks. The investor who avoids risk all together is doomed to below average results.

Higher Market Risk

One of the first arguments against international investment is the higher degree of volatility of returns (or market risk) in the international markets. Clearly, certain individual international markets fluctuate to a much greater extent than the U.S. market and many individual markets have a higher market risk than the U.S. market. The Hong Kong market, for example, has a much higher volatility of annual returns than the U.S. market, as shown in Table 2. While the market risk is greater, the rewards are also greater. This is demonstrated over the fifteen years to 1984, during which the Hong Kong market provided a total return of 17.1 percent per annum compared with 7.8 percent per annum for the United States. The main point, however, is that the low correlation of returns between the international markets reduces market risk while enhancing return.

Marketability and Dealing Problems

A widely cited disadvantage, for institutional investors in particular because of the size of their transactions, is the limited marketability and dealing problems in executing international transactions. This argument assumes that the institution does not have the intelligence or flexibility to adapt to difficult circumstances. It is certainly true that an institutional investor cannot place an order for $10 million of a particular security in the Australian market, for example, and necessarily expect to have the deal executed on the same day. That does not mean that such an amount cannot be bought, it simply means that thoughtful tactics have to be employed and that some patience may be required. It is particularly important that the international investor take the time and trouble to understand the peculiarities of dealing in each market.

TABLE 2 CAPITAL INTERNATIONAL INDEXES IN U.S. DOLLARS WITH GROSS DIVIDEND REINVESTED EACH MONTH-END

	Year-to-Year Change																Compound Average
	1970	1971	1972	1973	1974	1975	1976	1977	1978	1979	1980	1981	1982	1983	1984	% Change 15 years	Annual Rate of Return
Australia	−19.2%	− 1.6%	+ 21.1%	− 12.1%	−33.2%	+ 50.9%	−10.2%	+12.0%	+22.0%	+ 43.9%	+54.5%	−23.8%	−22.5%	+56.1%	−12.5%	+ 87.8%	4.3%
Austria	+11.5	+ 8.5	+ 37.8	+ 25.1	+15.0	− 2.9	+15.6	+ 5.7	+15.6	+ 19.5	−12.5	−20.7	−12.5	− 1.4	− 4.3	+124.8	5.5
Belgium	+ 7.2	+22.3	+ 32.1	+ 14.6	−14.3	+ 13.9	+ 9.6	+ 8.3	+28.8	+ 16.9	−19.0	−15.1	+ 9.6	+25.6	+13.3	+271.0	9.1
Canada	+15.8	+14.2	+ 33.2	− 3.1	−26.6	+ 15.2	+ 9.8	− 1.9	+20.6	+ 52.1	+22.6	−10.8	+ 2.5	+33.4	− 7.6	+294.3	9.6
Denmark	− 6.5	+10.2	+112.7	+ 5.4	−10.8	+ 23.9	+ 7.2	+ 2.3	+ 9.4	− 2.3	+18.0	+25.4	+ 2.9	+69.4	−35.4	+398.0	11.3
France	− 5.2	+ 1.6	+ 24.9	+ 3.8	−22.6	+ 45.2	−20.1	+ 6.0	+73.4	+ 28.8	− 2.1	−28.7	− 4.1	+33.2	+ 5.1	+149.0	6.3
Germany	−23.8	+24.7	+ 18.6	− 4.5	+17.3	+ 30.0	+ 6.7	+25.8	+25.3	− 4.1	−11.1	− 6.4	+10.2	+24.1	− 5.1	+185.9	7.3
Hong Kong	+45.4	+61.4	+162.6	− 39.1	−56.8	+111.2	+40.9	−11.3	+18.6	+ 83.9	+72.7	−16.0	−44.4	− 2.8	+47.0	+973.8	17.1
Italy	−17.6	−11.9	+ 14.8	+ 10.2	−33.5	− 8.7	−26.6	−18.7	+46.4	+ 17.4	+80.4	−10.1	−18.8	+ 3.9	+ 9.3	− 14.3	Negative
Japan	−11.4	+54.9	+126.9	− 20.2	−15.6	+ 20.0	+25.7	+15.9	+53.4	− 11.8	+30.3	+15.9	− 0.5	+24.9	+17.1	+990.2	17.3
Netherlands	− 6.6	+ 1.7	+ 29.7	− 4.8	−15.7	+ 50.3	+16.9	+16.4	+20.8	+ 19.8	+13.1	−13.8	+16.6	+38.4	+11.5	+413.7	11.5
Norway	+34.2	+18.7	+ 9.0	+128.8	−40.1	− 15.0	+15.1	−23.3	+ 6.6	+183.9	−18.6	−15.9	−28.2	+82.2	+ 0.9	+388.4	11.2
Singapore	− 3.9	+63.7	+218.5	− 32.9	−48.3	+ 63.8	+13.9	+ 5.9	+45.1	+ 28.6	+62.8	+18.3	−16.7	+31.7	−26.9	+890.9	16.6
Spain	− 3.7	+26.3	+ 41.2	+ 25.3	− 8.5	+ 0.1	−36.2	−34.3	+ 7.7	+ 5.4	+ 4.3	+13.1	−29.1	− 4.7	+41.7	+ 5.9	0.3
Sweden	−19.0	+36.9	+ 16.9	+ 2.8	+11.8	+ 21.2	+ 6.4	−21.4	+23.9	+ 2.6	+22.8	+38.7	+24.4	+50.3	−21.1	+380.1	11.0
Switzerland	−13.2	+27.5	+ 28.7	− 3.8	−12.5	+ 41.3	+10.5	+28.8	+21.9	+ 12.2	− 7.3	− 9.7	+ 3.5	+19.3	−11.1	+203.0	7.7
United Kingdom	− 5.8	+48.1	+ 3.9	− 26.0	−50.6	+116.0	−12.5	+58.3	+14.7	+ 22.3	+41.5	−10.5	+ 9.4	+17.4	+ 5.7	+282.1	9.4
United States	+ 4.8	+12.5	+ 17.6	− 16.2	−27.7	+ 35.8	+23.2	− 8.0	+ 6.0	+ 14.4	+30.0	− 4.1	+22.1	+22.0	+ 6.0	+208.9	7.8

Source: Based on Morgan Stanley Capital International stock market indexes and yields published on a regular basis in *Morgan Stanley Capital International Perspective* as cited by Morgan Stanley, *Investing Internationally*, undated.

Information Deficiencies

The shortage and lack of timeliness of information in most of the markets outside the United States is another frequently cited disadvantage, but it should not be a major problem to those with reasonable analytical capability who make an effort to understand the companies in which they might invest or the environment in which those companies are operating. This perceived disadvantage is, in fact, a cause of market inefficiencies which provide opportunities to investors who are diligent and perceptive enough to identify opportunities before they become widely known.

Exchange Rate Risk

Over one hundred years ago Benjamin Disraeli said, "The one thing that drives more men mad than love is the currency question." There is no doubt that foreign exchange risk is a very real concern, but it should be kept in perspective. For example, Bruno Solnik and Bernard Noetzlin have suggested that exchange rate risk amounts to only about "15 percent of the aggregate risk involved in equity investments and 50 percent of that involved in bonds."[3] The low exchange rate risk for equity investments is, to a large degree, the product of a very low or even negative correlation between security price and exchange rate movements.

To give an example based on an Australian copper stock, a depreciation of the Australian dollar against the U.S. dollar would result in a comparable depreciation of the U.S. dollar value of the investment, but this would be offset—and often exceeded—by the opposite exchange rate effect on the earnings of the Australian company whose revenues come mainly from exports and are denominated primarily in U.S. dollars. Depreciation of the Australian dollar would therefore lead to appreciation of the Australian dollar earnings of the company which, in turn, would be reflected in its share price. In such a situation it is not unusual for an exchange rate loss of 10 percent to be offset by a gain in the share price stock of 30-40 percent or even more.

Nevertheless, exchange rate risk can be managed. There are many tools available to hedge completely or partially the exchange rate risk if that risk is judged to be high or of increasing significance. Hedging by means of forward contracts, options or futures is sensible from time-to-time, as exchange rates have become highly volatile in the short term and subject to wider swings over the medium to long term. The day-to-day or even week-to-week fluctuations in currency values are random in the same way that very short-term movements in stock markets are random. The prime need is to make a reasonable assessment of the likely medium-term trend in the currency, which is less difficult than short-term market timing.

Finally, it is important to remember that the exchange rate impact on an investment can be positive as well as negative. From early 1985, exchange rate gains have been an important contributor to the superior returns in U.S. dollar terms provided by the international stock and bond markets.

Accounting Differences

Different accounting methodologies are frequently cited as a major disadvantage for U.S. investors. The average U.S. analyst should, however, be capable of applying the basic principles of security analysis to somewhat different circumstances and should have the necessary open-mindedness and flexibility to understand different approaches to the basic issue of valuation of a company.

A notable absurdity occurs in attempting to deal with the issue of accounting differences. This is the conversion of foreign company balance sheets and income statements into U.S. dollars. The argument in support of this practice is that it provides for standard comparisons between companies. The gross error is to overlook the fact that fluctuations in exchange rates are totally independent of the basic business activity of a company. The adjustment of a financial statement into U.S. dollars obscures and distorts the underlying trends of the business and also ignores the fact that foreign exchange rate gains or losses incurred by the company have already been taken into account in the local currency denominated statements.

The earnings per share of a French company, when translated into U.S. dollars, will fluctuate according to changes in the French franc/U.S. dollar exchange rate which may have absolutely nothing, or very little, to do with the earnings of the company. That company will then be seen as having significant fluctuations in earnings per share in U.S. dollar terms when it may have very steady growth in French franc terms. Similarly, the translation of a balance sheet into U.S. dollar terms will introduce fluctuations in balance sheet items which are totally unrelated to the business of the company and misrepresent its true position.

Political Risk

The issue of political risk assumes that there is no political risk in the U.S. market. The extremes of political risk such as revolution and/or nationalization typically are highly unlikely since most investors are likely to invest in politically low-risk countries such as those of the OECD. In practical terms, the assessment of political risk in major OECD countries such as Japan and Germany is no more difficult than assessing the political risk in the United States, and not much different in terms of magnitude. Once the rhetoric is ignored, a change in government in a democratic society rarely results in extreme changes of basic economic policy. A Democratic administration in the United States may be more inclined to promote social expenditure and a Republican government may be more inclined to promote defense expenditure, but the underlying political realities are such that the changes are likely to be marginal. Furthermore, changes of policy usually take considerable time to implement, with considerable warning as to the likelihood of implementation.

The most dramatic example of maturation of political risk in recent years was probably the election of the Socialist Mitterand government in France. Mitterand came to power with a program to socialize the French economy and proceeded to implement that policy. Shortly thereafter, however, the underlying economic realities forced a return to policies that were virtually indistinguishable from those followed by the former government. In fact, these policies were probably more free-market-oriented than those that could have been implemented by the former government. The days after the election of Mitterand actually marked the low point of the French market and represented an unusual buying opportunity.

The main points are, first, that governments reflect the underlying trends in an economy, they do not determine those trends; and second, politial risk is a two-sided coin, with change as likely to be positive as negative.

Taxation

Finally, there is the perceived disadvantage of taxation. Again the issue is more serious in perception than in reality. Although many governments impose stamp duties or transaction taxes on the purchase or sale of securities, these taxes are usually very low and fade into insignificance when compared with the market gains or losses that are being risked by the investor. Dividend or interest withholding taxes are often applied, but rarely amount to more than ten or fifteen percent of dividends, or about 0.5 percent of the funds invested. Although investors theoretically invest for a stream of dividends over time, most investors anticipate capital gains in their quest to maximize total returns. Income returns are not usually a significant part of the total return. While withholding taxes are an irritation, they should not deter international investment.

A PHILOSOPHICAL APPROACH TO INTERNATIONAL INVESTMENT

The key to optimizing returns from international investments, as with domestic investments, is the asset allocation decision. In the case of international investing, the asset allocation decision goes beyond the simple stock/bond/real estate/cash equivalents ratio to include within each of these main categories the allocation between various markets and the currency exposure.

The essence of our approach is to devote considerable resources to strategic decisions which concern appropriate asset allocation mix, including market and currency selection. Further, in a constantly changing environment it is essential to anticipate significant developments and to provide for and maintain the flexibility necessary to adjust the asset allocation mix accordingly. In following a relatively active allocation policy, a combination of fundamental analysis and technical analysis appears to provide the best results.

Although asset allocation is the main determinant of the total return, it is also important to devote resources to stock selection. Poor stock selection can offset much, or even all, of the gain from good asset allocation decisions. Furthermore, good stock selection, or value assessment of stocks, can be a useful tool in determining intelligent market selections. Careful stock analysis helps determine whether particular markets are undervalued or overvalued and thus confirm or call into question the broader asset allocation decision. It is therefore important to have a discipline in place which will enable reasonable cross-market comparisons of value.

THE FUNDAMENTAL APPROACH TO ASSET ALLOCATION AND STOCK SELECTION

The fundamental approach involves "top down," or macro, assessments of both secular and short-term political and economic developments as part of the determination of the relative attractiveness of economies and markets. The assessment of currency risk should also be part of this process. Secondly, an evaluation system for equities is required to facilitate reasonable cross-market comparisons of value in a "bottom up," or micro, assessment. Finally, the assessment and comparison of expected real interest rates and likely trends in nominal interest rates in the various markets is important for fixed-income securities.

The institutional investor clearly needs to devote some resources to these tasks. The private investor, however, is more likely to rely on research studies produced by stock brokers and other secondary sources. In an institutional setting it is best to encourage the existing domestic macroeconomic analyst or analysts to expand their horizons, particularly as a notable failing of many analysts has been a lack of understanding of the impact of the increasing internationalization of the United States on the domestic economy.

Desk Research is Important

The approach to assessing secular and short-term political and economic developments should be two-fold. The first phase of the preparation process is "desk research," which involves the assessment and synthesizing of a large volume of material published by a wide range of sources.

The sources available include publications from supranational organizations such as the United Nations, the World Bank, the International Monetary Fund, the OECD, the European Economic Commission as well as the central banks and finance ministries of specific countries. Although much of this material is too dated to have immediate value, the historical data can provide important perspectives on developing secular trends. Other useful sources of information include the commercial banks in various countries, local and international stock brokers and publications such as the *Economist*, the *Far East Economic Review* and the *London Financial Times*. While the listing of these sources may intimidate the neophite, it does belie the assertion that there is a shortage of information. The main problem is not a shortage of information; it is, rather, the ability to effectively sort through data to identify and separate the germane from the irrelevant.

Travel to Investment Centers

Desk research is the essential background for the next step of the assessment process, which involves visits to key policy makers, bankers, stockbrokers and company managements. Visits are an important part of the process of synthesizing information, and institutions should be prepared to fund a regular program. Government policy makers will rarely provide information that is not otherwise available, but it is important to develop an understanding of their thought processes and the issues that concern them. This helps form a judgment as to the sequence of likely policy developments. Visits to bankers, stock brokers and company managements also help develop an understanding of the subtleties at work within a particular economy and are an indispensible aid to understanding the approach of domestic investors to their own market. They enable the investor with an open and receptive mind to understand the important differences that exist between particular economies and markets. It is by comparison of strengths and weaknesses that the investor ultimately arrives at a judgment of the relative attractiveness of the markets available for investment.

Securities Valuation

An important part of a system of assessing relative attractiveness of markets is a valuation method for equity securities. A sensible valuation system also provides a disciplined framework for stock selection. We prefer a simple earnings discount model which is driven by expected growth in earnings per share for the next three years and price/earnings multiples that are related to norms that might be expected for particular stocks in their own market. The methodology used assesses companies in their own environment rather than according to arbitrary standards, and enables a reasonable assessment of relative values across markets. An important element in the model is the statistical phenomenon of regression to the mean: a stock that is priced substantially above its mean price/earnings multiple has a high probability of returning to and falling below its longer-term mean (or average) price/earnings multiple.

A three-year time horizon is used for earnings estimates because expectations are more likely to be realized over a longer period than over a short one. Three-year earnings growth estimates are likely to be more accurate than one- or two-year earnings estimates, but less accurate than estimates for five or ten years. Although the accuracy of estimates for the trend rate of growth is likely to be higher over five or ten years, the period is of much less relevance for investors who are geared to short-term quarterly or yearly performance targets.

Assessment of Bond Returns

Apart from being of value in cross-market comparisons of equity securities, an earnings discount model is useful in the comparison of relative valuations between fixed income securities and equities. In the assessment of fixed income securities emphasis should be placed on the expected real, or inflation adjusted, interest rate. The expected real interest rate depends primarily on anticipated inflation rates. The relative attractiveness of fixed income securities will depend on an assessment of the likely trends in interest rates and the likely movement in foreign exchange rates.

Exchange Rate Trends

The assessment of fundamental trends in foreign exchange rates is much simpler and more reliable over periods of two to three years. Over such periods, indicators such as purchasing power parity calculated on both wholesale prices and consumer prices is a reasonable guide to the equilibrium level of exchange rates. Similarly, trends in terms of trade become important. Since exchange rates became free to float in accordance with market forces in the early 1970's, fundamental analysis has become of less value for short-term assessments. This is largely because capital account transactions have grown to greatly exceed trade transactions and capital flows between countries are often short-term and even speculative. The result is that foreign exchange rates are now priced in a manner similar to equity securities. In other words, short-term fluctuations in exchange rates are now determined by a whole host of factors, including the intangible factor of confidence. In recent years, the technical analysts of foreign exchange rates appear to have a far better record of success than the fundamentalists.

TECHNICAL ANALYSIS

Academics and pure fundamentalists regard technical analysis as akin to witchcraft. There is no shortage of studies that prove that technical analysis has as much predictive value as reading the entrails of a goat. A spirited defense of technical analysis is not intended, however, our experience is that technical analysis can be an aid to intelligent decision making, if it is clearly related to sound fundamental assessment.

Timing of Decisions

Technical analysis can help with the timing of decisions arrived at on the basis of a careful assessment of the fundamentals. It can also provide an alert to changing fundamental trends in the short term as well as early warning of major trend changes. If fundamental analysis suggests that a particular security should be bought but a technical assessment suggests the contrary, a reexamination of the assumptions underlying the fundamental assessment should be made before making a decision. Conversely, if the initial fundamental analysis was negative but the technical assessment suggested that strength was coming into a particular market, a reexamination of assumptions would be in order before making a decision.

A number of technical analysis systems are available to international investors, and institutions can use these services or develop their own systems. Morgan Stanley Capital International, for example, publishes a chart book every quarter which also includes summary fundamental data. A sample is shown on the next page. Charting and technical analysis services covering specific markets are also available from a variety of sources.

USE OF OUTSIDE RESOURCES

Although an investment management organization may produce a considerable amount of in-house research, use of research from outside sources can prevent the problems that arise from inbred think-

HITACHI LTD JAPAN YEN

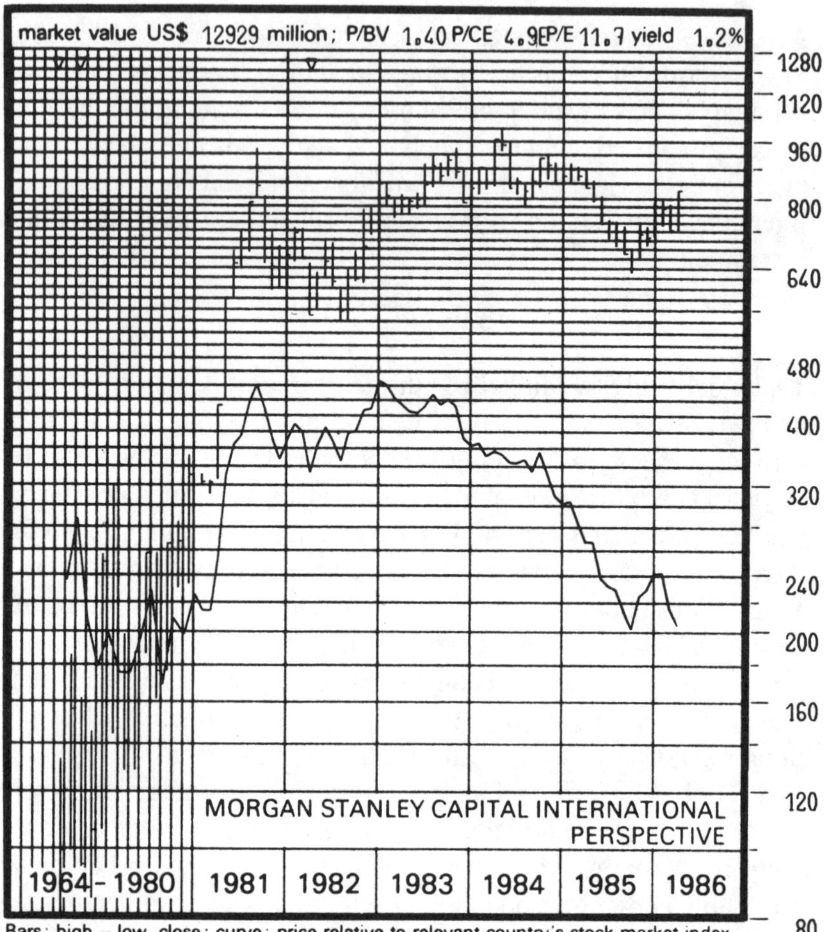

Bars: high — low, close; curve: price relative to relevant country's stock market index

ELECTRICAL & ELECTRONICS
HEAVY DUTY ELECT. MACHINERY, HOUSEHOLD APPLIANCES, COMMUNICATIONS EQUIPMENT
OWNS MAJORITY OF HITACHI CABLE, CREDIT, MAXELL AND METALS
6 MONTHS TO 30 SEPT 85:
SALES +3%, EARNINGS -14%
CURRENT DIVIDEND RATE: YEN 9.50
CAPITAL: 2.80 BILLION SHARES (YEN 50)

balance sheet at 31 MARCH 85 (YEN BILLION)			
fixed assets	1095	book value (BV)	1637
investments	393	other liabilities	323
other assets	267	long term debt	609c
current assets	3319	current liabilities	2505

year to: 31 MARCH	1981	1982	1983	1984	1985	
sales	3359	3699	3944	4367	5013	YEN BILLION
CE = earnings + depreciation	245	277	318	389	486	
earnings	129	137	151	167	210	
earnings	48.39	49.68	53.72	59.64	74.97	YEN PER SHARE
dividends	7.00	7.00	7.00	7.50	9.00	

Source: *Mogran Stanley Capital International Perspective*, April 1986. Reprinted with permission.

ing. In addition to publications by the United Nations, the IMF, World Bank, central banks of individual countries, commercial banks and stock brokers, various types of research services may be purchased from specialist organizations. These services provide research findings ranging from data bases of macroeconomic information to financial data on individual companies.

One of the major difficulties for investors is assimilating the amount of information that is available. The temptation is to read or study too much and to attempt to retain too many details. The essential skill to develop is the ability to separate the relevant from the irrelevant and to identify the major underlying trends. It is therefore important to avoid the trap of confusing quantity with quality and to focus on irrelevant short-term factors while ignoring the more important medium- to long-term trends. This is, of course, much easier said than done.

Warner Prince Incorporated publishes a weekly global technical analysis system based on momentum and trend analysis (see illustrations on the following pages). This service covers twentyone stock markets, twentyfour currencies, several commodity markets and a number of interest rate markets. The momentum analysis incorporates a number of different time series to provide assessments of short-term momentum, intermediate-term momentum and long-term momentum. Another feature of this system is formulations which help to make changes of trend quite definitive. A quantitative assessment is also incorporated. It provides a comparative ranking of the various markets from the most attractive down to the least attractive.

Momentum Rankings

The momentum ranking numbers and portfolio action recommendations shown in the preceding example are determined by an interpretation of the charts. Momentum ranking values are first assigned to the individual charts in the upper right-hand corner. They are then consolidated, totaled and averaged on the cover sheet to show the relative attractiveness of each market. The numerical scale of +5 to −5 depicts the slope of the trend line in a positive or nega-

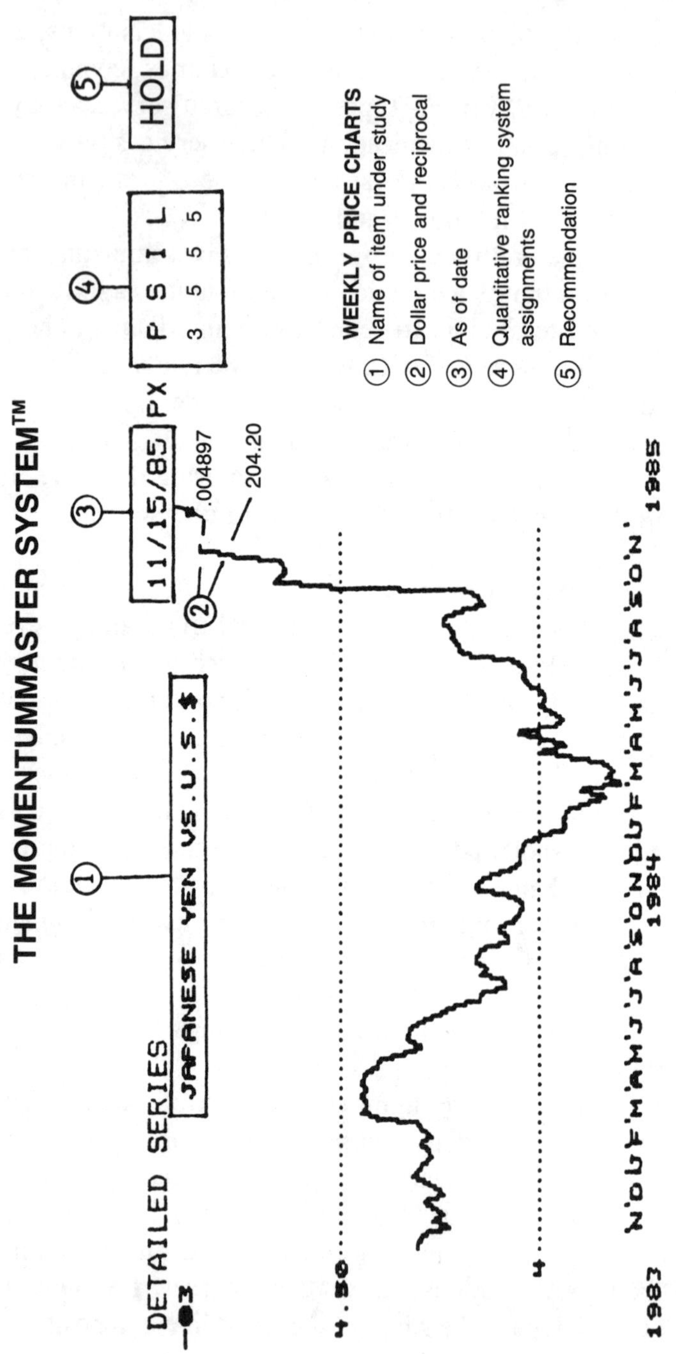
THE MOMENTUMMASTER SYSTEM™
DETAILED SERIES
-03
JAPANESE YEN VS. U.S. $
11/15/85
PX
P S I L
3 5 5 5
HOLD
.004897
204.20
4.50
4
N D J F M A M J J A S O N D J F M A M J J A S O N
1983
1984
1985
WEEKLY PRICE CHARTS
1 Name of item under study
2 Dollar price and reciprocal
3 As of date
4 Quantitative ranking system assignments
5 Recommendation

SHORT-TERM MOMENTUM

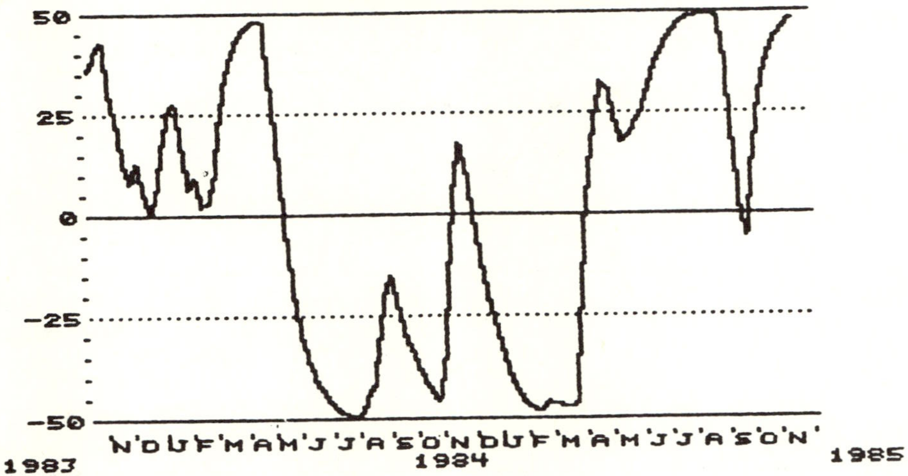

SHORT-TERM MOMENTUM

- Cannot exceed +50 or −50
- Sensitive to all but very minor trend changes
- Leads turns in intermediate-term momentum
- Reaffirms intermediate-term momentum
- Gives clear indications of price trend changes

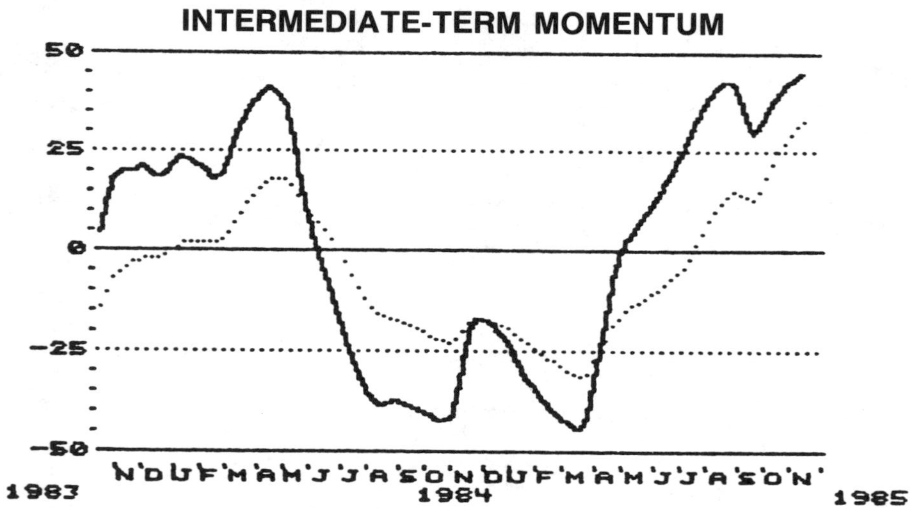

INTERMEDIATE–TERM MOMENTUM

- Cannot exceed +50 or −50
- Charts two series
  Fast (Sensitive)
  . . . Slow (Less Sensitive)
- Crossovers are important confirmations of trend.
- Failures to cross indicate trend failures.
- Above zero reference line is bull market; below is bear market.

HARMONICS

- Simultaneous turn ups/downs of short- and intermediate-term momentum often precede big moves.

tive direction. A value of +5 or −5 depicts the greatest rate of change and/or a major trend reversal. A value of zero indicates neutral momentum.

The coding for the ranking system is as follows:

P = Last week's price movement. Ranking is of very short-term changes in direction of price.

S = Short-term momentum. Ranking is of trend changes of at least short-term duration that may warrant action.

I = Intermediate-term momentum. Ranking is of confirmed short-term changes that may warrant more significant portfolio action.

L = Long-term momentum. Ranking is of the latest long-term month-end momentum chart which confirms long-term trends.

Portfolio Action Recommendations

There are nine recommendations that can be made. The definitions are as follows:

1. *Buy:* A "buy" recommendation is usually made only once in a market cycle upon a reversal from a very over-sold position.
2. *Buy More:* Maintains a "buy" recommendation and reflects the fact that both the intermediate-term and short-term momentum indicators are rising. If P is coded in a contrary direction with a large value, buying more with caution is warranted.
3. (a) *Stop Buy/Hold:* Usually reflects the fact that short-term momentum has turned down while the intermediate-term remains in an uptrend.
   (b) *Hold:*
4. *Sell 1/2:* Reflects the turn down (reversal) of both the short-term and the intermediate-term momentum indicators. If P is coded in a + direction with a large value, one might proceed to sell slowly.

5. *Hold 1/2:* Short-term momentum or price has turned positive with intermediate-term in downtrend.
6. *Sell Rest:* Both short-term and intermediate-term momentum indicators are in downtrends; there is no evidence of support near current price levels, and long-term momentum is peaking or is a downtrend.
7. *Sell Short:* Same condition as #6, but short-term indicator is now through zero on downside. The intermediate-term indicator is also expected to decline through zero.
8. *Stay Short:* Above condition continues.
9. *Cover Short:* The short-term indicator has turned up from an oversold condition. The intermediate-term indicator remains in a downtrend. N/L means do not buy yet (not long).

An asterisk on the left side of a recommendation indicates a change from the prior week's recommendation.

An asterisk on the right side alerts the reader to look for further amplification in comments at below right.

DECISION MAKING

The approach to investment decision making in an international environment is essentially the same as that in a domestic environment. Most important for an institution is a well thought out set of disciplines and adherence to them. The art of good investment decision making rests to a large degree on a reasonably accurate assessment of the future. The future is, however, by definition unknowable with certainty. Investment decision making is therefore largely related to managing the risks associated with uncertainty in such a way that the probability is high that downside is minimized and upside is maximized.

In an institutional setting there is often a premium put upon appearing to be knowledgeable, which encourages the recitation of trivial detail at great length. It is therefore incumbent upon the investor to ensure that questions asked are designed to establish the significance of developments. Similarly, it is the role of the investor to discourage an undue focus on day-to-day fluctuations in markets and encourage a deliberate, careful assessment of the basic trends.

The combination of positive fundamental and technical assessments gives a high degree of confidence that the judgment arrived at is correct. Similarly, the combination of positive "top-down" and "bottom-up" assessments gives a high degree of confidence in an action being contemplated.

Decisive action should be taken when the level of confidence in an assessment is high. When there is a low degree of confidence, or a high level of uncertainty in general, action should be taken to protect the value of the portfolio. Most people can make money in a bull market, but a much smaller proportion of investors manage to preserve a substantial part of their gains when the bull market inevitably turns to a bear market.

No individual has a monopoly on wisdom, particularly in investment management. It is therefore important to receive input from one's collegues and to subject one's views to constructive criticism. The best approach to investment decision making is a collegiate one which encourages frank discussion and exchange of views. In the final analysis, however, one decision maker must accept responsibility. Decisions should be made, however, only after hearing arguments on all sides.

CONCLUSION

This chapter has shown how international portfolio investors can increase investment returns and reduce overall risk. International investment offers a substantial broadening of opportunities through exploitation of differing comparative advantages between countries, market inefficiencies and faster growth rates in many economies. This chapter has also provided some perspective in assessing the perceived disadvantages. In particular, it should be remembered that many perceived disadvantages also offer opportunity and that the superior investor is likely to be the one who takes sensible, well-judged risks rather than a completely risk averse posture.

Because a substantial proportion of total return is accounted for by the asset allocation decision, considerable resources should be devoted to strategic decisions. In this respect, a combination of fundamental and technical analysis, applied in a pragmatic fashion, is likely to lead to the best results. Perhaps the most important skill to develop is the ability to review data from a wide variety of sources and to differentiate between the germane and the irrelevant. Finally, decision making is most effective when it is based on high levels of confidence. As in domestic investment, international investors will benefit from an open-mindedness that welcomes ideas from a range of sources and a determination to act decisively when the level of confidence in a course of action is high.

NOTES

[1]Source: Datastream International:
Japan: Economic Planning Agency
United States: Department of Commerce.
OECD: National Accounts on OECD Countries.

[2]George Santayana, *The Life of Reason*, 1905-1906.

[3]B. Solnik and B. Noetzlin, ''Optimal International Asset Allocation,'' *International Investing*, P. L. Bernstein. ed. New York: (Institutional Investor Books, 1983.)

CHAPTER TWENTY-EIGHT

MICHAEL R. ROSENBERG is Director of International Fixed Income Research for Merrill Lynch. The international fixed income research group publishes a weekly review of global bond market and currency trends (including recommended global portfolio strategy), a bi-weekly review of yield curve and yield spread developments in all major bond markets, and a monthly international economic and financial calendar.

Mr. Rosenberg joined Merrill Lynch in August 1984. Prior to joining Merrill Lynch, he was Director of International Bond Management for Prudential Insurance Company of America (1982-84). At Prudential he managed a $400 million multi-currency bond portfolio. Prior to joining Prudential, he was an international economist for Chase Manhattan Bank (1976-77) and a senior currency and international money market analyst for Citibank (1978-81).

Mr. Rosenberg holds a Bachelor of Science degree in accounting from the State University of New York at Albany, a Master of Arts degree in economics from Queens College, and a Ph.D. in economics from Penn State University.

Global Bond Portfolio Management

Michael R. Rosenberg
Vice President
Merrill Lynch Capital Markets
New York, New York

INTRODUCTION

Investment managers are increasingly taking an international perspective in their asset allocation decisions. Our purpose here is to provide globally-minded investors, particularly new entrants in the international arena, with general guidelines for setting up and constructing an international bond portfolio, and a framework for designing active global bond portfolio strategy.

Managing a global bond portfolio is more complex than managing a domestic bond fund. Variations in government regulations, market practices, settlement procedures, yield conventions, and secondary market liquidity means that the international investment manager must be thoroughly knowledgable of numerous institutional details. Moreover, transaction costs in the form of commissions, taxes, bid/offer spreads, custody fees, and settlement charges differ widely among markets, thereby requiring that the international investment manager have a thorough understanding of trading, regulatory and accounting practices, as well. Finally, and perhaps most importantly, the international fixed income strategy process requires that the investment manager evaluate the complex interaction of currency movements, interest rate changes, inter- and intra-market yield spread developments, and yield curve shifts in all of the major markets.

GETTING STARTED: SETTING UP AN INTERNATIONAL BOND PORTFOLIO

The first step in setting up an international bond portfolio is to determine the investor's financial objectives. Is the portfolio to be designed to maximize return or to minimize risk, or is some risk level tolerable, whereupon the portfolio can be actively managed to maximize return subject to a predetermined risk constraint. Once this is decided the international investor should select an optimal time horizon to make his investment decisions, both to achieve his stated total return goals and for performance measurement purposes. For instance, investors may select either a short-term investment time horizon so as to catch short-run swings in exchange rates and interest rates, or a long-term time horizon to capture the general trend in currency and bond market movements. To a large extent, the investment time horizon decision will be dictated by:

1) the general objective of the fund;
2) one's views as to the relative merits of aggressive, active and passive management; and
3) the time and resources investors can and will devote to the active management of the international bond portfolio.

In the initial stages of setting up an international bond portfolio, the investment manager should draw up a delegation of authority list. Such a list should indicate which foreign markets and credits will be approved for purchase. Based on an assessment of country and credit risk, as well as an assessment of tax and liquidity considerations, an approved list of issuers should be drawn. Names can be added or dropped over time as conditions warrant. For example, a risk-averse fund may choose to invest only in government and government-guaranteed issues. Another fund may approve the purchase of AAA and AA corporate issues, and so forth. The delegation of authority list also should detail what percentage of the fund's assets can be assigned to any single credit.

Once it is clear which markets and credits will be approved, the international investor should select a global custody service (usually a large international bank with an extensive overseas branch and correspondent banking network) to arrange for the delivery and settlement of bought and sold securities and foreign exchange, the collection of coupon income, the reclaiming of any coupon tax due the investor because of double taxation treaties, maintaining cash balances in various markets on deposit, and the receipt of comprehensive and timely reports on portfolio activities and the valuation of total assets under management. It would be wise for the investment manager to set up an internal bond operations unit to review all trade details (i.e., price, settlement date, and accrued interest), specify delivery instructions, and contact the global custody service to arrange for settlement and safe custody.

ESTABLISHING PORTFOLIO MANAGEMENT GUIDELINES

Once these housekeeping duties are taken care of, the international investment manager should turn his attention to the establishment of portfolio management guidelines for the distribution of the global bond fund's assets. These self-imposed asset allocation guidelines should assign minimum, normal, and maximum positions that can be held in any single currency bloc or market. The purpose of the guidelines is to underscore the desire for diversification and at the same time provide ample latitude for active management. For example, Table 1 below highlights the asset distribution guidelines for a hypothetical global bond fund. The guidelines define the proportion of the portfolio's funds which can be assigned to the major currency blocs: U.S. Dollar, German Mark, Japanese Yen, and British Pound.

TABLE 1 ASSET ALLOCATION GUIDELINES FOR STRUCTURING A HYPOTHETICAL GLOBAL BOND PORTFOLIO

Currency Bloc	Minimum Position	Normal Position	Maximum Position
U.S. Dollar*	25%	50%	75%
German Mark**	10%	20%	60%
Japanese Yen	10%	20%	60%
British Pound	5%	10%	55%

*Includes U.S. and Canadian Markets.
**Includes German, Dutch, Swiss, French, and ECU Markets.

The normal weights chosen should reflect the approximate relative current market value of each of the major markets in the total world bond market, or perhaps even better, reflect the relative liquiity and tradeability of each market. If investors use a widely followed external benchmark (or bogey) for performance evaluation purposes, they might want to use the benchmark's fixed weights as the normal weights.

The minimum and maximum guideposts should reflect the operational constraints facing the active portfolio manager. Within the limits defined by the minimum and maximum position guideposts, the portfolio manager should be free to allocate funds among currencies and maturities. Within the assigned portfolio constraints, the investment manager then can decide which currency blocs (and which markets and sectors within each bloc) will be overweighted, which will be underweighted, in which markets funds will be invested long, and in which markets funds will be invested short. These decisions can only be made by assessing what direction exchange rates and interest rates will take.

TOTAL RETURN ANALYSIS

Although management styles differ, it generally holds that the active management of multicurrency bond portfolios lends itself much more to a top/down rather than a bottom/up approach. That is, investors find that the rewards from choosing the right currencies and maturities to invest in far outweigh the rewards from individual bond selection. This is not to say that individual bond selection should be dismissed as unimportant; if done correctly, it can add valuable incremental return to a portfolio. What it does suggest is that the allocation of an investor's time and resources should be handled carefully so that those areas representing the greatest sources of return, as well as risk, receive the greatest attention.

A top/down assessment of total return outcomes in the various markets requires that the projected return on multicurrency bond investments be made comparable in terms of a single base currency. That is, from a dollar based investor's perspective, the projected returns on dollar and non-dollar bond investments must be translated in dollar terms first before a ranking based on dollar-adjusted performance can be made. In dollar terms, the principal sources of return on multicurrency bond investments are:

1) currency changes versus the dollar;
2) coupon income;
3) interest on interest; and
4) changes in local currency bond prices.

Mathematically, the total return in dollar terms on a non-dollar bond investment for a single period is shown below:

$$(1 + R\$) = (1 + LC) * (1 + \$) \text{ or}$$

$$R\$ = LC + \$ + (\$ * LC)$$

The equation states that the total return in dollar terms (R$) on a foreign bond investment equals the local currency return (LC), plus the currency gain or loss ($), plus a small product term which measures the impact of the currency change on the local currency return ($ * LC). For example, if the local currency return on a foreign bond is 10 percent and the respective foreign currency appreciates by 5 percent, the total return in dollar terms on the foreign investment would be 15.5 percent. The reason that the total return is not 15 percent (LC + \$ = 10% + 5% = 15%) is that the currency gain applies to both the principal and to the local currency return. Thus, in the example above, a \$1,000 investment in a foreign bond would yield a 5 percent currency gain on the initial \$1,000 investment (\$50) and a 5 percent currency gain on the \$100 local currency return (\$5). Totalling the different sources of return would yield \$100 (10 percent local currency return on the initial \$1,000 investment) plus \$50 plus \$5 to equal \$155, which amounts to a 15.5 percent total return.

The ranking of markets according to projected total return outcomes requires a careful assessment of what direction exchange rates and interest rates will take over the relevant investment time horizon. The interest rate forecasts should include projections of government note and bond yields for all relevant maturities in all markets. The initial focus should be on government note and bond yields, after which an analysis of key sectors could be made to search for incremental yield opportunities.

A straightforward procedure to derive total return projections is to first estimate what local currency returns will be along all points on each of the major government bond yield curves, then translate these local currency return forecasts in terms of a single base currency, such as the dollar. For example, in Chart 1, a projected local currency return curve (solid line) is constructed for a hypothetical foreign bond market. The local currency return curve plots projected local currency returns against each of the relevant points on the foreign bond yield curve. In the chart, the local currency return curve is drawn with an upward slope, indicating that the longer maturities in the foreign bond market are expected to outperform the shorter maturities. If the longer maturities were expected to underperform the shorter maturities, the local currency return curve would be drawn with a downward slope.

Translating local currency projections for each market into a single base currency such as the dollar is a fairly straightforward exercise, using the total return equation described above. Given one's assessment of the change in the relevant foreign currency versus the base currency, total returns in terms of the base currency can

CHART 1 INVESTING IN A HYPOTHETICAL FOREIGN BOND MARKET PROJECTED TOTAL RETURNS (IN LOCAL CURRENCY AND DOLLAR TERMS) ALONG DIFFERENT POINTS ON THE FOREIGN BOND YIELD CURVE

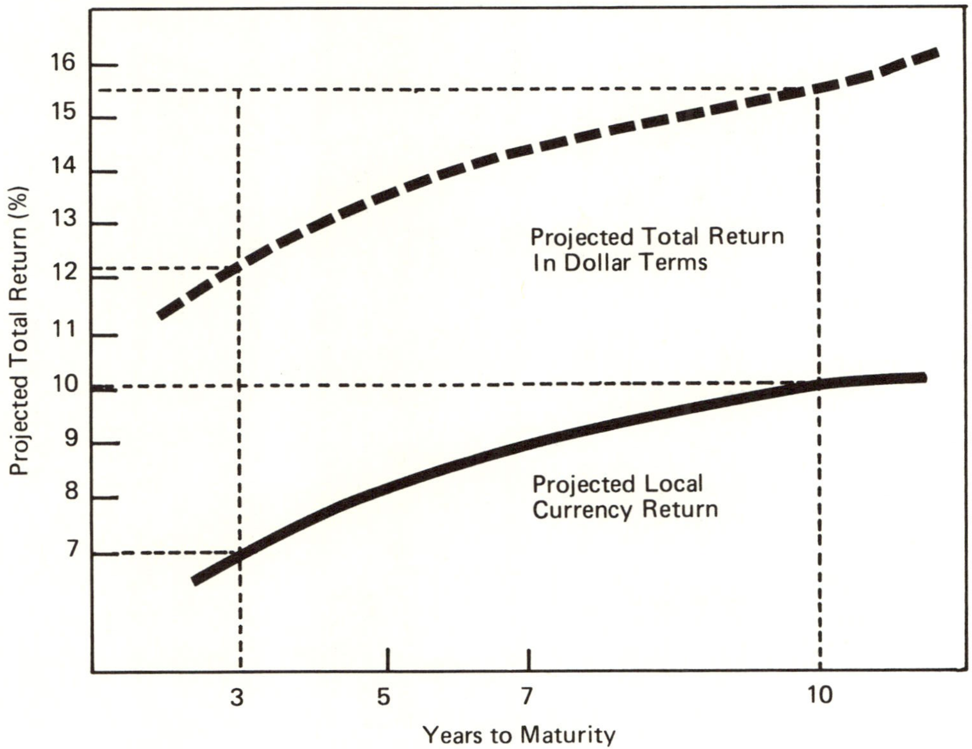

be calculated. In Chart 1, a projected total return curve in dollar terms for our hypothetical foreign bond market (dashed line) is drawn on the assumption that the relevant foreign currency is expected to appreciate against the dollar. The total return curve lies above the local currency return curve because the expected appreciation of the foreign currency versus the dollar raises the total return on the foreign bond in dollar terms to a U.S. investor. Had the foreign currency been expected to depreciate, the total return curve would instead have laid below the local currency return curve.

It should be noted that although the gap between the projected total and local currency return curves reflects the contribution of the expected currency change, the two curves are not parallel. As we showed in the total return equation above, the contribution of the currency change to total return affects not only the value of the principal but the local currency return as well. Thus, if the longer maturities are expected to outperform the shorter maturities in local currency terms, the contribution of the currency change will be more heavily felt at the long end of the yield curve. For example, assume that the projected local currency return on a hypothetical short-term foreign note is 7 percent and on a similar but longer-term foreign bond is 10 percent (see Chart 1). Then, if the relevant foreign currency is projected to rise by 5 percent against the U.S. dollar, the projected total return in dollar terms for short- and long-term foreign securities would be 12.35 percent and 15.5 percent respectively. Since the gap is wider at the longer end than at the shorter end, the curves are not parallel.

Once total return projections in terms of a single base currency are calculated for all markets, the international manager must begin the process of ranking the markets according to best expected performance. At times, the ranking process will be fairly straightforward—i.e., the best performing markets will be associated with the best performing currencies. For example, in Chart 2, hypothetical projected total return curves for the U.S. and two foreign bond markets are drawn. Foreign bond market #1 is expected to post the strongest performance in the U.S. dollar terms because its currency is expected to gain ground on the dollar. Foreign bond market #2

CHART 2 HYPOTHETICAL PROJECTED TOTAL RETURNS IN DOLLAR TERMS ON U.S. AND FOREIGN BONDS

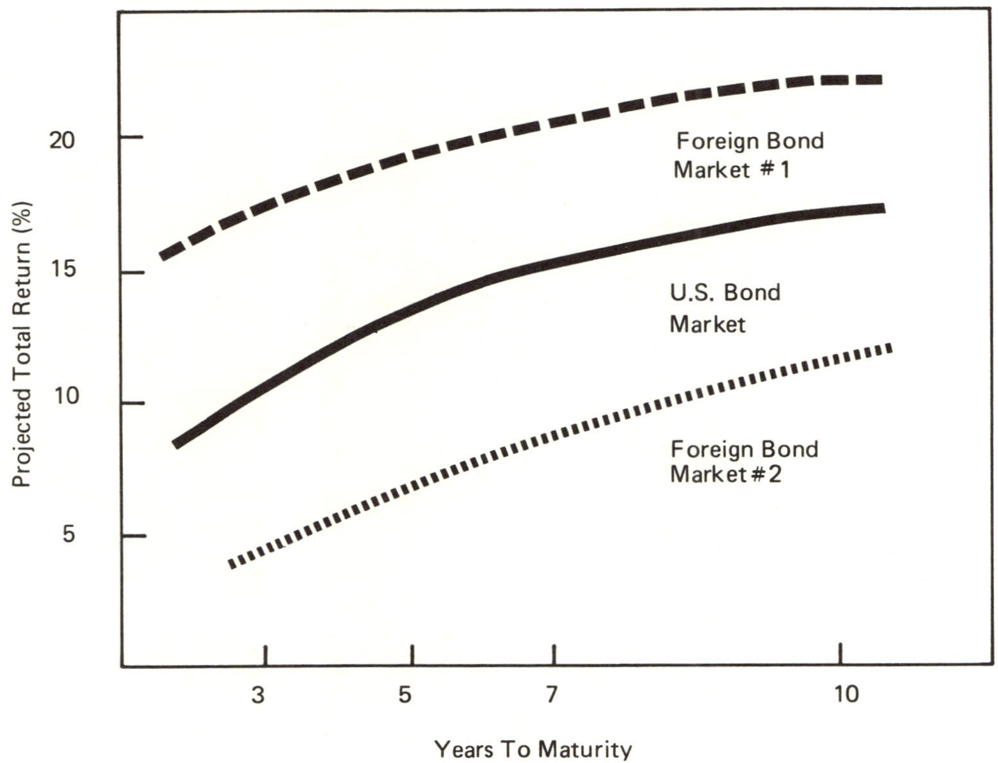

is expected to post the weakest performance in U.S. dollar terms because its currency is expected to lose ground to the dollar. Based on a simple ranking according to expected performance, an international manager would overweight foreign bond market #1, normally weight the U.S. bond market, and underweight foreign bond market #2 in his global bond portfolio.

However, there will be many occasions when the ranking process will be more complex. It is not always true that the best performing markets are associated with the best performing currencies. For example, in Chart 3, the projected total return curve for foreign bond market #1 is drawn on the assumption that the currency is expected to appreciate against the dollar, but the bond market in local currency terms is projected to experience a sharp setback. As a result, the total return curve slopes downward, with the highest projected returns being at the short end of the maturity spectrum. The projected total return curve for foreign bond market #2 is drawn on the assumption that the underlying currency is expected to depreciate against the dollar, but a strong performing bond market in local currency terms lifts the projected returns on longer-term securities. As shown, despite the weakness of the currency, long-term bonds in foreign bond market #2 are expected to perform favorably in U.S. dollar terms because of the strong local currency performance. In terms of establishing a ranking according to projected performance, the international manager would recommend overweighting the short end of foreign bond market #1 and the long end of foreign bond market #2, and underweighting the U.S. market.

MANAGING CURRENCY AND INTEREST RATE RISK

The precise assignment of portfolio weights in a global bond fund will be dictated largely by the investment manager's assessment of currency and interest rate trends. However, since there are significant risks inherent in any currency or interest rate forecast, prudent managers should ensure that minimum diversification standards are

CHART 3 HYPOTHETICAL PROJECTED TOTAL RETURNS IN DOLLAR TERMS ON U.S. AND FOREIGN BONDS

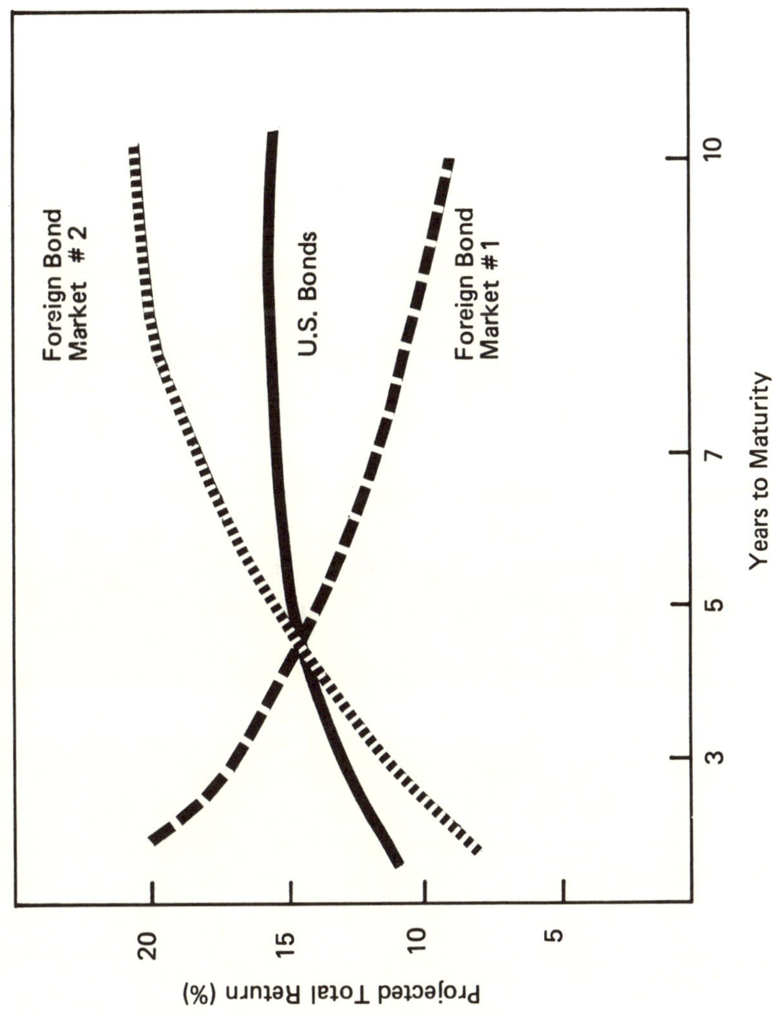

met—i.e., that all or most of the fund's assets are not allocated to a single currency or market. Instead, by requiring that the precise assignment of portfolio weights conform to prescribed asset allocation guidelines, the fund manager can be certain that minimum international diversification requirements are met and at the same time be confident that ample scope exists to overweight and underweight the various currency blocs and markets.

The establishment of internal portfolio management guidelines should be accomplished before the actual currency and security selection process begins. Table 2 is similar to Table 1 in that it highlights how internal guidelines can be structured for a hypothetical global bond fund. These guidelines define minimum, normal and maximum positions that a global bond fund can assign to each of the major currency blocs. The selection of appropriate portfolio weights for each currency bloc (and the markets and sectors within each currency bloc) along the min-norm-max spectrum in Table 2 should involve a two-stage process. First, based on an analysis of underlying economic fundamentals, the investment manager should rank each of the markets according to its projected total return performance. This ranking will dictate which range along the min-norm-max spectrum each market's weights should fall. Those markets

TABLE 2 GLOBAL BOND PORTFOLIO STRATEGY TO DETERMINE THE OPTIMAL ASSET MIX FOR AN ACTIVELY MANAGED GLOBAL BOND FUND

	Fundamentally Bearish	Fundamentally Bullish	
Currency Bloc	Minimum Position	Normal Position	Maximum Position
U.S. Dollar*	25%	50%	75%
German Mark**	10%	20%	60%
Japanese Yen	10%	20%	60%
British Pound	5%	10%	55%

*Includes U.S. and Canadian markets.
**Includes German, Dutch, Swiss, French and ECU markets.

projected to post the strongest total return performance will be assigned portfolio weights in their prescribed norm-max ranges, whereas those markets projected to record the weakest total return performance will be assigned portfolio weights in their prescribed min-norm ranges.

The second stage of the active management decision process should require the investment manager to integrate his longer-run fundamental view with his shorter-run technical view of currency and interest rate trends. Based on the investment manager's technical reading of market trends, he can determine how much to overweight or underweight a particular market. For example, if the fund manager's technical reading of the market confirms a generally bullish fundamental assessment, then the assigned portfolio weight to that market should lie closer to the maximum position along its prescribed norm-max range. Likewise, if the fund manager's technical reading of the market confirms a generally bearish fundamental assessment, then the assigned portfolio weight to that market should lie closer to the minimum position along its prescribed min-norm range. If the technical reading does not confirm the fundamental assessment, then the assigned portfolio weight should gravitate closer to the normal position along the relevant min-norm or norm-max range.

The only time a fund manager would recommend the maximum allocation to a particular market or currency bloc would be when he is both fundamentally and technically bullish on that market's prospects, and at the same time, is both fundamentally and technically bearish on the prospects for all other markets. Otherwise, the actual portfolio mix should fall somewhere between the prescribed minimum and maximum guideposts for each market.

Active international bond managers must constantly assess and reassess the fundamental and technical outlook for the major courrencies and respective bond markets. Total return projections should be reviewed on a frequent basis, perhaps monthly. This is because unforeseen developments may alter the fundamental outlook for currencies and interest rates, and also because the workout time required for a total return projection to be realized may have to be shortened or lengthened.

There will be many instances when new developments may contribute to a cloudy picture for the currency and interest rate outlook, and at such times the portfolio manager's mettle is truly tested. Fortunately, many avenues are open to the global portfolio manager to hedge short-term currency and interest rate risk. Futures and options markets are available in many currencies, and the investor can use such markets to temporarily protect a heavily overweighted or underweighted position in one or more currencies. For example, if a portfolio manager wishes to hold onto an overweighted Deutschemark bond position but is nervous about the near-term outlook for the currency (not the underlying bond), he can hedge the currency risk in the short-run by selling the nearby Deutschemark futures contract (or by selling Deutschemarks forward in the interbank forward market), or he can hedge himself by buying a put on the nearby Deutschemark options contract. There are fewer futures and options contracts available to protect against interest rate risk in all of the major bond markets, but the more volatile bond markets such as the U.S., U.K., Japanese and Canadian markets do have such hedging vehicles available.

For those markets where no adequate interest rate hedging vehicle is available, the portfolio manager is always free to alter the maturity/coupon profile of his portfolio. However, investors will probably find that those markets which do not offer adequate interest rate hedging vehicles also exhibit considerably less volatility than those markets that do. When markets exhibit little overall volatility it often proves expensive to adjust the maturity/coupon mix too finely. In most cases, it may be preferable to ride out any storms that do develop in such markets, rather than to try to fine tune the portfolio too exactly.

MONITORING PORTFOLIO PERFORMANCE

The only way a fund manager can accurately evaluate portfolio performance and design portfolio strategy is by monitoring his asset mix through carefully constructed security valuation and asset allocation reports. Table 3 shows a security valuation report for a hypothetical global bond fund. The report provides the fund manager with a snapshot of his security holdings, broken down by market. The report reveals both the local currency and dollar value of each security held, the purchase price and current price, the par value (i.e., the total amount) of each issue held, and the share that each security comprises in the total portfolio. Such a snapshot is valuable for fund managers who seek diversification across currencies, markets and credits and for investors who attempt to periodically upgrade their holdings to enhance coupon income or yield.

TABLE 3 HYPOTHETICAL GLOBAL BOND FUND
Security Valuation Report For The Week Ending:

Market	Issue	Par Value	Purchase Price	Current Price	Local Currency Value	U.S. Dollar Value	Percent of Portfolio
U.S.	XXXXX						
	XXXXX						
	XXXXX						
	XXXXX						
	XXXXX						
Japan	XXXXX						
	XXXXX						
	XXXXX						
	XXXXX						
	XXXXX						
Germany	XXXXX						
	XXXXX						
	XXXXX						
	XXXXX						
	XXXXX						
United Kingdom	XXXXX						
	XXXXX						
	XXXXX						
	XXXXX						
	XXXXX						

Table 3 is a useful tool for monitoring the fund's security holdings, but in order to get a clear and concise snapshot of the fund's exposure to currency and interest rate risk, a more compact, less comprehensive report is needed. A fund manager may wish to construct a report similar to Table 4, which shows the broad currency/bond market mix profile for a hypothetical global bond fund. Such a table indicates the net currency exposure that the global fund has in each of the major currency blocs, any currency positions that are hedged, the cash/bond mix that the portfolio holds in each market, and the maturity structure and sector breakdown of the bond holdings in each market. The table can be drawn to show how the portfolio weights stand in regard to the weights of a benchmark performance index (or bogey). This would then indicate which currencies, maturities and sectors are being over and underweighted.

CONCLUSION

Only through active global bond portfolio management can fund managers be successful in enhancing return above the level that can be earned on a pure domestic bond portfolio. In fact, without the benefit of active management, there is no reason to believe that over the long-run the returns on passively managed foreign bond funds should outperform the returns on passively managed domestic bond funds, and this is borne out by the facts. What active management attempts is to exploit the existence of sizable difference in the year-to-year total return performance among the various bond markets around the globe, which should provide the international manger with significant opportunities to enhance return if he correctly adjusts currency and market weightings. This also means that there are great risks if asset allocation is done incorrectly. The steps outlined here should help investors to manager such risk.

TABLE 4 HYPOTHETICAL GLOBAL BOND FUND—ASSET MIX REPORT

	Currency Decision		Market Decision			Composition of Bond Portfolio								
						Maturity Structure						Sector Breakdown		
Currency Bloc	Net Currency Position	Currency Hedge	Gross Currency Position	Cash Equiv.	Bonds	1-3 Years	3-5 Years	5-7 Years	7-10 Years	10-15 Years	Long	Gov't.	Euro	Foreign
US$ *	- ( )	-	-	-	-	- ( )	- ( )	- ( )	- ( )	- ( )	- ( )	- ( )	- ( )	- ( )
DM **	- ( )	-	-	-	-	- ( )	- ( )	- ( )	- ( )	NA	NA	- ( )	- ( )	- ( )
YEN	- ( )	-	-	-	-	- ( )	- ( )	- ( )	- ( )	NA	NA	- ( )	- ( )	- ( )
STG	- ( )	-	-	-	-	- ( )	- ( )	- ( )	- ( )	- ( )	- ( )	- ( )	- ( )	- ( )
TOTAL	100	0	100	-	-	- ( )	- ( )	- ( )	- ( )	- ( )	- ( )	- ( )	- ( )	- ( )

- Portfolio Weight
( ) Performance Benchmark Weight

* Includes U.S. and Canadian Markets
** Includes West German, Dutch, Swiss, French and ECU Markets

SECTION VI

Peripheral Issues

CHAPTER TWENTY-NINE

FRED CHOI (Ph.D., University of Washington) is Professor of Accounting and International Business at New York University. He is former chairman of NYU's Area of Accounting, Taxation and Business Law and former Director of the Vincent C. Ross Institute of Accounting Research. Professor Choi is a frequent journal contributor, the author of ten books on the subject of international accounting and control, and a recipient of the American Accounting Association's 1986 Wildman Medal. A consultant to CPA firms, multinational corporations, and financial and academic institutions on exchange risk management, performance evaluation, and international financial analysis, he is a frequent lecturer in excutive programs in the United States and abroad.

THE EFFECT OF ALTERNATIVE ACCOUNTING PROCEDURES ON INTERNATIONAL INVESTMENT PERFORMANCE

Frederick D.S. Choi
Professor of Accounting
New York University
New York, New York

The rise of international equity markets, described in an earlier chapter, reflects a growing interest among both individual and institutional investors in the fortunes of foreign business enterprises. This enthusiasm for international equities is attributable to more than just increasingly cosmopolitan attitudes among international investors. For one thing, political climates around the world are becoming more congenial to foreign investors. Concommitant with this development is the easing of capital controls by more and more countries as increasing recognition is accorded the potential of external finance to accelerate economic development timetables. Inflation, the driving force behind currency instabilities, has also subsided in many countries [Sibley, 1986].

On a more microlevel, a major incentive for international equity investors is the attractive returns available overseas. Studies have shown, for example, that foreign equities frequently outperform domestic securities in the United States, even when the effects of currency risks are taken into account [Warfield, 1985]. Foreign shareholdings also afford domestic investors a means of diversifying their investment portfolios internationally, thus reducing the risks associated with "holding one's eggs in a single basket" (Warfield, Chapter 25).

Whether investors purchase foreign shares listed abroad or traded on domestic exchanges, their buy or sell decisions are premised, for the most part, on information contained in the investee's published financial statements. Here lies the rub! Readers typically removed from the local scene must analyze and interpret financial statements prepared in an environmental context that is often very different from their own.

PROBLEMS CONFRONTING READERS OF FOREIGN FINANCIALS

Disregarding problems of data accessibility and timeliness, readers of foreign financial statements must often contend with differences in language and terminology, statement format, currency of denomination, statement orientation, extent of financial disclosure and accounting measurement rules. Consider first the language barrier. Companies located in non-English speaking countries publish their accounts in the national idiom. Readers unskilled in the particular language must attempt language translations. Whether these translations are personally undertaken—utilizing language lexicons and the like—or done professionally, one should exercise caution. Cursory translations often lead to message distortions. For example, the word "current"—translated to Japanese—reads similar to "present." While the two words convey the same basic meaning, when used in the context of asset valuation the meanings are quite distinct. Thus, valuing a non monetary asset at *current* value does not connote the same message as valuing the asset at *present* value. The former implies a market valuation concept, the latter implies a discounted cash flow measure. Both, of course, could yield very different valuations. Similar considerations apply to accounting terminology differences.

Differences in financial statement formats also can prove troublesome. In their elementary accounting courses, U.S. analysts learn to prepare balance sheets according to the account form, with assets appearing on the left and liabilities and owners' equity on the right. In the United Kingdom and most Commonwealth countries, the reporting format employed is just the opposite. North American readers are also accustomed to seeing assets listed in decreasing order of liquidity and liabilities listed in increasing order of maturity. This practice, which is intended to provide statement readers with a feel for a company's liquidity position, is seldom followed in European and Commonwealth countries. Equally bothersome are differences in financial statement classifications. For example, reacquisition of a firm's own shares (treasury stock) is reported as a contra-account to shareholders' equity in U.S. balance sheets. It is often shown as an asset in countries such as Italy and Portugal. And, whereas the time frame distinguishing a current and a noncurrent liability is a year in the United States and Canada, in a country such as West Germany it is often four years.

To a U.S. reader accustomed to dealing in dollars, analysis of accounts expressed in foreign currencies may be confusing. The normal inclination is to translate foreign currency balances to domestic currency. Aside from questions of convenience and personal preference, however, foreign currency reports are largely troublesome in appearance only. Financial ratios that transform nominal (interval) measurements to percentage relationships are independent of the currency of denomination. Readers preferring a domestic currency framework when analyzing foreign currency financial statements may use year-end exchange rates to effect the *convenience* translations. Care, however, must be exercised when translating time-series data. Use of year-end rates to translate foreign currency trend data can distort underlying financial patterns when exchange rates fluctuate between reporting periods. This problem can be avoided by scaling prior-year data for exchange rate differentials between years. Alternatively, foreign currency data can be translated to domestic currency using a single base year's exchange rate.

Problems such as the above, while troublesome, are seldom critical. At most, they cause analysts some initial disorientation. Problems of greater import relate to statement objectives, extent of disclosure and differences in the accounting principles (GAAP) employed.

Accounting exists to serve some decision process. Accordingly, to the extent that decision processes differ from country to country, so will the content of accounting reports. In this regard, the majority of accounting systems can be broadly classified into two types: those that primarily serve more macro-oriented decision models versus those that serve more atomistic decisions. The former tend to emphasize more uniform accounting systems, which also share a legalistic and conservative bent. Accounting practices in countries such as Belgium, Denmark, France, Germany, Italy, Norway, Spain, Sweden and Switzerland are examples in this regard [Spicer and Oppenheim, 1984]. Accounting systems in countries such as Australia, Canada, Hong Kong, the Netherlands, New Zealand, the Philippines, the United Kingdom and the United States, in contrast, are oriented more towards private investors. Here, accounting practices are much more adaptable to changing business circumstances and are not dictated by taxation requirements. Analysts aware of such differences in national reporting philosophies are better positioned to interpret and reconcile disparities between major systems.

Differences in corporate financial disclosure are also of grave import to security analysts. Unfortunately, disclosure levels taken for granted when reading American, British or Canadian annual reports are seldom found elsewhere. As examples, Singaporean companies rarely disclose cost of sales or operating expenses in their income statements or notes thereto. Funds flow statements, which provide useful insight into a company's investing and financing activities, are rarely provided by reporting entities in countries such as Denmark, Germany and Switzerland. Descriptions of accounting policies customarily disclosed in the "notes" section of Anglo-American annual reports are limited or non-existent for most Italian, Spanish and Korean companies.

Although corporate disclosure levels have not been very high in the past, this is changing. Institutional pressures for increased corporate transparency are increasing at the local, regional and international levels. At the same time, market forces appear likely to succeed where bureaucrats are likely to fail. Spurred by the need for external money capital, competition for access to limited supplies of external finance is forcing more and more companies to climb aboard the disclosure bandwagon [Choi, 1973]. A good example of this trend is Sweden. For a long time Swedish financial statements, influenced by tax requirements, have conveyed a distorted picture of a company's actual operating performance. In the face of limited domestic supplies of needed capital, Sweden's largest multinationals, such as Volvo and L.M. Ericsson, voluntarily evolved a reporting format providing income numbers conforming to both the U.S.-style and the generally accepted Swedish accounting principals. New electronic information systems allowing for easy access and retrieval of financial information on a global basis also is contributing to an improved disclosure picture.

One of the major hurdles readers of foreign financial statements confront is the need to reconcile significant differences in measurement principles when comparing financial statement data between countries. As a result of the diversity that characterizes national accounting measurement rules, observed differences in accounting-based financial ratios between countries may be influenced as much by differences in accounting principles as by differences in the underlying attributes that those ratios are trying to measure.

A perfect example in this regard—one that constitutes the major theme of this chapter — is the differing foreign currency translation methods employed by business entities around the world and the differential statement effects of these variations. The principal measurement issues associated with the currency translation process and their implications for financial statement readers are discussed in the following section.

FOREIGN CURRENCY TRANSLATION ISSUES

Companies translate foreign account balances from one currency to another to record foreign-currency transactions (foreign-currency denominated purchases, sales, borrowing or lending) in their financial statements, and to prepare combined or consolidated statements coupled with accounting for foreign investments under the equity method.

Translation is not synonymous with conversion. The latter involves a physical exchange of one currency for another, as when a French franc receivable or payable is actually paid off with U.S. dollars. Gains or losses associated with such currency conversions generally constitute *transaction* gains or losses. Translation, however, is simply a change in monetary expression. No physical exchange of currencies occurs. Accordingly, exchange gains or losses resulting therefrom (i.e., *translation* gains or losses) are simply the result of a restatement process, and have no immediate cash flow consequences.

If foreign exchange rates were relatively stable, as they were prior to the early 1970's, the currency translation process would be a straightforward matter. Widespread adoption of floating exchange rates, however, has complicated this restatement procedure. In translating foreign currency transactions of importing and exporting companies, there may be major disagreements as to whether foreign exchange gains and losses thereon should be treated as separate gains or losses, or as adjustments to the underlying transactions. In translating foreign currency financial statements, major issues relate to 1) which exchange rates to employ in translating various financial statement accounts, and 2) the accounting disposition of translation gains or losses [Choi and Mueller, 1984].

FOREIGN CURRENCY TRANSACTIONS

Foreign currency transactions occur whenever an enterprise purchases or sells goods for which payment is made in a foreign currency or when it borrows or lends foreign currency. Translation is necessary to maintain the accounting records in the currency of the reporting entity. On this basis, a foreign exchange gain or loss arises whenever the exchange rate prevailing as of the transaction date and used to book the event differs from the exchange rate prevailing when the transaction is settled. Should financial statements be prepared prior to settlement, the accounting adjustment would equal the difference between the amount originally recorded and the amount presented in the financial statement.

Disagreement exists as to the accounting treatment accorded these gains or losses. Those favoring a "single-transaction" perspective treat the gain or loss as an adjustment of the original transaction balances. The assumption here is that the transaction and its subsequent settlement are a single event. An unfavorable exchange rate change, for example, would be treated as a decrease in accounts receivable and a decrease in revenues associated with a credit sale invoiced in foreign currency. Those favoring a "two-transactions" perspective treat transaction adjustments as exchange gains or losses. Here, a transaction is considered a separate event from its settlement. This fact should be remembered when comparing gross profits and bottom lines of a U.S.-based MNC with counterparts in countries such as Italy, Portugal or Spain, as the latter generally adopt a single-transaction perspective [Fitzgerald, et. al., 1979].

A closely related issue is the matter of when transaction adjustments should be recorded. Possibilities include 1) when the foreign currency payable or receivable is settled, 2) when the exchange rate changes, or 3) when the exchange rate changes more than a specified percentage from the rate previously used. The first possibility avoids the problem of intermittant rate fluctuations but delays recognition of any exchange adjustment until a foreign currency transaction is settled. The second possibility gives immediate effect to all rate changes, even though unrealized. The third delays recognition of minor rate changes that could reverse themselves prior to settlement. Underlying the latter two approaches is the belief that financial statement readers are afforded more timely information when the results of an event are reported in the period of the exchange rate change rather than when it is subsequently settled.

Companies in the United States are required to adhere to the second option. While the practice is also subscribed to internationally, it is not consistently applied to transactions. For example, in Australia, exchange adjustments on short-term transactions are generally recorded in the period of the exchange rate change when unsettled foreign currency payables or receivables relate to purchase or sale transactions. Similar adjustments on long-term items, however, are generally amortized over the period between the change in the exchange rate and the settlement date. Statement readers, beware.

FOREIGN CURRENCY FINANCIAL STATEMENTS

At present, companies operating internationally use a variety of methods to express, in domestic currency, transactions, assets, and obligations that have been stated or been quantified in a foreign currency. Two general approaches to foreign currency translation can be distinguished. One employs a single translation rate to restate foreign currency balances to the domestic currency equivalents. The other uses multiple rates. Each is premised on a different concept of foreign operations and translation objectives. Exhibit 1 summarizes the treatment of specific balance sheet items under these methods and their variations.

Single-Rate Method. Long popular in continental Europe, Asia and many Commonwealth countries, use of a single rate to translate foreign currency financial statements is considered appropriate when foreign entities are viewed from the perspective of the local as opposed to the parent company. This method recognizes a foreign-based operation as a separate unit doing business in a foreign currency and retains the foreign currency as the appropriate unit of measure. Original financial statement relationships are preserved in the reporting currency by translating all foreign currency accounts by a constant; namely, the current or year-end exchange rate. Moreover, exchange gains and losses resulting from the restatement process bypass income and appear instead in shareholders' equity or some balance sheet reserve account. Accordingly, only the form, not the nature, of the foreign accounts is changed under this single rate method.

For all its simplicity and conceptual appeal, the single or current

EXHIBIT 1 EXCHANGE RATES EMPLOYED IN DIFFERENT TRANSLATION METHODS FOR SPECIFIC BALANCE SHEET ITEMS

	Single-Rate Method	Multiple-Rate Methods		
	Current-Rate	Current-Noncurrent	Monetary-Nonmonetary	Temporal
Cash	C[a]	C	C	C
Accounts receivable	C	C	C	C
Inventories				
Cost	C	C	H	H
Market	C	C	H	C
Investments				
Cost	C	H	H	H
Market	C	H	H	C
Fixed assets	C	H	H	H
Other assets	C	H	H	H
Accounts payable	C	C	C	C
Long-term debt	C	H	C	C
Common stock	H[b]	H	H	H
Retained earnings	*c	*	*	*

C[a] = Current rate.
H[b] = Historical rate.
$*_c$ = Residual, balancing figure representing a composite of successive current rates.

rate method is often faulted for violating a long-standing principle underlying the construction of consolidated statements. This is the reporting of the results of both domestic and foreign operations to the parent company's shareholders from a single currency framework: i.e., U.S. dollars in the case of a U.S. multinational enterprise. By subjecting parent currency equivalents to fluctuations every time exchange rates (current rates) change, the current rate method signals that all foreign currency assets and liabilities are subject to exchange rate risk. This, however, is seldom the case, as inventory and fixed asset values abroad are generally supported by local inflation. There is also concern that while stockholders' equity or reserve adjustments shield an MNC's bottom line from translation gains and losses, such adjustments may lead to confusion among statement readers, further detracting from the credibility of financial statements.

Multiple Rate Methods. As their name suggests, multiple rate methods employ a combination of both historical and current exchange rates. Premised on a *parent company* perspective, foreign operations are viewed as extensions of the parent company, as opposed to independent reporting entities. Here, the object of translation is to change the unit of measure from the foreign currency to the reporting currency of the parent (i.e., U.S. dollars). A related object is to have foreign currency financial statements conform to accounting principles adhered to by the parent. Thus, if the parent company values its nonmonetary assets at historical cost, translation of a subsidiary's foreign currency fixed assets at the historical rate (i.e., the exchange rate prevailing when the foreign currency asset was first acquired) preserves their historical cost in the consolidated statements. There are three historical rate methods in use today.

Under the *current-noncurrent* method, once popular in the United States and favored by Iranian, Pakistani and Zambian entities, a foreign subsidiary's current assets and liabilities are translated into its parent company's reporting currency by the current rate. Noncurrent assets and liabilities are translated at historical rates. Income statement items, except for depreciation and amortization charges, are translated at average rates applicable to each month of operation, or on the basis of weighted averages covering the whole period to be reported. Depreciation and amortization charges are translated at the historical rates in effect when the related assets were acquired.

While it protects reported gross margins from the distorting effects of currency gyrations, this translation option is not without shortcomings. First, little conceptual justification exists for using a balance sheet classification to determine the exchange rate used in translation. Moreover, using the year-end rate to translate current assets implies that foreign currency cash, receivables and inventories are equally exposed to exchange risk, regardless of their form. But in those instances where local price increases are possible following a devaluation of the local currency, inventory values are protected from currency erosion. On the other hand, translation of long-term debt at the historical rate protects interim periods from the impact of fluctuating currencies, while burdening the year of settlement with possibly significant currency gains or losses. Many consider this to be at odds with economic reality.

The *monetary-nonmonetary* method, once a favorite of many U.S. concerns and still popular in Central America, Taiwan, Finland and Sweden, also uses a balance sheet classification scheme to determine appropriate translation rates. Foreign currency monetary assets and liabilities such as cash, receivables and payables (including long-term debt) are translated at the current rate. Nonmonetary items—fixed assets, long-term investments, and inventories—are translated at the historical rate. Income statement items are typically translated by average rates, with the exception of depreciation and cost of sales, which are translated using appropriate historical rates.

In contrast to the current-noncurrent method, this translation option relates exchange rate risk to the composition of a firm's current assets. It also reflects changes in the domestic currency equivalent of long-term debt in the period in which they occur, producing what many consider to be more timely indications of exchange rate effects. Unfortunately, this method masks inventory risk when local pricing adjustments, following a currency devaluation, are constrained by governmental price controls or by competitive pressures. Another perceived distortion arises from matching sales at current prices and translation rates against cost of goods sold measured at historical costs and translations rates. Exchange rate changes often result in distorted profit margins, owing to the lag in inventory turns. In recognizing translations gains and losses currently, a company increases its earnings volatility and perceived riskiness.

Under the *temporal rate* method, once mandated in the United States by Financial Accounting Standard (FAS) 8, foreign currency assets and liabilities retain their original measurement bases. Cash, receivables and payables are translated at the current rate. Assets carried in foreign financial statements at historical cost are translated at the historical rate (i.e., historical cost times a historical exchange rate preserves historical cost in parent currency). Assets carried at current values, such as inventories under the lower-of-cost-or-market rule, are translated at the current rate (i.e., current cost times a current rate preserves current cost in parent currency). Revenue and expense items are translated at rates prevailing when the underlying transactions took place, although average rates are suggested when revenue or expense transactions are voluminous.

Being a variant of the monetary-nonmonetary method (under historical cost valuation), this translation approach shares most of its advantages and disadvantages. In deliberately ignoring local inflation as part of the translation process, the temporal translation method shares a limitation common to all the above methods.

Exhibits 2 and 3 highlight the financial statement effects of the various translation methods described. The balance sheet of a hypothetical Swiss subsidiary of a U.S.-based multinational appears in the first two columns of Exhibit 2. The third column depicts the U.S. dollar equivalent of the Swiss franc (SF) balances when the exchange rate is $1/SF2.0. Should the franc appreciate by 33⅓ percent against the dollar (now $1/SF1.50), a number of different accounting results are possible. (Bracketed expressions in the exhibit identify those foreign currency balances affected by exchange rate changes, which give rise to translation gains or losses). Income statement effects of an appreciating franc appear in Exhibit 3.

Clearly, reported results of multinational enterprises can vary markedly depending on the translation method utilized. Liquidity positions can deteriorate significantly under the monetary-

EXHIBIT 2—TRANSLATION GAINS AND LOSSES UNDER DIFFERING METHODOLOGIES ASSUMING AN APPRECIATING FOREIGN CURRENCY[a]

Swiss Subsidiary Balance Sheet in Swiss Francs		U.S. Dollars Before Franc Appreciation ($1/SF2.0)	U.S. Dollar Equivalents After Swiss Franc Appreciation ($1/SF1.5)			
Amount(000's)	Item		Current-Rate	Current-Noncurrent	Monetary Nonmonetary	Temporal
	Assets					
SF 900	Cash	$ 450	$ 600	$ 600	$ 600	$ 600
900	Accounts receivable	450	600	600	600	600
	Inventories					
	Cost					
1,800	Market	900	1,200	1,200	900[b]	1,200
4,500	Fixed assets, net	2,250	3,000	2,250	2,250	2,250
SF 8,100		$4,050	$5,400	$4,650	$4,350	$4,650
	Liabilities and owners' equity					
SF 1,800	ST payables	$ 900	$1,200	$1,200	$1,200	$1,200
3,600	LT debt	1,800	2,400	1,800	2,400	2,400
2,700	Owners' equity[c]	1,350	1,800	1,650	750	1,050
SF 8,100		$4,050	$5,400	$4,650	$4,350	$4,650
	Translation gain (loss)		$ 450	$ 300	$ (600)	$ (300)

[a] Note that if the exchange rate remained unchanged over time, the translated statements would be the same under all translation methods.

[b] Under some interpretations, this item would be reclassified as a monetary item and translated at the current rate.

[c] In the translated statements, Owners' Equity is a residual balancing figure.

EXHIBIT 3—SWISS SUBSIDIARY INCOME STATEMENT
(in thousands)

			U.S. Dollar After Franc Appreciation ($.66 2/3=SF1)			
	Swiss Francs	U.S. Dollars Before Franc Appreciation ($.50=SF1)	Current Rate	Current-Noncurrent	Monetary Nonmonetary	Temporal
Sales	SF 8,000	$4,000	$5,334	$5,334	$5,334	$5,334
Cost of sales	4,000	2,000	2,667	2,667	2,000	2,000[a]
Depreciation[b]	450	225	300	225	225	225
All other expenses	1,600	800	1,067	1,067	1,067	1,067
Income before tax	1,950	975	1,300	1,375	2,042	2,042
Income tax (40%)	780	390	520	520	520	520
Translation gain (loss)	—	—	450[c]	300[d]	(600)[d]	(300)[d]
	SF 1,170	$ 585	$ 780	$1,155	$ 922	$1,222

Note: This example assumes that the income statement is prepared the day after revaluation.

[a]Assumes that inventories were written down to market at period's end.
[b]Estimated life of fixed assets is assumed to be ten years.
[c]Translation gains or losses are reflected in consolidated equity.
[d]Assumes that translation gains and losses are immediately reflected in current income.

nonmonetary method in comparison to the current rate method. Similarly, solvency ratios under the latter can be inferior to those generated by the current-noncurrent method. Moreover, the effect of currency translation on bottom lines is conditioned by the accounting dispositions of translation adjustments. While the example in Exhibit 3 assumed immediate recognition of translation gains or losses, balance sheet deferrals or direct adjustments to consolidated equity could significantly alter reported outcomes.

How then should translation effects be treated? Many analysts are generally opposed to inclusion of translation adjustments in current income on the grounds that they are merely the product of a restatement process. Changes in the domestic currency equivalents of a foreign subsidiary's net assets are "unrealized," having no effect on local currency cash flows generated by the foreign entity. Inclusion of such adjustments in current income would, therefore, be misleading. Under these circumstances translation adjustments should be accumulated separately as part of consolidated equity.

Some analysts oppose equity adjustments, however, on the grounds that exchange rates often do not reverse themselves. Even if they did, deferral of exchange adjustments are premised on exchange rate predictions, in practice a most difficult undertaking. Situations could arise where operating results are misstated due solely to forecasting errors. To some analysts, deferring translation gains or losses masks the behavior of exchange rate changes: i.e., rate changes are historical facts and financial statement users are best served if the effects of exchange rate fluctuations are accounted for when they occur.

A contrasting viewpoint favors deferring translation gains or losses and amortizing these adjustments over the life of related balance sheet items. One example here is to include any exchange loss, stemming from translating a foreign currency liability, as part of the related asset's cost. This assumes that an asset's cost includes the sacrifice required to discharge related obligations. Another alternative is to include such translation gains or losses as an adjustment of the carrying value of foreign currency liabilities. Amounts so deferred would be amortized over the remaining life of the long-term debt by treating deferred translation gains or losses as an adjustment of interest expense. Such treatment is defended on the grounds that management typically assesses the likelihood of exchange rate changes when evaluating the costs and benefits of domestic versus foreign currency borrowings.

Still another option in accounting for translation gains and losses is to recognize them in the income statement immediately. Deferral of any kind is widely regarded as artificial and misleading. Moreover, deferral criteria are attacked as impossible to implement and internally inconsistent. Thus, the traditional approach has been to recognize losses as soon as they occur but to recognize gains only to the extent realized. While conservative, deferring a translation gain solely because it is a "gain" denies that a rate change has occurred. Moreover, deferring translation gains while recognizing translation losses is internally inconsistent. Another problem with this approach has been the absence of any explicit criteria to determine when realization of a translation gain occurs. In addition, those favoring deferral of translation gains are at a loss to determine how much should be deferred.

Immediate recognition of translation gains and losses, however, introduces a random element to earnings, possibly resulting in significant gyrations every time exchange rates change. Moreover, inclusion of such bookkeeping gains and losses in reported earnings could easily mislead. Such adjustments are seldom compatible with the expected economic effects of rate changes on an enterprise's cash flows.

Evidence regarding national practices suggests that more and more countries are opting for use of either the temporal method or the current rate method [Business International, 1982]. With regard to accounting for translation gains and losses, diversity is still the order of the day. In many countries, practices appear divided between immediate recognition of translation gains and losses and deferral. Equally popular is the practice of taking such gains and losses to consolidated equity [Choi and Sondhi, 1985].

In the United States, all the foregoing treatments were permitted prior to 1976. To end this diversity, the Financial Accounting Standards Board (FASB) issued, in 1976, FAS. No. 8 [FASB, 1975].

In addition to mandating use of the temporal principle, this pronouncement required immediate recognition of exchange gains and losses, both transaction and translation. This latter feature proved more controversial than any other. Leading national currencies fluctuated widely during the 1970's, producing the so called "yo-yo effect" on the bottom lines of MNC's. Fearful that such earnings patterns would affect their cost of capital, managements often expended large amounts of resources to minimize what were often noncash (translation) losses.

Dissatisfaction with FAS No. 8 led to the issuance of a new translation pronouncement, FAS No. 52 [FASB, 1981]. Whereas FAS No. 8 adopted a parent company point of view, FAS No. 52 adopted a situational approach and recognized a local company perspective as a valid reporting framework. The new translation rules were designed to:

1. reflect in consolidated statements the financial results and relationships measured in the primary currency in which each consolidated entity conducts its business (its functional currency), and
2. provide information that is generally compatible with the expected economic effects of an exchange rate change on an enterprise's cash flows and equity.

These objectives were premised on the notion of a "functional currency," which mirrors the currency perspective adopted by management for consolidated entities. The functional currency of a particular foreign entity is defined as the currency of the primary economic environment in which it operates and generates cash flows. If a foreign entity's operations are relatively self-contained and integrated within a foreign country (i.e., an operation that is not an extension of the parent company), its functional currency would ordinarily be its local currency (i.e., lira in the case of an Italian subsidiary of a U.S. parent). If a foreign entity is merely an extension of a U.S. parent company, its functional currency would be the U.S. dollar.

Determination of the functional currency is a key feature of FAS No. 52, as it determines the choice of translation method and disposition of exchange gains and losses. If the foreign currency in which the foreign entity's records are maintained is deemed to be the functional currency, its financial statements are *translated* to dollars using the current rate method. Translation gains or losses arising therefrom are disclosed in a separate component of consolidated equity. This preserves the financial statement ratios as measured in the local currency statements. However, if the U.S. dollar is determined to be the functional currency, a foreign entity's financial statements are *remeasured* to dollars using the former temporal method prescribed by FAS No. 8. Here all translation gains or losses arising from the translation process are included in determining current income. If a foreign subsidiary's records are not maintained in its functional currency, remeasurement into the functional currency is required prior to dollar translation. Thus, if a Belgian subsidiary's functional currency is French francs but it maintains its records in Belgian francs, remeasurement from Belgian francs to French francs would be necessary prior to dollar translation at the current rate. Remeasurement into the functional currency (i.e., French francs) employs procedures identical to the temporal method.

Use of the current rate method for operations located in hyperinflationary environments (environments in which the cumulative rate of inflation exceeds 100% during the three preceeding years) is deemed not to provide meaningful results. Accordingly, FAS No. 52 requires that the U.S. dollar be used as if it were the functional currency in operations located in: Argentina, Brazil, Chile, Colombia, Ghana, Iceland, Israel, Peru, Somalia, Sudan, Turkey, Uruguay, Yugoslavia and Zaire [Business International, 1982].

While transaction (conversion) gains and losses continue to be recognized in current income, as they were under FAS No. 8, two major exceptions are now peritted for MNC's adopting the local currency as functional. First, gains or losses on foreign currency transactions deemed to be hedges of a foreign affiliate's balance sheet exposure (i.e., those balance sheet accounts that in the aggregate would yield a net translation loss or gain when translated at the current rate) may now be included as a separate component of shareholders' equity. This component of equity is where losses or gains from translating foreign currency financial statements under the current rate method are disclosed. Second, gains or losses on intercompany transactions for which settlement is not planned or anticipated in the forseeable future may also bypass current income and appear in consolidated equity.

IMPLICATIONS OF FAS NO. 52 FOR FINANCIAL ANALYSTS

Does FAS NO. 52, intended to overcome many of the criticisms leveled at its predecessor—FAS No. 8, promise to ease the life of financial analysts? Probably not. Despite the current rate method's simplicity, its preservation of local currency relationships in the consolidated results, and its ability to shield reported earnings from "paper" gains and losses, this reporting methodology introduces a whole new set of reporting problems for financial statement analysis.

For starters, the current rate methodology implies that all of a foreign operation's resources and obligations are exposed to exchange rate risk, a point raised earlier. However, is this really the case when property, plant and equipment values, for example, are normally offset by local inflation? Concluding that all assets and liabilities are so exposed on the basis of translated results may lead to incorrect assessments of environmental risk. Current rate translation of original transactions values abroad also produces parent currency equivalents that defy interpretation. To wit, translation of a historical cost-based fixed asset by a historical exchange rate yields a dollar equivalent that can be interpreted as historical cost in dollars. Translation of the same historical cost item by a current exchange rate, however, results in a dollar figure representing neither historical cost nor current cost. Adding this translated valuation to a parent company's other fixed asset accounts contaminates what would otherwise be useful consolidated figures.

The situational posture adopted by FAS No.52 also abandons a long-standing consolidation principle in the United States: consolidated statements are designed to report to U.S. shareholders the results of all foreign operations from a U.S. dollar perspective. Adopting the notion of functional currencies accomodates a multiple currency perspective. A likely outcome is increased reader confusion. Suppose a U.S. parent company possesses foreign subsidiaries in Belgium and Ireland. The functional currency of the Belgium affiliate is deemed to be the franc, while the functional currency of the Irish affiliate is the U.S. dollar. Translation gains or losses, resulting from restating Belgian financials using the current rate method, would bypass income and appear in consolidated equity. In contrast, translation gains or losses stemming from translation of the Irish statements by the temporal method would be reflected in current earnings. Question: Does a translation gain or loss generated under the current rate method differ in substance from a translation gain or loss generated under the temporal method? If the answer is no, does it make sense to disclose some translation gains and losses in equity while disclosing others in income? Unfortunately, for analysts, most companies preparing foreign consolidations do not identify what functional currency designations are being employed for their major affiliates.

Another major critiscm of FAS No. 52 relates to foreign inflation. Owing to the inverse relationship between a country's internal inflation rate and the external value of its currency, use of the current rate to translate historical cost-based nonmonetary assets located in inflationary environments could produce dollar equivalents far below their recorded values. Such translated results could mislead rather than inform. Lower dollar equivalents would understate the actual earning power of foreign assets. Moreover, rate of return statistics of foreign operations would be biased upwards, creating false expectations of profitability. The FASB attempts to mitigate this problem for hyper-inflationary environments by requiring use of the dollar as the functional currency. This procedure holds constant the dollar equivalents of foreign currency nonmonetary assets as translated by the historical rate in accordance with the temporal method.

This accounting procedure, however, also has its limitations. For one thing, translation by the historical rate is meaningful only if differential rates of inflation between the subsidiary's host country and parent country are perfectly negatively correlated with exchange rates. Failing this, the dollar equivalents of foreign currency assets will be misleading. It is precisely in hyper-inflationary environments that historical cost measures prove misleading. Further, should the FASB treatment be followed, and should inflation rates in the hyper-inflationary economy eventually subside (i.e., fall below a compounded annual rate of 26 percent per annum), switching to the current rate method (the local currency would now become functional) could produce a substantial hit to consolidated equity as exchange rates will have changed markedly during the interim. Under these circumstances, charging stockholders' equity with translation losses on foreign currency fixed assets could have a significant effect on financial ratios employing stockholders' equity in the denominator. Although the dollar at present remains relatively weak in relation to the foreign currencies of many of its trading partners, subsequent strengthening of the dollar could put many companies in technical violation of indenture provisions specifying minimum debt to equity ratios and the like.

Analysts also dislike the idea of "burying" translation gains and losses, heretofore disclosed, in stockholders' equity. Aside from potential reader confusion, critics argue that such treatment violates the all-inclusive (clean surplus) concept of income. Long adopted in the United States, this concept requires companies to disclose not only operating revenues and expenses but also unusual nonoperating and infrequently occurring items in the income statement, separately disclosed. This provision, in contrast to the operating (dirty surplus) concept of income, was designed to enlighten statement readers on all items bearing on a firm's profitability.

Preference for the all inclusive concept is prompting some analysts to impute the translation adjustments appearing in consolidated equity to the bottom line. In carrying out such adjustments, however, analysts need to back out any translation gains (losses) related to translation of foreign currency fixed assets at current rates. Failing this, adjusted earnings will appear better (worse) than prior to the adjustment.

FAS No. 8's treatment of exchange gains and losses was intended, among other things, to minimize the use of balance sheet reserves to cushion the impact of fluctuating currency values on reported earnings. Several features of FAS No. 52 reintroduce such smoothing opportunities. As an example, assume the functional currency of a U.S. parent company's Swiss subsidiary is the U.S. dollar. If the Swiss subsidiary was in a net monetary asset position, devaluation of the Swiss franc relative to the dollar would give rise to a translation loss. To avoid this, the U.S. parent could designate a previous Swiss franc long-term borrowing as an effective hedge of that exchange risk exposure. In this instance, a transaction gain incurred on the Swiss franc borrowing would flow to consolidated equity as an offset to the translation loss stemming from consolidation. Alternatively, a Deutsche Mark borrowing could achieve a similar result if movement in Deutsche Mark and Swiss franc were positively correlated.

A final reporting problem relates to the statement of changes in financial position. The problem stems from the fact that currency gyrations and the current rate translation method often produce changes in reported assets and liabilities that are at odds with both the direction and magnitude of the underlying transactions. A direct consequence is that statement readers may receive a distorted picture of a multinational company's financing and investing activities. It is not always clear whether fund sources and uses reflect the result of an operational decision or simply the result of an exchange rate change. As an example, local funds may have been used to retire a significant portion of a foreign subsidiary's foreign currency debt, thus reducing its exposure to exchange rate risk should the borrowed currency revalue. Nevertheless, the reported results could suggest a significant increase in local currency debt giving rise to a *source* rather than a *use* of funds owing to the translation effect. Similar interpretive problems surface with respect to capital expenditures and other items of working capital. A separate evaluation of the combined effect of exchange rate fluctuations and translation methodology is essential in ferreting out the actual flows being depicted in the funds statement and their relationship to other financial statements [Choi and Sondhi, 1984]. However, the FASB did not mandate preparation of such an analysis. Neither did it require disclosure of details regarding the reported changes in financial position for individual foreign subsidiaries or for consolidated operations.

CONCLUSION

Readers of foreign financial statements must contend with a number of reporting problems not faced by those who confine their analyses to domestic investments. These obstacles arise because someone removed from the local scene must read and interpret financial reports that have been prepared on the basis of different languages, currencies, disclosure levels, business and financial practices, and accounting measurements.

An especially troublesome measurement issue stems from the need to translate financial accounts from one currency framework to another. It is unlikely that accounting standard setters will ever formulate the ideal currency translation pronouncement. FAS No. 52, as we have seen, is a case in point. Although it offers a number of improvements over its predecessor, it raises as many questions as it answers. Until a reporting standard that recognizes the interdependence between currency translation and accounting for inflation is fashioned, the currency translation controversy will likely continue.

In the meantime, analysts should familiarize themselves with the nature of alternative currency translation methods so as to facilitate meaningful reconciliations between U.S. and foreign-based MNC's. The complexity of attempting such reconciliations will vary depending upon such factors as 1) the nature and extent of a firm's foreign operations, 2) the composition of its net assets, 3) the character of its foreign currency transactions, 4) the flexibility of local pricing policy to offset exchange losses, 5) governmental constraints on strategic positioning of corporate funds, 6) the extent and direction of exchange rate movements, 7) features of the currency translation method employed, and 8) accounting dispositions of exchange gains and losses, both transaction and translation.

BIBLIOGRAPHY

Business International Corporation, *New Directions in Managing Currency Risk: Changing Corporate Strategies and Systems Under FAS No. 52* (New York: BI, 1982)

Choi, Frederick D.S. "Financial Disclosure and Entry to the European Capital Market," *Journal of Accounting Research,* (Autumn 1973), pp. 159-75

, and Gerhard G. Mueller **International Accounting** (Englewood Cliffs, N.J.: Prentice-Hall, Inc., 1984)

, and Ashwinpaul Sondhi "Accounting for Floating Currencies: An International Perspective," *Journal of Accounting, Auditing, and Finance* (Summer 1985), pp. 335-40

, and Ashwinpaul Sondhi "SFAS No. 52 and the Funds Statement," *Corporate Accounting* (Spring 1984), pp. 46-56

Financial Accounting Standards Board "Accounting for the Translation of Foreign Currency Transactions and Foreign Currency Financial Statements," *Statement of Financial Accounting Standards No. 8* (Stamford, Connecticut: FASB, October 1975)

, "Foreign Currency Translation," *Statement of Financial Accounting Standards No. 52* (Stamford, Connecticut: FASB, December 1981)

Fitzgerald, R.D., A.D. Stickler, and T.R. Watts *International Survey of Accounting Principles and Reporting Practices* (Ontario: Price Waterhouse International, 1979)

Sibley, Angus, "Investing in Global Equities," *Accountant's Magazine* (May 1986) pp. 27-29.

Spicer and Oppenheim *Understanding Financial Statements Around the World* (New York: Spicer and Oppenheim, 1984)

Warfield, Gerald *How To Buy Foreign Stocks and Bonds* (New York: Harper and Row Publishers, 1985)

CHAPTER THIRTY

FRANCIS J. GREY is the Managing Partner of Tax Services in the Philadelphia office of Coopers & Lybrand. Mr. Grey has authored several books, including *Tax Planning for Real Estate Transactions; Pennsylvania Taxation of Corporations;* and *Planning, Financing and Constructing Health Care Facilities.* In addition, he was a contributing author to *Taxation of Individuals,* Warren Gorham, Lamont, Inc.

Mr. Grey is chairman of the Philadelphia Chamber of Commerce Taxation Committee. He is a member of the Advisory Board, University of Pennsylvania Tax Conference, and has chaired several committees on various professional associations, including the American and Pennsylvania Institutes of CPAs. He is presently adjunct professor of law for the Graduate Tax Program at Villanova University.

DOUGLAS W. NAKAJIMA is a Tax Manager in the Philadelphia office of Coopers & Lybrand. He is actively involved in domestic and international tax planning for both U.S. multinationals and foreign entities operating in the United States and is a member of Coopers & Lybrand's International Tax Group in Philadelphia. He has co-authored several articles, including "The President's Tax Proposal: A Failure to Reform," *Pennsylvania Outlook.*

Mr. Nakajima received a B.A. degree from the University of Pennsylvania in 1977; and J.D. and L.L.M. (Taxation) degrees from the Villanova University School of Law in 1980 and 1984 respectively. He is a member of the Pennsylvania and American Bar Associations.

TAXATION AS AN INCENTIVE OR IMPEDIMENT TO INTERNATIONAL PORTFOLIO INVESTMENT

Francis J. Grey
Douglas W. Nakajima
Coopers & Lybrand
Philadelphia, Pennsylvania

INTRODUCTION

Portfolio investors seeking profit in the international marketplace must broaden their perspective beyond the pure business and economic sense of the deal to the potential tax benefits and costs inherent in the specific investment vehicle. The variety and diversity of tax treatment mandated in each country of potential investment create a seemingly endless series of issues. This basic confusion is exacerbated by the obligatory interaction of tax provisions affecting both the *investment* and the *investor*. The veracity of the cliched certainty of death and taxes proven yet again, it falls to the distinguished cadre of investment advisors to fashion order from such confusion, and to do so at a good rate of return.

The following discussion provides an overview of the essential tax issues which should be addressed by U.S. portfolio investors investing abroad (''outbound investment'') and foreign investors entering the U.S. market (''inbound investment''). Additional caution must be exercised with regard to provisions implemented with the recent U.S. tax reform act. Absent prior experience or regulatory authority of any kind, these sections could be a trap for the unwary.

FOREIGN PORTFOLIO INVESTMENT IN THE UNITED STATES

The primary tax concern of foreigners purchasing U.S. portfolio investments is whether and to what extent earnings generated by the investment will be subject to U.S. taxation. The tax consequences will vary, based upon three factors: (1) the investor's residency status under U.S. tax law; (2) the country where the income will be "sourced" for tax purposes; and (3) the form of the investment and the character of any income generated. Individuals who are not citizens of the United States are divided for U.S. tax purposes into two categories: residents and nonresidents. There is a significant difference in the manner each category is taxed.

Generally, a *resident* foreign individual will be taxed on his worldwide income, regardless of source. As such, the foreign national who is deemed "resident" in the United States will, in all significant respects, be taxed on the same basis as a U.S. citizen. By comparison, however, the nonresident foreign investor will be taxed only upon business income "effectively connected" with the active conduct of a U.S. trade or business, or permanent U.S. establishment (at graduated rates), and upon passive or investment income from U.S. sources not "effectively connected" (at a flat rate which may be reduced by tax treaty). Capital gains from U.S. sources which are not "effectively connected" are not taxed unless the foreign individual meets the substantial presence test (discussed below).

Determination of Residency

In general, foreign individuals who are neither citizens nor "residents" of the United States will avoid being taxed in the United States. However, a foreign individual who enters the United States on a nonimmigrant visa will be considered a United States resident if he is present on at least thirty-one days during the current year and the total number of days of presence during (1) the current year; plus (2) the first preceding year multiplied by one-third; plus (3) the second preceding year multiplied by one-sixth, equals at least 183 days. This is known as meeting the "substantial presence test." Thus, a foreign individual who is present in the United States for at least 183 days in a calendar year will generally be considered a United States resident. However, a foreign individual who is present for *less* than 183 days in a particular year may still be considered as resident in that year if his presence in either of the preceding two years will bring him to the 183-day level.

Exemptions from this substantial presence test are available if the foreign individual's tax home is in a foreign country *and* the individual has a closer connection with such country than the United States. Special exceptions are also made for certain residents of Canada and Mexico.

Foreign individuals becoming "permanent lawful residents" of the United States at any time during the year are deemed residents for tax purposes as well. A permanent lawful resident is one who has been granted such status under United States imigration laws. Typically, these are holders of immigrant visas or "green cards."

Foreign individuals who are residents of certain countries with which the United States has an income tax treaty may obtain relief from United States taxation as a "resident." Treaty provisions generally set forth residence criteria, as agreed by the two countries, to avoid any onerous impact on taxpayers. Certain types of investment income, such as interest, dividends, or royalties, are often excluded from treaty coverage or are subject to special tax withholding provisions.

SOURCING RULES

After first distinguishing what persons will be subject to U.S. tax, the next consideration is what income will be subject to U.S. tax. The elaborate source of income rules become of paramount importance to nonresidents, who may avoid U.S. taxes on earnings not sourced or deemed to be sourced to the United States.

Resident Aliens

As discussed earlier, resident aliens receive no favor under U.S. tax law. Absent specific exception, their gross income will include all income from whatever source derived, U.S. or foreign. After reduction for certain allowances and deductions, their remaining income is currently taxable under the rate schedules set by the Tax Reform Act of 1986 (TRA) (see Table 1). Additionally, most states and some localities impose an income tax.

Passive income for U.S. residents is generally subject to U.S. tax at the usual rates whether from U.S. or non-U.S. sources. Once again, however, this general rule may be altered by applicable tax treaty provisions.

Capital Gains and Losses

When an investment asset has been held by an individual for more than six months (one year for assets acquired before June 23, 1984), the asset is deemed a long-term capital asset and will be subject to the rules governing long-term capital gain and loss. Investment assets held less than six months are taxable as short-term assets, i.e., taxed as ordinary income (or losses).

Gain or loss on disposition is determined by taking the difference between the amount realized and the asset's adjusted basis (generally, cost of the asset plus any expenses incurred in connection with the purchase, less distributions attributable to the asset). Under the TRA, capital gains will be taxed at the same rate as ordinary income. Previously, a 60 percent exclusion of capital gain subject to tax was available to reduce the effective rate of tax on capital gains. However, beginning in 1988, no advantage will result from capital gain characterization.

TABLE 1 PERSONAL INCOME TAX RATES UNDER THE 1986 ACT

1987 Taxable Income	Tax Rate	1988 Taxable Income	Tax Rate
Married filing jointly			
$ 0 — 3,000	11%	$ 0 — 29,750	15%
3,000 — 28,000	15	29,750 — 71,900	28
28,000 — 45,000	28	71,900 — 149,250	33
45,000 — 90,000	35	over 149,250	28
over 90,000	38.5		
Single			
$ 0 — 1,800	11%	$ 0 — 17,850	15%
1,800 — 16,800	15	17,850 — 43,150	28
16,800 — 27,000	28	43,150 — 89,560	33
27,000 — 54,000	35	over 89,560	28
over 54,000	38.5		

Taxable income is income after all deductions (including either itemized deductions or the standard deduction) and exemptions.

Nonresident Aliens

Nonresidents are taxed only on income from U.S. sources and certain business income associated with U.S. businesses. U.S. source passive investment income, such as dividends, interest, annuities, and rents unrelated to a U.S. business are generally subject to U.S. tax at a flat rate of 30 percent of the gross amount paid. The 30 percent rate may be reduced or eliminated by treaty. (See Table 2 and 3).

Special rules apply to interest paid on certain types of obligations issued by a U.S. corporation or the U.S. government and held by a nonresident. Generally, interest on such investments will not be subject to U.S. tax if the obligations were first issued after July 1984.

TABLE 2 WITHHOLDING TAX RATES ON INTEREST BETWEEN SELECTED COUNTRIES

From \ To	Australia	Belgium	Canada	Denmark	France	Germany	Ireland	Italy	Japan	Luxembourg	Netherlands	Spain	Sweden	Switzerland	United Kingdom	United States	Statutory (Montreaty)
Australia	—	10	10	10	10	10	10	10	10	10	10	10	10	10	10	10	10
Belgium	10	—	15	15	15	0	15	15	15	0	0	15	15	10	15	15	25
Canada	15	15	—	15	15	15	15	15	15	25	15	15	15	15	15	15	15
Denmark	0	0	0	—	0	0	0	0	0	0	0	0	0	0	0	0	0
France	10	10	10	0	—	0	0	10	10	10	10	10	0	10	10	10	45
Germany	10	15	15	0	0	—	0	25	10	25	0	10	0	0	0	0	25
Ireland	10	15	35	0	0	0	—	10	10	0	0	35	0	0	0	0	35
Italy	15	15	15	15	15	0	10	—	10	10	15	12	15	12.5	15	15	15
Japan	10	15	15	10	10	10	10	10	—	20	10	10	10	10	10	10	20
Luxembourg	0	0	0	0	0	0	0	0	0	—	0	0	0	0	0	0	0
Netherlands	0	0	0	0	0	0	0	0	0	0	—	0	0	0	0	0	0
Spain	18	15	15	10	10	10	18	12	10	18	10	—	15	10	12	18	18
Sweden	0	0	0	0	0	0	0	0	0	0	0	0	—	0	0	0	0
Switzerland	10	10	15	0	10	0	0	12.5	10	35	5	10	0	—	0	5	35
United Kingdom	10	15	15	0	10	0	0	30	10	0	0	12	0	0	—	0	30
United States	10	15	15	0	10	0	0	30	10	0	0	30	0	5	0	—	30

Source: *International Tax Summaries 1986, A Guide for Planning and Decisions,* Coopers & Lybrand International Tax Network, Jon D. Jacobs, Editor, John Wiley & Sons, Inc. (1986)

TABLE 3 WITHHOLDING TAX RATES ON DIVIDENDS BETWEEN SELECTED COUNTRIES

From \ To	Australia	Belgium	Canada	Denmark	France	Germany	Ireland	Italy	Japan	Luxembourg	Netherlands	Spain	Sweden	Switzerland	United Kingdom	United States	Statutory (Montreaty)
Australia	—	15	15	15	15	15	15	15	15	30	15	30	15	15	15	15	30
Belgium	15	—	15	15	10/15	15	15	15	15	10/15	5/15	15	15	10/15	15	15	25
Canada	15	15	—	15	15	15	15	15	15	25	15	15	15	15	15	10/15	25
Denmark	15	15	15	—	0	10/15	0	15	10/15	5/15	0/15	10/15	5/15	0	0/15	5/15	30
France	15	10/15	15	0	—	0	10/15	15	10/15	5/15	5/15	10/15	0	5/15	5/15	5/15	25
Germany	15	25/15	15/25	25/15	25/15	—	20/15	25	25/15	25/15	25/15	25/15	25/15	15	20/15	15	25
Ireland	0	0	0	0	0	0	—	0	0	0	0	0	0	0	0	0	0
Italy	15	15	15	15	15	32.4	15	—	10/15	15	0/32.4	15	10/15	15	5/15	5/15	32.4
Japan	15	15	15	10/15	10/15	10/15	10/15	10/15	—	20	10/15	10/15	10/15	10/15	10/15	10/15	20
Luxembourg	15	10/15	15	5/15	5/15	10/15	5/15	15	15	—	2.5/15	15	5/15	15	5/15	5/7.5	15
Netherlands	15	5/15	10/15	0/15	5/15	10/15	0/15	0	5/15	2.5/15	—	5/15	0/15	0/15	5/15	5/15	25
Spain	18	15	15	10/15	10/15	10/15	18	15	10/15	18	5/15	—	10/15	10/15	10/15	18	18
Sweden	15	15	15	5/15	0	5/15	0	10/15	10/15	5/15	0/15	10/15	—	5	0	5/15	30
Switzerland	15	10/15	15	0	5/15	5/15	10/15	15	10/15	35	0/15	10/15	5	—	5/15	5/15	35
United Kingdom	0	0	0	0	0	0	0	0	0	0	0	0	0	0	—	0	0
United States	15	15	10/15	5/15	5/15	15	5/15	5/15	10/15	5/15	5/15	30	5/15	5/15	5/15	—	30

Source: *International Tax Summaries 1986, A Guide for Planning and Decisions,* Coopers & Lybrand International Tax Network, Jon D. Jacobs, Editor, John Wiley & Sons, Inc. (1986)

Additionally, interest paid to nonresidents on deposits in U.S. banks and certain other financial institutions is generally free of U.S. tax.

Income "effectively connected" to a U.S. trade or business is sourced to the U.S. and taxed at regular rates. If income is "effectively connected" to a U.S. trade or business, tax credits or deductions may be available to the nonresident alien.

U.S. source capital gains of nonresidents are generally not subject to U.S. tax if unrelated to a U.S. business *and* if the nonresident is not physically present in the United States for 183 days or more.

APPLICATION OF THE SOURCE RULES

Dividends

Generally, dividends from U.S. corporations are U.S. sourced income, and dividends paid by foreign corporations are foreign sourced income. However, as with most tax provisions, the difficulty is not with the general rule, but with the interpretation and application of the exceptions.

Domestic corporations are permitted to exclude income received from sources outside the United States, if within a three-year period immediately preceding the close of a tax year, at least eighty percent of the gross income is derived from sources outside the United States.

Dividends from foreign corporations are generally foreign source income unless 50 percent or more of its gross income for a three year period preceding the declaration of the dividend was effectively connected with a U.S. trade or business.

Interest Income

U.S. sourced interest income generally includes interest from interest-bearing obligations assumed or issued by a resident of the United States, as well as by the United States, its agencies and instrumentalities, states, political subdivisions, the District of Columbia, and

U.S. territories. For purposes of the interest source rules, the term "resident of the United States" includes (1) individuals who are U.S. residents at the time of the interest payment; (2) U.S. corporations; (3) U.S. partnerships which at any time during their tax year are engaged in trade or business in the U.S.; and (4) any foreign corporation or partnership which at any time during its taxable year is engaged in a trade or business in the United States.

Interest received by nonresident aliens and foreign corporations on deposits in banks, savings and loan associations, and insurance companies which is not effectively connected with a U.S. trade or business is not sourced to the United States. Exceptions are also made for interest received from a resident alien or domestic corporation where less than 20 percent of the payor's total gross income during the three preceding tax years was received from U.S. sources, and for interest on deposits with foreign branches of U.S. banks or savings and loan associations.

Interest on foreign obligations is generally foreign source income except where interest is paid by a foreign corporation which had 50 percent or more of its gross income for the preceding three-year period effectively connected with a U.S. trade or business. A prorata portion of such income is treated as being sourced in the United States.

Royalties

Royalties from property located in the United States or from an interest in such property are U.S. source income. This category would include U.S. patents and copyrights.

Gain from Sales of Portfolio Investment Property

Gain from the sale of portfolio investment property not effectively connected to a U.S. trade or business is treated as derived from the country where the property is sold. However, if such property is sold within the United States, any resulting gain would be U.S. source income. The "place of sale" is defined as where the rights, title, and interest pass to the buyer. In the event the seller retains bare title to the property, then the time and place that beneficial ownership and risk pass to the buyer governs the place of sale. The Internal Revenue Service has the authority to examine a transaction to determine if it has been manipulated primarily for tax avoidance purposes; in such cases, the IRS can establish the time and place of sale at the point where the substance of the sale occurred, considering all facts and circumstances of the transaction.

TAX CONSIDERATIONS FOR U.S. CITIZENS AND RESIDENT ALIENS INVESTING OUTSIDE THE U.S.

U.S. portfolio investors must focus their planning efforts on the reduction of their global tax liability. This requires a two-pronged approach. U.S. tax planning will focus on foreign tax credits and available deductions which can offset the income generated by the investment; foreign planning efforts will be directed at obtaining a full understanding of local tax laws and available means to reduce potential double taxation of portfolio earnings.

U.S. TAX CONSIDERATIONS

Since U.S. taxable income is determined on a worldwide basis, U.S. investors with foreign investments are exposed to double taxation on foreign earnings. The foreign tax credit (FTC) provisions attack the second tier, or foreign level, of tax. As a result, the U.S. tax provisions assure that the FTC cannot bestow additional benefits on the U.S. taxpayer (i.e., provide a credit for foreign taxes paid in excess of the U.S. taxes which would have been paid on an equivalent amount of domestic income). Generally, an FTC is allowed to the extent of any income taxes or payments in lieu of income taxes, paid or accrued to any foreign country or to any possession of the United States. Alternatively, an election is available to take a deduction for such foreign taxes paid as an itemized deduction. However, the benefit attributable to the tax deduction is generally less than could be obtained by taking a tax credit. Under certain circumstances, discussed below, the deduction may still be advisable.

Resident aliens are allowed the FTC in most cases. However, use of the FTC by citizens of certain countries may be denied if reciprocal credits are not afforded U.S. citizens residing in the alien's country. Additionally, individuals who are entitled to exclude income from sources within the U.S. possessions cannot take the FTC.

Foreign Tax Credit Mechanism

In order to obtain the FTC, the qualified U.S. taxpayer must elect to forego claiming the itemized deduction for all foreign taxes paid. That is, either all foreign taxes paid in a given year are claimed for FTC or all are claimed as a deduction. However, the election is revocable for the period in which a claim for credit or refund must be filed (usually three years from the later of the due date of the return or actual filing date).

Cash basis taxpayers generally claim the FTC for the year the foreign taxes were paid. However, an election can be made to claim foreign tax credits for foreign taxes *accrued.* Accordingly, in the year of such accrual election, the investor can obtain an FTC for taxes paid in the current year *and* for taxes accrued for a subsequent year. The election is binding on all future years and to the extent of any variance between accrual amounts and actual tax payments, the IRS must be notified. The adjustment will be computed and any additional tax payment due, or overpayment to be refunded will be determined by the IRS.

The FTC to be applied to U.S. tax liability must be translated to a U.S. dollar figure. The rate of exchange on the date the foreign tax is paid is used by cash method taxpayers; accrual basis FTCs are computed utilizing the exchange rate as of the last day of the tax year.

Foreign Tax Credit Limitations

The credit claimed for foreign taxes paid or accrued cannot exceed the U.S. income tax liability attributable to the taxable income from all sources outside the United States. Generally, operating losses in one foreign country will offset income from another foreign country. However, separate limitation categories, or "baskets" limit the credit allowable on certain income categories. The passive income basket includes the following foreign source income items:

- Dividends
- Interest
- Rents and Royalties (except business rents and royalties from unrelated parties)
- Gains from the disposition of noninventory property that give rise to passive income (e.g. patents) or nonincome producing property (e.g. gold)
- Undistributed foreign personal holding company income of a foreign personal holding company
- Income *equivalent* to interest
- Passive foreign investment company inclusions
- Gains from commodities transactions (except hedges and active business gains of a producer, processor, etc.)
- Foreign currency gains from transactions in financial assets and liabilities (except hedges)

Although the passive income basket appears to cover most forms of portfolio income, there are some significant exceptions. For example, a separate FTC basket is established for foreign interest that is subject to a 5 percent or greater foreign withholding tax.

As a result of the overall limitation and separate basket limitations, excess FTCs may be created. The excess credits may be carried back two years and forward five years. However, the total of unused credits carried to another year plus the current year FTCs, are subject to the FTC limitation for that current year. Excess credits in each basket are subject to the same limitation and carryback/forward rules. In the event excess foreign tax credits are expected to fall victim to the five-year carryforward limit, the alternative of claiming an itemized deduction for foreign taxes paid may salvage at least some value for the foreign taxes paid.

Foreign Personal Holding Companies

U.S. resident shareholders in foreign personal holding companies (FPHCs) may have to include a portion of the FPHCs earnings in their U.S. taxable income even though a dividend is not actually paid. A FPHC is a corporation over half of whose shares are owned by five or fewer U.S. citizens or residents. At least 50 percent of the FPHC's income must consist of dividends, interest, royalties, annuities, and certain other passive income.

FPHCs are taxed in a manner similar to U.S. personal holding companies (PHCs). Generally, a tax is imposed on undistributed FPHC income. The undistributed income subject to tax is calculated by making several adjustments to the corporation's regular taxable income, including deductions for capital gains. Under TRA provisions, the adjustment for net capital gains is allowed only if they are effectively connected with the conduct of a U.S. trade or business.

Controlled Foreign Corporations

Investors holding stock in a controlled foreign corporation (CFC) could be liable for U.S. tax on certain types of *undistributed* foreign source investment income. In essence, the CFC provisions eliminate the tax deferral benefit which could otherwise be enjoyed by the foreign corporation; however, it is the U.S. shareholders and not the CFC who are taxed on such undistributed income.

A CFC is a foreign corporation with over 50 percent (voting power or value) of its shares owned by citizens or residents of the United States, domestic partnerships, domestic corporations, or any non-foreign estate or trust that is deemed to be a "U.S. shareholder" under the CFC rules. To meet the definition of "U.S. shareholder," a U.S. citizen must own at least 10 percent of the voting power of the foreign corporation. As such, a foreign corporation owned 100 percent by unrelated U.S. citizens not one of whom controlled 10 percent or more of the stock in such corporation, would not be a CFC. The requisite share ownership may result from direct ownership, indirect ownership (via attribution rules which designate constructive ownership of shares owned by certain related parties), or through a combination of both direct and indirect ownership. Therefore, the investment group itself becomes a potential source of tax liability.

U.S. shareholders, as defined for CFC purposes, are required to include in income their prorata share of "Subpart F income" (generally, income from insurance of U.S. risks, foreign income of certain foreign personal holding companies and sales corporations, the CFCs income other than income which is included in the gross income of a U.S. citizen other than by reason of the CFC rules), previously excluded Subpart F income, and the increase of any earnings invested in U.S. property.

Passive Foreign Investment Companies

Formerly, foreign income of a foreign corporation that was not a controlled foreign corporation or a foreign personal holding company would escape U.S. tax consequences regardless of the character of the income or the nature of the shareholders. Tax on the undistributed earnings and profits was generally deferred, subject to tax at ordinary rates only upon disposition of stock in the foreign investment company. This rule applied to foreign corporations that were previously in the business of investing in securities or commodities if 50 percent or more of the corporation's value was held by U.S. citizens.

The TRA limits substantially the deferral benefit for "passive foreign investment companies" (PFICs). Generally, a PFIC is defined as any foreign corporation that derives 75 percent or more of its income from passive investments or any foreign corporation at least half of whose assets are passive assets. Except in the case of a PFIC that becomes a "qualified electing fund,"a U.S. shareholder of a PFIC must pay a special tax plus an interest charge on gain realized from the disposition of PIFC stock, or upon the receipt of an "excess distribution"(the shareholder's prorata portion of a total corporate distribution in excess of 125 percent of the prior three-years' distributions).

U.S. shareholders in "qualified electing funds" at any time during the fund's taxable year must include in income for their taxable year within which the taxable year of the fund ends, their prorata share of the fund's ordinary earnings and net capital gain for the fund's taxable year. These current inclusions will result in current tax unless the investor makes (subject to an interest charge) an election to defer U.S. tax on amounts included in income for which no current distribution is made.

FOREIGN COUNTRY TAX CONSIDERATIONS

The preceding discussion raises only the U.S. side of the tax analysis necessary to any investment decision. A thorough understanding of the foreign tax exposures associated with the foreign investment must be considered in conjunction with the U.S. provisions. The interaction of the foreign and domestic tax provisions, primarily as a result of the foreign tax credit, will result in the ultimate global tax cost.

Although analysis of each foreign country's tax laws is beyond the scope of this discussion, the same fundamental considerations outlined for U.S. purposes must be addressed in the foreign context: (1) the basis upon which each taxing jurisdiction imposes tax; (2) the tax rate structure(s) applicable to income generated by the investment; and (3) the issue-oriented tax provisions designed to address particular local country concerns and policies.

Generally, taxing jurisdictions can be grouped into one or more of the following categories:

- Source of Income—only income taxed is income derived from sources within the country, regardless of residence.
- Territorial Basis—all income derived from domestic sources and exempt foreign source income is taxed.
- Residence Basis—tax is imposed on a worldwide basis for all residents.

- Citizenship Basis—citizens of a country are taxed on their worldwide income.

The categories are by no means exclusive and are often combined. As can be seen from our prior discussions, the United States manages to use variations of all the tax bases.

CHAPTER THIRTY-ONE

OLIVIA P. ADLER is an associate in the Washington, D.C. office of Dechert Price & Rhoads, a Philadelphia law firm. Prior to joining the law firm, she was assistant counsel of the Investment Company Institute, the United States national trade association for open-end investment companies. She holds an A.B. from Radcliffe College and an LL.B. from Harvard Law School.

ANTHONY L. BARTOLINI is a partner with Dechert Price & Rhoads, where he specializes in U.S. taxation of international operations. Mr. Bartolini has served as chairman of the Mid-Atlantic Region of the International Fiscal Association and of the Tax Section of the Philadelphia Bar Assocation. Mr. Bartolini holds a B.A. from St. Barnard's Seminary and College and a J.D. from Villanova University.

ALLAN S. MOSTOFF is a partner in the Washington, D.C. office of Dechert Price & Rhoads. Prior to joining the firm in 1976, he was director of the Division of Investment Management Regulation of the United States Securities and Exchange Commission. He holds an undergraduate degree from Cornell University, an M.B.A. from New York University and an LL.B. from New York University Law School.

DAVID J. RACHOFSKY is a partner with Dechert Price & Rhoads. His corporate tax practice includes specialties in taxation of international operations, financial institutions and investment companies.

LEGAL IMPLICATIONS OF INTERNATIONAL PORTFOLIO INVESTMENT

Olivia P. Adler

Anthony L. Bartolini

Allan S. Mostoff

David J. Rachofsky

Dechert Price & Rhoads
Philadelphia, Pennsylvania

INTRODUCTION

An investor in securities of foreign issuers should be aware of a variety of issues which confront him not at all, or to only a small degree, when investing in U.S. securities. This chapter will touch on the types of legal issues which an investor should consider when contemplating portfolio investment in foreign securities. The discussion is not designed to be exhaustive but rather to highlight the most commonly encountered types of restrictions and to identify areas in which foreign practices are most likely to differ from those in the United States. The chapter does not deal with restrictions related to "direct investment"—investment or other action involving a control position in a foreign issuer.

GENERAL RISKS OF FOREIGN INVESTMENT

In addition to more specific legal issues which are discussed below, investors in foreign securities should be aware of a variety of political and economic factors which can affect their investments. The prospect of war, insurrection, economic terrorism, economic sanctions, or political changes leading to significant shifts in economic policy would, of course, make any investment extremely risky. In certain countries, the risk of expropriation, nationalization, or confiscatory taxation may be significant. Political or economic factors may also suggest that restrictions directed at foreign investors in general, or from certain countries, might be a possibility. In addition to these larger political and economic concerns, investors should be aware that the cost of conducting transactions in foreign securities is greater than in the United States. Not only are there communications and currency exchange expenses that are not entailed in domestic transactions, but commissions and custodian fees are often higher in other countries than in the United States. Finally, a variety of other economic factors, regulatory arrangements, and securities practices can significantly affect the cost of investing in foreign securities.

EXCHANGE CONTROLS

The United States currently has no exchange control regulations. Although at one time it did impose controls on foreign direct investment as well as an excise tax on foreign portfolio investments (Interest Equalization Tax), these have now been dropped. Many other countries, however, do currently have exchange control regulations of various types, as discussed below.

Exchange Rates

The value of securities or bank deposits denominated in currencies other than the U.S. dollar may be affected favorably or unfavorably by changes in the exchange rates between such currencies and the U.S. dollar. Changes in foreign currency rates will also affect the value of dividends and interest earned on foreign securities, the value of gains and losses realized on the sale of securities, and various transaction costs payable in foreign currency. The free market rate of exchange between the U.S. dollar and other currencies is determined by the forces of supply and demand in the foreign exchange markets. These forces are affected by factors such as the international balance of payments, inflation, speculation, and other economic and financial conditions.

Exchange rates are also affected by regulations adopted by specific countries to moderate or negate the impact of free market forces. Some countries may fix exchange rates or peg their rates to a "basket" of specified currencies. In Latin America, where complex exchange controls are common, different exchange rates may be applicable to different types of transactions, as has been the case, at times, in Mexico.[1] Governments may also intervene on an ad hoc basis to influence the exchange rates for their currencies or engage in planned longer-term programs to raise or lower the value of their currencies relative to those of other countries, such as key trading partners. Members of the European Economic Community (EEC) have established a European Monetary System designed to stabilize exchange rates within the EEC. However, the rates are subject to periodic realignment within the system. Investors may engage in currency transactions, including the use of forward currency contracts, in an attempt to hedge against currency fluctuations. Such techniques may be particularly helpful in countries where the settlement period for securities transactions is protracted.

Other Exchange Controls—General

In addition to direct action regarding exchange rates, countries may impose other types of exchange controls which affect the conduct of international transactions. France, for example, has an extensive system of exchange controls designed to control transactions affecting the French franc and capital movements in and out of

France.[2] All trading in francs, as well as capital movements in and out of France, must be conducted through banks registered to operate in France.[3] Transactions in francs outside France[4] or with nonresidents[5] are sharply limited and all payments of dividends and interest by residents to nonresidents must be made through an authorized intermediary.[6] Borrowings from nonresidents, including issuance of debt securities, must also comply with exchange control regulations.[7]

Germany and the United Kingdom, by contrast, have few restrictions on international investment or currency movement,[8] though Germany does require Bundesbank approval of certain loans which either involve foreign currencies or are indexed on a basis other than DMs.[9] Reports concerning various international transactions must also be filed with the Bundesbank,[10] though the transactions are not regulated.[11]

Other types of exchange controls are enforced by means of restrictions on foreign investment and on repatriation of capital and earnings. These are described below. Investors should be aware that regulations in this area are subject to change and that some countries change their rules quite frequently. Moreover, the imposition and alteration of exchange controls is regarded, in international law, as an inherent governmental power and any damages resulting from these actions are ordinarily not recoverable.[12]

Restrictions on Foreign Portfolio Investment

The United States does not generally restrict foreign portfolio investment in U.S. companies but does attempt to monitor significant foreign investment positions in publicly traded U.S. companies by requiring reporting by owners of 5 percent or more of a class of an issuer's equity securities.[13] Similar reports are required from institutional investors exercising investment discretion over accounts holding, in the aggregate, over $100 million in equity securities.[14] Additional rules regulate tender offers for U.S. companies, establishing procedural and disclosure requirements.[15] These provisions apply to all investors, and are not specifically directed at foreigners.

Many foreign countries, however, set limits on the extent to which non-nationals can invest in their securities, or require prior government approval for investment by foreigners. Some may also close sensitive industries to foreign investment. This general type of restriction is common in Latin America, the Far East, and Scandinavia. Mexico, for example, limits the percentage of voting stock of Mexican corporations which can be owned by non-Mexican nationals. Moreover, Mexican law generally is implemented to reserve ownership of expansions of business to Mexicans, so that the opportunity for foreign investment does not increase with industrial growth.[16] Since non-Mexican affiliates of Mexican companies own and retain most of the stock available to non-Mexicans, most of the stock currently traded in Mexico is not available to foreign investors. Moreover, certain sectors of the Mexican economy, including petrochemicals, minerals, and utilities, are reserved for the Mexican nation and are not available for foreign investment.[17] In Argentina, investment in certain key sectors requires prior government approval, which is difficult to obtain,[18] and Brazil either prohibits or limits foreign investment in certain industries.[19]

Among the Far Eastern countries, Korea permits foreign investors to purchase securities issued in Korea only with permission from the Korean Ministry of Finance, though certain Korean companies are permitted to make limited types of offerings abroad.[20] Foreign investment in Taiwan is similarly restricted.[21] In Singapore, Malaysia, and Thailand, investment by foreign investors may be subject to percentage limitations, while in the Philippines, foreigners may own only Class B shares.[22] Until 1980, Japan required that foreigners obtain prior governmental approval for a securities purchase. Prior approval now is required only under exceptional circumstances. Japan does, however, require prior notice for some types of foreign purchases of Japanese securities.[23]

Finland, Sweden, and Norway prohibit foreign purchases of debt securities and sharply limit the proportion of an issuer's equity securities which may be owned by foreigners, as well as the extent to which foreigners can exercise voting rights. Moreover, exchange control policies in some Scandinavian countries require foreign investors in certain instances to obtain central bank permits before investing in securities. Those equity securities which are available to foreigners often trade at a premium, and the market for such shares—because it is more limited—is thus more volatile and less liquid than the market for such securities available to Scandinavian nationals.[24] Some Scandinavian countries may also prohibit foreigners from investing in certain key or sensitive industries. Denmark, for example, does not permit foreign investment in companies engaged in arms trading,[25] while Sweden prohibits foreign investment in banks, finance companies and stockbrokers.[26]

While restrictions of this type are not prevalent in Europe, Italy requires that an Italian bank review the reasonableness of the price in any securities sale between an Italian resident and a non-resident.[27]

Many countries require that existing shareholders have preferential rights to subscribe to new issues of a company's shares. Certain countries, such as Norway, may also require that foreign investors, if prohibited by applicable percentage limitations on foreign ownership from exercising their rights, sell their rights or the securities to nationals, or agree to limits on voting the shares. Norway also gives company employees the right to subscribe for shares not subscribed to by shareholders.[28] Policies of this type not only restrict the rights of foreign investors but serve to further limit their investment opportunities.

Restrictions on Repatriation of Investment and Earnings

Countries may impose controls limiting the extent to which the proceeds of investments may be repatriated by a foreign investor. The following examples merely suggest the variety of forms such controls may take. In Korea, for example, conversions of Won into foreign exchange, transfers of funds out of Korea, and repatriation of capital are subject to considerable restrictions and require government approval.[29] Venezuela requires registration of foreign investments and requires prior approval of repatriation of profits, with only specified portions permitted to be repatriated annually.[30] Brazil permits repatriation but imposes progressively higher taxes on withdrawals exceeding certain percentages.[31] Restrictions on repatriation in other countries, by contrast, may simply require that the initial investment be registered with or approved by the appropriate authorities (e.g. Spain)[32] or that repatriation be via an approved intermediary (e.g. France)[33] or reported to an appropriate authority (e.g. Germany).[34] Repatriation is often subject to clearance as to payment of any required taxes. Other restrictions may permit repatriation only up to certain annual percentage limits (e.g. Italy)[35] or to the extent sufficient foreign exchange is available (e.g. Argentina).[36] Restrictions may also relate to whether payments are proceeds from sale of a capital investment or interest and dividend payments (e.g. India).[37] Some countries may require that interest or other payments due to foreigners be placed in "blocked accounts" under certain conditions (e.g. India, Greece, Egypt).[38] Assets placed in such accounts can often be used locally but their withdrawal from the country is prohibited or subject to certain approvals, annual limits, or other conditions. Where assets in such accounts are invested, investment income may, or may not, be subject to the same restrictions as capital assets.

Another additional complication for foreign investors is that certain countries which impose withholding taxes on dividends and other securities-related payments may retain an excess amount with respect to foreign investors—particularly institutional investors. The United Kingdom, Holland, and Switzerland, for example, retain amounts in excess of taxes for which the investor is actually liable (the excess being the tax credit available to the investor under the relevant tax treaty with the United States), and investors can recover the excess only upon application. Recovery of these amounts, on which no interest is paid, can take several months to a year.

Non-Resident Accounts

Exchange rate risks and, in some countries, risks of currency blockage or other government action may make maintenance of non-resident accounts unattractive. Foreign investors who do wish, nevertheless, to maintain cash in local bank accounts to facilitate their investment activities should inquire as to the authority of local banks to provide such accounts, as well as restrictions applicable to nonresident accounts. Some countries may limit the balances in these accounts or impose restrictions as to the use of funds held in such accounts. Chile, for example, permits such accounts to be used only for conversions to local currency, or to cover imports.[39] Restrictions may also depend on whether the deposit is in local or foreign currency, whether transactions are for local or foreign activities, or whether the funds on deposit are from capital or other types of transactions (e.g. Finland).[40] Some countries may set different interest rates for "nonresident" and "resident" accounts.

SECURITIES MARKETS

Compared to the high standard set by U.S. securities markets, the quality of securities markets in foreign countries varies widely. Foreign stock and bond markets are generally not as developed or efficient as in the United States, and there is greater price volatility. The following chart lists the ten largest securities markets based on total market capitalization of listed equity securities on September 30, 1985.

MARKET CAPITALIZATION
September 30, 1985

Rank	Market	(In Billions)
1	United States	U.S. $1,711
2	Japan	817
3	United Kingdom	290
4	Canada	134
5	West Germany	133
6	Australia	64
7	Switzerland	63
8	France	57
9	Italy	50
10	Netherlands	42

Source: *Capital International Perspective* (Issue IV) 1985, Capital International Perspective S.A., Geneva, Switzerland.

By contrast, the following charts provide comparable statistics for Scandinavian and Far Eastern markets.

MARKET CAPITALIZATION
March 31, 1986

Rank	Market	(In Billions)
1	Sweden	U.S. $ 51.2
2	Denmark	16.0
3	Norway	9.5
4	Finland	7.1
*	United States	2,630.0

Source: *The Scandinavia Fund, Inc.* prospectus dated June 17, 1986.

MARKET CAPITALIZATION
December 31, 1985[41]

Rank	Market	(In Billions)
1	Hong Kong	U.S. $34.50
2	Malaysia	16.46[42]
3	Singapore	11.07
4	Taiwan	10.34
5	Korea	7.38
6	Thailand	1.86
7	Philippines	.87

Source: *The Asia Pacific Fund, Inc.*, preliminary prospectus dated September 2, 1986.

Market capitalization is not necessarily indicative of market liquidity however. Markets in some countries may be characterized by low float—i.e., significant portions of shares listed may not be actively traded. This is true, for example, in Italy.[43]

Trading may be carried on over a variety of exchanges as well as in the over-the-counter market. For example, the United States has ten stock exchanges, compared with West Germany (eight), Japan (eight), France (seven), Switzerland (seven), and Canada (five), while the United Kingdom, the Netherlands, Belgium, Luxembourg, Denmark, Sweden, Norway, Italy, Singapore, Hong Kong,

Malaysia, South Africa, Indonesia, Kuwait, Australia, Mexico, Brazil, Israel, and Bahrain all have at least one exchange.[44]

Exchanges may differ considerably in the types of securities they list. While some exchanges, as in the United States, are used predominantly for equity securities, other exchanges, such as the Amsterdam exchange, are used largely for bonds. The Stock Exchange in London lists a large number of government bonds as well as equity securities. The Luxembourg Exchange lists 70 percent of all Eurobond issues.[45] Hong Kong, on the other hand, has a well-developed equity market, but had only eight interest-bearing securities as of July 31, 1986.[46]

The role of large institutions and the degree to which they dominate the market in general, or specific types of securities, varies widely. In Japan, for example, the four leading securities firms are responsible for a significant portion of market transactions, including transactions for their own accounts, having significant impacts on prices.[47]

Additionally, most countries do not prevent commercial banks from engaging in investment banking, so banks are likely to play a more significant role in foreign securities markets than they do in the United States. In West Germany, for example, banks are members of stock exchanges and often maintain significant long-term equity positions in publicly traded securities.[48]

SETTLEMENT PROCEDURES

Investors used to the seven-day settlement procedures in the United States may be startled by the time required to settle purchases abroad. Italy, for example provides for monthly settlement of transactions in exchange-listed equity securities, and settlement may take considerable longer in fact. Moreover, foreign purchasers of Italian securities are required to deposit amounts up to 100 percent of the purchase price until settlement occurs and when selling securities must similarly deposit those securities until settlement.[49] In France, securities are traded either in the cash, or "spot," market, the monthly settlement market, or the conditional settlement market.

In the last instance, the purchaser's obligation becomes firm only at his option upon the fulfillment of certain conditions. Then the transaction becomes a monthly settlement transaction and collateral deposits of 20-40 percent are required.[50] Securities transactions in the Scandinavian countries generally settle in three to seven days,[51] while transactions in West Germany settle on the second business day following trading.[52]

REGULATION OF BROKER-DEALERS AND INVESTMENT ADVISERS

The United States imposes an extensive system of licensing and compliance regulations on broker-dealers, which is enforced through the joint efforts of the Securities and Exchange Commission, state securities commissions, stock exchanges, and self-regulatory groups. A similar but less extensive system is in place for investment advisers. Few other countries regulate these activities as strictly.

Most countries with developed securities markets regulate broker-dealers to some degree. Regulation in Japan, Canada, and Australia is by means of registration with a government agency which is also empowered to deny registration.[53] The United Kingdom requires securities dealers to obtain a license from the appropriate government agency, except that members of the Stock Exchange are regulated exclusively by that exchange.[54] France regulates dealers through a combined government agency and self-regulatory process.[55] The Asterdam Exchange is the sole regulator of broker-dealers in the Netherlands.[56]

Regulation of investment advisers is much less prevalent. The United States, Canada, and Australia are the only countries with a regulatory process for this industry.[57]

SECURITIES REGULATION

The securities regulatory systems of different countries vary widely in style, from minimal to comprehensive. Regulation may be administered by government agencies, as in the United States, or through the stock exchanges or other self-regulatory organizations.

France, Italy, and Mexico, for example, administer their securities laws through national commissions along the lines of the U.S. Securities and Exchange Commission.[58] In the Netherlands and West Germany, on the other hand, securities regulation is conducted almost entirely by the stock exchanges.[59] Canada and, to a lesser extent, Australia resemble the United States in having certain securities laws and regulations administered by their various states.[60]

Much of what is accomplished through securities laws in some countries is done through laws governing corporations in others.

Disclosure Documents

Few countries have prospectus disclosure requirements comparable to those of the United States, though most countries where capital is raised through securities offerings do require disclosure documents meeting certain standards. Requirements are often set by stock exchanges. Securities listed on the Stock Exchange of London must publish a full prospectus in the financial press. Prospectuses are also published in West Germany in connection with offerings of exchange-listed securities.

Continuous Reporting

There is wide variation in the degree of continuous disclosure required in foreign countries. Canada, Australia, and Japan are similar to the United States in requiring the filing of annual and other periodic reports with relevant regulatory authorities. West Germany, France, the United Kingdom, and the Netherlands are among the countries which impose annual and periodic reporting requirements.[61]

Countries requiring reporting of material developments include various Canadian provinces, France, the United Kingdom, the Netherlands, Australia, and Japan.[62]

The European Economic Community has taken some steps to develop common minimum disclosure and continuous reporting requirements for community members, though practices in these countries still vary widely.

ACCOUNTING AND AUDITING

One area of continuing diversity worldwide is in standards of accounting. Some of the principle areas of foreign contrast with U.S. practices are as follows:

— Consolidated statements. They may not be required or are prepared on a basis different from that used in the United States;
— methods for valuing inventories, investments, and fixed assets;
— accounting for contingencies and estimated liabilities;
— accounting for stock dividends;
— accounting used for mergers and acquisitions;
— statements of sources and applications of funds;
— standards regarding the timing and recognition of income.[63]

With growing internationalization in securities transactions, some of these differences may diminish. For example, in 1987 standards in Germany were changed to conform with Council Directive Nos. 4, 7, and 8 of the European Economic Community. These changes bring German standards closer to U.S. standards.[64]

Foreign auditing practices may differ from U.S. practices regarding confirmation of receivables and observation of physical inventories. Also, foreign auditors are in many cases not required to be independent of the issuers which they audit.[65]

INSIDER TRADING

Most countries with well-developed capital markets recognize that control of insider trading is necessary to maintain investor confidence in the markets. However, none has controls as extensive as those in the United States and some, such as Italy,[66] the Netherlands, and Belgium have no controls at all.[67] Hong Kong has regulations in this area but no enforcement mechanism.[68] Insider trading is not currently a crime in Switzerland, but bankers and company officials can be prosecuted under bank secrecy or business secrets laws for passing inside information to third parties.[69] Switzerland has now given preliminary approval to a bill which would make insider trading itself a crime.[70]

In the United Kingdom, it is a crime to trade in a Stock Exchange listed security using inside information which would materially affect the price. A recently enacted law permits Government-appointed inspectors to examine persons suspected of being involved in the illegal use of insider information to trade shares for personal gain.[71] Directors of companies are required to report their holdings and those of their immediate families, as well as changes in such holdings.[72] Trading on inside information in certain limited categories is a crime in France, but only with respect to stock exchange transactions.[73] West Germany deals with insider trading pursuant to a voluntary regulatory scheme. Participating companies adopt rules preventing certain insiders from engaging in stock exchange transactions using inside information.[74] The prohibitions in these countries do not extend to major stockholders or auditors and do not cover tipping.

Most of Canada's provinces regulate insider trading and Ontario, in particular, has more far reaching rules in the area than the United States.[75] Rules in Australia are also extensive.[76] Those in Japan, however, are relatively ineffective.[77]

Bank secrecy laws in countries such as Switzerland and the inability to pierce nominee accounts have impeded efforts to regulate insider trading throughout the world. Switzerland, as noted above, appears to be responding to some extent to pressures to be more accommodating to needs of foreign enforcement authorities.

TAKE-OVER REGULATION

The United Kingdom, the Netherlands, Canada, Australia, France, Hong Kong, and Japan all have rules governing takeovers. Canada,

Australia, and France also have rules either restricting or requiring special approval for takeovers by foreign investors. West Germany has no takeover rules. This is probably due to the fact that large blocks of stock in the leading companies are held by banks and other entities so that takeovers cannot easily be attempted without their cooperation.[78]

SHAREHOLDERS' RIGHTS

The corporate laws of most countries provide for annual shareholders' meetings and voting by proxy, and the solicitation of proxies is generally undertaken to meet legal quorum requirements. Few countries regulate this process as extensively as the United States and Canada. In countries where companies commonly issue shares in bearer form, communication with shareholders is difficult in any event. In France and West Germany, for example, quorum requirements are generally met by soliciting the banks or brokers who hold customers' securities. Japan regulates the solicitation of proxies for listed securities and has experienced several hotly fought proxy contests. Australia, the United Kingdom, the Netherlands, and Switzerland, on the other hand, have virtually no proxy regulations.[79]

It should be noted that voting rights for shares held by non-nationals may be restricted. For example, Sweden[80] and Finland[81] have specific percentage limits as to shares which may be voted by non-nationals.

While foreign countries generally do not extensively protect shareholders' voting rights, shareholders' preemptive rights to new issues of shares by a company whose stock they own is much more widespread abroad than in the United States, as has been noted earlier. And employees may have subscription rights prior to those of the general public, as is the case in Norway. Preemptive rights may be somewhat circumscribed for non-nationals, however, due to restrictions otherwise applicable to their ownership of shares.

Many foreign countries permit the issuance of shares in "bearer" form. While this permits individual shareowners' identities to be kept secret, it also inhibits communication with shareholders on various corporate matters. Thus, countries where "bearer" shares are common have generally relied on publication in the press for communicating with shareholders and announcing dividends, while shareholders arrange for the banks and stockholders holding their shares to track and communicate such notices and collect dividend payments on their behalf.

LIMITATIONS ON DIVIDENDS

Corporation laws of some countries may place specific limitations on a company's payment of dividends. In the Scandinavian countries, for example, dividends must be authorized at an annual shareholders' meeting and, except in Finland, may be reduced by legal reserve requirements of up to 10 percent of a company's annual net profits.[82] The Danish and Swedish governments have at various times enacted more restrictive rules.[83] Sweden also requires companies to contribute 20 percent of annual profits above a certain level to wage earners' funds used to purchase company shares.[84]

SUMMARY

Investment in international securities entails considerations far more comprehensive and complex than investing in domestic securities. Many of the variations in the legal environments adopted by nations represented in typical internationally diversified portfolios have been addressed in this chapter. Discussion of the legal constraints deployed by certain other countries makes clear why they are not candidates for most international investors. While admittedly not exhaustive, the sources cited in the footnotes may provide interested investors with additional material regarding the legal implications of international portfolio investment.

NOTES

[1]*The Mexico Fund, Inc.*, prospectus dated November 17, 1983, p. 19

[2]Law No. 66-1008 of December 28, 1966 (*Journal Officiel,* December 29, 1966)

[3]Decree 68-1021 of Nov. 24, 1968 (*Journal Officiel,* Nov. 25, 1968), Articles 1-2; Circular of Aug. 9, 1973 (*Journal Officiel,* August 10, 1973)

[4]Bank of France letter to Monsieur le Delegue General of the French Banking Association, May 31, 1978. See Arrete of Aug. 9, 1973 (*Journal Officiel,* August 10, 1973), Article 10.

[5]Bank of France letters Nos. 155 A.F. (June 24, 1970), 234 A.F. (April 7, 1982) and 238 A.F. (August 26, 1982)

[6]Arrete of Aug. 9, 1973 (*Journal Officiel,* August 10, 1973), Articles 2 and 5

[7]See, e.g., Circular of Jan. 19, 1974 (*Journal Officiel* January 20, 1974), Title I

[8]See Section 1 of the Foreign Trade Law (Aussenwirtschaftsgesetz) of April 28, 1961, as amended; Exchange Control Notice EC84, October 24, 1979.

[9]Currency Law (Wahrungsgesetz) of June 20, 1948, Section 3

[10]Foreign Trade Law, Section 26, and Regulation implementing the Foreign Trade Law (Aussenwirtschaftsverordnung) of Aug. 31, 1973, as amended, Sections 55-69

[11]Regulation implementing the Foreign Trade Law, Sections 55-58. See also, generally, "Capital Controls Within the Common Market," Claude C. Kelly, Jr. *International Financial Law*, 2d Ed., R.S. Rendell, Editor, Vol. 2

[12]"Capital Controls in Latin America," Richard C. Allison, *International Financial Law,* note 11, supra, p. 31

[13]Sections 13(d) and 13(g) under the Securities Exchange Act of 1934, and related rules

[14]Section 13(f) and Rule 13f-1 under the Securities Exchange Act of 1934

[15]Section 14(d) of the Securities Exchange Act of 1934, and related rules

[16]See note 12, supra, pp. 34-35

[17]*Id.*, p. 34

[18]See note 12, supra, p. 32

[19]*Id.*, p. 33

[20]*The Korea Fund, Inc.*, prospectus dated May 23, 1986, p. 7

[21]*The Asia Pacific Fund, Inc.*, preliminary prospectus dated September 2, 1986, p. 14

[22]*Id.*

[23]"Capital Controls Within Japan," by Ken Tsunematsu, *International Financial Law,* Note 11, supra, pp. 51-55

[24]*The Scandinavia Fund, Inc.*, prospectus dated June 17, 1986, pp. 9-10

[25]*The Nordic Fund Inc.*, prospectus dated May 16, 1986, pp. 25
[26]*Id.*, p. 35.

[27]*The Italy Fund Inc.*, prospectus dated February 26, 1986, p. 9

[28]*The Nordic Fund Inc.*, preliminary prospectus dated May 16, 1986, pp. 23-24

[29]*The Korea Fund, Inc.*, prospectus dated May 23, 1986, p. 7

[30]See note 12, supra, p. 35

[31]*Id.*, p. 33

[32]*Foreign Exchange Information—A Worldwide Summary* (1985 Edition), Price Waterhouse Information Guide ("Price Waterhouse"), p. 133

[33]*Id.*, p. 50

[34]*Id.*, p. 53

[35]*Id.*, p. 65

[36]See note 32, supra, p. 1

[37]*Id.*, p. 60

[38]*Id.*, pp. 60, 55, 45

[39]See note 32, supra, p. 27

[40]*Id.*, p. 48

[41]Unless otherwise noted

[42]Due to significant overlap between the Kuala Lumpur Stock Exchange and The Stock Exchange of Singapore, data are only for those companies which are both listed and registered in their respective countries.

[43]*The Italy Fund Inc.*, prospectus dated February 26, 1986, p. 9

[44]*Bloomenthal, International Capital Markets and Securities Regulation* (1986), p. 122

[45]*Id.*, p. 123

[46]*The Asia pacific Fund Inc.*, preliminary prospectus dated September 2, 1986, p. A-6

[47]*The Japan Fund, Inc.*, prospectus dated May 15, 1975, pp. 40-41

[48]*The Germany Fund, Inc.*, preliminary prospectus dated May 9, 1986, p. 12

[49]*The Italy Fund, Inc.*, prospectus dated February 26, 1986, p. 10

[50]*The France Fund, Inc.*, prospectus dated May 30, 1986, p. 17

[51]*The Scandinavia Fund, Inc.*, prospectus dated June 17, 1986, p. 20

[52]*The German Fund, Inc.*, preliminary prospectus dated May 9, 1986, p. 31

[53]Bloomenthal, note 44, *supra*, pp. 1-140

[54]*Id.*, pp. 1-141

[55]*Id.*

[56]*Id.*

[57]*Id.*

[58]Bloomenthal, note 44, supra, p. 1-65

[59]*Id.*, p. 1-66

[60]*Id.*, p. 1-65 to 1-66

[61]Bloomenthal, note 44, supra, pp. 1-69 to 172

[62]*Id.*

[63]Mostoff and Spencer, ''United States Regulation of International Securities Transactions,'' *International Financial Law* (2d. Ed., 1983), Euromony Publications, edited by Robert S. Rendell, p. 2

[64]*The Germany Fund, Inc.*, preliminary prospectus dated May 9, 1986, p. 16

[65]Mostoff and Spencer, note 63, supra, p. 2

[66]*The Italy Fund, Inc.*, prospectus dated February 26, 1986, p. 19

[67]Bloomenthal, note 44, supra, p. 1-98

[68]*The Asia Pacific Fund, Inc.*, preliminary prospectus dated September 2, 1986, p. A-6

[69]*The Washington Post,*October 8, 1986, p. Gl

[70]*Id.*

[71]*The New York Times,* November 17, 1986, p. D4

[72]Bloomenthal, note 44, supra, pp. 1-90 to 1-91

[73]*Id.*, p. 1-92

[74]*Id.*, pp. 1-93 to 1-94

[75]Bloomenthal, note 44, supra, pp. 1-94 to 1-96

[76]*Id.*, pp. 1-97 to 1-98

[77]*Id.*, p. 198

[78]*Id.*, p. 1-101 et. seq.

[79]Bloomenthal, note 44, supra, p. 1-133 et. seq.

[80]*The Nordic Fund, Inc.*, preliminary prospectus dated May 16, 1986, p. 35

[81]*Id.*, p. 28

[82]*The Nordic Fund, Inc.*, preliminary prospectus dated May 16, 1986, pp. 24-26

[83]*Id.*, p. 25 et. seq.

[84]*Id.*, p. 36

SECTION VII

Summary

CHAPTER THIRTY-TWO

KATHLEEN P. WEBER is a Project Leader in the Trading Analytics Group of Information Services at Salomon Brothers Inc in New York. Currently, she is responsible for providing analytical programming support to the fixed-income trading areas. Prior to joining Trading Analytics, Ms. Weber was an Analyst in the International Bond Market Research Group and was responsible for the monthly publication "International Bond and Money Market Performance Indices." Ms. Weber received a BS in Computer Applications and Information Systems from New York University in 1961.

SUSAN BADYNA is an analyst in the International Bond Market Research Group at Salomon Brothers Inc in New York. She follows both the dollar and nondollar bond markets and is responsible for publishing the monthly report *International Bond and Money Market Performance Indices*. Ms. Badyna holds a Bachelor of Arts Degree in Economics.

INTERNATIONAL BOND AND MONEY MARKET PERFORMANCE 1978-85: EIGHT-YEAR REVIEW

Kathleen P. Weber
Susan Badyna
Salomon Brothers Inc
New York, New York

INTRODUCTION

As bond market performance has become more important on a worldwide basis, the need has arisen for an accurate, replicable fixed-income benchmark. Increasingly, index returns are being used as a comprehensive representation of "market performance." Broad market indexes are also used for many asset allocation decisions. These considerations have heightened the importance of the replicability of index returns. This need is particularly important in situations where a portfolio manager desires to "buy the index" and consistently match the market's performance.

The Salomon Brothers International Bond and Money Market Performance Indexes provide a comprehensive measure of the total return performance of high-quality securities in major sectors of the bond and money markets. The indexes were introduced in September 1981 and contain historical information dating back to January 1, 1978.[1] Separate total rate-of-return indexes, in local currency and U.S. dollar terms, are updated monthly for bond and money market sectors in ten of the major international currencies, including the

U.S. dollar.[2] The Australian Government and Euro-ECU bond markets were added to the system on October 1, 1984.

In order to provide an overall measure of international fixed-income performance, the total return indexes for individual sectors were combined to form the World Bond Index and World Money Market Index. The bond index is calculated on both a weighted and unweighted basis. The World Bond Index (weighted) is a weighted average of the total-rate-of-return indexes for twenty-one fixed-rate bond markets denominated in ten currencies. The actual weights are based on the market value of bonds outstanding in each market, measured in U.S. dollars. The Salomon Brothers World Market Index is calculated on an unweighted (that is, equally weighted) basis, reflecting the lack of comprehensive data on relative market sizes. For example, domestic and Euro-Deutschemark deposits together receive 1/8 of the total weight of the World Money Market Index. (The unweighted Salomon Brothers World Bond Index is calculated in the same manner.)

In this chapter, we review the eight-year period since the inception of the indexes.

BEST AND WORST PERFORMANCES SINCE 1978

On a compound annual return basis, the U.S. dollar-denominated securities were the top performers since 1978. In U.S. dollar terms, Eurodollar floating-rate notes topped the eight-year best-performance list for both bonds and money market instruments, with a return of 13.0 percent.[3] Returns among the other top performers were similar—within a range of about 100 basis points. Foreign dollar and Eurodollar bonds posted returns of 10.9 percent and 10.8 percent, respectively. The Japanese Government sector and the U.S. Government market held fourth and fifth place, respectively, with returns of 10.4 percent and 9.8 percent.

Among the shorter-maturity instruments within the indexes, the U.S. dollar-denominated money markets also took the top four places. Returns on U.S. Treasury bills, domestic certificates of

TABLE 1 FIVE BEST AND WORST PERFORMERS, 1978-85
(Compound Annual Rate of Return in U.S. Dollar Terms)

Best

Bond Market		Money Market	
Eurodollar FRNs	13.0%	U.S. Dollar Eurodeposits	12.3%
Foreign Dollars	10.9	Eurodollar CDs	12.1
Eurodollars	10.8	U.S. Dollar Domestic CDs	11.7
Japanese Governments	10.4	U.S. Dollar Treasury Bills	10.6
U.S. Governments	9.8	Japanese Yen Eurodeposits	9.7

Worst

Bond Market		Money Market	
Swiss Governments	3.5%	Swiss Franc Eurodeposits	4.1%
Foreign Swiss Francs	4.1	Swiss Franc Domestic Deposits	4.2
West German Governments	5.4	Deutschemark Eurodeposits	5.2
Euro-Deutschemarks	5.4	Deutschemark Domestic Deposits	5.5
French Governments	5.7	Dutch Guilder Eurodeposits	5.7

deposit (CDs), Euro-CDs and Eurodollar deposits were 10.6 percent to 12.3 percent, and the rankings reflect the usual interest rate relationship among these instruments. The superior performance of the yen versus the U.S. dollar over the past eight years relative to other currencies put Japanese yen Eurodeposits in fifth place with a return of 9.7 percent.

The list of worst performers over the eight-year period was denominated by the Swiss and West German markets. The Swiss franc-denominated bond sectors posted returns of 3.5 percent to 4.1 percent, while the West German bond markets followed with 5.4 percent returns. Despite posting the largest currency decline (5.7 percent) on a compound annual basis over the past eight years, French Government bonds were the best of the worst with a 5.7 percent return in U.S. dollar terms. Swiss franc- and Deutschemark-denominated instruments were also the poorest performers in the money markets, recording returns of 4.1 percent to 4.2 percent and 5.2 percent to 5.5 percent, respectively. Dutch guilder Eurodeposits did slightly better with a 5.7 percent return.

The total rates of return in both local currency and U.S. dollar terms of individual market sectors on a year-by-year basis have differed substantially from the compound annual returns produced over the eight-year period. Since 1982—when performances in most of the bond markets finally outpaced their related money markets—annual total rates of returns in the bond markets continued to surpass, almost uninterrupted, the returns in the corresponding shorter-maturity markets. (Table 2 shows the annual total rates of return, in local currency and U.S. dollar terms, since 1978 for all the individual bond and money market subsectors, as well as the composite world indexes.) However, since this reversal in performance is fairly recent, in many cases, the compound annual returns still reflect the strength of the money markets in the earlier years.

Figure 1 illustrates the monthly levels of the total rate-of-return indexes of Government bonds measured in U.S. dollar terms for the period since 1978. As the top panel indicates, the U.S. and Canadian Government markets consistently moved together, reflecting the close interest rate and exchange rate relationship that exists

FIGURE 1 TOTAL RATE-OF-RETURN INDEXES OF GOVERNMENT BONDS, 1978-85
(U.S. Dollar Terms)

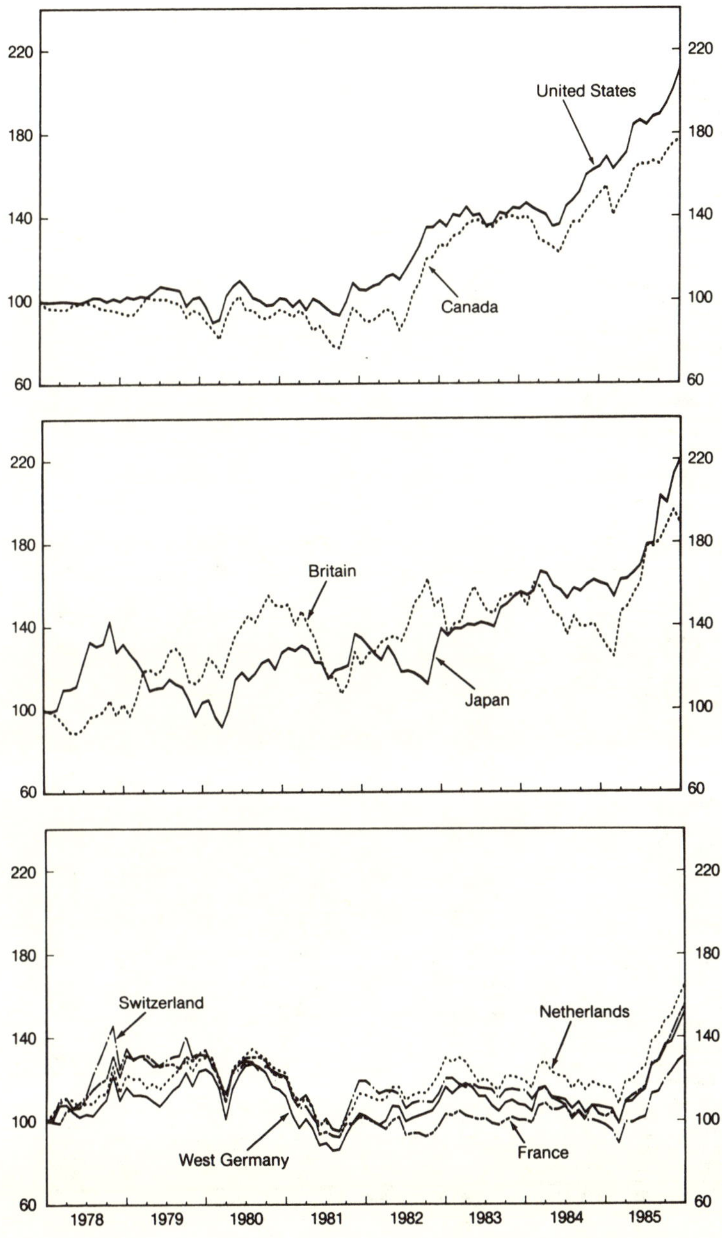

TABLE 2 TOTAL RATES OF RETURN OF INTERNATIONAL BOND AND MONEY MARKETS[a], 1978-85

	Local Currency Terms								
	1978	1979	1980	1981	1982	1983	1984	1985	1 Jan 78-31 Dec 85[b]
U.S. Dollar									
U.S. Government Bonds	-0.1%	1.9%	-0.8%	4.0%	31.3%	4.1%	14.3%	28.5%	9.8%
Foreign Dollar (Yankee) Bonds	3.0	-2.3	-1.3	0.7	40.1	10.0	15.9	27.9	10.9
Eurodollar Bonds	2.9	0.5	4.6	4.5	30.5	11.2	14.7	20.6	10.8
Eurodollar FRNs	9.2	13.3	14.4	20.1	15.2	10.5	12.7	9.3	13.0
Eurodollar Zeros[c]	—	—	—	—	—	9.4	11.3	36.5	23.4
U.S. Treasury Bills	7.3	10.5	12.1	15.8	11.7	9.1	10.4	8.1	10.6
Domestic CDs	8.1	11.6	13.3	18.0	13.6	9.4	11.4	8.4	11.7
Euro CDs	8.5	12.0	13.9	18.7	13.9	9.6	11.5	8.6	12.1
Eurodeposits	8.6	12.2	14.7	18.4	14.3	10.0	11.5	8.8	12.3
Canadian Dollar									
Canadian Government Bonds	2.2%	-1.7%	3.7%	-3.0%	41.4%	10.4%	15.2%	24.8%	10.8%
Euro-Canadian Dollar Bonds	3.2	1.4	6.2	11.0	20.0	16.2	15.5	17.5	11.2
Canadian Treasury Bills	8.2	11.6	12.6	20.0	15.0	9.5	11.7	9.7	12.2
Eurodeposits	8.7	12.1	13.7	19.5	16.2	10.1	11.6	10.2	12.7
Deutschemark									
West German Government Bonds	1.1%	1.6%	1.8%	5.1%	20.8%	5.1%	14.7%	10.9%	7.4%
Euro-Deutschemark Bonds	6.2	-0.7	0.7	6.7	19.1	6.6	12.4	10.0	7.5
Domestic Deposits	3.8	6.2	10.0	12.9	9.8	6.0	6.3	5.7	7.6
Eurodeposits	3.4	5.9	9.5	12.4	9.5	5.7	6.0	5.6	7.2
Japanese Yen									
Japanese Government Bonds	7.3%	-3.3%	4.4%	14.3%	10.4%	10.9%	11.5%	9.1%	7.9%
Samurai Bonds	6.7	-5.2	7.3	7.3	11.7	12.8	10.4	7.6	7.2
Euroyen Bonds	6.0	-6.4	4.7	12.3	12.5	9.7	10.9	7.5	7.0
Domestic CDs	5.4	5.5	11.4	8.4	7.0	6.9	6.8	6.7	7.2
Gensaki	5.4	5.6	11.0	8.2	7.1	6.7	6.5	6.6	7.1
Eurodeposits	5.4	5.9	11.8	8.3	7.2	6.7	6.6	6.6	7.3
U.K. Sterling									
U.K. Government Bonds	-2.7%	3.2%	19.7%	1.6%	49.3%	12.6%	8.9%	12.5%	12.2%
Eurosterling Bonds	-2.6	8.1	8.0	8.6	32.0	16.0	13.9	10.5	11.4
U.K. Treasury Bills	8.1	13.5	17.1	14.1	13.3	10.5	10.1	12.3	12.3
Domestic CDs	8.4	13.7	18.1	14.6	13.4	10.6	10.2	12.2	12.6
Eurodeposits	10.0	14.2	18.0	14.7	13.7	10.6	10.3	12.4	12.9
Swiss Franc									
Swiss Government Bonds	10.3%	-2.4%	0.8%	-0.3%	12.4%	3.4%	2.4%	5.8%	3.9%
Foreign Swiss Franc Bonds	5.7	-2.9	1.3	0.8	14.1	4.5	6.6	7.2	4.5
Domestic Deposits	1.4	1.4	6.1	9.2	6.1	4.1	4.3	5.1	4.7
Eurodeposits	1.1	1.2	5.9	9.2	6.0	4.1	4.4	5.2	4.6
Dutch Guilder									
Dutch Government Bonds	6.4%	2.8%	5.6%	6.4%	23.2%	6.4%	13.2%	10.2%	9.1%
Foreign Dutch Guilder Bonds	6.2	3.4	5.5	7.2	24.7	8.0	14.9	10.2	9.8
Euroguilder Bonds	6.5	3.2	7.2	8.5	22.6	9.1	12.6	9.8	9.8
Domestic Deposits	6.3	9.5	11.6	12.1	9.4	5.8	6.4	6.6	8.4
Eurodeposits	6.0	9.1	11.5	12.1	9.4	5.8	6.4	6.5	8.3
French Franc									
French Government Bonds	17.0%	-3.5%	3.7%	6.0%	20.2%	19.8%	18.0%	18.2%	12.1%
Euro-French Franc Bonds	17.0	-2.4	5.3	5.8	22.7	23.1	18.3	13.0	12.5
Domestic Deposits	8.9	9.3	13.2	16.1	16.1	13.2	12.6	10.7	12.5
Eurodeposits	11.1	11.1	13.7	19.0	20.7	17.5	13.7	11.4	14.7
Australian Dollar									
Australian Government Bonds[d]	—	—	—	—	—	—	—	6.6%	6.4%
European Currency Unit									
Euro-ECU Bonds[d]	—	—	—	—	—	—	—	11.1%	15.4%
World Bond Index (Weighted)	2.1%	0.5%	4.0%	6.3%	27.0%	8.4%	12.9%	18.7%	9.6%
World Bond Index (Unweighted)	5.5	-0.4	4.8	5.4	24.3	11.1	12.7	12.6	9.3
World Money Market Index (Unweighted)	6.5	8.8	12.2	14.2	12.1	8.9	9.2	8.7	10.0

[a] Including reinvestment of income. [b] Compound annual rate. [c] 1 Mar 82 = 100. [d] 1 Oct 84 = 100.

TABLE 2 TOTAL RATES OF RETURN OF INTERNATIONAL BOND AND MONEY MARKETS[a], 1978-85 (cont.)

U.S. Dollar Terms								
1978	1979	1980	1981	1982	1983	1984	1985	1 Jan 78-31 Dec 85[b]
-0.1%	1.9%	-0.8%	4.0%	31.3%	4.1%	14.3%	28.5%	9.8%
3.0	-2.3	-1.3	0.7	40.1	10.0	15.9	27.9	10.9
2.9	0.5	4.6	4.5	30.5	11.2	14.7	20.6	10.8
9.2	13.3	14.4	20.1	15.2	10.5	12.7	9.3	13.0
—	—	—	—	—	9.4	11.3	36.5	23.5
7.3	10.5	12.1	15.8	11.7	9.1	10.4	8.1	10.6
8.1	11.6	13.3	18.0	13.6	9.4	11.4	8.4	11.7
8.5	12.0	13.9	18.7	13.9	9.6	11.5	8.6	12.1
8.6	12.2	14.7	18.4	14.3	10.0	11.5	8.8	12.3
-5.5%	-0.6%	1.7%	-2.4%	35.8%	9.5%	8.8%	17.5%	7.4%
-4.6	2.5	4.2	11.7	15.3	15.3	9.1	10.6	7.8
-0.1	12.8	10.4	20.8	10.5	8.7	5.5	3.3	8.8
0.4	13.3	11.5	20.3	11.6	9.3	5.4	3.7	9.3
16.2%	7.3%	-10.6%	-8.4%	14.2%	-8.1%	-1.0%	43.4%	5.4%
22.1	4.9	-11.6	-7.0	12.5	-6.7	-2.9	42.2	5.4
19.3	12.2	-3.4	-1.6	3.8	-7.2	-8.2	36.7	5.5
18.9	11.8	-3.9	-2.0	3.4	-7.5	-8.5	36.5	5.2
31.8%	-21.5%	22.9%	5.5%	3.3%	12.6%	2.7%	37.3%	10.4%
31.2	-23.0	26.4	-0.9	4.5	14.5	1.7	35.5	9.6
30.3	-24.0	23.3	3.6	5.4	11.3	2.1	35.4	9.4
29.6	-14.3	31.2	0.0	0.2	8.4	-1.7	34.4	9.6
29.6	-14.2	30.7	-0.1	0.2	8.2	-1.9	34.2	9.5
29.6	-14.0	31.6	-0.1	0.3	8.3	-1.9	34.2	9.7
3.2%	12.4%	28.9%	-18.9%	26.4%	1.1%	-13.1%	40.6%	8.3%
3.3	17.7	16.3	-13.4	11.8	4.1	-9.1	38.1	7.5
14.7	23.6	26.1	-8.9	-4.0	-0.8	-12.1	40.4	8.4
15.0	23.8	27.1	-8.6	-4.0	-0.7	-12.0	40.3	8.7
16.7	24.3	27.1	-8.5	-3.8	-0.7	-12.0	40.5	9.0
34.7%	-0.6%	-9.6%	-1.6%	1.2%	-4.8%	-14.6%	34.3%	3.5%
29.0	-1.1	-9.1	-0.5	2.7	-3.8	-11.1	36.0	4.1
23.8	3.3	-4.9	7.7	-4.5	-4.2	-13.1	33.3	4.2
23.5	3.1	-5.1	7.8	-4.6	-4.2	-13.0	33.4	4.1
22.1%	6.8%	-5.8%	-8.5%	15.8%	-8.6%	-2.6%	42.7%	6.5%
21.9	7.5	-5.8	-7.9	17.2	-7.2	-1.2	42.7	7.2
22.2	7.2	-4.3	-6.8	15.3	-6.2	-3.2	42.3	7.2
22.0	13.8	-0.4	-3.7	2.9	-9.0	-8.5	38.1	5.8
21.7	13.3	-0.5	-3.7	2.8	-9.1	-8.5	38.0	5.7
31.1%	0.1%	-8.1%	-16.0%	1.9%	-2.8%	1.5%	52.8%	5.7%
31.2	1.3	-6.7	-16.1	4.0	-0.1	1.8	46.0	6.1
22.0	13.4	0.4	-8.0	-1.7	-8.1	-3.0	43.1	6.1
24.5	15.3	0.8	-5.7	2.3	-4.6	-2.1	44.1	8.2
—	—	—	—	—	—	—	-12.5%	-9.2%
—	—	—	—	—	—	—	40.2%	34.4%
9.4%	-1.8%	7.8%	-1.0%	20.2%	5.7%	5.7%	32.3%	9.3%
17.0	0.2	1.3	-5.4	14.2	2.3	-0.3	30.6	6.9
17.7	9.3	8.8	2.3	3.0	0.7	-2.4	26.4	7.9

between the two countries. The often independent and sometimes opposite movements of the Japanese and British Government markets are illustrated in the second panel. Movements in the Swiss, West German, Dutch, and French Government sectors were highly correlated over the eight-year period, reflecting not only the close relationship of their local markets but also the similar movements of their currencies versus the U.S. dollar. Figure 2 presents the World Bond Index (both weighted and unweighted) and the unweighted world money market index for the same period.

DISPERSION OF ANNUAL RETURNS

The dispersion of annual U.S. dollar returns in the Government and shorter-maturity Eurodeposit markets is depicted in Figure 3. In general, no single market dominated either the best- or the worst-performance list on an annual basis. For the most part, during the first half of the eight-year period, the money markets outpaced the bond markets. However, since 1982, the top returns in the bond markets consistently bettered those in the money markets. In the Government bond rankings, the U.S. Treasury market was the top performer only once during the past eight years. However, in the shorter-maturity markets, the U.S. dollar-denominated Eurodeposit sector posted the second-best return in 1981 and was the top performer in the 1982-84 period.

As a result of foreign currency fluctuations versus the U.S. dollar, as well as timing differences in the economic cycles of the various international markets, major swings in performance were reported by most of the markets during the eight-year period.

In 1978, the appreciation of the Japanese and European currencies generated large foreign exchange gains for U.S.- and Canadian dollar-based investors in these markets and forced the U.S. dollar-, Canadian dollar- and sterling-denominated markets to the bottom of the performance rankings. This situation reversed itself in 1979, as the second oil crisis weakened the yen and strengthened sterling. For U.S. dollar-based investors, returns in the Japanese

FIGURE 2 SALOMON BROTHERS WORLD BOND AND MONEY MARKET PERFORMANCE INDEXES, 1978-85
(U.S. Dollar Terms)

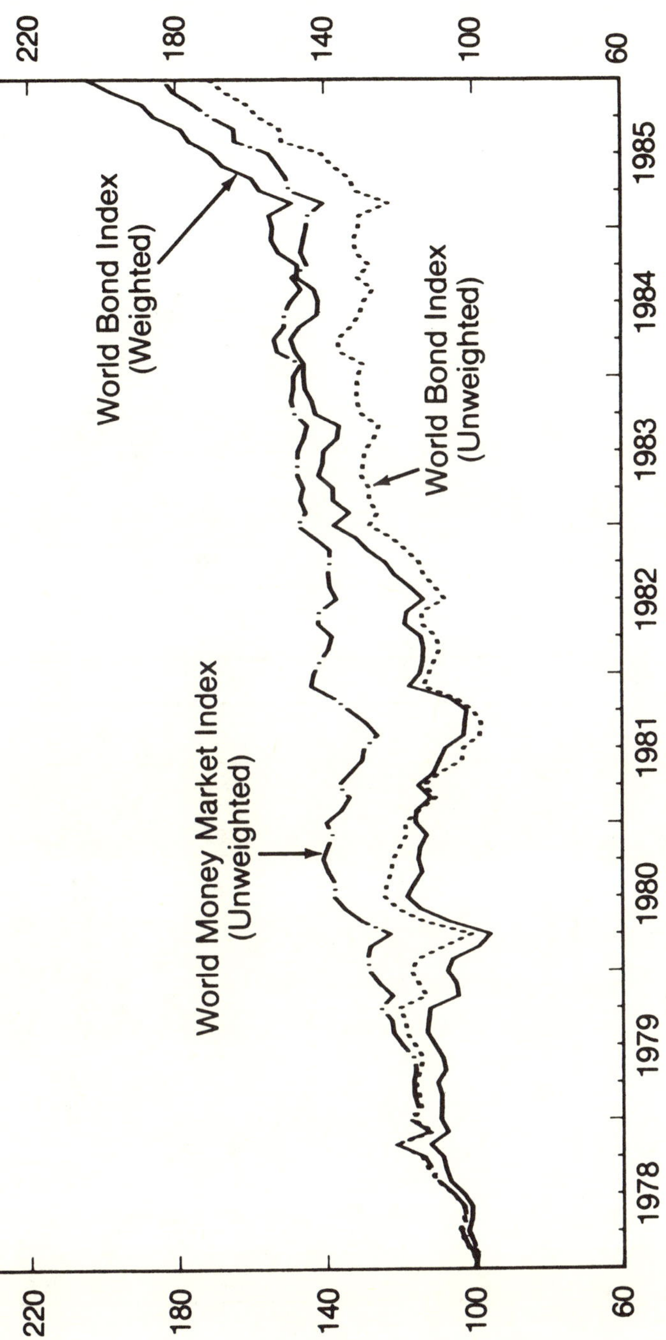

FIGURE 3 DISPERSION OF ANNUAL RETURNS, 1978-85
(U.S. Dollar Terms)

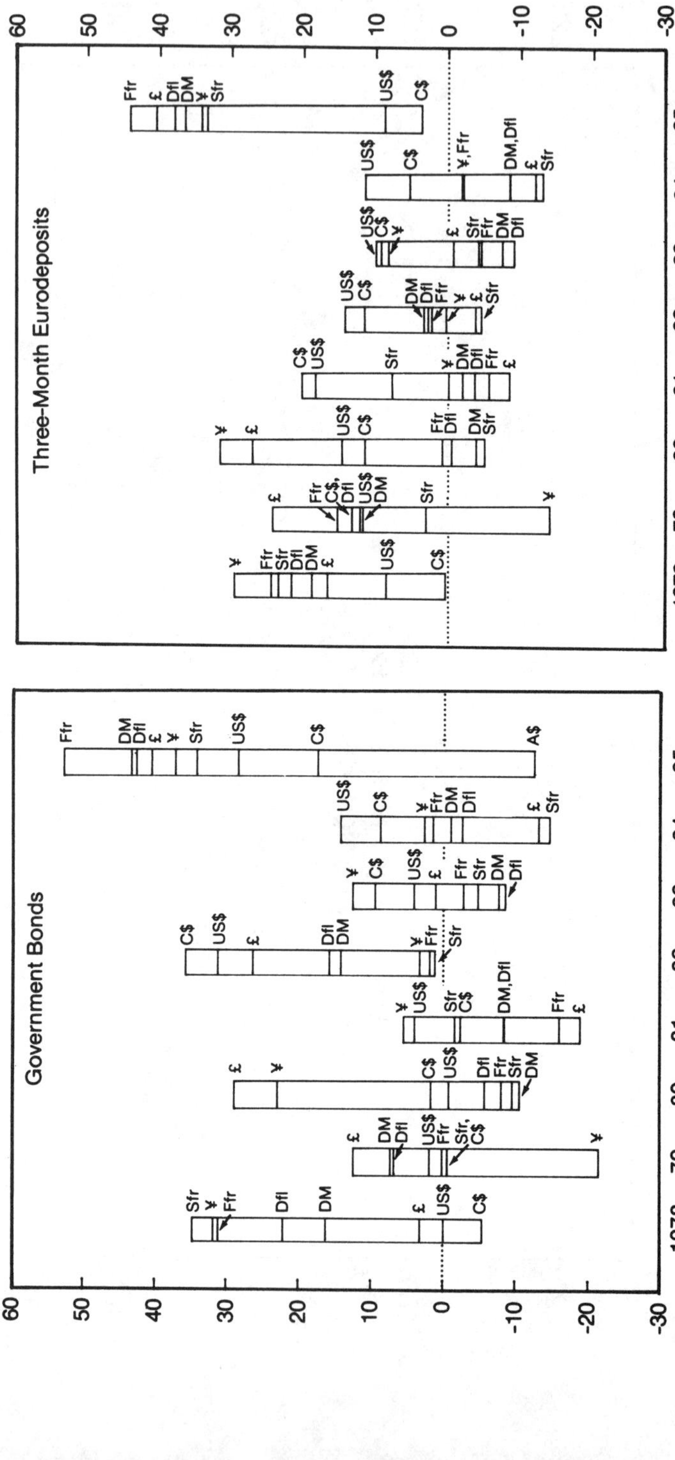

bond markets plummeted to the lowest levels recorded in the eight-year period (−21.5 percent to −24.0 percent) as the yen declined by 18.8 percent versus the U.S. dollar. Returns in the other international Government markets ranged from 12.4 percent in Britain to −0.6 percent in Canada and Switzerland (all in U.S. dollar terms). In 1980, sterling continued to improve, and the yen recovered, moving the British and Japanese Government markets to the top of the performance list. In contrast, the European Government markets all produced negative returns in U.S. dollar terms during 1980.

The dollar's strength in 1981-84 pushed the Canadian- and U.S. dollar-denominated markets to the top or near the top in both the Government and Eurodeposit markets. In 1981, Japanese and U.S. Government bonds were the only Government sectors that posted positive returns in U.S. dollar terms (5.5 percent and 4.0 percent, respectively). Returns ranged from as low as −18.9 percent for the British Government market. The money markets fared slightly better; returns were as high as 20.8 percent for Canadian Treasury Bills. However, in many of these markets, returns were negative.

In 1982, the bond markets finally outpaced the money markets. The top Government sector—Canada—returned 35.8 percent; a large decline in yields was diminished only slightly by the 3.9 percent depreciation of the Canadian dollar against the U.S. dollar. Swiss Government bonds ended the year at the other end of the spectrum—with only a small positive return of 1.2 percent. However, 1982 was the only year in the eight-year period when all the Government markets posted positive returns in U.S. dollar terms.

Total return performance deteriorated markedly in 1983. Japanese Government bonds again rose to the top of the Government list, recording a 12.6 percent return in U.S. dollar terms, as the yen was the only currency to appreciate against the U.S. dollar. Eurodollar deposits topped the list in the money markets, reflecting the overall strength of the U.S. dollar and high U.S. interest rates. Dutch guilder bond and money market instruments were the big losers, as the guilder depreciated by 14.1 percent versus the U.S. currency.

In 1984, the U.S. Government bond market—with a return of 14.3

percent—topped the annual performance list of Government bonds for the first time since the inception of the indexes. The rally that took place in the U.S. dollar bond markets in the second half of that year, combined with the declines posted by all of the foreign currencies, placed the U.S. dollar markets at the top of the performance list. Returns ranged from 11.3 percent in the Eurodollar zero-coupon market to 15.9 percent for foreign dollar (Yankee) bonds. Swiss Government bonds and U.K. gilts ended the year where they had spent most of it: at or near the bottom of the performance rankings. This showing reflected the large declines of the Swiss franc and British pound (16.7 percent and 20.3 percent, respectively) versus the U.S. dollar.

Performance results in 1985 were just the opposite of those posted in 1984. The sharp reversal of the U.S. dollar's exchange value against most foreign currencies began with its dramatic plunge in March; by the end of 1985, some of these currencies had posted gains of nearly 30 percent versus the U.S. dollar. French Government bonds far outdistanced the other Government markets in 1985, with an annual total rate of return in U.S. dollar terms that exceeded 50 percent. West German and Dutch Government bonds were next, with returns of 43.4 percent and 42.7 percent, respectively. Despite the weakness of the U.S. currency, the U.S. dollar-denominated bond markets fared relatively well on a local currency basis, posting returns of 20.6 percent to 28.5 percent in the coupon markets and a spectacular 36.5 percent return in the Eurodollar zero-coupon sector. The only other market that performed in this range was the Canadian Government sector. At the other end of the spectrum, the Australian Government bond sector generated a negative return of 12.5 percent in U.S. dollar terms, as the Australian dollar tumbled by 17.9 percent against the U.S. currency over the year.

CORRELATION AND VARIABILITIY OF RETURNS

The correlation of monthly returns between the major international bond markets for the period January 1, 1978 to December 31, 1985

TABLE 3 CORRELATION MATRIX
MONTHLY RETURNS OF INTERNATIONAL BONDS, 1978-85

Local Currency Terms

Dollar Bloc

Deutschemark Bloc

	US$ Govt	US$ For	US$ Euro	US$ Zero[a]	C$ Govt	C$ Euro	DM Govt	DM Euro	Sfr Govt	Sfr For	DFL Govt	DFL For	DFL Euro	Ffr Govt	Ffr Euro	ECU Euro[b]	£ Govt	£ Euro	¥ Govt	¥ Sam	¥ Euro	A$ Govt[b]
U.S. Dollar																						
Govt	1.00																					
Foreign	0.90	1.00																				
Euro	0.90	0.95	1.00																			
Euro-Zero[a]	0.75	0.74	0.79	1.00																		
Can. Dollar																						
Govt	0.79	0.83	0.84	0.75	1.00																	
Euro	0.64	0.76	0.76	0.65	0.68	1.00																
Deutschemark																						
Govt	0.51	0.62	0.61	0.54	0.57	0.50	1.00															
Euro	0.62	0.70	0.71	0.43	0.62	0.59	0.88	1.00														
Swiss Franc																						
Govt	0.34	0.46	0.46	0.44	0.43	0.42	0.48	0.45	1.00													
Foreign	0.61	0.68	0.71	0.43	0.61	0.61	0.67	0.77	0.67	1.00												
Dutch Guilder																						
Govt	0.55	0.64	0.67	0.47	0.53	0.55	0.75	0.76	0.47	0.70	1.00											
Foreign	0.51	0.64	0.65	0.41	0.53	0.60	0.74	0.77	0.47	0.71	0.94	1.00										
Euro	0.47	0.57	0.57	0.38	0.51	0.59	0.64	0.68	0.43	0.64	0.81	0.89	1.00									
French Franc																						
Govt	0.18	0.36	0.34	0.21	0.40	0.35	0.39	0.45	0.25	0.41	0.50	0.51	0.42	1.00								
Euro	0.23	0.34	0.33	0.38	0.37	0.36	0.32	0.37	0.27	0.37	0.37	0.42	0.48	0.53	1.00							
ECU																						
Euro[b]	0.26	0.21	0.27	0.06	0.28	0.35	0.54	0.62	-0.13	0.12	0.60	0.63	0.29	0.43	0.38	1.00						
U.K. Sterling																						
Govt	0.33	0.39	0.38	0.24	0.32	0.30	0.30	0.31	0.32	0.21	0.33	0.27	0.27	0.16	0.12	0.34	1.00					
Euro	0.41	0.54	0.54	0.07	0.43	0.57	0.45	0.48	0.29	0.39	0.43	0.42	0.41	0.22	0.26	0.21	0.68	1.00				
Japanese Yen																						
Govt	0.35	0.46	0.40	0.18	0.35	0.47	0.58	0.59	0.37	0.48	0.46	0.52	0.55	0.23	0.37	0.48	0.26	0.32	1.00			
Samurai	0.49	0.61	0.57	0.20	0.49	0.55	0.64	0.71	0.36	0.63	0.66	0.75	0.72	0.45	0.39	0.63	0.24	0.38	0.73	1.00		
Euro	0.44	0.57	0.52	0.18	0.43	0.56	0.64	0.73	0.36	0.64	0.60	0.69	0.68	0.37	0.43	0.63	0.23	0.44	0.74	0.85	1.00	
Australian Dollar																						
Govt[b]	0.25	0.26	0.26	0.04	0.27	0.32	0.48	0.46	0.01	0.23	0.47	0.43	0.41	-0.03	-0.07	0.32	0.06	-0.27	0.58	0.64	0.36	1.00

[a] 1 Mar 82-31 Dec 85.
[b] 1 Oct 84-31 Dec 85.

TABLE 3 CORRELATION MATRIX
MONTHLY RETURNS OF INTERNATIONAL BONDS, 1978-85 (cont.)

U.S. Dollar Terms

	Govt	For	Euro	Zero[a]	Govt	Euro	Govt	Euro	Govt	For	Govt	For	Euro	Govt	Euro	Euro[b]	Govt	Euro	Govt	Sam	Euro	Govt[b]
	US$				C$		DM		Sfr		DFL			Ffr		ECU	£		¥			A$
U.S. Dollar																						
Govt	1.00																					
Foreign	0.90	1.00																				
Euro	0.90	0.95	1.00																			
EuroZero[a]	0.75	0.74	0.79	1.00																		
Can. Dollar																						
Govt	0.75	0.79	0.79	0.73	1.00																	
Euro	0.60	0.69	0.69	0.67	0.79	1.00																
Deutschemark																						
Govt	0.37	0.41	0.36	0.34	0.47	0.40	1.00															
Euro	0.40	0.43	0.39	0.29	0.46	0.39	0.98	1.00														
Swiss Franc																						
Govt	0.31	0.34	0.31	0.28	0.42	0.35	0.86	0.86	1.00													
Foreign	0.40	0.42	0.40	0.27	0.46	0.39	0.87	0.89	0.97	1.00												
Dutch Guilder																						
Govt	0.39	0.43	0.40	0.36	0.45	0.38	0.95	0.95	0.85	0.87	1.00											
Foreign	0.38	0.43	0.39	0.34	0.46	0.40	0.95	0.95	0.85	0.87	0.99	1.00										
Euro	0.35	0.38	0.34	0.32	0.44	0.38	0.95	0.95	0.84	0.85	0.97	0.98	1.00									
French Franc																						
Govt	0.25	0.33	0.30	0.31	0.38	0.35	0.86	0.87	0.77	0.78	0.87	0.87	0.85	1.00								
Euro	0.28	0.33	0.30	0.34	0.39	0.37	0.82	0.84	0.73	0.74	0.84	0.85	0.85	0.93	1.00							
ECU																						
Euro[b]	0.16	0.06	0.11	0.27	0.40	0.50	0.96	0.97	0.97	0.97	0.96	0.96	0.95	0.91	0.97	1.00						
U.K. Sterling																						
Govt	0.35	0.36	0.34	0.28	0.45	0.45	0.51	0.52	0.51	0.49	0.51	0.49	0.50	0.44	0.44	0.86	1.00					
Euro	0.39	0.44	0.41	0.21	0.49	0.54	0.54	0.55	0.55	0.56	0.52	0.51	0.51	0.44	0.46	0.82	0.89	1.00				
Japanese Yen																						
Govt	0.28	0.36	0.31	0.14	0.31	0.37	0.56	0.59	0.59	0.59	0.57	0.59	0.59	0.60	0.62	0.70	0.39	0.40	1.00			
Samurai	0.33	0.42	0.37	0.14	0.35	0.39	0.59	0.63	0.62	0.64	0.61	0.63	0.63	0.64	0.64	0.76	0.39	0.42	0.97	1.00		
Euro	0.33	0.44	0.38	0.14	0.35	0.42	0.59	0.63	0.62	0.65	0.61	0.63	0.62	0.62	0.64	0.77	0.40	0.46	0.96	0.98	1.00	
Australian Dollar																						
Govt[b]	0.38	0.35	0.40	0.21	0.52	0.57	0.67	0.65	0.58	0.59	0.67	0.67	0.66	0.51	0.62	0.60	0.41	0.35	0.48	0.53	0.47	1.00

Dollar Bloc

Deutschemark Bloc

[a] 1 Mar 82-31 Dec 85.

[b] 1 Oct 84-31 Dec 85.

is presented in Table 3. U.S. and Canadian securities—which comprise the dollar bloc—acted as a group, as did securities denominated in Deutschemarks, Dutch guilders, Swiss francs, French francs, and the European Currency Unit—the Deutschemark bloc—in local currency and U.S. dollar terms.

Among the dollar-bloc markets, the correlation between the Canadian and U.S. markets is slightly higher in local terms than in U.S. dollar terms. The fluctuation of the Canadian currency versus the U.S. dollar occasionally offset the close interest rate relationship that exists between the two countries. On the other hand, the correlations of returns among the Deutschemark-bloc markets is strengthened considerably, when returns are expressed in U.S. dollar terms. This reflects the close relationship of exchange rate movements in these currencies versus the U.S. dollar. As expected, the Euro-ECU market is highly correlated with the rest of the Deutschemark-bloc markets—especially in U.S. dollar terms.

Table 4 presents the variability of returns within each of the individual bond and money markets in local currency and U.S. dollar terms. The Eurodollar zero-coupon bond market recorded the highest annualized standard deviation of monthly returns in local currency terms, reflecting the longer average duration of this sector. Among the major Government markets, the Canadian Government sector was the most volatile in local currency terms, and the Swiss Government market was, by far, the least volatile.

In U.S. dollar terms, the Australian Government market recorded the highest variability of all the markets, as a result of the volatility in the Australian dollar exchange rate versus the U.S. dollar during the 15-month period ended December 1985. Among the markets for which we show eight years of data, however, the British Government bond market posted the highest volatility. The Japanese bond markets and the foreign Swiss franc bond sector registered standard deviations of monthly returns (annualized) in the 16.6 percent to 17.6 percent range, reflecting the high volatility of the yen and the Swiss franc versus the U.S. dollar. Excluding actual dollar-denominated bonds, the least volatile returns in U.S. dollar terms were recorded in the Euro-Canadian bond market, among the international sectors,

TABLE 4 VARIABILITY OF RETURNS IN INTERNATIONAL BOND AND MONEY MARKETS, 1978-85

	Annualized Standard Deviation of Monthly Return		Annualized Standard Deviation of Monthly Exchange Rate Fluctuations vs. U.S. Dollar
	Local Currency Terms	U.S. Dollar Terms	
U.S. Dollar			
U.S. Government Bonds	11.6%	11.6%	
Foreign Dollar (Yankee)Bonds	11.9	11.9	
Eurodollar Bonds	8.3	8.3	
Eurodollar FRNs	1.4	1.4	
Eurodollar Zeros[a]	13.0	13.0	
U.S. Treasury Bills	0.9	0.9	
Domestic CDs	1.3	1.3	
Euro CDs	1.4	1.4	
Eurodeposits	0.9	0.9	
Canadian Dollar			4.6%
Canadian Government Bonds	12.7%	15.0%	
Euro-Canadian Dollar Bonds	7.2	9.6	
Canadian Treasury Bills	1.1	5.2	
Eurodeposits	1.0	4.9	
Deutschemark			12.5%
West German Government Bonds	6.2%	16.3%	
Euro-Deutschemark Bonds	5.9	16.2	
Domestic Deposits	0.8	12.5	
Eurodeposits	0.8	12.5	
Japanese Yen			13.3%
Japanese Government Bonds	5.7%	16.6%	
Samurai Bonds	6.0	16.7	
Euroyen Bonds	7.2	17.4	
Domestic CDs	0.7	13.5	
Gensaki	0.7	13.5	
Eurodeposits	0.6	13.5	
U.K. Sterling			12.1%
U.K. Government Bonds	10.9%	18.1%	
Eurosterling Bonds	8.5	16.1	
U.K. Treasury Bills	0.9	12.4	
Domestic CDs	1.2	12.4	
Eurodeposits	0.8	12.3	
Swiss Franc			14.6%
Swiss Government Bonds	4.1%	16.1%	
Foreign Swiss Franc Bonds	5.4	17.6	
Domestic Deposits	0.7	14.7	
Eurodeposits	0.8	14.7	
Dutch Guilder			12.6%
Dutch Government Bonds	6.0%	15.2%	
Foreign Dutch Guilder Bonds	6.2	15.5	
Euroguilder Bonds	5.1	14.6	
Domestic Deposits	0.7	12.7	
Eurodeposits	0.7	12.6	
French Franc			12.4%
French Government Bonds	5.6%	14.1%	
Euro-French Franc Bonds	5.6	13.9	
Domestic Deposits	1.0	12.3	
Eurodeposits	1.2	12.4	
Australian Dollar			16.5%
Australian Government Bonds[b]	5.6%	20.3%	
European Currency Unit			12.5%
Euro-ECU bonds[b]	4.5%	14.3%	
World Bond Index (Weighted)	7.1%	10.4%	
World Bond Index (Unweighted)	5.3	11.7	
World Money Market Index (Unweighted)	0.7	8.4	

[a] 1 Mar 82-31 Dec 85.
[b] 1 Oct 84-31 Dec 85.

and in the French Government bond market, among the Government sectors. The annualized standard deviation of the Canadian dollar's monthly fluctuation versus the U.S. dollar is, by far, the lowest of the nine foreign currencies included in the review.

In the money markets, the lowest volatility, in local currency terms, was recorded by the Japanese and Dutch instruments. U.S. dollar-denominated markets, on the other hand, posted the highest volatility. The volatility of the Swiss franc and yen was also evident in the money markets, as issues denominated in these two currencies were the most volatile in U.S. dollar terms.

THE CURRENCY FACTOR IN INTERNATIONAL RETURNS

Currency fluctuations have played a major role in international bond and money market returns over the past eight years. Figure 4 shows the fluctuations of nine major currencies against the U.S. dollar since January 1, 1978. The Canadian dollar has been the most stable by far against the U.S. dollar, while the Japanese yen and Swiss franc have been the most volatile. The pattern of U.S. dollar returns generated by the Deutschemark-bloc Government markets (see Figure 1, bottom panel) is reinforced in Figure 4 (right panel), which illustrates how the Deutschemark-bloc currencies also moved in a synchronized fashion over the past eight years. As expected, the European Currency Unit moved in tandem with the other Deutschemark-bloc currencies.

Table 5 shows the portion of annual returns in U.S. dollar terms that is attributable to currency movement. Currency gains or losses account for a large percentage of the total return for most markets in most years—frequently overwhelming local currency performance. Despite some major swings on a year-by-year basis, the Japanese yen was the only currency to post a gain (2.2 percent) versus the U.S. dollar on a compound annual basis over the eight-year period. The other currencies generated declines of 0.5 percent to 5.7 percent.

During the period from 1978 through mid-1980, the weakness of

FIGURE 4 CURRENCY FLUCTUATIONS AGAINST THE U.S. DOLLAR, 1978-85

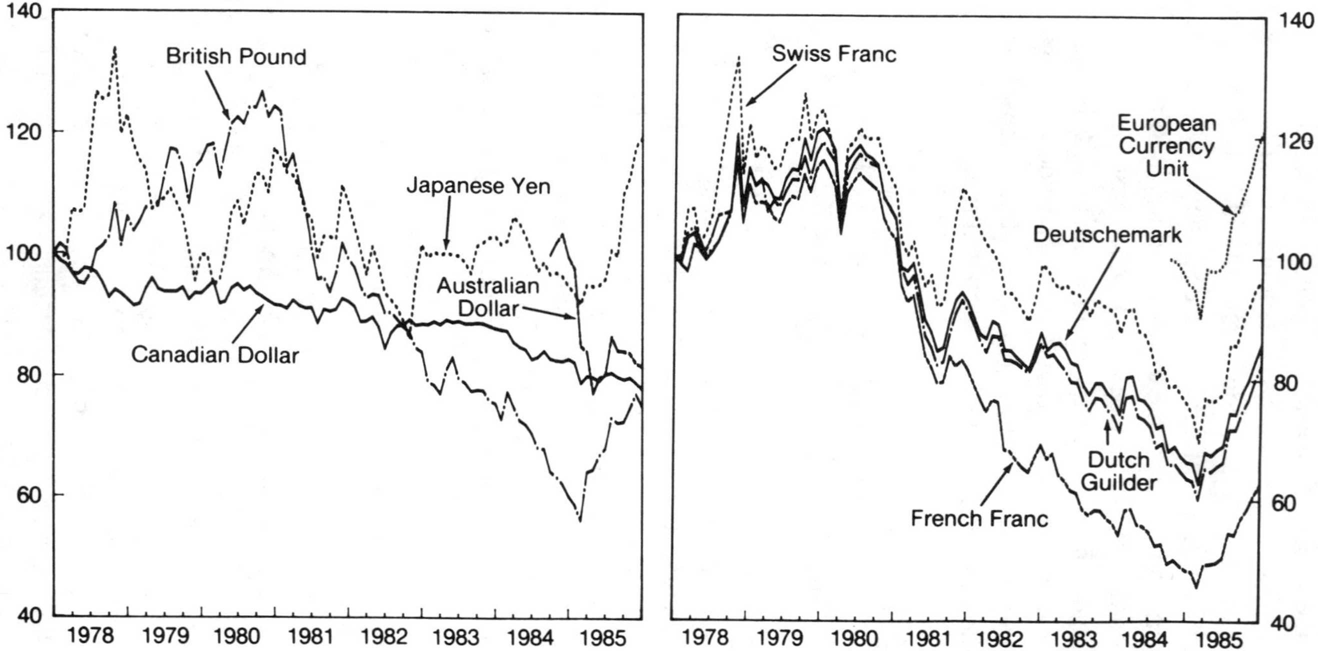

TABLE 5 CURRENCY FACTORS IN INTERNATIONAL MARKET PERFORMANCE, 1978-85

	1978		1979		1980		1981	
	Total US$ Return	**Currency Return Portion**	**Total US$ Return**	**Currency Return Portion**	**Total US$ Return**	**Currency Return Portion**	**Total US$ Return**	**Currency Return Portion**
Canadian Govt. Bonds	-5.5%	-7.6%	-0.6%	1.1%	1.7%	-1.9%	-2.4%	0.7%
Euro-C$ Deposits	0.4	-7.6	13.3	1.1	11.5	-1.9	20.3	0.7
W. German Govt. Bonds	16.2	15.0	7.3	5.6	-10.6	-12.2	-8.4	-12.9
Euro-DM Deposits	18.9	15.0	11.8	5.6	-3.9	-12.2	-2.0	-12.9
Japanese Govt. Bonds	31.8	22.9	-21.5	-18.8	22.9	17.8	5.5	-7.7
Euro-¥ Deposits	29.6	22.9	-14.0	-18.8	31.6	17.8	-0.1	-7.7
U.K. Govt. Bonds	3.2	6.1	12.4	8.9	28.9	7.7	-18.9	-20.3
Euro-£ Deposits	16.7	6.1	24.3	8.9	27.1	7.7	-8.5	-20.3
Swiss Govt. Bonds	34.7	22.2	-0.6	1.8	-9.6	-10.4	-1.6	-1.3
Euro-Sfr Deposits	23.5	22.2	3.1	1.8	-5.1	-10.4	7.8	-1.3
Dutch Govt. Bonds	22.1	14.8	6.8	3.9	-5.8	-10.8	-8.5	-14.1
Euro-Dfl Deposits	21.7	14.8	13.3	3.9	-0.5	-10.8	-3.7	-14.1
French Govt. Bonds	31.1	12.1	0.1	3.8	-8.1	-11.4	-16.0	-20.8
Euro-Ffr Deposits	24.5	12.1	15.3	3.8	0.8	-11.4	-5.7	-20.8
Aust$ Govt.	—	—	—	—	—	—	—	—

TABLE 5 CURRENCY FACTORS IN INTERNATIONAL MARKET PERFORMANCE, 1978-85 (cont.)

	1982		1983		1984		1985		1978-85 Compound Annual	
	Total US$ Return	Currency Return Portion	Total US$ Return	Currency Return Portion	Total US$ Return	Currency Return Portion	Total US$ Return	Currency Return Portion	Total US$ Return	Currency Return Portion
Canadian Govt. Bonds	35.8%	-3.9%	9.5%	-0.8%	8.8%	-5.6%	17.5%	-5.8%	7.4%	-3.0%
Euro-C$ Deposits	11.6	-3.9	9.3	-0.8	5.4	-5.6	3.7	-5.8	9.3	-3.0
W. German Govt. Bonds	14.2	-5.5	-8.1	-12.5	-1.0	-13.7	43.4	29.4	5.4	-1.9
Euro-DM Deposits	3.4	-5.5	-7.5	-12.5	-8.5	-13.7	36.5	29.4	5.2	-1.9
Japanese Govt. Bonds	3.3	-6.4	12.6	1.4	2.7	-7.9	37.3	25.8	10.4	2.2
Euro-¥ Deposits	0.3	-6.4	8.3	1.4	-1.9	-7.9	34.2	25.8	9.7	2.2
U.K. Govt. Bonds	26.4	-15.3	1.1	-10.1	-13.1	-20.3	40.6	25.1	8.3	-3.5
Euro-£ Deposits	-3.8	-15.3	-0.7	-10.1	-12.0	-20.3	40.5	25.1	9.0	-3.5
Swiss Govt. Bonds	1.2	-10.0	-4.8	-7.9	-14.6	-16.7	34.3	26.8	3.5	-0.5
Euro-Sfr Deposits	-4.6	-10.0	-4.2	-7.9	-13.0	-16.7	33.4	26.8	4.1	-0.5
Dutch Govt. Bonds	15.8	-5.9	-8.6	-14.1	-2.6	-13.9	42.7	29.6	6.5	-2.4
Euro-Dfl Deposits	2.8	-5.9	-9.1	-14.1	-8.5	-13.9	38.0	29.6	5.7	-2.4
French Govt. Bonds	1.9	-15.3	-2.8	-18.8	1.5	-13.9	52.8	29.1	5.7	-5.7
Euro-Ffr Deposits	2.3	-15.3	-4.6	-18.8	-2.1	-13.9	44.1	29.1	8.2	-5.7
Aust$ Govt.	—	—	—	—	—	—	-12.5	-17.9	-9.2[a]	-14.8[a]

[a] 1 Oct 84 = 100.

the U.S. currency allowed U.S. dollar-based investors who had invested in nondollar-denominated instruments to enjoy significant gains when they converted their returns into U.S. dollars. In mid-1980, however, the U.S. dollar began to strengthen. From that point through to early 1985, U.S. dollar-based investors who had ventured into nondollar-denominated markets experienced losses on most of their currency translations back into U.S. dollars. This situation was reversed in March 1985, when the foreign exchange value of the U.S. dollar plummeted versus the other major currencies. This falloff continued almost uninterrupted throughout most of the year and made the nondollar markets attractive, once again, to U.S. dollar-based investors. Figure 5 illustrates the effect of these currency fluctuations on the returns earned by U.S. dollar-based investors who invested in nondollar-denominated markets.

The West German and British Government bond markets (depicted in the first and fourth panels, respectively, of Figure 5), show the currency gains earned by U.S. dollar-based investors who owned these securities prior to 1981. However, since that time, U.S. dollar-based investors in these markets experienced losses when converting returns back to U.S. dollars. The second panel shows that since the yen has not always demonstrated a clear trend relative to the U.S. dollar, the currency portion of U.S. dollar returns on Japanese Government bonds fluctuated more frequently than the European Government markets throughout this eight-year period. On the other hand, the Canadian dollar posted frequent losses versus the U.S. unit during the past eight years. As a result, the translation of local currency returns on Canadian Government bonds into U.S. dollars produced a currency loss for U.S. investors that widened cumulatively over time (see third panel of Figure 5).

The bottom panel of Figure 5 highlights the local currency and U.S. dollar returns of a weighted portfolio of all nondollar bond markets (Government, foreign, and Euro) contained in the Salomon Brothers Indexes. Note the dollar's general shift from a pattern of weakness to one of strength and back to one of weakness versus the nine other currencies. As in most of the individual markets, prior to 1981, U.S. dollar-based investors received additional return in

FIGURE 5 CURRENCY GAIN OR LOSS FOR U.S. DOLLAR-BASED INVESTORS, 1978-85

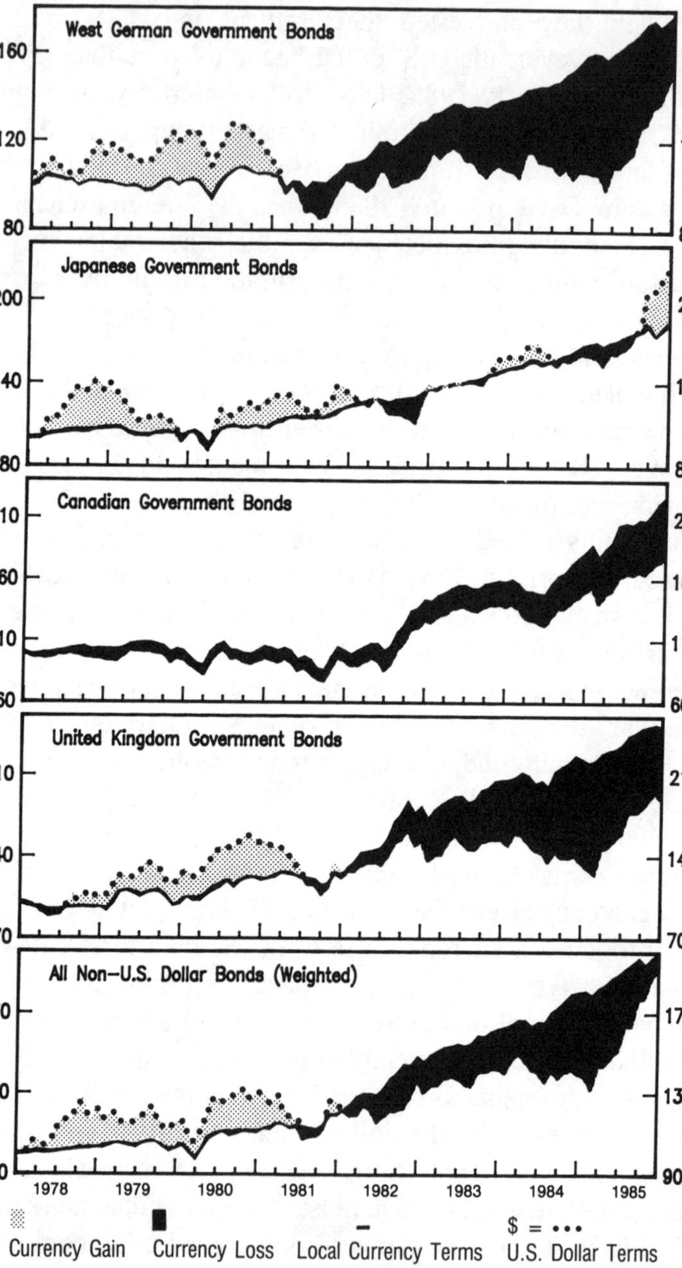

the form of a currency gain when converting the local returns on the nondollar portfolio into U.S. dollars. From 1981 to March 1985, this trend reversed, as the strength of the U.S. dollar caused the gap between the local and U.S. dollar indexes to widen considerably in favor of the local market returns. Since March 1985, however, the slope of the curves expressed in U.S. dollar terms steepened sharply, reflecting the rapid decline in the exchange value of the U.S. dollar that continued throughout the year. In the last ten months of 1985, the non-U.S. dollar bond index, expressed in U.S. dollar terms, recouped most of the declines that it suffered since mid-1980.

THE EFFECTS OF INTERNATIONAL DIVERSIFICATION

International investors can reduce currency risk, as well as interest rate risk, by diversifying across markets. Because international fixed-income markets are not perfectly correlated, internationally diversified portfolios generally lower risk by reducing the volatility of returns relative to that on single-currency portfolios (see Table 3). In some instances, this reduction in volatility is achieved at the expense of a smaller average return on the diversified portfolio. However, diversifying out of a weak currency can improve base-currency returns and reduce portfolio volatility.

Table 6 illustrates the effects of diversification on U.S. dollar-based portfolios made up of 100 percent U.S. Treasury securities during four time periods within the eight-year period. On a compound annual basis over the eight years, the highest U.S. dollar returns were earned on a portfolio composed of 100 percent of U.S. Treasury issues. However, by diversifying approximately 40 percent into a portfolio that includes all the nondollar markets (Government, foreign, and Euro) in our index, on a weighted basis, the annualized standard deviation of returns decline from 11.6 percent to 10.4 percent.

During the January 1978-June 1980 period, when the U.S. dollar was weak, by diversifying 20 percent to 30 percent into the nondol-

TABLE 6 EFFECTS OF DIVERSIFICATION ON A U.S. DOLLAR-BASED PORTFOLIO, 1978-85

	Jan 78-Dec 85		Weak Dollar Period Jan 78-Jun 80		Strong Dollar Period Jul 80-Feb 85		Weak Dollar Period Mar 85-Dec 85	
	Compound Annual Return	Annualized Standard Deviation	Compound Annual Return	Annualized Standard Deviation	Compound Annual Return	Annualized Standard Deviation	Compound Annual Return	Annualized Standard Deviation
100% U.S./0% Non-U.S.	9.8%	11.6%	3.7%	12.4%	8.8%	11.4%	36.3%	10.1%
90% U.S./10% Non-U.S.	9.6	11.1	4.3	11.9	8.1	10.8	38.0	9.6
80% U.S./20% Non-U.S.	9.5	10.7	4.9	11.7	7.3	10.3	39.7	9.1
70% U.S./30% Non-U.S.	9.4	10.5	5.5	11.7	6.5	10.0	41.5	8.9
60% U.S./40% Non-U.S.	9.3	10.4	6.1	11.9	5.7	9.8	43.5	8.9
50% U.S./50% Non-U.S.	9.1	10.5	6.6	12.3	5.0	9.7	45.5	9.2
40% U.S./60% Non-U.S.	9.0	10.8	7.2	12.8	4.2	9.7	47.5	9.7
30% U.S./70% Non-U.S.	8.9	11.3	7.8	13.4	3.4	9.9	49.7	10.4
20% U.S./80% Non-U.S.	8.7	11.8	8.3	14.2	2.6	10.2	52.0	11.4
10% U.S./90% Non-U.S.	8.6	12.5	8.9	15.0	1.9	10.5	54.4	12.6
0% U.S./100% Non-U.S.	8.5	13.2	9.4	15.9	1.1	11.0	56.9	14.0

lar markets, a decline in volatility was enhanced by an increase in return from 3.7 percent to 5.5 percent. The results in the ensuing period of dollar strength, July 1980-February 1985, resemble those of the eight-year period: Returns slid as investors diversified into the nondollar markets, but so did the volatility of returns.

In the March-December 1985 period spectacular results were attained at both ends of the spectrum. The 36.3 percent return (annualized) on portfolios containing 100 percent U.S. Treasury issues is attributable to the strong rally in the U.S. bond market. However, as U.S. dollar-based investors diversified into the international markets, returns increased to as high as 56.9 percent (100 percent diversification into the non-dollar markets), reflecting the plunge in the exchange value of the U.S. dollar. During this time period, the lowest volatility was seen at a level of approximately 30 percent to 40 percent diversification into the nondollar markets, with a corresponding annualized return of 41.5 percent to 43.5 percent in U.S. dollar terms.

SUMMARY

This chapter has presented historical data on returns to international fixed-income instruments in terms of local currency and U.S. dollar returns. Indices have been developed to use as reference returns for specific market portfolios. Dispersion, correlation and variability of returns have been analyzed in periods of dollar strength and weakness. The currency factor in overall returns has been isolated and the effects of diversification across currencies has been highlighted. To complete the story on historical returns on fixed income instruments, the appendix to Chapter 32 contians end-of-month historical data on rate of return indices on all appropriate instruments by currency for the period 1978-1985; where the index for each series is set at 100 for December 1977.

NOTES

[1]The introduction of the Salomon Brothers International Total Rate-of-Return Indexes in September 1981 was accompanied by a report, *Performance Indexes of International Bond and Money Markets,* Jeffrey Hanna, which reviewed performance for the period 1978-mid-1981.

[2]See *International Bond and Money Market Performance,* published monthly.

[3]Throughout this report, returns are in U.S. dollars terms on a compound annual basis, unless otherwise noted.

APPENDIX

Historical Total Rate-of-Return Indexes,
by Currency, 1978-85
(End-of-Month Data, Dec 1977 = 100.0)

TABLE A1

U.S. Dollar

	Govt.	Yankee	Euro$	Eurodollar FRN	Eurodollar Zero	T-Bill	Dom. CD	Eurodollar CD	Eurodollar Dep.	Non-US$ in US$ Bond	Non-US$ in US$ Money
1978											
Jan	99.5	99.5	99.8	100.9	NA	100.5	100.6	100.6	100.6	99.8	100.2
Feb	99.7	99.9	100.3	101.9	NA	101.0	101.1	101.1	101.2	101.3	102.7
Mar	99.9	100.9	101.5	102.8	NA	101.6	101.7	101.8	101.8	104.0	104.4
Apr	99.9	101.3	102.4	103.8	NA	102.1	102.2	102.3	102.4	102.0	102.8
May	99.5	100.8	102.0	104.3	NA	102.7	102.9	102.9	103.1	102.1	103.2
Jun	99.1	101.1	102.0	105.1	NA	103.2	103.5	103.5	103.7	107.3	106.4
Jul	100.2	102.2	103.2	105.3	NA	103.9	104.2	104.3	104.4	113.3	110.8
Aug	101.7	104.4	103.7	106.2	NA	104.4	104.9	105.0	105.2	114.1	112.8
Sep	101.5	104.8	103.7	107.0	NA	105.0	105.5	105.7	105.9	116.1	115.0
Oct	99.8	103.1	101.5	107.1	NA	105.7	106.2	106.3	106.7	124.9	123.9
Nov	101.2	104.0	103.7	108.1	NA	106.5	107.1	107.3	107.6	113.3	113.2
Dec	100.0	103.0	102.9	109.2	NA	107.2	108.1	108.5	108.6	118.5	110.0
1979											
Jan	102.1	104.2	104.6	110.9	NA	108.1	109.3	109.6	109.7	115.3	116.3
Feb	101.2	103.6	104.0	111.9	NA	108.9	110.1	110.5	110.7	116.1	117.5
Mar	102.3	104.6	105.7	113.2	NA	109.8	111.0	111.4	111.7	117.0	117.4
Apr	101.8	105.2	106.3	114.3	NA	110.7	111.9	112.4	112.7	113.0	116.6
May	104.3	106.3	107.3	115.4	NA	111.6	112.9	113.4	113.7	112.5	117.0
Jun	106.9	109.0	107.9	115.4	NA	112.5	113.9	114.4	114.6	114.3	120.4
Jul	106.2	108.6	107.5	117.6	NA	113.4	114.8	115.3	115.7	118.9	123.2
Aug	105.6	108.8	107.2	119.3	NA	114.2	115.6	116.2	116.8	118.5	123.5
Sep	104.9	107.6	106.3	120.6	NA	115.1	116.6	117.2	117.8	118.5	126.8
Oct	97.5	98.7	101.2	121.2	NA	116.0	117.5	118.1	119.1	110.6	122.9
Nov	101.1	100.0	103.2	122.6	NA	117.3	119.3	120.1	120.4	108.8	126.8
Dec	101.9	100.7	103.3	123.7	NA	118.5	120.6	121.5	121.8	112.6	129.7
1980											
Jan	96.9	96.8	99.9	125.5	NA	119.7	121.9	122.9	123.4	113.7	130.1
Feb	89.3	86.8	93.1	126.5	NA	120.6	122.8	123.7	124.8	107.1	128.9
Mar	90.7	86.5	95.3	127.7	NA	122.0	124.2	125.1	126.4	100.0	122.5
Apr	102.4	97.3	104.8	130.2	NA	124.0	127.2	128.5	128.2	110.0	130.9
May	106.9	105.1	109.7	132.4	NA	125.4	129.3	130.8	129.9	121.2	135.8
Jun	109.6	110.2	112.9	133.4	NA	126.2	129.9	131.3	131.5	125.2	139.1
Jul	106.1	108.4	111.3	134.8	NA	127.0	130.5	132.0	132.8	124.4	138.3
Aug	101.3	101.6	106.1	135.7	NA	127.7	131.1	132.6	133.8	124.6	140.6
Sep	100.0	99.7	104.8	137.2	NA	128.7	132.1	133.7	135.0	127.7	142.0
Oct	97.6	98.4	105.2	138.3	NA	129.9	133.5	135.1	136.4	128.5	140.4
Nov	98.0	97.3	106.0	139.6	NA	130.9	134.4	136.0	137.8	125.0	138.7
Dec	101.1	99.4	108.1	141.5	NA	132.8	136.6	138.4	139.8	128.0	140.3
1981											
Jan	100.5	98.9	108.0	143.5	NA	134.3	139.0	140.9	141.7	127.2	135.4
Feb	97.0	97.2	105.8	145.6	NA	135.9	141.1	142.9	143.6	122.8	132.6
Mar	100.1	99.0	108.5	148.4	NA	137.9	143.3	145.3	145.7	126.7	135.7
Apr	95.3	96.6	106.0	150.0	NA	139.1	144.1	146.1	147.7	122.6	131.9
May	100.8	96.0	106.6	151.9	NA	140.7	145.9	148.0	149.6	116.1	128.0
Jun	99.1	98.7	109.6	154.3	NA	142.8	148.2	150.5	151.7	113.7	126.9
Jul	96.2	95.7	107.5	156.5	NA	144.5	150.3	152.6	154.0	107.2	122.7
Aug	93.5	92.0	105.0	159.0	NA	146.4	152.7	155.0	156.3	108.8	125.8
Sep	92.6	90.9	104.3	162.9	NA	148.5	155.2	157.8	158.7	108.8	130.6
Oct	99.3	93.3	107.6	164.8	NA	150.4	157.6	160.3	161.0	112.4	135.1
Nov	108.3	103.5	114.5	168.6	NA	152.4	160.1	163.3	163.4	124.8	141.7
Dec	105.0	100.0	112.9	170.6	NA	153.8	161.2	164.2	165.4	122.1	140.6

NA Not available.

TABLE A1 (Continued)

U.S. Dollar

				Eurodollar			Dom.	Eurodollar		Non-US$ in US$	
	Govt.	Yankee	Euro$	FRN	Zero	T-Bill	CD	CD	Dep.	Bond	Money
1982											
Jan	104.7	97.7	111.6	172.3	NA	154.9	162.4	165.4	167.2	121.0	138.6
Feb	106.7	101.0	114.0	174.3	100.0	156.5	164.2	167.4	168.9	118.9	135.6
Mar	107.8	103.6	116.8	176.8	97.9	158.1	166.3	169.4	171.1	119.2	134.3
Apr	111.1	107.7	120.8	179.3	105.3	160.0	168.5	171.7	173.2	124.1	138.2
May	112.3	110.1	123.0	181.3	105.2	161.7	170.6	173.8	175.2	121.9	138.2
Jun	109.8	106.2	120.2	183.3	100.4	163.3	172.2	175.6	177.6	115.9	132.1
Jul	114.9	110.1	124.3	186.3	104.3	165.5	175.3	178.7	179.7	118.7	133.8
Aug	120.3	118.4	130.5	188.8	109.3	167.3	177.5	181.1	182.0	121.4	133.9
Sep	126.1	123.7	133.3	190.4	117.8	168.5	178.6	182.2	183.9	121.6	133.3
Oct	134.7	133.8	141.2	191.6	129.4	169.5	180.3	184.0	185.7	122.9	132.9
Nov	134.8	138.4	143.4	194.5	128.2	170.5	181.8	185.6	187.5	128.3	137.5
Dec	137.9	140.1	147.3	195.9	135.0	171.8	183.1	187.1	189.1	136.6	142.5
1983											
Jan	135.1	140.4	149.0	197.3	140.5	173.0	184.5	188.5	190.7	130.2	139.8
Feb	140.8	144.8	153.1	199.6	142.6	174.1	185.8	189.9	192.1	133.8	141.1
Mar	139.9	147.0	153.6	201.1	142.8	175.2	186.8	191.0	193.5	134.1	140.0
Apr	144.5	152.5	157.2	203.0	149.7	176.5	188.4	192.6	195.0	137.5	141.7
May	140.2	151.7	157.3	204.1	143.0	177.8	189.7	194.0	196.5	138.3	141.5
Jun	141.0	150.7	157.3	205.7	142.7	179.0	191.0	195.4	198.1	137.5	141.1
Jul	135.4	147.4	155.0	207.6	138.8	180.3	192.4	196.8	199.5	134.8	139.0
Aug	136.3	147.2	156.2	209.8	138.2	181.8	194.1	198.6	201.3	133.4	137.8
Sep	141.7	151.8	160.7	211.8	146.6	183.3	195.9	200.5	203.0	140.6	141.4
Oct	140.8	152.2	162.1	213.6	148.5	184.7	197.4	202.0	204.7	140.7	142.2
Nov	144.0	154.5	162.8	215.0	147.7	186.0	198.9	203.5	206.4	141.9	141.3
Dec	143.5	154.2	163.8	216.5	147.7	187.4	200.3	205.1	208.0	142.5	141.2
1984											
Jan	146.3	158.4	166.2	219.7	153.2	188.9	202.1	206.9	209.8	140.0	138.5
Feb	143.9	157.3	165.5	221.2	149.0	190.2	203.6	208.4	211.4	146.1	145.7
Mar	142.2	153.5	164.5	223.3	144.3	191.6	205.0	209.9	213.2	149.8	146.5
Apr	140.7	153.4	164.6	225.3	144.8	193.3	206.8	211.8	215.0	146.3	143.0
May	135.0	147.0	160.9	227.3	144.9	194.9	208.6	213.6	216.9	142.1	142.8
Jun	136.1	148.4	162.6	229.6	145.7	196.4	210.4	215.4	218.9	140.5	140.6
Jul	144.7	156.4	167.2	231.9	148.0	198.1	212.7	218.0	221.1	135.7	137.0
Aug	147.7	160.7	172.6	234.3	155.5	199.8	214.8	220.1	223.3	141.2	139.5
Sep	151.6	165.1	174.0	236.4	157.8	201.5	216.9	222.3	225.4	137.9	134.5
Oct	159.8	173.0	179.4	239.0	161.6	203.6	219.5	225.0	227.8	140.9	136.0
Nov	162.3	176.0	185.6	241.6	165.3	205.4	221.4	227.1	229.8	141.8	134.9
Dec	164.0	178.7	187.9	244.0	164.3	206.9	223.1	228.8	231.8	139.7	133.8
1985											
Jan	168.7	184.8	191.2	246.1	168.0	208.3	224.6	230.3	233.6	138.1	133.1
Feb	162.8	178.9	187.3	247.3	157.0	209.6	225.7	231.5	235.2	131.6	128.1
Mar	166.8	182.1	190.2	249.5	163.3	211.0	227.4	233.4	236.9	143.5	138.4
Apr	170.8	186.8	194.8	251.6	173.7	212.7	229.5	235.5	238.8	144.3	139.0
May	183.9	201.0	203.1	253.9	187.4	214.2	231.3	237.5	240.6	148.5	141.4
Jun	186.1	203.2	205.4	255.5	185.5	215.5	232.5	238.7	242.2	151.9	144.1
Jul	184.0	201.1	205.7	257.2	184.3	216.8	233.9	240.0	243.9	163.7	154.3
Aug	188.0	206.3	210.2	259.4	191.9	218.1	235.4	241.8	245.5	164.3	154.3
Sep	189.0	206.8	211.0	261.2	189.9	219.5	237.0	243.6	247.2	176.7	161.4
Oct	194.3	212.2	214.5	263.0	199.7	220.8	238.7	245.2	248.9	178.1	166.2
Nov	201.2	218.6	220.4	264.6	216.6	222.1	240.1	246.7	250.5	187.5	172.1
Dec	210.7	228.5	226.5	266.5	224.4	223.7	241.8	248.5	252.3	191.6	174.9

TABLE A2

Canadian Dollar

	Gov't. Bonds		Euro-C$ Bonds		C$ T-Bills		C$ Eurodep.		Non-C$ in C$	
	C$	US$	C$	US$	C$	US$	C$	US$	Bond	Money
1978										
Jan	98.0	96.8	99.6	98.3	100.6	99.4	100.7	99.4	101.0	101.7
Feb	98.3	96.5	99.8	97.9	101.1	99.2	101.2	99.3	102.6	105.0
Mar	99.4	96.1	99.6	96.2	101.7	98.3	101.8	98.4	105.8	108.5
Apr	99.5	96.0	100.0	96.5	102.2	98.6	102.4	98.8	105.0	107.1
May	100.8	98.2	102.0	99.4	103.0	100.4	103.2	100.6	103.6	106.2
Jun	101.4	98.7	103.0	100.3	103.7	100.9	103.8	101.1	106.3	109.7
Jul	102.7	99.4	104.4	101.0	104.4	101.0	104.6	101.2	110.6	115.0
Aug	103.6	98.5	103.5	98.4	105.1	99.9	105.3	100.1	113.9	119.4
Sep	104.2	96.7	102.7	95.2	105.8	98.1	106.1	98.3	117.8	125.2
Oct	101.9	95.8	100.0	94.0	106.6	100.2	106.9	100.5	119.9	132.7
Nov	102.4	95.5	102.4	95.5	107.3	100.1	107.8	100.5	115.5	122.4
Dec	102.2	94.5	103.2	95.3	108.2	100.0	108.6	100.4	118.7	130.0
1979										
Jan	102.1	93.3	104.2	95.2	109.2	99.8	109.7	100.3	119.9	128.7
Feb	102.0	93.5	104.5	95.8	110.1	101.0	110.6	101.4	119.5	129.5
Mar	103.4	97.5	106.5	100.4	111.1	104.7	111.6	105.2	117.3	125.5
Apr	106.3	101.9	107.5	103.1	112.1	107.5	112.6	108.0	112.8	122.3
May	107.3	101.0	109.1	102.7	113.1	106.5	113.7	107.0	115.8	125.2
Jun	107.6	100.8	108.9	102.0	114.1	106.9	114.7	107.4	118.7	129.6
Jul	107.5	100.7	108.2	101.4	115.1	107.9	115.8	108.5	120.9	132.5
Aug	106.0	99.3	107.2	100.4	116.1	108.8	116.9	109.5	120.5	132.8
Sep	104.5	98.6	105.7	99.8	117.1	110.5	117.9	111.3	119.2	135.2
Oct	99.6	92.0	100.6	92.9	118.1	109.1	119.2	110.1	113.5	134.2
Nov	102.1	95.5	101.4	94.8	119.3	111.5	120.4	112.6	112.7	136.7
Dec	100.5	93.9	104.6	97.7	120.7	112.8	121.8	113.8	115.4	139.9
1980										
Jan	94.9	89.6	101.9	96.2	122.2	115.3	123.2	116.3	112.9	138.7
Feb	90.2	86.0	96.7	92.2	123.5	117.8	124.5	118.7	104.1	135.9
Mar	88.8	81.6	97.9	89.9	124.7	114.6	126.0	115.7	104.7	134.8
Apr	99.7	91.8	105.9	97.5	125.9	116.0	127.4	117.4	116.6	143.8
May	105.1	99.1	112.0	105.6	128.2	120.9	129.0	121.7	122.2	145.2
Jun	107.6	102.3	113.8	108.1	130.0	123.6	130.5	124.1	124.9	147.2
Jul	101.4	95.2	113.7	106.8	131.1	123.1	131.9	123.9	124.5	148.4
Aug	101.0	95.6	110.5	104.6	132.0	124.9	133.1	125.9	121.1	149.4
Sep	98.4	92.0	110.2	103.1	133.0	124.4	134.3	125.6	123.8	153.0
Oct	98.0	91.0	111.4	103.4	134.0	124.5	135.6	125.9	124.2	152.5
Nov	100.7	92.8	111.0	102.3	135.0	124.4	136.8	126.1	123.1	152.0
Dec	104.2	95.5	111.1	101.8	135.9	124.5	138.4	126.8	127.1	154.9
1981										
Jan	103.0	94.3	113.8	104.2	137.8	126.1	140.1	128.2	127.1	149.7
Feb	101.0	91.9	115.1	104.8	139.8	127.3	141.8	129.0	123.5	147.6
Mar	103.0	95.2	116.3	107.4	142.1	131.3	143.9	133.0	125.4	148.5
Apr	100.6	92.0	116.7	106.7	143.7	131.4	145.9	133.4	122.0	146.1
May	93.7	85.3	114.1	103.9	145.4	132.4	147.8	134.7	120.9	142.4
Jun	96.1	87.6	115.3	105.1	147.7	134.7	150.1	136.8	118.9	141.2
Jul	93.2	82.6	113.3	100.3	149.7	132.6	152.4	135.0	116.9	141.2
Aug	86.0	78.2	111.8	101.6	152.4	138.6	154.9	140.9	113.6	140.3
Sep	85.1	77.1	110.6	100.2	155.4	140.8	157.6	142.7	113.6	146.2
Oct	95.7	87.1	112.2	102.1	158.2	143.9	160.2	145.7	118.2	150.5
Nov	103.9	96.3	118.2	109.6	161.1	149.4	163.0	151.1	127.6	154.3
Dec	101.1	93.2	123.3	113.7	163.1	150.4	165.4	152.5	125.1	154.1

TABLE A2 (Continued)

Canadian Dollar

	Gov't. Bonds		Euro-C$ Bonds		C$ T-Bills		C$ Eurodep.		Non-C$ in C$	
	C$	US$	C$	US$	C$	US$	C$	US$	Bond	Money
1982										
Jan	97.8	89.4	123.8	113.2	164.6	150.5	167.6	153.2	125.7	153.3
Feb	101.1	89.9	121.8	108.3	166.2	147.8	169.6	150.8	128.6	154.9
Mar	104.0	92.6	123.8	110.2	168.3	149.8	171.9	153.0	129.3	153.3
Apr	106.7	95.7	124.3	111.5	170.5	152.9	174.1	156.2	133.1	156.3
May	106.6	93.8	125.9	110.8	172.3	151.6	176.2	155.0	135.1	156.3
Jun	101.0	85.4	122.1	103.2	174.4	147.4	178.8	151.1	135.5	160.1
Jul	105.0	91.5	123.3	107.4	177.1	154.3	181.1	157.8	135.6	156.6
Aug	116.3	102.7	125.6	110.9	179.8	158.8	183.7	162.2	138.2	154.3
Sep	122.7	108.5	133.2	117.8	181.9	160.9	186.0	164.6	140.7	153.2
Oct	133.9	119.6	139.3	124.4	183.9	164.3	188.2	168.1	144.3	151.0
Nov	136.3	120.5	144.8	128.0	185.7	164.2	190.3	168.2	149.6	157.9
Dec	142.9	126.5	148.0	131.1	187.6	166.1	192.3	170.3	156.0	163.3
1983										
Jan	141.7	125.4	151.1	133.7	189.0	167.3	194.1	171.8	151.1	160.3
Feb	146.6	130.5	153.6	136.8	190.4	169.6	195.6	174.2	155.1	160.7
Mar	148.9	131.8	155.5	137.6	191.9	169.8	197.3	174.6	156.0	160.5
Apr	152.3	136.0	158.2	141.3	193.3	172.6	198.8	177.5	159.0	160.7
May	154.9	137.7	160.9	143.0	194.7	173.1	200.4	178.2	158.3	161.3
Jun	155.0	138.2	161.6	144.0	196.3	175.0	202.0	180.1	157.6	160.4
Jul	152.2	135.0	162.6	144.3	197.7	175.4	203.6	180.6	154.1	159.0
Aug	151.9	134.8	162.7	144.3	199.3	176.8	205.3	182.1	153.4	157.6
Sep	156.1	138.7	164.9	146.5	200.8	178.4	206.9	183.8	160.7	161.5
Oct	157.2	139.5	168.3	149.3	202.4	179.6	208.5	185.0	161.8	162.7
Nov	158.6	140.0	170.7	150.7	203.8	179.9	210.1	185.4	164.3	162.7
Dec	157.7	138.6	171.9	151.1	205.3	180.5	211.7	186.1	165.0	163.3
1984										
Jan	159.8	140.1	174.0	152.5	207.1	181.6	213.4	187.2	165.3	160.8
Feb	156.4	136.9	174.5	152.7	208.7	182.7	215.1	188.2	168.6	169.4
Mar	150.3	128.7	173.5	148.6	210.1	180.0	216.8	185.7	173.9	174.7
Apr	149.9	127.3	175.5	149.0	212.0	180.0	218.6	185.7	172.6	172.4
May	148.0	125.1	175.3	148.1	213.8	180.7	220.5	186.4	167.6	173.1
Jun	147.7	122.5	177.7	147.4	215.4	178.6	222.4	184.5	170.5	174.5
Jul	156.3	130.2	179.6	149.6	217.6	181.4	224.7	187.2	170.9	169.2
Aug	162.6	137.1	183.0	154.3	220.3	185.8	227.0	191.4	174.2	169.8
Sep	165.4	137.3	184.9	153.5	222.3	184.6	229.1	190.3	176.8	167.0
Oct	172.3	142.5	190.4	157.5	224.8	185.9	231.7	191.6	183.7	169.6
Nov	177.3	146.3	196.0	161.8	227.2	187.6	234.0	193.2	186.1	168.7
Dec	181.7	150.8	198.6	164.9	229.4	190.5	236.2	196.2	184.4	166.2
1985										
Jan	187.5	154.5	202.2	166.6	231.2	190.5	238.3	196.4	187.1	166.9
Feb	177.7	140.4	195.7	154.7	232.2	183.5	240.2	189.8	187.5	169.1
Mar	184.8	148.2	201.6	161.6	234.7	188.2	242.1	194.2	195.6	179.0
Apr	190.1	152.1	206.5	165.2	237.1	189.7	244.4	195.5	199.1	180.2
May	203.9	162.0	212.3	168.6	239.0	189.9	246.6	195.8	209.9	184.8
Jun	205.4	165.2	216.1	173.8	240.7	193.7	248.5	199.9	210.9	185.3
Jul	204.0	164.7	217.9	176.0	242.8	196.1	250.6	202.4	217.6	197.2
Aug	208.0	166.6	222.1	177.9	244.6	195.9	252.5	202.3	222.2	199.1
Sep	207.4	165.2	221.1	176.1	246.5	196.4	254.5	202.8	232.7	209.2
Oct	213.7	170.9	224.6	179.6	248.4	198.6	256.4	205.1	235.6	214.4
Nov	221.4	175.0	229.9	181.7	249.9	197.5	258.2	204.1	248.9	224.8
Dec	226.7	177.2	233.3	182.4	251.6	196.8	260.2	203.5	260.0	231.2

TABLE A3

Deutschemark

	Govt. Bonds		Euro-DM Bonds		DM Dom. Dep.		DM Eurodep.		Non-DM in DM	
	DM	US$	DM	US$	DM	US$	DM	US$	Bond	Money
1978										
Jan	101.4	100.6	101.3	100.5	100.3	99.6	100.3	99.5	100.3	101.1
Feb	104.1	107.6	102.6	106.0	100.6	104.0	100.5	103.9	96.6	98.9
Mar	103.7	107.9	103.6	107.7	100.9	105.0	100.8	104.9	97.5	99.9
Apr	103.2	104.3	103.2	104.3	101.2	102.3	101.0	102.2	99.7	101.7
May	102.3	101.9	103.2	102.8	101.5	101.2	101.3	101.0	101.2	103.9
Jun	102.3	103.2	103.8	104.7	101.8	102.7	101.6	102.5	102.4	105.6
Jul	100.0	102.6	102.9	105.6	102.1	104.9	101.9	104.6	104.4	107.9
Aug	101.4	106.7	104.9	110.4	102.5	107.8	102.2	107.6	102.6	106.8
Sep	102.4	110.3	106.1	114.3	102.8	110.7	102.5	110.4	100.7	106.1
Oct	101.6	122.0	106.4	127.7	103.1	123.8	102.8	123.4	92.4	101.2
Nov	101.2	109.8	105.5	114.5	103.4	112.3	103.1	112.0	98.5	103.6
Dec	101.1	116.2	106.2	122.1	103.7	119.3	103.4	118.9	94.2	102.2
1979										
Jan	100.4	112.3	106.6	119.2	104.1	116.5	103.8	116.1	97.0	103.0
Feb	99.7	112.5	105.9	119.6	104.4	117.8	104.0	117.4	96.1	103.1
Mar	99.9	111.9	106.4	119.3	104.8	117.4	104.4	117.0	97.9	104.0
Apr	99.5	109.4	104.3	114.6	105.2	115.6	104.7	115.1	98.0	105.7
May	97.6	107.1	104.6	114.8	105.7	115.9	105.2	115.4	99.1	106.3
Jun	98.0	110.8	105.9	119.8	106.1	120.1	105.6	119.5	97.7	105.7
Jul	100.0	114.7	107.0	122.7	106.7	122.4	106.2	121.8	98.0	106.5
Aug	102.3	117.1	107.2	122.8	107.3	122.9	106.8	122.2	97.6	107.0
Sep	102.9	123.1	106.2	127.1	107.9	129.1	107.3	128.4	92.5	104.5
Oct	100.4	116.7	102.9	119.6	108.6	126.2	108.0	125.5	88.7	104.7
Nov	102.5	123.8	104.6	126.3	109.3	132.0	108.7	131.3	85.4	103.6
Dec	102.7	124.8	105.5	128.1	110.2	133.8	109.5	133.0	86.8	105.3
1980										
Jan	101.9	122.1	103.4	123.9	111.1	133.2	110.3	132.3	87.1	107.2
Feb	98.1	115.5	98.2	115.5	111.9	131.7	111.1	130.7	82.7	108.6
Mar	93.9	100.8	95.5	102.4	112.8	121.0	111.9	120.1	88.7	114.7
Apr	99.3	115.2	102.9	119.3	113.7	131.8	112.8	130.8	91.3	112.4
May	103.8	121.9	106.6	125.2	114.6	134.6	113.6	133.5	96.9	115.0
Jun	106.5	126.4	108.3	128.6	115.6	137.2	114.6	136.0	98.8	116.3
Jul	108.5	127.1	109.9	128.7	116.5	136.4	115.5	135.2	98.4	117.5
Aug	107.8	125.6	108.4	126.3	117.5	136.8	116.3	135.5	97.0	120.1
Sep	106.4	122.9	105.8	122.1	118.4	136.7	117.2	135.3	99.0	122.5
Oct	105.6	116.1	104.6	115.1	119.3	131.3	118.1	129.9	104.1	128.0
Nov	105.8	114.8	105.6	114.5	120.2	130.4	118.9	129.0	103.8	128.5
Dec	104.6	111.6	106.2	113.2	121.2	129.2	119.9	127.8	108.9	132.8
1981										
Jan	104.0	102.5	106.1	104.5	122.2	120.3	120.8	119.0	118.5	140.2
Feb	98.5	96.5	101.9	99.8	123.1	120.5	121.7	119.1	115.4	138.5
Mar	101.6	100.9	105.6	104.9	124.3	123.5	122.8	122.0	117.1	139.5
Apr	101.4	96.2	105.4	100.0	125.6	119.3	124.0	117.7	118.2	142.8
May	98.1	88.1	103.1	92.7	127.0	114.1	125.3	112.6	123.6	147.6
Jun	101.4	89.1	105.0	92.3	128.5	112.9	126.7	111.4	124.3	150.2
Jul	100.9	85.6	105.6	89.5	129.9	110.1	128.0	108.5	123.1	151.7
Aug	100.8	86.1	104.5	89.2	131.4	112.1	129.4	110.5	121.7	154.2
Sep	103.5	93.2	106.5	95.8	132.8	119.5	130.7	117.6	114.2	150.9
Oct	106.0	98.8	108.8	101.3	134.2	125.0	132.1	123.1	115.2	150.0
Nov	109.4	103.4	112.7	106.5	135.6	128.1	133.4	126.1	125.6	154.9
Dec	109.9	102.2	113.3	105.3	136.9	127.2	134.7	125.2	124.5	156.8

TABLE A3 (Continued)

Deutschemark

	Govt. Bonds		Euro-DM Bonds		DM Dom. Dep.		DM Eurodep.		Non-DM in DM	
	DM	US$	DM	US$	DM	US$	DM	US$	Bond	Money
1982										
Jan	110.6	99.9	114.0	103.0	138.1	124.8	135.8	122.7	127.6	159.6
Feb	111.9	98.0	114.8	100.6	139.2	122.0	136.9	120.0	131.1	161.8
Mar	115.3	100.0	118.1	102.5	140.5	121.9	138.2	119.9	133.2	162.3
Apr	119.3	107.0	121.6	109.1	141.7	127.1	139.3	125.0	133.4	160.8
May	119.6	106.6	121.9	108.6	142.8	127.2	140.3	125.0	133.6	160.8
Jun	117.3	99.6	121.9	103.5	144.0	122.3	141.4	120.1	135.1	164.1
Jul	119.4	101.3	122.9	104.3	145.1	123.1	142.5	120.9	139.8	166.6
Aug	122.4	102.5	124.9	104.6	146.3	122.5	143.6	120.2	146.7	169.4
Sep	125.2	103.6	126.4	104.6	147.3	121.9	144.6	119.6	151.7	171.0
Oct	128.3	104.8	129.8	106.1	148.3	121.2	145.5	118.9	159.6	173.1
Nov	129.2	109.4	130.9	110.9	149.4	126.5	146.5	124.1	157.7	171.7
Dec	132.8	116.6	134.9	118.5	150.3	132.0	147.4	129.5	158.7	170.7
1983										
Jan	133.0	112.9	134.3	114.0	151.2	128.3	148.3	125.8	159.1	174.3
Feb	135.0	116.0	135.7	116.6	152.0	130.6	149.0	128.0	162.3	173.5
Mar	136.9	117.9	138.1	118.9	152.7	131.6	149.7	128.9	161.8	171.9
Apr	136.6	115.9	138.8	117.8	153.4	130.2	150.3	127.6	169.3	176.9
May	134.8	111.7	139.0	115.1	154.2	127.7	151.0	125.0	172.3	181.7
Jun	135.6	111.7	139.0	114.5	154.8	127.6	151.6	124.9	172.9	182.5
Jul	135.5	107.1	138.9	109.8	155.5	123.0	152.2	120.4	175.7	188.6
Aug	134.9	104.6	139.7	108.3	156.3	121.2	153.0	118.6	178.5	191.4
Sep	136.7	108.7	141.1	112.2	157.0	124.8	153.6	122.1	182.5	190.9
Oct	138.3	109.9	143.0	113.6	157.8	125.4	154.4	122.7	183.4	192.0
Nov	138.6	107.8	143.4	111.5	158.6	123.4	155.1	120.7	190.0	195.8
Dec	139.6	107.2	143.8	110.5	159.4	122.5	155.8	119.8	192.6	198.4
1984										
Jan	140.6	104.4	145.5	108.0	160.3	119.0	156.7	116.4	199.5	202.6
Feb	143.3	115.3	148.2	119.2	161.1	129.6	157.4	126.7	186.0	194.4
Mar	144.0	116.2	149.3	120.5	161.9	130.7	158.2	127.7	186.9	194.9
Apr	144.8	111.3	149.6	114.9	162.7	125.1	159.0	122.2	193.4	201.4
May	144.7	110.8	149.3	114.3	163.5	125.2	159.7	122.3	187.5	202.2
Jun	146.3	109.9	150.0	112.7	164.3	123.5	160.4	120.6	190.6	203.8
Jul	147.1	105.8	149.2	107.3	165.2	118.9	161.3	116.1	201.5	209.1
Aug	150.5	109.0	152.7	110.6	166.0	120.3	162.1	117.4	206.6	211.4
Sep	152.3	103.8	154.6	105.3	166.8	113.7	162.8	110.9	220.2	219.3
Oct	155.3	107.2	157.3	108.6	167.7	115.8	163.6	113.0	225.0	218.6
Nov	158.8	106.9	160.1	107.8	168.5	113.5	164.4	110.7	233.7	223.4
Dec	160.0	106.1	161.7	107.2	169.4	112.4	165.2	109.6	236.7	225.7
1985										
Jan	159.5	105.5	161.3	106.6	170.2	112.6	166.0	109.8	239.3	225.7
Feb	157.1	98.6	159.5	100.1	171.0	107.3	166.7	104.7	242.4	231.3
Mar	160.0	108.8	162.5	110.5	171.8	116.9	167.5	114.0	236.1	226.8
Apr	162.1	109.3	164.4	110.8	172.7	116.5	168.4	113.6	242.1	230.2
May	164.7	112.7	167.1	114.3	173.6	118.8	169.3	115.8	250.1	230.3
Jun	166.8	115.1	168.3	116.2	174.4	120.5	170.0	117.4	252.2	232.1
Jul	169.8	126.5	171.5	127.7	175.4	130.7	170.9	127.3	240.8	227.1
Aug	173.6	129.0	174.6	129.7	176.2	131.0	171.6	127.6	244.4	227.9
Sep	175.0	136.3	175.0	136.3	176.9	137.8	172.3	134.2	242.4	225.7
Oct	172.2	137.7	172.7	138.1	177.7	142.1	173.0	138.4	240.1	225.3
Nov	174.7	145.2	175.3	145.7	178.3	148.2	173.7	144.4	240.9	223.1
Dec	177.5	152.1	177.9	152.5	179.1	153.6	174.4	149.6	240.9	218.8

TABLE A4

Japanese Yen

	Gov't. Bonds		Samurai Bonds		Euro-¥ Bonds		¥ Dom. CDs		¥ Gensaki		¥ Eurodep.		Non-¥ in ¥	
	¥	US$	¥	US$	¥	US$	¥	US$	¥	US$	¥	US$	Bond	Money
1978														
Jan	100.6	99.4	101.3	100.1	101.8	100.6	100.6	99.5	100.6	99.5	100.6	99.5	100.9	101.5
Feb	100.8	100.6	101.6	101.5	101.6	101.5	101.0	100.8	101.0	100.8	101.0	100.8	100.7	102.9
Mar	102.5	110.0	102.9	110.4	103.2	110.7	101.6	109.0	101.6	109.0	101.6	109.0	93.5	96.3
Apr	103.4	110.3	104.0	111.0	102.2	109.0	102.1	108.9	102.1	108.9	102.1	108.9	92.9	95.5
May	104.0	111.6	103.2	110.7	101.1	108.5	102.5	110.0	102.5	110.0	102.5	110.0	92.0	95.5
Jun	104.4	122.3	103.5	121.2	103.6	121.2	102.9	120.5	102.9	120.5	102.9	120.5	84.7	88.8
Jul	105.0	132.9	104.2	131.8	104.2	131.9	103.4	130.8	103.4	130.8	103.4	130.8	80.0	84.6
Aug	104.3	130.8	105.4	132.2	104.7	131.4	103.8	130.2	103.8	130.2	103.8	130.2	82.1	87.0
Sep	104.8	132.0	105.3	132.6	106.4	134.0	104.2	131.3	104.2	131.3	104.2	130.3	82.4	88.4
Oct	106.4	142.6	107.3	143.8	107.8	144.4	104.7	140.4	104.7	140.4	104.7	140.4	78.7	88.8
Nov	106.8	127.9	106.0	126.9	106.1	127.1	105.0	125.7	105.0	125.7	105.0	125.7	85.9	92.3
Dec	107.3	131.9	106.7	131.2	105.9	130.2	105.4	129.6	105.4	129.6	105.4	129.6	84.9	94.3
1979														
Jan	107.6	127.1	106.7	126.0	105.2	124.2	105.9	125.1	105.9	125.1	105.9	125.1	88.2	96.5
Feb	107.0	123.5	104.2	120.2	100.4	115.9	106.2	122.6	106.2	122.6	106.2	122.6	91.1	100.2
Mar	103.8	118.3	104.3	118.8	100.7	114.7	106.6	121.5	106.6	121.5	106.6	121.5	94.7	101.7
Apr	101.9	109.4	102.8	110.3	99.6	106.9	107.1	115.0	107.1	115.0	107.1	115.0	100.2	108.2
May	101.9	110.6	102.5	111.2	99.5	108.0	107.6	116.8	107.6	116.8	107.6	116.8	99.8	107.3
Jun	101.6	110.9	100.5	109.7	99.1	108.2	108.0	117.9	108.0	117.9	108.0	117.9	101.6	109.9
Jul	103.7	114.9	102.6	113.7	100.7	111.6	108.6	120.3	108.6	120.3	108.6	120.3	101.4	110.5
Aug	103.7	112.5	103.1	111.8	102.3	110.9	109.0	118.2	109.0	118.2	109.0	118.2	103.8	113.6
Sep	104.7	111.0	103.4	109.7	101.6	107.8	109.3	116.0	109.5	116.2	109.5	116.2	105.9	119.6
Oct	104.2	104.9	101.9	102.6	98.4	99.1	110.0	110.8	110.1	110.9	110.2	111.0	103.6	123.0
Nov	101.6	97.1	101.0	96.5	97.9	93.6	110.5	105.6	110.6	105.7	110.9	105.9	112.3	134.7
Dec	103.7	103.6	101.2	101.0	99.2	99.0	111.2	111.0	111.4	111.2	111.6	111.4	108.6	131.2
1980														
Jan	105.1	104.8	101.9	101.6	99.2	98.9	112.0	111.7	112.3	112.0	112.4	112.1	106.7	131.8
Feb	101.9	96.7	94.6	89.8	92.8	88.0	112.7	106.9	112.6	106.8	113.2	107.4	105.1	138.3
Mar	95.8	91.7	91.4	87.4	86.4	82.6	113.0	108.1	113.1	108.2	114.0	109.1	101.5	130.5
Apr	100.6	100.3	99.9	99.6	96.5	96.2	114.0	113.7	114.8	114.5	115.1	114.8	109.3	133.1
May	107.1	114.5	104.9	112.1	101.8	108.8	115.5	123.5	115.9	123.9	116.3	124.3	107.3	127.8
Jun	108.6	118.1	107.5	116.9	104.8	114.0	117.1	127.3	117.1	127.3	117.7	128.0	108.7	128.2
Jul	109.1	114.2	106.9	111.9	104.8	109.7	118.3	123.8	118.1	123.6	118.9	124.5	111.7	133.0
Aug	108.0	117.5	108.1	117.6	106.0	115.2	119.2	129.6	119.1	129.5	120.1	130.6	103.9	129.5
Sep	108.1	122.5	107.4	121.6	105.2	119.3	120.5	136.5	120.2	136.2	121.3	137.5	99.5	124.8
Oct	109.7	124.1	107.9	122.0	105.2	119.0	121.6	137.5	121.8	137.7	122.5	138.6	98.7	123.6
Nov	108.2	119.3	107.8	118.8	105.0	115.7	122.8	135.4	122.6	135.2	123.6	136.2	100.5	125.7
Dec	108.3	127.3	108.6	127.7	103.8	122.1	123.8	145.6	123.6	145.4	124.7	146.7	95.4	118.2
1981														
Jan	111.9	129.6	106.5	123.4	108.4	125.5	124.9	144.7	124.9	144.7	125.7	145.7	95.7	116.1
Feb	113.0	128.3	107.1	121.6	108.1	122.7	125.8	142.8	125.5	142.6	126.6	143.8	93.5	116.5
Mar	115.6	130.6	108.0	122.1	110.3	124.6	126.8	143.3	126.6	143.0	127.6	144.2	97.3	120.0
Apr	115.9	128.7	109.0	121.0	110.5	122.7	127.6	141.7	127.6	141.6	128.4	142.6	94.7	119.1
May	114.7	122.5	107.6	114.9	108.7	116.0	128.3	136.9	128.0	136.7	129.2	138.0	98.3	121.0
Jun	115.6	122.4	108.1	114.5	109.8	116.3	129.1	136.7	128.9	136.5	130.1	137.8	97.1	121.4
Jul	115.4	114.7	109.0	108.3	111.0	110.3	129.9	129.1	129.7	128.9	130.9	130.1	99.6	126.5
Aug	115.4	118.8	109.3	112.6	110.6	113.9	130.8	134.6	130.4	134.2	131.7	135.7	94.3	124.6
Sep	116.4	119.7	109.8	112.9	111.6	114.7	131.6	135.2	131.1	134.8	132.5	136.2	93.6	129.8
Oct	118.2	121.0	111.1	113.7	111.4	114.0	132.4	135.5	132.1	135.2	133.3	136.5	99.6	134.9
Nov	122.1	136.1	115.1	128.4	115.7	129.0	133.2	148.5	132.8	148.1	134.2	149.6	99.9	128.5
Dec	123.7	134.3	116.6	126.5	116.5	126.5	134.2	145.6	133.7	145.1	135.0	146.5	99.6	131.7

TABLE A4 (Continued)

Japanese Yen

	Gov't. Bonds		Samurai Bonds		Euro-¥ Bonds		¥ Dom. CDs		¥ Gensaki		¥ Eurodep.		Non-¥ in ¥	
	¥	US$	¥	US$	¥	US$	¥	US$	¥	US$	¥	US$	Bond	Money
1982														
Jan	124.7	130.4	118.4	123.8	118.0	123.4	134.8	141.0	134.3	140.4	135.7	142.0	103.8	135.4
Feb	125.7	126.6	119.5	120.4	118.7	119.6	135.4	136.4	135.0	136.0	136.4	137.4	108.4	138.5
Mar	128.0	123.7	121.7	117.6	121.5	117.4	136.2	131.6	135.8	131.2	137.2	132.6	115.2	144.1
Apr	128.8	130.3	122.3	123.7	121.7	123.1	136.9	138.5	136.4	138.0	138.0	139.6	113.5	140.8
May	127.5	125.1	123.1	120.8	122.3	120.0	137.6	135.0	137.0	134.4	138.7	136.1	117.9	140.8
Jun	126.0	117.9	121.3	113.5	121.4	113.6	138.5	129.6	138.0	129.2	139.5	130.6	119.9	147.6
Jul	128.0	118.5	122.7	113.6	122.7	113.6	139.3	128.9	138.9	128.6	140.4	129.9	126.4	151.6
Aug	128.6	117.3	123.4	112.6	122.9	112.1	140.2	127.9	139.7	127.4	141.2	128.8	134.8	154.4
Sep	129.3	115.0	124.1	110.4	123.2	109.6	141.0	125.4	140.6	125.1	142.1	126.4	143.0	158.3
Oct	129.9	112.0	125.0	107.7	125.5	108.2	141.9	122.3	141.3	121.8	142.9	123.2	156.1	163.7
Nov	133.0	127.3	127.6	122.1	128.8	123.3	142.7	136.6	142.2	136.1	143.8	137.6	139.6	150.3
Dec	136.5	138.7	130.2	132.3	131.1	133.2	143.6	145.9	143.2	145.5	144.6	147.0	135.4	145.4
1983														
Jan	135.9	135.2	132.6	131.9	133.3	132.7	144.6	143.8	143.9	143.1	145.5	144.7	133.6	146.3
Feb	138.1	138.7	133.7	134.2	132.7	133.2	145.2	145.8	144.7	145.3	146.3	146.8	137.1	146.2
Mar	138.8	138.6	134.6	134.4	133.8	133.6	146.0	145.8	145.6	145.4	147.1	146.9	137.9	146.0
Apr	140.2	140.6	135.3	135.7	134.8	135.2	147.0	147.4	146.4	146.8	147.8	148.3	141.8	147.0
May	140.3	140.2	136.7	136.6	136.7	136.6	147.8	147.7	147.1	147.0	148.7	148.6	140.9	147.5
Jun	141.9	141.6	137.2	136.9	135.9	135.7	148.4	148.2	147.7	147.5	149.4	149.2	140.2	147.4
Jul	142.5	140.8	138.9	137.2	137.6	135.9	149.2	147.4	148.6	146.8	150.2	148.4	137.0	147.2
Aug	143.9	139.4	139.8	135.4	138.5	134.2	150.1	145.4	149.5	144.8	151.0	146.3	139.3	149.4
Sep	146.4	148.5	142.3	144.3	139.8	141.8	151.0	153.1	150.3	152.5	151.8	154.0	138.7	145.4
Oct	147.5	150.5	143.5	146.5	141.7	144.6	151.8	154.9	151.3	154.4	152.7	155.8	138.3	145.3
Nov	149.5	153.8	145.1	149.3	143.4	147.5	152.7	157.0	152.0	156.3	153.5	157.8	137.7	143.2
Dec	151.4	156.1	146.9	151.4	143.7	148.2	153.5	158.2	152.8	157.5	154.3	159.0	136.6	142.8
1984														
Jan	151.8	154.5	149.0	151.6	146.9	149.5	154.4	157.0	153.7	156.3	155.2	157.9	138.8	142.5
Feb	153.0	156.6	150.0	153.5	147.3	150.7	155.1	158.7	154.4	157.9	156.0	159.6	140.5	148.7
Mar	156.0	166.0	152.1	161.8	149.4	158.9	156.1	166.0	155.2	165.1	156.8	166.8	133.8	143.0
Apr	156.7	165.0	152.3	160.3	148.2	156.0	157.0	165.2	156.1	164.3	157.7	165.9	132.6	141.5
May	154.2	159.0	149.9	154.6	146.0	150.6	157.7	162.6	156.9	161.7	158.5	163.4	131.1	144.9
Jun	156.1	156.9	150.9	151.8	148.6	149.5	158.6	159.4	157.7	158.5	159.3	160.1	134.6	147.1
Jul	157.0	152.8	152.6	148.6	149.7	145.7	159.5	155.2	158.6	154.3	160.2	155.9	141.8	149.2
Aug	159.8	157.9	154.4	152.6	151.9	150.2	160.4	158.5	159.4	157.5	161.0	159.1	144.2	149.3
Sep	161.3	156.3	156.1	151.2	153.0	148.2	161.2	156.1	160.2	155.1	161.8	156.6	147.4	147.9
Oct	164.4	159.8	160.1	155.6	156.3	151.9	162.1	157.5	161.1	156.5	162.7	158.0	152.7	149.0
Nov	167.7	161.9	161.1	155.5	158.0	152.5	163.1	157.3	161.9	156.2	163.5	157.8	155.6	149.3
Dec	168.9	160.3	162.2	153.9	159.4	151.2	163.9	155.4	162.8	154.4	164.4	156.0	158.2	151.2
1985														
Jan	169.9	159.3	163.1	152.9	159.5	149.5	164.8	154.4	163.7	153.3	165.3	154.9	162.0	152.8
Feb	166.9	153.6	160.7	147.9	157.9	145.2	165.6	152.3	164.4	151.2	166.1	152.7	158.1	150.7
Mar	170.1	162.0	163.0	155.3	161.3	153.6	166.4	158.4	165.2	157.3	166.9	158.9	161.8	157.7
Apr	171.2	162.5	164.0	155.7	160.7	152.5	167.4	158.8	166.2	157.7	167.8	159.2	165.8	157.2
May	173.9	165.4	166.7	158.5	162.6	154.7	168.3	160.1	167.0	158.8	168.7	160.4	174.6	159.4
Jun	175.8	169.0	167.9	161.3	164.3	157.9	169.1	162.5	167.9	161.3	169.5	162.9	175.7	160.4
Jul	177.3	179.0	170.0	171.6	165.5	167.1	170.1	171.6	168.8	170.3	170.5	172.0	171.9	161.8
Aug	179.4	179.3	171.1	171.0	167.3	167.2	171.0	170.8	169.7	169.5	171.4	171.2	176.3	163.7
Sep	183.4	202.4	172.4	190.2	168.3	185.6	171.9	189.6	170.6	188.1	172.3	190.0	162.0	152.5
Oct	176.0	199.1	169.3	191.4	166.6	188.3	172.5	195.0	171.2	193.6	173.2	195.7	162.3	152.6
Nov	180.1	212.8	169.9	200.8	169.5	200.2	173.6	205.0	172.2	203.3	174.1	205.6	160.9	150.0
Dec	184.2	220.1	174.6	208.6	171.4	204.8	174.9	208.9	173.5	207.2	175.2	209.3	164.2	150.4

TABLE A5

U.K. Sterling

	Gov't. Bonds		Euro-£ Bonds		£ T-Bills		£ Dom. CDs		£ Eurodep.		Non-£ in £	
	£	US$	£	US$	£	US$	£	US$	£	US$	Bond	Money
1978												
Jan	97.9	99.4	102.3	103.9	100.6	102.2	100.6	102.2	100.6	102.1	98.2	98.4
Feb	96.6	97.2	102.6	103.2	101.0	101.6	101.0	101.6	101.1	101.7	100.5	102.0
Mar	96.7	93.5	100.8	97.4	101.5	98.1	101.6	98.2	101.7	98.3	107.0	108.5
Apr	93.8	89.2	98.4	93.6	101.9	96.9	101.9	96.8	102.3	97.2	108.4	108.9
May	93.7	88.9	97.5	92.5	102.4	97.2	102.5	97.2	103.1	97.8	108.4	109.6
Jun	94.1	91.0	98.2	94.9	103.1	99.6	103.2	99.8	103.9	100.4	108.9	110.6
Jul	96.3	96.7	100.6	101.0	103.9	104.3	104.2	104.6	104.8	105.2	108.0	110.3
Aug	96.6	97.7	101.1	102.3	104.8	106.0	105.2	106.4	105.8	107.0	108.3	111.3
Sep	96.9	99.4	102.2	104.8	105.5	108.2	105.9	108.6	106.7	109.4	107.6	111.7
Oct	96.7	105.0	93.1	101.1	106.2	115.3	106.5	115.6	107.8	117.0	104.4	112.9
Nov	96.5	97.6	94.4	95.5	107.0	108.3	107.3	108.5	108.9	110.1	107.7	111.6
Dec	97.2	103.2	97.3	103.3	108.0	114.7	108.3	115.0	110.0	116.7	103.9	111.2
1979												
Jan	94.0	97.4	95.6	99.0	109.2	113.1	109.6	113.5	111.2	115.2	107.0	111.6
Feb	100.7	106.0	100.3	105.6	110.2	116.0	110.6	116.5	112.3	118.3	104.1	110.7
Mar	110.2	118.7	106.5	114.7	111.4	119.9	111.9	120.5	113.5	122.2	101.2	107.8
Apr	111.3	119.6	107.6	115.6	112.5	120.9	113.1	121.5	114.8	123.3	98.9	107.2
May	108.8	117.4	108.3	116.9	113.6	122.5	114.1	123.1	115.9	125.1	99.7	107.0
Jun	106.2	119.8	106.6	120.2	114.4	129.1	114.8	129.5	117.0	132.0	97.1	104.7
Jul	109.2	128.2	107.9	126.7	115.8	135.9	116.2	136.4	118.3	138.9	94.3	102.2
Aug	110.6	129.6	109.0	127.7	117.2	137.2	117.7	137.8	119.7	140.2	93.9	102.7
Sep	109.9	125.6	106.5	121.7	118.4	135.3	119.0	136.0	121.0	138.3	96.3	108.4
Oct	105.1	113.9	101.5	110.0	119.8	129.8	120.4	130.4	122.5	132.7	95.1	111.7
Nov	98.5	112.6	101.5	116.0	120.9	138.2	121.4	138.7	124.0	141.7	91.0	108.4
Dec	100.4	116.0	105.2	121.6	122.6	141.7	123.2	142.3	125.5	145.1	91.8	109.5
1980												
Jan	106.0	125.0	105.7	124.6	124.3	146.6	124.9	147.3	127.2	150.0	87.4	107.1
Feb	103.0	121.7	100.2	118.4	125.9	148.8	126.5	149.5	128.9	152.4	80.7	105.8
Mar	103.1	116.0	99.1	111.6	127.7	143.7	128.4	144.6	130.9	147.3	82.3	106.2
Apr	108.0	126.5	106.0	124.2	129.4	151.6	130.5	152.9	132.8	155.6	88.7	108.6
May	111.5	135.5	113.9	138.4	131.2	159.4	132.3	160.8	134.8	163.7	91.7	108.0
Jun	114.5	140.4	114.7	140.7	133.1	163.2	134.2	164.6	136.7	167.7	93.6	109.3
Jul	119.5	145.2	117.2	142.4	135.0	164.1	136.4	165.7	138.7	168.5	92.0	109.7
Aug	114.1	142.0	115.6	143.8	136.6	169.9	137.7	171.2	140.5	174.7	88.2	108.3
Sep	119.6	148.5	114.6	142.2	138.5	171.8	139.7	173.4	142.4	176.8	88.6	109.6
Oct	122.1	154.9	117.1	148.5	140.2	177.8	141.4	179.3	144.3	183.1	85.4	105.5
Nov	122.5	150.3	115.6	141.8	141.9	174.1	143.7	176.2	146.1	179.2	87.3	108.2
Dec	120.2	149.5	113.7	141.4	143.6	178.7	145.4	180.9	148.2	184.3	88.9	107.7
1981												
Jan	121.8	150.4	117.1	144.6	145.3	179.4	147.2	181.8	150.0	185.3	89.2	104.6
Feb	122.9	140.5	117.9	134.8	146.8	167.8	149.1	170.4	151.7	173.3	93.8	112.3
Mar	126.3	147.3	118.8	138.5	148.4	173.1	150.6	175.5	153.5	178.9	94.4	112.4
Apr	125.5	140.0	120.6	134.6	149.9	167.3	152.0	169.6	155.1	173.0	95.4	114.9
May	124.5	134.0	118.8	127.9	151.2	162.8	153.4	165.2	156.6	168.6	98.0	116.3
Jun	122.0	123.2	118.1	119.3	152.8	154.3	155.0	156.5	158.3	159.8	104.3	124.5
Jul	120.5	115.4	116.6	111.7	154.1	147.6	156.1	149.5	160.0	153.2	105.4	128.2
Aug	120.0	115.5	117.5	113.1	156.0	150.1	156.1	150.2	161.7	155.6	104.5	130.8
Sep	114.8	107.6	114.7	107.5	157.4	147.6	159.6	149.6	163.5	153.3	108.0	140.0
Oct	116.2	112.5	117.1	113.4	159.6	154.4	161.9	156.7	165.5	160.2	109.4	139.5
Nov	125.2	127.5	124.4	126.7	162.1	165.0	164.8	167.7	167.7	170.7	114.0	138.0
Dec	122.1	121.1	123.3	122.4	163.9	162.6	166.6	165.3	169.9	168.7	114.6	141.2

TABLE A5 (Continued)

U.K. Sterling

	Gov't. Bonds		Euro-£ Bonds		£ T-Bills		£ Dom. CDs		£ Eurodep.		Non-£ in £	
	£	US$	£	US$	£	US$	£	US$	£	US$	Bond	Money
1982												
Jan	129.7	126.9	125.8	123.0	166.1	162.5	168.8	165.2	172.0	168.3	114.6	140.3
Feb	134.6	127.5	128.7	121.9	167.9	159.0	170.8	161.7	174.0	164.7	117.7	143.6
Mar	142.4	132.2	136.6	126.8	170.1	157.8	173.0	160.5	176.3	163.5	120.3	145.7
Apr	143.6	134.1	136.9	127.9	171.8	160.4	174.7	163.1	178.3	166.4	124.5	148.8
May	144.9	135.1	139.8	130.3	173.6	161.8	176.5	164.5	180.1	167.9	123.8	148.8
Jun	146.8	132.6	140.4	126.8	175.8	158.7	178.7	161.4	182.3	164.6	122.5	148.0
Jul	154.7	140.0	144.6	130.9	177.8	160.8	181.0	163.7	184.3	166.7	125.7	149.6
Aug	169.3	151.2	154.4	137.9	179.7	160.5	183.0	163.5	186.3	166.5	131.0	152.0
Sep	175.9	155.0	156.3	137.7	181.2	159.7	184.5	162.6	188.1	165.8	135.5	153.8
Oct	186.5	162.6	163.2	142.3	182.9	159.4	186.2	162.3	189.8	165.4	141.8	155.3
Nov	176.6	149.6	162.8	137.9	184.1	156.0	187.4	158.8	191.5	162.2	152.6	166.0
Dec	182.3	153.2	162.8	136.8	185.7	156.1	188.9	158.8	193.1	162.3	161.3	173.6
1983												
Jan	171.7	135.8	164.6	130.2	187.1	148.0	190.2	150.4	194.7	154.0	168.3	182.8
Feb	179.5	141.1	167.9	132.0	188.8	148.4	192.1	151.0	196.3	154.3	174.9	185.8
Mar	184.2	142.0	173.5	133.8	190.6	146.9	194.1	149.6	198.2	152.7	178.1	188.5
Apr	187.9	152.5	178.5	144.8	192.3	156.0	195.9	159.0	199.9	162.2	172.8	179.7
May	191.0	158.9	180.0	149.8	194.0	161.4	197.5	164.4	201.8	167.9	165.8	174.3
Jun	191.4	152.4	182.4	145.2	195.7	155.8	199.3	158.7	203.5	162.0	174.1	183.0
Jul	185.8	146.8	181.2	143.2	197.1	155.7	200.7	158.6	205.1	162.1	171.2	182.0
Aug	188.1	146.0	182.0	141.3	198.8	154.4	202.5	157.2	207.0	160.7	173.4	184.2
Sep	196.5	152.9	183.6	142.9	200.4	156.0	204.2	158.9	208.6	162.3	181.3	188.5
Oct	198.6	154.3	185.8	144.4	202.1	157.0	205.9	160.0	210.3	163.4	182.8	189.8
Nov	204.2	155.2	188.4	143.2	203.6	154.8	207.4	157.7	212.0	161.2	189.3	193.5
Dec	205.2	154.8	188.8	142.4	205.2	154.8	208.9	157.6	213.6	161.1	191.0	195.1
1984												
Jan	205.6	149.6	191.3	139.3	206.8	150.6	210.5	153.3	215.3	156.8	198.7	199.6
Feb	207.5	160.7	194.7	150.7	208.3	161.3	212.1	164.3	216.9	168.0	188.5	195.3
Mar	211.6	158.5	197.7	148.1	209.9	157.3	213.8	160.3	218.5	163.8	196.9	203.9
Apr	208.8	151.7	197.8	143.7	211.4	153.6	215.4	156.6	220.2	160.1	200.5	206.6
May	202.1	145.5	194.2	139.8	212.7	153.2	216.7	156.1	221.9	159.8	195.9	208.5
Jun	204.5	144.1	197.4	139.1	214.5	151.3	218.5	154.0	223.5	157.6	199.8	210.8
Jul	199.2	135.3	196.9	133.7	215.8	146.6	219.3	149.1	225.3	153.1	211.0	214.8
Aug	212.5	144.4	203.6	138.4	218.2	148.4	222.3	151.2	227.3	154.6	216.7	218.4
Sep	217.2	139.3	206.1	132.2	219.9	141.1	224.3	143.9	229.2	147.1	230.5	225.8
Oct	220.2	139.5	208.5	132.1	222.0	140.7	226.3	143.5	231.5	146.8	242.4	231.5
Nov	226.3	140.8	213.9	133.1	224.1	139.5	228.5	142.2	233.5	145.4	250.0	234.8
Dec	223.4	134.5	215.0	129.4	225.8	136.0	230.3	138.7	235.6	141.9	258.9	242.1
1985												
Jan	220.1	129.3	211.5	124.2	227.0	133.4	231.2	135.9	237.6	139.6	268.7	247.9
Feb	222.4	125.0	217.7	122.4	229.0	128.8	233.0	131.0	239.5	134.7	269.2	251.7
Mar	228.4	146.5	220.3	141.3	231.8	148.7	236.2	151.6	241.8	155.2	246.5	232.4
Apr	230.9	149.1	222.4	143.5	234.5	151.5	239.3	154.5	244.6	157.9	248.9	231.7
May	232.4	155.3	224.4	150.0	236.9	158.4	241.6	161.6	247.3	165.3	251.8	226.2
Jun	236.1	160.7	228.0	155.2	239.1	162.8	243.8	166.0	249.6	170.0	251.2	225.5
Jul	243.5	178.3	231.0	169.2	241.9	177.3	247.1	181.0	252.4	185.0	239.6	220.8
Aug	246.1	178.0	232.5	168.1	244.1	176.6	249.1	180.2	254.9	184.5	246.1	224.1
Sep	250.0	181.4	235.1	170.5	246.5	178.9	251.4	182.5	257.4	186.9	255.8	233.0
Oct	251.6	188.5	236.9	177.4	248.9	186.5	253.7	190.1	259.9	194.7	251.3	231.0
Nov	252.9	195.5	238.9	184.7	251.1	194.2	256.1	198.1	262.2	202.8	254.2	230.2
Dec	251.3	189.1	237.5	178.8	253.6	191.0	258.5	194.6	264.8	199.4	271.5	241.1

TABLE A6

Swiss Franc

	Gov't. Bonds		Foreign Bonds		Sfr Dom. Dep.		Sfr Eurodep.		Non-Sfr in Sfr	
	Sfr	US$	Sfr	US$	Sfr	US$	Sfr	US$	Bond	Money
1978										
Jan	101.8	101.9	101.2	101.4	100.2	100.4	100.2	100.3	99.5	100.1
Feb	102.4	110.6	100.2	108.1	100.3	108.3	100.3	108.3	92.9	94.1
Mar	102.8	111.1	100.1	108.1	100.4	108.5	100.4	108.4	94.3	95.7
Apr	103.7	106.1	101.1	103.5	100.5	102.8	100.4	102.7	98.8	100.4
May	104.1	108.5	100.5	104.8	100.6	104.8	100.4	104.7	96.8	98.8
Jun	104.9	112.2	101.1	108.2	100.7	107.7	100.5	107.5	96.4	98.9
Jul	106.7	121.9	101.9	116.4	100.8	115.1	100.6	114.9	93.3	95.7
Aug	107.4	129.5	103.2	124.6	100.9	121.8	100.8	121.6	89.1	91.5
Sep	107.8	137.7	103.9	132.6	101.1	129.0	100.9	128.8	84.8	87.5
Oct	109.5	145.5	105.0	139.7	101.2	134.6	101.0	134.3	83.8	90.2
Nov	109.6	124.9	103.7	118.2	101.3	115.5	101.0	115.2	93.9	98.3
Dec	110.3	134.7	105.7	129.1	101.3	123.8	101.0	123.4	89.0	95.6
1979										
Jan	110.9	129.1	107.9	125.6	101.4	118.0	101.1	117.6	93.4	98.8
Feb	110.6	131.0	106.7	126.4	101.4	120.2	101.1	119.8	91.7	97.9
Mar	110.4	129.2	105.5	123.4	101.4	118.7	101.1	118.3	93.9	99.4
Apr	109.8	126.1	105.0	120.6	101.5	116.5	101.1	116.1	93.7	101.0
May	110.0	126.5	104.3	119.9	101.5	116.8	101.1	116.3	94.4	101.3
Jun	108.5	129.0	105.4	125.3	101.7	120.9	101.2	120.4	92.9	100.4
Jul	109.2	130.7	106.7	127.7	101.8	121.8	101.4	121.3	94.1	102.2
Aug	109.7	131.2	107.0	127.9	102.0	121.9	101.5	121.4	93.8	102.6
Sep	110.6	140.5	107.8	137.0	102.1	129.8	101.6	129.1	87.7	98.3
Oct	109.3	130.6	103.1	123.2	102.3	122.1	101.8	121.5	87.1	102.4
Nov	107.1	132.4	102.4	126.6	102.5	126.7	102.0	126.1	84.6	101.8
Dec	107.7	133.9	102.6	127.6	102.8	127.9	102.3	127.2	86.0	103.5
1980										
Jan	104.2	125.8	98.8	119.2	103.2	124.5	102.7	123.9	87.6	107.5
Feb	104.6	121.6	95.3	110.8	103.6	120.5	103.1	119.8	84.8	111.3
Mar	101.8	108.9	94.2	100.8	104.1	111.4	103.6	110.8	89.4	116.3
Apr	103.9	123.0	101.1	119.7	104.7	124.0	104.1	123.3	90.0	111.0
May	104.4	124.4	103.4	123.1	105.2	125.3	104.6	124.6	96.2	114.6
Jun	105.7	128.5	104.2	126.6	105.8	128.6	105.2	127.9	97.1	114.6
Jul	107.0	127.9	104.7	125.2	106.4	127.2	105.7	126.4	97.1	116.2
Aug	103.3	123.8	103.3	123.9	106.8	128.1	106.2	127.3	95.0	117.7
Sep	105.3	126.2	102.6	122.9	107.4	128.6	106.7	127.8	95.9	119.0
Oct	107.0	123.8	103.8	120.1	107.9	124.9	107.2	124.1	99.0	122.4
Nov	107.5	122.1	103.5	117.5	108.4	123.1	107.7	122.3	99.3	123.7
Dec	108.6	121.0	104.0	115.9	109.1	121.6	108.3	120.7	103.8	127.9
1981										
Jan	107.9	111.1	103.8	106.8	109.6	112.8	108.8	112.0	112.5	135.2
Feb	105.3	105.9	100.4	100.9	110.1	110.7	109.3	110.0	111.3	136.2
Mar	104.1	107.0	101.7	104.5	110.8	113.9	110.0	113.1	112.2	136.1
Apr	103.3	101.6	98.9	97.3	111.5	109.7	110.7	108.9	113.1	139.2
May	101.8	97.2	98.0	93.5	112.3	107.1	111.5	106.4	114.9	140.0
Jun	104.0	101.2	101.7	99.0	113.2	110.2	112.4	109.4	110.9	136.0
Jul	104.1	95.9	100.9	92.9	114.1	105.1	113.3	104.4	111.9	140.3
Aug	102.4	95.1	98.3	91.3	115.1	106.8	114.2	106.1	110.7	142.6
Sep	102.1	102.5	97.7	98.1	116.0	116.4	115.1	115.6	101.8	135.7
Oct	103.2	111.2	100.7	108.5	116.9	125.9	116.1	125.1	99.1	129.6
Nov	106.6	119.1	103.5	115.6	117.9	131.8	117.1	130.9	105.3	130.5
Dec	108.2	119.0	104.8	115.2	119.0	130.9	118.2	130.0	104.2	131.9

TABLE A6 (Continued)

Swiss Franc

	Gov't. Bonds		Foreign Bonds		Sfr Dom. Dep.		Sfr Eurodep.		Non-Sfr in Sfr	
	Sfr	US$	Sfr	US$	Sfr	US$	Sfr	US$	Bond	Money
1982										
Jan	108.6	116.3	105.0	112.4	119.9	128.4	119.1	127.5	106.5	134.0
Feb	108.4	113.1	104.1	108.6	120.8	126.0	119.9	125.1	108.9	135.2
Mar	111.8	114.4	107.3	109.8	121.7	124.5	120.8	123.6	111.9	137.2
Apr	113.1	114.3	108.8	110.0	122.5	123.8	121.5	123.8	117.6	143.1
May	113.9	112.9	110.9	110.0	123.0	122.0	122.1	121.0	119.2	143.1
Jun	112.5	105.9	109.8	103.4	123.5	116.3	122.6	115.4	120.9	148.8
Jul	115.1	108.5	110.9	104.6	124.0	116.9	123.0	116.0	124.6	150.7
Aug	117.7	109.4	112.2	104.3	124.5	115.7	123.5	114.8	131.0	153.5
Sep	119.6	109.1	113.9	103.9	124.9	114.0	124.0	113.1	136.3	156.3
Oct	121.4	108.9	116.4	104.4	125.4	112.4	124.4	111.6	143.9	159.0
Nov	121.2	113.1	117.4	109.6	125.8	117.4	124.8	116.5	141.7	157.1
Dec	121.6	120.4	119.6	118.4	126.2	125.0	125.3	124.0	139.6	152.3
1983										
Jan	122.7	120.4	121.4	119.1	126.6	124.2	125.7	123.3	136.3	151.3
Feb	122.5	117.6	120.5	115.7	126.9	121.8	126.0	120.9	144.1	156.6
Mar	122.1	116.0	120.8	114.7	127.2	120.8	126.3	119.9	145.6	157.4
Apr	123.0	117.7	121.4	116.1	127.5	122.0	126.6	121.0	148.7	158.0
May	122.5	115.7	121.0	114.3	128.0	120.9	127.0	120.0	149.3	160.1
Jun	122.6	115.5	121.7	114.6	128.4	121.0	127.5	120.1	149.5	160.5
Jul	123.6	114.8	122.3	113.6	128.9	119.7	128.0	118.9	147.6	160.9
Aug	121.9	110.4	122.4	110.9	129.5	117.3	128.5	116.4	150.8	164.3
Sep	122.8	114.6	122.8	114.6	129.9	121.3	129.0	120.5	153.3	162.9
Oct	124.5	115.1	123.0	113.7	130.4	120.6	129.5	119.7	156.3	165.8
Nov	124.7	114.5	123.7	113.6	130.9	120.2	130.0	119.3	159.0	166.2
Dec	125.6	114.6	124.9	113.9	131.3	119.7	130.4	118.9	160.2	167.5
1984										
Jan	125.5	110.2	126.0	110.6	131.8	115.7	130.9	114.9	166.5	171.9
Feb	125.4	114.7	126.8	115.9	132.2	120.8	131.3	120.0	162.4	172.4
Mar	125.9	115.8	127.5	117.3	132.6	121.9	131.7	121.1	162.6	172.3
Apr	125.7	110.8	127.9	112.8	133.0	117.2	132.1	116.4	167.1	176.8
May	124.8	109.3	126.4	110.6	133.4	116.7	132.5	116.0	162.6	178.1
Jun	126.4	107.4	128.0	108.7	133.8	113.6	132.9	112.8	167.3	181.9
Jul	125.8	100.9	128.2	102.8	134.2	107.6	133.4	106.9	179.2	189.6
Aug	126.7	104.3	129.8	106.9	134.7	110.9	133.9	110.2	180.0	187.5
Sep	126.7	99.8	130.2	102.6	135.2	106.5	134.3	105.8	188.2	190.8
Oct	126.6	100.4	130.7	103.6	135.8	107.6	135.0	106.9	193.8	191.8
Nov	128.0	99.3	132.0	102.4	136.3	105.7	135.5	105.1	200.7	195.4
Dec	128.6	97.8	133.1	101.2	136.9	104.1	136.1	103.4	204.2	198.4
1985										
Jan	128.6	95.2	133.1	98.5	137.5	101.7	136.7	101.1	211.5	203.6
Feb	127.9	89.0	132.4	92.2	138.0	96.0	137.2	95.5	215.9	210.7
Mar	128.6	99.5	133.1	103.0	138.6	107.2	137.8	106.6	205.3	201.1
Apr	129.8	99.1	135.0	103.0	139.2	106.2	138.4	105.6	211.6	205.2
May	130.7	100.7	136.2	105.0	139.9	107.8	139.1	107.2	219.6	206.4
Jun	130.8	101.9	136.8	106.6	140.4	109.4	139.7	108.8	221.1	207.6
Jul	131.3	113.0	137.6	118.4	141.1	121.3	140.3	120.7	206.9	198.1
Aug	132.8	113.8	139.3	119.4	141.7	121.4	140.9	120.8	210.2	199.0
Sep	133.3	119.9	140.0	125.9	142.3	127.9	141.5	127.2	208.4	196.8
Oct	134.2	123.7	140.3	129.3	142.8	131.6	142.0	130.9	206.8	197.0
Nov	135.1	128.4	141.4	134.4	143.3	136.2	142.6	135.5	209.2	196.8
Dec	136.2	131.4	142.7	137.6	143.9	138.8	143.1	138.0	212.9	196.6

TABLE A7

Dutch Guilder

	Gov't Bonds		Foreign Bonds		Euro-Dfl Bonds		Dfl Dom. Dep.		Dfl Eurodep.		Non-Dfl in Dfl	
	Dfl	US$	Dfl	US$	Dfl	US$	Dfl	US$	Dfl	US$	Bond	Money
1978												
Jan	103.8	104.1	103.7	104.0	103.3	103.6	100.5	100.8	100.5	100.8	99.3	99.9
Feb	104.5	108.9	104.6	108.9	104.9	109.2	100.9	105.1	100.9	105.1	96.4	98.0
Mar	105.4	110.7	105.4	110.8	105.9	111.3	101.4	106.6	101.4	106.5	96.9	98.6
Apr	107.0	110.0	106.4	109.4	107.2	110.2	101.8	104.6	101.8	104.6	98.3	99.7
May	106.0	106.5	107.2	107.6	107.8	108.2	102.3	102.7	102.2	102.7	100.4	102.8
Jun	107.1	108.5	107.8	109.2	108.3	109.8	102.7	104.1	102.6	104.0	101.8	105.0
Jul	105.5	108.3	106.6	109.4	106.7	109.5	103.1	105.8	103.0	105.7	104.0	107.8
Aug	107.4	112.6	108.3	113.6	107.5	112.8	103.5	108.6	103.5	108.5	103.0	107.0
Sep	105.3	112.9	106.1	113.8	105.3	112.8	104.0	111.5	103.9	111.4	101.5	106.5
Oct	104.5	126.0	106.2	128.0	106.0	127.8	104.7	126.3	104.5	126.0	92.9	100.4
Nov	104.8	113.7	105.7	114.7	106.6	115.6	105.4	114.4	105.2	114.2	98.9	103.4
Dec	106.4	122.1	106.2	121.8	106.5	122.2	106.3	122.0	106.0	121.7	95.0	102.0
1979												
Jan	107.3	120.1	108.4	121.4	109.1	122.2	107.3	120.1	106.9	119.7	97.3	102.5
Feb	106.3	120.3	107.8	122.0	109.5	123.9	108.0	122.3	107.7	121.8	96.2	102.3
Mar	107.8	116.1	109.4	117.7	110.7	119.1	108.8	117.1	108.4	116.6	102.3	108.3
Apr	107.7	118.0	109.7	120.2	111.0	121.6	109.5	120.0	109.0	119.4	98.4	105.5
May	106.2	115.1	107.9	116.9	109.1	118.3	110.2	119.5	109.7	118.9	100.3	107.1
Jun	106.9	118.6	108.1	120.0	108.6	120.5	110.9	123.1	110.3	122.5	99.8	107.4
Jul	107.9	122.0	109.6	123.9	109.4	123.7	111.7	126.3	111.1	125.6	99.8	107.6
Aug	110.4	124.6	111.7	126.1	112.0	126.5	112.6	127.1	111.9	126.3	99.5	108.0
Sep	110.7	129.2	112.1	130.9	111.1	129.7	113.3	132.4	112.7	131.6	95.8	106.7
Oct	109.2	123.7	110.6	125.3	110.7	125.4	114.3	129.6	113.7	128.8	91.9	107.0
Nov	110.1	129.2	110.7	129.9	110.0	129.1	115.2	135.2	114.5	134.4	89.3	106.2
Dec	109.3	130.3	109.8	130.9	109.9	131.0	116.4	138.8	115.6	137.9	89.8	106.7
1980												
Jan	109.4	128.4	109.8	128.8	111.3	130.7	117.6	138.1	116.8	137.1	90.0	108.9
Feb	102.8	119.1	102.1	118.2	106.5	123.4	118.8	137.6	117.9	136.5	85.2	109.6
Mar	102.6	108.8	100.7	106.8	104.6	110.9	120.0	127.3	119.1	126.3	90.1	115.2
Apr	110.2	125.0	109.7	124.4	113.0	128.2	121.2	137.5	120.2	136.4	94.0	114.2
May	111.0	128.4	111.5	129.0	115.1	133.2	122.3	141.5	121.4	140.4	98.9	115.9
Jun	112.2	131.5	113.0	132.5	115.8	135.7	123.5	144.7	122.5	143.6	100.7	116.9
Jul	115.6	134.4	116.7	135.6	117.1	136.1	124.6	144.8	123.6	143.7	99.8	117.3
Aug	113.9	131.7	114.9	132.9	117.0	135.3	125.6	145.3	124.6	144.1	98.4	120.0
Sep	112.6	129.7	113.6	130.9	117.2	135.0	126.7	146.0	125.7	144.8	99.7	121.7
Oct	114.0	125.6	114.3	125.9	117.4	129.4	127.8	140.8	126.8	139.7	103.8	126.6
Nov	114.5	124.0	115.5	125.1	117.1	126.8	128.8	139.4	127.8	138.4	104.0	127.6
Dec	115.4	122.8	115.9	123.3	117.8	125.3	129.9	138.2	128.9	137.2	108.7	131.8
1981												
Jan	115.5	113.7	116.5	114.7	119.6	117.8	130.9	128.9	129.9	127.9	117.5	139.0
Feb	112.4	107.6	114.5	109.6	118.5	113.5	131.9	126.2	130.8	125.3	116.8	140.7
Mar	114.1	110.9	115.3	112.1	118.5	115.3	133.0	129.4	132.0	128.4	118.5	141.6
Apr	114.3	105.7	116.2	107.4	119.9	110.8	134.1	124.0	133.1	123.1	120.1	145.8
May	112.6	98.4	114.5	100.0	119.3	104.2	135.3	118.2	134.2	117.2	125.4	151.1
Jun	116.4	99.4	117.5	100.3	119.7	102.2	136.6	116.6	135.6	115.7	126.4	154.0
Jul	116.4	96.1	117.4	96.9	120.7	99.6	138.0	113.9	136.9	113.0	124.8	155.1
Aug	114.1	94.9	115.6	96.1	118.1	98.1	139.4	115.9	138.4	115.0	123.5	157.7
Sep	114.8	100.6	116.2	101.8	118.4	103.7	140.9	123.5	139.9	122.5	116.6	154.2
Oct	115.9	105.7	117.9	107.4	120.8	110.1	142.5	129.8	141.4	128.9	117.2	152.6
Nov	121.3	113.1	122.2	114.0	124.6	116.2	144.1	134.3	143.0	133.3	126.2	156.0
Dec	122.8	112.3	124.1	113.5	127.7	116.7	145.6	133.1	144.5	132.1	125.4	158.4

TABLE A7 (Continued)

Dutch Guilder

	Gov't Bonds		Foreign Bonds		Euro-Dfl Bonds		Dfl Dom. Dep.		Dfl Eurodep.		Non-Dfl in Dfl	
	Dfl	US$	Dfl	US$	Dfl	US$	Dfl	US$	Dfl	US$	Bond	Money
1982												
Jan	124.5	110.9	126.3	112.5	128.9	114.8	146.9	130.9	145.8	129.9	128.1	160.7
Feb	126.9	109.7	128.2	110.8	130.4	112.7	148.1	128.0	147.0	127.0	131.5	163.0
Mar	130.4	110.3	132.8	112.3	135.4	114.5	149.5	126.4	148.4	125.5	135.3	165.6
Apr	132.9	116.1	135.5	118.3	136.5	119.2	150.6	131.5	149.5	130.5	136.0	164.4
May	133.3	116.1	138.0	120.2	136.1	118.6	151.7	132.1	150.5	131.1	135.6	164.4
Jun	131.9	109.8	133.9	111.5	137.6	114.6	152.8	127.2	151.7	126.3	136.5	166.4
Jul	134.8	112.2	136.3	113.4	139.5	116.1	153.9	128.1	152.7	127.1	141.1	168.9
Aug	137.2	113.5	139.3	115.2	141.7	117.2	155.1	128.3	153.9	127.3	147.0	170.4
Sep	138.4	113.3	140.3	114.9	143.8	117.7	156.2	127.9	155.0	126.9	151.6	171.7
Oct	144.6	117.2	144.5	117.1	147.9	119.9	157.3	127.5	156.1	126.5	158.9	173.2
Nov	146.9	122.3	149.6	124.6	151.8	126.4	158.3	131.8	157.0	130.7	158.6	173.7
Dec	151.3	130.1	154.7	133.0	156.6	134.6	159.3	136.9	158.0	135.8	160.5	173.5
1983												
Jan	152.6	127.9	158.7	133.0	159.5	133.7	160.1	134.2	158.8	133.1	159.3	175.4
Feb	154.8	130.3	159.2	134.0	160.5	135.1	160.8	135.4	159.5	134.2	164.0	176.3
Mar	154.7	128.2	159.8	132.4	162.5	134.6	161.5	133.8	160.2	132.7	166.6	178.2
Apr	150.9	123.1	156.9	128.0	162.4	132.4	162.1	132.2	160.8	131.1	174.2	183.6
May	148.8	118.5	155.9	124.2	161.9	128.9	162.8	129.7	161.5	128.6	177.0	188.5
Jun	151.3	120.2	157.4	125.1	162.3	129.0	163.6	130.0	162.2	128.9	177.0	188.6
Jul	152.9	117.1	159.8	122.4	164.2	125.8	164.4	125.9	163.0	124.8	178.9	193.9
Aug	152.9	114.5	160.8	120.5	165.5	124.0	165.2	123.8	163.8	122.7	182.1	197.4
Sep	157.5	121.2	164.0	126.2	168.1	129.4	166.0	127.8	164.6	126.7	185.7	196.4
Oct	158.0	121.3	165.8	127.3	168.5	129.3	166.9	128.1	165.4	127.0	187.3	198.2
Nov	160.4	120.3	166.9	125.2	169.4	127.1	167.7	125.9	166.3	124.7	193.7	202.4
Dec	160.9	118.9	167.1	123.5	170.9	126.3	168.6	124.6	167.1	123.5	196.8	205.7
1984												
Jan	162.2	115.7	169.4	120.7	172.6	123.1	169.5	120.8	168.0	119.8	203.9	210.6
Feb	164.0	126.5	171.9	132.6	174.2	134.3	170.3	131.3	168.8	130.2	191.4	202.4
Mar	165.8	128.4	173.5	134.4	176.0	136.3	171.1	132.5	169.6	131.4	192.1	202.7
Apr	166.7	123.2	174.7	129.0	177.6	131.2	172.0	127.1	170.5	126.0	198.2	209.0
May	165.5	121.6	174.7	128.3	178.7	131.2	172.9	127.0	171.4	125.9	192.8	210.3
Jun	167.4	120.8	175.4	126.6	179.6	129.6	173.7	125.4	172.2	124.3	195.7	211.8
Jul	167.4	115.2	175.8	121.0	180.7	124.4	174.7	120.2	173.1	119.2	207.2	218.2
Aug	171.4	119.1	179.0	124.4	182.4	126.8	175.6	122.1	174.1	121.0	211.8	219.8
Sep	174.6	114.6	182.8	120.1	184.3	121.1	176.5	115.9	174.9	114.9	224.0	226.8
Oct	178.9	118.3	188.6	124.8	186.9	123.7	177.5	117.4	175.9	116.4	230.3	227.5
Nov	180.2	116.8	190.6	123.5	189.8	123.0	178.4	115.6	176.8	114.6	238.0	231.5
Dec	182.1	115.8	192.0	122.1	192.4	122.3	179.3	114.0	177.7	113.0	242.1	235.1
1985												
Jan	182.8	115.6	193.0	122.1	193.6	122.4	180.2	114.0	178.6	113.0	245.1	235.5
Feb	179.2	107.9	188.3	113.3	188.9	113.7	181.0	109.0	179.4	108.0	247.3	240.7
Mar	182.4	118.9	192.0	125.2	192.4	125.5	181.9	118.7	180.3	117.6	241.4	236.0
Apr	184.1	119.2	194.9	126.2	194.4	125.8	183.0	118.5	181.4	117.4	228.3	239.2
May	188.0	123.4	199.0	130.6	197.4	129.6	184.1	120.9	182.5	119.8	255.3	239.4
Jun	189.5	125.6	200.5	132.9	199.6	132.3	185.1	122.7	183.4	121.6	257.3	241.0
Jul	192.5	138.0	203.4	145.9	201.6	144.6	186.2	133.6	184.6	132.4	245.7	235.2
Aug	196.5	140.9	207.7	149.0	205.7	147.5	187.3	134.3	185.6	133.1	248.8	235.4
Sep	197.5	147.6	209.0	156.2	207.6	155.2	188.2	140.7	186.5	139.4	248.3	234.4
Oct	195.9	150.3	207.7	159.4	208.3	159.8	189.2	145.2	187.5	143.8	245.9	234.1
Nov	198.2	158.4	209.9	167.7	209.6	167.5	190.1	151.9	188.3	150.5	246.4	231.3
Dec	200.6	165.2	211.5	174.2	211.4	174.0	191.1	157.3	189.3	155.9	246.8	227.1

TABLE A8

French Franc

	Govt. Bonds		Euro-Ffr Bonds		Ffr Dom. Dep.		Ffr Eurodep.		Non-Ffr in Ffr	
	Ffr	US$	Ffr	US$	Ffr	US$	Ffr	US$	Bond	Money
1978										
Jan	100.8	99.4	100.8	99.5	100.8	99.5	101.1	99.7	101.0	101.7
Feb	101.1	98.9	99.2	97.0	101.6	99.3	102.1	99.8	102.9	105.3
Mar	102.7	104.9	103.4	105.6	102.4	104.6	103.2	105.5	99.9	101.7
Apr	104.5	106.0	109.1	110.8	103.2	104.7	104.2	105.7	99.6	100.9
May	105.0	106.3	109.3	110.7	104.0	105.4	105.2	106.5	99.7	101.5
Jun	107.0	110.9	109.3	113.3	104.8	108.6	105.9	109.8	99.6	101.9
Jul	107.6	115.1	111.4	119.2	105.5	112.9	106.8	114.3	99.8	102.3
Aug	110.1	118.2	114.1	122.5	106.2	114.0	107.6	115.6	100.5	103.7
Sep	111.6	120.1	113.4	122.0	106.9	115.0	108.4	116.7	101.1	105.5
Oct	112.7	131.4	113.2	131.9	107.6	125.4	109.4	127.5	96.2	103.8
Nov	114.5	121.0	115.3	121.9	108.2	114.4	110.2	116.5	101.5	106.0
Dec	117.0	131.1	117.0	131.2	108.9	122.0	111.1	124.5	97.4	104.3
1979										
Jan	119.1	129.7	120.8	131.6	109.6	119.4	112.0	122.0	100.0	105.2
Feb	120.0	131.1	120.9	132.1	110.1	120.3	112.8	123.2	99.7	106.0
Mar	120.9	131.5	121.5	132.2	110.7	120.5	113.6	123.5	101.1	106.5
Apr	120.9	128.9	122.2	130.2	111.4	118.7	114.3	121.9	101.2	108.3
May	118.9	125.9	121.7	128.9	112.1	118.7	115.1	121.9	102.6	109.5
Jun	116.6	126.9	119.5	130.0	112.7	122.7	116.0	126.2	101.7	109.3
Jul	115.5	127.3	116.4	128.4	113.6	125.2	117.0	129.0	102.3	110.1
Aug	114.0	125.1	118.7	130.2	114.5	125.6	118.2	129.7	102.4	111.0
Sep	114.9	130.8	117.6	133.8	115.4	131.3	119.3	135.7	98.4	109.3
Oct	116.0	128.7	116.8	129.5	116.6	129.3	120.6	133.8	94.0	109.0
Nov	114.9	131.8	113.8	130.6	117.7	135.1	122.0	140.0	91.4	108.2
Dec	112.9	131.3	114.3	132.9	119.0	138.4	123.4	143.6	92.2	109.0
1980										
Jan	113.8	130.1	115.2	131.7	120.2	137.4	124.9	142.7	92.6	111.6
Feb	107.6	120.4	114.3	127.9	121.4	135.9	126.3	141.3	88.2	113.2
Mar	108.3	112.7	111.0	115.5	122.8	127.8	127.7	132.9	91.8	117.0
Apr	111.5	123.7	115.8	128.3	124.1	137.6	129.2	143.2	96.3	116.4
May	112.6	127.0	118.0	133.0	125.5	141.4	130.6	147.2	101.6	118.5
Jun	114.0	130.1	119.4	136.2	126.9	144.8	132.1	150.7	103.4	119.6
Jul	115.4	130.4	122.0	137.8	128.2	144.9	133.5	150.9	102.8	120.2
Aug	116.4	130.5	122.8	137.7	129.4	145.1	134.8	151.1	101.6	123.3
Sep	115.6	128.6	121.4	135.0	130.8	145.5	136.2	151.5	103.3	125.6
Oct	114.8	122.5	121.6	129.7	132.1	141.0	137.6	146.9	107.3	130.2
Nov	116.0	121.1	122.7	128.1	133.3	139.2	138.9	145.1	107.9	131.8
Dec	117.1	120.7	120.3	124.1	134.7	138.9	140.3	144.7	112.2	135.4
1981										
Jan	118.0	112.7	123.9	118.4	136.0	129.9	141.7	135.3	121.1	142.7
Feb	118.1	109.7	122.2	113.5	137.2	127.5	142.9	132.8	120.3	144.3
Mar	119.5	112.3	123.2	115.8	138.7	130.4	144.5	135.8	122.6	145.9
Apr	119.5	106.5	123.9	110.4	140.1	124.9	146.0	130.1	124.6	150.7
May	111.2	93.5	118.1	99.3	141.6	119.0	147.5	124.0	130.4	156.4
Jun	115.2	94.7	116.1	95.5	143.4	117.9	149.5	122.9	131.3	159.1
Jul	116.6	92.7	117.6	93.5	145.4	115.6	151.9	120.7	129.7	160.2
Aug	115.6	92.1	116.6	92.9	147.6	117.7	154.6	123.3	128.9	163.5
Sep	117.4	98.6	118.4	99.5	149.8	125.8	157.7	132.4	121.6	159.9
Oct	119.8	98.6	122.6	100.9	152.0	125.2	160.9	132.5	129.9	169.0
Nov	121.9	101.6	124.7	104.0	154.3	128.6	164.1	136.8	141.3	174.5
Dec	124.0	101.3	127.3	104.0	156.4	127.8	166.9	136.3	140.5	177.3

TABLE A8 (Continued)

French Franc

	Govt. Bonds		Euro-Ffr Bonds		Ffr Dom. Dep.		Ffr Eurodep.		Non-Ffr in Ffr	
	Ffr	US$	Ffr	US$	Ffr	US$	Ffr	US$	Bond	Money
1982										
Jan	125.6	99.6	128.8	102.2	158.3	125.6	169.1	134.2	144.1	180.6
Feb	127.2	97.8	132.2	101.6	160.2	123.1	171.2	131.7	148.0	183.2
Mar	128.4	95.9	130.7	97.6	160.3	121.2	173.7	129.7	153.5	187.6
Apr	130.6	100.2	132.6	101.7	164.3	126.1	176.3	135.3	155.0	187.2
May	133.4	101.8	136.5	104.1	166.3	126.9	179.0	136.9	155.1	187.2
Jun	136.1	93.1	138.6	94.8	168.7	115.4	182.8	125.1	166.5	203.9
Jul	138.1	94.0	140.8	95.8	170.9	116.3	186.1	126.6	172.9	207.7
Aug	141.0	93.9	143.3	95.6	173.3	115.4	189.3	126.1	183.0	213.0
Sep	141.3	92.4	144.0	94.2	175.4	114.7	192.1	125.6	190.4	216.5
Oct	145.4	93.9	148.9	96.2	177.4	114.5	194.9	125.8	200.2	219.0
Nov	145.6	97.7	153.1	102.7	179.5	120.4	198.2	133.0	197.6	216.6
Dec	149.1	103.2	156.2	108.1	181.5	125.6	201.4	139.4	200.0	216.2
1983										
Jan	153.5	102.5	161.5	107.9	183.5	122.6	205.1	137.0	200.7	220.9
Feb	154.9	104.9	163.3	110.6	185.3	125.5	208.4	141.1	204.5	219.4
Mar	159.6	102.5	166.3	106.8	187.3	120.3	212.4	136.4	215.7	231.0
Apr	160.6	101.5	171.2	108.2	189.2	119.5	215.4	136.1	225.6	237.9
May	163.2	100.6	172.5	106.3	191.3	117.9	218.5	134.6	229.4	244.2
Jun	165.2	101.2	174.8	107.0	193.2	118.3	220.8	135.2	230.4	245.4
Jul	168.7	98.6	177.4	103.7	195.1	114.1	223.2	130.5	235.0	254.8
Aug	170.0	98.0	181.7	104.7	197.3	113.7	226.0	130.3	237.3	256.8
Sep	171.6	100.2	185.0	108.1	199.3	116.4	228.7	133.6	245.4	259.4
Oct	174.3	101.6	188.0	109.6	201.4	117.5	231.5	135.0	247.3	261.2
Nov	176.0	100.3	190.6	108.6	203.5	116.0	234.1	133.5	255.8	266.4
Dec	178.7	100.3	192.3	108.0	205.5	115.5	236.7	133.0	259.6	270.5
1984										
Jan	182.7	98.9	197.1	106.7	207.7	112.5	239.3	129.7	269.2	276.9
Feb	183.5	107.1	199.4	116.4	209.7	122.5	241.8	141.3	253.5	266.9
Mar	185.2	108.4	200.2	117.2	211.9	124.1	244.7	143.4	254.8	267.5
Apr	188.0	105.2	202.2	113.1	214.1	119.9	247.8	138.8	262.4	275.2
May	189.3	105.4	203.5	113.4	216.4	120.6	251.0	139.9	254.6	276.1
Jun	195.7	106.9	206.1	112.6	218.5	119.5	253.7	138.7	258.9	278.4
Jul	194.9	102.2	209.4	109.9	220.9	115.9	256.5	134.6	272.3	284.7
Aug	198.8	104.8	213.0	112.3	223.1	117.7	259.2	136.7	279.7	288.1
Sep	204.2	101.0	216.3	107.0	225.1	111.5	261.5	129.5	298.0	299.4
Oct	214.6	107.7	220.6	110.7	227.4	114.2	264.2	132.7	303.8	297.9
Nov	209.5	103.1	225.1	110.7	229.4	112.9	266.7	131.3	314.2	302.8
Dec	210.8	101.9	227.4	109.9	231.5	112.0	269.2	130.2	319.0	306.7
1985										
Jan	215.8	104.0	230.8	111.2	233.6	112.7	271.6	131.0	322.1	306.3
Feb	216.3	98.8	232.4	106.1	235.5	107.6	273.9	125.1	326.4	314.6
Mar	221.5	109.3	234.3	115.7	237.5	117.3	276.2	136.5	319.0	309.0
Apr	226.5	111.9	236.9	117.1	239.7	118.5	278.8	137.9	323.8	310.2
May	229.4	114.0	240.7	119.6	241.8	120.2	281.4	139.9	337.5	313.3
Jun	230.6	116.3	241.8	122.0	243.8	123.0	283.7	143.2	338.4	313.5
Jul	233.8	127.6	243.3	132.8	246.0	134.4	286.3	156.4	322.9	305.5
Aug	236.1	128.3	245.2	133.2	248.1	134.8	289.1	157.2	328.7	307.4
Sep	236.4	134.6	246.7	140.5	250.2	142.5	292.1	166.4	326.1	303.9
Oct	241.3	141.4	250.0	146.4	252.2	147.9	295.0	172.9	321.9	302.6
Nov	245.1	149.0	254.8	154.9	254.1	154.6	297.4	180.9	323.7	299.9
Dec	249.1	155.6	256.9	160.5	256.2	160.2	300.0	187.6	325.1	295.1

TABLE A9

Australian Dollar

	Gov't. Bonds		
	A$	**US$**	**Non-A$ in A$ Bond**
1984			
Sep	100.0	100.0	100.0
Oct	100.2	102.3	101.5
Nov	101.1	104.7	101.2
Dec	101.4	101.1	104.9
1985			
Jan	103.6	101.3	107.7
Feb	101.5	86.5	118.8
Mar	102.0	86.0	127.2
Apr	102.8	79.5	141.0
May	105.4	84.2	142.9
Jun	107.8	86.8	144.3
Jul	110.7	96.1	138.4
Aug	109.1	92.1	144.1
Sep	110.1	92.9	150.2
Oct	107.3	90.2	153.3
Nov	106.7	87.8	163.5
Dec	108.1	88.6	169.6

TABLE A10

European Currency Unit

	Euro-ECU Bonds	
	ECU	**US$**
1984		
Sep	100.0	100.0
Oct	104.5	104.0
Nov	106.1	104.0
Dec	107.7	103.2
1985		
Jan	108.0	102.8
Feb	108.6	98.1
Mar	111.2	109.4
Apr	112.6	110.2
May	114.8	112.7
Jun	115.0	114.6
Jul	117.8	126.1
Aug	117.8	125.5
Sep	118.4	131.5
Oct	117.4	134.3
Nov	118.9	141.1
Dec	119.6	144.7

TABLE A11

World Indexes

	Weighted World Bond		Unweighted World Bond		Unweighted World Money	
	Local Curr.	US$	Local Curr.	US$	Local Curr.	US$
1978						
Jan	99.7	99.6	100.9	100.6	100.5	100.2
Feb	100.0	100.5	101.2	102.7	101.0	102.5
Mar	100.6	102.0	102.0	104.5	101.5	104.0
Apr	100.4	101.1	102.5	103.3	102.0	102.7
May	100.3	101.0	102.5	103.2	102.5	103.2
Jun	100.3	103.3	103.1	106.3	103.0	106.1
Jul	101.2	106.8	103.7	110.3	103.5	110.0
Aug	102.1	108.0	104.9	112.8	104.1	111.8
Sep	102.3	108.8	105.0	114.5	104.6	113.8
Oct	101.6	112.2	104.3	121.2	105.2	121.7
Nov	102.3	107.4	104.7	111.5	105.8	112.4
Dec	102.0	109.3	105.4	116.9	106.5	117.6
1979						
Jan	102.9	109.1	106.1	114.6	107.2	115.4
Feb	103.1	109.1	106.3	115.2	107.8	116.5
Mar	104.4	110.2	107.8	116.1	108.5	116.6
Apr	103.9	108.0	107.8	114.8	109.2	116.0
May	104.5	108.8	107.5	114.1	109.8	116.5
Jun	105.3	110.8	107.2	116.2	110.5	119.6
Jul	106.1	112.9	107.8	118.5	111.3	122.1
Aug	106.2	112.5	108.4	118.8	112.1	122.5
Sep	105.9	112.1	108.0	120.6	112.9	125.5
Oct	101.1	104.5	104.8	113.1	113.8	122.2
Nov	101.5	105.1	104.5	115.2	114.7	125.9
Dec	102.5	107.4	105.1	117.2	115.8	128.5
1980						
Jan	101.1	106.0	104.1	115.4	117.0	129.0
Feb	95.6	98.9	99.3	106.3	118.0	128.2
Mar	94.4	95.7	97.7	100.9	119.1	122.7
Apr	102.6	106.9	104.8	113.8	120.5	130.4
May	107.5	114.6	108.8	120.7	121.9	135.0
Jun	110.0	118.2	110.7	124.3	123.1	137.9
Jul	109.4	116.3	111.5	123.7	124.3	137.4
Aug	105.9	114.1	109.7	122.5	125.3	139.4
Sep	105.8	115.1	109.1	122.0	126.4	140.8
Oct	105.5	114.6	109.5	120.2	127.6	139.5
Nov	105.5	112.8	109.8	118.3	128.7	138.2
Dec	106.6	115.8	110.1	118.7	130.0	139.9
1981						
Jan	107.7	115.6	111.0	114.8	131.3	135.8
Feb	106.1	111.7	109.5	110.4	132.6	133.6
Mar	108.9	115.2	111.2	113.5	134.0	136.6
Apr	106.8	111.0	110.7	109.3	135.2	133.4
May	107.7	109.4	108.5	103.4	136.5	130.2
Jun	107.7	107.8	109.9	103.0	138.1	129.6
Jul	106.2	102.9	109.3	98.6	139.6	126.2
Aug	104.5	102.6	107.7	98.2	141.3	129.1
Sep	103.8	102.1	107.5	100.5	143.1	133.6
Oct	107.8	106.7	110.4	105.1	144.9	137.8
Nov	114.6	117.6	115.5	113.7	146.8	143.9
Dec	113.3	114.7	116.1	112.2	148.4	143.1

TABLE A11 (Continued)

World Indexes

	Weighted World Bond		Unweighted World Bond		Unweighted World Money	
	Local Curr.	US$	Local Curr.	US$	Local Curr.	US$
1982						
Jan	114.3	113.8	117.0	110.8	149.9	141.6
Feb	116.4	113.6	118.7	109.3	151.3	139.2
Mar	119.3	114.4	121.9	110.3	152.9	138.3
Apr	121.6	118.7	123.9	114.1	154.4	142.0
May	122.3	118.1	125.2	114.0	155.9	141.8
Jun	120.7	113.6	124.1	107.9	157.5	137.1
Jul	124.8	117.3	126.9	110.6	159.2	138.9
Aug	129.9	121.5	131.4	113.6	160.8	139.3
Sep	133.8	124.0	134.2	114.8	162.2	138.9
Oct	140.1	128.6	139.5	118.2	163.6	138.8
Nov	140.2	131.9	140.9	122.1	165.0	143.0
Dec	143.8	137.8	144.2	128.2	166.3	147.5
1983						
Jan	141.6	133.5	145.0	125.9	167.6	145.3
Feb	145.9	137.9	147.4	128.2	168.8	146.7
Mar	146.8	137.9	149.3	128.1	170.1	145.9
Apr	149.8	141.8	151.1	130.3	171.2	147.5
May	148.7	140.6	151.6	129.7	172.5	147.5
Jun	149.5	140.4	152.4	129.3	173.6	147.3
Jul	146.7	136.7	152.3	126.8	174.8	145.7
Aug	147.5	136.1	153.1	125.5	176.1	144.8
Sep	152.3	142.6	156.0	130.2	177.4	148.2
Oct	152.7	143.5	157.7	131.4	178.7	149.1
Nov	155.2	145.4	159.3	131.4	179.9	148.5
Dec	155.8	145.7	160.2	131.2	181.1	148.5
1984						
Jan	157.7	145.6	162.2	129.7	182.4	146.4
Feb	157.3	148.0	163.1	136.1	183.6	152.9
Mar	157.6	149.2	163.6	136.6	184.9	153.8
Apr	157.0	146.8	164.0	133.0	186.3	151.0
May	152.9	142.0	162.2	130.6	187.6	151.0
Jun	154.5	141.7	164.1	129.7	188.9	149.3
Jul	158.6	142.9	165.8	127.0	190.3	146.4
Aug	162.8	147.5	169.8	131.3	191.9	148.9
Sep	165.8	147.3	172.1	128.0	193.3	144.8
Oct	171.4	152.5	176.3	131.6	194.9	146.4
Nov	174.7	154.4	179.3	132.3	196.4	145.7
Dec	176.0	154.0	180.6	130.9	197.8	144.9
1985						
Jan	178.5	155.0	182.2	130.7	199.1	144.5
Feb	174.7	148.8	180.1	122.8	200.3	140.3
Mar	178.4	157.5	183.3	132.9	201.8	149.5
Apr	181.4	159.8	185.8	133.2	203.4	150.3
May	189.1	167.6	190.3	137.8	204.9	152.6
Jun	191.3	170.5	192.2	140.7	206.3	155.1
Jul	191.8	176.4	194.6	151.4	207.8	164.2
Aug	195.1	178.7	196.7	152.0	209.3	164.4
Sep	197.0	185.9	197.9	157.9	210.7	170.8
Oct	197.9	189.0	197.9	161.0	212.1	175.2
Nov	202.9	197.2	200.6	167.0	213.4	180.6
Dec	208.9	203.6	203.4	170.9	214.9	183.2

CHAPTER THIRTY-THREE

ROGER G. IBBOTSON is Professor in the Practice of Finance, Yale School of Management. He is also President of Ibbotson Associates, Inc. in Chicago and New Haven. Among his many publications, Professor Ibbotson is co-author (with Rex Sinquefield) of *Stocks, Bonds, Bills, and Inflation* and co-author (with Gary Brinson) of *Investment Markets: Gaining the Performance Advantage.* He previously taught at the University of Chicago, where he was Executive Director of the Center for Research in Security Prices.

LAURENCE B. SIEGEL is Managing Partner of Ibbotson Associates, Inc, where he advises money management professionals on investment stategies and historical rates of return, and where he consults with corporate finance departments and regulated industries on cost of capital, valuation, taxation, and investment issues. He is also Instructor in Economics at Keller Graduate School of Management. Mr. Siegel is the author of numerous articles in financial journals and has contributed to several books on finance.

INTERNATIONAL EQUITY MARKETS AND RETURNS*

By Roger G. Ibbotson
Professor
in the Practice of Finance
Yale University
New Haven, Connecticut
and
Laurence B. Siegel
Managing Partner
Ibbotson Associates
Chicago, Illinois

The Japanese economy has captured the world's attention. Japanese cars outsell American- and European-made cars in many parts of the United States. Japanese consumer goods—from electronic devices and microchips to motorcycles and musical instruments—dominate world markets. American workers lose jobs to workers in some Japanese plants whose efficiency—*not* wage-adjusted—is reportedly twice that of the Americans. These results are from a country which lost a world war and which, in 1946, had one of the world's lowest per capita incomes: $29 a year.

Can this economic success be discerned in the stock market? The answer is an emphatic yes. From 1960 to the mid-1980's, a dollar invested in Japanese equities would have grown to about $50, including reinvestment of dividends. This performance has far outshone any other country. U.S. and European equities were practically tied, with a dollar growing to about $11 in the United States and Europe.

*This chapter is adapted with permission from a chapter in Roger G. Ibbotson and Gary P. Brinson, *Investment Markets: Gaining the Performance Advantage* (New York: McGraw-Hill Book Company. Copyright © 1987, McGraw-Hill, Inc.)

INTERNATIONAL STOCK MARKET RETURNS SINCE 1960

International equities have provided healthy returns to investors in the past quarter century, primarily because of Japan's spectacular performance and the large size of the Japanese market. Figure 1 shows the results that would have been obtained if a dollar had been

FIGURE 1 GROWTH OF A DOLLAR INVESTED IN WORLD EQUITIES 1960-1985 (1960 = $1.00)

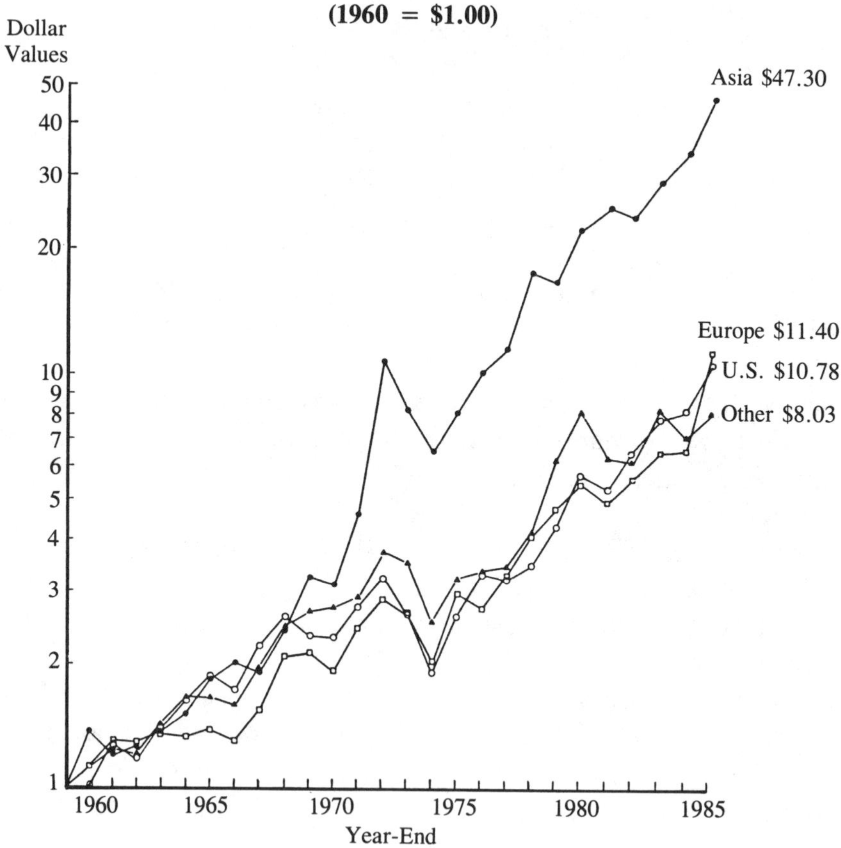

Source: Roger G. Ibbotson, Richard C. Carr and Anthony W. Robinson "International Equity and Bond Returns," *Financial Analysts Journal,* July-August, 1982, with updates by the authors of this chapter.

invested in portfolios of Asian, European, U.S., and other stocks at the beginning of 1960. Asia was clearly the big winner, while the other regions were tied for a poor second place. Over 1960-69, the Asian index consisted exclusively of Japan, but beginning in 1970, Hong Kong and Singapore were given a small weight in the index. Though small, these growing markets also have had spectacular returns. The portfolio of "other" countries in Figure 1 includes Canada and Australia.

In this chapter, international equity returns are converted to a common denominator—U.S. dollars. For most of the twentieth century, U.S. gross national product was a large component of the world's output, and U.S. dollars were the principal world currency. In addition, dollar-adjusted returns represent realizable returns after accounting for currency fluctuations but before transaction costs and taxes.

Total returns vary widely among countries and are annualized for five-year periods in Table 1. Japan's returns were amongst the highest for every half-decade. On the other hand, Italy had three out of five half decades with negative average annual returns. The largest five-year average gain was 40 percent per year in Hong Kong in 1975-79. The largest drop was 11.2 percent per year in the United Kingdom in 1970-74.

The smallest and largest annual returns (not shown) occurred in the newly developed Asian countries: the highest was +211 percent in Singapore in 1972, the lowest −60 percent in Hong Kong in 1974. But annual returns (not shown) were volatile in the established industrial countries too, ranging from +183 percent in Norway in 1979 to −50 percent in the United Kingdom in 1974.

Table 2 details summary statistics of foreign equity returns since 1960. A country's standard deviation provides the variability of its returns, and thus is a measure of risk. Two markets with the highest returns, Singapore and Hong Kong, were extremely risky, as was Norway, which had only average returns. Japan and the United Kingdom were riskier than average. The remainder of the countries had a level of stock market risk comparable to that of the United States.

In Figure 2 the size of each major international equity market is shown as a percentage of the total. The United States makes up nearly

TABLE 1 INTERNATIONAL EQUITIES
U.S. DOLLAR ADJUSTED TOTAL RETURNS FOR 5-YEAR PERIODS,* ANNUALIZED 1960-1985 (FOR SUMMARY STATISTICS, SEE TABLE 2)

	EUROPE								
PERIOD	AUSTRIA %	BELGIUM %	DENMARK %	FRANCE %	GERMANY %	ITALY %	NETHER-LANDS %	NORWAY %	SPAIN %
1960-64	13.3	7.2	8.9	2.6	6.5	−0.7	7.2	4.4	14.7
1965-69	0.9	2.5	4.9	3.8	9.6	10.7	7.1	7.3	18.1
1970-74	19.5	13.7	15.5	−0.6	4.8	−9.4	−0.2	19.0	14.5
1975-79	8.3	18.9	7.7	22.2	16.3	−1.4	23.9	17.6	−10.2
1980-85	8.6	15.8	17.0	10.7	18.0	22.3	18.3	7.4	8.4

	EUROPE			ASIA			OTHER		
PERIOD	SWEDEN %	SWITZER-LAND %	UNITED KINGDOM %	HONG KONG %	JAPAN %	SINGAPORE %	AUSTRALIA %	CANADA %	U.S. %
1960-64	11.8	10.1	6.6		8.8		8.8	12.7	11.2
1965-69	6.1	9.9	11.2		16.4		15.4	5.9	7.0
1970-74	8.2	3.7	−11.2	4.1	15.9	11.2	−10.7	4.6	−1.8
1975-79	5.1	21.7	32.8	40.1	18.8	29.5	21.5	18.0	17.7
1980-85	24.7	11.0	16.4	8.7	20.7	2.2	5.4	7.7	18.2

*Note: Sample includes one six-year period, 1980-85. Returns are compound annual (geometric mean) returns over the period indicated.

Source: Constructed by the authors using capital appreciation returns and dividend yields from Morgan Stanley Capital International Perspective, New York. U.S. returns computed using Ibbotson Associates' *Stocks, Bonds, Bills & Inflation 1986 Yearbook*, Chicago 1986.

TABLE 2 WORLD EQUITIES: SUMMARY STATISTICS 1960-1985

Asset	Annual Returns in U.S. Dollars: Compound Return (%)	Arithmetic Mean (%)	Standard Deviation (%)	Year-End Wealth Index 1959=1.00 $	1985 Year-End Value in Billions U.S. $
Europe					
Austria	9.9	13.6	35.9	11.63	4.0
Belgium	11.6	12.9	17.4	17.35	20.9
Denmark	10.9	13.8	27.8	14.90	13.1
France	7.6	10.1	25.2	6.66	78.5
Germany	11.2	14.3	29.9	15.62	179.0
Italy	4.4	8.8	34.6	3.06	64.7
Netherlands	11.2	12.8	19.4	15.79	51.6
Norway	10.8	18.1	48.1	14.48	9.8
Spain	8.6	10.9	21.7	8.52	18.7
Sweden	11.5	13.4	20.6	16.79	29.8
Switzerland	11.1	14.1	27.9	15.62	90.3
United Kingdom	10.5	14.5	31.2	13.27	328.3
Asia					
Hong Kong*	16.1	29.5	56.8	10.90	38.0
Japan	16.2	19.2	28.9	49.72	909.1
Singapore*	13.0	24.2	59.5	7.05	20.4
Other					
Australia	7.4	10.2	24.9	6.40	62.5
Canada	9.6	10.9	17.3	10.81	146.9
United States	9.6	11.2	16.9	10.78	1955.4

*1970-1985

Source: Returns, wealth indices, and year-end values from *Morgan Stanley Capital International Perspective*, New York.

FIGURE 2 MARKET VALUES OF INTERNATIONAL EQUITIES (Year End 1985 Values)

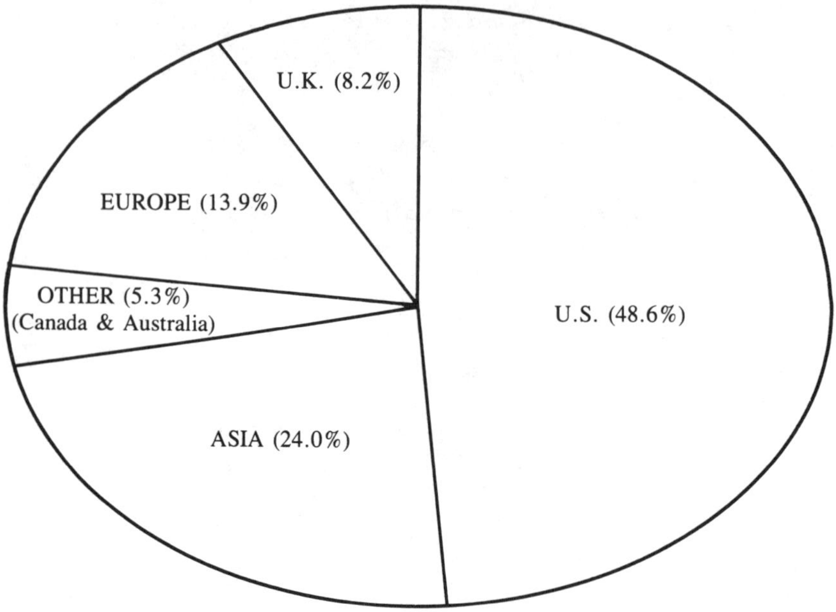

Source: Chart based on market values from Morgan Stanley, *Capital International Perspective,* New York.

half the world market. The United States aside, Japan dominates the market with a 22.6 percent share. Other large markets include the United Kingdom, Canada, Germany, France, Switzerland and Australia.

MARKETS THAT MOVE TOGETHER: EQUITY RETURN "BLOCS"

Correlations of dollar-adjusted total returns show which countries' stock markets move together (i.e., have high cross-correlations) and which go their own way. Table 3 displays "blocs" of countries whose stock markets have had high cross-correlations. Substantial

TABLE 3 EQUITY RETURN BLOCS: CROSS-CORRELATIONS OF U.S. DOLLAR-ADJUSTED TOTAL RETURNS 1960 1985

Central Europe

	Germany	Netherlands	Switzerland
Germany	1.000		
Netherlands	0.654	1.000	
Switzerland	0.839	0.716	1.000

East Asia

	Japan	Hong Kong	Singapore
Japan	1.000		
Hong Kong	0.690	1.000	
Singapore	0.848	0.796	1.000

Anglo-Pacific

	U.S.	Canada	Australia
United States	1.000		
Canada	0.691	1.000	
Australia	0.627	0.656	1.000

United Kingdom and the United States

	United Kingdom	United States
Australia	0.611	0.630
Belgium	0.352	0.431
Canada	0.374	0.701
France	0.475	0.268
Germany	0.331	0.264
Hong Kong	0.484	0.654
Japan	0.202	0.197
Netherlands	0.663	0.741
Singapore	0.297	0.521
Switzerland	0.485	0.467
United States	0.629	1.000

comovement might be expected among countries related by such factors as geographical proximity, currency arrangements, trading partnerships or cultural similarity.

In fact, several central European countries form a distinct equity return bloc: Germany, Switzerland and the Netherlands are each correlated with the others at a level above 0.5. (Perfect comovement, or identical returns, is represented by a correlation coefficient of 1.0; no relationship, 0.0; precise opposite movement, −1.0.) France and Belgium are less distinctly associated with this bloc, although the Netherlands and Belgium are highly correlated, as might be expected due to their proximity and their past political ties (not shown on Table 3).

Proximity or cultural similarity, though, does not determine an equity bloc. Germany and Austria share a language, a border and many cultural traits, but have a correlation below 0.3 (not shown). Sweden and Norway, which used to be one country, have an extraordinarily low correlation, −0.2 (not shown), perhaps because Norway is largely a resource economy while Sweden is heavily industrial. Confirming this conjecture, the other two resource-dominated economies in the group, Canada and Australia, have correlations of 0.5 and 0.2 (not shown) with Norway, respectively.

The Asian equity bloc is remarkable for its high correlations across what are actually very dissimilar countries. Japan, Hong Kong, and Singapore comprise this bloc: each country is correlated with the other at a level above approximately 0.7. Note that these three countries are geographically very far apart; Tokyo and Singapore are about as distant as London and New York. The countries in the Asian bloc all have heavily industrialized, export-oriented economies.

The United States, Canada, and Australia also form a bloc, with all cross-correlations exceeding 0.6. These countries are all English speaking, were once British colonies, cover very large land areas, have high per capita incomes, and are rich in natural resources. In addition, they are strong political allies. The United States, however, is a service economy first and a manufacturing economy second, while Canada and Australia are resource economies with large agricultural export sectors. The massive volume of U.S.-Canadian trade helps to explain the high correlation of these two countries. Australia, though, is far away; the point on the Earth's surface directly opposite Perth, Australia, lies between Florida and Bermuda. Australia also trades heavily with East Asia as well as with the North American countries. While not studied due to the small size of its equity market, New Zealand has many similarities to Australia and western Canada and can be included in this bloc, called the Anglo-Pacific group of countries.

The United Kingdom cuts across all regions and national boundaries to form a bloc of its own. The United Kingdom is correlated to some degree with every country of economic importance, including the United States (0.6), France (0.5), Germany (0.3), and even Japan (0.2). Correlations of the United Kingdom with its present and former Asian colonies are also high: 0.5 for Hong Kong, which is still a British colony, and 0.3 for Singapore. This extraordinary association of the United Kingdom with the rest of the world's equity markets indicates that extent to which the United Kingdom dominated world trade, politics and culture for more than a century, affecting the capital markets as well as other institutions of diverse countries throughout the world.

Risk-Adjusted Returns

Table 4 displays the alphas and betas for each country and regional portfolio. Alphas are risk-adjusted returns relative to the world stock market, and betas are a measure of risk, where the beta of a country having an average risk is equal to one. The alpha of a country is expressed in percent per year and is positive for countries that beat the world market on a risk-adjusted basis. Countries beaten by the world market have negative alphas.

Asian countries had the highest alphas. Hong Kong, which was studied over fifteen years, as compared with twenty-five years for most of the countries, had the highest alpha of any country, 13.2 percent. Of the countries studied for twenty-five years, Japan's very high alpha, 8.9 percent, was second only to Norway. Hong Kong and Singapore were very risky as measured by their betas, which

TABLE 4 DOLLAR-ADJUSTED EQUITY RETURNS: REGRESSIONS ON WORLD EQUITIES, 1960-1984

	Excess Return Regressions of Country Equities on World Equity Portfolio			
Country or Region	**Alpha (%)**	**Alpha T-statistic**	**Beta**	**Unadjusted R^2**
Austria	0.34%	0.08	0.17	0.02
Belgium	2.39	0.93	0.51	0.31
Denmark	3.02	0.56	0.69	0.16
France	−1.44	−0.34	0.65	0.22
Germany	1.20	0.31	0.54	0.18
Italy	−4.05	−0.77	0.46	0.08
Netherlands	1.13	0.50	0.96	0.67
Norway	9.62	5.06	0.08	0.05
Spain	3.17	0.68	0.01	0.00
Sweden	3.52	0.95	0.50	0.17
Switzerland	0.68	0.17	0.93	0.39
United Kingdom	1.36	0.28	1.43	0.51
Europe Total	−0.63	−0.30	0.84	0.65
Hong Kong*	13.21	1.22	2.60	0.58
Japan	8.93	1.54	0.78	0.17
Singapore*	12.60	1.03	2.46	0.49
Asia Total	8.65	1.43	0.89	0.20
Australia	−0.99	−0.26	1.20	0.54
Canada	1.21	0.47	0.87	0.56
Other Total	0.26	0.11	0.97	0.66
Non-U.S. Total	1.34	0.71	0.88	0.71
United States Total	−0.25	−0.25	1.07	0.93

*1970-1984.

Note: All returns are excess returns, i.e., total returns in excess of the U.S. Treasury bill return.

Sources: Table 1 for year-by-year returns by country; *Stocks, Bonds, Bills, and Inflation 1986 Yearbook,* Ibbotson Associates, Chicago, for Treasury bill returns; Roger G. Ibbotson, Laurence B. Siegel, and Kathryn S. Love, "World Wealth: Market Values and Returns," *Journal of Portfolio Management,* Fall 1985 for returns on portfolios (regional and world) of countries' equities. See the latter article for the methodology used in this table.

were 2.60 and 2.46 respectively. Japan was less risky than the world market, with a beta of 0.78.

The performance of the European countries was widely varied, with Norway (alpha of 9.6 percent) being the standout. Excepting Norway, alphas ranged from −4.1 percent in Italy to 3.5 percent in Sweden. Betas were low except for that of the United Kingdom, which had a beta of 1.43. The European portfolio had negative risk-adjusted performance, with an alpha of −0.6 percent and a beta of 0.84 on the world market.

Canada outperformed Australia, with alphas of 1.2 and −1.0 percent respectively. Canada also had a lower beta than Australia.

The non-U.S. portfolio, containing all seventeen countries, outperformed the United States in risk-adjusted terms. The non-U.S. portfolio had an alpha of 1.3 percent and a beta of 0.88, while the U.S. portfolio had an alpha of −0.3 percent and a beta of 1.07. As noted before, investors would have both improved risk-adjusted performance and reduced economy risk by holding a global rather than a U.S. only portfolio over the last twenty-five years.

LONG-RUN RETURNS ON INTERNATIONAL EQUITIES

The past quarter century of international equity returns is of great current interest. This modern period does not, however, tell a complete story. Since 1960, the world has enjoyed a period of relative *political* stability, with no major wars, no large changes in borders, and no shifts in economic systems of the important economic powers. Also, by starting at 1960, the rapid growth phases of Europe, the United States, Canada and, to some extent, Asia are missed.

Divergence Between Asset and Claim Values: The Japanese Experience

When ranked by the size of returns, Japanese stocks were shown as the unchallenged winner over the period starting in 1960. But returns in prewar and postwar Japan exemplify the divergence that can occur in values of assets and the claims on those assets, such as stocks. Suppose an investor had brought Japanese stocks in the 1860s. What would have been the result?

Japan's Meiji Restoration in 1867 brought a pro-capitalist government into power and opened Japan to world trade. Japanese equity returns were high, similar to those in the other high-growth countries of that time—the United States and Britian. Any investor would have fared well buying Japanese stocks in the 1860's and holding them. But during World War II, investors from Allied countries would have lost all claims to Japanese stocks, making their Japanese equity portfolios worthless. After the war, international investors would have had to invest new capital in Japanese equities to reap the high postwar returns.

Even in economically "winning" countries having high long-term returns, international investors face the risk of losing their equity claims. Let's now turn to the risk of investing in "losing" countries.

Interrupted Markets and the Winner-Loser Country Phenomenon

Eighteenth- or nineteenth-century investors who bet on the United States, Canada or Britian would have been prodigious forecasters of the world economy. Investors ordinarily cannot expect to have such foresight. In 1900, an international investor might well have bought Austro-Hungarian, Russian and German stocks instead of U.S. and British issues. The Austro-Hungarian equities would have lost all value by the end of World War I. The Russian equities would have been rendered worthless by the Communist government, which nationalized firms shortly after the Russian Revolution of 1917. And German equity claims were destroyed by World War II.

Table 5 shows summary statistics of long-term equity returns for a wide variety of countries. Many of these countries' returns were interruped by war, or were terminated by Communism or a country's loss of sovereignty. Long-term investors may expect growth in the overall world ecomomy, yet if they do not diversify, international investors run a very substantial risk of choosing a country that will prove to be a "loser."

TABLE 5 SUMMARY STATISTICS ON WORLD EQUITIES

US Dollar Adjusted Returns	Number of Years of Data	Compound Annual Return	Arithmetic Mean Return	Standard Deviation	1982 Cumulative Wealth Index Value	1982 Agg. Mkt. Capitalization in Billions $US
1926-1982 Total Returns						
United Kingdom	57	8.1%	11.2%	28.0%	113.53	$ 181.6
United States (NYSE)	57	9.2	11.4	21.6	136.89	1294.7
1926-1982 Capital Appreciation						
Uninterrupted Series						
Canada	57	4.2	6.7	22.5	14.28	105.0
Sweden	57	4.7	7.0	20.9	17.02	17.1
Switzerland	57	5.8	7.7	21.1	25.40	41.4
United Kingdom	57	3.1	6.6	28.0	10.73	181.6
United States (NYSE)	57	4.4	6.6	20.8	10.26	1294.7
1929-1982 Capital Appreciation						
Interrupted Series						
Australia	54	2.9	–	–	4.75	41.4
Belgium	54	1.2	–	–	1.94	8.1
Denmark	54	2.8	–	–	4.52	6.0
Finland	54	2.5	–	–	3.77	N/A
Italy	54	−0.6	–	–	0.71	19.7
Japan	54	−1.3	–	–	0.49	410.2
Mexico	54	−3.0	–	–	0.19	1.1
Norway	54	3.0	–	–	4.87	1.6

Sources: Morgan Stanley, *Capital International Perspective,* New York, for all countries for 1960-1982 except Finland and Mexico; various government, United Nations, and private sources collected by the authors for the other years and for Finland and Mexico for all years.

Diversification: The Key to Intelligent International Investing

While investors cannot avoid the risk of picking losing countries or being separated from their claims, diversification minimizes this risk. If a hypothetical investor of 1900 had held U.S. and British equities as well as those of the fallen European powers, much of the risk would have been diversified away, and the investor would have substantial capital today. Diversification across countries is analogous to diversification across stocks within one country. While investors may not be able to predict which stock, or which country, will win and which will lose, by holding a diversified portfolio investors are virtually guaranteed some winners over the long run. This diversification argument is the primary reason for investing internationally. Let's now examine the logic of international equity investing in greater conceptual detail.

WHY INVEST INTERNATIONALLY

As national economies gradually meld into an interdependent world economy, investing across national borders has become a strategy of great interest. The Europeans, living in small, specialized countries, have been investing in each others' capital markets—as well as other world markets—for decades or longer. Today, investors in the United States are beginning to realize that their country, too, is becoming a specialist in the world economy; that self-sufficiency is a path to inefficiency while specialization leads to economic success; and that, therefore, international investing to achieve diversification makes sense.

Investing in foreign equities is justified for three reasons:

- the size of foreign markets
- the performance and diversification available in foreign markets

- the increasing integration or interdependence of the world economy.

Each reason will now be treated in turn.

Size and Opportunity

For many years, non-U.S. equity markets have constituted a large share of world equity value. Furthermore, these markets have been increasing in relative importance. U.S. stocks made up roughly two-thirds of the world's equity value in 1960, with foreign countries constituting the other third. But by 1985, although the U.S. market had grown considerably, its share of the world market had fallen to 49 percent.

This observation alone makes a case for international investing. By holding only U.S. equities, an investor eliminates over half of the world's equity markets. Of course, accounting and other inputs to stock analysis differ among countries both in form and accuracy, putting the U.S. analyst of foreign companies at some relative disadvantage.

Performance and Diversification

As noted earlier, high returns in foreign countries—especially Japan—and low correlations with U.S. equity returns have provided investors with an opportunity both to make money and to diversify their portfolios. The need for diversification is made clearer by once-promising foreign markets where investors lost all their capital to war, Communism, or conquest. Investors run the same risks today, and they can only minimize them by diversifying across the world equity markets.

An Interdependent World

The final reason for investing internationally is the interdependence of national economies. The world is in a state of transition from a set of nation-states, each striving for self-sufficiency, to a community of trading nations that specialize according to their comparative advantages. Japan has become the consumer-goods manufacturer of the world, Switzerland the world's banker, Germany the purveyor of luxury automobilies. The United States also is losing its highly diversified character and is becoming a specialist in service and information technologies: including banking, brokerage, money management, as well as computers, telecommunications, education, medicine and agriculture. Therefore, to discover the successful companies in these diverse fields, investors must search across national borders.

HOW TO INVEST INTERNATIONALLY

The world's stock exchanges are compared in Table 6 (pages 868-869). A country may have numerous stock exchanges (Germany) or no active exchange (Ireland, whose equity trading is done in England). Also, some countries classified as emerging markets have sizable stock exchanges.

The equity capitalization of a country cannot be computed by adding the capitalizations of its stock exchanges. This is because stocks are frequently listed on more than one exchange, and sometimes on exchanges in different countries. For example, the New York Stock Exchange, (NYSE) lists dozens of foreign stocks. Likewise, the Tokyo and Osaka exchanges have approximately the same capitalization since they list roughly the same stocks; yet almost all trading occurs on the Tokyo exchange. Switzerland has three exchanges with almost identical listings, including a large proportion of non-Swiss stocks. Let's now briefly describe the world's principal equity markets.

The International Equity Arena

United States. The U.S. equity market can be broken into three parts—national exchanges, regional exchanges, and the over-the-counter (OTC) market. In the mid-1980's, the NYSE was the dominant player in equity trading. This exchange was over six and a half times the capitalization of the OTC market and did twice as much trading, while the AMEX, the other national exchange, ranked a distant third. Of these three, the OTC market is growing most quickly. The regional exchanges have traditionally functioned as secondary markets for nationally listed stocks and primary markets for regional stocks. Now, with the advent of computerized trading linking them to major markets, the regional exchanges have become more important.

Canada. Canada's dominant marketplace is the Toronto Stock Exchange. While the Toronto exchange has traditionally served as a haven for penny mining and energy stocks, the list has become much more industrial in past years.

Mexico. Following decades of decentralized capital markets, the Mexican government in the 1970's established a central stock exchange at Mexico City, the Bolsa de Valores de Mexico. In addition, international investors may easily buy and sell most Mexican securities through U.S. brokers, or may purchase shares of mutual funds specializing in Mexican investments.

United Kingdom and Ireland. The Stock Exchange, named as if it were the only one in the world, is the central securities marketplace for the United Kingdom and the Republic of Ireland. It resulted from the 1973 consolidation of all regional stock exchanges with the old London Stock Exchange. The Stock Exchange is one of the oldest exchanges in the world, dating to the 1600's. This exchange lists thousands of issues, by that measure the world's largest. The list is large because almost any reputable security in any developed country can be listed. In fact, the list includes more than one hundred NYSE and AMEX stocks. Moreover, fixed-income issues outnumber equities on the Stock Exchange. Thus, the number of issues on The Stock Exchange vastly overstates the size of the British stock market. Although the largest in Europe, in equity value the British market is only about one-eighth as large as the U.S market.

Germany. Germany's publicly traded stock market is small compared with its huge debt market, the private equity market, and the integrated commercial and investment banking houses. Yet Germany's public stock market is the second largest in Europe and

TABLE 6 STOCK EXCHANGES AROUND THE WORLD

Country	Exchange(s)	1982 Trading Volume (Bil US $)	1982 Number of Issues Listed: Domestic	1982 Number of Issues Listed: Foreign	12/31/1982 Market Capitalization (Bil US $)	Principal Share Price Indices
Argentina	Buenos Aires	0.2	247	1	1.0	Buenos Aires Stk. Exch. Index – 248 issues
Australia	Total of 6	5.1	931	20	41.5	Australian Share Price Index – 260 issues
Austria	Vienna	0.1	62	35	1.5	Wiener Borsehammer index – 43 issues
Belgium	Brussels	1.9	212	139	8.6	Indice General du Comptant – 67 issues
Brazil	Rio de Janiero	3.7	607	0	N/A	IBV Index – 30 issues
	Sao Paulo	2.2	478	0	10.3	BOVESPA Index – 109 issues
Canada	Montreal	2.2	387	18	167.9	General Index – 85 issues
	Toronto	14.3	759	60	103.5	TSE 300 Composite Index – 300 issues
Denmark	Copenhagen	0.1	206	4	5.5	Copenhagen Stock Exchange Index – 38 issues
France	Paris	9.6	535	164	38.1[3]	CAC Index – 262 issues
Germany	Total of 8	16.6	450	177	69.0	Frankfurter Allgemeine Zeitung – 100 issues
Hong Kong	Total of 4	N/A	N/A	N/A	24.0	Hang Seng Index
Israel	Tel Aviv	6.7	212	1	15.9	General Share Index – all listed issues
Italy	Milan	2.8	138	0	19.9	MIB Historial Index – 129 issues
Japan	Osaka	18.4	1009	0	370.6	300 Common Stock Index
	Tokyo	146.9	1427	12	417.4	Tokyo Stock Price Index; Nikkei Dow Jones
Korea	Seoul	2.7	334	0	4.4	Korea Composite stock Price index – 334 issues
Luxembourg	Luxembourg	N/A	88	138	4.7	Domestic Share Price Index – 7 issues
Malaysia	Kuala Lumpur	1.4	194	67	13.9	Kuala Lumpur Stk Exch Indust. Index – 30 issues

Country	Exchange(s)	1982 Trading Volume (Bil US $)	1982 Number of Issues Listed		12/31/1982 Market Capitalization (Bil US $)	Principal Share Price Indices
			Domestic	Foreign		
Netherlands	Amsterdam	5.1	216	260	25.7	ANP-CBS General Index – 51 issues
Norway	Oslo	0.1	112	6	2.4	Oslo Bors Stock Index – 52 issues
Singapore	Singapore	2.4	112	176	31.2	SES Industrial and Commercial Index – 32 issues
South Africa	Johannesburg	2.6	470	24	77.8	JSE Actuaries Index – 141 issues
Spain	Barcelona	0.2	426	1	11.5	General Index of Barcelona Stk Exch – 73 issues
	Madrid	1.1	448	0	11.2	Madrid Stock Exchange Index – 69 issues
Switzerland	Basel	18.6	101	157	33.2	Societe' de Banque Suisse – 90 issues
	Geneva	N/A	106	172	36.8	Societe de Banque Suisse – 90 issues
	Zurich	N/A	119	155	38.7	Societe de Banque Suisse – 90 issues
United Kingdom	London	32.7	2279[1]	485[2]	196.2[4]	Financial Times All Ordinaries Index
United States	American	19.7	784	50	45.0	AMEX Market Value Index – over 800 issues
	New York	488.4	1482	44	1258.7	NYSE Composite; S&P 500; Dow Jones
	OTC (NASDAQ)	100.2	3008	268	153.1	NASDAQ OTC Composite Index – over 3000 issues
	Regionals	67.8	N/A	N/A	N/A	None

Notes: 1. Includes some companies with fixed income issues only.
2. Includes Ireland.
3. 12/31/1981
4. Excludes Ireland.

Source: *FIBV Statistics* 1983 (Federation Internationale des Bourses de Valeurs, Paris, France); additional information by authors.

provides important investment opportunities. The market is decentralized, with the Frankfurt exchange dominant in fixed-income and international securities and the Dusseldorf exchange dominant in domestic industrial stocks. An over-the-counter market flourishes and is competitive with the exchanges.

France. The French equity market is the third largest in Europe and one of the world's oldest. The Paris Bourse, or exchange, originated in the 1500's, but equity trading was not its major activity until two hundred years later. In the twentieth century, French stocks have assumed a substantial role in world markets. Despite nationalizations in the early 1980's, the French economy provides substantial opportunities to U.S. investors.

Switzerland. The Swiss stock market, while playing a secondary role to its credit markets, ranks fourth in size in Europe and has an aggregate market value far out of proportion to its population. The three principal stock exchanges, Zurich, Geneva and Basel, function essentially as one, since trades are executed wherever terms are most favorable. The Swiss exchanges list a large number of fixed-income issues and foreign securities. Of the few hundred Swiss equities, only several dozen have large enough markets for institutional trading.

Belgium and Luxembourg. Belgium's principal stock exchange, the Brussels Bourse, is a dynamic market where foreign investment is welcomed. Most domestic Belgian stocks are industrials. An approximately value-weighted portfolio of Belgian equities can be held by purchasing the shares of one company, Société Générale de Belgique, which is said to own 30 percent of the value of all publicly traded Belgian stocks. Nearby Luxembourg, a small grand-duchy, is closely tied to but independent of Belgium. Unlike Belgium, Luxembourg does not tax security trades, so some investors employ its brokers to buy and sell Belgian and other securities.

Italy. Until recently, Italy has not generally been considered to be a major stock market. Situated in Milan, this market was in an almost unbroken decline from 1962-1979. The 1980's have seen a dramatic resurgence in Italian stocks, although they remain at the bottom of the pack in long-run performance.

Netherlands. The Netherlands, historically a world trading and financial center, houses a major equity market. The principal exchange is at Amsterdam, where shares of the Dutch East India Company were first listed in 1602. The Dutch were pioneers in international investing since their domestic market is so specialized. Robeco, a global investment trust formed in the 1930's, is the country's largest shareowner and a model international equity portfolio. Robeco is listed on 19 stock exchanges, more than any other firm in the world.

Norway. Resource-rich Norway became financially prominent in the 1970's, when rising energy prices pushed Norwegian stock prices to dizzying heights. Much of the market value of Norwegian stocks is represented by Norsk Hydro, the national electric company.

Spain. Despite the autocratic rule of Francisco Franco, Spain emerged in the 1960's and early 1970's as a growing economy with a rapidly rising stock market. After 1959, considerable economic and political liberalization occurred, causing an influx of foreign capital. From the mid-1970's until recently, however, returns were poor. Foreign investment on the Madrid, Barcelona, and Bilbao stock exchanges is welcomed and traditional corporate secrecy is giving way to fuller disclosure.

Sweden. Sweden is the industrial powerhouse of the Scandinavian group, with the best historical equity returns in Europe. Interestingly, Sweden's adoption of certain aspects of socialism does not preclude very large, profitable private enterprises. The stock market is open to foreigners willing to abide by various complex rules.

Japan. Japan's equity market, like its population and overall economy, is roughly half the size of the United States and is by far the most important non-U.S. equity market in the world. The Tokyo Stock Exchange (TSE), Japan's principal trading venue, has about 1400 stocks, making it only slightly smaller than the NYSE in the number of stocks listed. The exchange has two tiers, or categories, of listings. The "first section" of the TSE corresponds very roughly with the NYSE in listing requirements and the "second section" with the AMEX. In trading volume, the TSE ranks first in the world. The price of an average share is under $5, and consequently daily trading is measured in the hundreds of millions of shares. The market is also extremely liquid, with a high trading volume as a percentage of its aggregate value.

Japanese business tradition encourages companies doing business with one another to hold each other's shares. Thus corporate holdings of corporate stocks form an appreciable portion of Japan's aggregate equity value. This portion is not nearly enough to cut into the liquidity of the market, but it creates a double-counting problem in estimating the size of the market.

Hong Kong. Hong Kong has a highly volatile stock market, subject to extreme price swings. Stock prices rose twentyfold in the early 1970's and then came crashing down in 1973-74. After another surge in the late 1970's, the market plunged in 1983 when diplomatic talks between the United Kingdom and Communist China over the colony's future stalled. When an agreement was reached, specifying that Hong Kong will become part of China in 1997 with the right to retain a capitalist economy for at least fifty years, the stock market soared once again in the mid-1980's.

Singapore. Following its separation from the Malay Federation in 1965, Singapore emerged as the richest Asian country outside Japan. Banking is the largest industry and the principal vehicle for stock investment. While Singapore's stock market has fluctuated wildly in the past, like that of Hong Kong, Singapore's market has become more stable in recent years as the country has become more developed.

Australia. Australia is a resource-rich country with a standard of living comparable to that of the United States and Canada. Despite the wealth of its mining regions, the principal Australian stocks are industrial and financial companies. The largest Australian company, Broken Hill Proprietary, is a diversified conglomerate offering a cross-section of the Australian economy.

Implications for Investors

Institutional investors have a number of strategies to cope with the high information and transaction costs associated with international equities. One popular approach is using money managers from other countries, particularly those in Japan, the United Kingdom and Switzerland. Institutions may also build relationships with brokers in countries with large equity markets. One drawback to trading in some foreign markets is that commissions are at high rates. Also, bid-asked spreads are large, and the thin markets are subject to price pressure effects.

While active stock selection may yield superior results for some managers, a passive strategy reduces trading costs and avoids the costs of gathering and evaluating information on foreign stocks. As a quasi-passive strategy, institutions may achieve diversification by holding shares of global investment companies, such as Robeco, or regional investment companies, such as Société Généràl de Belgique.

Individual investors seeking a diversified international portfolio can choose from a number of open-end mutual funds. Since no-load international stock funds exist, investors should avoid "load" funds. For those who favor a particular country, regional portfolios are available either as open-end or closed-end mutual funds. Since almost all international equity funds available to individual investors are actively managed, fees will probably be high.

REFERENCES

Bernstein, Peter L. ed. *International Investing* (New York: Institutional Investor, Inc., 1983) Diverse readings on the subject, compiled by a master editor and writer on finance.

Esslen, Rainer. *The Complete Book of International Investing: How to Buy Foreign Securities and Who's Who on the International Investment Scene* (New York: McGraw-Hill Book Company, 1977) Although dated due to the rapid changes in the field, Esslen provides a flavor of the ''hands-on'' side of foreign equity investing.

Lessard, Donald R., ed. *International Financial Management: Theory and Application,* 2d, ed. (New York: Wiley, 1985) This book of readings includes some of the best articles on the subject.

INDEX

A

B

D

E

H

I

J

L

M

N

O

P

R

S

T

U

W

Y